Sites of Gender

Sites of Gender

WOMEN, MEN AND MODERNITY
IN SOUTHERN DUNEDIN,
1890–1939

EDITED BY BARBARA BROOKES,
ANNABEL COOPER AND ROBIN LAW

AUCKLAND UNIVERSITY PRESS

To the memory of our friend Robin Law
1956–2003

First published 2003

Auckland University Press
University of Auckland
Private Bag 92019
Auckland
New Zealand
www.auckland.ac.nz/aup

© The contributors, 2003

ISBN 1 86940 301 0

Publication is kindly assisted by the History Group, Ministry for Culture and Heritage and by the History Department (School of Liberal Arts) and the Anthropology Department (School of Social Sciences), University of Otago

National Library of New Zealand Cataloguing-in-Publication Data
Sites of gender : women, men and modernity in Southern Dunedin 1890-1939 /
edited by Barbara Brookes, Annabel Cooper and Robin Law.
Includes bibliographical references and index.
ISBN 1-86940-305-3
1. Sex role—New Zealand—Dunedin—History—20th century. 2. Sex role—New Zealand—Dunedin—History—19th century. 3. Dunedin (N.Z.)—Social conditions—20th century. 4. Dunedin (N.Z.)—Social conditions—19th century.
I. Brookes, Barbara L. (Barbara Lesley), 1955– II. Cooper, Annabel. III. Law, Robin, 1956–
305.30993920904—dc 21

This book is copyright. Apart from fair dealing for the purpose of private study, research, criticism or review, as permitted under the Copyright Act, no part may be reproduced by any process without prior permission of the publisher.

Front cover photograph: The preparing room at Donaghy's Rope and Twine factory in South Dunedin in the early twentieth century. Courtesy of Donaghy's Industries and the Hocken Library
Back cover photograph: Women lifesavers at St Clair, c.1920. Courtesy of Otago Settlers Museum

Cover design: Christine Hansen
Printed by Astra Print Ltd, Wellington

Contents

Preface and Acknowledgements		vii
List of Maps		xii
One	Situating Gender *Barbara Brookes, Annabel Cooper and Robin Law*	1
Two	The Landscape of Gender Politics: Place, People and Two Mobilisations *Annabel Cooper, Erik Olssen, Kirsten Thomlinson and Robin Law*	15
Three	Working Gender, Gendering Work: Occupational Change and Continuity in Southern Dunedin *Erik Olssen*	50
Four	Schooling for a Gendered Future: Gender, Education and Opportunity *Dorothy Page, Howard Lee and Tom Brooking*	91
Five	Producing and Consuming Gender: The Case of Clothing *Jane Malthus and Chris Brickell*	123
Six	Spare Time? Leisure, Gender and Modernity *Barbara Brookes, Erik Olssen and Emma Beer*	151
Seven	Down and Out on the Flat: the Gendering of Poverty *Annabel Cooper and Marian Horan*	190
Eight	To and From, There and Back: Gender in Spatial Mobility *Brian Heenan and Sarah Johnsen*	226
Nine	On the Streets of Southern Dunedin: Gender in Transport *Robin Law*	258

Ten	The Risk to Life and Limb: Gender and Health *Barbara Brookes*	285
Eleven	God, the Devil and Gender *John Stenhouse*	313
Endpiece	Marriage: The Gendered Contract *Barbara Brookes*	348

Appendices
I   Chronology of Significant Events *Robin Law* — 356
II Qualitative and Quantitative Databases of the Caversham Project
    David Hood — 362
III List of Pseudonyms — 371

Notes — 372
Select Bibliography — 419
Notes on Contributors — 426
Index — 428

Preface and Acknowledgements

It is now a truism that gender, like other categories of social analysis, cannot properly be studied in isolation. Although gender difference shows consistencies across similar societies, it emerges and is changed through its interactions with the institutions, technologies, belief systems and daily practices of particular societies at particular historical moments. In addressing these complexities, this volume seeks to analyse gender by 'setting it deep' in a place and a time: the suburbs of southern Dunedin between 1890 and 1939. To that end, we set out the processes of settlement and development of the southern suburbs early in the book, but subsequent chapters addressing specific aspects of gender also attend to the history of the place. Parts of the book will therefore read as much like social history as gender history; parts of it as historical geography. In this interdisciplinary study we have also sought to embed our discussions of gender in analyses that derive from our various disciplines – history, geography, gender studies – although several of us also address the shortcomings of existing work in our disciplines. It is our view that, if we are to explore our topic carefully, this kind of depth, both in terms of setting and in terms of scholarly practice, is necessary.

This collection has been long in the making. It grew out of what has come to be known as 'the Caversham Project', initially a quantitative and statistical study of social and geographical mobility, in the borough of Caversham in southern Dunedin. It started there because Erik Olssen lived there when he returned to Dunedin from North America and began to think that he could apply the methods of historical sociology to the complex historical space he occupied. The project developed, over twenty-five years, with the support of many students, several departmental research assistants, grants from the now-defunct Social Science Research Fund and the University of Otago, and then the Foundation for Research, Science and Technology, until it had developed the largest social history database in Australasia. The first phase of the project produced numerous working papers and articles, and Erik's own book,

Building the New World. Much of that work began to reveal the persistent and specific gendering of the database, based as it was on historical records. Erik then initiated the formation of the Sites of Gender group in order to address that bias.

The Sites of Gender group – the authors represented in this collection – began meeting in 1995. Thanks to a number of University of Otago research grants and further generous support from the Foundation for Research, Science and Technology, we were able to expand the research programme. In order to accumulate evidence about women, and evidence about men that allowed greater discussion of their gendering, the project's database was substantially extended to cover a longer time period (1890 to 1939) and a larger geographical area (now encompassing two more boroughs). A new set of oral histories, bringing the total to around 140, was commissioned. This further work on the database has, to date, provided the basis for a series of working papers, articles by several authors, numerous scholarly presentations and talks to community groups, and a highly successful exhibition curated by Seán Brosnahan and Peter Read at the Otago Settlers Museum. As this volume approached publication, we received financial assistance from the Departments of History and Anthropology, the New Zealand and the Pacific Centre for Research Excellence, the Division of Humanities at the University of Otago, and the History Group, Ministry of Culture and Heritage.

Little could have been achieved without the money. But the project has depended on people, of whom there are so many to acknowledge. There are the many people of southern Dunedin who gave up their time to speak to us about their lives, their families and the places they grew up in and were formed by. They have contributed to an oral-history collection whose surface has only been touched in this book – it is a rich source, both for us and for future researchers. We are grateful to all those who spoke to us.

There are the research fellows and research assistants, who are becoming the 'Caversham alumni' as they travel the globe, meeting each other in unlikely places. In the earlier period, Judi Boyd, David Thomson and Tony Ballantyne made outstanding contributions as research assistants. From 1995 to 1999 the project was very fortunate to have a team of dedicated researchers who helped significantly in giving the Sites of Gender phase cohesion and momentum: Hamish James, who was full-time, and part-timers Megan Cook, who – among other things – undertook an astonishing number of interviews, Maureen Hickey and Shaun Ryan. Subsequently, the project benefited from the commitment of Emma Beer, Shaun Broadley, Sandy Brown, Fiona Carter-Giddens, Karen Duder, Claire Gooder, Marian Horan, Alison Holmes, Andrew Joel, Sarah Johnsen, Emma Liddell, Eva Lubcke, Anne Marie Nielson, Kate

Smith and Andrea Watson. We are indebted to Sandy Brown, who oversaw the construction of the new database, and David Hood, the last of the database managers, who handled the pressures of final production with skill and remarkable goodwill. Paula Waby transcribed many of the oral histories while Dr Jens Hansen's assistance with NUDIST software enhanced our ability to use them.

We were lucky to have Professor Clyde Griffen of Vassar College visiting during the early stages of Sites of Gender, and are grateful for his contributions. In 2000, we organised a symposium to discuss work in draft. Happily, we asked Professors Desley Deacon, then of the University of Texas (now at the Australian National University), and Miles Fairburn, University of Canterbury, to participate as commentators: we are indebted to them also for their insights and their critiques of draft work.

This is a project that could not have succeeded without the active support of librarians and archivists. We are particularly grateful to the staff of the Hocken Library, National Archives, Dunedin, and the Otago Settlers Museum, many of whom have assisted this project over the years. It is a particular sadness that we cannot now thank David McDonald, a reference librarian with an incomparable knowledge of the Hocken's collections and an indefatigable willingness to go as many extra miles as the humblest research assistant requested. Several generations of Caversham assistants discovered the essential technique for bending Hocken rules ('Tell David it's for Caversham'). His untimely death shocked us all. Sean Brosnahan, Peter Read and Valmai Shaw of the Settlers Museum supported – indeed, carried out – our desire to 'take the project home' to many of the people of Dunedin through the exhibition 'The Birth of Modern Times', which was based on the project's research as well as the Settlers' own collections. We are grateful to all three institutions for their permission to reproduce images and to quote from archival sources. Seán Brosnahan of the Settlers Museum and Mary Lewis of the Hocken both gave us great assistance as we searched for photographs. We also wish to thank the Otago Hospital Board for permission to quote from the Otago Benevolent Institution archives. Anna Blackman, then of the DCC Archives, was also very helpful to us. A project that involves so many people and runs through many years incurs numerous debts, and very many other people and organisations have also given such permissions. They are acknowledged in credits and references, but we wish to record our thanks here also.

We wish to thank the authors, who have been persuaded or beleaguered into many changes in the interest of a coherent volume, and for their particular assistance, Dorothy Page and Chris Brickell. David Hood produced draft after draft of the maps amid many other tasks. We are also grateful to

Brian Heenan and Les O'Neill for their comments on the maps, and Patricia Sargison for creating the index.

Marian Horan, Penny Isaac and Kirsten Thomlinson contributed by tackling significant MA topics and creating valuable databases. Howard Baldwin, who also completed a valuable MA, returned to the project as a Royal Society Teaching Fellow in 2002. His energy and enthusiasm helped keep everyone moving forward. Countless History, and some Gender and Women's Studies, students have also contributed by tackling topics relevant to the project.

A project of this size also requires efficient and proactive administration. For this, we wish to thank Cathy Thomson and Sue Lang. Elizabeth Caffin and the staff of the Auckland University Press, including the anonymous reader, have also been unfailingly helpful.

There are two special debts to record. Erik Olssen initiated the Caversham project and the databases that underpin it are the result of his work over many years. He established the Sites of Gender group and wrote the grant applications that brought in the money. In the preparation of this volume, he has done a great deal more than contribute to the chapters that carry his name: he also read and commented on drafts of all the chapters, suggesting where pertinent evidence was to be found, recalling the conclusions of long-ago class essays, writing an extra sentence (or more) when needed, spending days unearthing photographs at the Hocken and other more obscure sources. But he also helped substantially to lay the broader groundwork for histories of the southern suburbs. He was the architect, and for most of its history the coordinator, of the History Department's fourth-year dissertation programme, under the rubric of which many of the research essays that appear in the notes were carried out. He also taught, initially with Tom Brooking and later with Barbara Brookes, research-based courses using the Caversham database. He and other members of the History Department supervised many of the resulting essays and dissertations. His knowledge of the study area is prodigious. On one occasion, as we discussed how we might characterise the range of methods the project deployed, Robin Law suggested that we list the 'Ask Erik' method. It wasn't such a bad idea.

Robin Law contended with cancer throughout the creation of this book, and died in March of this year. As both an author and one of the editors, and as an articulate and enthusiastic participant in discussions, she has contributed enormously to this project. Until her last few days, she made the contributions so characteristic of her: capturing the 'big picture' succinctly and precisely, reframing an argument so that it proceeded logically and smoothly, redrafting an anecdote to bring out its point, sketching out her diagrams ('famous', we learned at her funeral service) to illuminate a debate, and – always – making us laugh at the quirky, particular, closely observed detail. She was generous and astute, brilliant and unexpected. Always, she found the perfect metaphor. When she spoke at her farewell from the university at the beginning of this year, anchored to a wheelchair and an oxygen inhaler, she talked about collaborative research relationships that – you find – turn into friendships. You work away, and think that all the time you're making an oyster, she said, and then you realise that what you have made is a pearl. And how right she was. We miss our colleague greatly, but we miss our friend far more.

Annabel Cooper and Barbara Brookes
Dunedin, August 2003

List of Maps

All maps were drawn by David Hood.

Designing maps for a 50-year period, in which the area under study developed considerably, presented us with some dilemmas. We decided to use the 1938 street plan, in order to include all the streets that existed by the end of our period. Many of the industries, institutions, churches, halls, and many other sites displayed in the maps, however, existed in the area for only part of the period. The maps are not intended, therefore, to be accurate for any particular moment. Furthermore, the maps include the significant features named in the text, but make no claim to comprehensiveness.

Many of the southern suburbs' street names have changed since the 1890s, mostly but not always as a result of the boroughs' amalgamation with Dunedin city. Most confusingly, the names of some streets were reallocated (so that Hillside Rd, for example, once named the present King Edward St). In order to avoid confusion, we use the street names of 2003, both in the maps and text (except occasionally, where we specify otherwise).

As the cadastral map provided the basis for our maps, street lines retain their irregularities.

2.1 Location of the study area
2.2 The suburbs of southern Dunedin
2.3 Male occupational class by suburb, 1891–1939
2.4 Kensington
2.5 Northern Caversham Borough: Caversham township, Rockyside, Calderville and Parkside through to the Glen and Caversham Rise
2.6 South Dunedin
2.7 Southern Caversham Borough, including St Clair and Kew
2.8 St Kilda
3.1 Major workplaces for the residents of southern Dunedin within 15 minutes' walk of Kensington, c. 1922

LIST OF MAPS

- 4.1 State primary schools of the southern suburbs
- 5.1 Drapers, dressmakers, milliners, outfitters and tailors from the 1912 Stone's trade directory
- 6.1 Sites of organised leisure, 1890–1939
- 7.1 Households receiving outdoor relief, 1905
- 8.1 Location of sub-areas
- 8.2 A sample of circular mobility pathways traced by Rachel Grimmett between Faringdon Villa and selected activity sites in Dunedin
- 8.3 A sample of circular mobility pathways traced by Richard Grimmett and sons
- 8.4 A sample of circular mobility pathways between Faringdon Villa and selected activity sites outside Dunedin
- 9.1 Electric tramway routes and opening dates, 1890–1939
- 10.1 Indexed locations of infant mortality, 1900–20
- 11.1 Selected sites of worship, 1891–1939

One Situating Gender

BARBARA BROOKES, ANNABEL COOPER AND ROBIN LAW

'The only way to find a larger vision is to be somewhere in particular.'[1]

In 1893, pairs of respectably dressed women walked the streets of southern Dunedin, bearing a petition for female suffrage in their gloved hands. As these determined canvassers knocked on the front doors of the homes in the area, public debate about the role of women in the New World entered private households with the force of a fresh southerly wind off the nearby Pacific Ocean. The petition asserted the justice of extending the franchise to women and saw its denial as a 'grievous wrong'. Maude Hooper, a 23-year-old clerk living in the seaside suburb of St Clair; Ellen Hopkinson, a machinist from working-class South Dunedin; and Mary Ellen Burgess, a tailoress from Caversham, were among the women willing to challenge a gender order that reserved the world of political debate for men. More than half of the women of the southern Dunedin area supported this claim, a strikingly large share, and a contrast to the national rate of support, which was just under 25 per cent. Here, the winds of gendered change blew strong.[2]

The right of men to citizenship entailed a responsibility denied to women: the duty to bear arms. The manager of the Hillside Workshops, together with ten other employees, served in the Boer War and their images presided over the workspace, reminding the men of their duty to a larger imperial community, bound by ties of language and culture. It was a duty readily taken up by the 110 men from the workshops who volunteered to serve in the First World War. The continuity of links with Britain ensured more volunteers for the Second

World War. By that time a former boot clicker from Caversham, Frederick Jones, headed the martial arm of government as Minister of Defence.[3] War reinscribed masculinity with the role of defender of women and children.

This volume shows how the system and meaning of gender relations was crucial yet contested in one community in the years 1890–1939. Normative styles of masculinity and femininity were reshaped over this period in which women asserted their right to citizenship. For a brief time prior to the granting of the vote in 1893, those opposed to enfranchisement feared that the world would be turned upside down: that emasculated men would be forced to mind babies while masculinised women took to politics. Their fears were unrealised, but they indicate the apparent fragility of understandings of gender. Our interest here is in exploring the ways in which the practices and meanings of gender relations, and the performance of gender identities, were played out in a variety of social sites in one urban setting. A close analysis of these sites of gender indicates that, as the pace of social change quickened, masculinity and femininity were redefined – the latter more dramatically than the former – but in ways which often reaffirmed difference and inequality.

We seek here to complement and extend earlier historical and social geographical research on gender relations and on the social history of urban settlements in this country. The suburbs of southern Dunedin, especially the formerly independent borough of Caversham, have been the focus of an intensive long-term collaborative research project, resulting in a detailed social-history database.[4] The earlier stages of this work highlighted difficulties in obtaining certain kinds of gender-specific data, most notably relating to the occupational status of women, and the marital status of men. These 'gender gaps', as well as the common interests of researchers, precipitated the formation of a 'Sites of Gender' group within the larger project. Its members, whose work is collected in this volume, have been meeting and working together for five years. This intense collaboration – involving regular seminars, collaborative writing teams and discussions of draft chapters – provided an unusually rich and stimulating environment for research. One of the significant features of the group was the interdisciplinary mix: it included scholars with backgrounds in history, human geography, urban planning, gender studies and clothing technology.

In chapters one and two, we set the context for this volume as a whole. This introductory chapter provides the theoretical underpinning and situates the volume in relation to international and New Zealand debates. Chapter two traces the processes of settlement of the southern suburbs, gives an outline of its populations, and introduces the question of gender through two case studies. It also includes the book's reference maps. Chapters three to twelve examine gender in relation to particular 'sites' of change and constitute the main body of our study.

The period 1890–1939, beginning during the Long Depression and ending as the Great Depression evaporated and the Second World War began, was chosen for various reasons. As Claire Toynbee has remarked, 'the social and economic foundations of modern New Zealand were already in place, and industrialisation was proceeding at a rapid pace'.[5] Urbanisation and industrialisation, the engines of modernity, dominated the period at a national level. These two processes both formed New Zealand's earlier suburbs and created them 'modern', not just in their technologies and their workforces, but also in the home lives of their inhabitants.

The construction of new familial forms was one of several intersecting and interrelated changes occurring across this turbulent period. The fertility transition ('the Mothers' Mutiny', as James Belich has called it)[6] saw a great reduction in family size. At the same time expectations about the conditions deemed necessary to the health and education of children rose sharply. A fast-expanding proportion of the young began attending secondary school. Even as this transformation in the value placed on family life took place, home production and self-employment fell, and women's work made a partial move beyond the household. Men, however, strengthened their ties to the home. The advent in the 1890s of the 'New Woman' marked a rupture with femininities of the past. The 'New Man' was as likely to be found in the home in his leisure time as the 'New Woman' was outside of it.

State involvement in people's lives increased, and some attributed Liberal innovations, such as pensions for the elderly (1898) and widows (1911), to the new influence of women in the electorate.[7] The male-breadwinner wage was reinforced by the Arbitration Court established by the Liberals in 1894. The National Provident Fund (1911) and the Family Allowances Act (1926) increased support to the elderly and to families respectively. The Labour Party's Social Security Act 1938, at the end of our period, consolidated and expanded this emerging system of state assistance.[8] Even so, the 1920s saw a contestation over economic citizenship that began the erosion of the male-breadwinner ideal.[9] By 1933, despite the view that 'the difficulties of the country are too great for women to grapple with', Elizabeth McCombs had taken a seat in Parliament.[10] The House at the centre of this more organised and integrated state was no longer an exclusively male domain, although it was to be many years before women achieved a numerically significant presence there.

A focus on gender complicates the story of New Zealand as a social laboratory based on ideas of equality, independence, security and opportunity.[11]

The contemporary rhetoric of equality was sustained by a belief in 'natural' differences between the sexes, a view that had crystallised only in the early nineteenth century.[12] Men asserted their independence as breadwinners, claiming wages that enabled them to support dependants: wives and children. They claimed security in their employment in order to create stability for their families, and they sought opportunities for advancement.

Women's claims for equality in citizenship were contested, though partially granted in 1893. From that date they had the right to vote but not to sit in Parliament. Independence in the exercise of a political voice was not matched by independence in the home. Women were depended upon to sustain the family but were dependent for their livelihood on male breadwinners.[13] Because of inequality in wages and the shape of family life, women's security lay in marrying a good provider. Organisations such as the Benevolent Institution and the Society for the Protection of Women and Children sought to ameliorate the condition of women who made a bad bargain. The most dramatic shift over the period – the decline in family size – suggests that women took new opportunities to attain better health for themselves and their families and, in turn, initiated new desires in their daughters and sons.

A fine-grained analysis of multiple sites of gender in one locality has the potential to illuminate the operation of gender in the past and to reveal the intense labour necessary to sustain 'natural' differences between the sexes. Our multidisciplinary team has been challenged by Joan Scott's provocative questions: 'How does gender work in human social relationships? How does gender give meaning to the organisation and perception of historical knowledge?'[14] In the course of our research, seminars and discussions we have become convinced that a focus on gender transforms our understanding of the period 1890–1939 in important ways. Everything from behaviour in the bedroom and the pew, to domestic technologies such as telephones and washing machines, public trams and private motor cars, movie theatres and lipstick, contributed to a reworking of gender relations, the re-coding of objects in a gendered system of meaning and the emergence of different ways of being masculine and feminine. As these changed, so did the patterns and textures of people's lives. Modernity was not exterior to people's existence, but was literally embodied in their bodies and psyches, and that embodiment was profoundly gendered.

Using the lens of gender

The term 'gender' as an analytic category has now been in use for long enough to attract attempts at a genealogy: that is, stories about the origins and shifting usage of the term.[15] The story told by these chroniclers of usage is of an ever-widening frame as the object of study has been redefined and taken-for-granted categories called into question. In brief, we can trace a shift over time from a concern with 'women' to 'gender' to 'difference'. Understanding the way that gender is used in this collection requires some understanding of this theoretical trajectory and the place of our work within it. For historians, the most significant contribution is Joan Scott's influential essay, 'Gender: A Useful Category of Historical Analysis', which both traces the usage of the term and puts forward a way to use gender as a concept in historical – and other – research. Scott's approach has profoundly influenced this collection and so is discussed in some detail here in relation to New Zealand research on gender.

Intellectual genealogies can be seen as waves in which each phase supersedes its predecessor, each paradigm addressing the weakness of the last and effectively ousting it. Or – and this is the way we prefer to see the intellectual inheritance we are working with – each phase can be understood to have developed from former phases, often partly in critical response to perceived limitations, but primarily as a cumulative process. Indeed, we suggest that, in many examples of feminist history, several of the supposedly 'successive' phases are in fact evident in any one piece of work, as they are in most of the chapters in this volume.

The key project of feminist history as it emerged in the late 1960s and early 1970s was a compensatory one: to recover and write histories of women. Inspired by a feminist politics, it addressed the neglected terrain of women's experience, with the documentation and explanation of women's subordination to men as one of its aims. The legacy is twofold. First, committed feminist researchers explored the lives of women in the past, generating the new sub-discipline of women's history. Second, many scholars, even those who might not have identified themselves as feminists, were alerted to the need to attend to gender variations, to disaggregate data by gender, to recognise silences and missing information and to avoid generalising from the experiences of men.

For historians of women in New Zealand, the fight for women's enfranchisement was an obvious starting point, explored in Patricia Grimshaw's *Women's Suffrage in New Zealand*. Two volumes of essays under the title *Women in History*, edited by Barbara Brookes, Charlotte Macdonald and Margaret Tennant, made available the most recent research being done in women's history and signalled the directions in which research was moving. The centennial of women's suffrage in 1993 saw a number of publications that foregrounded women's experience, including Charlotte Macdonald's *The Vote, the Pill and the Demon Drink*, Sandra Coney's *Standing in the Sunshine*, and *Suffrage and Beyond: International Feminist Perspectives*, a collection edited by Caroline Daley and Melanie Nolan.[16]

The most significant theoretical developments from this impetus were the identification of gender as a social construction distinct from biological sex, and the justification of the study of gender as a social category. They directed attention to the commonsense social categories of men and women and how their patterns of behaviour and experience differed. Nevertheless, at the outset the study of gender tended to be seen as 'the study of things related to women',[17] a conflation that remained more or less unexamined until the 1980s.

The problems that drove this compensatory research, though mitigated now by a body of research on women, have not disappeared. In the Sites of Gender research project, our exploration of gender began by examining the male and female categories in aggregate data sources such as electoral rolls, school attendance records, church membership and medical records.[18] The limits placed on researchers by contemporary methods of recording, however, continue to render much information on women less accessible than that on men. Erik Olssen's previous study of the relationship between social structure and the organisation of work identified a resounding silence on the subject of women.[19] That silence in the local record helped prompt the increased size of our database; such information is otherwise hard to find. Jane Malthus and Chris Brickell's chapter on the gendered structure of clothing manufacturing is also compensatory work. So is their attention to consumption, a whole field of study once considered too 'trivial' for scholarly work, because of its association largely with women, and now accorded the status of serious study as a result of the work of feminist researchers. John Stenhouse's chapter on the activities of women in churches is similarly a foray into an under-researched area: churches as a field of women's endeavours, but also church life at the level of everyday parish activity, which, as the key area of women's contribution, has attracted the least attention in church history. Nor did the activities of women in creating and maintaining cleanliness and providing good nutrition in their homes always attract attention for their contribution to the great transition in public health over the nineteenth and early twentieth centuries. The main focus of scholarly work was once on the well-known public-health crusaders, rather than the women who carried their teachings into specific household practices. Barbara Brookes's chapter shows how these practices changed. In these and other chapters, compensatory research can be shown still to be an important component of work on gender. But it is not all.

As feminist theory developed in the 1980s and beyond, the focus expanded from the experiences of women to include two interrelated approaches:

masculinities, or men studied not as a gender-neutral norm but as men; and gender as a relational concept. The first, and still the only, book-length study of the history of masculinity in New Zealand, Jock Phillips's *A Man's Country?*, explored the image of the Pakeha male and raised important questions about gender and nationhood. It has been followed more recently by the collection edited by Robin Law, Hugh Campbell and John Dolan, *Masculinities in Aotearoa/New Zealand*, which includes some historical work.[20]

As gender has developed as a relational concept, it has come to be recognised as an integral element in the organisation of social institutions, the allocation of material resources and the operation of power. Margaret Tennant's *Paupers and Providers* is one of the earlier examples of this shift.[21] Recent work in the area of gender relations includes Caroline Daley's study of the rural town of Taradale, *Girls & Women, Men & Boys*.[22] Melanie Nolan's *Breadwinning: New Zealand Women and the State*, which looks closely at the way the state negotiated gendered concepts of providers and dependants, is an interesting example: its subtitle, marking it as a study of women and the state, in part belies its content, which deals as much with the implications of the state for men and reveals the way in which the study of women now increasingly incorporates the study of gender relations.

In the present study, several chapters examine manhood. Although the meanings of Pakeha masculinity were undergoing an important transition during this period, especially as a largely rural or frontier society became predominantly urban and suburban, and as the focus of many men's lives increasingly included home and family, there were significant continuities too: financial provision remained a key determinant of masculinity. As with femininity, masculinity was negotiated in all areas of life. Erik Olssen discusses the entrenchment of the male-breadwinner wage, and he and others consider its implications. John Stenhouse attends to the reasons for the relative absence of men from the churches and the negotiations around the meanings of Christianity for those who stayed. Barbara Brookes looks at the ways in which men's work made them especially vulnerable to severe injury. Annabel Cooper and Marian Horan discuss the expectations of men who could not support their families for reasons of injury or failure to find employment.

The theme of gender relations has also become central. Brian Heenan, for example, tracks the daily circulation pattern of the women and men of the Grimmett family, showing the very different journeys that emanated from one household, and also explaining that, even where they converged, gendered relationships dictated a demarcation of responsibilities. Robin Law's work on the development of new transport technologies shows how gendered patterns both formulated and were shaped by such new phenomena as the tram (where the sexes had their allocated spaces without particular privilege attached) and the private car (where hierarchy, rather than a simpler separation of spaces, prevailed). Chapter three on work and chapter four on education demonstrate how, over one short generation, the school and working lives of girls prepared them to be women unlike their mothers in important respects – to know different things and to hold different expectations – while boys were more likely to continue to follow in their fathers' footsteps. Barbara Brookes, Erik Olssen and Emma Beer discuss the fundamentally gendered meanings of the very concept of leisure, as well as the actual leisure pursuits of the women and men of the area. Jane Malthus and Chris Brickell's study of the production/consumption nexus shows how central gender was to the modernisation of these interrelated processes. Annabel Cooper and Marian Horan discuss the complex family dynamics associated with the earning and allocation of income within families, and the ways in which changing welfare policies helped to shape these dynamics.

As the cultural turn swept through the social sciences, increasing attention was paid to gender as a symbolic construct, a framework of difference by which meaning and value are ascribed to much more than women, men and relations between the sexes. Joan Scott's article on gender offers, as well as a genealogy of the term, a definition that seeks to explore this more recent attention to gender as a system of meaning. According to Scott, gender is both 'a constitutive element of social relationships based on perceived differences between the sexes' and 'a primary way of signifying relationships of power'.[23] In the first part of her definition, she shows how gender, like class or ethnicity, is implicated in the organisation of social relationships. In this process, symbolic representations (for example, the Virgin Mary) are invoked, normative concepts are articulated (for example, in scientific, legal and religious doctrines), social institutions are structured (for example, kinship, the labour market, education, the polity) and subjective identity is constructed.[24] In the second part of her definition, she discusses gender as a 'primary field within which or by means of which power is articulated'. Explaining this second part, Scott argues that gender is more than a concept that addresses the relative position of men and women; it 'provides a way to decode meaning' in a wider field of human interaction. Gender is drawn on to articulate power and to structure many aspects of social life beyond those that are immediately apparent as the domain of relations between men and women. She quotes Maurice Godelier, who contends that 'sex-related differences between bodies are continually summoned as testimony to social relations and phenomena that have nothing to do with sexuality. Not only as testimony to, but also testimony for – in other words, as legitimation.'[25] Recent historical work in New Zealand influenced by these developments – but drawing also, we argue, on the earlier phases – includes Caroline Daley and Deborah Montgomerie's collection *The Gendered Kiwi* and Bronwyn Dalley and Bronwyn Labrum's collection *Fragments*.[26]

Scott's category of 'subjective identity' has been the subject of intensive recent research. The cultural turn has also initiated the attention in many disciplines to questions of identity, subjectivity, memory and experience. This has long been the stuff of oral history (a source from which much of our work draws), but, as issues of language and discourse have come to the fore, oral history is seen less as a kind of immediate access to the past and more as material for interpretation: how, for example, might we interpret the language of femininities and masculinities? Discussions of experience and identity, such as those by Joan Scott and Denise Riley, question what it is to 'have' experience and how categories of identity change over time so that, for example, the term 'woman' might mean very different things at different times and places. Identity, including gender identity, has come to be seen less as a direct expression of an authentic inner self, and more as a culturally and historically shaped set of practices or performances.[27]

Although the authors of this volume have been influenced to varying degrees by the theoretical debates and the historical work outlined above, we have all used a multi-faceted definition of gender that directs attention to social relationships, symbolic representations and subjective identity. We have scrutinised historical records for what they say about differences in the ways that men and women or boys and girls behaved, about the norms that governed their behaviour and the doctrines that shaped their access to society's resources and participation in social institutions. We have searched for evidence about the way that gender operates as a binary pair, and the way that this binary was applied to many aspects of social life, gendering activities and objects as diverse as knitting needles and motorcycles. In the words of oral-history informants and the traces left in written documents, we have looked for insight into how dominant ideas of what it meant to be a woman or a man were accepted, contested, or transformed in people's sense of themselves as individuals.

The different authors of this volume share some elements of a common approach (and have tolerated many editorial interventions in the interests of producing a coherent volume rather than a series of unrelated chapters), but the perceptive reader will observe variations in emphasis and style. In part these are derived from the various disciplinary traditions that each author has brought to the shared project; the interplay of these differences has been one of the pleasures of collaboration. The variations are also the result of different kinds of historical sources and of different authors' positions in relation to gender politics. As editors, we have not tried to mute the different voices, but have left their variety intact in the hope that each has something worthwhile to offer to a diverse audience.

Situating the study in place

The approach taken in the Caversham project has been shaped by the historical and geographical parameters of the study. We have examined the operation of gender in a particular urban setting: southern Dunedin. Our focus has been on the neighbourhood or locality, and how that may be related to larger spatial entities such as city, nation-state and empire. Although the locality may be formally demarcated and mapped as a distinct, bounded territory within space, it is more than that. It is also a place created by socio-spatial practices that operate at a range of scales, but are expressed at the local level.

This notion of place as constituted by relationships and practices draws on recent work in human geography and anthropology.[28] The prevailing concepts in geography of space as a container and place as a territory defined by a set of coordinates on a map have been challenged. Places are now more often understood in terms of fluid and overlapping boundaries (social and spatial) created and maintained by practices of power and exclusion. These practices, which define places such as a locality, may occur at any scale (global, national, regional and so on). In Linda McDowell's words, places 'touch the ground as spatially located patterns and behaviours'.[29]

One of the ways in which places are constructed is through the practices and meanings of gender. As Louise Johnson observes, 'geographical space has come to be seen not as a neutral container of social and bio-physical relations but as a medium which registers and expresses power and sexual difference'.[30] Feminist geographers have argued that place and gender must be seen in dialectical relationship, as mutually constitutive. Linda McDowell and Joanne Sharp explain it thus:

> The spaces in which social practices occur affect the nature of those practices, who is 'in place', who is 'out of place' and even who is allowed to be there at all. But the spaces themselves in turn are constructed and given meaning through the social practices that define men and women as different and unequal. Physical and social boundaries reinforce each other and spatial relations act to socialise people into the acceptance of gendered power relations – they reinforce

power, privileges and oppression and literally keep women in their place. But one can also 'push against oppressive boundaries' . . . to challenge dominant power, taking it on from the margins.[31]

A range of work in feminist geography has explored the many ways in which place and gender interact.[32] For example, a recent book by N. Laurie *et al.* explores notions of femininity, arguing that gendered identities are constituted in and through particular sites.[33] Gender history, too, has been attentive to the interaction of gender and place. Dean Wilson argues that gender defined the nature of community in nineteenth-century central Auckland, with women's networks of tight mutual dependence rooted firmly in their immediate neighbourhood, and those of men operating in much more diffuse patterns both socially and spatially.[34]

In this book, we examine the dialectical relationship between gender and place over the decades. Our focus is on the spatial scale of neighbourhood or suburb – what we call locality. Southern Dunedin provides the bounded frame within which we trace change over time in a variety of interlinked activities. This locality is inserted into a larger set of spatial structures, notably Dunedin city, Otago province, the New Zealand nation state (the last seen both as distinctive and as representative of New World settler societies) and the British Empire. This work complements other place-specific studies in New Zealand, such as Daley's study of the small rural town of Taradale. The locality is discussed in greater detail in the next chapter.

Within the locality of southern Dunedin we discuss particular places, such as the Grimmett family home 'Faringdon Villa', the Hillside Workshops, the Otago Benevolent Institution and the churches and schools. The built environment of southern Dunedin included homes, streets, churches, schools, parks, pubs, lodges, sports clubs, factories, offices and shops. These were the sites within which the residents of southern Dunedin made their daily lives and which helped to give meaning to their existence, and they were 'sites of gender' where gender was performed. Each of these sites was used and occupied in ways that were shaped by the dominant understandings of gender at the time; but gender might also be performed differently according to specific sites.

The term 'site' is used in this book in two ways. First, it refers to the kinds of places described above, which were physical entities in socially and culturally mapped space. The particularity of this locality, containing both industrial and residential areas – and often combining the two – is part of our focus. Sites in this usage are the contexts of gendered behaviour; they bear gendered cultural meaning and they are the frameworks against which men, women, girls and boys develop a sense of their own gendered subjectivity. Second, 'site' also refers to a domain or a cluster of social practices and ideas that are expressed in a variety of physical spaces. The broad domains of work, education, consumption, leisure, poverty, mobility, transport, health, religion and (more briefly) marriage, which are the subjects of the chapters in this volume, are key arenas of social life in which gender was enacted, and which both shaped and were shaped by gender. The authors have examined these domains as sites in which the various interrelated levels of gendered practice as elaborated by Scott can be seen in operation. In each of these sites, whether physical or social, it becomes clear that the gendered story is by no means a simple or a single one: at any of these interrelated levels, more than one narrative might be in train.

The interrelation of these two meanings becomes apparent if we consider some of the spaces within our locality. We might begin at the micro-level of the different rooms of the house – generally areas where women were most 'in place', to adopt McDowell and Sharp's terms. The kitchen, the laundry and the bathroom were the rooms in which a mother's responsibilities for her family's nutrition and the long labours needed to keep clothes, bedding and bodies clean and germ-free were undertaken. Kitchen and laundry were indisputably a mother's territory and their systems and routines, though shaped by the practices of her family and neighbours, were managed by her. Other rooms might not be so specifically under her control, but 'inside' was, almost always, a woman's responsibility. The border between house and street marked the boundary between family privacy and public space, and for many women that space was deployed to signify (one's own) or to interpret (another's) domestic capability: the cleanliness of the front step was a widely understood sign of the level of domestic order within.

The demarcation between inside the house and outside was commonly understood to mark the point where men's domestic activities began, although many fathers' responsibilities included such tasks as mending the family's shoes, or carpentry in and around the house, as well as the maintenance of sometimes extensive vegetable gardens outside. Yet, as we go on to argue, the pattern of widespread home ownership and the suburban values of domesticity and neighbourhood oriented a majority of men as well as women in these communities towards the home. Our evidence confirms the view that the period saw a broad domestication of masculinity: even while the home remained primarily a woman's domain, the 'family man' became typical, less and less 'out of place' in the home.[35]

Men, women and children all passed through the next set of spaces, the streets, at different times of the day and for different purposes (as Brian Heenan relates, tracing the daily paths of one family). The populations of these physical 'sites' were determined by their differing participation in social 'sites': work, domestic production, education, consumption and leisure. Early in the morning, the streets were full of men whistling their way to work, mostly on foot or bicycle, with some working women (mostly young and unmarried) among them – they might be on their way to the tram if they were among the many women employed in the clothing or other manufacturing businesses in the city. A little later, school children walked together on their way to school, and as the morning wore on housewives might venture forth to carry out household business, visit nearby family, or shop – the last an activity which, over our period, took on greater importance as home production dropped and was replaced with greater reliance on store-bought goods. Most women would be back home again, however, in time to prepare the midday dinner for the men and children, who dashed home, ate, and took off again for work or school. Before the dominance of the private car, as Robin Law demonstrates, walking, cycling and the trams made the streets sites of relatively egalitarian mingling.

Neighbourhood streets were in many respects the domain of children, who could be said to have lived in them while adults only traversed them. Here (as well as in families and in schools) gender was reproduced: boys formed gangs and perhaps made forays off to fight other streets' gangs, 'big girls' minded their baby sisters and brothers, girls played girls' games with girls, and boys with other boys. Boys might range over a wider area, being less likely to be called on to help in the house, or to generate anxiety for their safety. Many of our oral informants saw the streets as safer spaces than they are now, even quite late at night: in the age of frequent walkers, there were usually plenty of people about. They might also be the location of behaviour that 'push[ed] against oppressive boundaries', such as the loud and rackety Friday night 'yahooing' of the 'matchy tarts' from the Wax Vesta match factory, who were ticked off when they returned to the more disciplined site of their workplace (as Robin Law relates in chapter nine).

Among the area's institutions, some were sites of convergence, where people of both sexes met. Even these sites, however, participated in the organisation of gender. For children, the schools were the obvious example. Dorothy Page, Howard Lee and Tom Brooking show how the extended schooling more common after the turn of the century meant an increasing similarity between the lives of older girls and boys – though schooling practices might have ensured that their school experiences differed. For adults as well as children, the churches were the focus of regular social gathering. Though they were ostensibly united in common purpose, John Stenhouse's closer inspection reveals that commonality to be marked by different activities and alliances;

and, even though women made up most of the church members, men dominated the pulpit. Locations such as the Grimmetts' garden plot were the sites of separate activities, engaged in by women and men alongside each other.

Other sites separated the sexes more formally. Pubs, lodges, sports clubs and the larger workplaces were the most significant of these (with the exception of some lodges and sports clubs, these were all masculine spaces, either by regulation or custom). From 1910 legislation banned women from working in the all-male environments of pubs.[36] Large employers of men such as the Hillside Workshops were, as Erik Olssen has argued in *Building the New World*, the site of significant developments in the way masculinity was understood in the context of work, although the effects extended beyond the workplace into politics and back into the home. It was seldom that a woman entered this masculine terrain, although men did work in several occupations in the largely female workforce of the Wax Vesta Factory. However, most women in the paid workforce were employed in smaller workplaces that were more likely to be mixed, especially where there was a male employer.

Most of these sites – those we have mentioned above, such as the streets, schools and churches, and of course the largely owner-occupied homes – were being replicated in very similar forms across the rest of New Zealand as cities 'grew' suburbs. But others – or rather the high concentration of them – marked our area as distinctive. The southern suburbs' concentration of heavy industry in parts of a predominantly residential area produced large employers of men and the all-male communities that formed in and from them. The area's concentration of charitable institutions such as the Benevolent Home (with its largely elderly and male inmates) and the Industrial School (with its population of 'problem' children) also produced gender- or age-specific groups readily identified by the rest of the community. In the next chapter, we discuss the southern suburbs' distinctiveness as a locality.

Two The Landscape of Gender Politics: Place, People and Two Mobilisations

ANNABEL COOPER, ERIK OLSSEN,
KIRSTEN THOMLINSON AND ROBIN LAW

This chapter is designed to set the scene for those that follow: to give an account of Dunedin's southern suburbs and their development after 1840, of their patterns of settlement and how these differed from the rest of Dunedin and among the different suburbs. The final section of the chapter anticipates the argument of the book as a whole – that gender is both 'embedded' in place and helps to constitute it – in discussing two distinctly gendered events from the beginning of our period. Both events unfolded nationally, but both can be shown to have had deep roots in the southern suburbs of Dunedin.

In the 1880s and 1890s, working men mobilised on a scale unprecedented in New Zealand. Although this was a national – in fact a trans-Tasman – movement, the activity in New Zealand was at its most intense in the Dunedin-Port Chalmers area. The *Otago Workman*, produced in the heart of working-class southern Dunedin, was its radical mouthpiece, and workplaces, pubs and homes across the southern Dunedin Flat hummed with talk of unions and united action. The elected representatives of these working men played a decisive role in forging the legislative conditions for the 'wage workers' welfare state'. At the same time, as we have signalled in our introduction to this volume, women were mobilising in support of a different goal: the right to vote. A series of petitions circulating in the early 1890s demanded adult female suffrage, and increasing numbers of women of voting age added their names to the list. The third of these petitions, and the pro-suffrage activity that surrounded it, was successful and women voted for the first time in 1893. As we go on to show, southern Dunedin women supported this petition in astonishingly high numbers. This chapter, then, has two functions: first, it draws an outline of the geographical character and the settlement of this area, in order to survey the ground for the volume as a whole. Second, using some of the evidence produced by this 'groundwork', it concludes by addressing the two mobilisations at the beginning of the period under study. Why were the supporters of these political movements particularly active in this place? Can we complicate the stories that are usually told about these mobilisations: in one case, a narrative of class and, in the other, a narrative of gender? Were they more closely related than they at first appear? And what part did they play in establishing the setting for the transitions in gender that were to play out over the next fifty years?

When we focus on streets and neighbourhoods we quickly note what Mark Granovetter calls 'embeddedness' – individuals in households are embedded in networks of association just as economic life is embedded in social life.[1] As Hanson and Pratt have argued, the notion of embeddedness has a distinct geographical resonance. Indeed, the consideration of locality as central to determining the meaning of social and cultural practices has obtained significant salience among geographers over the last fifteen years.[2] As this volume contends, it has a powerful bearing on the emergence of specific gendered patterns. In order to open up these questions, and in order to sketch out the scene for the rest of this book, we need to consider the nature of the territory: the land itself, its settlement processes, and the changes in its developing society before our period begins in 1890. Although the lie of the land created the area's topographical boundaries, the people of the southern suburbs forged a complex set of interwoven and contrasting identities within those boundaries. Each suburb acquired a distinct character, defined by the interactions between topography, the division and ownership of land, the timing and processes of settlement, the siting of large and small industries, and the occupational class, religion, age and origin of the settlers. This part of the chapter owes an important debt to the work of G. N. Stedman, whose MA thesis on the southern Dunedin Flat has saved us – and other authors in the volume – a great deal of work.[3]

In the nineteenth century, the area covered by this study linked the Otago Peninsula to the mainland, and separated Otago Harbour from the Pacific Ocean. (Extensive reclamation has since altered the harbour edge dramatically.)[4] The area includes the once independent boroughs of Caversham, South Dunedin, and St Kilda (which amalgamated with Dunedin in 1904, 1905 and 1989 respectively). Caversham, the largest and, topographically and socially, the most complex of the boroughs, included the suburbs of Kensington, Kew and St Clair as well as Caversham itself. South Dunedin also included the area

THE LANDSCAPE OF GENDER POLITICS

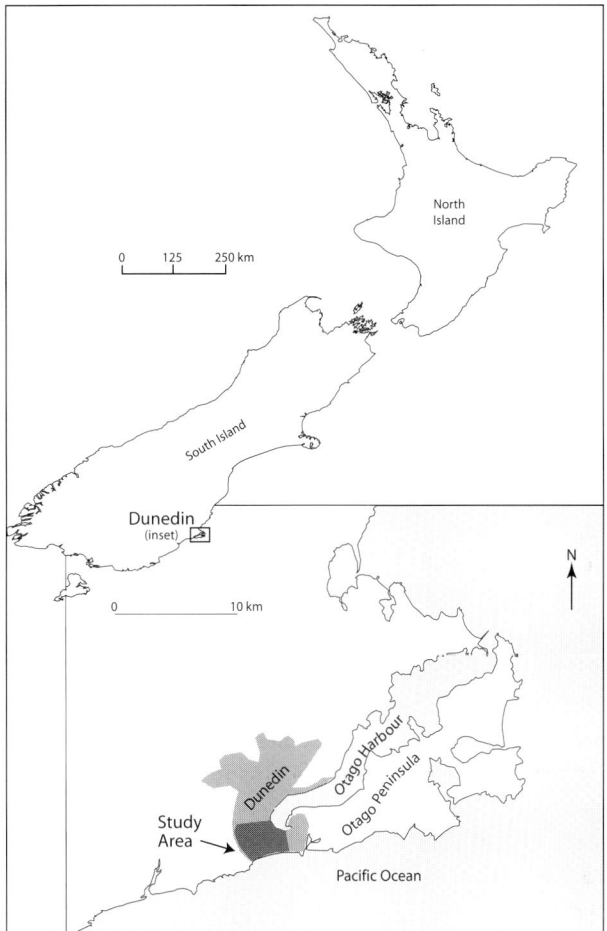

MAP 2.1 Location of the study area

known as Forbury.[5] The chapters in this volume all rely on the Caversham Project Database, whose population consists of more than 70,000 people who registered to vote or who lived on a street within the boundaries of these three former boroughs during the period 1890–1940.[6] We refer to the area as a whole as 'the southern suburbs', 'southern Dunedin' or 'the study area'. 'South Dunedin' refers specifically to the suburb and borough of that name. 'The Flat', a name still widely used, includes all of South Dunedin, St Kilda, and the area of Caversham Borough to the south of the Main South Rd and east of Playfair St. 'The Flat' – not surprisingly – excludes the hilly areas of St Clair, Kew, Rockyside, Caversham Rise and Caversham Extension.

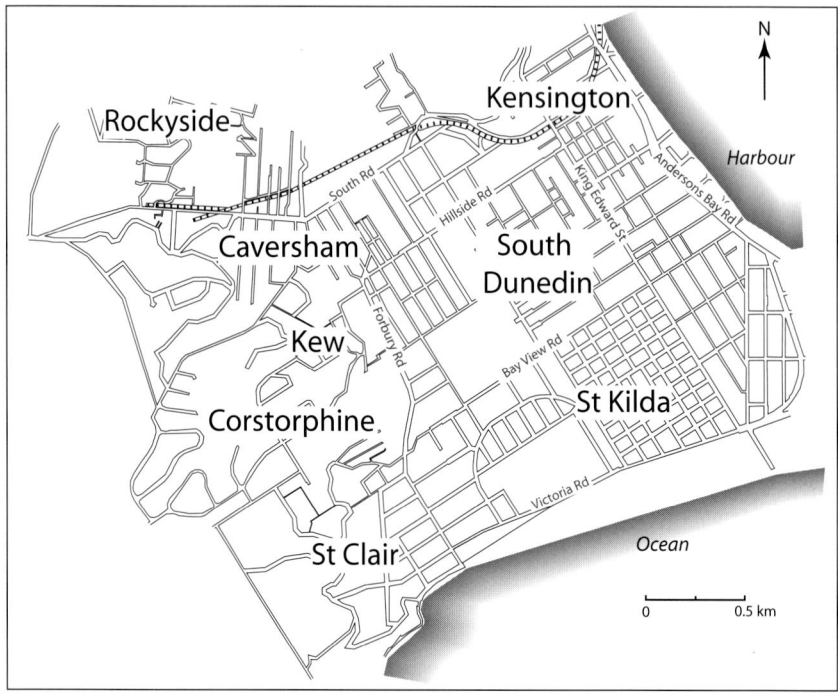

MAP 2.2 The suburbs of southern Dunedin

From 'the Swamp' to 'the Flat': the rise of the southern suburbs

Prior to European settlement, the area now known as the Flat was mostly low-lying swampy land that had been part of the territory of the Ngai Tahu people. Although they regularly used the rich resources of the area, it had not been a site of permanent occupation. They travelled from the settlement at Otakou near the mouth of the harbour to catch eels, crayfish, fish, pukeko, ducks and weka.[7] To travel past the swamp on the main pre-European coastal route south, they took a path that ran along the inside of extensive sandhills bordering the ocean.[8] In 1844 the area was purchased as part of the Otago block and passed into British jurisdiction. Although some of our interviewees had childhood memories of seeing Maori using the old path south, or of amateur archaeological finds, Pakeha settlement effectively destroyed the resources Maori had drawn on and all but erased the visible presence of Ngai Tahu in the area.[9] Within fifty years the immigrants' drainage, reclamation and horticultural practices had transformed the salt-marshes. Almost 12,000 years of Eurasian history was compressed into a couple of generations, and the uses of the land changed forever.

Thomas Litchfield Stanley, first vicar of Caversham, captured this view of the 'swampy flat' in 1869. It looks from the bottom of Caversham Rise to the sand dunes and the ocean, across what would become the suburbs of South Dunedin, Caversham, St Kilda and St Clair. The early farms and the beginnings of settlement on the slopes and the higher ground of the Flat, in the middle foreground, are evident. W. H. Valpy's farm, 'The Forbury', covered the lighter area of flat ground in the centre right of the picture, and the Benevolent Institution can just be seen at the centre right edge. HOCKEN LIBRARY

The transformation of wildlife-rich swamp into farmland, and then suburban and industrial land, was not immediate, however. Beyond the western and northern slopes and the strip of elevated land skirting them, Pakeha settlement was scattered and farming predominated until the 1880s. Although market gardens and nurseries remained important throughout the period, the Central Otago gold rushes, from 1861, saw Caversham township established as the first stop for travellers heading either south or into Central Otago. The township grew up at the foot of the Caversham Valley, close to the 'Swamp Rd', the main route south and thence inland. With a slightly higher elevation than the rest of what was to become 'the Flat', a pub, a post office and a school, it offered the nucleus for urban settlement.[10] A limeworks exploited the local sandstone, and the first few dwellings and small industries were established. With the completion of the first section of the main trunk railway south, and stations at Kensington and Caversham, not to mention relocation of the Otago immigration barracks to Caversham in 1873, those two areas (Caversham and Kensington) became the hub for a rapid expansion of industry and population.[11]

The settlement of the northern and southern halves of the Flat developed quite differently. In the north, the urbanisation of Caversham, South Dunedin and Kensington took place in the last quarter of the nineteenth century; the greater part of the expansion of St Clair, Kew and St Kilda, the southern half of the Flat, occurred in the twentieth. From the 1870s industry and commercial enterprises dominated the northern part, and were often mixed higgledy-piggledy with residential houses. People who lived here also often worked here. St Clair, St Kilda and Kew, by contrast, were developed exclusively as residential suburbs, with the pattern of streets of houses surrounded by the considerable number of parks and recreational facilities. Most residents in paid work (except for those employed in other people's houses) travelled out of these suburbs for the purpose. By the time the entire area was urbanised (around 1930), the traces of these differences marked the character of each.[12] Where Dunedin itself was an early Victorian city, therefore, the southern suburbs straddled the late Victorian era and the emergence of modernity.

The infrastructure developed piecemeal. In the 1880s gas pipes were laid along the main streets of Caversham and South Dunedin boroughs for lighting. Some gas was reticulated to private homes, and water was reticulated through Caversham, South Dunedin and parts of St Kilda.[13] Although dairying had largely retreated to the hills surrounding the Flat, most of the southern half of the Flat still retained a rural character. Substantial nurseries occupied some of the sunnier slopes, and Chinese market gardeners, mostly ex-gold miners, worked about 20 hectares straddling Caversham and South Dunedin.[14] Extensive gardens and orchards also surrounded the Benevolent Institution and the Industrial School (two important regional institutions established in 1862 and 1869 respectively). Horses grazed extensive areas around Forbury racetrack. As subdivisions were built, the main roads and streets were formed, then paved and lit, and from 1880 horse-drawn trams linked most of the Flat, including St Clair and St Kilda, to the city. Because of the high cost of widening the streets to allow electric tramlines to be laid, Caversham Borough's ratepayers voted to amalgamate with Dunedin City in 1904. South Dunedin followed suit in 1905. Attempts to deal with the drainage problem were sluggish: until 1910–11 high tide and spring tides saw the open drains of South Dunedin and Caversham reverse themselves so that the human effluent and rubbish floated back up the Flat towards the Kew–St Clair Rise. Only after the great flood of 1923 was significant progress made in ensuring that South Dunedin and Caversham were waterproofed. St Kilda took even longer.[15]

'The Flat' acquired much of its distinctive character precisely because it *was* flat. The stretch of land between harbour and ocean was by far the largest

The rapid expansion of the Hillside Railway Workshops saw them invade and consume whole Kensington streets. In this 1926 photograph the cheek-by-jowl proximity of the industrial and the residential, typical of parts of the northern Flat, is evident. The King Edward Theatre on King Edward St near Cargill's Corner is the large building in the left background. ALEXANDER TURNBULL LIBRARY, F 92604 1/2

area of flat land close to the city. The higher land, which was also close to the railway and the Main South Rd (as 'Swamp Rd', the southern route out of Dunedin, became known), was quickly identified as some of the city's best land for industry. Its proximity to the sea attracted residents seeking a healthy environment, and the higher flat land, close to the railway and close enough to the port, attracted industry. Both arrived, and the industry provided a livelihood for many of the residents. The industry that did most to define the northern part of the area as an industrial suburb arrived early, in 1874, when the government railway workshops were relocated to Hillside. Over the next ten years, other large industrial concerns followed. As noted, the two main loci, Kensington and Caversham, were close to the railway. In Kensington, W. M. White's pipe factory (subsequently Lambert's and later McSkimming's), a flour mill, and Smith and Fotheringham's brickyards were established close by the Hillside Workshops. McKinlay's bootmaking factory overlooked them from the bottom of the Caversham Rise. The city's gasworks, close by in South Dunedin, made this one of Dunedin's most industrial areas.

In the Caversham township area were a tannery and quarry, the Wax Vesta match factory, Briggs's and Cowie and Co's breweries, several large bakeries and clothes-making workshops, and the first gasworks. Other sizeable industrial establishments were scattered. Donaghy's rope works ran along the edge of Bathgate Park in South Dunedin; a tannery and Fox's substantial quarry were established at the Glen, at the foot of the Mornington hill; George

Methven's large factory for manufacturing plumbing supplies dominated the foreshore; and the Shiel brothers' large quarry and brickfield, first situated near the township, dominated Forbury for most of the period under study. Other industries came and went more briefly, including Fletcher Brothers Construction (1911–23), Alfred Morris's Dubbin factory (1902–20) and various lolly and cordial factories.

As G. N. Stedman notes, these industries gave the area 'its distinctive character. [They] dominated the urban scene ... on account of both their physical extent and the size of the labour force working in them.'[16] The industrial infrastructure changed little after 1890 (some industries moved site, but very few left the area). Industry played a major part in producing a distinct occupational structure and a distinctively gendered urban society. By the turn of the twentieth century the Hillside Railway Workshops had expanded to occupy over 7 hectares, swallowing up a number of streets and employing over 400 men.[17]

The occupation of southern Dunedin

The workforce followed the industries, occupying first the northern half of the area and then expanding into the southern half and occupying the hills. It is a relatively straightforward exercise to describe the male occupational structure.[18] By 1900 manual workers and self-employed tradesmen comprised more than half of the inhabitants of the oldest southern boroughs, Caversham and South Dunedin, and roughly one-third of the emerging new borough of St Kilda. Across the entire study area, skilled tradesmen – the artisans and mechanics of the pre-war period – constituted the largest single occupational class. In 1902 13 per cent of all skilled men worked in the metal trades and another 12.5 per cent worked in the building trades (forty years later the figures had dropped to 9 per cent for each of the two industries). Most of the self-employed and small employers had graduated from the ranks of the skilled tradesmen, shared their core values and belonged to the same churches, friendly societies and sports clubs. Allegiance to craft cut across class and linked 'middle-class' masters – artisans who had set up on their own account – to the working-class journeymen and apprentices they employed. Most of the unskilled – around 25 per cent of the population – also worked alongside skilled men and shared their values.

The dramatic growth of white-collar occupations during the period 1890–1939 constituted the most important change in the occupational structure, both locally and nationally. This growth contributed to the decline in the proportion of self-employed in handicraft trades from just over 12 per

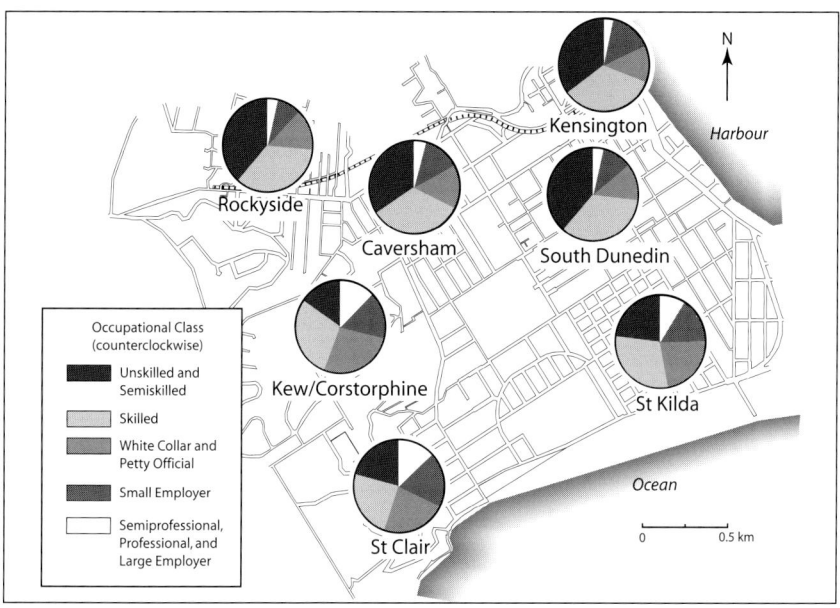

MAP 2.3 Male occupational class by suburb, 1891–1939

cent to just under 7 per cent across the period 1902–38. The growth of white-collar occupations also reduced the proportion of skilled tradesmen across the period from 37 to 29 per cent. In absolute terms, however, the numbers of skilled, self-employed and small businessmen grew.[19]

Evidence about the female occupational structure is much more limited. Electoral rolls – the main source for the figures on male occupational structure – ignored women's occupations from 1902 onwards. The Registrar of Births, Deaths and Marriages followed suit. But there were significant developments. Quite apart from the remarkable growth in employment for unmarried women, first in factories and then in shops and offices, discussed in chapter three, many women ran businesses or subcontracted work from their own homes. For most women and men, marriage represented entry into the world of adults, but for women it also marked a career change, and almost always departure from paid work. The housewife's domestic work – a full-time job for most married women – freed her husband and later her dependent children to take full-time work. As we discovered in the first phase of the oral-history project, most housewives also contributed substantially to the family's income through various forms of self-provisioning – making jams and preserves, sewing and knitting, and so on.[20] High levels of per capita income for men, however, here as elsewhere, made the male-breadwinner wage critical in determining the material well-being of most households in the southern suburbs.[21] Therefore, although the male occupational structure is a problematic way of defining the class structure, it is by far our most detailed and reliable source here.[22]

In the period 1900–40 the demographic characteristics of the southern suburbs changed more than the occupational structure. The total population grew steadily. Caversham and South Dunedin boroughs grew rapidly in the last quarter of the nineteenth century, boasting populations of 5266 and 5363 respectively in 1901. St Kilda grew most rapidly, from 383 persons in 1881 to 1700 in 1901. (Together these three boroughs comprised almost 25 per cent of greater Dunedin's population.) Over the next forty years the population continued to grow, with South Dunedin reaching roughly 6680 and Caversham more than 9000 in 1936. Over that period St Kilda also continued to grow until it reached almost 8000 in 1926, at which point it was the most densely settled borough in the country (South Dunedin and large parts of the old Caversham borough were even more densely settled, but no longer enjoyed the legal status of boroughs).[23] Steady growth was not the only significant change. Between the 1870s and the First World War, the sex ratio changed: an excess of males gave way in the 1880s and 90s to an excess of females, in common with most urban areas. The excess of females became quite marked because of high male mortality rates in the war.[24]

Over the same period, the predominantly youthful population of the 1870s acquired a more mature age distribution. Indeed, the population aged with dramatic speed during the 1890s, both in the study area and in Otago. Because of the Benevolent's role in caring for old men, residents in Parkside and Caversham township were particularly conscious of this change.[25] Equally striking is the fact – the significance of which has been less fully explored – that a population of immigrants, mainly from Britain, had become a society of New Zealanders. Both the census data and the information on place of birth in our marriage database confirm that in 1891 most adults had been born in Britain, but most of those under 21 had been born in New Zealand. During the next twenty years the native-born became a majority of adults also. The marriage database, which includes 10,000 persons, reveals the trend. Over 80 per cent of those marrying in the 1880s had been born in Britain; in the 1890s about half were New Zealand-born; and in the 1900s more than 80 per cent of brides and almost 70 per cent of grooms were New Zealand-born. By the 1930s the natives were 91 per cent of brides and almost 88 per cent of grooms.[26] (Variations existed across the area, to which we shall return.)

Most of the men and women who lived in the southern suburbs married and had children. Around 10 per cent of all women were widows, a figure that remained consistent across the period. Possibly as a result of the changing sex ratio, the proportion of women who married fell locally across the period (although the shift was slight).[27] The rapid expansion of women's employment in the semi-professions, a marked feature nationally across the period, probably in part reflects this urban demographic reality. The project's marriage-register database indicates that men married for the first time, on average, at just over twenty-seven years old and women at twenty-five years old. Within the southern suburbs, the average age of first marriage does not appear to have changed significantly across the period, despite the downward national trend, partly because of a dramatic shift in the local age-specific distributions, especially for women.[28] The proportion of southern Dunedin brides who were younger than twenty-one when they married fell dramatically (from more than 25 per cent in the 1880s to less than 12 per cent in the 1900s and each successive decade). Not only did the proportion of brides under twenty-one decline, but the proportion in their thirties also grew from a negligible 3.3 per cent in the 1880s to more than 12 per cent in the 1910s and thereafter (around 20 per cent of men waited until their thirties before marrying for the first time). The census tables confirm these trends.[29]

When women postpone marriage, fertility typically declines. The national decline in Pakeha fertility during this period has been well established. As Brian Heenan has observed, urban fertility in New Zealand peaked in 1881 and then began a period of 'prolonged decline' that lasted until the end of the 1930s. Two sharp falls punctuated this long-term fall, the first occurring during the 'Long Depression' of the 1880s and 90s, and the second taking place during the so-called 'Great Depression' of the late 1920s and 1930s.[30] We lack data for the Great Depression, but census data for the three southern boroughs through the Long Depression confirms that the fertility rate halved between 1881 and 1901 (although the southern boroughs still had the Dunedin urban area's highest rates).[31] Over the next twenty years the fertility rate continued to fall both in Dunedin and New Zealand and, though census data is not available for the study area in this period, we assume that the same trend continued in the southern suburbs. According to Miriam Vosburgh, women with issue who married in 1880 had averaged 6.9 live births; women with issue who married for the first time in 1920 would average just over three births during their fertile years. Although Vosburgh found that working-class couples lagged behind the late nineteenth-century trend, by the end of our period the differential had disappeared.[32] As a result, parents invested more both financially and emotionally in their children; the impact of repeated pregnancy and childbearing on the time and health of married women was substantially limited; the need for help in the house declined; and the burden of expectation on many daughters was dramatically reduced. The crashing fertility rate resoundingly signalled a fundamental transformation in the lives of women and relations between the sexes. The meaning of bodily difference had been radically altered.

Suburban variations

The demographic and occupational characteristics of the three boroughs varied, and significant variations existed within Caversham Borough (which now comprises five modern suburbs). Map 2.3 summarises the variations in occupational structure. Before 1901 the census allows us to sketch the variations of importance to this study. Thereafter we rely on the Caversham Project's database, which has been derived from several sources (see Appendix II). Although much of our work has shown how complex local society was, thus defying the tendency to generalise, it is helpful to start by recognising the

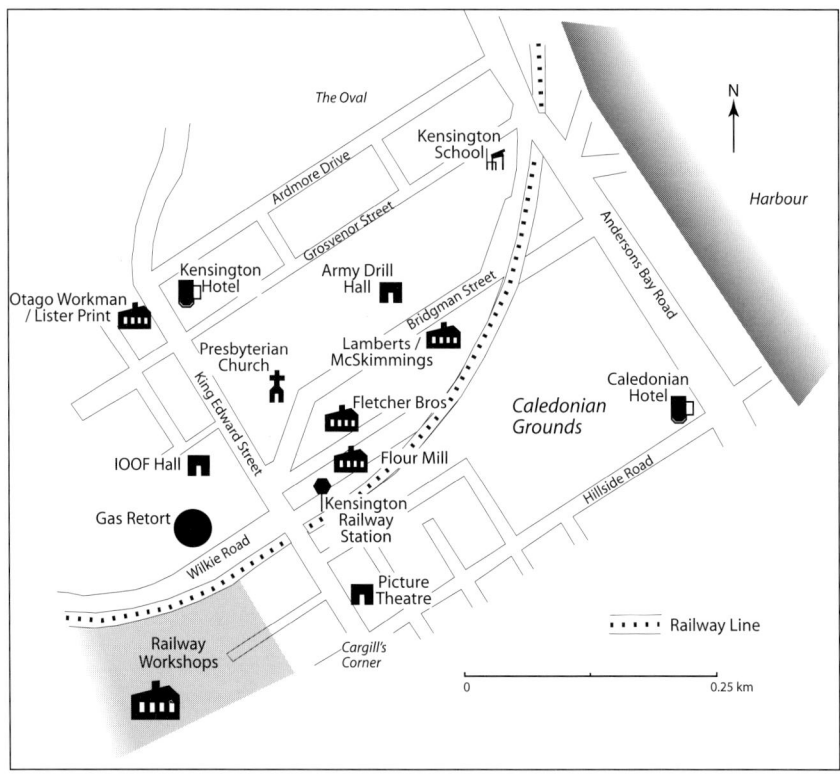

MAP 2.4 Kensington

THE LANDSCAPE OF GENDER POLITICS

Kensington east of King Edward St, with South Dunedin in the background, 1901. Sections were small and houses close together. In the left foreground is the edge of the Oval. Beyond Kensington's houses open space remains, with the railway, not visible here, running through part of it. The nearer part of this ground would be subdivided in the following decade. Beyond that is the Caledonian Ground with its grandstand. Behind the Caledonian, the gasworks in South Dunedin are just visible. To the right of the Caledonian, east Kensington's industry is concentrated. The Hillside workshops are out of the picture, to the right. Anderson's Bay Rd runs along the (as yet unreclaimed) harbour's edge. HOCKEN LIBRARY

major contemporary (and current) images of the three boroughs. As we have seen, the northern half of the Flat (most of Caversham Borough and all of South Dunedin) was dominated by industries and was widely seen as working class. South Dunedin had a greater concentration of low-value housing than Caversham. The housing stock in the oldest settled parts, particularly Kensington and the area of South Dunedin adjacent to it, deteriorated across the period. When the 1936–37 Housing Survey undertook an inventory of the city's slums, most of the substandard housing was concentrated in those older areas.[33] As we have noted, the southern half of the Flat, St Clair and St Kilda, was exclusively residential and dominated by larger houses, more recently built, and higher average property values. It was widely seen as more affluent and had a higher proportion of white-collar workers. In these newer suburbs, home and family were truly enclaves, separate from the working world and the smoky grime that often blew across the older areas.[34]

These images were not unrelated to reality. Caversham Borough contained three identifiably different, and geographically distinct, broad areas, two of which were at the foot of the hills that bounded the Flat to the north. These two areas, Kensington and Caversham township, were the first settled parts of the Flat. Kensington was a relatively self-contained suburb, separated from Caversham township by empty paddocks and Carisbrook. In some respects Kensington was closer to adjacent South Dunedin. Industries dominated

27

this suburb – now largely displaced by motorways and light industries – and it was within easy walking distance of the concentration of industries and businesses immediately to the east. Most of the houses were four- or five-roomed wooden cottages, increasingly grimy thanks to the smoke from the nearby gasworks and the railway running sheds on the other side of the Oval. In 1922 most of the houses were rental rather than owner-occupied. In 1902 more than 40 per cent of all residents were skilled and 24 per cent unskilled, another 11 per cent being self-employed. Only 11.5 per cent of residents had white-collar jobs, one of the lowest proportions in the study area. By the end of the period, the unskilled (now 32 per cent) had supplanted the skilled (26 per cent) as the dominant group. A slightly higher proportion of white-collar workers now lived in Kensington and there was still around 3 per cent who were large-businessmen, professionals and semi-professionals. In the 1890s Kensington strongly opposed no-licence (that is, prohibition) and always gave strong support to Liberal–Labour and later independent Labour Party candidates.[35] In 1902 some 19 per cent of the study area's population lived here; by 1938 that figure had fallen to 13.4 per cent.

Caversham township, comprising one-third of the study area's population at the start of the period, was topographically and socially complex. Apart from the township, which centred on the business and retail strip, the area known as Caversham included some distinct sub-areas (see Map 2.5). The most important were Rockyside (to the north of the valley), Calderville (at the bottom of the valley) and Parkside (the area between the Benevolent Institution and Carisbrook). Caversham Rise and Caversham Extension, the

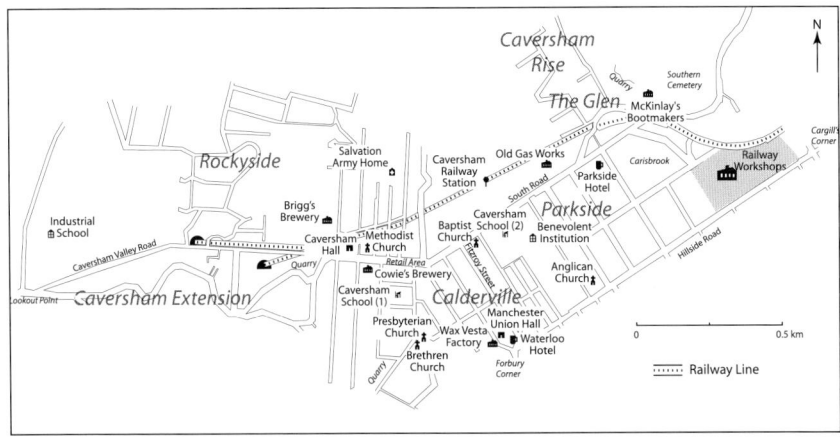

Map 2.5 Northern Caversham Borough: Caversham township, Rockyside, Calderville and Parkside through to the Glen and Caversham Rise

The northern part of Caversham Borough, taken from Caversham Extension. The South Rd runs through the centre of the image, then disappears as it beomes Caversham Valley Rd and passes through the two-storeyed buildings of the Caversham retail strip at the left of the image. Rockyside lies on the hill above the valley, with the chimney of the old gasworks (long disused by this time), Fox's quarry, and Caversham Rise visible before the harbour. Calderville and Parkside occupy the area to the right of the South Rd. HOCKEN LIBRARY

latter topographically contained but linked by a footpath to the township, completed this geographical essay in complexity. In the 1920s substantial growth also occurred in Calton Hill, a new subdivision lying on the hill between Kew and Caversham Valley.

The skilled and the unskilled dominated Caversham at the start and the end of the period. White-collar workers also settled in the suburb (12 per cent in 1902 and 17 per cent in 1938) and small businessmen, many of them in handicraft trades, often lived near their workshops or businesses in the area (13 per cent in 1902 but just under 6 per cent in 1938). In those parts of the suburb covered by the Housing Survey of 1936–37, most of Calderville and some of Parkside, home ownership was high. So was the proportion of English-born immigrants (they outnumbered Scots, a rare occurrence in Dunedin). One or two interviewees thought Caversham the heartland of the English presence in Dunedin.[36] There is anecdotal evidence to suggest that this idea had some truth to it. Many of the more prominent Scots had spent many years in England before migrating to the colony; the Presbyterian minister for most of the period was an Englishman; and distinctively English churches, notably the Baptists and the Wesleyans, were present in much greater strength than in Dunedin or New Zealand as a whole. Politically, the voting booths in Caversham suburb were staunchly pro-Liberal–Labour and then narrowly preferred Labour or Socialist candidates from 1914 onwards (the township became part of Dunedin Central in 1911 and by 1922 much of the borough belonged to that electorate). In the 1890s the polling booth at Caversham Hall, close by a rowdy pub, gave stronger support to no-licence than most booths in the southern suburbs, although the majority preferred continuance of the status quo. In Calderville and Parkside – particularly Parkside – well over half favoured reduction or no-licence, even in the 1890s.

South Dunedin, lying between the boroughs of Caversham and St Kilda, was geographically the centre of the Flat, and of the southern suburbs. The streets adjacent to Hillside Rd, many of them narrow, linked by even more narrow lanes and dominated by small wooden cottages, were settled first. The streets to the south and west, settled later, were wider and small wooden cottages were fewer. South Dunedin contained the second substantial retail strip, on King Edward St (in fact it was Dunedin's second most significant retail area). In 1902 30 per cent of the study area's population lived in South Dunedin; in 1938 it was 21.5 per cent. It was also in many respects symbolically central, for it came to be synonymous with the working class, both for

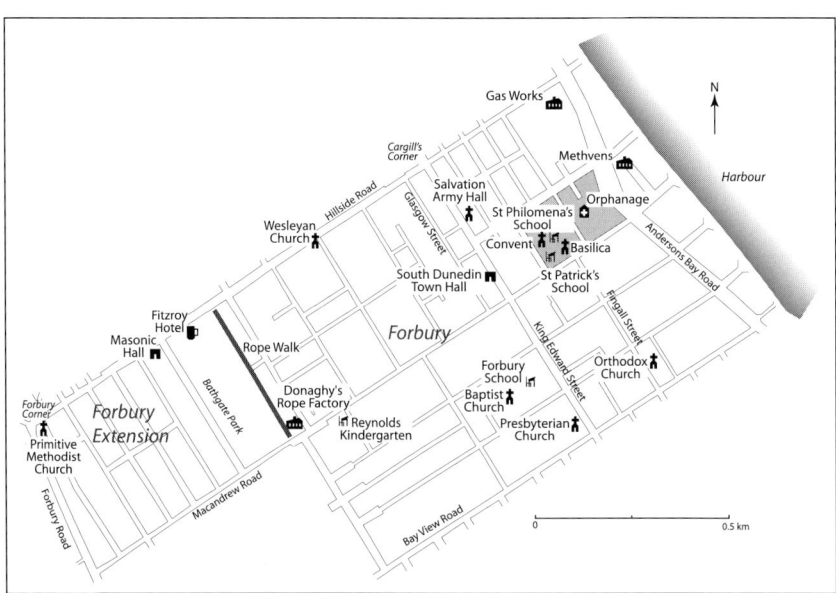

Map 2.6 South Dunedin

South Dunedin in 1910, with Macandrew Rd running diagonally from the bottom left of the image. The cluster of large buildings on its right is Macandrew Rd School. Market gardens still occupy much of the area in the foreground, part of Caversham Borough. Bathgate Park, with the Donaghy's rope walk – one of the area's landmarks – bisects the image horizontally through left and centre. Beyond it lies the most closely packed area of the Flat, with the poorest housing stock. The gasworks chimney is visible near the harbour, and Dunedin city and the wharves lie beyond at the left of the image. MUIR AND MOODIE, HOCKEN LIBRARY

its inhabitants and others in Dunedin. Other social classes lived in South Dunedin, including 14.6 per cent white-collar workers in 1938, but no other borough was 80 per cent working class. In 1902 the skilled outnumbered the unskilled, but that changed over the period (as it did in Kensington).

Across the entire suburb, 58 per cent owned their own homes. Although mean property values rose as one travelled from east to west, along with the proportion of owner-occupied homes, the Housing Survey of 1936–37 included the entire area when it set out to identify Dunedin's slums.[37] The gasworks dominated the eastern area, lying between the harbour and Fox St. Small wooden four-roomed cottages predominated, with the exception of one or two small tenements. Sections were small, property values low, and even small employers tended not to live close to their workshops and businesses here.[38] The substantial size of South Dunedin's Irish-Catholic population, to which the convent and orphanage contributed, also made the area distinctive. Between 1905 and 1915 the arrival of a small number of 'Syrians' – Lebanese – compounded the sense of difference. The main South Dunedin polling booth, invariably near Cargill's Corner and always by far the largest in the entire study area, strongly supported Liberal–Labour, divided evenly between T. K. Sidey and the Labour Party from 1911 until 1928, and then became a Labour Party stronghold. In the 1920s the South Dunedin Labour Party became one of the major community institutions on the Flat. Not surprisingly, the biggest polling booth always voted strongly against no-licence, although a growing number wanted reform. The booth at the Wesleyan schoolroom, seven blocks to the west, overwhelmingly preferred either reduction or no-licence, although it also often preferred a Labour candidate.

St Clair was the first and most affluent beachhead in the occupation of the southern half of the Flat, for it was already lightly settled by 1880 when the first horse-tram service started. Although St Clair, like Kew, was part of Caversham Borough, everyone always recognised that it represented a superior residential address, even if its beaches provided all the citizenry with recreational opportunities. St Clair (and later Kew) became suburbs with substantial concentrations of large employers, managers of substantial businesses and public-sector organisations, professionals and semi-professionals

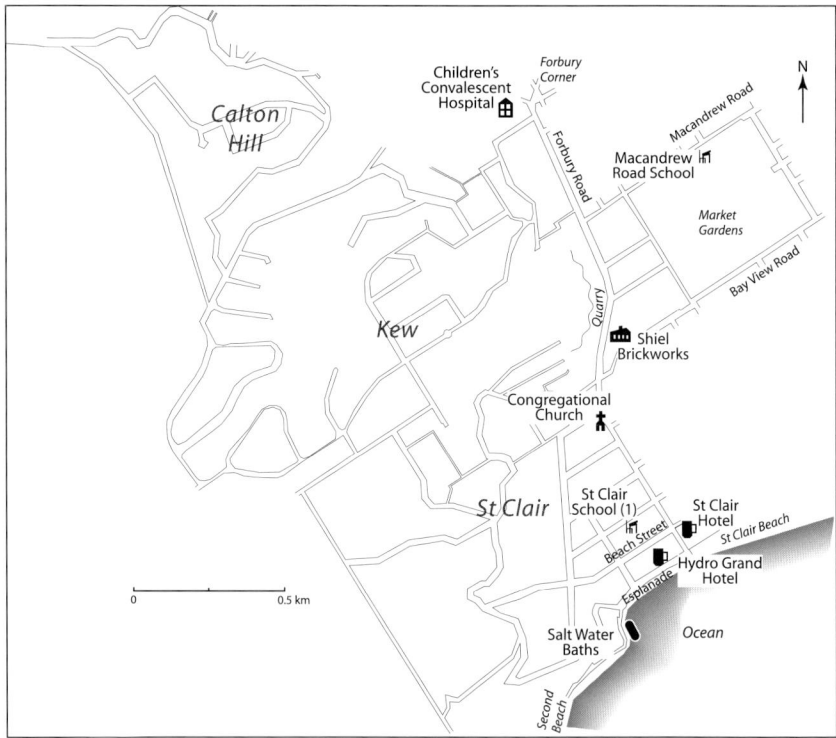

Map 2.7 Southern Caversham Borough, including St Clair and Kew

THE LANDSCAPE OF GENDER POLITICS

Henry Gore, one of the country's outstanding photographers and first film-makers, took this panorama centred on Beach St around 1910. The first St Clair School is on the right, although by this time the building was the Post Office. The recreational character of the beach is evident in the large structure at the left, and the salt-water baths are perched on the rocks under the headland. The substantial homes of the wealthy occupy the St Clair slopes. The Kew rise is to the far right of the picture. HENRY GORE, OLVA MANSON COLLECTION

(around 11–12 per cent at the start and end of the period compared to 4–5 per cent for the study area as a whole). Many of the houses were very large by colonial standards and boasted tennis courts, stables and substantial areas of lawn and garden. The mean value of houses was substantially higher than in other parts of the borough, although values ranged considerably. Levels of home ownership were very high. Roughly 25 per cent of the suburb's adult male population were skilled men and another 25 per cent were white-collar. Unskilled comprised 11 per cent at the start and 13 per cent at the end of the period, a considerably lower figure than any other suburb in the study area. Warehousemen and clerks also lived in the area.

The census does not allow us to say whether St Clair was demographically distinctive, but the absence of hotels, the presence of three churches (including one of Dunedin's two Congregational churches) and the existence of a croquet and a bowls club underline the suburb's reputation as a home for the better off. St Clair was also distinctive in its voting behaviour, preferring more conservative candidates. Kew, which was settled in the 1910s and 20s, shared many of these characteristics. Oral-history informants often noted that St Clair and Kew were not to be confused with Caversham (one or two were horrified to realise they had once belonged to Caversham Borough). Many also used St Clair as a synonym for wealth, upper-class status or pretension.[39] In the 1890s and 1900s it became a local version of a garden suburb. No industries were located within it, and residents in paid work generally commuted out of the area. Shiel's quarry and brickfield, together with several large market gardens, separated St Clair from the rest of the borough. In 1902 just over 10

33

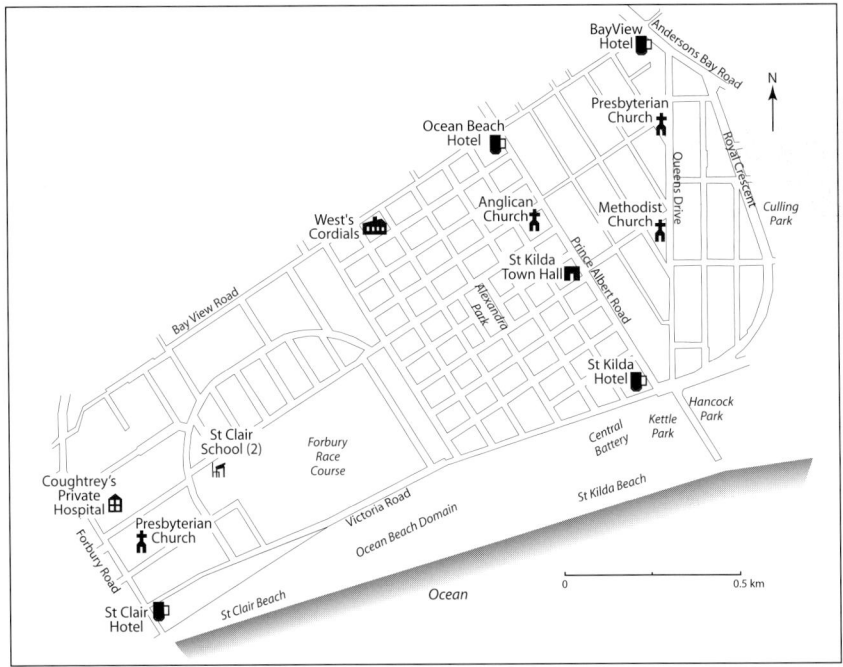

Map 2.8 St Kilda

per cent of the population of the southern suburbs lived in St Clair or Kew; by 1938 the figure was 19 per cent.

St Kilda, settled last, also differed most. In 1902 only some 6 per cent of the study area's population lived here; by 1938 the proportion had exploded to 26 per cent. Initially, the skilled dominated, bringing their families to this suburban frontier. White-collar men, less numerous then than skilled, both in the southern suburbs and the colony, were the only class substantially over-represented, however, and the unskilled were under-represented. Sections and houses were large, cottages almost unknown, and even in the 1890s the New Zealand-born dominated. In the 1890s almost everyone was married and in the process of forming families. Home ownership was also widespread. By the time of the Housing Survey, some 81 per cent of families lived in homes they owned. The fact that 34 per cent of the borough's households owned their own fowls in 1901 conveys something of its *rus in urbe* character (by 1936 the proportion had fallen to 15 per cent).[40] Sports grounds, parks and reserves abounded instead of the industries of the older areas of the Flat. (West's Cordials, on the boundary of St Kilda, was the exception to this.) Over the next forty years St Kilda became more attractive to white-collar men and

'Talking of the Flat reminds me that there is some land advertised for sale . . . this week the auctioneers went out in a boat to mark out the allotments . . .' wrote an *Otago Witness* wit on 6 November 1874. St Kilda did not usually require the method of transport pictured here during the great flood of April 1923, but its aftermath saw improved drainage and protection from high tides. St Kilda's tidy and respectable villas can be seen weathering the onslaught in the background. OTAGO SETTLERS MUSEUM

their families until, as in St Clair, they heavily outnumbered the unskilled (who were concentrated in the borough's central area). By 1938 large employers and managers, professionals and semi-professionals comprised over 7 per cent of the borough's population, most of them living in the handsome streets adjacent to St Clair. By 1914 churches outnumbered pubs, and the area's overwhelming support for reducing the number of licences still further, and feeble support for continuance, underlines a broad consensus about moral issues.[41]

The rapid growth of St Clair, Kew and St Kilda tilted the demographic balance away from the predominantly blue-collar older suburbs of the old Flat: South Dunedin, Kensington and Caversham township. In a sense, the manual working class, proud of blue collars and honest dirt, became a minority within its own heartland, for 45 per cent of the people in the southern suburbs lived in St Clair, Kew or St Kilda by 1938 (in 1902 the figure had been 16 per cent). Young families and their children dominated the newer suburban areas, such as Calton Hill and other subdivisions of the interwar period. Although St Kilda's fertility rate fell proportionately as much as Caversham's or South Dunedin's, it started and ended at a higher level. Yet the data on the occupational character of the various suburbs reminds us to be wary of easy generalisations or structural explanations. The unskilled were found everywhere, although only nineteen out of more than fifty streets in Caversham Borough had a majority of that class (only a handful had more than 60 per cent and none more than 80 per cent).⁴² Likewise, as far as we can tell, different religious groups, though sometimes concentrated in particular boroughs, never concentrated in particular subdivisions, let alone streets. As one can see from studying either election results or the results of the triennial referendum on licensing, every option and every candidate won some support at every booth. It was as if the people who settled the area, and their children (and subsequent newcomers), shied away from making manifest in their spatial arrangements the Old World divisions of class and religion. When it came to ethnicity, however, distinctions continued to prevail (as they did, of course, with gender).

Against the overwhelming British origins of the majority, three small but important ethnic groups were perceived as 'different'. The Chinese constituted a tiny minority – forty-eight men and two women in 1891 – but occupied a much more central place in symbolic terms. The Chinese population by 1901, when Chinese women could not legally enter the country, was an almost exclusively masculine community, consisting largely of ex-gold miners. Some were market gardeners, also selling door-to-door and supplying local greengrocers, and there were a couple of Chinese laundries. Others were residents of the Benevolent Institution, although in 1907 some of the Benevolent's trustees sought to have them repatriated to China.⁴³

Like the Chinese, the Lebanese community constituted an extremely small but ethnically 'visible' group, in part because they also frequently traded as hawkers, and because they preferred to live in close proximity to other Lebanese. There were only about a dozen families, who had originally settled, along with the majority of Dunedin's Lebanese immigrants, in the Walker St (now Carroll Street) area of the city in the 1890s. Between 1900 and 1915, however, the Orthodox Lebanese left to settle in South Dunedin: religious differences with the Catholic majority appear to have been the reason. Most moved to the terraced housing in Mafeking Terrace, off Glasgow St, and the tiny St Michael's Orthodox church was established in Fingall St in 1911.⁴⁴ Their 'difference' and their deviance from norms of working-class respectability was often regarded with suspicion. Mabel Cartwright, a Presbyterian deaconess working in the area in 1908, described Glasgow St as having 'such a lot of Assyrian folk about. It makes one sad to see them sitting about in gutters, and to hear some of their talk.'⁴⁵

The third significant minority is remarkable not for its visibility but its invisibility. Maori did not move into the area in substantial numbers until the 1970s and 80s. In our period, most Maori lived in rural communities. The 1908 electoral roll for Southern Maori yields only four Dunedin addresses, and none in the study area. Only twenty-one persons identified themselves

THE LANDSCAPE OF GENDER POLITICS

as Maori in the 1936 census (ten in South Dunedin, seven in Caversham and two in St Clair/Kew). Tracking those who did live in the area, furthermore, is complicated by the pattern of Maori–Pakeha intermarriage in the South Island, which presumably resulted in, among other things, an assumption of Pakeha surnames. Atholl Anderson demonstrates a pattern of:

> rapid assimilation towards the Pakeha population and into European culture. One reason is that, from as early as the 1820s, the families were mainly patrilocal; that is, the Maori women partners left their communities and went to live in European or mixed-race settlements, where they brought up their children in predominantly European ways. The trajectory of intermarriage accordingly angled sharply away from the Maori and towards the European side. Post-European southern Maori history was, as a result, one of largely unremarked racial and cultural assimilation.[46]

Charlie Williams, known as a senior player to members of the Southern Rugby Club between 1908 and 1920, or as an Otago representative in 1910,

Most southern Dunedin residents, overwhelmingly of British descent and living in a period where assimilationist policies were the norm, came into contact with Maori culture primarily through 'display' events such as the Maori carnival at Dunedin's choral hall. Many citizens attended this event to see a 'whare with an elaborate painted front', and a scene 'of a fortified village', 'a number of Maoris – men, women, and children – wearing Maori garments and head-dresses'. The haka performed by the boys was a crowd favourite, and stalls were stocked with 'articles of native handiwork'. The 'poi girls' are pictured here. OTAGO WITNESS, 2 AUGUST 1902

37

revealed a different identity when he played for the Maori All Blacks in 1910, 1911 and 1913 – as Charlie Tipene.[47]

If the general southern pattern of assimilation prevailed in southern Dunedin – and there is no reason to think otherwise – it is not surprising that in our interviews Maori are most notable by their absence. A few references are more suggestive, however. Although most people, when asked whether they knew any Maori families, spoke of visits to or from people in Broad Bay, Moeraki or other places out of Dunedin, one informant said:

> There weren't many Maori about then. I would say the Chinese were the prominent non-Kiwi [sic] people. You know, Maoris weren't... what – I was going to say scarce but that's not the right word. They weren't predominant.... But there were enough of them around that everybody knew, well, they're of Maori descent. [Interviewer: So were there any Maori families living near you?] I can't remember a Maori family living near us. Dunedin has been, up until recent times, I think [it] was the whitest city in New Zealand.[48]

Marion Cooper, whose great grandmother was Maori and who described herself as 'dark', recounted a family life that bore no obvious cultural trace of this side of her ancestry. But she recalled:

> When I was little, eh, I had to go up to College Street School.... I can remember standing outside the back gate and I didn't want to go because the kids called me Maori, and I was – but whether it was just a good excuse, because I didn't want to go to school or not I don't know.... That was the only time I ever remember anything like that.... When we were at Caversham School there was one Maori boy there, and he's the only Maori boy I ever remember come – just a little boy he was, but I remember Mr Burns, the headmaster, had the whole school lined up, somebody must have said, you know, something to this wee boy, and we all got a lecture that you, you know, treat him the same as everybody else.[49]

It is possible that the predominant nuclear family pattern of settlement was also unattractive to Maori. It is worth adding a note here about this aspect of the locality and its settlement. Even where the density was highest – among the highest in New Zealand – there were very few 'row houses', with the most commonly noted in Glasgow St and the adjacent Mafeking Terrace, South Dunedin. There were also some residences above the shopping precincts in South Dunedin and Caversham. Apart from these exceptions – and they were perceived to be exceptional – no one ever seems to have thought of establishing anything but single-family units on separate titles, with their own garden space, no matter how tiny. Although the area was not formally planned, its subdivisions all conformed to a ruling idea: that of one family living in one dwelling, its privacy sheltered by the space surrounding it. In poorer parts of the area, smaller sections diminished this privacy, but there appears to have been no thought of European-style apartment dwelling as a model for cheaper housing. This kind of development lent itself to the high levels of home ownership characteristic of the area as a whole. It also both reflected and anchored the idea – an important one, this volume contends – of the male-breadwinner norm. A husband's prime function was to earn (although as time went on his duties at home were to become greater); a wife was a homemaker. In these dwellings and their gardens, domestic production could take on substantial proportions. This pattern of suburban life – an earning husband, a wife occupied in the home – both drove and was driven by the pattern of separate, predominantly owner-occupied, dwellings.

In the old Flat – Kensington, Caversham suburb, South Dunedin – the predominance of large industries in close proximity to a residential area, and particularly the influence of their largely male workforces (the Wax Vesta match factory and Donaghy's Rope and Twine Co. were the most notable exceptions), defined the character of the area in both class and gender terms. Masculine bonds tied the Flat as a whole, but the 'old' Flat particularly, together. From these very local workplaces, large or small, men formed various kinds of union: craft and trade unions, but also lodges, drinking affiliations and sports clubs. The strength of these networks was an important part of what made the area distinctive rather than typical. (The concentration of these workplaces and their corresponding affinities in Caversham and South Dunedin may explain the fact that the term 'the Flat', though it technically covers all of the flat land, is most strongly associated with these areas.)

Women, in a fashion perhaps specific to this area, formed networks both further afield and closer to home. Some young, unmarried women worked on the Flat, but many more – especially as domestic work fell more and more from favour – travelled into the city to work, meeting perhaps on the trams, or as they walked into town, and certainly as they worked together in factories, department stores, and offices. The more common historical pattern, as Robin Law notes in chapter nine, is for men to travel further to work sites than women.[50] It seems likely that southern Dunedin reversed this tendency, usually retaining most of its working men within the residential locality, and sending many of its young women off to employers in the city. Married women, and others whose work kept them in the household, had different networks, much more characteristic of their peers elsewhere: their links were likely to be neighbourhood-based, much more tightly local than those of either men or women in the paid workforce. It was they who held together more immediate communities, through daily conversation (or conflict), by exchanges of children's clothes or food across back fences, by mutual child-minding, or by such income-earning practices as fostering the illegitimate child of a neighbour's daughter.[51] It was married women, too, who carried the burden of maintaining links between family members, whether by regular visits to those who lived nearby, or letter-writing to those far away.

Place and gender politics: the working men's mobilisation and the women's suffrage petition

'Embeddedness' of society and culture in place is a reference for the themes that run through this volume. We go on to explore relationships between place and gender through a series of 'sites' – work, education, leisure, mobility and so on. Because the matter of locality is so central, it has been important to give attention to southern Dunedin itself and to the shaping of its population. In this final section, to set the theme at the beginning of our period, we discuss two compelling – and, as we shall argue, related – events: the working men's mobilisation of the 1880s and 90s, and the support for the 1893 petition for women's suffrage. Both, as we shall show, were public matters that linked questions of gender and class. Both, we argue, took on local form: each event was marked not only by its vigour within the area under study, but also by particularities that can be identified as emerging from the character of the place. Why did each of these mobilisations flourish so strongly, though variously, in this locality and its sub-areas? We seek here to show gender and class 'in location' at the outset of the study period.

The most important source for the large database underpinning this book is the electoral rolls. The electoral rolls give a full name and address for everyone registered to vote. For men they give occupational status. For women, from 1905 onwards, they give marital status. Their particular value is that they provide information about almost all individuals of voting age, not just heads of household. Our study begins in the 1890s for good reason: women were only included in the electoral rolls from 1893, the first year of female suffrage.

And yet, of course, the question of gender in southern Dunedin predates 1893. The 'working men's mobilisation' of the 1880s and 1890s, discussed elsewhere by Erik Olssen and Bruce Scates, may not have been seen in terms of gender at the time but – as the following chapter makes even more clear – changes in men's work over the period are significantly illuminated by analysis in terms of gender.[52] Some of the broader picture is necessary here. By 1890 Dunedin was the colony's most industrialised city and one of its two major commercial centres. Dunedin and Port Chalmers were still the leading ports,

THE LANDSCAPE OF GENDER POLITICS

The blacksmiths of Hillside workshops. The symbolism of the rolled-up sleeve and the well-muscled forearm is already well understood by these men and their photographer. Masculine bonds, often deriving from the large industrial workplaces on the 'old' Flat, tied men, as men, in ways that underpinned their sporting, drinking, or neighbourly affiliations. The system of apprenticeship brought boys entering a trade into not only a world of work, but the larger masculine social world of the craft. *OTAGO WITNESS*, 2 SEPTEMBER 1903

and home to the Union Shipping Company, the largest in Australasia. The regular weekly shipping service between Dunedin and the major Australian ports – and the strong connections with Australian unions – meant that the great upheaval that erupted in Brisbane, Sydney and Dunedin, the Maritime Strike of 1890, was in some respects one trans-Tasman mobilisation. After the launching of the Maritime Council in Dunedin in 1889, unions quickly multiplied in numbers and size. Several Imperial unions (that is, local branches of British unions) were powerful, notably the Amalgamated Society of Engineers and the Amalgamated Society of Carpenters and Joiners. Most skilled trades unionised. Wharf lumpers and labourers unionised. Thanks to the local furore over whether the Old World curse of 'sweating' existed, a Royal Commission strongly endorsed the widespread view that unionism provided an antidote. As a result much of middle-class Dunedin came to accept the need for unions and a group of prominent men organised the country's first union for women, the Dunedin Tailoresses' Union. A radical-cum-socialist critique of capitalist society became widely accepted. Samuel Lister's *Otago Workman*, published first from his home in Bathgate St, South Dunedin, and then from premises in Hillside Rd, Kensington, became the voice of the new labour movement.⁵³ The local Trades and Labour Council (T & LC) bought a daily newspaper, *The Globe*, and even the *Evening Star* (often known as the *Twinkler*) swung into a mood of impatient reformism. Such works as Edward Bellamy's *Looking Backward* (1888), a socialist evangel, went through several local editions.

The ferment was more potent in Dunedin than elsewhere in New Zealand, although many of the South Island's industrial towns were caught up in the new mood.⁵⁴ Branches of the Knights of Labour sprang into existence. In the spring of 1890, on the eve of a general election based on universal manhood suffrage, an industrial dispute in Sydney burst across the Tasman. At Port Chalmers, seamen and wharf lumpers walked off the job. The Maritime Strike, as it was known, closed all of New Zealand's major ports, though Dunedin and Port Chalmers were closed the longest. Unionists throughout the city became involved and contributed financially. Vast public meetings backed the cause of labour (a term that, despite its associations with birth, was effectively monopolised by the activities of men).⁵⁵

Months of dissent and deprivation for workers and their families concluded in a rout, at least in the short term, and the men returned to work. Bruce Scates, writing of the strike in the wider Australasian context, has discussed both the participation of women in the strike and the ways in which, in their participation but also in more complex ways, some (or many) working men viewed women as posing a threat to the gender order as the mobilisation proceeded. When women participated in riots or attacks on scabs (such as when 'the "inflammable" women of Dunedin lined the wharf and spat on the scabs'), such departures from the role of dependant were viewed uneasily. The 'respectable artisan leadership' of urban unions, 'who defined their masculinity in terms of providing for wives and families and who believed implicitly in the separation of politics from the home', were likely to see such public women as a threat to their goals.⁵⁶ As the strike rolled on to its sorry conclusion, and as debate in the homes of the strikers began to turn against staying 'out', 'women became a convenient scapegoat, bearing the blame for the failure of men'.⁵⁷ Here is a compelling reason why, as Scates contends, 'The Great Strike has long been seen as a crisis in class relations; it is time it was understood as a crisis in gender relations as well.'⁵⁸

Even as the strike was unfolding and then failing, however, local city unionists decided to contest certain seats in the House of Representatives and formed a 'Labour Party'. All unions sent delegates and the local T & LC put forward three working men and gave its blessing to three radical liberals. In the election the Labour slate swept the city, capturing all three seats, and also won Caversham and Peninsula (which included South Dunedin). Dunedin had become a pro-labour stronghold. In 1891 the T & LC organised a Workers' Political Committee and this organisation remained a powerful force in Dunedin politics until it was eventually replaced by a new national organisation, the Independent Political Labour League (1905–8).

As Erik Olssen explained in *Building the New World*, the local labour movement and the Liberal–Labour Members of the House (MHRs) played a critical role in the 1890s in drafting and enacting the legislation that created the 'wage workers' welfare state'. From 1893 onwards the local Labour MHRs, all of them strong unionists, sat on the Labour Bills Committee. David Pinkerton, the Dunedin bootmaker who helped translate the mobilisation of 1888–90 into permanent political power, chaired the committee. William Pember Reeves, the first Minister of Labour, was undoubtedly the key figure in envisaging the Liberal–Labour social programme. He was quite clear, however, in acknowledging the importance of the little Labour caucus of six MHRs, four of them from Dunedin and two of them from the study area, in helping to push through the legislation that made New Zealand 'the world's social laboratory'. When the first generation of Labour MHRs resigned or lost their seats, other unionists and socialists replaced them (T. K. Sidey, who represented most of the study area from 1901 until 1928, was a Liberal, but identified with that party's 'left wing' and carefully cultivated the railway workers' vote).[59]

In one sense, the political mobilisation of working men in the late 1880s provided a congenial context in which their wives and daughters, some of whom had participated in strike activity, could develop their own demand for equality. Pinkerton and the other Labour–Liberal MHRs all strongly supported female suffrage. So, too, did Robert Stout, once the MHR for Caversham and one of the key architects of the new politics. The wives of these men were also prominent. Yet this mobilisation of working men, insisting on their rights and attacking the existing social order as exploitative and unjust, was in itself a deeply gendered programme. As the next chapter explains more fully, the male-breadwinner wage and the concept of the manly independence of labour, critical to the larger mobilisation of the era, were fundamental to the 'wage workers' welfare state'. That these concepts were – in the terms then imaginable – inherently exclusive of any claims women might have to a living wage, and reliant on the support of unpaid women at home, was a point that never entered mainstream discourse.

One brawny arm of the 'men's mobilisation' was actively hostile to women's suffrage. As Kenneth Turner has argued, Samuel Lister's *Otago Workman* spoke to this constituency in its persistent and satirical opposition to the movement, and in its frequent support for the views of the most passionate and colourful anti-suffrage campaigner, Dunedin MHR Henry

Smith Fish. (The *Workman* supported Fish until he objected violently to being satirised himself. Thenceforth they were enemies.)⁶⁰ The *Workman* – a paper that had emerged out of southern Dunedin to speak for the working man – stood staunchly against the franchise. Its tone on the issue was jocular, but its ridicule reflects anxiety about the stability of the gender order, about the place of the working man if women were to change, and about the threat to men's jobs as women entered the paid workforce in unprecedented numbers. Women would neglect 'that place for which [they were] created', drive their husbands to the public house, would 'forfeit . . . all claim to chivalry'; suffrage supporters were a terrifying 'female army'.⁶¹ Women's inferiority to men was sustained in many a witty quotation and anti-suffrage candidates were backed for election with their views widely reported in the *Workman*'s pages. Many anti-suffragists saw the dominance of the Women's Christian Temperance Union (WCTU) in the pro-suffrage campaign as a sign that women would swing the national vote in favour of prohibition, and identified this alliance as a core threat to the domestic independence of working men, at just the time when they sought to reassert their power in the workplace. (It should be noted, in passing, that the Franchise League distanced itself from the WCTU and was more the instrument of the Tailoresses' Union.)⁶² Turner argues, however, that it was precisely – and unintentionally – the *Workman*'s promotion of the vociferous anti-suffrage views of Henry Fish that in turn reinvigorated Dunedin's strong agitation in favour of suffrage. According to the *Otago Workman*'s local correspondent, 'The Chiseler' (almost certainly Lister himself), when it became clear that Fish had been defeated in 1893, the vast crowd of women watching the results go up 'indulged in a war dance, fast and furious, reaching from Garrison Hall to the Octagon . . .'.⁶³ The conflicts in the gendering of the culture of working men, we suggest, were made manifest here. Such conflict provoked many to hold fast to the gender order, but it inspired many others to rethink it: the latter, among women, were in the majority when it came to the question of female suffrage.

It has long been recognised that Dunedin was the primary centre of women's suffrage agitation.⁶⁴ In the rest of this section we consider a remarkable fact about the women of southern Dunedin in particular: whereas just under 25 per cent of New Zealand women of voting age signed the suffrage petition of 1893, a staggering 57 per cent of those in the study area put their names to the call for the vote. This contrasts with support in Christchurch (22.5 per cent), Wellington (17.23 per cent) and Auckland (8 per cent), where both the WCTU and unionism were admittedly weak.⁶⁵ It seems unlikely that the result can be attributed to unusually persistent canvassers, although they were evidently thorough within the area – Marion Hatton, one of the

THE LANDSCAPE OF GENDER POLITICS

Anxieties about just what would change if women gained the vote sometimes ran riot, as this cartoon from the *New Zealand Mail*, 29 December 1893, reveals.

two presidents of the Dunedin Women's Franchise League, lived in St Clair. Support for suffrage across the area was high. Among some social groups, and in some areas and streets, it was significantly higher again. In discussing these data, the interactions identified earlier in this chapter – of place, settlement, family patterns, religious affiliation and occupational class – direct us to the complexities underlying gender patterns and gender change. In this place, the majority of women loudly and independently recorded their support for gender change and for the participation of women in public life. What formed such women?

As national studies, particularly Patricia Grimshaw's *Women's Suffrage in New Zealand*, have demonstrated, support for the vote was rising for a number of reasons: Grimshaw identifies increasing participation by women in education and paid work and also points to the significance of nonconformist churches.[66] Kirsten Thomlinson has analysed the information that can be gleaned about southern Dunedin signatories to the last, successful suffrage petition (only women of voting age were invited to sign). It has not been possible to establish the educational levels of the signatories, but other factors can be examined. Like Grimshaw in her national study, Thomlinson rejects the primary importance of any one factor in explaining the enthusiasm that southern Dunedin women showed for the vote. Several factors – religious

45

denomination, occupational class and neighbourhood[67] – can be shown to have played a major part.

Southern Dunedin had more than its share of evangelical Protestant churches (as John Stenhouse shows in chapter eleven). In particular, it boasted four times as many Baptists as the national average. These churches accorded women greater equality than did the Anglicans or Catholics.[68] Record linkages between the petition and church membership show the women of these congregations to be over-represented among the signatories, and Baptist women were the most likely of all denominations to sign. Presbyterians, too, were frequent signers. The picture is complicated, though, by the responses of Anglican and Catholic women. Like the Presbyterian church, the Anglican church was divided over suffrage, yet, in contrast to Presbyterian women, Anglican women of the area were relatively unlikely to sign. Many Catholic women, however – and this is undoubtedly the most interesting finding of this part of the investigation – signed in the face of ferocious opposition from Bishop Moran and his clergy. The most strongly Catholic areas were also the areas of greatest neighbourhood support. So, although the churches appear to have played their part in shaping attitudes to female suffrage, the clergy's influence on many of the flock had its limits.[69]

Women in paid work do not appear to have been especially instrumental in the petition's success: indeed, there is some slight indication that married women wholly occupied in work at home were more likely to sign.[70] When we consider occupational class, however, both that of working women and that of men (which is much easier to establish), the differences are marked. Middle-class women were the least likely of the area's socio-economic groups to sign. Difficulties of occupational classification preclude a detailed analysis of the class of signatories in paid work, but it is clear that working-class women supported the petition in considerably greater numbers than middle-class women. A more specific analysis can be done when the occupational class of husbands and fathers is considered. Women belonging to the families of skilled men were the most enthusiastic supporters of suffrage, but those from unskilled and semi-skilled families were only marginally less so.[71]

We might speculate that the powerful masculine working-class socio-political cultures of the Flat, emerging out of the work culture of both the large industries and the smaller operations of the skilled tradesmen, may have operated in a twofold fashion to produce this climate of working-class women's support for women's suffrage. It may be that the power of men's public associations was all too evident, as men had the final say over family money, made their own decisions about their leisure time, chose whether or not to work or strike, and whether or not to physically abuse their kin or to erode the family fortunes through drink. Amelia Broadley, deserted with three children, and Jessie Barlow, whose husband seldom supported her and their children and was 'in the habit of coming home drunk and ill-treating her and the children', both signed.[72] Even if a woman was satisfied with her own marital luck in these respects, she probably did not need to look far to see an example of a much worse fate. In a climate in which the flexing of men's political and domestic muscle may often have been closely intertwined, many women who signed undoubtedly felt that some political muscle of their own would redress some of these imbalances. The curtailing of manly independence, which female suffrage seemed to threaten, was the source of much of the masculine opposition to female suffrage. But there may have been more than a few women who signed in the face of anti-suffrage husbands and fathers, as did Jane Lister, the wife of the *Workman*'s editor himself![73]

But – *pace* Scates – the political culture of the skilled men of the area may also have contributed in a much more positive fashion to southern Dunedin women's wish for change. In a study of societies where women gained the franchise early, Patricia Grimshaw discusses the matter of 'specific political culture, aspects of which were conducive to women's rights'. She points to the importance of:

> an exploration of the intersection of women's rights with the processes by which men in these communities were seeking to establish an identity for themselves in some ways in contra-distinction from men in the metropolitan cultures from which they had separated. . . . Gender divided men and women. But kinship and community also bound them together. For Mid-Westerners, Australasians, *their* women were sturdy pioneers, *their* women were the mothers of the new generation of citizens, *their* women were able and smart.[74]

Not all the skilled men of southern Dunedin held the *Workman*'s view of the place of men and women. The ethos of the skilled was – broadly – egalitarian, cooperative and future-oriented. Their affiliation with the evangelical churches was high. As is demonstrated later in this volume, the skilled sent their daughters to secondary school in high numbers, and they encouraged them to acquire marketable skills themselves. At least as important as any inclination towards gender equality, however, is their belief in politics as an effective means for social change: for the skilled in particular, activity in the public arena mattered. Both skilled and unskilled, right at the beginning of our period, would have been aware of the political agitation over the sweated labour of women. The protest that was to culminate in the Sweating Commission of 1890 began just a few streets away from the borders of the study area in the Reverend Waddell's church in Walker St. Such agitation paved the way for women's greater participation in public life.

Religious affiliation and occupational class, then, appear to have played a part in shaping women's response to the petition. The third factor we consider here, neighbourhood, is at least as striking. Thomlinson's analysis of the 1893 petition is of particular interest in its demonstration, not only that the southern suburbs as a whole were fertile ground for the suffrage petition, but also that some sub-areas supported it much more vigorously than others.

Table 2.1 Petition signatories by suburb, 1893

	Number signatories	Percentage total number	Adult female population*	Percentage adult female signatories
Caversham	432	31.3	711	60.8
Kensington	127	9.2	161	78.9
South Dunedin	635	45.9	961	66.1
St Clair/Kew	99	7.2	211	46.9
St Kilda	89	6.4	229	38.9
Total	1382	100	2273	60.8

* The adult female populations for Caversham, Kensington and St Clair are estimated from the 1891 census.

Neighbourhood is shown to be a surprisingly important factor in suffrage support. To a significant extent, place interacts with occupational class, with areas dominated by the skilled showing strongly, but it also appears to operate independently. Where you lived helped to shape whether or not you supported suffrage. Kensington, numerically dominated by the skilled working class, stood out with 78.9 per cent of adult women signing. South Dunedin with 66.1 per cent was not far behind. Support was particularly strong in its south ward, which like Kensington had a high concentration of skilled male workers. Caversham's 60.8 per cent was underpinned by the sub-area of Calderville, around Caversham township, another core of intense support, where skilled tradesmen predominated. Similarly, place interacts with religious denomination: Anglican-dominated St Kilda was an area of lower support.

But, though variations in levels of support across the area can be distinguished to some extent by occupational class and religion, they also have in common length of settlement and relative density of settlement. The newest area, St Kilda, showed the lowest support, with 38.9 per cent signing. St Kilda had hardly begun to develop in 1893, and many streets had only a few homes. There were no institutions such as schools and churches to provide a community focus. Besides, in 1893, St Kilda consisted of three distinct residential clusters that were quite separate from each other. By the same token, St Kilda and St Clair were the areas least affected by the sweating furore, the Maritime

Strike and the associated working-class mobilisation. All the areas of strongest support are among the oldest and most closely settled parts of the southern suburbs. Kensington, South Dunedin and Calderville, the areas where women supported suffrage most vigorously, are the earliest communities in the area. Although this does not mean that the residents were necessarily of long standing, it does suggest that established institutions (such as churches, schools and lodges) and the consolidation of close neighbourhood and extended family networks – exactly the networks that married women characteristically form – are likely factors in the effect of neighbourhood. As Brian Heenan shows in chapter eight, Caversham suffrage supporter Rachel Grimmett was at the heart of just such close family and neighbourhood networks. In a parallel to the rapid organisation of masculine labour, we might say that these networks provided the means by which women, too, were 'organising'.

Conclusion

In this chapter we have sought to prepare the ground for the more specific analyses that follow. Much of what we have described marks the southern suburbs of Dunedin as typical of New Zealand urban development at the time: a society consisting almost entirely of British immigrants or their descendants in the process of becoming 'native' while still responding to the large international trends of modernity. The older pattern of industrial suburbs gave way to the twentieth-century 'garden' suburb. Patterns of marriage and fertility were in keeping with those of the rest of urban New Zealand. In some respects, southern Dunedin stood out, however, and we have sought to point to its distinctiveness in addressing the 'two mobilisations'. On the one hand, working men's protest concealed a deep reliance on the older gender order; on the other, gender change was afoot in the homes of women who appended their names firmly to the petition. Change was in the air of the trams and factories, too, where the daughters of those women took up new access to public space and earned their own incomes; it was happening in the backyards of married men who were spending more time tending the vegetables and less time in the pub. These changes were happening throughout the country, as they were, broadly, in other New World societies. But the southern suburbs' distinctive mix of artisan radicalism, evangelicalism, Scottish commitment to education and high levels of work opportunities for young women disposed them to become something of a vanguard. Few of these changes made an obvious splash: it was the kind of change that happens incrementally, working its way into the norms, assumptions and identities of the people who enacted it, little by little, until something new has acquired the status of the given.

Three Working Gender, Gendering Work: Occupational Change and Continuity in Southern Dunedin

ERIK OLSSEN[1]

The gendered division of labour was fundamental to the organisation of production between the 1880s and the Second World War, but the meaning of sexual bodily difference changed, and changed considerably. The Hillside Railway Workshops' piercing whistle, which signalled the start and end of the working day, represented one of the continuities, the separation of home and work, private and public spheres, women's and men's domains.[2] At any one time, hundreds of men worked at the Hillside Workshops, the largest single work site on the Flat. Many whistled or sang as they walked to work, confident in the worth of their skills, their industry and their claim to public space. To the east of the workshops were several other large engineering workshops, notably Shacklocks and Methvens, where hundreds of local residents worked. As noted in chapter two, the men of the metal trades and the building trades constituted around 25 per cent of the workforce in 1902 and 18 per cent in 1938. Both industries were exclusively male and a vigorous system of apprenticeship ensured that the next generation of workers was initiated into the crafts and their shop cultures, their customs, and their hierarchies of age and skill. Where women were brought into factories, as in bootmaking, they were not part of the social and political life of the male artisans.

Rapid urbanisation, which accompanied the industrial revolution in Britain and New Zealand, coincided with the growth of a strong belief in fundamental biological difference between the sexes. Between the 1770s and the 1830s, urbanisation also generated apprehension about women's capacities and proper activities.[3] The apprehensions accompanied the migrants from

Britain to New Zealand and, inevitably, raised issues about the capacities and roles of men. Between the 1880s and the 1930s, many of these questions played themselves out for the immigrants, and later their New Zealand-born children, in the context of the southern suburbs, which included one of New Zealand's earliest and most densely settled industrial areas.

This chapter focuses on several major changes and shifts that altered 'the knowledge which established meanings for bodily differences'.[4] First, the process of re-defining work and skill that accompanied the establishment of the male-breadwinner wage as normative: although it had its origins in Britain, it was only completed by the immigrants and their children once here. At that point, sometime in the 1900s, the breadwinner was also the head of household (in Britain, unlike the colony, it remained a matter of complaint that many working-class families had at least two breadwinners, making the definition of 'head' arbitrary).[5] Second, the declining importance of the artisanal handicraft trades and the area's shrinking need for navvies, together with an attack on work subcultures in which alcohol was integral, contributed to the triumph of a new model father and husband for whom domesticity and family were of central importance. These shifts were related in complex ways

Large numbers of navvies found employment locally in the period 1903–14, first working on the tramlines, then the double railway track (seen here) and the new tunnel through to Burnside, and macadamising the main roads and laying proper foul water drains. Many also picked up work on such large-scale Council projects as stabilising the sandhills. This photograph was taken from near the bottom of Caversham Rise. OTAGO WITNESS, 6 FEBRUARY 1907

to the rapid growth in employment opportunities for women, particularly young and unmarried women. The changing division of labour, particularly the rapid expansion of 'white-collar' and semi-professional occupations from the 1900s onwards, helped reconstitute the meanings of masculinity and femininity and relationships between the sexes.

Manual workers – masters, journeymen, apprentices and the unskilled – dominated the study area's occupational structure and, with their families, most of its suburbs, although the proportions varied from suburb to suburb and from street to street. The skilled men of the handicraft trades – such as lapidaries, coopers, coachbuilders, brewers and maltsters, confectioners, bakers – were also present in large numbers. Craft cut across class, uniting some of the most successful businessmen, such as the Shacklocks, the numerous small masters, and the journeymen and apprentices they employed. The power of craft – sustained by local product markets and the democratic traditions of artisan radicalism that flourished among the area's skilled workers – also survived in the larger industrial establishments, such as the Hillside Workshops. The fact that few significant changes occurred in the organisation of men's work within the study area's sizeable industrial sector underpinned the stability of this residential pattern and the conservatism of the male workforce.[6]

A high proportion of the numerous self-employed and small employers were skilled artisans. Their small workshops, together with numerous retailers, many of whom made what they sold, dominated Caversham township, the area around both Forbury Corner and Cargill's Corner, and parts of Prince Albert Rd. Most of the area's unskilled men were, in fact, 'skilled labourers', men who worked alongside the skilled and by and large shared their values. Most of those employed in the building trade also worked for themselves or fairly small enterprises. Fletcher Brothers Construction Co., with about twenty-five employees, was the largest firm in the local building industry between 1911 and 1923 (when it relocated its headquarters to the city). Their factory on Wain St manufactured joinery.[7] Most of the handicraft trades, and most of the industrial occupations, were exclusively male worlds. Bootmaking was an exception locally, and women dominated the stitching room of McKinlay's factory (which overlooked Kensington until it moved into the city in 1912). The mechanisation of bootmaking also put pressure on self-employed bootmakers during this period, forcing them to rely more on factory-made parts, repairs and sales. Wives and daughters in the handicraft sector often managed the finances and any paperwork. Richard Grimmett, a bricklayer who became a successful building contractor, taught his wife to read and write so that she could undertake that role.[8]

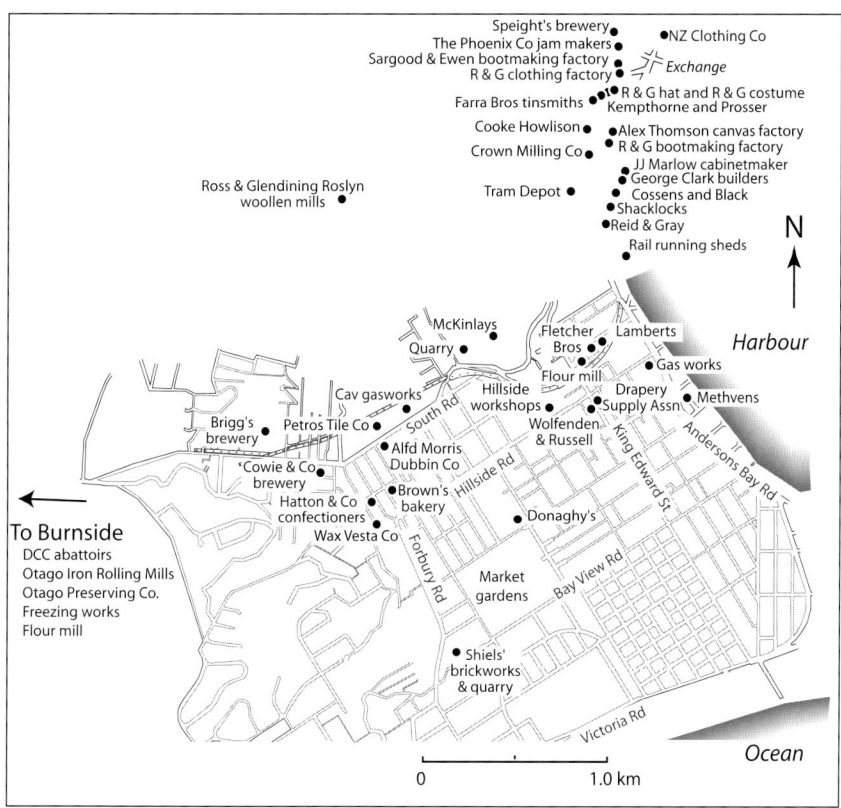

Map 3.1 Major workplaces for the residents of southern Dunedin within 15 minutes' walk of Kensington (plus Burnside, a 30-minute walk, and the Roslyn Mills), c. 1922. The map identifies only factories in the district between the Exchange and the Oval. There were also numerous agents, stock and station agents, government offices, warehouses and insurance companies with their head offices around the Exchange.

When the Hillside whistle summoned men to work, the only males left at home were the sick, the disabled, those too young to be at school or work, a growing number of pensioners and a handful who avoided work like the plague. The colonists believed in work and by the 1890s, for able-bodied men, a job and a wage sufficient to support a family had become central to their identity as husbands, fathers and heads of household, or, as the census put it from 1901 onwards, 'Breadwinners'. According to the *Oxford English Dictionary*, masculinity meant virility, vigour and power. Among workers, if not colonists generally, it also meant toughness, strength and the ability to look after yourself (an idea that stretched from 'holding' your drink to protecting your wife and children). Among artisans, skill and control of the labour process were also important to their manly independence, which meant, among other things, freedom from dependence on any patron or employer. An assertive egalitarianism was the dominant local ethos.[9]

Simultaneously another change, originating in Britain, became widely accepted, although it failed to conceal entirely an alternative perspective. The word 'work' came to be used increasingly only of the world of paid employment. In other words, what men did came to define work and what women did came to be viewed as something other than work: hardly work, or not really work. Unpaid activities, whether at home or in the rapidly expanding world of voluntary activities, came to be viewed as non-work, while paid work became a 'discrete activity in a distinct "economic" realm'.[10] David Ricardo, the great political economist, had provided the theoretical proofs, although his demonstration that labour itself constituted a form of capital had become central to mid-Victorian radicalism and socialism. (In a complex process, the idea of craft increasingly denoted skill in an unpaid or non-economic sphere.)[11] This fundamental reconceptualisation of the meaning of work and skill was both reflected in and articulated by the census, which in 1901 began defining all those who did domestic work as 'Dependants' rather than 'Breadwinners'.[12] On the Flat the new conventions struggled to win legitimacy, for everyone recognised the fundamental importance of the wife's economic contributions. Still, the new conventions, backed with the state's authority, destabilised the inherited traditions of the family economy.

The crucible of change
The 'Long Depression', which lasted locally from the late 1870s until the mid-1890s, brought widespread misery. People began leaving the colony, and particularly Dunedin, 'like migratory rats that are starved out.... This movement is known in the Colony's history as "the Exodus".'[13] In the 1880s skilled men from the Flat – and Dunedin and Otago – reshaped the traditions of British artisan radicalism to meet colonial conditions. As was noted in chapter two, in 1888–90 thousands of workmen on the Flat and in Dunedin took industrial and political action in order to sweep away abuses, reform society and guarantee industrious working men both employment and a 'fair wage'. There were positive and egalitarian aspects to the mobilisation, one of the largest in the Australasian colonies, but the desire to protect the interests of working men had implications for other groups. The men were determined to resist the threat that employers might sack them and hire boys, girls, skilled labourers, 'aliens', or even women in order to cut labour costs and obtain a more docile workforce (it was widely believed that men needed a higher stan-

dard of living than women). Fear that Chinese workers would be allowed into the colony and hired to break down the colonial standard of living acted as a major catalyst for the mobilisation of the 1880s; the fear that women and children might also supplant men was no less important. Indeed, the prospect of a war between the sexes threatened every married man's sense of prospective well-being. Even in industries where women and men contributed to production, such as bootmaking, women were banned from the union.[14]

These fears came to a head in the late 1880s. South Dunedin's Sam Lister established the *Otago Workman* in 1887. Lister's lively advocacy of artisan radicalism made him enormously influential. He particularly feared that unscrupulous employers would use women to supplant men and thus upset the 'natural order'. To what extent this was happening is now unclear; that it was feared and widely considered undesirable is obvious. The Reverend Rutherford Waddell, whose inner-city parish included a church in Kensington, where he preached regularly, won colony-wide fame with his denunciation

When women and men worked alongside each other, as they did in the preparing room at Donaghy's Rope & Twine Co. in South Dunedin, the possibility that women would take men's jobs was always present. The men in the foreground are placing hanks of hard fibre – probably sisal – on a machine which prepared the fibre for carding. The women in the background are supervising the carding machines. In the 1920s Donaghy's became the country's largest manufacturer of yarn and rope. COURTESY OF DONAGHY'S INDUSTRIES AND THE HOCKEN LIBRARY

of 'sweated labour' and his attack on his better-off parishioners for sustaining such an iniquitous system because of their desire for bargains. Waddell's sermon prompted the government to establish a Royal Commission, to which he was appointed, and when the commission took evidence in Dunedin several workers testified. The overwhelming complaint from the men, however, was about the threat to their jobs from 'boys' and 'youths'. Implicit in their testimony was the threat to the family that came when sons supplanted fathers and mothers competed with their children for low-paid jobs. John A. Millar, president of the powerful Maritime Council (which had its headquarters in Dunedin), complained to the Sweating Commission that he opposed 'the employment of boys because . . . it does away with the employment of the legitimate breadwinner of the family – the father'.[15] As the colony's most famous fitter and publican, Richard Seddon, later said, when Premier and Minister of Labour, 'Shall the fathers of this colony be put in the position to maintain their families and hold their heads up as men, or be made dependent, be degraded, and have to live on the earnings of their children . . . ?'[16]

In the late 1880s trade unionism appeared to promise deliverance from the consequences of the 'Long Depression'. Even Dunedin's middle classes were sympathetic to unionism, for the Sweating Commission had concluded that, where unions exist, 'the condition of the operatives has improved, wages do not sink below a living minimum, and the hours of work are not excessive'.[17] The message proved catchy. The *Otago Daily Times* estimated that by June 1890 the city had some 10,000 unionists (almost half the adult males).[18] The entire furore over sweating had largely focused on the exploitation of women and as a result a group of public-spirited men set up and recruited several hundred members for the country's first union for women, the Dunedin Tailoresses' Union. All the officers were men, although male clothing workers rejected an invitation to join.[19] With a parliamentary election due in December – the first to be held on the basis of 'one man one vote' – a group of male unionists, prominent among them Bob Slater of Caversham, formed a Workingman's Political Committee (WPC) to ensure that one or two workers were elected to the House of Representatives to speak on behalf of organised labour.[20] A succession of industrial disputes, culminating in the disastrous Maritime Strike, heightened class consciousness and helped the 'Labour Party', as it became known, to sweep the three-member city electorate, which included Kensington and Parkside, and pick up the suburban seats of Caversham and Peninsula (which included most of South Dunedin).[21]

Although women could not vote, in 1891 a young tailoress, Harriet Morison, contested the secretaryship of the Tailoresses' Union and organised a public campaign to compel the male candidate, Slater, to withdraw.

The first New Zealand Federated Tailoresses' Union Conference, Christchurch, 1891. Harriet Morison is seated to the left of the male president. She helped create the Dunedin Tailoresses' Union as both the largest women's union in the country and the backbone and fundraiser for the NZ Federation of Tailoresses. Morison, a lay preacher for the Bible Christian Church and also a Unitarian, devoted her life to helping working women, and in particular to unionising them. She and her DTU executive played a key role in building non-sectarian support for women's suffrage. EDEN GEORGE PHOTO, HOCKEN LIBRARY

Although men invariably talked of unionism and later socialism in terms of brotherhood, a process that marginalised women, the male mobilisation was proving more contagious than some men liked.[22] As the mobilisation gathered force, as we shall see in the chapter on leisure, union and Labour leaders urged their followers to behave in a sober and respectable fashion, a plea that required many men to alter their behaviour drastically. As we note in chapter two, antagonism towards women appears to have deepened in some male quarters. The *Otago Workman*'s anonymous columnist, 'The Chiseler', even blamed wives for the defeat of the Maritime Strike (striking men always depended upon women's support on the home front).[23] The Maritime Strike and the battle over women's suffrage were 'important battle[s] in the "sex war" of the nineties . . . [involving] an inversion of masculine and feminine, a challenge to male privilege and prerogatives . . .'.[24] In 1893 Slater, who hoped to be the Workingman's Political Committee (WPC) candidate for Caversham, omitted to invite the Tailoresses' Union or the local Franchise League to the critical meeting (although women's suffrage was now in effect). Both organisations promptly requested a new selection ballot, but the WPC refused. A well-attended meeting of the Tailoresses' Union unanimously concluded that 'there is now no necessity for any affiliation on our part with that body, and we claim the right to take an independent stand at the ensuing election'. Even the usually misogynist 'Chiseler' protested that 'they [the WPC] have not only cut their own throats, but also that of the Labour Party . . .'.[25]

The Labour members' legislative programme, particularly those elements that helped to ensure that all breadwinners had work and a rate of pay that would allow them to discharge their duty as breadwinners, was reinforced by a complex range of further measures: enforcement of compulsory schooling and immigration restrictions, especially on 'aliens'; new legislation governing conditions in factories, shops and offices that, among other things, limited the hours that women and children could work, thus rendering them less competitive with men; and the Industrial Conciliation and Arbitration Act, finally enacted in 1894, which afforded both protection and encouragement to unionism.[26] The newly formed Department of Labour also organised various forms of assistance for unemployed men – half the relief wages were paid to their wives on request. In 1895, following protests from women's groups, the department also began an employment service for women. The Dunedin branch – like the others – mainly served as a labour exchange for domestic servants.[27]

By 1901 most of the Flat's skilled men saw the arbitration system as the key to their right to a job, control of the labour process and a fair wage.[28] The court had already defined the maximum hours per week and penalty rates for overtime; determined which trades had the right to undertake what work; and limited (often very precisely) what work women could undertake in those industries, such as bootmaking, where they traditionally had a presence; solved the 'youth problem' by imposing ratios of apprentices and improvers to journeymen and women; and, in its awards to the tailoresses and female operatives in bootmaking, given legal force to the gendered wage (the minimum for women in bootmaking and clothing industries was about half a man's wage).[29] Later, as we shall see, the court tried to define a 'living wage', but until the rising cost of living became a political issue, around 1905, most people assumed that membership of a union would guarantee that wages did not fall below a 'living minimum', as the Sweating Commission had said.

From the late 1880s on, union leaders urged workmen to modify their own behaviour as part of their campaign to achieve and be worthy of these new rights, particularly their right to be represented by men of their own class in

Parliament. The debate over alcohol, which was central to this behavioural change, is investigated further in chapter six on leisure, and John Stenhouse looks at new forms of masculinity central to the process in chapter eleven on religion.

A fundamental consensus about the importance of the male-breadwinner wage and full employment for men shaped both the Liberal–Labour legislative programme and the transformation of working-class male behaviour. A few problems remained. Although the Liberal–Labour Government (1891–1912) succeeded in making the male-breadwinner wage normative, not all families had a breadwinner, not all breadwinners earned enough to support a family, and not all breadwinners were either employed by the government or under the Arbitration Court's jurisdiction. As Cooper and Horan show in chapter seven, poverty was the fate of those with irregular employment or an inadequate wage, the sick and disabled, and women with dependent children who lacked a male breadwinner, not to mention widows with dependent children. (Widows and widowers usually remarried if they had dependent children and wanted to keep them.)[30] By 1914 a local consensus also insisted that girls ought to serve a *de facto* apprenticeship in housekeeping and motherhood before they left school, and then take paid work for between eight and fifteen years of their lives. Even the daughters of the well-to-do went to work, although they tended to prefer such semi-professions as teaching or nursing. In the small Lebanese community, which strongly believed that women were born to be married, most women married well before their twenty-first birthday.[31]

The desirability of staying at school longer and of seeking paid employment, other than domestic service, occasioned controversy. In 1909–10 doctors Frederic Truby King and Ferdinand Batchelor denounced the trends, while doctors Emily Siedeberg and Agnes Bennett argued that paid work better prepared women to be partners and companions to their husbands. The debate doubtless attracted attention out on the Flat, but young women's behaviour had changed forever. Taking a paid job between leaving school and marrying had become the norm for most young women by the early 1890s. In the 1920s the first young Lebanese women, New Zealand-born and educated, kicked over the traces and took jobs, postponing marriage until the same age as most of their classmates. A few young women – famous then and now – even knocked on the doors of the older professions, such as law and medicine.[32] There is no doubt that work was rigidly segmented by gender, but gender was also being reconstructed by the changing division of labour and the experiences of paid work that were becoming the norm for women. Before looking at that process, however, we need to examine the male-breadwinner wage more carefully.

The breadwinner wage and the family economy

The ideal of the male-breadwinner wage – a modern form of a much older idea – required that 'the wage earned by a husband ought to be sufficient to support his family without his wife and young children having to work for pay'.[33] This was quite distinct from what Tilly and Scott have called 'a family wage economy', where the wages of several family members were essential to the family's survival.[34] Before Europeans colonised New Zealand, the collapse of the family wage economy in Britain, and the individuation of women's (and men's) wages, advantaged single women, disadvantaged married women, and resulted in most gainfully employed women being paid no more than they needed to support themselves (that is, an individual wage). Compulsory education, instituted in New Zealand in 1877 and enforced locally from the 1890s, also limited the ability of families to rely on the earnings of children younger than thirteen years old, but many families still depended on their labour and their post-school earnings. This worried working-class men and women less than the importance of the wife not having to work.[35] The male-breadwinner wage and its corollary, the marriage bar (the convention that women stopped working when they married), together with the demand for equal pay, was one of several techniques for structuring the labour market and, in particular, excluding women or rendering them uncompetitive.[36] The New World, with its generous abundance of land, also allowed rural and working-class families to reinstate several forms of self-provisioning that had become impossible in urban–industrial Britain.[37]

By 1914 most married men in New Zealand considered it a humiliating confession of their inadequacy if their wives had to accept paid work. By the same token, a wife's respectability, and her husband's, had come to depend upon her not having to seek paid work. Not all colonists accepted such views in the 1870s and 80s, presumably depending on which region or economic sector of Britain they had come from[38], but by the 1890s dissent had almost disappeared in New Zealand, at least in public. Within the study area most women gave up their paid jobs when they married (the 1878 Royal Commission into women's employment indicates that this was already a common colonial practice).[39] The reason that the *de facto* ban on married women taking paid employment became so widely accepted has more to do with ideas about respectability and the ideal life than with capitalist cunning or working-class male oppression.[40] Higher male wages in the colony allowed couples to decide that the wife need not work for income. Among the New Zealand-born, who comprised an increasing proportion of the area's adult population and largely dominated the new suburbs of St Kilda and Kew, this idea seems to have been very widely accepted.[41]

Aerial photograph of central South Dunedin, 1947. To the best of our knowledge the first aerial photographs of Caversham were taken as part of the first national photographic survey. Bathgate Park and Donaghy's factory and rope walk are seen at the bottom left, and the western end of the railway workshops at the top. The photograph also shows the way in which the houses ring each block, leaving a large area available for gardening. DUNEDIN CITY COUNCIL ARCHIVES

The male breadwinner's wage paid for '*two* labours, conducted at two separate sites . . . [but] in the wage form only one of them is recognised, only one is rewarded with payment . . .'.[42] Not that married women on the Flat objected, although if they had to support a family with their own earnings they doubtless resented their limited choices and the low pay. The widespread convention among colonial manual workers that the husband handed over his pay packet to his wife, keeping back enough money for his pleasures, mitigated the way in which the gendered division of labour entrenched the subordination of women in some parts of the world. Even 'The Chiseler', the voice of unreconstructed manliness, confessed that he gave his pay packet to Mrs C. because, when Chancellor of the Exchequer, he had run up a great deficit.[43] Rising real wages for men across the period made it easier for married women to retire from paid employment. When household earnings reached a certain level – probably around thirty shillings a week in 1914 – the value of a wife investing all her time in unwaged domestic production would usually have outstripped the value of any wage she might earn. The conversion of cash income into consumable goods required most of the housewife's attention. This was especially the case for families with children under the age of thirteen, for this period of high expenditure coincided with the family's lowest income.[44] Every union official who testified before the Cost of Living Commission, which sat in 1911–12, made these points. And both the housewife and her family gained status from her competence in managing resources. She also often gained pleasure, love and self-respect from her success in this domain, not to mention the chance to carve out an independent physical space in which her level of control was significant.[45]

The Liberal–Labour Government of the 1890s and 1900s accepted the ideal of the male-breadwinner wage and slowly identified the means for making it the norm. In the 1890s the Labour Party MHRs from Dunedin, including Caversham's Arthur Morrison and South Dunedin's Bill Earnshaw, dominated the Labour Committee of the House and played a decisive role in making the male-breadwinner wage central to the government's policy. Their successors, James Arnold (Dunedin Central, 1899–1911) and T. K. Sidey (Dunedin South, 1901–28), shared the same view and also served on the Labour Committee. Bob Slater of Rockyside, the workers' assessor on the Arbitration Court from 1896 until 1908, by trade a presser, regarded the male-breadwinner wage as fundamental to a civilised society.[46] These men, Methodists and Baptists for the most part, never doubted the moral legitimacy of the male-breadwinner wage. As workers began complaining about the rising cost of living, which meant that award rates no longer provided a minimum wage that would support a family, the Liberals grappled with the issue. In 1908 the government introduced a minimum wage for manual workers employed by the state. Partly in response to the government's signal and partly because of the famous Australian Harvester case, in which the Australian court spelled out formally what a breadwinner wage ought to be, the New Zealand court tackled the issue. William Sim, who had presided over the Otago Conciliation Board for several years before becoming Judge of the Arbitration Court (1906–14), decided in 1908 that 'anything less than 7s per day is not a living wage, where a worker has to maintain a wife and children'. He then set a minimum rate of eight shillings a day for unskilled men.[47]

In New Zealand, as in the study area, high wages and low differentials for skill meant that from the late 1890s until the Great Depression almost all able-bodied men earned enough to support their families. The practice of paying penal overtime rates, which the court made normative as it steadily introduced the 44-hour week for unionised urban workers in the decade before the First World War, further reduced the pressure on families. Particular events could suddenly increase the pressure – the high rate of inflation during the war, for instance – and the loss of a breadwinner's wage could be devastating. Powerful conventions among the skilled limited the impact of unemployment, which was severe at the start and end of the period. As a rule single men were laid off first and then, if necessary, married men went on to short-time, thus sharing the available work.[48] In industries dominated by female workers, such as the woollen mills, it is noteworthy that the Arbitration Court early ruled that if short-time became necessary then married women ought not to be favoured, and the work ought to be 'distributed . . . evenly amongst all classes of workers . . .'.[49] Some industries that depended on retaining a skilled workforce, notably the railway workshops, actually began constructing rolling stock and locomotives in order to retain their skilled workers. H. E. Shacklock

The weaving room, Roslyn Woollen Mills, Kaikorai Valley, 1921. By the 1920s it was usual for men and women to work alongside each other, although they occupied parallel worlds of work. Some jobs were for men, others for women. This appears to have been rarely if ever questioned. Ross & Glendining's large mill boasted several large departments – carding, spinning, warping, darning, scouring, drying, teasing – besides weaving. There were 50 machines in the weaving room when this photograph was taken in 1921, with another 30 about to start producing tweeds, rugs, and blankets. Each machine needed a female attendant. The supervisors were men. *OTAGO DAILY TIMES*, 15 NOVEMBER 1921

began making his famed 'Orion' coal ranges for much the same reason. Stable employment, largely achieved by the men at Hillside, came to be seen as an entitlement on the Flat and even in the more affluent hill suburbs of St Clair and Kew, and made the male-breadwinner wage a reality.[50]

While the male-breadwinner wage required full employment, and preference to married men when economic downturns occurred, it also required the segmentation of the labour market on the basis of sex and enforcement of the marriage bar. Informal procedures dealt with the marriage bar, and considerable variation appears to have existed, but the Arbitration Court increasingly used awards to segment the labour market. In industries where both men and women were employed, as in woollen mills or McKinlay's bootmaking factory, the gendered segmentation was embedded in pay rates, authority relations and the division of labour, with men and women undertaking quite distinct branches of the work (usually in separate rooms).[51] At the Mosgiel and Roslyn Woollen Mills, outside the area, but important sources of employment for locals, women usually made up around 58–65 per cent of the workforce. In emergencies, such as the war or the 'Great Depression', some of these rules were broken, but, though women were occasionally brought on to men's work, the reverse almost never occurred.

Ideas about gender and work were woven into the very tissue of people's deepest emotions. Marion Cooper recalled that, although her father was often out of work – 'it was depression time' – he refused to countenance his wife's return to work, even though the grandmother of the family was willing to take over managing the house. '[D]ad went mad and said if you are going into work then I am staying home.'[52] A local murder, perhaps, best shows the extent to which these rather abstract notions of political economy could become woven into the physiological fabric of being. Robert Turner, a butcher much given to strong drink, 'had neglected his family [of four boys and three girls] who . . . had to work at an early age' while his wife had 'to go out washing'. He lived mainly in the stable, where he had a locked room in which he stored various items that he collected, including firearms. As the children became older and more resentful, Robert's refusal to work caused increasingly angry 'family broils'. Tensions between the father and his oldest son, Percy, a 25-year-old traveller, became much worse after Robert's release from Seacliff Asylum (he had been committed for threatening some members of the family with a pistol). Percy now sometimes assaulted his father and threatened to leave if his father would not look for work. 'I was frightened of him . . .' the father told the Court. 'It was because I would not work he got on me.' On the day of the murder Mrs Turner gave her husband lunch early, hoping to have him out of the way before Percy got home. When Percy returned he wanted to know 'where father was and whether he had gone to work or not'. Mrs Turner told him that his father was in the stable. Percy went, taking a revolver with him (it was not illegal to carry revolvers until 1921). After an argument a shot was fired and Robert ran into the street, where a neighbour disarmed him. He then went to the Ocean View Hotel and ordered a beer: '. . . it will be the last I'll have; I've shot my son.'[53] Most of the murders that occurred on the Flat – and there weren't many – involved the failure of either a husband or a wife to fulfil the marriage contract.

Despite the potency of this consensus, the male-breadwinner wage concealed and repressed powerful cross-currents and contradictions. As several scholars have argued, in legislating for women's rights the state undermined the traditional female role and threatened the male role of breadwinner.[54] The Sweating Commission's recommendation that women should be paid a 'living wage' led to certain forms of subcontracting being outlawed, but before the First World War women's wages remained about half that of men's in most industries.[55] Wage rates for women remained predicated on the assumption that they had no dependants. The two unions that represented factory and shop tailoresses, the Federated Tailoresses and the Dunedin Tailoresses, did not object, for their members were usually young and unmarried. The plight of married women who had to work to support dependants remained unrecognised (the Widows' Pension of 1911 marked the first exception).[56] Few agreed with the first National Council of Women's plea that a portion of the male's breadwinner wage should be paid directly to wives.[57] Nor did the mid-Victorian tendency to pay single and married men different wage rates, which also became the practice in countries such as France, survive the Arbitration Court's passion for uniformity. Although the judge and his two assessors had no trouble accepting gendered pay differentials, they refused to tolerate any difference between the rates for married and single men. The growth of unionism made any such differential politically unacceptable, for unionists vehemently opposed differentials for fear that it would weaken the labour movement.[58]

In 1920 Parliament stipulated that all awards should provide for 'a fair living wage'. Over the next few years, Justice Francis Frazer, Judge of the Arbitration Court (1921–34), grappled with the implications of this policy. In 1922 he concluded that wage policy alone could not establish minimum living standards for all, not least because men varied – some had families and some had none; some had one or two children and others had many more. In 1925 he backed away from the complex implications of that position and decided that every man ought to be paid enough to 'maintain himself, a wife, and two children'.[59] This ruling created a storm of controversy. In 1926, convinced that social need was best addressed by targeted assistance, the Reform Government enacted a Family Allowances Act. Although this provided some limited aid to married couples with dependants and an inadequate wage, it did not address the fact that large numbers of men were paid to support families they did not have. Not only did the male-breadwinner wage create powerful anomalies and injustices, it was always in some respects a fiction. The state adopted contradictory policies on the subject, as Melanie Nolan has shown. It allowed women's pay rates to gain rapidly on men's, especially in the state sector. Family Allowances, first introduced in 1926, also eroded the male-breadwinner wage by providing for children outside the wage packet.[60] The fact that many women lived independently of men and outside family households also created a disjunction between the ideal and the reality supposedly reflected in the male-breadwinner wage. Over the period some 20 per cent of all households on the Flat had female heads; around 25 per cent of all businesses were owned and run by women; and roughly 25 per cent of all properties and 33 per cent of all rental properties were owned by women.[61]

The debate between women who privileged economic opportunities and those who emphasised the primacy of women's familial role meant that the meaning of domesticity – and its significance as a site of contestation – shifted over the period.[62] Some very well-known local women – Helena Sidey (née Baxter) and Mabel McIndoe (née Hill) – had given up careers to marry. Others, such as the Sisters of Mercy and some well-known teachers, had chosen a vocation other than marriage.[63] Jane Runciman, the long-serving secretary of the Tailoresses' Union (1908–43), grew up in South Dunedin and lived on the Flat until the early 1920s. She played a prominent role in several organisations and the United Federation of Labour.[64] Well-known Dunedin women, such as the flamboyant and 'unladylike' headmistress of Otago Girls' High School between the wars, Miss Mary King, provided a more representative model of a career woman.[65] The issue became very contentious during the Great Depression. Many women believed that even unmarried women ought to give up paid work while male breadwinners were unemployed. The Dunedin branch of the National Council of Women, and women like Runciman, demanded some form of relief for unemployed single women and vigorously championed the economic rights of married women. During both wars, however, most people favoured women working, including married women. In the Second World War, some women even worked in engineering shops for the first time, but not at Hillside.[66]

Despite success in achieving the male-breadwinner wage, most working-class households with two or three children younger than fourteen years old were only comfortably off if the breadwinner's income could be supple-

Jane Runciman (1873–1950). The eldest daughter of a clerk/accountant, Runciman lived on Hillside Rd in the 1890s and attended Macandrew Rd School. She became Secretary of the Tailoresses in 1908 and retained the position until her retirement in 1943. In the 1900s she was active in various welfare organisations, in the 1910s she took a prominent role in the United Federation of Labour and the Otago Women's Patriotic Association, and in the 1920s and 1930s was active in local politics, serving on the Otago Hospital Board 1927–38. She was also one of the first four women to be appointed JPs and in 1931–39 took an active role in the Dunedin Women's Unemployment Committee.
OTAGO WITNESS, 1 FEBRUARY 1927

mented. The self-employed, especially in the handicraft trades, often needed the labour input of their children, and truancy rates were highest among these people.[67] When new employment opportunities opened up for young and unmarried women in the 1870s, most working-class breadwinners doubtless concluded that the potential rewards outweighed the challenges. Some evidence suggests that mothers were at first upset when daughters spurned domestic work for the factory, 'but sweet seventeen loves her liberty and will have none of the drudgery of domestic service . . .'.[68] In the late 1870s observers also claimed that at least some heads of household sent wives and daughters to earn the household's bread, being themselves unemployed or preferring idleness. The 1878 Royal Commission investigated this issue carefully and concluded that the practice was uncommon.[69] A profound shift was under way within the working-class household economy. As fertility fell and new domestic technologies became available – starting with piped clean water and flush toilets in the 1900s and expanding in the 1920s with the use of electricity for lighting, heating and cooking – it became worth more to the family to send their daughters to work than to keep them at home.[70] The fact that the household ceased to be the primary site of production and became the primary site of consumption, a marked trend across the period, especially in more affluent households, also gave daughters more choice.

Whatever the norm of the male-breadwinner wage concealed, there is little doubt that it consolidated the self-esteem and authority of the male as head of household and compensated men for the declining importance of the family wage economy. The wide acceptance of the male-breadwinner wage also limited the threat posed by technological change to the very identity of manual workers as men. This is clear in retrospect; in prospect, however, men may be excused for fearing the worst. In the skilled trades, as we noted earlier, masculinity had long been firmly rooted in the possession of skill and the independence that this bestowed. But the pressure on the handicraft sector, which declined sharply across the period, made artisans nervous about the future. Men in skilled trades undergoing a shift from workshop to factory, particularly in bootmaking, were especially anxious to prevent women

Alex Thompson and Son Ltd, Princes St South, manufacturers of canvas products. Thompson's manufactured horse covers, tents, and later folding chairs, successfully adapting to the dramatic fall in the number of horses used for transport by targeting the new leisure pursuits of New Zealanders. As the canvas used in the new products became lighter, and the sewing machines more robust, work once done by men could be tackled by women and women could also be brought on to new lines of work. E. A. PHILLIPS, C. 1946, HOCKEN LIBRARY

from expanding their traditional positions in the industry as mechanisation diluted male skill. (Over the next twenty-six years, nationally, the proportion of women among the skilled shrank from 16 to 11.3 per cent.)[71]

Locally, and in New Zealand more generally, unions borrowed the tactics used in Britain to contain the threat that dilution would allow less skilled women (or men) to supplant them. The demand for the male-breadwinner wage, the bar on married women working, equal pay, protective laws that limited the hours that women could work, and limits on what sort of tasks women might undertake all featured. It may be, as Sonya Rose argued for Britain, that 'the ideology of the family wage developed as part of an attempt to revitalize a traditional notion of masculinity'.[72] And yet, as far as we can tell from oral histories in which people recollect their childhoods, that traditional notion had begun adapting to the new idea of equality within marriage, an idea not unrelated to women's franchise, a reform which enjoyed overwhelming support in the southern suburbs, as chapter two explains. The high local rate of female support for the suffrage, no less than the idea of equality within marriage, owed much to the fact that although a very high proportion of women from the area preferred to be full-time wives and mothers, before marrying they had spent about a decade working for wages. That, as historians have long recognised, constituted a revolution. As our local evidence indicates, however, the social and cultural consequences of that revolution have often been assumed rather than spelled out. Young and unmarried women became the driving force behind social change, the foot soldiers of modernity. The relationship between men and work, by contrast, changed little, which is not to say that younger men did not side with their sisters and girlfriends.

Women in paid work

The rapid growth of women's participation in the labour market fundamentally changed the social and cultural meanings attached to bodily difference. Daughters, more than sons, began challenging the authority of their mothers and fathers. In the 1870s and 80s many families sent all but one or two of their daughters to work in the new factories in order to increase the family's income. By the 1900s daughters were making their own choices and keeping more of their earnings for themselves. In many families, such as the Roberts, one daughter went into service, another trained as a tailoress or milliner, and yet another did two years at secondary school and entered a white-collar or even a semi-professional job.[73] A handful of married women worked in the new mills and factories, but most married women with dependent children

'The Henry Potts Mission . . . Employees [at the Roslyn Woollen Mill] listen . . . .' Messrs Henry and Potts were Baptist evangelists from the United States who toured New Zealand in 1910. Local employers of young women had a strong tradition of assuming paternal responsibility for the moral and physical well being of their charges. This photograph reminds us that the employer became an alternative source of moral guidance and standards to the traditional authority of parents and especially fathers. OTAGO WITNESS, 20 JULY 1910

who needed an income usually subcontracted to do work at home.[74] Thanks to the Employment of Females Act (1873), and various subsequent amendments, hours were limited and working conditions were good. Although some married mill-workers complained about the limit placed on their hours, because it made them uncompetitive with males, most of the colonists shared the contemporary British view that women in industry, like children, required protection from exploitation.[75] As questions about racial fitness became more urgent in the last decades of the century, these concerns deepened, because the health of women, it was thought, determined the health of both nation and race. Dissent, never strong, disappeared.[76]

In the 1870s and 80s thousands of young women took jobs in the city's new clothing and bootmaking factories, the rapidly expanding bespoke sector, and the Mosgiel and Roslyn Woollen Mills (both within thirty minutes of Caversham Station).[77] Mechanisation, an increasingly complex subdivision of the labour process, and feminisation went together, as they did elsewhere. The

NZ Clothing Factory, Head Office, Dowling St. By the early 1900s few offices tried to segregate men and women at work. Here we see the ledger clerks of both sexes bending over their ledgers – enormous heavy books – while the typists sit behind them. By the end of the period the service sector in Dunedin employed twice as many women as the manufacturing sector, yet to judge from the extant photographs the opposite was the case. HOCKEN LIBRARY

smaller tailoring and dressmaking workshops, several of which were located in Caversham Valley and King Edward St, were less mechanised, but mechanisation also allowed an increasingly complex division of labour, which in turn permitted women to be brought on to all work except cutting and pressing – physically demanding skilled jobs that many women disliked doing. Slater told the Sweating Commission that only two women worked as pressers at the height of the 'Long Depression'. 'It is work women ought not to do,' he added.[78] In the woollen mills, by contrast, 'technological innovations were not fast enough to cause more than passing concern to workers' and the basic structure of the gendered division of labour did not alter over the period.[79] As far as we can tell, mechanisation in bootmaking did not affect the gendered division of labour either.

From the 1900s thousands nationally joined the rapidly expanding service class – sometimes referred to as the new middle class – by entering one of the semi-professions or a job in the fast-expanding white-collar stratum (the female participants in this process are usually referred to as 'white-blouse' or 'pink-collar'). According to national figures, the 1910s saw dramatic growth in the numbers of shop assistants, clerks, cashiers, typists and stenographers.[80] We lack precise local figures for this 'white-blouse' revolution, but most of the women who were interviewed, especially those born after 1910, had at least two years at secondary school and later picked up further qualifications. Miss Shiel trained to be a kindergarten teacher, for instance, and Jocelyn Dean attended night school to improve her qualifications.[81] In the manual working class, unions spearheaded the defence of men's right to men's work, and (as we saw) the proportion of women in skilled manual jobs fell sharply between 1901 and 1936 (the 1923 Apprenticeship Act removed all legal recognition and protection from female apprenticeships).[82] Small-scale retailers and manufacturers, such as Joseph Braithwaite the bookseller, often first hired women to be shop assistants, cashiers, clerks, typists and stenographers. The expanding frontier of semi-professional jobs such as nursing and teaching was equally important. Although the women in these occupations tried to achieve professional status and power, they were invariably thwarted (thus making the concept of a semi-profession analytically useful). Semi-professional women formed their own organisations, such as the Women Teachers' Association.[83]

The public service played a critical role in segmenting the labour market in ways that protected the status, pay superiority and authority of men.[84] Few women were employed by the state before 1912, except as cleaners and cooks, although Seddon's decision that cadets ought to be appointed on merit, regardless of sex, brought a slight change. In 1913 the Public Service Commissioner, established under the Public Service Act of 1912, excluded young women from the examinations, which effectively barred women from permanent positions, and ruled that any women employed by the state had to resign on marriage. In the following year he decided that 'female employees were to have maximum salaries lower than those of males' and that it was inappropriate for women to supervise men.[85] The annual D-3 list for the Railways Department, which provides every permanent employee's name and classification, had fewer than five women's names.[86] In many departments a dramatic increase occurred during the First World War, but the Post and Telegraph Officers' Association spearheaded a fearful reaction.[87] Even the Public Service Association, long committed to equal pay as a principle of fairness, failed to resist the post-war drive to restore pre-war gender relations.[88] Although we lack New Zealand studies, and the local evidence is rather slight, it seems likely that by the 1920s the gendering of work and pay in the service class fundamentally underpinned the careers, and the authority, of many middle-class males. Although new systems of segmentation quickly emerged, confining women (by and large) to the lower reaches of the service class, this 'white-blouse' frontier, like other new frontiers, subtly changed those who occupied its terrain and began shaping new understandings of femininity and masculinity. This was especially true of women born during the 1910s and 20s, who educated themselves to seize such opportunities and entered the labour market as the first Labour Government dramatically expanded the public service. For example, Miss I. B. Paine and Miss Dorothy Meder, both born in 1922, became quite senior public servants.[89]

By the 1890s domestic work had become unpopular with younger women, especially the New Zealand-born. It remained the major source of female employment nationally, however, especially for married women. The substantial homes of St Clair, Caversham Rise and City Rise always needed one or two servants and often subcontracted out such work as washing and ironing. Older women could easily get work if respectable (that is, good housekeepers, sober and well spoken, clean and tidy in their own person). Old-fashioned young women enjoyed working in such homes because they could learn about the social norms of the refined. Helena Sidey, the wife of T. K. Sidey (the local MP, 1901–28, and then Legislative Councillor, 1928–31), never had difficulty hiring women from Caversham township to work as waitresses for her grand garden parties. Those who took such work often remembered their former employers with respect thirty and forty years later.[90] Such local institutions as the Benevolent Institution, the Industrial School and the Salvation Army Home also needed cleaners, laundrywomen, charwomen, cooks and waitresses. The Sisters of Mercy, who ran an orphanage from 1897 onwards, also placed girls in service, although few of them ended up working for families in the southern suburbs (St Clair excepted).[91]

All households sometimes needed additional assistance. Such life-cycle events as births and sicknesses required extra support for the wife–mother. If kin networks were unavailable, someone had to be hired. Once the eldest daughter had left school, of course, she could be called upon. If a mother died, the eldest daughter usually took over her familial role, if she was old enough. Jane Runciman became sole parent for her three siblings when both her parents died (one of her younger sisters later became her housekeeper).[92] Rose Roberts's sister, in service, came home to run the house when her grandmother died (they had been brought up by their grandparents): 'So that was her job.' Rose was quite old before she had to cook her first meal. Vera Horder (née Newton) had to leave school to help in the fruit shop when her father was ill.[93] Boys, too, were usually taken from school and sent to work if the father became sick or died. This happened to Alexander Davidson, later one of Macandrew Road School's most famous heads, because his mother could earn no more than £1 a week in the Roslyn Mill.[94] Yet most families only had a daughter (or less often a son) available for a brief period. When all the children were under fourteen, most families needed help. Hence union secretaries and workingmen were just as likely to bemoan 'the servant problem' as anyone else. The first meeting of the Dunedin Women's Branch of the Labour Party, over half of whose members lived in the study area, discussed 'the servant problem' (although they wanted them brought under the Arbitration Court's jurisdiction).[95] Younger women kept avoiding service. As one Beatrice Tracey explained in a letter to the *Otago Daily Times*, factory work was greatly preferable to domestic work's 'humiliation, loneliness and infinite monotony'.[96]

Two sources allow us a partial insight into the extent to which local women had entered the labour market towards the start of the period. After women were enfranchised, and for the following three elections, the Registrar of Electors recorded women's occupations (officials in Wellington were interested in women's occupations because of the sweating inquiry). Table 3.1 thus constitutes a unique snapshot near the start of our period, though a distorted one, because young women between the ages of fourteen and twenty-one (voting age) – around 60 per cent of the female workforce – are omitted. Although the table clearly shows that the great majority of women older than twenty-one were 'at home', it also indicates the extent to which important sectoral shifts in the pattern of women's employment had started to become apparent in the study area.

Table 3.1 Women's electoral roll entries by occupational group and number and percentage of women at home, 1893–1905[97]

	1893	1896	1899	1902	1905	Total (all years)*	%
Occupational Group							
Semi-professional	17	52	56	60	11	196	8.2
Self-employed/small employer	5	34	40	44	12	135	5.7
Petty officials		4	3	5		12	0.5
White Collar	9	38	48	65	4	164	6.9
Skilled	30	228	226	219	13	716	30.1
Semi-skilled	6	60	63	77	3	209	8.8
Unskilled	122	250	219	306	49	946	39.8
Women at home:							
as number	304	1892	2300	2470	3449	10415	
as per cent†	62	74	78	76	97	81	
Total women	493	2558	2955	3246	3541	12793*	

† as a percentage of all women registered to vote
* some women are counted more than once
Source: Caversham Project Electoral Roll Database, 1893–1905.

Shop assistants were already quite common, but female clerks, typists, cashiers and secretaries were still relatively uncommon. The only semi-professional group present in strength during the 1890s was religious, thanks to the Sisters of Mercy Convent in South Dunedin, although a handful of midwives, the matrons of the major local institutions, and an occasional irregular medical practitioner featured. Skilled and unskilled, not surprisingly, were the largest strata in the 1890s. Dressmakers and tailoresses, plus a handful of bootfitters and bookbinders, dominated the ranks of the skilled. Smaller numbers worked as milliners, mantle-makers and makers of other specialised garments. Machinists dominated the semi-skilled, an expanding stratum nationally and locally. No women became large employers, higher managers, or professionals. Eighty-eight storekeepers dominated the petty proprietors.[98] The occupations of women who belonged to the local Miriam Rebekah Lodge of the IOOF (1905–30) – our third source – also indicate that national trends had a strong local presence. Apart from 41 machinists, 33 dressmakers and 7 milliners, there were also 16 saleswomen, 16 typists, 13 shop assistants and various other white-collar or semi-professional women (22 in all, including 5 clerks and 5 waitresses).[99]

The rapid expansion of the semi-professions, especially teaching and nursing, created significant opportunities for young women and destabilised the traditional gendering of work. (At the national level, the semi-professional stratum was the third largest occupational class for women, employing around 16 per cent of all gainfully employed women, compared to 3 per cent of men).[100] Teachers and nurses, not to mention women doctors and the matrons of the Flat's various welfare institutions, exercised visible social authority. They were among the most educated members of local society, many having had four or five years of secondary education and occasionally a university degree. Although there were not large numbers of female semi-professionals living on the Flat – it was not a large class nationally – the social visibility of teachers and nurses, not to mention matrons and nuns, gave the change symbolic weight. So, too, did Rebecca Glanvill, Caversham's highly efficient postmistress for most of the period. This stratum became the largest one for women, with local growth reflecting the national trend that saw the proportion of females working in 'white-blouse' occupations expand from 7.2 per cent in 1901 to 29.7 per cent in 1936. One suspects that the shared experience of secondary school, and of the shared journey to and from, helped forge the 'new middle class' or service class.

There were few local employment opportunities for women. The Wax Vesta Factory in Caversham township employed about fifty women, including some married women. Women dominated the matchbox-making room and the packing room (over the period 1900–10 the proportion under twenty years old fell sharply from 68.5 per cent to 48.4 per cent).[101] McKinlay's bootmaking factory, on Eglinton Rise, overlooking the Glen and Carisbrook, also employed between thirty and forty girls and young women as machinists in the stitching department. Donaghy's Rope and Twine factory, which ran along Bathgate Park, employed women too, mostly for sorting and carding flax fibre. Many of these factories and smaller workshops also employed a few women in the office, as did many of South Dunedin's shops. The South Dunedin branch of the Drapery Supply Association, and the Flat's only department store, Wolfenden and Russell, not only employed women as sales and clerical staff, but also ran sizeable dressmaking workshops.[102] Along Hillside Rd, King Edward Rd, Prince Albert Rd and the Main South Rd there were also several tailoresses' shops, one or two milliners, larger firms such as the Direct Distributing Co. and Dominion Tailoring & Mercery Co. and, from the 1920s, hairdressers and toilet specialists.

Throughout the period most employment opportunities for women were in the city. Until 1905, when electric tramways linked Caversham, St Kilda and St Clair to the Exchange, Dunedin's transport hub, most young women from the southern suburbs took the train into the city or walked, as discussed in chapter nine. Around the Exchange and the railway station (about ten minutes' walk away), young women from the study area joined the throngs who poured into the city every morning of the working week. Males of all ages – merchants, retailers, solicitors, travelers, cadets, delivery boys – mingled with the girls and young women who worked in the clothing and bootmaking factories, the clothiers and drapers, offices and shops, not to mention the city's thirteen department stores. (Few male manual workers from the Flat journeyed into the city's centre to go to work.) The boot factories of the central city – such as Sargood and Ewen, or Ross and Glendining – employed women as machinists. When Elizabeth McMillan left school in the early 1920s, her job was putting eyelets in shoes and boots at Ross and Glendining's, 'about 500 pairs a day'.[103] Hallenstein's New Zealand Clothing factory, Ross and Glendining's various factories, Hudson's biscuit and confectionery factory and Irvine and Stephenson's food processing factory all employed increasing numbers of young women and were within ten minutes walking distance of the railway station or the Exchange.[104]

In the 1900s the city's major department stores, such as Brown Ewing and the Drapery and General Importing Company (DIC), started employing women in large numbers (as chapter four discusses in more detail). The success of the department stores in employing women as typists, clerks and cashiers helped open opportunities for them in other branches of business as

The box room at the NZ Wax Vesta factory, c. 1937. The 'girls' are tending the various machines for making the insides and outsides of the rectangular and circular boxes for wax vesta matches, including the process of sticking the sandpaper to the sides. They were provided with work uniforms and the forewoman, Mrs Francis, insisted that they had to dress as smartly as shop workers. In 1939 over 30 women worked in this room and another 10 or 11 in the wax room. Mavis Liverpool recalled that the girls sang as they worked in the 1920s. Around 15 men were also employed by the factory. Throughout the Depression the factory regularly worked overtime. The Maher 'girls' had no trouble getting work, unlike their brothers (notes supplied by Mr Randall and interviews with Mavis Liverpool and Hilda Maher). PHOTOGRAPH COURTESY OF HILDA MAHER

well. In the 1900s some insurance companies and then the public service began employing small numbers of women. During the Great Depression there was a backlash against women retaining jobs when men were jobless, but young women such as Jocelyn Dean and Dorothy Meder planned their schooling to prepare them for office jobs and took their chances when prosperity returned and created new opportunities. Others, such as Gertrude Shiel, the daughter of C. W. Shiel, who owned the area's largest brickmaking works and quarry with his older brother, trained for a semi-profession, in her case kindergarten teaching.[105] (Like many of these career women, she used her initials, as most men did, rather than her first name.)

The rapid expansion of semi-professional and 'white-blouse' opportunities placed considerable strain on nineteenth-century gender relationships in the wider society, at home and at work. These young women, often from the homes of artisans or tradesmen, had usually finished at least two years of high school and were often more educated than their brothers who left school to take up apprenticeships.[106] Their employers required them to pay attention to self-presentation and a range of businesses emerged to assist, including toilet specialists, hairdressers and the specialist departments of the city's department stores. Just as these well-dressed and well-behaved young women commuted to and from the city by themselves, they also increasingly went shopping for clothes, and then for amusement on the late shopping nights, either by themselves or, more commonly, with a girlfriend.[107] Many travelled the country and in some cases went to Australia or Britain to work. As Gertrude Shiel said, recalling the extent of her travels, 'I was quite emancipated.'[108]

In the 1890s and 1900s, codes of respectability were strictly enforced in offices, even to the use of glass partitions and separate doors for entering the workplace. After the initial shock, new codes of etiquette and decorum, less rigid and formal, were elaborated to govern relationships between men and women sharing the same work space, coming and going through the same doors and often eating in the same tearooms or staff rooms. Employers expected their employees to behave respectably (in return, no doubt, for paternalistic rewards). As Robin Law notes in chapter ten, the 'matchy tarts', who worked at the Wax Vesta factory in David St, would get into trouble with Mr Rutherford, the owner, if they misbehaved in public. Mavis Liverpool recalled that she and her sister, as Wax Vesta workers, were told to 'be punctual, had to be clean and tidy, and conduct ourselves in a manner that would bring credit to the factory'.[109]

Although women entered a world of unequal pay, the gender gap narrowed considerably across the period. In the 1890s and 1900s there was considerable talk of equal pay for equal work. Employee associations in the public sector, notably the Public Service Association and the Educational Institute, remained committed to the principle, even when many male members were unsettled by its implications.[110] In the period from the 1880s until the end of the First World War, women's pay rose, in the semi-professions (such as teaching), from around 50 per cent of men's to around 60 per cent and continued to gain in the interwar years. Tailoresses also earned, on average, around 60 per cent of the male tailor's wage by 1914, although in many manual jobs women earned no more than 50 per cent of the male rate.[111] Piece-rates, common in the clothing industry, make it very difficult to know how much money skilled workers took home at the end of the week. According to the 1878 Royal Commission into the subject, most young women, once trained, earned between twenty and thirty shillings a week, although wages ranged from thirteen to forty shillings. Rose Roberts, a dressmaker, proudly recalled ending on £2 10s a week in the 1920s. 'That was the top wage.'[112] The average weekly earnings for a man until 1914 would have been around £3 a week, assuming that neither the weather nor the state of the market reduced his earnings. In 1905 the Arbitration Court awarded Dunedin's shop tailoresses twenty-five shillings a week minimum, but in January 1906 local employers told 116 tailoresses that they would be fired unless their union negotiated under-rate permits for them. The 'girls' struck and won their point.[113]

Although rapid change, whether precipitated by depression or war, usually called into question the permanence of the gendered division of labour, unequal pay provided the coping stone for the gendered division of labour, just as the gendered division of labour justified unequal pay. Women invariably received less for the same work or similar work in the same industry, but many young women earned more than their male siblings (the lower the skill, as a rule, the more quickly one earned an adult wage, with the result that unskilled and semi-skilled females in the manufacturing sector earned more than male apprentices for the first five to seven years). R. W. Maskell, a teacher, had no doubt that his future wife, Sir Percy Sargood's personal

The second strike at Ross & Glendining's Roslyn Woollen Mills, Kaikorai Valley. Convinced that some male staff in positions of authority were guilty of favouring certain girls in return for sexual favours, hundreds of 'girls' walked out. The company and the strikers quickly agreed to appoint the mayor and J. T. Paul, a prominent Methodist and union leader, and also a Member of the Legislative Council, to arbitrate. After taking extensive evidence the arbitrators found no evidence of immorality, although 'there have certainly been indiscretions committed' and clear evidence of favouritism. The company promptly agreed to the recommendation that the offending males be removed to other parts of the factory and the strikers unanimously agreed to return to work. *OTAGO WITNESS*, 12 JULY 1911; PHOTOGRAPH *OTAGO WITNESS*, 19 JULY 1911

secretary, earned considerably more than he did (although she left work on marrying).[114] In the woollen mills, as Bartlett showed, girls on time rates in the late nineteenth century earned virtually as much as boys under twenty-one, and then earned substantially more until the 1920s, when boys gained a slight margin.[115]

Women employed in 'white-blouse' or semi-professional jobs often earned more than manual workers, especially those in occupations that were liable to see earnings disrupted by wet weather or seasonal patterns. The dramatically rapid expansion of 'white-blouse' and semi-professional occupations for women created among many men a strong sense of a world out of kilter. High rates of unemployment (or under-employment) and rapid inflation compounded the unease. For instance, during the war, a period of rapid inflation, almost all unionised occupations lost ground rapidly because they could not return to the Arbitration Court for a new award until three years had elapsed (the government finally remedied this in 1918 by giving the court authority to issue general wage orders). Before that date the Arbitration Court's unpredictably arbitrary response to wage demands, caused partly by the complete lack of proper statistics, compounded many men's sense of a world out of kilter.[116] Men also knew that in many countries employers substituted women for men in order to lower their costs. Local men's fears were not unfounded, although there were no local instances of employers substituting women for men or *vice versa*. In the Wax Vesta factory men always undertook the more dangerous jobs. During the First World War, despite the strong recommendations of the Efficiency Board, nobody willingly challenged existing patterns of gendered segmentation.[117] Deep customary beliefs and values undoubtedly explain this situation, together with the cultural homogeneity of the population. The only racial minorities were so small and vulnerable that even their menfolk were excluded from most occupations (and the Chinese, of course, were mainly a community of males). The leaders of the almost exclusively male and white union movement saw no reason to question either the gendered or the racial segmentation of the labour market, let alone the pay differentials. That they increasingly declaimed about manhood suggests the depth of their unease.[118] However, segmented labour markets were not necessarily an effective method of male domination, either at work or at home, because from the First World War onwards they often created opportunities for women.[119]

In the 1920s young single women began invading the entrepreneurial frontier. The confidence derived by participating in the labour market, and capturing new jobs, armed women with the skills to set up on their own account; their success enhanced women's confidence and independence. Although the fact has been long overlooked by historians of women's work,

A Chinese market gardener working the treadle. The Chinese ability to live frugally, and work very hard, upset many white workers, especially in the late nineteenth century, when they feared that employers would cheerfully employ the cheapest labour available. By 1914 a local accommo-dation had been reached. The Chinese, in return, made no effort to enter most lines of skilled work, confining themselves to market gardening, the greengrocery trade, and laundry work. For most of our period the Chinese market gardens were on land leased from the Shiel brothers, and Charles Shiel's children, Gerald and Gertrude, were often invited to major festivals, such as the Chinese New Year, and allowed to help on the treadles. COURTESY OF THE RECTOR, KING'S HIGH SCHOOL. OTAGO SETTLERS MUSEUM

women were active in business and enjoyed a strong position in certain lines of activity, such as the grocery trade (around 40 per cent of all grocers in the study area across the period were women). Entrepreneurial opportunities for self-employment declined across the period, relative to the area's population, but women in the southern suburbs owned a higher proportion of all businesses than was the case in Dunedin or the province. Whether this reflected working-class attitudes or the study area's ethnic mix is not clear. Confectioners, music teachers, retail drapers, not to mention milliners and dressmakers, were usually women. Many were married women or widows, but from 1920 onwards a growing proportion were young women who had not yet married. To what extent this reflected an opportunity created by the terrible casualty rates of the First World War is not known, but the pattern is consistent with all the evidence that points to the growing freedom and opportunities enjoyed by young unmarried women.[120]

The list of businesses run by women in Otago and Southland also indicates areas where women established themselves long enough to be listed in the directories, but then disappeared, not to be replaced. Whether these businesses mark the lines of an early twentieth-century battle between the sexes for control of certain lines of work, or merely represent forays by women identifying economic opportunities that would not provoke male hostility, is not yet clear.[121] Women newsagents do not seem 'unnatural', but the lonely woman who began importing motor cars and selling them may have found the struggle too much, especially in a society that assumed women were mechanically inept. The maker of artificial fishing flies did not disappear, but remained alone in a man's world. The commission agent and the mining agent appeared only once. Cab proprietors also appeared briefly in 1903, then disappeared. Achieving an entry in a directory constituted a significant achievement. Many women doubtless tried their hand at a line of work, but gave up before obtaining the cachet of a directory entry. As we saw previously, much short-term casual work was entrepreneurial rather than waged.[122]

The new sectors in which women established themselves further illuminate the gendering of paid work. In the interwar years, women – mainly unmarried – established a monopoly over two areas relating to appearance: the business of retailing beauty products (they were known as toilet specialists) and hairdressing. Hairdressing provides a valuable case study, and one central to the changing norms of femininity. The bob and the permanent wave facilitated the feminisation of this new trade. They also made women's hairdressing more technologically skilled than the men's barber trade, thus allowing women hairdressers to charge more.[123] Just as the absence of unions made it easier for women to gain entry to an occupation, so the absence of regulation in the field of ladies' hairdressing allowed women to get a foothold in the industry. Rita Grimmett, daughter of a well-known local builder, Roland (a son of Richard and Rachel Grimmett), nicely illustrates these trends. In 1926, staked by her parents, she opened her own hairdressing salon for ladies (her father transformed the shop into a salon). She was twenty-four years old and had learned the trade at a large inner-city salon, Isles and Poole. She soon had more than enough work to keep her busy and enjoyed having greater responsibility. Within a few years she had to bring in her sister, Louise, to cope with the work. Partnerships between sisters or family members remained very common across this period and the Grimmett girls prospered.[124] Louise also enjoyed the new independence. 'I didn't have a real boss . . . . I could please myself. If I wanted to go and buy some chocolate next door I could.'[125]

The young single women who set up successful businesses, like those who sold their skill and labour for a regular wage, enjoyed relative affluence

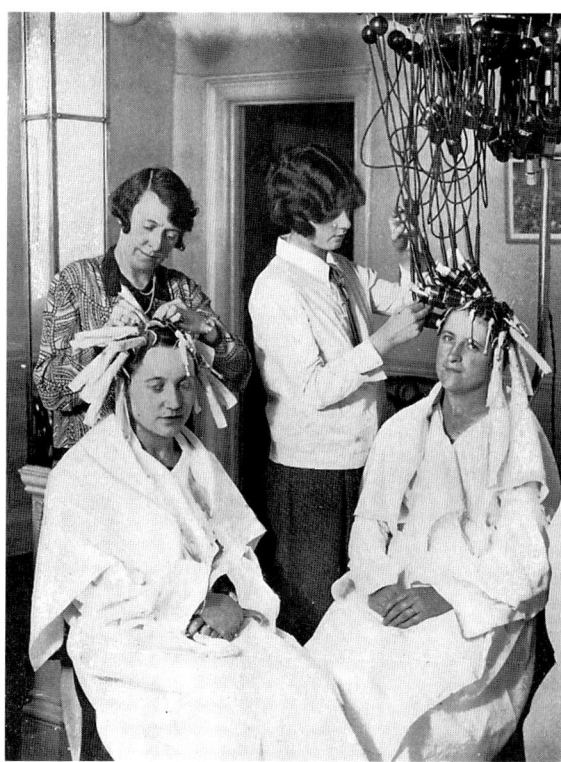

Women hairdressers provide their clients with permanent waves. The fashion for permanent waves helped to redefine the appearance of femininity in the interwar period and made women's hairdressing more skilled and more lucrative than barbering men. Hairdressing thus became a fast-expanding source of opportunities for young women. Several large salons in the city offered apprenticeships and many young women, like the Grimmett girls, set up in business. In 1933 a customer took Rita and Louise Grimmett to court, claiming that she had been scalded during the waving process. Rita was about to marry and give up work, but Louise closed the business shortly after and went to work for another hairdresser.
OTAGO WITNESS, 18 DECEMBER 1928

and freedom. Factory girls, shop girls and office girls – as they were known – may have viewed each other askance, but they took pride in contributing to the well-being of their parents' household and saving for the day that they married and set up a home of their own. They also enjoyed working with other young women and being paid a wage of their own. They had better working conditions than those of women in service, freedom from parental control and supervision and a legitimate right to be in public. Quite apart from their opportunities for promotion and pay increases, they often enjoyed work-based sporting teams and social outings. 'We had a lot of fun together ...' Marion Cooper recalled.[126] The absence of thousands of young men during the First World War saw young women exploit their bridgeheads in several 'white-collar' jobs, since the absence of unions in this sector made it hard for employers to resist market demand.

Young women became visibly confident in public. Many bought Helena Rubinstein's cosmetics, a recent fashion. Some even smoked. In the 1920s they enjoyed having their hair bobbed or permed. As the chapter on leisure shows, they also now went to dances, the local beaches, films and the theatre. Young women's organised leisure and sporting activities took off. Money of their own underwrote the new freedoms. Many still saved to equip their glory boxes, but they would have fewer children than their mothers and many fewer than their grandmothers. When they did marry, they retained their sense of confidence and entitlement. Often, too, they had saved a substantial contribution to the cost of setting up their new home.[127]

These occupational opportunities severed the continuity of experience that once linked the generations. Neither the grandmothers nor the mothers of the young women entering the workforce in the 1880s and 90s had worked outside the home – their own mother's or someone else's – let alone enjoyed a sizeable income of their own. Those who took part in the so-called 'white-blouse' revolution entered an even less familiar world – one of department stores, offices and government departments. These sorts of work were quite unrelated to women's traditional domestic duties. By the 1930s, the revolutionary break had become normative, at least among families that remained in the area for two or three generations. The significance of gender as a constitutive element in identity, and as a way of signifying power, was fundamentally altered by these young women who entered the labour market. Their experience and pleasure in their independence, no less than their sizeable network of acquaintances and friends, led them to expect more of life and marriage, insist more upon equality within marriage, and create more spaces for a life of their own. If Bennett and Siedeberg were right, experience of paid work outside the family context enhanced the equality of wives and husbands.

Before leaving the world of women's paid work, however, it is important to note that the marriage bar – the convention that women stopped working when they married – was often honoured in the breach. The marriage bar undoubtedly imposed a new confinement, but married women in the southern suburbs enjoyed many opportunities in the new economy. Although only about 3.5 per cent of married women in New Zealand are recorded as having paid work in our period, the proportion locally would have been at least double that and probably higher.[128] We need to consider the possibility that the rhetorical vehemence with which the principle was espoused may have reflected the fact that it had no legal authority and was often flouted. It was not uncommon for married women with a trade skill to supplement the family's income by working at their trade, usually but not always from home. Despite the Sweating Commission's report, subcontracting remained very common. Marion Cooper took in work, some of it for a large firm, even though her husband would not tolerate her going out to work. Elizabeth McMillan, to take another example, also took in sewing and occasionally worked as a waitress or undertook door-to-door selling 'for extra money'.[129] Others, such as Janet Frame's mother, the wife of a locomotive engine driver who lived in St Kilda during the 1920s, wrote poetry, printing it herself on a hand-set press, then hawking it from door to door.[130] As the number of women with educational qualifications grew, many also continued to work, despite the conventions, especially once their children had grown up. Urban society provided many opportunities to earn money.

Gendered work and the work of gender

The sudden widening of employment opportunities for women who lived in the study area, including entrepreneurial opportunities, made women more visible and important as workers and consumers. The Electoral Office may have stopped recording women's occupations, but nobody read electoral rolls. The 'feisty' traditions of independent womanhood, alive and well in many provincial and peripheral regions of Britain, remained visible in these predominantly working-class communities of Dunedin's southern suburbs well into the twentieth century. The prominence of such local midwives as Catherine Cardno, a graduate of the Aberdeen Lying-in Hospital, who delivered almost every baby born in Caversham between the 1890s and the 1920s, also reminds us that women continued to dominate the world of birth and small infants (see also chapter ten). The sizeable number of women who headed households, owned and rented property, and ran businesses both reflected and strengthened that tradition. The invasion of the new frontier of factory work by young unmarried women in the late nineteenth century, followed by the invasion of the city's shops and offices and the rapid growth of such semi-professions as nursing during the next thirty years, meant that by the 1930s most women had worked for wages for around ten years, as had their mothers and even their grandmothers. Most of the women interviewed for this project who were born after the First World War reported that their mothers had also worked in jobs other than domestic service. Working with other young women outside the domestic sphere armed successive generations of women with a new sense of freedom, entitlement and independence, not to mention new skills that could stand their families in good stead if the breadwinner's earnings stopped. And, by and large, both the local community and the state actively encouraged these trends.

The rigid segmentation of the labour market, the normative status of the marriage bar and gendered pay differentials helped to ensure that women could not threaten men's dominance within the labour market. Although the strength of shop culture among skilled men and their skilled labourers, no less than the power of their unions, effectively contained any threat that women might have posed in the manual trades, the price of male victory was eternal vigilance. In un-unionised sectors of the economy, the contest for control of new jobs, such as typing, was won by women and men vacated. As a result it became easier to locate these jobs towards the bottom of a hierarchy. A broadly similar process happened when women became dominant in occupations such as nursing. When young women stepped into white-collar clerical occupations during the First World War, it was far from apparent that they would leave when the young men came home, though they did. The diffuse anxiety that women – or disabled servicemen, or 'aliens' – might be used by employers to attack the jobs and conditions of white males persuaded many unions to back a national Labour Party, despite strong reservations about the ideological extremism of some northern leaders. In the post-war period one of the main concerns of the new Labour Party, formed in 1916, was to re-establish male security in paid employment. In the post-war years the Public Service Association led the charge, urged on by the Post and Telegraph Officers' Union (which confined women to the job of switchboard operator).[131] Neither the unions nor the various Labour parties[132] that contested the southern electorates challenged the ban on married women working, although many married women had to work; nor did either favour public provision for unemployed single women, let alone unemployed married women with dependants.

It is symptomatic of this tension that not only did women flock into the un-unionised white-collar sector, but hardly any women joined the local branches of the Labour Party. When 'some of the wire-pullers' on the WPC rushed through candidate selection without inviting the Franchise League or the Tailoresses' Union to participate, they revealed the extent to which many unionists thought women marginal to the new politics of social class. Both organisations disaffiliated when their complaints were ignored (according to the *Otago Workman*, three-quarters of the 4000 women registered to vote belonged to one or other organisation).[133] The respectable artisans who dominated the WPC, who defined their masculinity in terms of their ability to provide for wives and families 'and who believed implicitly in the separation of politics from the home', saw women as dependants or victims.[134] From the 1900s on, socialist women, often the wives or daughters of union leaders, began organising female-only institutions to deal with issues affecting women and especially mothers. In 1923 some sixteen women attended the first meeting of the Dunedin Women's Branch of the Labour Party. Mary McCarthy, the branch's first president, an experienced teacher who lived in St Clair for much of the period, tried to persuade the Labour Party to address issues relevant to women's economic citizenship, such as the motherhood endowment and family allowances. In 1925 the branch urged the national conference to make '"Motherhood Endowment" . . . the Chief Plank in the coming Election . . .'.¹³⁵

The ideology of separate spheres, and the breadwinner wage, profoundly influenced women of all political persuasions. When 'Big Jim' Roberts, national secretary of the Alliance of Labour, complained to a subsequent meeting of the local women's branch that the 'basic wage' was insufficient for a man to support his family, not a single woman challenged him (and this despite the fact that most career women needed a sister, mother or aunt to be their housekeeper).¹³⁶ The women's branch was also expected to organise morning and afternoon teas for the Labour Representation Committee, not to mention social events such as dances, bazaars and Queen Carnivals. In such ways did political parties help men regain control of politics after the suffrage.¹³⁷ Significantly, the South Dunedin Branch of the Women's Christian Temperance Union boasted as many members. Although the Temperance Union preferred moral to economic explanations for poverty, the two organisations maintained formal ties and some women belonged to both.¹³⁸ The fledgling Communist Party in Dunedin, strong in the metal trades and the building trades, tried hard to recruit women in the 1930s, but made little progress, in part because the party considered class the only source of inequality and injustice. For that reason, local Communists, strongly supported by the South Dunedin Branch of the NZLP, persuaded the local Tailoresses to give up their separate existence and merge with a male-dominated Clothing Workers' Union.¹³⁹

These shifts in the gender order help explain the sudden popularity among the unskilled, and manual workers generally, of a new 'macho' image of manliness – tough, pugilistic, assertive, muscular and brawny – proletarian in a word. Nor is it coincidental that such sports as rugby league, boxing and wrestling became popular among men in the interwar period. It is, as I discussed in *Building the New World*, more than possible that Sidey's success in holding Dunedin South owed a lot to his gentlemanly manners and gentle physical presence. The brawny arm that symbolised male union power after the Red Fed moment in 1912–13, alive and well among tramway workers, for instance (as Robin Law shows), must have conveyed a double message to many women. Simultaneously, if paradoxically, *Truth*, the most popular weekly in the country, increasingly portrayed 'pen-pushers' as both economic parasites and sexual hybrids. These were not local cultural productions. As women, strongly supported by active Christians of both sexes, successfully domesticated male behaviour, men – especially the hard drinkers and the hard doers – sought symbolic recompense.¹⁴⁰ Indeed, the communities on the Flat reworked many of these tensions and conflicts into a new consensus

'Stevo' Boreham (1857–1925). 'I say if a man likes to take the risk and drink water it's no business of ours . . . .' Son of a Tasmanian farmer, he spent his teens at sea then settled in New Zealand. A 'gun' shearer and unionist, he claimed to have organised several trades in 1889–90 and played a key role in organising the Shearers' Union. In 1902 he and his wife and several children settled in Dunedin. As secretary of the Agricultural and Pastoral Workers' Union he tried to organise and represent the navvies who built the city's new tramlines. He later helped organise the Dunedin Labourers' Union. A great stump orator, his lack of administrative ability hindered his career as a union bureaucrat, but this enhanced his reputation for straight shooting. He became a very model of the Australasian bushman. FRED RAYNER'S SKETCH, *THE SKETCHER*, DECEMBER 1914

about the meaning of masculinity. It is too early to claim that the women and men of the southern suburbs played an important role in articulating a consensus about gender for the entire country, in the way that they certainly did for key elements of the wage workers' welfare state (as I showed in *Building the New World*).[141] The fact that masters and journeymen remained numerically important in all suburbs – around 45–50 per cent in 1902 and around 35 per cent in 1938 – and that the service class recruited strongly from skilled men, not to mention their sons and daughters, meant that the dominant ideology of gender remained one acceptable to skilled men. A married man's ability to provide for his family lay at its heart.[142]

The rise of the ideology of the male-breadwinner wage ran parallel to the emergence of the 'suburban family man' – a domesticated husband and father who could control both his sexual desires and his temper. Temperance, as almost everyone agreed, was the key. As a subculture of work characterised by hard drinking, gambling and fighting fell into disrepute, other forms of activity provided new templates for masculine behaviour. At the same time, a growing proportion of men entered white-collar jobs that were not congruent with traditional images of masculinity. The centrality of breadwinning to married men's sense of themselves as men partially obviated these threats.

In a predominantly working-class community, pride in skill, the capacity for hard work and the ability to provide for their families continued to outweigh the symbolic importance of clothes or money, at least for men. By 1915 so, too, did the fact that young unmarried men of all classes had proven their manhood in the firing line. Apart from organised sport – discussed in chapter six – 'do-it-yourself' activities around the home, together with some hobbies (including the new world of cars and motor cycles), created new ways of articulating masculine identity. Toughness and strength remained important, but so, too, did skill and dexterity, tidiness and patience. Men such as Sir Donald Cameron, a long-term resident of St Kilda who became Otago's most famous example of the rise from office boy to general manager, helped prove that tidiness and refinement entailed no loss of manhood. Slowly, across the period, the level of privation and discomfort, not to mention danger, that men would tolerate at work fell away. Few criticised those men who, in the 1930s, refused to leave for the work camps or those single men who, having no choice, complained about sleeping on the frozen ground in such places as Lindis Pass.[143]

Shifts in the division of labour unbalanced the Victorian gender order, both in the colony and in other advanced societies. Although work and skill

The Godber family. Albert Percy Godber, foreman in the tinsmiths' shop, was transferred to Hillside in 1925. He and his wife, Laura, bought this house at 9 Baker St, close to the workshops, in a recent subdivision dominated by handsome villas and elegant bungalows, wide grass verges, and two rows of plain trees. Their only child, Phyllis, clearly asserts her independence. Godber's passion for Maori design can be seen above the front door and thanks to his passion for photography we have an unrivalled collection of workshop photographs. The Godbers here represent the new model family. GODBER COLLECTION, G1049, ALEXANDER TURNBULL LIBRARY

were increasingly defined as male, and women's contribution to the family economy was increasingly ignored by public servants and scholars, the meanings attached to female and male bodies shifted dramatically. A consensus had emerged in the 1840s that women ought not to undertake the most physically demanding occupations – and they were banned from working in mines – but they did perform an increasing number of paid jobs and put paid to the stereotype of 'anaemic' or 'hysterical' femininity. In the 1870s and 80s the discontinuity between the generations created some tensions, but by the 1910s a high proportion of the female paid workforce had mothers who had also gone out to work before marrying. Although daughters were more reliable than sons in contributing to the family economy, the individuated wage also gave them both an income of their own and a sense of entitlement. The increased autonomy and independence of a growing proportion of young women enabled them to seek more education and to attack yet further stereotypes of female incompetence or inadequacy. Men's behaviour either shifted to accommodate these changes, or disadvantaged them in finding a wife.

Although the household became less important as an actual site of production across the period, its symbolic value increased. Family-oriented males of the southern suburbs increasingly modified their wildness before marriage and tried to eliminate it once married. The proportionate decline in the handicraft trades, the dramatic expansion of white-collar occupations, and the virtual disappearance of navvies once the major public works had been completed (1908–12) all reinforced this important shift. Work may have been a refuge from home for forty-four hours each week, and the pub, too, but most married men increasingly spent much of their free time with their families, doing up their houses and cultivating their vegetable gardens. The on-going role of the family economy – a sort of ironic counterpoint to the norm of the male-breadwinner wage – also meant, as was the case with most feminised entrepreneurial domains, that it is impossible to identify a fixed boundary that separates home from marketplace, the private from the public sphere. In short, a peculiar double movement occurred: men became more domesticated and dependent upon family support while their masculinity became more dependent upon having a job that paid enough to support the wife and family. By the 1930s, domesticity won for married men when the two imperatives came into conflict. The new frontier of paid work for unmarried young women also subtly changed those who occupied its terrain. The life histories of young women who left school between the 1870s and 1930s changed much more than did those of their male peers; and because of this they were less accommodating to tradition, more pushy in demanding change, and initiated a profound transformation of the traditional roles of wife and mother.[144]

Four Schooling for a Gendered Future: Gender, Education and Opportunity

DOROTHY PAGE, HOWARD LEE AND TOM BROOKING

The fondest memory of some of the early pupils of Caversham Primary School related to break-up day. On the preceding afternoon, a half-holiday, the boys would raid the bush across the railway line for greenery to decorate the old grey stone classroom for the prize-giving. The girls added flowers: brightly coloured lilies, lupins and gladioli, and fragrant cabbage roses. After the ceremony, on this one day of the year, the girls ventured into the boys' playground for a daring game of 'Kiss-in-the-Ring'. They all formed a big circle, around which one of the boys would chase one of the girls. If he caught her before she got back to her place, he kissed her – unless the headmaster happened to come by first. Thus the segregated worlds of boys' and girls' play came together for a brief, illicit moment on the threshold of adulthood.[1]

This chapter seeks to investigate the opportunities awaiting boys and girls leaving Caversham and the other state primary schools of southern Dunedin in the 1880s and how far they changed over the next half-century. We want to assess how far the differing roles men and women were expected to play as adults were already moulding the experience of boys and girls at primary school, and the extent to which these differing expectations influenced them when they left school to enter paid or unpaid employment or continue their education at secondary school.

The years from 1880 to 1939 were a time of dramatic social change in New Zealand. Its characteristic features – urban and industrial development, expanded transport systems, increased bureaucracy – have been summed up in the term modernisation. There were significant demographic changes, too. In Dunedin, while the population as a whole doubled, individual family size reduced from an average of more than six children to two or three. Although the changes affected both men and women, their effect was most striking on younger working-class women. Girls leaving primary school were less often required to stay home to look after younger siblings and could look forward, for a time, to the independence of paid employment, in factories or in the burgeoning clerical, secretarial and retail sectors. As Erik Olssen has shown, about 39 per cent of young women aged between fifteen and twenty-four were in the paid workforce in 1891. By 1921 this proportion had grown to 50 per cent and continued to rise.[2]

For the desirable fields of white-collar employment – as secretaries or shorthand-typists – that were opening up to women, they needed education beyond primary school level. At the beginning of the twentieth century, girls' secondary schools, newly democratised by free places, were buffeted by conflicting demands. On the one hand, educational administrators urged training in domestic skills for all girls, and medical men warned against the stress of a demanding academic curriculum on female adolescent bodies. On the other, parents and pupils demanded, with considerable success, specialised training in commercial subjects. Although the issue of providing appropriate education for New Zealand's future citizens, taking into account both sex and class, was most hotly contested in the secondary schools and new technical colleges, the groundwork for futures predetermined by gender was laid in the primary schools. Our investigation into the schooling of southern Dunedin children thus falls into two parts, as we examine, through the lens of gender, their primary and post-primary experience.

Whether the experience of southern Dunedin school children was typical of children elsewhere in New Zealand is not easy to determine. The role of gender in our educational system has not been a primary focus of educational historians, whose interest has lain rather in the history of educational provision and the development of a national system of education. Primary schools, especially, have received little attention. The exceptions tend to focus on girls' experiences, although those of the boys do appear – to provide contrast, or to establish the norm. In 'White Pinafores, Slates, Mud and Manuka', for example, Kay Matthews uses oral evidence to back up her claim that primary schooling for girls in Hawke's Bay between 1880 and 1918 was 'a relatively short-term experience curtailed by the more pressing demands of the family economy'.[3] In her history of the curriculum in girls' schools between 1900 and 1975, Ruth Fry argues that, though girls had a better chance of functioning on an equal footing with boys at primary school than they were likely to have at work or in the family, they were still receiving messages in keeping with the gendered expectations of society.[4] Like Fry, Anne-Marie O'Neill includes both primary and secondary teaching in her article on

'The Gendered Curriculum', but directs most of her attention to the latter.⁵ Margaret Tennant's discussion of the New Zealand movement for sexual differentiation in education in the early twentieth century focuses on the 'education in womanly qualities' in high schools. Revisiting the 'domestic education debate', Melanie Nolan also relies on evidence from secondary education to cast doubt on the commitment and effectiveness of the state's promotion of domestic education for girls.⁶

The promotion of masculine values in schools has received less direct attention from historians than the attempts to inculcate womanliness. Colin McGeorge's depiction of the 'moral curriculum' in primary schools as being 'aimed at habits of industry, obedience and respect for lawful authority through unswerving discipline and strict routines' is a useful pointer to the accepted ideal of masculinity. Jock Phillips, tackling the question, 'What role does New Zealand society expect of its males and when and how did that role evolve?', makes passing reference to the contribution of boys' schools to establishing the male stereotype. Sport historian Greg Ryan, who has examined the role of rugby in New Zealand boys' high schools between the 1880s and the 1930s, suggests that we should revise some stock assumptions about the role of the game in defining that stereotype.⁷

Virtually no writers on education, other than those setting down the narratives of individual schools, deal with the local. Caroline Daley is not primarily concerned with school in her study of the Hawke's Bay community of Taradale, but, because her work has a strong sense of locality and because it uses gender – in Joan Scott's terms – as a category of historical analysis we have found it a valuable point of comparison with our own study of southern Dunedin.⁸ It is our contention that at primary school the experience of southern Dunedin children reflected that of children in other New Zealand cities, and that our narrative provides a useful case study in a comparatively neglected area. At secondary level, on the other hand, we have found more than merely a reflection of national trends. The special characteristics of southern Dunedin, a predominantly skilled working-class area of a city with a Scottish respect for education, enabled both boys and girls to gain enhanced social and economic advancement through post-primary education. In our period, we argue, this enhancement of opportunities was more striking for girls.

Girls and boys at primary school
'How have social institutions incorporated gender into their assumptions and organization?' asks Joan Scott.⁹ In the case of primary schools, the

This photograph of Caversham School about 1909 (above) shows a spacious play area, in which the separate play of well-dressed boys and girls is overseen by the teachers to the left of the picture. The impression of order is reinforced by the church-like architecture of the buildings in the background. In contrast, Kensington school (below) the second state school on the Flat and located in a more impoverished area, appears cramped and bleak. HOCKEN LIBRARY

answer is multi-layered and not always clear-cut. The little, enclosed world of the school is a microcosm of the society it serves, performing the roles and relationships pupils will meet in the adult world, as well as instilling its values. To the Scottish founders of Dunedin, education for both girls and boys was a serious matter. Even on the predominantly working-class Flat, where the standard of most parents' education was not high, three large primary schools predated the introduction of compulsory schooling and attendance figures were well above the national average. With minor exceptions, boys and girls followed the same basic curriculum and sat the same examinations. But schools teach by example, as well as by the formal transmission of information, and children were shown a teaching hierarchy that replicated the gender order of the patriarchal Victorian family. Like a traditional family, the primary school had its paterfamilias in the headmaster, who wielded authority and commanded respect. Men taught the senior classes. The infant mistress, holding the highest position to which a woman could aspire, took charge of the youngest children. Like a well-run family, the well-run school was orderly; in 1891 all the southern Dunedin schools were pleased to receive a 'very good' from the inspectors for order, discipline and manners.[10] The well-run school demonstrated familial stability. William Milne headed Caversham School for more than forty years and one infant mistress, Miss Donald, presided over the youngest children for thirty-two years. Like a father ambitious for his children, Milne aimed for a 96 per cent pass rate in examinations for his pupils. 'We were always a happy family at Caversham School,' is how his first assistant remembered it many years later.[11]

Caversham, which opened in 1861, was the first of the five state primary schools to be established in southern Dunedin in the late nineteenth century. It was followed by Kensington (1874), Forbury (1875), Macandrew Road (1883) and St Clair (1896). By 1900 they had a combined roll of just over 2000. Musselburgh, just beyond the study area but taking children from within it, opened in 1905. Although all the schools recruited some children from across the class structure, different classes were predominant in different schools and this determined their standing in the community. Thus Caversham was perceived as serving a skilled working-class community, Forbury, rough working-class, St Clair middle-class and Musselburgh lower middle-class.[12] These state schools were regulated by the 1877 Education Act, which made education to age thirteen free, compulsory and secular. Catholic boys and girls on the Flat were catered for by St Patrick's School, established first as a school–chapel in 1878, then, from 1882, placed under the care of Dominican sisters, who travelled daily from their priory in the centre of town, until in 1896 it was taken over by the Sisters of Mercy, whose convent was adjacent.[13]

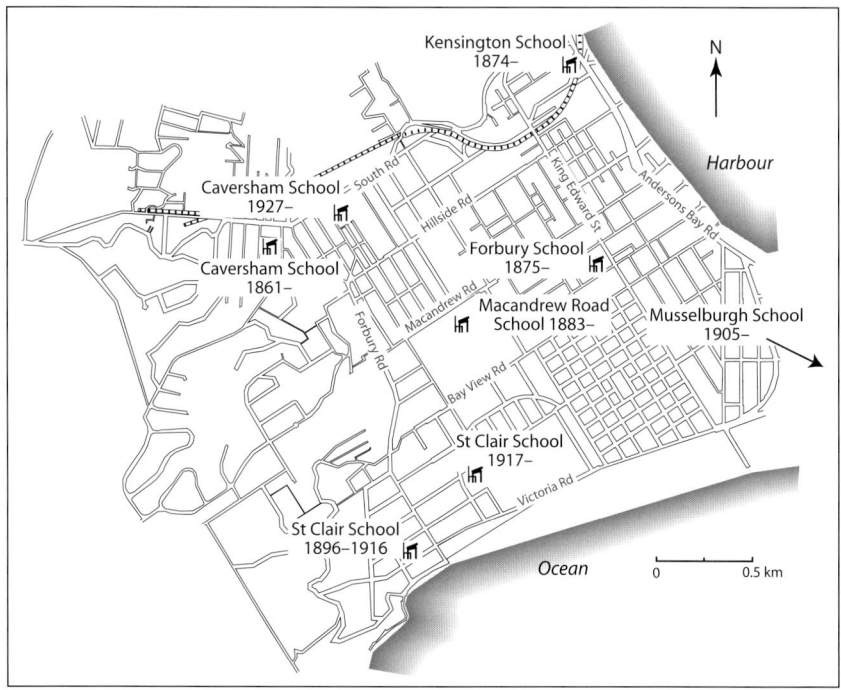

Map 4.1 State primary schools of the southern suburbs

By the turn of the century, New Zealand parents had wholeheartedly accepted the concept of compulsory state-funded primary education for their children. From a base of 748 schools, with 65,040 pupils in 1878, the primary school population had more than doubled, to 130,744 pupils, taught in 1707 schools, in 1900. The average attendance had risen from 74.6 per cent in 1880 to 84.1 per cent in 1900.[14] A good proportion of Otago's early settlers came from Scotland, where elementary education was universal, and they placed a high value on education. The attendance rate of the southern Dunedin schools exceeded even the high national average. Caversham School began 1890 with 610 pupils, increasing the roll to 665 by the end of the year; the average attendance is recorded as 609.25, a remarkable 95.4 per cent. There was no significant difference between truancy rates for boys and girls – the received wisdom was that girls were more often kept at home to help mother, as Kay Matthews found in rural Hawke's Bay – but the problem of absenteeism was evidently not significant. All the schools in southern Dunedin increased their rolls during 1890. All but Forbury had a slightly higher proportion of boys, as was the case throughout the country: in 1900, nationally, there were

48 per cent schoolgirls to 52 per cent schoolboys. The ratio of girls to boys was lower in the five to seven age group, suggesting that parents were anxious to protect their little daughters from the rigours of school, or perhaps from the long walk to get there.¹⁵

Although the basic primary school curriculum was not differentiated according to gender, and differences in the educational experience of boys and girls were less marked at primary level than at secondary, they were nevertheless entrenched from the beginning. Important formal and informal distinctions between boys' and girls' schooling, in the subjects taught, in discipline and in play, looked ahead to what it was accepted would be their separate futures in the workplace and the home. Ruth Fry maintains that it was the perceived need to teach home-related subjects to girls that provided the main argument for differentiation in the curricula for girls and boys. The 1877 Education Act required that all girls be taught sewing, which was allocated special importance by the framers of policy, as an essential skill for adult life. All women teachers were expected to teach it. While the girls learned sewing, the boys were supposed to do military drill, but this requirement was often ignored, until the Boer War produced a wave of patriotism that resulted in a standard scheme of primary school cadet training. Sometimes the boys did gardening, but often they were given extra arithmetic. This was a subject with a covert gender dimension. At first, girls were allowed to pass the sixth standard examination in arithmetic with only two and a half sums right out of five, while boys had to have three. The impression that mathematical expertise was not for girls was reinforced by their being excused geometrical drawing. In 1899 school inspectors were instructed to judge other work done by girls 10 per cent more leniently than that done by boys. Topics in the curriculum, as well as the general ethos and environment of the schools, were masculine in tone. Readers in English and history, for example, celebrated heroes of the Empire. At the turn of the century, special manual training centres were set up, with specialist instructors and the facilities to teach standard five and six boys woodwork and girls cooking, a gendered training in practical skills that went unchallenged right through to the 1970s. Macandrew Road School became the manual training centre for the schools of southern Dunedin.¹⁶

Physical activities and playground games differed for boys and girls. Segregated playgrounds were at first the norm, the separation sometimes enforced by a solid wall, as Daley describes at Taradale School. At Caversham, there was an 'established division' of the playground into boys' and girls' areas. Traditionally, boys played marbles and tops, and rougher games, some with names now unfamiliar. A booklet produced for the sixty-fifth anniversary celebrations in 1926 of Caversham School listed shinty, fly-the-garter, prisoner's

Academic achievement at primary school, assessed by annual examination and carefully recorded, was scrutinised by school inspectors and parents alike. The record card of Minnie Sutherland, who attended Caversham School between 1892 and 1897, shows her satisfactory progress through the school. CAVERSHAM PROJECT COLLECTION

base, goosey and buck-buck, while noting casually that the girls were content with hopscotch and skipping. Tops and marbles remained staple activities for boys at least to the 1920s, together with bar-the-door, a boisterous chase from one side of the playground to the other. From the start, Caversham boys had more organised physical activities, too. Discipline was a key element of the masculine ethos and physical training was primarily disciplinary. According to the 1904 syllabus, a class at drill was to perform exercises with military precision to set commands. Military drill was instituted at the school in the 1870s, taken on Wednesday afternoons by a caustic sergeant-major, who would bawl out a boy with poor posture as a 'rotten cabbage in a wheelbarrow'.[17] Sport was called on to help develop masculine character; a keen pupil teacher got together the first rugby team as early as 1884. From 1879 boys could march in a fife and drum band, probably the first school band in Otago. Both girls and boys, however, regarded the gymnasium as their territory, alike enjoying the horse, dumb-bells and clubs.[18]

That the nineteenth-century classroom was strictly regimented may be taken for granted. Teachers, coping with very large classes, followed narrowly interpreted prescriptions in an atmosphere of tightly imposed order. There was a heavy emphasis on examinations, especially the final Proficiency exam.

The culmination of the examination system was the Proficiency exam, taken in Standard 6. Between 1902 and 1937 the Certificate of Proficiency testified that the holder had two years' secondary education. Walter Little of Musselburgh passed his Proficiency in 1925. CAVERSHAM PROJECT COLLECTION

With this qualification, even if they had not reached the age of thirteen, pupils could leave school.[19] The proportion of examination passes, constantly scrutinised as proof of the quality of education, was high for both sexes. In 1882, for example, Caversham achieved a 91 per cent pass rate and a group of standard six pupils – three girls and one boy – took out four of Otago's forty-six junior scholarships to high school.[20]

Schooling on the Flat in the nineteenth century is well beyond the reach of oral history, but from the early years of the twentieth century we have been able to capture, in an extensive series of interviews begun twenty years ago, what southern Dunedin children thought of their primary schooling. The recollections were generally happy ones – Caversham was a 'dandy school', one said. Several proudly remembered the Caversham choir performing in the spacious elegance of His Majesty's theatre in the centre of town. Former pupils were happy to return to the school for the monthly dances held in the gymnasium.[21] The recollections highlighted differences in the school experiences of boys and girls, tending, indeed, to focus on the subjects they had been taught separately. Hugh Mercer, for example, who went to Forbury and Musselburgh schools and left to work in his parents' shop, named agriculture as his favourite subject. Jessie Cumming, of Caversham School, received her only prize, a copy of *Little Women*, for 'sewing on hooks and eyes and domes and making a buttonhole'. Sadly, she was too busy looking after her younger siblings to read the book. Manual training, in woodwork and cooking, was fondly recalled. When they were in standard four, girls hand-sewed an apron and cap to wear at their cooking classes the next year. The half-day spent at the manual training centre at Macandrew Road School was regarded as a welcome break in the weekly routine. Provision of the required ingredients could be a problem for girls from poorer families. Jessie Cumming, one of a family of eleven children, whose father had been killed in an industrial accident and whose mother was ill, had to rely on her cooking partner to bring such items as an egg or some butter. Although the girls were supposed to take their baking home, she ate all of hers on the way. The walk – or in the case of a few privileged St Clair boys by the 1920s, the bike ride – to and from the manual centre was a rare time for socialising, during which both boys and girls shared what the girls had baked in class.[22]

Corporal punishment featured prominently in the memories of the men and women interviewed. The punishment meted out to boys and girls was different. The perception was that girls were more compliant, boys naughtier. A former pupil of St Patrick's described with a frisson of delighted disapproval how the boys in her class had used rulers to flick ink-soaked bits of blotter at the ceiling and how they had yelled their times tables.[23] Daley found the same attitude at Taradale: 'Keeping rules was associated with femininity; breaking rules was a masculine pursuit,' is the way she sums it up. Administering and receiving the strap or cane was a man-to-man ritual, recalled in later years with bravado. The strap was a traditional part of school life for boys, an important element in the code of masculinity. To take a strapping without betraying any pain was admired as taking your punishment like a man. 'Are we to raise a race of cowards . . . a set of hypochondriacal weaklings?' the editor of a Dunedin magazine fulminated in 1889, in response to a suggestion that corporal punishment might be harmful.[24] The attitude persisted, but a teacher who strapped too often or without due cause was bitterly resented. At least three former Caversham pupils remembered the regular strapping they received at the hands of the notorious 'Stringy' Wilson for incomplete homework or incorrect sums. One mother transferred her children to St Clair for their final year rather than have them in his class. Occasionally, the cane was used. Hugh Mercer described bending over a desk to be caned on his backside. Former St Clair pupils remembered boys repeatedly strapped on

SCHOOLING FOR A GENDERED FUTURE

The well-turned-out Caversham School Cadet Corps drilling in the school grounds in 1909 illustrates the strong militaristic element in boys' education at all levels in the early years of the twentieth century, an element intensified during the First World War. The figures of two girls watching from the play-shed remind us of the contrasting roles of men and women in wartime. HOCKEN LIBRARY

the hand by one particular teacher. One woman related how upset she and the other girls in her class had been by the daily strapping of a hard core of half a dozen boys who regularly had up to seventeen spelling errors (the teacher unmoved by one who, each morning, would snivel and back away the width of the classroom) and more than one recalled how much the boys feared the strap of the first assistant. One widely admired teacher 'strapped the boys when or if absolutely necessary, but never the girls'.[25] Boys, it was accepted, had to be toughened.

The First World War sharply increased children's awareness of their divergent future roles. Primary school readers made this clear. 'Into her sacrificial role, the waiting woman, the sad heroine, sister of a soldier killed at the front, the school girl was initiated early,' writes Fry. Girls joined their mothers in knitting, fundraising, farewelling soldiers and waiting, while boys' patriotism found an outlet in the cadet corps, now compulsory in most schools. Certainly, the Minister of Education, J. A. Hanan, was careful to refer to both boys and girls when he spoke at St Clair School in 1917 of the need to build children up mentally and physically to replace the men who had 'given their lives in fighting for the noblest cause that men could strive for'. Both boys and girls joined eagerly in the unrestrained shouting and banging of desks permitted at the armistice, but the school Rolls of Honour and memorial gates erected in the post-war period were an ongoing, sobering reminder of an exclusively masculine activity.[26]

Organised sport – football for boys and basketball for girls – was an established part of primary school life by the 1920s, but our interviewees said surprisingly little about it. St Clair pupils enjoyed an hour of sport every Wednesday and remembered warmly the teachers who coached rugby or cricket – 'Mr McMullan was our hero,' one said. Athletics was especially strong in the school in the interwar period and both boys and girls participated in the annual Primary Schools Athletics Sports at Logan Park, where St Clair won the shield most years in the 1920s. Girls' playground games had evidently become more boisterous, too; the girls of at least one class 'played soccer with a tennis ball at lunch-time'.[27]

In summary, then, though the core primary school curriculum was the same for boys and girls, the schools as institutions actively participated in

This 1917 class of Standard 2 girls from Musselburgh School are shown doing their patriotic duty, knitting socks for soldiers. REPRODUCED, BY PERMISSION, FROM HEATHER NICHOLSON, *THE LOVING STITCH*, P.90. PHOTO COURTESY JAN KETTINK

the teaching of gender. They took it for granted that boys were rougher, were better at arithmetic and were destined for leadership roles and active lives. For girls the future was assumed to lie in home and motherhood. Although the women teachers provided alternative role models for the academically inclined, girls would have been aware that the top positions in the teaching hierarchy were a male preserve. In the classroom, as well as in the playground, the two sexes tended to keep to themselves. A former St Clair boy, who had clear recollection of many things from his schooldays in the 1920s, confessed that he could not recall the names of any of the twenty or so girls who had been in his class from the first through to the sixth standard. Gender distinctions at primary school may not have been so sharply delineated as they would be at secondary school, but they were already securely in place.[28]

Crossing the boundary to secondary school
The idea of boundaries is a recurring theme in Caroline Daley's study of gender relations in the Taradale community, whether they took the form of the real iron fence that divided the boys' and girls' playgrounds at the school, or less tangible constraints on men and women: they were gendered boundaries, to be accepted, negotiated, sometimes challenged.[29] When they left their primary school days behind, the boys and girls of Dunedin's southern suburbs clearly felt they were widening the boundaries of their experience. The break-up day tradition of girls entering the boys' playground to play a kissing game symbolised the new freedoms of young adulthood. For many boys in the early part of our period, especially those who had passed the Proficiency examination in their final year at primary school, formal education had ended and they prepared to enter apprenticeships, very likely in the southern Dunedin area, which would assure their future livelihoods. For girls in this period, leaving primary school was a less straightforward step towards independent adulthood. For some the boundaries became more constricting. Most returned home to unpaid domestic duties and whether this role was a subordinate or an adult one depended on individual families. From the early twentieth century there was a striking change, as the proportion of both boys and girls who moved on to secondary education rose dramatically. As they travelled daily beyond their familiar neighbourhood, they also extended the boundaries of their experience and ambitions.

In the nineteenth century the great mass of New Zealand children were not expected to advance beyond the primary school. A few annual local Education Board or Board of Governors' scholarships, which allowed them to attend secondary school free of charge, facilitated mobility for a small group of pupils towards university study. For boys, this eventually led on to careers in professions such as medicine or law, or at least a respectable white-collar job; for girls, it led to teaching. This route was taken by very few southern Dunedin children. Rather, ambitious boys and their parents learned to use the primary schools' annual standards examinations as a ladder to economic and social advancement.[30] For example, apprentices at the huge Hillside Railway Workshops in Kensington, which employed 400 men in 1904, had to have passed standard four.[31] The Standard Six Proficiency Certificate proved to be a particularly attractive credential for those boys leaving school with ambitions to enter desirable employment, such as the civil service.[32]

In the new century this pattern changed. Richard Seddon, swept back into power in 1902 on a wave of egalitarianism, responded to the mood by opening up the secondary schools to 'free-place scholars' with Proficiency.[33] The number of children newly eligible to go to secondary school was not great: 7168 children throughout the country passed the Proficiency examination in 1902. Nevertheless, the change was momentous.[34] Among those who, from 1903, crossed the primary–secondary boundary were a significant number of children from southern Dunedin. Which of them actually made it to secondary school, however, was often determined by factors other than success in their Proficiency exam. Where the family income was marginal, a father's loss of employment, or the untimely death of a parent, could suddenly throw the family into penury. When Annie Norman's husband became ill with 'phossy jaw' from his work in the Wax Vesta match factory, she had to rely on the Charitable Aid Board and neighbourly kindness to feed herself and her three children. When he died, she had no option but to return to live with her own parents.[35] If children lost a mother, a daughter would be likely to have to stay at home, as happened in the case of Pat Donnelly's two eldest sisters. Jessie Cumming had to leave school at fourteen when her mother became a semi-invalid after the accidental death of her father; she had to look after the five youngest of the eleven children in the family.[36] In marked contrast to families who could not afford secondary education for all their children, both the sons and daughters of the wealthy and prominent family of Robert Rutherford, founder of the Wax Vesta factory, received substantial high school education and some went on to university as well.[37]

Where did most boys and girls from southern Dunedin go when they left primary school, and how did this change over the period? The intended destinations of standard six and seven pupils are entered on the pupils' school records and in the table below we have summarised this information from Caversham, Forbury, Musselburgh and St Clair schools, for the period 1881–1929. The figures are not available for each school over the whole period. They are incomplete, especially for the earlier part of the period, and especially for Forbury School. The records of Kensington and Macandrew Road schools have not survived. In the early years, the destination column is frustratingly often left blank, more often in the case of girls, and more often in the case of those who did not pass the Proficiency exam than in the case of those who did. To simplify the table, the insignificant categories of 'ambiguous', 'misfortune' and 'moved out of district' have been incorporated with the blanks as 'unknown'.

Table 4.1 Destinations of primary school leavers from southern Dunedin (percentage)

	1881–1902		1903–1918		1919–1928	
	Boys	Girls	Boys	Girls	Boys	Girls
Education	9	12	47	49	73	75
Home	5	22	3	25	1	7
Work	44	6	42	12	18	6
Unknown	42	60	8	14	8	12
Total per cent	100	100	100	100	100	100
Total number	441	349	457	348	305	262

Source: Caversham Project Primary School records: Caversham, 1881–1929, Forbury 1885–1925, Musselburgh 1906–1928, St Clair 1887–1929.

The most obvious trend illustrated in the table is the strong increase in the numbers of both boys and girls going on to secondary school. Conversely, there is a decline in the number of boys moving straight from primary school to paid employment and, even more markedly, in the number of girls citing 'home' as a destination. The 'unknown' category decreases sharply over the period, presumably because of better record-keeping. In the case of girls, this category is likely to have included those who were returning to help at home. Despite their omissions, the figures provide interesting insights, clearly identifying gender differences and, perhaps more significantly, commonalities in trends over the period. By the end of the 1920s roughly three-quarters of the pupils of both sexes from these four major southern Dunedin schools were enjoying secondary education, a proportion that would increase from 1936 when the Proficiency examination was abolished as an entry requirement. What kind of secondary education could they expect?

Choice of secondary school

Melanie Nolan argues convincingly that the most important movement in New Zealand education over the whole period between 1870 and 1930 was egalitarian: 'the extension of a liberal education to girls in the same way as boys and to the working class in the same way as to the upper and middle classes'.[38] But there was more at issue, as Nolan acknowledges, than making the traditional curriculum more widely available. Strong pressures were at work in favour of a 'modern' secondary education, considered more suited to the new student population, and taking into account gender and class. In our investigation into the secondary education of southern Dunedin children we found that considerations of gender and class continually modified the trend towards an egalitarian, modern education for all children.

To understand fully the significance of free places at secondary school for southern Dunedin children it is helpful to set the Dunedin high schools in the context of their social class origins. Otago Boys' High School (OBHS) had been founded in 1863 to provide an academic education to privileged sons of the well-to-do, who were destined to become leaders in the professions and the business community. Its dominance was scarcely challenged by Protestant denominational schools, although Catholic boys usually went to Christian Brothers', which opened in 1876. There was no high school for boys in southern Dunedin until King's High School opened in 1936.[39] A few boys from southern Dunedin primary schools attended OBHS before 1903, mainly on scholarships, but a detailed study has established that schooling there was 'overwhelmingly the domain of those who lived close to the school itself' and that parents of southern Dunedin could not, on the whole, afford to send their children there.[40]

When Otago Girls' High School (OGHS), the first state secondary school for girls in New Zealand, opened in 1871, it offered a curriculum similar to that of the boys' school, with a light dusting of feminine accomplishments. Initially it was housed in the south wing of the Boys' High School building, and a high wall was put up to divide the playground.[41] The new girls' high school was not intended to challenge the traditional order of society. Its male advocates assumed that the future of well-educated women would be as wives

OPPOSITE: Pupils from primary schools in southern Dunedin could choose among three state secondary schools in this period. Each was designed by a leading architect and together they make a strong statement about the importance attached to education in the southern city. It was a value shared by families from South Dunedin. TOP: Otago Boys' High School (1863) moved to this building, designed by R. A. Lawson, in 1885. It offered a traditional academic education, expected to lead to employment in the professions. MIDDLE: Otago Girls' High School (1871) occupied this building, designed by Edward Anscombe and built on the site previously shared with the boys' school, in 1909. The original academic curriculum was broadened to include domestic and commercial courses. BOTTOM: King Edward Technical College (1913), designed by Henry Mandeno, was intended to offer practical training in trade skills to working-class boys and domestic skills to their sisters. It was popular with South Dunedin families, but the girls proved more interested in commercial than domestic training. ALL HOCKEN LIBRARY

SCHOOLING FOR A GENDERED FUTURE

for well-educated men. 'Such a cultivation of mind as will make a really good wife, sister or daughter to educated men' was the aim.[42] Later in 1871, however, acting on a petition from the same group of determined women who had brought the high school into being, the University of Otago agreed to accept women students. It took some years for the Girls' High School to attain the academic standard required to get pupils through the university entrance examination – Matriculation – but the school then took the lead in providing able university students, and by 1886 the first of a steady trickle of former pupils were graduating in arts and entering the teaching profession. A decade later they were moving into medicine and law as well.[43] Well-to-do Dunedin parents had more choice of secondary schools for their daughters than for their sons, thanks to a range of private girls' schools, usually denominational and with an emphasis on the teaching of ladylike accomplishments, such as Presbyterian Columba College and Anglican Saint Hilda's. From their primary school at Saint Patrick's in South Dunedin, Catholic girls could go either next door to Saint Philomena's, run since 1897 by the Sisters of Mercy, or, if they sought a more refined education, to St Dominic's in the city.[44]

In spite of the similarity of their curricula and initial sharing of site, the tone of the Otago Boys' and Girls' High Schools was very different. For the boys, school discipline, reinforced by corporal punishment, was strict; rugby, cricket and school cadets taught manliness, academic achievement was admired and a culture of pride in the school was maintained by its Old Boys. The girls' school, on the other hand, was a world of female authority and order where, as Muriel May recalled of her first day in 1911, all was 'comely and serene', just as her mother, a pupil of the 1870s, had described it to her. The difference is neatly illustrated by the Boys' High magazine of April 1899, which allocated four pages to Girls' High news. In the boys' section sport dominates – six pages are given over to football, six to athletics and fifteen to cricket – as well as Old Boys' news and an account of prize day. In the girls' section there are notes on examinations and a list of new pupils, but the focus is on womanly philanthropic activities: a good beginning for the Dorcas Society (which sewed for charity), the sending of flowers to the hospital and a competition for the best-dressed doll, the dolls to be donated to the hospital.[45]

When it opened in 1908, the co-educational King Edward Technical College represented something quite different. Its origins lay in the evening courses, run from 1889 by the Technical Classes Association, to enable primary school leavers, employed during the day, to carry on their education to Matriculation level. Academic subjects such as English and arithmetic were accompanied by practical ones such as plumbing, engineering and dressmaking. The classes were primarily aimed at males, but from the start girls proved eager to participate; there were more than 100 of them among the 457 attending in 1895.[46] As a day school, the King Edward Technical College was one of a series of technical schools, beginning with one in Auckland in 1905, to be established in all the main centres by 1910. Intended for 'those children who failed to benefit from the standard literary fare' they were originally intended to teach agricultural and domestic subjects. Viewed as non-academic schools with lower-class pupils, the 'techs' were both looked down on by the high schools and feared as competitors.[47]

Secondary school pupils from southern Dunedin

Once they left primary school, southern Dunedin pupils tended to become submerged in the general population of the city's secondary schools. In this section we aim to counter this dilution of the sense of locality by identifying secondary school pupils from southern Dunedin by gender, class (indicated by their father's occupational grouping) and the primary school they attended. We then take a case study, linking attendance at Caversham, Forbury, St Clair or Musselburgh schools with choice of secondary school, keeping in mind the differences between the academic curriculum and career expectations of the traditional single-sex high schools and the new commercially focused King Edward Technical College. Constrained by the availability of records, this case study focuses on the years 1906 to 1929.

We first consider the class background of the secondary school pupils from southern Dunedin, separating out boys and girls. In Figure 4.1 we identify the occupational classifications of the fathers of the 321 pupils (out of 883) for whom this information is available. Although the numbers are not large, it is striking how many fathers in skilled and semi-skilled occupations chose to send their daughters to secondary school. The apprenticeships and cadetships available to boys did not exist for girls and it seems likely that opportunities opening up in office work held a special appeal for families attached to the skilled trades. Professionals also sent more daughters than sons to secondary school, but all the other occupations were more likely to send sons. The biggest discrepancy by gender occurred amongst white-collar and small employers, who gave much more support to their sons' education; it seems that they were less ambitious for their daughters, at least in terms of paid employment. That such a small number of daughters of the 'large employer' class were being sent to state secondary schools encourages speculation that they might have been attending private schools instead. Fathers from this group certainly valued their sons' education: a study using

OBHS records relating to southern Dunedin pupils for the period 1911 to 1921 has found that most OBHS fathers came from the managerial and business elites and the skilled category.[48]

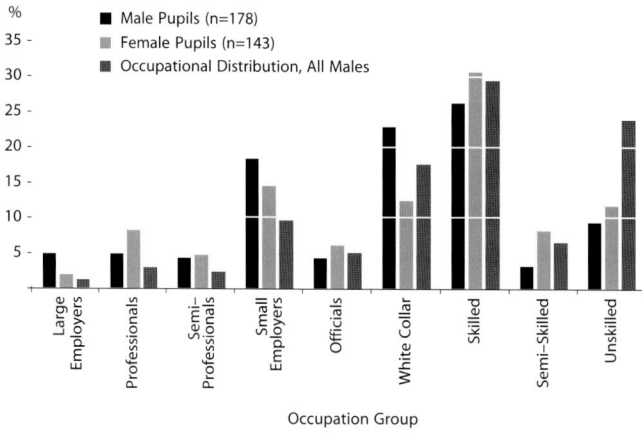

Figure 4.1 Occupations of fathers of Standard 6 and 7 pupils proceeding to state secondary education, Caversham, Forbury, Musselburgh, St Clair schools, 1906–1929

The pattern of attendance at secondary school was not dissimilar for boys and girls from southern Dunedin over our study period. Before the turn of the century, very few of either attended high school at all. Thereafter, right through to 1929, more boys than girls usually attended, although there were exceptions to this, for example, during the First World War. But it is noteworthy that, although southern Dunedin was a predominantly working-class area, the proportion of girls going on to high school was higher than for New Zealand as a whole.[49] In general, boys and girls went to separate institutions. Almost three-quarters of the southern Dunedin children who went to secondary school before 1929 attended single-sex schools, 840 as against 297, and even the apparently co-educational King Edward Technical College offered mainly separate courses for boys and girls. Single-sex secondary schooling was the dominant pattern elsewhere in New Zealand as well, no doubt stemming from the British Victorian tradition wherein boys and girls were educated separately for moral and religious reasons.[50] In the table below, we use information from the same four primary schools to deduce something of the pattern of secondary school attendance for southern Dunedin children.

Table 4.2 Secondary school destinations of Standard 6 and 7 pupils from selected schools, 1906–1929, showing number and percentage

Primary School		Secondary School				Total
		OBHS (boys)	OGHS (girls)	KETC (boys)	KETC (girls)	
Caversham	no	110	110	42	63	325
	%	34	34	13	19	100
Forbury	no	7	3	6	5	21
	%	33	14	29	24	100
Musselburgh	no	152	95	48	40	335
	%	46	28	14	12	100
St Clair	no	91	69	19	23	202
	%	45	35	10	11	100
Total	n=	360	277	115	131	883

Source: Caversham primary schools records database: Caversham, Forbury, Musselburgh, St Clair Schools.

If we assume that sending a child to secondary school was a mark of parental ambition, we find that the skilled working-class parents of Caversham shared this ambition with those from lower-middle-class Musselburgh and up-market St Clair. They also preferred the traditional academic education offered by the high schools. It would be tempting to assume, on the basis of the figures, that very few pupils from Forbury School went on to secondary education and that this was because the school served a rougher area, but it would be a rash assumption. Forbury, in fact, kept very poor records of the intended destination of its school leavers: for years on end, in some cases, this column in the pupils' records was left blank.

We can sharpen the focus by taking two sample years, 1911 and 1919, and matching up the names of pupils leaving these four primary schools with first-year class lists from Otago Boys' and Girls' High Schools and King Edward Technical College (KETC).

Table 4.3 Secondary school destinations of Standard 6 and 7 pupils from selected schools, 1911 and 1919

	1911				1919			
	OBHS	OGHS	KETC (boys)	KETC (girls)	OBHS	OGHS	KETC (boys)	KETC (girls)
Caversham	2	1	0	6	3	0	16	14
Forbury	1	2	5	5	0	2	6	15
Musselburgh	4	0	0	3	3	0	4	4
St Clair	14	10	0	1	11	8	0	1
Total	21	13	5	15	17	10	26	34

Source: Caversham Database; Class rolls, OBHS, OGHS, KETC.

Although the sample is small – just 140 children in all – it enables us to identify some trends over time in the broad pattern of educational choice set out in Table 4.2. It also gives the lie to any suggestion that the parents of Forbury School pupils were not interested in secondary education for their children, and it highlights the increasing popularity of KETC for primary school leavers, especially girls, from southern Dunedin.

For children from southern Dunedin, taking up a place at any of these secondary schools, all of which were situated on a steep hill overlooking the town centre, was facilitated by the extension of the city's electric tramway system to Caversham, St Clair and St Kilda in 1904–5. Cheap and frequent, trams were their main means of transport, offering them the independence of unsupervised travel and enlarging the physical boundaries of their lives, as they left their own neighbourhood and suburb each day for the public bustle of the city.[51] They were now identified by their uniform as a pupil of a particular school, rather than as someone's son or daughter, known locally. The wearing of school uniform, which developed over the period, reflected notions of gender and class. In 1911 pupils of girls' schools were distinguished only by the colour of their hatbands, but by the 1920s girls from OGHS and the private schools were wearing the gym tunic, blouse, tie and blazer (and, on the street, ladylike hat and gloves) that would characterise girls' high schools for decades to come. For boys from the High School, uniform was an outward expression of discipline. They wore shorts and blazers and were expected to have their ties straight, socks pulled up and caps on outside the school grounds. Attention to the niceties of uniform created another public distinction between the High Schools and the Tech, where uniform was less rigidly enforced. Some pupils took pride in their uniform, but others found it desperately constraining. It was, however, agreed to be a great leveller, preventing ready identification of children as coming from middle-class or working-class homes. The 'scruffy' children of both sexes who populated the primary school playgrounds were absent from the secondary schools.[52]

Class and gender in the curriculum

From 1899 New Zealand's new Inspector General of Education, George Hogben, set in motion a scheme to democratise the country's education. Central to his thinking was the ideal that no able child should be barred from secondary education by lack of money. We have noted that the free-place system, the cornerstone of his policy, opened up new worlds of secondary education to children from modest backgrounds. Equally, the coming of free-place pupils, for whom Hogben intended a less academic, more practical education, precipitated striking changes in New Zealand's secondary schools. In the early years of the twentieth century the implications of these changes were worked out in terms of class and gender.

New Zealand was one of the first countries in the Western world to embrace the doctrines of educational and social efficiency, with their twin tenets of differentiated schooling and a gendered curriculum.[53] Specific courses, such as academic, agricultural, commercial, domestic and industrial, were introduced to cater for the different pupils attending the three types of post-primary schools, secondary, district high and technical high schools. There were problems: on the one hand, it was no easy task to change an educational market long accustomed to stamping the 'socially inferior' label on anything remotely 'applied', 'manual', 'practical' or 'technical'; on the other, the high schools could not afford to relinquish the free-place scholars to the technical colleges.[54] The problem did not markedly affect boys' education, perhaps because the value to boys of a high school education was widely accepted, and because night classes in trade skills were well established, easing the transition to the idea of daytime technical colleges. In girls' education, on the other hand, there were significant changes, which proved sharply contentious. That girls should receive practical training was generally agreed, but what should be its focus? The options were domestic or commercial, and the contestation between the two reflected changes occurring in women's lives and expectations. It also reflected sharp disagreement between educational theorists, who placed emphasis on the training of future wives and mothers in domestic skills, and parents who wanted their daughters to be able to participate in the new vocational opportunities of the expanding economy. We can follow these issues further by contrasting the responses of the girls' and boys' high schools to the influx of free-place scholars from 1903.

At Otago Girls' High School, the experienced and charismatic Maria Marchant, principal from 1891 to 1911, recognised that the only way her school could survive in the new environment, in which some 70 per cent of the free-place holders left before the expiry of the two-year tenure permitted under the regulations, was to introduce short practical courses in line with the girls' immediate vocational needs:[55]

> [T]hese girls' parents cannot afford to keep them at school for more than two years as a rule. I foresee that if I am not allowed to supply what our pupils require, the girls will stay on at the primary schools, or go to the technical school, and the Girls' High School will fall to the ground. I have given up hoping ever to attract back the children of well-to-do parents . . .[56]

Marchant was threatened by competition from two sides: the private schools for the children of the well-to-do and KETC for those of more humble background demanding training for office jobs.[57] After debating the matter for several months, the Otago High Schools' Board of Governors agreed to appoint a commercial mistress to teach shorthand and bookkeeping during the school day, with typing offered as a chargeable extra to be taken after school hours. The new commercial course proved to be highly popular among free-place entrants.[58]

Without the threat of competition from private schools, Otago Boys' High School was affected by the advent of free-place students to a much lesser extent. Alexander Wilson, the rector when free places were introduced, was adamant that the traditional academic curriculum remain unchanged, arguing that 'those not ready to profit by the secondary school ought to attend a technical school'. His successor, William Morrell, who opposed offering commercial training in his school because he believed that this belonged in KETC – he called it 'a drill ground for the lower ranks of the industrial and commercial army'[59] – was nevertheless forced to concede the attractiveness of short courses in bookkeeping, commercial geography, commercial correspondence and shorthand for the less academically inclined students.[60] The basic curriculum, however, remained uncompromisingly academic and the culture strongly masculine. Otago Boys' High School continued to expect that its sons would

Members of the Otago Boys' High School Shooting Team, winners of the Silver Bugle Competition in 1914, may well have used their expertise in the war that began before the year was out. *OTAGO BOYS' HIGH SCHOOL MAGAZINE*, 1914, HOCKEN LIBRARY

be leaders in their community. An all-male staff accepted without question the value of physical punishment. Manliness was taught through sport, especially cricket and rugby, which was compulsory. Greg Ryan points out the extent to which New Zealand's elite boys' secondary schools helped establish rugby as a 'manly' and 'national' game by providing encouragement, coaching and playing opportunities. OBHS produced more All Blacks than any other school in New Zealand before 1914, exemplifying what Jock Phillips calls the 'centrality of rugby as a moral vision' in New Zealand boys' schools.[61] The ethos of masculinity was reinforced by the tragedy of the First World War: of the 167 former pupils killed, at least one had still been a schoolboy in 1914–15. The first magazine after the armistice urged secondary schools of the Empire to 'continue to inculcate in the boys that pass through them a genuine patriotism, high ideals and a true spirit of service . . . the best possible work for the Empire and for humanity'. A fine memorial arch to the fallen was dedicated in 1923.[62]

Disputes around girls' education were exacerbated from 1910 by a new government policy. What was an appropriate education for a woman? The question was a very old one, but it had new relevance at a time when the concept of femininity, traditionally defined in terms of marriage, motherhood and household management, was being challenged by the availability of new paid jobs for women. The Department of Education embarked upon a policy of imposing greater variation in the high school curriculum along strictly gender-based lines. Hogben was of the opinion that all girls should leave post-primary school with 'an intelligent grasp of the principles underlying household management', in particular practical and theoretical domestic science.[63] Several prominent Dunedin physicians, such as Truby King, Lindo Ferguson and Ferdinand Batchelor, all from the Otago Medical School, went further and declared that domestic instruction not only constituted the best preparation for marriage and motherhood, but also contributed to national fitness and a stable home environment.[64] Politicians frequently made reference to the national importance of having properly educated women knowledgeable in domestic matters. Despite strong dissent from those who claimed that in a modern society girls had to be trained to compete on an equal footing with males – and these dissenters included such prominent women doctors as Emily Siedeberg – two hours of home science a week became mandatory in 1917 for all third and fourth form girls, irrespective of the type of post-primary school they were attending. Melanie Nolan believes that the timing was significant. During the war there had been rapid changes as women took over male jobs, and the insistence on domestic education for girls was an attempt to put a brake on change.[65] For OGHS the legislation necessitated the appointment of a home science teacher, and caused a crisis in classroom accommodation, just when the commercial course was enjoying a boost from wartime conditions.[66]

The requirement to provide domestic training for girls cannot have caused anxiety to King Edward Technical College, which opened in 1908. In 1905 the dressmaking class had been the largest of all the evening classes of its parent body, the Dunedin Technical Classes – there were five classes with a total of 124 students – and cookery classes were also well established. The daytime occupations of the 722 Dunedin students listed at this time included 119 who described themselves as engaged in domestic duties, so it must have seemed safe to assume that domestic classes at the new college would prove popular. The experience of the evening classes also made the college confident of attracting day pupils into its commercial classes, to which the required domestic component could readily be added. The superintendent found the 'conspicuous success' of commercial subjects in the evening classes a source of pleasure and looked forward to extending the scope of the work to day classes, training young people before they entered employment, rather than part-time after work.[67]

The King Edward Technical College, then, began with high hopes for its domestic course. It soon became evident, however, that the girls, and their parents, did not share these hopes. They determinedly turned their backs on the domestic course in favour of commercial. In 1915 there were 155 girls taking the commercial course, together with thirty-eight boys; only fifty-one girls had opted for the domestic course. The following year, low numbers in the domestic course were a cause for concern: once again a full two-thirds of the girls enrolled for commercial. A number of these objected to the requirement that they take either sewing or cookery as part of their course. 'Strange as it may seem,' the principal reported, 'sometimes the mother of a girl applying for admission to the day school subjects objects to her daughter's learning either needlework or cookery.' When such a mother learned that this was compulsory, she would usually decide to send her daughter elsewhere. The (presumably under-utilised) KETC facilities were made available to pupils from private schools and even students of the University of Otago School of Home Science for cookery lessons.[68]

The principal's report in 1915 provides a vivid snapshot of the Technical College. The buildings, he explained with satisfaction, were debt-free and the facilities the best in New Zealand. There were 303 students, of whom fifty-eight were boys in the industrial course. The commercial course was growing each year and the principal was constantly being approached to see if any pupils were ready for positions in the workforce; over the last two or three months, thirty-three of the 194 commercial pupils had been called

From 1900 manual training was introduced for senior pupils in primary schools, cookery for girls, woodwork for boys. At secondary level, while Technical Colleges focused on such gendered practical courses, other schools were also expected to provide them. These photographs show a woodwork class at KETC in 1910 and a cookery class at Otago Girls' High School in 1925.
KING EDWARD TECHNICAL COLLEGE JUBILEE MAGAZINE, 1959 (TOP); OTAGO SETTLERS MUSEUM (BOTTOM)

in this way, the girls usually starting at a higher salary than the boys. The domestic course had fifty-one pupils, who through the year had prepared 8896 hot lunches for sale at 4d or 5d each. In 1916 a 20-page typed magazine produced by some of the girls adds to this picture in a jolly, if juvenile, way. 'Our brainy stenographers,' it reported, were being 'literally worked to death' for their Junior Government Examinations and the domestic girls had carried off prizes for pies at the recent Apple Show.[69] The KETC evening classes, always much larger than the day school, with 1277 students in 1915, catered primarily for young tradesmen. Pat Donnelly, for example, studied English, arithmetic and plumbing for a year while in the employ of the City Council Gas Department. Ian Martin, who had gone to OBHS for four years, and had failed Matriculation English (and so the whole exam), took the subject at night tech to enable him to go to university. A sample group of evening-class students who had been to primary school in southern Dunedin shows a sharp increase from 1911, when there were thirty, of whom eighteen were males, to 1919, when there were sixty-one, of whom forty-seven were males.[70]

By the 1920s secondary education for both sexes had become the norm. That boys now routinely attended secondary school did not fundamentally alter their expectations. The career paths of boys from southern Dunedin were still largely determined by class and they tended increasingly to opt for KETC training in the skilled trades. Only two of those interviewed went on to tertiary education: Stuart Sidey, the son of an elite family, who studied law, and Ian Martin, who used night tech as a bridge from OBHS to training in accountancy.[71] The rest took up apprenticeships and cadetships, often starting in humble jobs, such as errand boys, at the bottom of the employment ladder. Of the thirty-nine boys in our sample group from 1911 and 1919 who went to OBHS, twenty-four had left by the end of their second year, and only two stayed the four years that would enable them to sit Matriculation and proceed to tertiary education.[72]

Otago Boys' High School might go its own way, but Girls' High had to enter into direct competition with the Technical College for commercial students. The principal from 1922 to 1944 was the forceful and astute Mary King. She argued that, if her school was to survive, it had to demonstrate that it was so much more thorough in all aspects of its commercial teaching that its examination candidates surpassed those from KETC.[73] She also sought to differentiate her school on class grounds. 'As a general rule,' she explained, 'those who go to the Technical School belong to the labouring classes; those wanting a "nicer" education go to the High School.'[74] This perception of class difference was shared by our interviewees. One remarked that Girls' High pupils 'kind of looked down on' Tech pupils. There was no question about the quality of commercial training at KETC, however, and southern Dunedin girls who went there opted overwhelmingly for this course. None took an industrial or technical course. Of our sample group, eleven out of fifteen in 1911, and twenty-nine out of thirty-three in 1919 took commercial.[75] Helen Wilson, daughter of a former mayor of Dunedin, went to OGHS for three years, but then spent three years at KETC evening classes, because she considered the standard of the high school's commercial course was not up to that of the technical college. Alison Abraham, who took commercial at Girls' High, explained that it took longer to get through the course than at KETC, because there 'they just had straight commercial', without extras.[76] The majority of our interviewees who went to OGHS took a commercial course rather than an academic or domestic one. More personal factors than class background or employment aims could, of course, influence one's choice of

Girls, and their mothers, preferred commercial to domestic training, flocking to join typing classes, such as this one at KETC in 1931. By this time typing had become a feminised occupation. *KING EDWARD TECHNICAL COLLEGE JUBILEE MAGAZINE*, 1959

school. Frances Kenny was convinced that she only succeeded in getting to Girls' High because she was the youngest of six children and her parents were more financially secure than they had been when their older children were sent to KETC, with early employment in mind. Her reason for wanting to go to OGHS was to indulge her passion for tennis.[77] For those girls who chose to attend KETC rather than OGHS, the difference in social standing of the two schools appeared more illusory than real. Indeed, the popularity of KETC in the eyes of many primary school leavers from southern Dunedin suggests that it was an institution that offered vocationally useful training closely attuned to the practical realities of the Dunedin labour market.

Some of the women interviewees from southern Dunedin who attended secondary school in the 1920s looked back with resentment on what they saw as inadequacies in the nature or length of their secondary schooling. There was evidence of thwarted ambition. Yvonne Morris, for example, remained bitter that her wealthy photographer father had decided to make her his assistant at the 1926 Exhibition instead of sending her to the private school Archerfield, as promised.[78] Helen Wilson did well at Otago Girls' but was forced to work from the age of fifteen. She overcame her disappointment by taking three years of night classes.[79] Most stayed at high school for two years or less. Few went on to tertiary education: Kitty Brown gained an MA and became a high school principal, but she was exceptional in her academic achievement and subsequent career.[80] Helen Tweed, an ex-Archerfield pupil, did two years of a Home Science course at Otago University, intending to go nursing when she was eighteen, but instead left to work in the office of her father's flourishing dyeing and dry-cleaning business. There were stresses involved in working for her 'Victorian' father, but she enjoyed having virtually sole charge of the office.[81] Most of the women interviewed stressed that the employment options for girls were very narrow: teaching or nursing for the more academic and office, shop, sewing or factory work for those who were less academically inclined or came from less affluent families. As they relished, if only for a few years, the independence, companionship and wage packet of the modern shop or office, they seemed quite unaware of how far these options had widened from their mothers' generation.

Conclusion

Schools are a prime site for the reproduction of gender differences, but also, as our study has revealed, a site in which the complexities of gender change must be worked out. They prepare children for the adult roles they will fulfil as men and women. In southern Dunedin during our period, these roles were centred on the family, itself an evolving institution. Elsewhere in this volume, writers have traced the impact on predominantly working-class southern Dunedin of the changes that were affecting New Zealand society as a whole. Foremost among these was what Erik Olssen has called the 'spectacular' decline in the size of the family unit, with which came new ideals of marital and parental responsibility.[82] The family wage was enshrined in working-class culture, but as well as being a breadwinner a husband was increasingly expected to be a 'family man'. His wife was still expected to contribute to the family economy by caring for home and family. His son was expected to become a breadwinner in his turn, bringing home a family wage. For boys growing to manhood in our period, there was a basic continuity of experience. In the case of girls growing to womanhood, on the other hand, there was sharp discontinuity. It ceased to be necessary for a daughter leaving primary school to return home to look after younger siblings or help with domestic chores. She could look forward to some years of paid employment before returning to the domestic sphere as wife. At the same time, as New Zealand society modernised in the first third of the twentieth century, employment options for young women were transformed by growth in the clerical, secretarial and retail sectors. These options, together with the availability of cheap public transport, less constrictive clothing and a range of leisure activities, helped create for them a quite new lifestyle.

The task facing New Zealand's education authorities was how best to prepare its future citizens of both sexes for participation in this rapidly evolving society. Steadily democratic in concept, their provision went through two distinct phases, of which free compulsory primary schooling in 1877 introduced the first. The second began just after the turn of the century, with the extension of two years' free secondary education to able pupils and the establishment of technical colleges throughout the country. Looking back from the vantage point of 1935, a writer in the journal *National Education* summed up the principles of New Zealand education as it had developed over these decades as being 'based on the child's own interests and activities, with more flexible teaching methods and more practical work' and ending the 'unnatural isolation of the school from the world outside'.[83] The practical work was gender-specific manual training and the end of isolation was to be achieved through employment-related education.

How did parents and children from southern Dunedin respond to these educational changes? Inspectors' reports indicate that, right from the start, primary school attendance was above the New Zealand average and that boys were eager to use the school examination system for employment advantage.[84] We can surmise that this attitude derives from the Scottish tradition of universal primary schooling, brought over with Otago's first settlers and reinforced, in the case of southern Dunedin, by the high proportion of skilled workers and also, perhaps, by the high proportion of evangelical Protestants in the area. In the nineteenth century, few pupils from southern Dunedin went on to secondary school. Typically, boys took up apprenticeships or unskilled jobs and girls returned to help at home. Apart from the high attendance rates, we have no firm evidence that there was anything about primary schooling in southern Dunedin that was markedly different from that in working-class suburbs of other New Zealand cities.

Southern Dunedin boys and girls participated in roughly equal numbers, and increasing proportions, in secondary education when it became available to them. For boys, secondary education meant a later entry into the workforce, and many chose employment-related courses when the Technical College opened, but the change was not dramatic. For girls it was. As our researchers have found throughout this study of southern Dunedin, the changes in women's lives over the period were of greater scope and significance than those in men's lives. The readiness with which southern Dunedin girls entered secondary education after the turn of the century suggests that the mothers of the 1890s, who had signed the suffrage petition in such decisive numbers and who took a leading part in the life of their various churches, wanted more out of life for their daughters than they or their own mothers had experienced.

No longer was elementary schooling, followed by domestic service, paid or unpaid, enough. They wanted education for their daughters to enable them to earn their livings in shops and offices. It is ironic that the state should have attempted to impose domestic education on New Zealand girls at the very time when domestic concerns were assuming less importance in the lives of women. The determination with which southern Dunedin girls eschewed domestic training at secondary school to flock into the commercial courses that would equip them to participate in the modern economy is clear evidence of the futility of the attempt.

Our study has focused on the period from the 1880s to the end of the 1920s, for the practical reason that we have detailed primary school records from southern Dunedin for this period, but also because it forms a coherent whole. In these years, New Zealand's school system was consciously adapting to a modernising society. The following decade shows wilder fluctuations. As economic depression bit in the early 1930s, the perceived need for retrenchment in the education budget cut across the former democratising trend. Desperate to cut expenditure, the government discouraged secondary education, its attitude exemplified by the Prime Minister's dismissive comment that 'frills introduced in the years of prosperity [could] be done away with'. It suddenly raised the barrier of the Proficiency examination to reduce the numbers of pupils who could enter secondary school – the 79 per cent pass rate of 1931 was reduced to a 67 per cent pass rate in 1932.[85] It closed teacher training colleges, raised the age for commencing school to six years, forced married women teachers out of the workforce and 'rationed' employment for many others. After 1935 the Labour Government reversed these decisions. Indeed, it went much further, proclaiming a policy to develop the individual child: its credo was that 'every person, whatever his level of academic ability . . . has a right as a citizen to a free education of the kind for which he is best fitted, and to the fullest extent of his powers'.[86] The masculine tone of the language is striking, and no doubt the primary intention of the policy was to confront inequalities stemming from class rather than gender, but it nevertheless heralded a change of considerable portent for boys and girls alike. As the ideal of teaching each individual child blended with the ideal of equality of educational opportunity, the primary school curriculum was freed up, and the Proficiency examination abolished. It would be naïve to claim that education had become class- and gender-blind, but, for boys and girls from southern Dunedin, the equality of opportunity that had been the aim of the education system between 1902 and 1930 came a step closer to reality.

Five Producing and Consuming Gender: The Case of Clothing

JANE MALTHUS AND CHRIS BRICKELL

By the time Helen Tweed married, she had put together a trousseau that included half a dozen nightgowns, half a dozen petticoats and panties, suspender belt, bra, blouses – all new – silk stockings, shoes, hat, gloves, a handbag and two frocks for dinner wear. She also had a stylish navy blue going-away outfit, made by Matita of London and purchased from the Drapery Supply Association.[1] She had a comprehensive trousseau and continued after marriage to sew or buy three or four new frocks for each ball season. But the size and contents of a woman's trousseau depended on the wealth of individual women and their families. Mavis Liverpool had a blue going-away outfit, and suggested that larger trousseaux were the privilege of 'people with bigger wages'.[2] For their part, men would purchase a new suit of trousers, waistcoat and jacket for their wedding, if they could afford it, and these would provide good service in subsequent years. Suits were worn in offices or auction houses, tailoring or supervisory jobs and even foundry or carpentry work, and were also the masculine norm for dances, church services and other social activities.

In this chapter we explore clothing and its wider context in southern Dunedin between 1890 and 1940. As clothing is produced and worn in particular times and places, wider social processes of gender, consumption and production are involved. These processes interweave continually. The means through which clothing is produced and sold constrain and give meaning to particular practices of consumption, while men and women play particular roles in these processes.[3] The consumption of clothing and other goods for the home depends on the income earned through paid work. Trousseaux and glory boxes could be slowly built up while women were engaged in the paid workforce, before marriage heralded the loss of an independent income. Subsequently, women's unpaid domestic labour included the making and mending of clothing and textiles, and this home production complemented consumption in the marketplace.

Angela McRobbie describes the 'production-consumption chain', which connects the consuming of clothes with the productive activity that creates them.[4] Buying fabric to sew into clothes, for example, involves the labour of the farmer, the spinner, the weaver, the shop assistant and the sewer, as well as a series of purchases. In other words, production is central to consumption. This suggests an analysis that weaves together considerations of the work carried out in households as well as the public sphere. By requiring labour in the household as well as the paid workplace, clothing crosscuts notions of 'public' and 'private' spheres.

McRobbie's approach rejects the widespread tendency to romanticise consumption purely as a means of popular empowerment. Such a romantic view can erase the wider social processes through which the consumed goods are produced, the labour involved in selling and the monetary constraints on consumers' ability to spend.[5] Histories of poverty and exclusion cannot be ignored. In southern Dunedin, wage levels and class position were of critical importance, and these translated into particular understandings of egalitarianism and social difference.[6] For example, discussions about what others wore and the lending or gifting of clothes reveal the connections between notions of egalitarianism and reciprocity. Here the literature that examines cultural values, meaning and signification inherent in processes of consumption is important.[7] Clothing is a marker of social distinction, indicating status and/or conformity with social and community norms.[8] It may also mark the extent to which its wearers identify with their surroundings or push at their boundaries.[9] Clothing, then, can be understood as a key node in a whole range of social relationships, where individual concerns meet the broader, structured patterns of social organisation.

Gender lies at the heart of all these concerns. As Joan Scott suggests, gender constitutes a whole range of social relationships and is therefore a primary field through which power is articulated.[10] Practices of work and consumption are gendered in a myriad of ways – at 'home', in the factory, in the street. For example, we argue that specific clothing styles have delimited the activities and forms of movement considered appropriate for women's bodies in particular, and so styles have changed as expectations of these bodies have modernised. Scott argues that, in order to pursue social meanings in the historical study of gender, we need to examine social organisation and individual subjectivity together. It then becomes possible to articulate the complex relationships between the two more closely.[11] To this end, we have adopted a broad-brush approach to the collection of source material with which to tell the story of clothing, consumption and production in southern Dunedin over our time period. The fragmentary nature of the sources makes such an approach doubly necessary.

The records of the Otago Benevolent Institution (OBI) offer case studies of some individuals' material circumstances. Magazines such as the *Otago Witness* included local advertising that gives clues about the organisation of retailing through the period, although unfortunately there is more documentation of larger inner-city retailers than of small suburban operators. Photographs reveal the relationship between occupation and work clothing, and local appropriations of contemporary fashions. Oral histories offer some recollection of circumstances, relationships and popular discourses from the 1920s and 1930s.[12] These testimonies are particularly useful for illuminating the gendered ways in which clothing was maintained within the home. By discussing these sources, we can consider the connections between clothing, work and individual experiences in southern Dunedin – a specific setting with a particular mixture of industries, retailers and practices of home production. At the same time, we can offer insights that apply across a much wider geographical and cultural landscape.

The following sections address the gendering of clothing production and retailing, and subsequent discussions work through the changes in women's and men's clothing over the study period. Here we consider some of the relationships between shifting fashions, and clothing as a marker of social status. Having explored the importance of women's household production and its significance in the production-consumption chain, we conclude with a reflection on discourses of egalitarianism and what they reveal about popular understandings of clothing, gender and work in southern Dunedin over the 50-year period.

Making clothes: factories and workshops

The period between the 1880s and 1920s in the USA and Europe was characterised by an increasing shift from small-scale production of clothing toward mass production. Dunedin and New Zealand did not lag behind, although the scale of operations was necessarily smaller. The 1870s and 80s saw the first clothing factories and their accompanying retail stores established in Dunedin. Notable among these was Hallenstein's, which opened a clothing factory in 1873 to manufacture men's and boys' clothing and a retail outlet in 1876, and the

Drapery and General Importing Company (DIC), also established by Bendix Hallenstein, in 1884. Dunedin was the heartland for the colony's clothing industry, and the Mosgiel and Roslyn Woollen Mills were among New Zealand's best known. All provided employment for southern Dunedin women.

Methods of mass production began to develop following the introduction of sewing machines, which proved reliable and faster alternatives to hand sewing. Sewing machine engineers quickly developed the capabilities of their machines, so that by 1882 complex overlocking stitches and buttonholing had become possible.[13] By the mid-1890s all the large clothing factories had introduced 'machines for cutting out, for making both coats and shirt button holes, for sewing on buttons . . .'.[14] As Erik Olssen explains in chapter three, mechanisation went together with increasing employment of women in the factories. Ross and Glendining employed large numbers of local women in their various textile and apparel factories,[15] and the Hallenstein's New Zealand Clothing Factory was for some time New Zealand's largest employer of women.[16] By 1901, 27 per cent of Dunedin's workforce was employed in the clothing industry and 80 per cent of that proportion were women.[17] In the

Ross and Glendining's Roslyn Woollen Mill, c. 1910s. Surrounded by their hats and coats and protected by aprons or smocks, young women work at seaming bundles of knitted jersey into 'unshrinkable' underwear, such as undershirts, and long johns, and outerwear, for men, women and children. Wicker baskets between the linking machines hold full and empty yarn spools and other supplies. ROSLYN WOOLLEN MILLS ALBUM, OTAGO SETTLERS MUSEUM

smaller tailoring and dressmaking workshops, several of which were located in Caversham Valley and King Edward Rd, a degree of mechanisation was introduced and this permitted an increasingly complex division of labour.

Dressmaking establishments took longer to establish factory production methods than did producers of men's clothing. In part this was the result of the more complex demands of garment fit imposed by women's clothes. It can also be attributed to the fact that the production of clothing at home allowed women greater entrepreneurial flexibility, since it could be carried out in combination with the care of children. We will return to consider clothing production within the home in a later section of the chapter.

At the outset of our period, workers in Dunedin clothing factories were not immune to the problem of sweated labour, which sparked the nationwide Royal Commission of Inquiry (the 'Sweating Commission') of 1890.[18] As in most women's occupations, wages were low, as the number of women who had work but needed help from the Otago Benevolent Institution indicates.[19] During the 1890s work itself could be hard to come by, especially for married women. One mother of four was a trained tailoress and shirtmaker, but had difficulty in securing the employment that she thought would provide sufficient income to support the family.[20] Another woman, a widow, had five children to support. Along with her eldest daughter, she took work at Ross and Glendining while her mother looked after the other children. Mother and daughter had a starting wage between them of 13s 10d per week, which was insufficient to clothe and feed the rest of the family. The widow's second daughter obtained an apprenticeship at the DIC, but began on no wages at all.[21] In 1916 a 'soldier's wife' wrote to the *Evening Star* about an advertisement she had responded to in order to supplement her 'meagre pension'. She was offered what she called an 'astonishingly low rate of 1s 6d per dozen' for sewing together pre-cut blouses.[22] Shortages of young women to work in clothing factories and woollen mills were a matter of complaint quite often from the early 1900s on.[23]

Hierarchies of gender and skill persisted within the production houses and factories.[24] Male tailors sat at the top of the hierarchy and were paid the highest wages. They hired tailoresses to do routine sewing of men's garments, such as the long seams of trousers, and the piecing of jackets, but kept the shaping of fronts and lapels as their speciality. Marjorie Scott was employed by a tailor after she had no luck seeking an opening as a dressmaker. She hated it! She spent her days 'sewing buttons on men's flies'. She stayed only a few months, during which she did learn 'a bit' about tailoring.[25] 'Factory tailoresses' learned their trade in the production houses of Hallenstein's and Ross and Glendining,[26] while 'shop tailoresses' worked in workshops making

Male pressers, New Zealand Clothing Company Factory. The pressing of men's jackets and trousers in the New Zealand Clothing Company Factory was not only men's work but required specialised machinery and tools. The heavy irons were heated by electricity and the men who used them earned more than equally skilled women. HOCKEN LIBRARY

made-to-measure garments for female and/or male clients. Laura Boulton, for example, was apprenticed to a shop tailoress and went on to own her own business during the 1920s. She would take charge of interviewing customers, cutting, fitting and patternmaking (based on illustrations in imported French fashion journals) and employed a couple of women dressmakers to sew.[27] Laura Boulton was well aware of distinctions in status between shop tailoresses and factory tailoresses, regarding the work of the latter as often 'slipshod' and not up to standard.[28] Interestingly, she noted that male shop tailors received higher wages than did the women, but she still adhered to an egalitarian ideal, and did not see men as having higher status or greater ease of promotion.[29]

Dressmakers worked not only for factories or tailoring firms, but also in the drapers' shops or as outworkers sewing household textiles, men's shirts and children's clothes. Some dressmakers worked in other people's homes. Jean Darby, for example, remembered a woman coming to their home occasionally and spending the whole day sewing a number of garments for the family.[30] Other clothing workers included milliners, who specialised in hat,

A small tailor's shop. The cutters and pressers sit against the wall and the fireplace where they heated their irons is visible in the back left corner. The machinists are hard at work, probably using treadle machines, while the highly skilled seamstresses sit at their workbench. The place and date are not known but c. 1910 seems likely. Note that workers dress well for work. HOCKEN LIBRARY

cap and bonnet-making, and hosiers, who made underclothing and items for the feet.[31]

To some degree, the particular gendered division of labour varied from one company to another. Usually men carried out the pressing of completed clothing, for example, although Johanna Waterman, who started work at a men's tailor in High St about 1919, noted that women sewed and pressed, while men cut out the garments and worked in the warehouse and dispatch areas.[32] In Laura Boulton's workshop, women would press clothes, primarily because there was no male presser on site, although she took obvious pride in the task:

> [In my earlier employment] the girls made the job but the men did the pressing ... but when we had our own business we had to press ourselves. I had a little gas stove. I liked them better than an electric iron. You heated them up in the gas. We had a 14 pound one, a 16 pound one, and a 20 pound one. You don't get the weight in your shoulder, you do it on your wrist. I've got quite a weighty electric one here now that you would think is pretty heavy.[33]

As this quotation demonstrates, small workplaces required women to carry out a variety of tasks, paying no heed to notions of female frailty or strict divisions of labour.

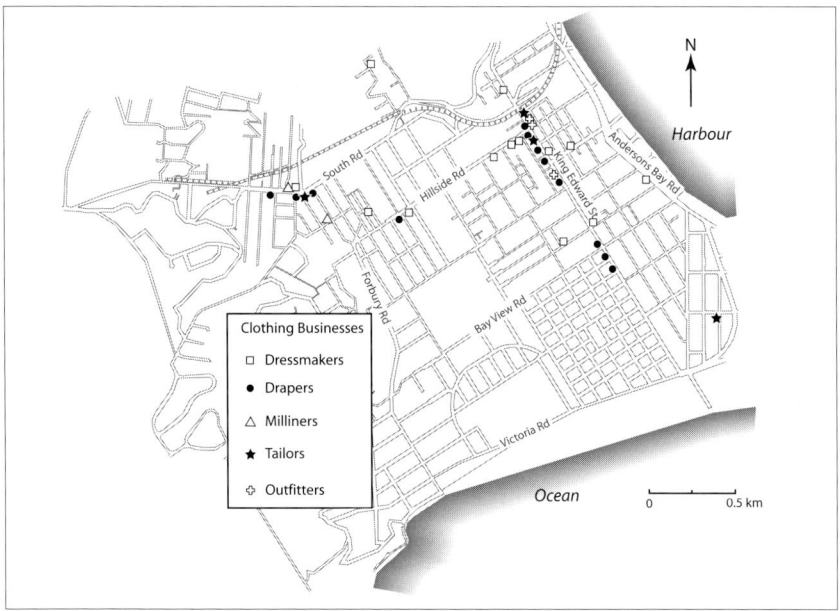

Map 5.1 Drapers, dressmakers, milliners, outfitters and tailors from the 1912 Stone's trade directory. The two distinct clusters of clothing businesses are concentrated in southern Dunedin's two main retail areas: the larger to the right at Cargill's Corner and King Edward St, and the smaller to the left along Caversham Valley Rd.

The growth in larger manufacturing businesses did not prevent small operations from retaining a market for their tailored or made-to-measure products. The output from the factories and the bespoke houses catered to different sections of society.[34] Some small clothing businesses still survived in southern Dunedin after the First World War. In 1920 there remained eighteen dressmakers, milliners and corset-makers, and five tailors, and by 1936 fourteen dressmakers or milliners, but no tailors.[35] There was clearly still a market for dressmaking and hats, even though the design of women's clothes had become much simpler than in the nineteenth century, and word-of-mouth advertising seems to have been sufficient for these businesses for the most part.[36]

Retailing: the organisation of consumption

Some of the businesses that made garments also sold them straight to the consumer. The major example in Caversham was Todd and Brown's tailoring business, where the owners dealt directly with the public. Another example is provided by the large firms: the DIC or Hallenstein's in the city, which manufactured their own goods and sold them through the retail shops they established. The DIC was aimed at middle-class consumers and sold a wide variety of goods, including sewing machines and clothing for both sexes and all ages. By 1900 the city boasted thirteen department stores, a figure that remained fairly constant over the next forty years. Southern Dunedin's only department store was Wolfenden and Russell, established in 1911 by W. E. Wolfenden, a grocer, and H. Russell, a draper. Like all department stores, it ran its own dressmaking shop, although most of its female staff worked in sales. By 1936 it employed some sixty people, mainly women.

Although Dunedin city's department stores were established from the 1870s, it was not until the 1900s that they started employing women in large numbers. Although some efforts were made to attract male customers, the stores appealed to women as the primary shoppers, and so women sales staff suited the culture of consumerism that the stores sought to promote. Women also found jobs as buyers, cashiers and clerks; some became managers of departments and directors of cosmetics. Although men were preferred for positions of authority, and so benefited most from the feminisation of the department stores' workforce, the young women also enjoyed prospects for promotion and pay increases.

A third type of small clothing business focused solely on retailing, with drapery the most prominent example.[37] Drapers' stores sold textiles for the home, such as sheets, towels and curtains, as well as clothing fabrics and haberdashery. There were thirty-five drapers' shops in Dunedin in 1890, including a number in southern Dunedin, many of which offered ready-to-wear and made-to-measure clothing for either men or women or both.[38] The Drapery Supply Association also established a branch in King Edward St at the turn of the century. The years that followed, however, saw the Dunedin central business area pick up an increasing proportion of the drapery trade,

Todd & Brown advertisement. Men who wished to look smart could have their suits tailormade at Todd and Brown Tailors on the Main Rd, Caversham. *THE SKETCHER*, DECEMBER 1914

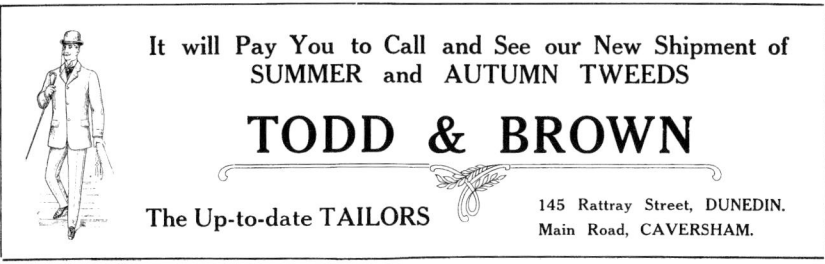

The Brown, Ewing and Co. department store displayed goods to attract customers in premises which made shopping a pleasurable activity. The menswear department had its own entrance, and offered ready-to-wear clothing and accessories as well as a made-to-order service for loose-fitting suits, morning suits and overcoats. The workrooms in Princes Street employed many girls and women who made up the garments ordered by customers. Much of the sewing was done by hand, perhaps to differentiate the service offered by a prestigious department store from that of the garment factories.
OTAGO WITNESS CHRISTMAS ANNUAL, 1907

and in the period following the First World War the total number of drapery stores in Dunedin started to decline.[39] This pattern of declining numbers of stores from 1920 was replicated across other operations, particularly tailors and clothing manufacturers. It can be explained by economies of scale, the amalgamation of smaller firms into fewer larger ones, the growing predominance of department stores, the effect of the First World War on labour availability and women's increasing willingness to venture further afield in public space.[40] Although the drapery stores declined in number, the 1920s saw the establishment of women's hairdressers, with a number to be found along Prince Albert Rd, King Edward St and the Main South Rd.

Proprietors of clothing businesses in Dunedin were much more likely to be men than women between 1894 and 1920: men made up 70 per cent or more of the proprietors over this period.[41] Men were more likely than women to own footwear, hat, tailoring and clothing manufacturing businesses. Women came closer to matching male ownership in drapery, perhaps not surprisingly, given that their customers were likely to be women. Only in dressmaking,

PRODUCING AND CONSUMING GENDER

Ready-made wear. Ready-mades were popular, although unattainable for those on low incomes and sometimes considered 'too common' for those of more affluent means. Here the first-floor women's costume showroom at Brown Ewing displays ready-made coats, jackets, skirts and blouses for day and evening wear. *OTAGO WITNESS*, 29 MAY 1907

millinery and corset-making concerns did women proprietors dominate the statistics. Even then, small but increasing numbers of men owned these types of business.

The First World War did not expand opportunities for married women to own or run clothing businesses. However, the number of women in business remained high relative to numbers in Dunedin overall. Of the women owners of dressmaking and millinery businesses, most were single.[42] When women married, they almost invariably left the formal labour market, although they may have continued to earn some income by sewing for neighbours and friends. However, a number of married women did run dressmaking and drapery businesses.[43] These women may have been widowed or had husbands who had deserted them and had therefore taken over a husband's business, although it appears that some were in stable marriages. These parts of the clothing industry were viewed as acceptable activities in which married women could participate: as Stana Nenadic observes, they had a 'deep social meaning which stressed images of family and community nurturing'.[44]

133

Daydream Corsets advertisement. Imported from England, Daydream Corsets offered to assist wearers to retain their youthful figures. Corsets were regarded as an essential item of clothing to present an elegant figure. The design of corsets and the fabrics they were made from altered over time, becoming less bulky and more comfortable. As fashion trends altered, so did the need for corsets. THE SKETCHER, MAY 1905

Changes in women's clothes and women's lives

As the organisation of the retailing scene changed over the period, so, too, did the clothing sold through these stores and the fabric that women would use as the basis of the garments they made themselves. In Dunedin in 1890 only some parts of a woman's outfit were available ready-made, although sewing machines and the slowly growing availability of patterns had democratised fashion to some extent. Skirts, corsets, hats, coats or capes and some underclothing could be purchased ready to wear, but much had to be ordered from a ladies' tailor, dressmaker or draper, or made by the woman or her friends. For the better off, Mollison, Mills and Co. of George St advertised cashmerette costumes for winter, 'beautifully made and handsomely trimmed with material for the bodice',[45] Brown Ewing had ladies' cream and white embroidered robes, and the Misses Brownlie in Princes St offered 'perfect-fitting, comfortable and durable corsets'.[46] Four dressmakers operated businesses in the southern Dunedin area in 1890, and thirty more in Dunedin's centre would have been relatively accessible to southern Dunedin residents.[47]

In the 1890s women's clothing was formal and restricting for bodily movement. The news of the formation of New Zealand's own Rational

PRODUCING AND CONSUMING GENDER

St Clair Beach, 1890s, when high levels of formality in dress still prevailed. External signifiers of fashionable appearance were followed as far as possible by all classes. Women wore boned dress bodices with high necklines, their tight waists emphasised by the fullness of sleeves and skirt. Skirts were flared with slight fullness retained at the back. Women's hair was usually long and pinned up in a roll or bun, while girls wore their hair either loose or in ringlets. Hats and parasols were essential to keep the sun off the skin. Either suits or jackets and trousers – along with a hat – were minimal public attire for all men. HOCKEN LIBRARY

Dress Association sparked a male writer for the *Otago Daily Times* to suggest that, although male dress had been rational for seventy years in colour and materials, women's 'instinctive fondness' for colour and the extravagance of fashion meant that they were 'about a century behind men'.[48] It seems possible that local women's clothing may have taken some heed of the movement for rational dress around the turn of the century, with the adoption of looser stays or corsets and slight shortening of hemlines.[49]

In the following decades, women's clothing became less formal and offered more room for movement. The growing informality and reduction in bodily constraint reflected other social changes for women. Women were bearing fewer children and so their bodies were more their own, and the image of the 'New Woman' became more widespread – she who had started to break away from stifling conventions of femininity and may even have taken up sport, smoking and motorcar driving.[50] Most would not have had access to cars, but bicycles and an extended electric tram service increased women's mobility.[51] The amount of time that young women spent unsupervised away from home increased as they travelled to school and then work. As Erik Olssen shows in chapter three, many more women spent some years in paid employment.

135

Violet Watson was a live-in domestic servant for Mrs Jefcoate of 'The Hollies', College Street, Caversham around 1900. She is still recorded as living at that address in 1911. Clearly proud of her crisp white uniform of apron, cap and cuffs, she illustrates the skill and toil of laundrywomen in keeping such items clean, starched and ironed. HOCKEN LIBRARY

Public toilets were built for women in the city, in the Botanic Gardens and at the beach, and this improved women's access to public spaces.[52]

For the women of southern Dunedin, who increasingly worked in local clerical, manufacturing or retailing positions, the evolution towards greater informality (although not always practicality) in dress must have been a blessing. By 1908 women could wear a long skirt, still at least ankle-length, with a separate bodice or blouse. Lighter colours became more fashionable, but waistlines were still restricted, although by now blouses pouched over them. It took some time for the changes led by Paul Poiret in Paris towards a much less restricted torso to filter through to New Zealand, but the fashion for large hats that spread in Europe around 1906 had certainly reached Dunedin by 1908.

At this time skirts, coats and paletots (a loose coat or jacket) were available ready-made, as was a range of underwear such as knickers, combinations and bloomers, 'knock about costumes' of navy cloth, and 'washable dresses'

PRODUCING AND CONSUMING GENDER

Images of the 'New Woman' and rational dress have perhaps influenced the young women of the Kensington Sunday School staff, who wear less formal and restrictive skirts and blouses in lighter colours, with masculine ties. Men's dress remains very formal: high collars with long ties, high buttoning waistcoats and jackets, fob watches and chains. ST ANDREWS PRESBYTERIAN CHURCH JUBILEE SOUVENIR, 1913, OTAGO SETTLERS MUSEUM

in the newest styles.[53] The range of prices for these garments (from 15s 6d to 69s 6d for the washable dresses) indicates that they were produced in various qualities of cloth and pitched at those of modest means as well as those with more money to spend. High necklines were still fashionable, although wrinkles were allowed to appear in the sides and front of the collar, with boning holding up the back portion only.[54] Bodily restraint for women was starting to loosen. The spread of organised sport, discussed in chapter six, accelerated the new freedom.

Improvements in communication and transport in the first two decades of the twentieth century granted international fashion trends an increasing influence on New Zealand styles. Radical changes in women's dress prior to and during the First World War saw hemlines rise, waistlines loosen and jackets become more sack-like, so that by the 1920s a major transformation had occurred. Women's bodies were considerably more free than they were at the turn of the century. The dress styles of the 1920s were also much easier to

Picnic, 1933. The radical changes in women's dress evident by the First World War continued into the 1920s. Women's bodies were less covered by dresses or bathing attire. Lower necklines, looser sleeves, freer waistlines and short hair were adopted by women of all ages and classes. Men's and women's swimsuits were very similar one-piece designs covering the torso and thighs. OTAGO DAILY TIMES AND WITNESS CHRISTMAS ANNUAL, 1933, OTAGO SETTLERS MUSEUM

construct than their predecessors, having fewer seams, using much less fabric and being less precise in their fitting. The most closely fitting outer garment was the cloche hat: snug on the crown and descending to the eyebrows. Corsets were still being advertised, but their shape had changed. No longer constricting the waist, the new corset was straight and boned to the hip, with attached suspenders to hold up the newly available rayon stockings.[55] Waistlines rose in the early 1920s, then fell below the natural waistline in the later part of the decade. Young women cut their hair to emulate the modern boyish look popularised by Gabrielle ('Coco') Chanel. Although wearing one's hair up signified adulthood for young women in the nineteenth century, by the 1920s short, shingled hair for all ages blurred the distinctions between the cohorts of women. All this reflected the changes afoot in other areas of women's lives.

By the 1930s southern Dunedin women of all ages and classes were wearing clothes radically different from those worn in the 1890s. Developments in textile technology, and production and marketing of clothing had expanded consumer choices, and shifts in fashion had changed women's appearance dramatically. Exposure to Hollywood movies also opened women's eyes to new possibilities in dress, hairstyle and cosmetics.

By the 1930s ready-made suits and dresses were widely available and the look was waisted, with a fitting bodice or blouse. Fabrics were now often patterned: floral prints, stripes, geometric patterns and polka dots were popular. Local people might purchase some items ready-made and make others themselves. An increase in the number of young women working in clothing

First Citizens' Ball, 1930. Had the glamour of the movies influenced these Dunedinites? Masculine attire included wing collars, black or white bow ties and waistcoats with dark suits, while women opted for satin, lace or tulle for their handkerchief hemline dresses. Their stockings could be held up with suspenders attached to corsets, or with elastic bands. Femininity could now include visible legs, arms and necks, short hair and make-up. *OTAGO WITNESS*, 25 FEBRUARY 1930

factories also had its influence: with their newly acquired dressmaking skills young women could make their own clothes in the more informal designs. Helen Tweed, whose family was reasonably prosperous, had three or four new garments each season. She made some of her own clothes on a Singer sewing machine, following Vogue or McCall's patterns, and had others made by a dressmaker, especially dresses of bias-cut georgette.[56]

Young women, apparently identified as more affluent and concerned with their appearance, were targeted with advertising about hair removal and cosmetics.[57] Fashion was continually featured in the *Otago Witness* from the First World War, though there remained an awareness of the financial difficulties some women faced. The *Witness*'s pages included hints and suggestions on maintaining garments, looking well dressed on a small clothing allowance and making accessories at home.[58]

Women's clothing differed according to the occasion. Work demanded a 'good' dress, with a hemline at mid-calf level, and a coat that might be purchased from London Mantles in George St.[59] Not all women possessed a range of clothing for wearing to work, and Mavis Liverpool noted that 'a lot of the girls would come in the same dress week after week'.[60] Another frock might serve for church, going to town and the weekly dance.[61] 'Special' dances such as balls demanded a more 'stylish' dress, ankle-length or longer. As Frances Kenny remembered, 'you would dress up more to go to a ball than you would to go to, say, a weekly dance'.[62] Weddings, too, required longer and more elaborate dresses. Hats and gloves were still compulsory wearing with a coat on the streets, to church, and on most other public occasions.[63]

Women's fashions had changed dramatically between 1890 and 1940, moving away from stiff corsets, boning and garments made of dark, heavy fabrics towards lighter fabrics and freer, more revealing dresses. This change in fashion followed a more general social widening of women's spheres of activity, as well as a modernising of the expectations placed upon women's bodies. So, what of men's appearances between 1890 and 1940?

Menswear: status markers and changing fashions

Two aspects of men's dress stand out as worthy of examination. First, though men's clothing underwent some changes over the period, these were not as dramatic as those of women's clothing. The lounge suit retained prominence, and its basic shape and fabric changed only marginally. Second, in its detail, men's clothing continued to transmit its wearer's status within the workplace, signifying distinctions between men. A man's place within the productive process was reflected in his consumption of particular styles of clothing.

In 1890s Dunedin, either suits or jackets and trousers – along with a hat – were minimal public attire for almost all men, regardless of class. Whether walking on the beach, at a picnic, in the streets, or at work, men were dressed in ways that would appear very formal to twenty-first-century eyes. For men in non-manual employment, all of these activities necessitated a bowler, derby, or wide-awake hat, a shirt with a starched collar of the wing or turned-down type, a bowtie or four-in-hand knotted tie, and a buttoned-up waistcoat with a watch-chain from buttonhole to left pocket. A high-buttoning jacket with narrow lapels was worn to and from work. In contrast, manual labourers were identified on the job by plain or striped shirts, with or without collars, rolled-up sleeves, neckerchiefs, wide-brimmed hats or caps and loose trousers held up with braces. Bakers dressed in white coveralls, while builders and carpenters wore white aprons over their shirts and waistcoats.

Ubiquitous masculine symbols included trousers, broad shoulders and waistcoats over shirts and braces. By the 1890s factory-made clothes for men and boys were widely available. Local retail drapers and tailors Herbert Haynes and Co. offered men's and boys' clothing of 'splendid workmanship guaranteed in this establishment as against the common factory slop-make so prevalent in the trade'.[64] Ross and Glendining, who were knitting manufacturers and woven fabric producers, with a factory in Stafford St, offered for sale knitted cardigans, jackets, football jerseys, boy's jersey suits, socks and lambswool shirts and pants.[65] Drapers J. Hardie and Co. sold ready-to-wear trousers, vests, coats, suits, engineers' jackets, overalls, Crimean shirts and drawers, and offered a made-to-order service for trousers and suits. The price differences between off-the-peg and made-to-measure garments (between 22s 6d and 35s, compared with 70s in the case of a suit) would have made the latter affordable only to a minority.[66]

By 1908 little outward change appeared in photographs of Dunedin men at leisure. Still in evidence were high-buttoned lounge suits or jackets and trousers, hats or caps, and even ties when playing the more sedate sports. Men at work exhibited some variety in attire. Whether leading hands or unskilled helpers, all the blacksmiths at Hillside Railway Workshops dressed in casual shirts with rolled-up sleeves, waistcoats and leather half-aprons. For their part, boiler-shop staff were all attired in three-piece lounge suits with ties. The lounge suit lost any association it might have had with leisure, just as it had elsewhere, and was by now considered a practical, multi-purpose work wardrobe.[67] As with the women of the period, status distinctions between men were communicated through differences in quality of cloth, cut and fit of jacket, and style of hat. Together with the wearing of accessories such as watch-chains, these differences make it possible to distinguish supervisors

Most of these boiler shop staff at Hillside Railway Workshops in 1903 dressed in coloured shirts, long ties, waistcoats, jackets, trousers and lace-up boots. Hardwearing moleskin fabric features in some trousers and jackets, and hat choices include wide-awakes, homburgs and caps. Bosses and supervisors can be identified by lighter coloured shirts, bowler hats and by the rather better cut and fit of their garments. CAVERSHAM PROJECT COLLECTION

or bosses from workers.⁶⁸ Pictures of boys at this time show them wearing short trousers and shirts with wide-collared overshirts or jackets in sailor-collar or puritan style, long black socks held up with garters, leather shoes and caps. The adoption of long trousers marked a rite of passage to manhood, and usually occurred with the beginning of full-time work.

International trends filtered through to men's dress during and after the First World War. The men's clothing industry in New Zealand had been galvanised by the war to introduce improved garment fit. It also adopted faster production methods that involved breaking down the production of ready-made clothes into discrete tasks. Further refinements continued following the war, and traditional tailors were slowly squeezed out of business by a higher quality of off-the-peg garments sold in retailers' menswear departments. Following overseas trends, southern Dunedin in the 1920s saw an increasing informality in men's dress styles. Knitted pullovers, lighter colours and fabrics for lounge suits, and more specialised sports dress – including white trousers, blazers trimmed with club colours for cricketers, and shorts and singlets for harriers – were all evident in local photographs.⁶⁹

Local retailers advertised men's clothing suitable for leisurely pursuits. Men's holiday wardrobes could be updated with tweed 'sports suits ... our own make' or dressing gowns, 'attractive paisley' and 'very suitable for travelling on your holidays'. These were priced from 25s to 95s.⁷⁰ Despite the range of price (and quality), it was clear from demobilised men's requests to the Otago Patriotic and Welfare Society for civilian clothing that having to purchase a whole suit of clothes at once put a severe strain on some household budgets.⁷¹

Hats continued as universal clothing items for men throughout the 1920s and 30s. All except young boys wore a hat in outdoor public spaces. As with suits, the particular style of hat worn marked out differences of class and status. A bowler, derby or 'bun' hat (the latter a local nickname) was worn by those who had professional, managerial, or authoritative positions and a reasonable income. One resident of Law St worked as a clothing buyer for Sargood, Son and Ewen in the 1920s and embarked upon overseas buying trips. 'A real dapper gentleman', he dressed in a bowtie, bun hat, spats, and carried a walking stick with a silver top.⁷² Homburg hats, made of stiff felt with a central crease and a rolled brim, were increasingly popular replacements for the bowler among the better off. Working-class men were likely to wear caps or felt hats, on and off the job.⁷³

Despite the move toward lighter colours and fabrics for men's suits, and a greater range of leisure clothing, men's dress changed relatively little over the period when contrasted with women's.⁷⁴ Restrictive and concealing garments for women had given way to outfits that were lighter, much more colourful and in many cases shorter. We have suggested that this reflects a number of other social changes affecting women's lives, including enhanced bodily mobility and greater possibilities for movement around the city.[75] The apparent slightness of changes to men's clothing is consistent with the wider finding of this volume: that their lives changed less than women's over the period.

Clothes at home: the production of consumption
So far we have concentrated on the changes in clothing styles and the items available in retail stores. As McRobbie suggests, however, gendered consumption is but one step in a 'whole chain of productive activity'.[76] Consumption and production came together for women in the home in at least two senses: women often worked for pay within the family home, and worked without pay when their labour was required to provide for the clothing needs of the family.

Some women took in work. The women seeking relief who appear in the casebooks of the Otago Benevolent Institution often took in knitting, sewing, crochet work, mat-making or washing.[77] The granting of relief underlines the fact that this was often an unreliable source of income, and insufficient to feed a family: earnings were typically between 2s and 5s per week. Knitting was by its nature slow, so earnings were of the order of 2s and 3s per week, and washing paid even less, unless a large volume could be managed. The amount of work procured and the speed with which it could be carried out were constraining factors. For those looking after sick children, or who were ill themselves, there was probably little choice but to take in whatever work was available, and outwork could always be organised around other household tasks.

For some women, however, taking in work could be more lucrative than some forms of factory labour. Phyllis Crossan, for example, always wanted to be a dressmaker. She had to wait until she was fifteen to get an apprenticeship with Dreavers, where she worked for three months for no pay, tacking, picking up pins and sweeping the floor, to see if she was suitable. Her first pay was 5s a week, and over time the wage increased to 10s a week: 'It was really nothing by the time you'd paid your tram fare. You might get a pair of stockings out of it.' Crossan found it more lucrative to set up on her own as a dressmaker, working from home.[78]

Taking in work provided an independent income for married women and the work could be juggled around other household demands. Working from home also satisfied societal demands that married women should spend most of their time in the domestic sphere.[79] Rosanna Paul's mother worked in the

Advertisement for 'White' sewing machine: sewing machines were still part of the ironmonger's stock in 1916, even though they were also fancy pieces of furniture. Alongside bicycles and lawn mowers, ironmongers carried mangles, wringers, carpet sweepers and other items central to the domestic domain. THE SKETCHER, JUNE 1916

millinery workroom at the DIC before she married, and afterwards carried on making hats for weddings and attending to 'old ladies [who] brought in jewellery to be put into their bonnets'.[80]

Women's sewing for their own families was facilitated by the availability of sewing machines, which were imported in large numbers by the beginning of our study period.[81] At this time the Drapery Supply Association in George St sold dress parcels containing 'one or more lengths of dress fabric for garments', as did Brown Ewing, while the Misses Brownlie in Princes St offered home dressmaking patterns from the USA.[82] Men's suits were usually not made at home, however, as suit fabrics were not generally available for public sale. The other requisite for home sewing was the mastery of sewing skills. Learning to sew was a part of growing up for young girls, who learned sewing and knitting at school, as well as from their mothers or other female relatives.[83] Given the high numbers of young women who worked in the clothing sector, many families had someone with formal training as a tailoress or dressmaker. This skill was very valuable in the home economy.

By the 1920s and 1930s, many southern Dunedin women may have purchased their 'best' dress or suit from a dressmaker or drapery store. This often required saving up, watching for sales, or using lay-by.[84] However, the practice of purchasing fabric for making into clothes at home was still very widespread. As McRobbie has observed, the buying of fabric was followed by further unpaid domestic labour.[85] Before marriage, Kitty Brown's mother had been a tailoress; afterwards she continued in an unpaid capacity by making all her children's clothes: 'frocks, coats, and we were well dressed'.[86] Home-made clothes were more affordable than off-the-peg garments and much cheaper than made-to-measure items. For those who could afford new fabrics, a range of attractive frocks, shirts and coats could be made for dances and other public events.[87] Mavis Liverpool noted that 'everybody dressed nice at those dances . . . I suppose materials being so cheap, you could make quite a lot of frocks'.[88] Some women made undergarments as well as outer clothing.[89]

Where families found themselves in a more perilous financial position, clothing and fabric circulated in a complex informal economy. Home sewing presented possibilities for reusing old clothes or, as Jean Darby describes it, 'cutting down old things, us[ing] big things to make small things and there was a lot of that went on'.[90] Similarly, clothing items would have their lifespan stretched: stockings would be darned in order to 'keep them going'.[91] Help was available from charities, churches and friends for those who struggled to provide even basic clothing for their families. The Sixpenny Clothing Club, presided over by Mrs Rachel Reynolds, spent over £38 in 1890 providing clothing and other textile goods for the needy in southern Dunedin.[92] One man was given underclothing by another, who also provided him with odd jobs at his stables.[93] Second-hand clothes were bought and sold: one couple who intermittently operated a little shop in the 1890s selling crockery and glassware also dealt in old clothes.[94] Later, the McKenzie sisters recalled their mother giving away dresses they had outgrown. They also remembered one laundry woman employed by their mother who would apparently slip things illicitly into her bag for her daughter and nieces. Rosanna Paul's family passed on used clothes to those less fortunate through their church or bazaars.[95]

Second-hand clothing was also passed along within and between families, and this was not necessarily seen as a demeaning practice.[96] From time to time Yvonne Morris's family in St Clair would be offered a 'nice frock', second-hand and at a discount price, by a more wealthy acquaintance living in a nearby 'mansion'.[97] Southern Dunedin women would also share clothes for special occasions. Mavis Liverpool remembered that:

> people used to swap things or loan things so that the kids would be nice. The kids had nothing so that if there was a school concert coming up, if you had a good dress somebody else would loan you a cardigan to go with it so you'd look nice. I always remember I had a striped blazer, where that ever came from I don't know.[98]

Once girls had grown into young women, clothes-swapping among friends would swell the variety of dresses a particular woman could wear to a dance, for example.[99] Weddings, too, occasioned the loan of accessories. Mavis Liverpool remembered that, when she got married, 'somebody lent me their veil and I had a headgear made. A girl I worked with lent me the pearls I wore.'[100] Adaptive reuse was another strategy: asked by a friend to be matron of honour at her wedding, Jean McFarlane attended in her own wedding dress, which had been dyed green for the occasion.[101]

Conclusion: sameness or difference?

Earlier we suggested that clothing can be understood as a node at which a range of social relationships connect, where the concerns of individuals meet the patterns of social organisation. Clothing provides one site where consumption and production meet and are transformed by gender, class and status. These connections can be further illustrated by examining the ways in which notions of egalitarianism circulated in southern Dunedin. Egalitarianism has long been held to be a defining characteristic of New Zealand social life. According to its ethos, all are entitled to the same life chances, regard, deference and social consideration.[102] However, this egalitarianism often pertained primarily to class, and the social position of women arguably constituted one of its greatest blind spots. In his discussion of work in chapter three of this volume, Erik Olssen documents the attempts of male-dominated unions to exclude women, their disinclination to question the gendered and racialised segmentation of the labour market and attendant pay differentials, and men's claims to public space.

The oral-history collection includes at least two views on clothing and expressions of egalitarianism. The most prevalent argued that there were few differences between people in the communities of southern Dunedin, and that people were either essentially the same in their clothing and material circumstances or tried to fit in with the consensus during dances and other gatherings. Mavis Liverpool argued that men and women were 'all the same' in dress: 'you had to fit in; you didn't dress any flasher than anyone else'.[103] Jean MacFarlane agreed that, though it was 'important to look smart' in public, 'you didn't like to be any different from anybody else really'.[104] In turn, Maureen Judge argued that 'you dressed up and looked smart in what you had; maybe some of them tried to keep up with the Joneses type of thing, but I can't recall that'.[105] This last statement implies the undesirability of appearing out of step with others, but also hints at the importance of being satisfied with one's income and social position or avoiding overt expressions of wealth.

PRODUCING AND CONSUMING GENDER

According to the second view, there was less of an egalitarian ethic among women when it came to dress for public occasions. When asked whether women tried to stand out from the crowd, Helen Tweed replied, 'Yes, definitely; particularly some of the flasher ones . . . wore very nice sophisticated frocks to the best of their purse I suppose you'd say.'[106] There is a certain ambivalence in Tweed's statement, however, given the reservation expressed later in her interview:

> there were people that could stand out, but normally, you know, we would all wear the same . . . but people didn't have a lot of clothes, like they do now. They would probably have one good outfit and then, you know, perhaps just one other thing.[107]

One possible way of interpreting such ambivalence would be to suggest that distinctions between 'us' and 'them' worked in such a way that 'our' group was understood as *internally* egalitarian, while the group itself was defined against those in a different class position, at least in part. Many of those interviewed, for example, drew a distinction between themselves and those who lived in 'mansions' in wealthier St Clair, at the same time as they asserted that those in their own social circles shared similar fashions and class background. Even Yvonne Morris, whose family lived in St Clair, distinguished between her own family and the 'snobby', 'different type of people', with their 'good jobs and nice homes', who resided there.[108] Others also felt that St Clair's residents were 'different': 'wealthier' or more 'well-mannered'.[109] This is not to say that class difference necessarily represented antagonism. Although Mavis Liverpool felt that 'you sort of kept to your own wage bracket people in those days', Pat Donnelly's family mixed with St Clair people on the sportsfield and saw them as helpful to the less well off in times of financial difficulty.[110]

Laura Boulton's thoughts on status came the closest to challenging the ideal of egalitarianism and it is noteworthy that she was talking about skill, not appearance. When asked whether she was conscious of the differences between the more skilled shop tailoress (which she was) and the factory tailoress, she replied: 'Oh yes, I was conscious. One or two people were very keen on these unions. I think they were jealous of us. We had a little room of our own. We were thought of as snobs I guess.'[111] Skill and the privileges that accrued to it ('a room of our own') were seen as the basis of social distinction, even if the implication is that to some extent the distinction was misplaced ('I think they were jealous'). Like some of the others interviewed, Laura Boulton saw class distinction as imposed by those outside her own group.

Views down rather than up the social scale were rare, but one further example demonstrates the tenuousness of egalitarian commitments and their apparent contradictions. The importance of notions of cleanliness and respectability to working-class communities has been noted by other authors,[112] and in the following schoolyard example egalitarianism and cleanliness are at odds:

> I can remember one slight incident about a girl being teased about something she was wearing, and I remember with shame that I just stood and watched. I realise now that I should perhaps have said something nice about her or to her . . . . It was something that she was wearing, a petticoat or something that she had, that had looked a bit grubby . . . she was a little girl, and I think she came from a fairly poor family.[113]

Those who did not conform to the community's standards of dress – or could not afford to – were cast by others as outsiders. However, though she singled out the above instance, Jean Darby reinforced the prevailing notion of egalitarianism by arguing that, 'as a whole I think children tended to mix very well'.

Certainly clothes held the ability to express social standing, helping to define the wearer and her or his relation to others. Those interviewed widely agreed that people consumed and produced clothing in very similar ways to their friends and acquaintances. However, we would suggest that, to some extent, distinctions between class groupings were themselves constructed through the forms of consumption in which their members participated. Reciprocity in the form of lending, mixing and matching clothing for special occasions was one characteristic of clothing consumption among the southern Dunedin working class. Ideals of egalitarianism were strong, and seemingly not in themselves challenged by the presence of those with 'bigger wages' who could afford to purchase more expensive clothes, and to forgo their own making and mending. It seems that many in southern Dunedin saw their own working-class circles as internally egalitarian, even when they recognised that wider Dunedin society was not. Such an egalitarian ethos could weather the discrediting of the truly poor who might transgress working-class ideals of cleanliness and respectability.

Although those interviewed for this chapter discussed distinction and egalitarianism with respect to class, they tended to be more circumspect when it came to gender. Although the oral histories and the other sources document differences between men's and women's dress, and accept the assumption that these should underline gender differences, gendered inequality was rarely explicitly mentioned. Only very occasionally was there any questioning of the

Wearing what could be a product from the Roslyn factory, this young woman epitomises the modern world of the 1920s. Her short hair and her fit and exposed body signify the complex social changes occurring, particularly for women. 'YOUTH AND BEAUTY AT THE BEACH', *OTAGO WITNESS*, 18 MARCH 1924, HOCKEN LIBRARY

ways in which a man might allocate his wage unjustly: for example, depriving his wife of spending money.[114] As we have already shown, Laura Boulton conceded that male tailors got 'much higher pay' than women undertaking the same job, but did not understand this as anything other than an unremarkable fact about the time. It appears as a mere difference between men and women of no real moment, and certainly she didn't think it translated into higher status or advantage for men.[115]

The notion of separate but equal spheres continued to hold significant purchase for southern Dunedin men and women of the time, with men wearing and selling (but not necessarily making) the trousers and most women leaving work to raise and care for a family after they married. Nor did anyone question the function of dress as a key signifier of gendered identity. Despite the transformations in women's dress, in particular, that these interviewees had witnessed in their later lives (the advent of trousers and other 'unisex' clothing), no one saw it as anything but right and proper that at that time clothing was the first means of distinguishing the sexes. During the period, women's clothing was clearly identifiable as women's, and men's as men's. This apparently unbroachable division directs us, perhaps, to the fact that, despite the fifty years of dramatic gender change between 1890 and 1940, no one yet questioned gender as a central distinction in the organisation of identity and of society. Yet the change in women's dress over our period, signifying a change in the prevailing understandings of femininity, was dramatic. Although the distinction between women and men was a given, the changes in what it meant to *be* a woman were reflected in the difference between the appearance of women in the 1890s and the – by comparison – unrestrained, comfortable and mobile appearance of women in the late 1930s. Modernity could not have been more strikingly embodied.

Six Spare Time? Leisure, Gender and Modernity

BARBARA BROOKES, ERIK OLSSEN AND EMMA BEER

On 22 June 1928 a great crowd gathered at the Hillside Workshops, the largest employers of men in the southern suburbs, for the official opening of the 'social block'. The mayor of Dunedin presided over the opening, accompanied by the mayor of St Kilda, the local MP, T. K. Sidey, the city librarian and the leading men at the workshops. The new facilities housed a library containing 15,000 volumes, a social hall that could seat 500 people, a dining room and apprentices' instruction room. 'Employees,' the *New Zealand Railways Magazine* noted, 'were thus supplied with food for the body, food for the mind, and means for social enjoyment.'[1] Constructive leisure was enshrined at the heart of Hillside. A working man could also be an avid reader in pursuit of self-improvement, he could play in the Hillside Orchestra, or dance in the hall. What he did not do was squander his spare time drinking. The community celebration marked, in a symbolic sense, the triumph of the campaign to tame male leisure pursuits.

Even before the 1900s, when the Arbitration Court began making the 8-hour day and the 44-hour week normative for unionised urban workers, almost all of them male, New Zealand had been famous for the 'four eights, that ideal of operative felicity . . .': 'eight to work, eight to play, eight to sleep, and eight shillings a day'.[2] Work and leisure for play defined a new way of thinking about time that had become normative in industrial societies during the nineteenth century, at least for men (because it cost money as well as time to enjoy many of the new leisure activities). The artisans and mechanics who dominated the southern suburbs understood the notion well. Although the young women who worked in factories enjoyed limited hours after the 1873

Employment of Women Act, at first they had few respectable avenues for play outside the home. In brief, leisure was a gendered notion, like equality, though it was usually presented in universal terms. Many men may have enjoyed the 'four eights', but for most women the distinction between work and leisure was irrelevant. Married women, daughters at home and domestic servants, like many rural workers, inhabited a pre-industrial world where work and play did not occupy separate periods of time, although housewives on the Flat had to heed the world of time. Male breadwinners had to be at work on time and children needed to be at school or work.[3]

Clare Langhamer, in her innovative approach to leisure history in England, emphasises the importance of context and meaning, asking, 'What did leisure mean to women [and men] and how did they experience it?'[4] Such an approach avoids scripting leisure history on previous male models and favours a non-hierarchical approach, where drinking tea and walking assume as much importance as more organised activities, which only slowly became available to young unmarried women. Recreation, in the sense of pleasurable self-refreshment, might be deeply embedded in women's lives. It might lie in the sensual pleasure of children and delight in their development, or in the sense of order when certain household tasks were completed. Because many women lacked free time, we can safely say that they lacked leisure, but such pleasurable activities as talking, visiting and sharing a meal, perhaps the most popular pastimes, could be done while working. Leisure alone was not the only thing associated with pleasure: both women and men found pleasure in their work, in each other and in their families. Indeed, play and work were not mutually exclusive, and pleasure, leisure and play were never synonymous. They became more at odds with each other across the period, however, as many forms of work came to be seen as drudgery, while fun, pleasure and play were thought to require leisure.

Historical studies of leisure in New Zealand are few.[5] Claire Toynbee's work on the family and Caroline Daley's work on Taradale's gendered leisure patterns are the important exceptions and both deal with much the same period as we do. Toynbee's analysis was based on oral histories with more than 100 New Zealand-born respondents, mostly born in Wellington province before 1912. Daley's was based on a close examination of a small provincial town. Toynbee's work identified the expansion of leisure activities in the towns, especially for men, but concluded that the growth of family-centered 'coupledom' was the most important change, especially among the middle classes (her class typology assumes a larger difference between middle and working classes than was usually apparent in our study area).[6] Daley explored communal leisure activities, such as picnics, and demonstrated that women and men did different things, even while doing them together: the tension between heterosocial and gender-specific leisure remained. Her study argued that men were better able than women to pay for and find the time for leisure pursuits, although a 'new breed of women', young and single and armed with an income, increasingly identified new organised and unorganised leisure activities for themselves.[7] Our research confirms the broad conclusions of Toynbee and Daley, especially the growing importance of 'coupledom' and of the various leisure activities of Daley's 'new breed of women'.

In the 1880s and 90s girls had few sports or leisure activities available outside the home, although, for those who found work in the factories, shops and offices, that had changed dramatically by the 1930s (as we shall see). Throughout the period boys who went to work promptly entered the world of men and began to take part in such male leisure activities as shooting and fishing. Most forms of leisure activity were homosocial, dancing and card games excepted, and, although men usually had more money to spend on their own amusements and pleasures, across the period some changes reduced and reformed men's leisure activities. '[I]n my Dad's day,' as one old timer reminisced, 'it was more men with men . . .' and the family came second.[8] Most men saw leisure as a reward for providing for their families or paying board, in the case of unmarried sons. In this period, indeed, one of the main sites of conflict over the meaning of both masculinity and femininity occurred in relation to particular forms of leisure. The fiercest battles raged over the behaviour appropriate to single women and married men, although the clamour generated as moral evangelists attacked 'the vestigial looseness, disorder and immorality of . . . colonising society' drowned out most other noise.[9] The commercialisation of many leisure activities, the construction of participants as admission-paying observers, went on in the background to these contests, slowly but surely reshaping the gendered meanings of leisure and the meanings of masculinity and femininity.

Reforming men

In the 1880s and 90s the numerous pubs and sly-grog shops of the southern suburbs provided important places for men to spend their leisure and reinforce their gendered identity. So, too, did friendly societies, not to mention the central city's brothels and the various places where men played two-up, an illegal gambling game. In South Dunedin, gangs of young men played two-up on almost any vacant section and drunkenness was common.[10] In the nineteenth century, alcohol was very widely used and often used to excess, especially by men. In the colonial period it was the drug of choice for all but 'wowsers' (a category that included most evangelicals). Quite a few women enjoyed a 'tipple' and a small minority were alcoholics. Mabel Cartwright, the Presbyterian deaconess in South Dunedin and Caversham early in the twentieth century, often came across signs of alcohol usage among the poorer housewives that she visited.[11] For many workmen in pre-industrial crafts it was also an integral part of work: a keg or jug was brought in during a lull in the work. The district's many pubs made it easy to obtain alcohol and they also offered ready companionship, if not the temporary oblivion of drunkenness. Before the 1890s most trade unions met in pubs.[12] Drunk men were common on the streets, especially near the pubs. Vera Horder, whose father ran a fruit-shop at Forbury Corner, right by the Waterloo Hotel, recalled that 'all those horrible ... drunk men used to come round [at closing time] and leer at me ...'. Gertrude Shiel, the oldest child of C. W. Shiel, one of two brothers who owned a large quarry and brickfield at Forbury, recalled 'men ... reeling out of the hotel, you had to watch yourself then'.[13] Not for nothing did some view alcohol as the Devil's ingenious means of promoting sin and wickedness. Gambling, licentiousness and violence often accompanied drinking. Family income was dissipated and violence often accompanied the drunkard home. In this sense the pub 'signalled men's power'.[14]

Yet, even in the 1880s, not all men drank. Under the 1881 Licensing Act, which empowered men and women in local communities to elect licensing committees that could determine how many hotels they wanted, support for reducing the number of licences grew rapidly.[15] The women who walked the streets of the southern suburbs in 1893, gathering signatures for the suffrage petition, as well as many of those who signed, shared a vision of a new model

Speight's advertisement, 1914. This advertisement captures the pleasure in drinking that men looked forward to after a hard day's work. Speight's is now synonymous with the 'Southern Man', but the relationship between masculinity and alcohol consumption is longstanding. It was the subject of great contention in Caversham as supporters of temperance and women's suffrage sought to reform male culture. Some men from Caversham worked in the Speight's brewery. THE SKETCHER, DECEMBER 1914, OTAGO SETTLERS MUSEUM

family centred on a virtuous and dutiful wife and a family-centred man who practised temperance and self-control in all spheres of life. As we saw, more than 50 per cent of local women signed, and in some neighbourhoods support exceeded 60 per cent. In winning the vote, these women helped define drunkenness as unacceptable (although the community remained more tolerant of unmarried young men's transgressions). In 1893 those who actively supported women's suffrage also often advocated prohibition, and vice versa. Many Protestant parishes throughout Dunedin strongly supported the cause, while Sam Lister's *Otago Workman* waxed wrathful in denunciation of 'the shrieking sisterhood' (his own wife signed the petition, nonetheless).[16] Despite Lister, one union after another banned alcohol from meetings and began ejecting any member who arrived drunk. Unions also began cooperating with employers to ban the use of alcohol at work.[17]

The sharp reduction in the number of licensed premises, not to mention increased support for prohibition, show that public attitudes and patterns of behaviour changed sharply in the period 1881–1919.[18] By 1900 most Baptists, Congregationalists, Primitives, Methodists, Brethren and 'Sallies' – about 25 per cent of the population – campaigned for prohibition. Many joined pro-temperance organisations such as the local Rechabites and the Band of Hope.[19] Several of those interviewed still remembered 'strike out the top line', the prohibitionist battle cry.[20] Between 1900 and 1919 most Presbyterians and many Anglicans joined them. Even in the areas most opposed to prohibition, Kensington and the east ward of South Dunedin, by 1919 about 40 to 45 per cent of the adults supported prohibition. Hundreds of activists devoted most of their leisure to this cause, especially at election time. Respectable women would not be seen in pubs, and in 1910 the law curtailed the employment of women as barmaids.[21] The local Catholic clergy and religious, although opposed to prohibition, strongly supported temperance, for they had no doubt of the ravages caused by alcohol. Alcohol was the major moral issue of the day and only faded once the prohibition movement had helped produce a more temperate society. The battle over the 'demon drink' symbolised wider and more complex moral issues relating to responsibility and pleasure, particularly among men.[22]

The strength of support for six o'clock closing of hotels on the Flat during 1916–17 in part reflected the community's virtual unanimity about the need for greater temperance and ensuring that all men went home for dinner. True, the desire to affirm solidarity with 'our boys at the front' set the agenda and doubtless ensured strong support. Only a handful of die-hard drinkers, led by the legendary Steve Boreham, opposed the measure (Lister had sold the *Otago Workman* to the Trades Council in 1901 and had died in 1913). Boreham, an

Australian by birth (as were about 5 per cent of the area's inhabitants before the war), was a keen unionist and socialist who had worked much of his life as a shearer and a labourer. Drinking and gambling were his main pastimes, although (like many manual workers) he was useful with his fists. His colourful language, strong views and commitment to intemperance made him a symbolic figure of considerable power. Although he raged at the rising tide of 'wowserism', and had the courage to defend his now unpopular cause in the public arena, he represented a passing form of masculinity, although one that many men secretly either admired or emulated. When he was killed in 1925 – he was hit by a motor cycle as he left an inner-city pub late at night – his funeral became a major civic event, and thousands of male mourners, including the mayors of Dunedin and St Kilda, accompanied him on the last journey.[23]

The campaign to domesticate men was legitimised by the breadwinner wage, with its expectation that the primary duty of married men was to support their families. The rise of a local variant of 'the cult of domesticity', centred on the suburban family man, saw married men increasingly give up or sharply limit their indulgences in order to devote their income and leisure to maintaining homes and cultivating vegetable gardens.[24] As early as the 1890s, younger members of all-male friendly societies preferred dances to drinking and even encouraged the formation of women's branches. The rage for dancing saw most societies build their own halls in the 1900s.[25] In the 1920s family-centred men also took their families to the pictures on a Saturday night, helped their wives organise and undertake holidays and presided over the family table. Family sing-songs, card games and dances, first popular in the 1890s, became well-nigh universal, even among the unskilled.[26] Signs of drunkenness in public places, common in the 1900s, had become less frequent by the 1930s. The pub became a strictly regulated refuge from domestic restraint, a sort of 'last hurrah' for unreconstructed masculinity, although from 1917 only for an hour. The national attack on many forms of gambling, which saw bookmaking become illegal in 1911, while far from being a complete success locally, paralleled the attack on alcohol.[27] This attack on once-common forms of male behaviour, largely successful, was also accompanied by other campaigns to reconstruct the norms of masculinity, particularly on the sportsfield.

Manly games
Until the final decades of the Victorian era, many young and single men spent much of their leisure drinking, gambling and playing games. Many married older men did the same. The various games were often mainly an

St Clair playground with hurdy-gurdy. As the growing number of cars made the streets less safe, and as adults increasingly wanted to supervise children at play, new-fangled equipment became popular, especially swings, slides, and hurdy-gurdies. Such equipment, together with supervision (either by parents or teachers), tamed boys' play but provided girls with a much wider variety of activities. The first playground at St Clair was opened in 1913, according to Aitken's *St Kilda*, p. 77. *OTAGO WITNESS CHRISTMAS ANNUAL*, 1927, OTAGO SETTLERS MUSEUM

excuse for gambling, but each sport had its devotees, who enjoyed the skills of such leisure activities as horse-racing, rowing, cricket, athletic contests of speed and strength, boxing, wrestling and the three main codes of football. Before the 1890s few rules existed for these sports: referees were almost unknown and sizeable sums of money often changed hands. Over the next generation a marked change occurred in most sports, with different outcomes for women and men. In one recreational activity after another, as in other spheres of life, people formed provincial and national organisations that codified the rules, set up enforcement procedures and penalties, and tried to provide adequate facilities. This impulse to organise, often in the name of efficiency, was paralleled by increased adult supervision of children's play and provision of purpose-built playgrounds. In the process, activities for men and women were sharply segregated, except in certain sports for the elite, notably tennis and golf, or the old, such as bowls or croquet. Bowls was very popular

> COMING BY SPECIAL TRAINS.
> ## WIRTH'S NEW, CIRCUS.
>
> WIRTH BROS.' (LTD.) GREATEST SHOW ON EARTH
> Will present a complete New Circus at
> DUNEDIN
> On MONDAY, JANUARY 5,
> For Six Nights Only.
>
> MATINEES WEDNESDAY AND SATURDAY.
>
> Location:
> CALEDONIAN GROUNDS
> (Cargill Corner Entrance).
>
> SENSATIONS THAT INTOXICATE THE SOUL WITH DELIGHT.
>
> Not only a Great Amusement Enterprise, but also an
> EDUCATIONAL INSTITUTION OF IMPORTANCE AND VALUE.
>
> PRICES: Reserved Seats at Jacobs's, 7s (including tax); 5s, 3s, 2s (plus tax).
>
> WIRTH'S HUGE ZOO open in the Afternoon from 4 to 5, when the Animals will be fed. Admission, 1s adults, Children 6d.

Advertisement for the circus at the Caledonian Grounds. The Caledonian Grounds hosted all types of community events from sports fixtures to circuses. Children and adults enjoyed the circus performances and the exotic animals on view at the zoo.
OTAGO DAILY TIMES, 2 JANUARY 1920, P. 1

before the war, and the greens and grandstand for the Caversham Club dominated David St. (The local coal merchant and local-body politician, John H. Hancock, played for New Zealand.)[28]

Some of the major changes can be identified by investigating more closely the history of the Flat's largest sporting event, the Caledonian Games. By the late 1860s the annual New Year's carnival had become the province's major sporting event (and part of an informal compromise between the Scots, who celebrated the New Year, and the English, who celebrated Christmas). In the nineteenth century, the Caledonian Games, held at the Caledonian Grounds in Kensington from 1876 onwards, consisted of dozens of contests and exhibitions, often for a modest purse or prize, with the spectators, if not the contestants, often gambling heavily on the outcome. John Ogg, the well-known publican of the Railway Hotel on Hillside Rd, was a household name because of his prowess at these contests (Cargill's Corner was widely known as

Ogg's Corner until the 1930s). Women competed in many events, often boisterously. Children set up their own parallel contests. Feasting and dancing were also central to the 'Cally Games', modelled as they were on recently invented Highland 'traditions'.[29] These games – a combination of circus, sports event and carnival – proved very popular until the early 1900s (although during the 1890s attendances fell from around 12–14,000 a day to 6–7,000). By the 1920s the popular cry, 'Where are you going on New Year's Day?' 'Oot to the Cale, oot to the Cale,' had become folklore. Although successfully reinvented in the 1920s as Scottish performance, which one paid to watch, the decline of the games as popular carnival coincided with the growing tendency to go on holiday over Christmas–New Year, the expansion of organised sport, and a vigorous attempt both to stop competitors gambling on the outcome of their own efforts and to eliminate the influence of bookmakers.[30]

Because large areas of the southern suburbs were settled during a period when physical fitness and sport became cults, particularly among men, the area boasted several major sports fields. The geographical spaces in which leisure activities were pursued permitted the display of male physical prowess and expressed male power and sexual difference.[31] In the 1880s many of the playing grounds were little more than open paddocks, but by 1900 local bodies accepted an obligation to provide improved grounds and facilities at such places as the Oval, the 'Cale', Carisbrook, Bathgate and Tonga parks in South Dunedin, and Tahuna, Kettle, Culling and Hancock parks in St Kilda. By the early 1900s young men from across the city used these grounds for organised sports. As the 44-hour week became common, on Saturday afternoons organised teams, almost invariably of men (usually unmarried), played such sports as rugby, cricket, league cricket and soccer.[32] Some of these grounds also hosted major events: harness racing at Forbury Park, circuses at the Oval and the Agricultural and Pastoral Society's annual summer show at Tahuna.

With the growth of public provision for organised sports a new debate began about the purpose of such activities, a debate that focused on the meaning of sportsmanship (a code for managing the more aggressive and competitive aspects of masculine behaviour). In the 1890s and 1900s the urban middle classes encouraged amateurism. There were two main reasons for this. First, the cult of games had become widely accepted among the educated middle classes in England, and the idea transplanted easily to the colony. Second, amateurism was seen as an antidote to two of the principal sources of corruption and unsportsmanlike behaviour, the payment of players and gambling on results.[33] The new man played sport for the love of the game, not for pecuniary gain. The colony's secondary schools became bastions of the

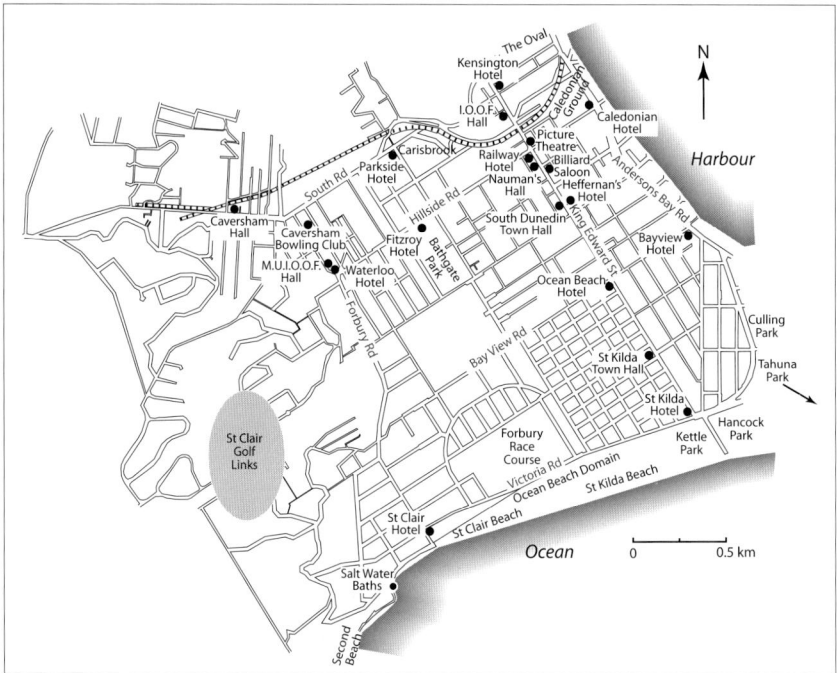

Map 6.1 Sites of organised leisure, 1890–1939. This map indicates the way in which men's leisure was catered for and commercialised in the southern suburbs, through sports grounds, hotels, lodges and a billiard saloon. Sports grounds and pubs signalled men's right to public space and time away from the domestic arena. Women's spare time was usually stolen from the round of daily tasks performed within the home. Young single women were more likely than their married sisters to have money to spend attending dances, the cinema or shopping for pleasure.

cult of games and the amateur ethos, and as they expanded rapidly after the introduction of free places in 1902 the proportion of young men socialised into this ethos gave it a significant advantage. By the war the amateur ethos was the norm in most sports.[34]

The amateur ethos made slower headway on the Flat than it did elsewhere because wagering on outcomes, and competing for a purse, were endemic in British and colonial culture, especially among working men. Boxing, wrestling, cycling and cricket all retained (or developed) a professional code, although the virtual abolition of bookmaking in 1911 constrained the role of money. The local battle was fought out most bitterly in the context of rugby union, the most popular sport for boys and men across the southern suburbs. Larger businesses fielded teams, as the Hillside Workshops did in most years, often for an annual contest against a team from Southland or North Otago.

However, most attention focused on the three local clubs that contested the city's premiership (Dunedin, Pirates and Southern).[35] Of those teams, Southern was the most important in creating a new model of masculinity for two reasons. First, it alone of the three clubs based in the area recruited almost all of its players locally and, at least in the pre-war years, virtually none of them had gone to Otago Boys' High, the major source of club players and amateurism in Dunedin. Second, and largely as a consequence, most of Southern's players were recruited from the working class. Southern thus contained within itself the sharpest conflicts over the payment of players, the ethics of players gambling on the result, and the forms of male aggression consistent with fair play – in a word, the meaning of sportsmanship.[36] These issues, together with that of alcohol, lay at the heart of the battle over the desired meaning of masculine behaviour, of what it ought to mean to be 'manly'.

Southern also had a special significance for the southern suburbs. Formed in 1899 by amalgamating the Caversham and Pacific clubs, both of which had strong local roots, it was predominantly recruited from the industrial working class and always practised on the Flat. When Southern adopted Bathgate Park as its headquarters in 1914, slap in the middle of the Flat, it became geographically as well as socially central. Even before then, its victories had become a matter of civic celebration. Games regularly attracted crowds of thousands and even before the First World War, when Southern contested the club final, more than 10,000 turned out to cheer. (As far as we can tell from photographs, until the 1930s it was rare to see women among the spectators.) Although Pirates had its fans, it never competed with Southern in Caversham and South Dunedin. Dunedin, by contrast, came to be the club preferred by Catholics, which gave it the advantage of fiercely partisan support – for around 20 per cent of South Dunedin's population was Catholic – but tended to limit its support to that minority.[37]

Until the end of the nineteenth century, rugby, both here and in England, was notable for its high levels of 'manly' violence. Following formation of the Otago Provincial Rugby Football Union in 1881, considerable progress was made in outlawing some of rugby's more violent practices. In the same period the codification of the rules, and the practice of appointing a referee, limited the risk that arguments over which rules were to be used, and how they ought to be interpreted, might erupt into open warfare.[38] The establishment of the New Zealand Union in 1893, which Otago only joined three years later, hastened the attack on excessive obstruction and violence and made payments to players the central issue on the agenda (the formation of the professional Northern Code of rugby league in England helped give the issue salience).

Alhambra v. Southern (in the black and white hooped jerseys). Although the two teams had played themselves to a standstill in drawing nil all only a few weeks earlier, before a crowd of 5000 at the Cally, Alhambra won the final 7–0. Southern was renowned for 'a vigour infrequently seen . . . these days'! In 1904 Southern triumphed, taking the Flag on points in the Premiership and winning the 2nd Division as well. The Flat rejoiced. The three southern mayors attended the celebratory 'smoke concert' in the South Dunedin town hall, an occasion punctuated by toast after liquid toast (A. R. Lawry, *From Inauguration to Premiers*, Dunedin, 1905, the first club history in New Zealand, provided a loving account of the events and Southern's history). OTAGO WITNESS, 4 JULY 1903

As we have noted, many working men saw no harm in taking payment for playing, especially if they had forfeited wages, and some saw no harm in betting on a game's outcome. Indeed, much of the interest in games centred on the substantial amounts at stake. Despite the best efforts of the Otago and the New Zealand Rugby Football Unions, payments under the table and gambling on matches was still rife on the Flat in the 1900s. The uproar over Southern's complicity in 'throwing' the 1915 championship against 'Varsity' helped settle matters. Those who wanted payments, or connived at 'throwing' games, could proceed down the path to professionalism. Not many made that journey and the two ringleaders were expelled.[39] Many club members considered the expulsion unjust, and the demand for their reinstatement served as a rallying cry for those who opposed the new ethos. Southern became more famous for its drinking, gambling and larrikinism. After the First World War many returned servicemen – most of them single – joined the club for that reason. The Fitzroy Hotel, by Bathgate Park, was their watering hole and the headquarters for the famous local bookmaker, 'Weasel' Donaldson.[40]

In the 1920s the respectable elements in the community, including some older committee men, recognised that reform was the precondition for Southern's survival.[41] In the mid-20s the campaign to reinstate the architects of the 'sold match' of 1915 finally ended and the club began to move forward. The sudden popularity of rugby league owed something to this outcome, however, for those who believed in remuneration and a more aggressive form of play found in the so-called Northern Code a game more to their liking. League, in Dunedin, was overwhelmingly a manual working-class game. No professionals or employers played. A sizeable proportion of the players in Dunedin worked at the Hillside Workshops, including Donald Crossan, whose death at the workshops (discussed in chapter ten) lost the Kaikorai Club a valued member. The participation of Hillside men was especially marked in the membership of the local City Club. The key figure at Hillside, E. Eckhoff, had been suspended from rugby for kicking an opponent, a charge he denied. As Charles Little pointed out, in his study of league's rise and fall, the game also recruited strongly among Catholics disaffected with the perceived sectarian bias of the Rugby Football Union (the State Primary Schools' Association's hostility to private and particularly Catholic schools fuelled sectarian tensions in the 20s). Although nobody now defended throwing games, clear differences of opinion concerning fair play, especially the degree of physical aggression that was acceptable, distinguished the views of masculinity held within different religious and occupational subcultures.[42]

League's fortunes soon faded and rugby, cleansed, soared to new heights of respectability and popularity. Southern's most famous player and coach, 'Old Vic' Cavanagh, had retired following the disgrace of 1915, although his promotion to manager of Ross and Glendining's clothing factory made the timing convenient. University ('Varsity') took advantage of its chance and persuaded Old Vic – a cutter by trade – to become their coach. Between 1923 and 1934 Varsity won the premiership ten times. Meanwhile, 'Young Vic', who had grown up in Playfair St and gone to Caversham School, distinguished himself as a cricketer and a rugby wing forward. When an injury forced him to retire from rugby, he in turn became Southern's coach. The oedipal contest between the Cavanaghs reflected and fed the traditional class rivalry between Southern and Varsity. Some sports-mad families split: Bert Grimmett's father backed Southern, so Bert backed Varsity.[43] The epic encounters between the two teams drew crowds of between 12,000 and 18,000. In 1935 Southern beat Varsity for the club championship. A. P. Gaskell immortalised the clash in 'The Big Game'. Not one woman appears in that story.[44] Some women

'Old Vic' and 'Young Vic' Cavanagh. The 'Professor of Rugby' and his son. In his first season as Southern's coach, 'Young Vic' asked his father, Varsity's coach, to 'come . . . and watch the Southern, sit beside me and give me a guide as to those particular things I wanted to get sorted out . . . . So he point blankly refused . . .'. His Mother stepped in: '"All these years you've spent . . . teaching other people Rugby surely to goodness you can help your own son . . ." So grudgingly, he couldn't fight that, he capitulated.' Fortunately, as O'Hagan remarked, they were as quick witted as they were short tempered, and combined to coach Otago to its first Ranfurly Shield triumph in 1935. OTAGO SETTLERS MUSEUM, COURTESY R. N. CAVANAGH

attended games, but they invariably sat in one of the grandstands. For test matches, starting with the first test against South Africa in 1921, a large party from Girls' High usually attended.[45]

The Southern meaning of manliness had become more self-controlled, though no less tough. Southern's sporting heroes of the interwar years, Jack Hore and Dave Trevathan, lived and played clean and hard. 'To Southern men [being Southern meant] . . . reward for labours; they do not seek special treatment because of their success; they do not brag of their achievements; and their relationships with others are unaffected.'[46] On the field each player did his job and placed the team's well-being ahead of his own. These values underpinned the Flat's commitment to egalitarianism and constituted attributes of a new man, a man who would make, in the fullness of time, a good husband and father.[47] Part of rugby's appeal to the middle classes had always been defined in terms of developing manliness through self-control; by the 1920s, not surprisingly, rugby was also seen as a training for war. Discipline and self-control were central to both activities.[48] Rugby, once a spawning ground for feckless violence, had become one of the principal means of socialising young men. Although drinking was still integral to the sport, the moment of excess had been confined to the post-game Saturday night party. In accommodating older traditions, amateurism locally, and in New Zealand, had become imbued with a passionate desire to win, fairly if possible, but, if the opposition refused to play fairly, then with whatever resort to surreptitious forms of manly skill was considered necessary.

The 'New Woman'

The 'New Woman', 'she who has discovered herself – not relatively as mother, wife, sister, but absolutely', was defined, above all else, by her leisure pursuits, whether smoking, cycling or dancing.[49] The 'anaemic spirit of femininity', never very strong in the colony, came under attack as a new generation of women sought autonomy and freedom from bodily constraint, symbolised most dramatically in dress reform.[50] Several oral-history informants remarked on the pleasures of walking and the new cult of physical fitness gave impetus to change.[51] The emergence of organised sports for women paralleled the growth of women's participation in the labour market. As with paid employment, for the most part unmarried single women led the way in enlarging women's leisured sphere and they benefited most. New laws limiting the hours of female factory workers (1873), shop assistants (1894) and office workers (1894) potentially gave many young women the time in which to pursue leisure pursuits if their work was not required at home. Although shopping alone rivalled reading as a leisure activity, from the 1890s some intrepid young women, in Dunedin and elsewhere, challenged traditional limits and constraints. In the 1890s, in Dunedin and throughout the Western world, bicycle riding became symbolic of the 'new woman'.[52]

An observer of a cycling procession at Tahuna Park in 1895 reported that, 'In the procession was a fair number of the members of the new Mirimo Club (ladies) who were greatly admired by the large crowd who watched them . . . . The notorious Dunedin larrikins did not put in an appearance, or else the large concourse of people restrained them, for there were no such jeers or boorish jokes such as Dunedinites are used to when lady riders are seen in the streets.'[53] Early women cyclists wished to maintain decorum while taking to the streets; they wanted to enjoy their new freedoms without jeopardising their respectability. By and large they succeeded, and in the early 1900s women took to motor cycling and automobile driving.[54] Emily Siedeberg, well-known throughout Dunedin as the first woman medical graduate and as medical superintendent of the St Helen's hospital, not to mention the doctor for the local Miriam Rebekah Lodge, was one of the first in Dunedin to own a car. In the interwar period some women flew, and Jean Batten, the 'aviatrix', became a national legend. As Charlotte Macdonald has observed, this quest for physical freedom and independence was part of the larger movement for 'full citizenship'.[55]

Until the 1890s the dominant code of respectability for colonial women allowed them to be physically active, but insisted that it was unfeminine for a woman to compete or make a spectacle of herself.[56] Yet attitudes were changing in complex ways. Dr Frederic Truby King, superintendent of Seacliff Asylum and a well-known lecturer at the Otago Medical School, denounced the effects of academic competition on secondary school girls, but insisted that women needed to be physically fit in order to discharge their reproductive duties.[57] Local debates about the declining birthrate and the 'evils of cram' – debates that won national attention – suggested that young women required healthy bodies, and should avoid too much study, for the future of the race. Yet anxiety remained that the competitive spirit, at work and play, might go too far, transforming independent 'bachelor women' into a third sex, 'combining in themselves so strongly the essentials of both men and women as to render them akin to neither'.[58] Fears of masculinised women were no doubt heightened by the sensational 1909 Dunedin trial of Amy Bock, who, under the alias of Percy Redwood, gained the affections of Agnes Ottaway and married her in an elaborate ceremony in South Otago attended by the local MP. The high court was packed for each day of the trial and the papers had a field day.[59]

Organising in quest of enjoyment was not only a relatively late priority for women, as Charlotte Macdonald noted, but one fraught with contention. '[S]mall enclaves of enthusiasts' blazed women's admission to the world of organised sports in the first half of our period.[60] Often women from upper-middle-class backgrounds led the way, whether playing croquet, tennis or golf, or climbing mountains ('women of leisure' were those with sufficient income to employ domestic help, although the scarcity of servants in the colony made every woman 'a Martha to a certain extent . . . .').[61] For most married women, the consuming nature of household and child care made time for sport a luxury. 'Golf,' declared the well-to-do captain of the North Otago Ladies' Golf Club, Mrs Percy Ward, 'is an ideal game for women – not too much exertion if played within reason, and in probably no other game can skill take so well the place of strength.' Mrs Ward, pictured walking in the bush on the pages of a Dunedin paper, camped for two months every summer, went 'in a great deal for rabbit shooting', tramping and 'practical gardening'.[62] Such a 'woman of leisure' had the time to take sport seriously, but it was not only wealthy women who engaged in such pursuits. Mabel Cartwright and her closest friend, 'my Darling Effie', often went on picnics, camped at Karitane and regularly 'walked a long way, then sat on the hills and read awhile'. She was practising deep-breathing exercises and reading Carlyle's *Heroes and Hero Worship*.[63]

Girls at primary school, and those proceeding to a secondary school, received some training in gymnastics from the mid-1880s. Otago Girls' High boarders formed a hockey team in 1899, the second in the city, but the school lacked any grounds other than two tennis courts, a situation that took years to improve and added considerably to the perils of hockey.[64] As far as we know, the Presbyterian Bible Class Union introduced basketball to Dunedin in 1906.[65] In basketball, as in hockey and tennis, in Dunedin as in the other towns, Bible Classes, primary schools, secondary schools and their Old Girls (including the Catholic ones) played a large role in the expansion of these sports. In the interwar period high school girls started to play cricket and a handful pioneered tramping and skiing.[66] Where women needed access to sports grounds, however, they often had to wheedle and beg. The numbers involved in most of these organised sports were rather small and none of the early teams were based on the Flat.

A ladies' hockey club: some snapshots of play at Anderson's Bay. Young women in their 'Tam o' Shanters' and wielding their 'formidable sticks' exemplified the physical freedom associated with the 'New Woman'. *OTAGO DAILY TIMES*, 22 AUGUST 1902

The women of the southern suburbs, with little time and opportunity to participate in organised sporting activities, could read about the achievements of the 'new woman' in twelve densely packed pages of the *Otago Daily Times & Witness Christmas Annual* in December 1907. 'Chronicles of the Enfranchised', written by 'One of Them', charted the contribution of women throughout the country to building the nation through philanthropy, education and the arts. The 'outdoor woman' loomed large. She was likely, the author wrote, 'to become a rapidly increasing expression of her sex in New Zealand'. The article reported on a great variety of sporting achievements, from hunting and fishing to tennis, golf and hockey. A number of hockey players were photographed proudly holding their 'formidable' sticks, which reportedly gave them a 'redoubtable' air as they caught their trams for the playing field. These new women were distinguished by their dress: 'Spick and span, ankles showing beneath well-cut skirts', hair tied back and 'eclipsed by serviceable motor caps or veils' or a 'Tam o' Shanter'. The hockey players represented the new woman's radiant health and good spirits as sport replaced concern with feminine trifles and vanity with 'frank and joyous freedom by the ease bred by entire absence of self-consciousness'. A local exemplar was to be found teaching at Otago Girls' High School. Flora Campbell, MA, Otago's lawn tennis champion, 1906–7, attributed her success to her Otago Girls' High training in 'physical culture' and 'to such girlish games as fives and hockey'.[67]

As competitive sports came to be accepted as consonant with femininity, 'girlish games' were now distinguished by their lack of body contact: wrestling, boxing and rugby were aggressive masculine sports. 'Ladylike' behaviour was also at odds with too much physical display. In fact, the onset of menstruation, residents of the southern suburbs remembered, might entail strict limitation of their physical activities. Joyce Jones recalled that, 'I used to be a beggar for standing on my head and turning cartwheels. Now I had to keep my feet on the ground and behave myself like a lady.'[68] One woman was not allowed to attend school when menstruating, while most were forbidden to swim or bathe.[69] In an editorial on 'The Emancipation of Women' in October 1919, the *New Zealand Medical Journal* echoed widely held ambivalence: '... liberal education and physical exercise for women are wholly commendable, provided that the first does not result in mental indigestion, and the latter in an attempt to incur physical strains, which the man's nervous fibre is better fitted to withstand'.[70]

Physical strain was part and parcel of life for the young women from the Flat who went to work in Dunedin's factories and that, in itself, might have been a disincentive to further sports activity. Many workplaces, such as Cadbury Fry Hudsons, offered the opportunity to join work-based sports teams by the interwar years. Despite the fact that the company required its employees to work three hours' overtime two nights per week, some found the energy for sport. The biscuit and confectionery factory employed more than 300 young women and sponsored three sports teams: two for basketball and a 'very keen' B-grade hockey team. Hilda Maher recalled that, at the Wax Vesta factory, 'we had a netball team, we had a marching team, we played tennis and that'.[71] Just as the Railway Workshops now saw constructive leisure as useful for its employees, companies employing women realised the benefits to health and worker loyalty (not to mention the free advertising) fostered by work-based teams. As Sutton-Smith pointed out many years ago, team games were also considered excellent for inculcating discipline and overcoming any inadequacies in upbringing.

Authorities such as Truby King regarded outdoor exercise and fresh air as much more beneficial for women than frequenting picture shows.[72] But it was in the moving pictures that the independent and autonomous 'new woman' was most often to be found. If the young women from the Flat could

Marching girls, 1937. Most factories that employed 'girls' fielded marching teams in summer and either basketball or hockey teams in winter. The Wax Vesta team of nine 'girls' is here photographed behind the Phoenix team, smartly turned out in the colours of the matchboxes (green, red and yellow). They practised on the lawn behind the factory after work each night and competed against the other city teams on Saturday afternoons. The factory provided the uniforms, a library, and a kitchen. Employees brought along what they wanted for lunch and the company employed a cook who then produced the meal. COURTESY OF HILDA MAHER

not emulate their heroines' lifestyles, they could, by the interwar years, adopt their shingled hair and shorter skirts, both of which offered a kind of physical liberation. However much moralists exhorted young women to pursue exercise to better prepare them for motherhood, time and energy for organised sport remained the prerogative of a select few. For any woman with domestic responsibilities, reading, the cinema and shopping fitted more easily into moments stolen from the necessary round of domestic chores. For the majority, the life of the new woman was more easily imagined than enacted.

Families at play

As the idea of the family as an ideal to live by diffused across all classes in the late nineteenth century, many came to believe that the leisure pursuits of the family marked the progress of the nation.[73] This new ethos nicely complemented the emergence of the suburban family man on the Flat, the new face of both manual and white-collar married men. Both sexes and all age groups often took their leisure together, even if they were interested in different activities. Wives, together with husbands and children, often attended functions and events as family groups. In the Edwardian period, on Sundays and public holidays, many families went for walks, promenading at St Clair and Second beaches, where the Garrison Band usually entertained. Locals in St Clair could sit in their own gardens, 'listening to the splendid band concerts that carried up the hill along with the barking of dogs and shouting of happy children, and the never-ending roar of the waves'.[74] On weekends many families took a harbour ferry to Broad Bay or Portobello to promenade or watch the yachts. (By the 1920s these yachting and rowing regattas were more popular

'Sunday afternoon at St Clair', 1926. A crowd gathered on the Esplanade listening to a band play. The brass band has been described as 'the working man's Symphony Orchestra', and the first national organisation was formed in 1889. The Salvation Army band took popular tunes into the arsenal of street evangelism, with some effect. HOCKEN LIBRARY

St Kilda Municipal Band 1920. The St Kilda Municipal Band began in Mornington but settled in St Kilda, whose Council outbid Mornington's proffered subsidy in 1912. In 1912 it won its first national contest, tying with Kaikorai. Brass bands were male musical enclaves but women musicians provided much of the musical education as piano teachers in the area. HOCKEN LIBRARY

than the Caledonian Games.) Often a local band, such as St Kilda's, provided musical accompaniments. Early in the new century the Sunday night sing-along around the piano, or a game of euchre or 500, became as common as the Sunday afternoon walk, and both eclipsed family prayer.[75]

City-wide community events, such as Summer and Winter A & P Shows, exhibitions (notably in 1889–90, and the Dunedin and South Seas Exhibition, 1925–26), the annual Labour Day and capping processions, the celebration of the monarch's birthday and the occasional Royal Visit, all attracted large crowds of both sexes and all ages. Admiral Byrd's expeditions, and the American fleet, drew tens of thousands. Circuses also attracted large crowds. Major races at Forbury Park, the home of harness and (more briefly) greyhound racing in Otago (like major rugby or cricket matches at Carisbrook), saw tens of thousands invade the area. Schools and churches, and most firms and voluntary organisations, held an annual picnic, often hiring a train or harbour ferry to take the crowds to the chosen spot. Such events usually saw entire families taking part. The fact that males and females were present at the same event did not mean that they did the same things, and even when they did their subsequent memories selected quite different aspects.[76] Within the boroughs of Caversham and South Dunedin there were regular annual events. The primary schools were the focus for end-of-year concerts and prize-givings, but before the First World War displays of gymnastics also drew sizeable audiences (in the interwar period, interschool sporting contests became common, thanks to the State Primary Schools' Association). The Caversham School Choir was so impressive that for some twenty years its annual concert was performed at His Majesty's, one of the city's largest theatres, and a fleet of trams ferried proud locals to and fro. Before the war, Caversham's Volunteer Fire Brigade often paraded by torchlight, accompanied by the Caversham Band, 'and the Chinese used to participate.... There'd be little firecrackers and they'd have a dragon...'.[77] Even in the 1930s and 40s, community sings proved enormously popular, especially among older folk. Robert 'Whang' McKenzie, South Dunedin-born and the most famous local journalist and radio commentator, led a weekly '"Whang" Community Sing' in South Dunedin's town hall throughout the Second World War.[78]

Summer holidays also became popular family pastimes, for the Christmas and New Year period allowed almost everyone the chance to get away (by 1900 the English holiday of Christmas had largely replaced the Scots' hogmanay, and Guy Fawkes was almost universally celebrated). Families now picnicked, camped and holidayed together. From the 1890s small clusters of holiday cottages, known as 'cribs', spread north and south along the coast. Holidays usually saw women's work of child care and cooking transposed to environments with fewer amenities and greater dangers for children. Families holidayed in Central Otago or the lakes, helped by state-owned bus services, railways and the SS *Earnslaw* on Wakatipu. The government organised train services to transport citizens to the nation's scenic wonders and offered family concessions (from early in the 1900s, railway workers received additional concessions).[79] On every public holiday before the First World War, special trains took thousands north and south to popular picnicking spots. By the 1930s, New Zealand Railways advertisements suggested that 'Mum' was entitled to leisure and should assert her claim: 'Woman's Right is a Trip by Train when she believes that a holiday is needed.'[80] Within Dunedin the DCC organised trams to take families to the city's parks, the botanical gardens and the rural fringes. Many in the southern suburbs headed south to Brighton beach or the Kaikorai River's estuary. Once the destination was reached, Dad and the boys might go and fish, or simply play beach cricket or quoits while the women prepared the food.[81]

The home itself became a site for new opportunities for leisure pursuits. The culture of the home handyman rapidly spread among the skilled, especially the growing proportion who owned their own homes. Gardening became a local passion. Aerial photographs from 1947 indicate the extent of the domestic vegetable gardens across most of St Kilda, South Dunedin, Caversham and Kew. Even in Kensington, where cottages on small sections abounded and freeholders were relatively few, a high proportion of house-

Advertisement for the Hermitage, 1933. Holidays at sites of natural beauty were promoted by the Government Tourist Bureau in association with Thomas Cook & Sons and New Zealand Railways. Mt Cook offered not only a first-class modern hotel but also a camping ground, the more usual holiday site for New Zealanders. *OTAGO DAILY TIMES*, 16 DECEMBER 1933

holds cultivated quite substantial gardens. (The Great Depression and the war had doubtless intensified this pattern.) Fathers often produced impressive vegetables to feed the family, while mothers grew flowers and ornamental shrubs. As a rule, the vegetable garden occupied most of the back section, whereas the flowers were confined to the small front garden, part of the house's public face.[82] Home beautification was reinterpreted in this era as a legitimate leisure pursuit, signifying the increased centrality of domesticity as a shared family interest.[83]

From the 1920s in Dunedin the radio also increasingly became a focus of family recreation. Professor Robert Jack's 4XD broadcasts of vocal and musical items could be picked up in most of St Kilda by 1923. By the end of that decade, six stations vied with each other in Dunedin, but only when the newly created Radio Broadcasting Company began transmissions locally in 1929 did

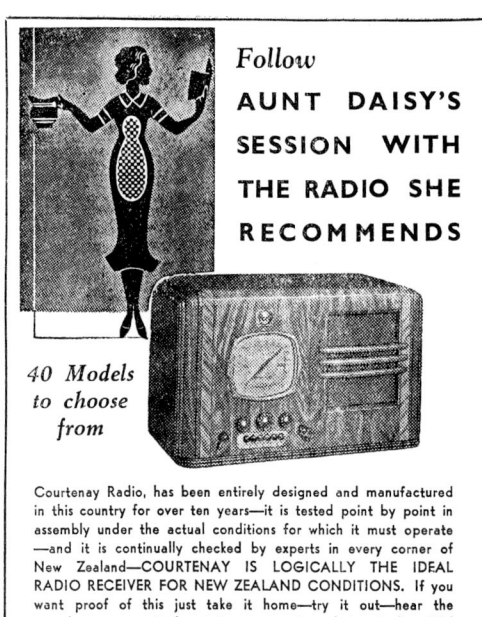

Courtenay radio advertisement. Radio scheduling took account of women's daily routine and brought the wider world into the home. Aunt Daisy gave cooking and household hints to housewives. The home was the main site of married women's leisure, and increasingly the place where married men spent their spare time. Radio programmes catered for many tastes and for all age groups at different times of the day. AUNT DAISY'S BOOK OF HANDY HINTS, WHITCOMBE AND TOMBS, C. 1946

radio achieve widespread popularity. Some local sporting events were now broadcast live. 'Whang' McKenzie became a household name because of his colourful rugby commentaries, and his broadcasts gave the housewife little option but to achieve some familiarity with this hitherto arcane male activity. (He also provided commentaries on racing, boxing and wrestling, the latter a very popular sport in the 1920s and 30s.) Radio allowed different markets to be provided for. While men got sport, especially on Saturday afternoons, women had their own programmes. By the late 1920s, 'Women's Hour' was a daytime staple and in the late 30s, following the introduction of the national commercial network, 'Aunt Daisy' began to win a local following. The late afternoon, after school, provided programmes for teenagers. Girls apparently followed serials more avidly than boys, although 'The Lone Ranger' was very popular with boys.[84] The entire family often shared listening in the evening, especially in winter. Reception often left much to be desired, however. ('All I remember is the crackling,' Christine King recalled.)[85] By the end of the 1930s listening to the radio came second only to the movies as a leisure activity. The family sing-song around the piano began to suffer the same fate that had overtaken family prayer.

Across the period families also became more child-centred. The rapid decline in family size, together with a new emphasis on the educational importance of play, meant that parents and schools increasingly organised activities for children and tried to regulate their play.[86] Some adults saw play as the key to socialisation. Early in the new century, Sunday Schools and Bible Classes increasingly offered various sports as an antidote to 'street corner loafing' – football and basketball teams, table tennis, tennis, harriers and badminton. By 1909, indeed, there were five church-based harrier clubs on the Flat, as well as the Caversham Harriers, a Civil Service Club and the St Kilda Harriers and Amateur Athletics Club.[87] By the 1920s the state primary schools fostered team sports for boys and girls and a lively programme of athletics. Interschool competitions flourished, with St Clair School regularly besting all others in the province at athletics. The Catholic schools, two of them on the Flat, were equally active in organising sports for their children. Organisations proliferated to transform play into a moral activity, notably Boy Scouts and Girl Guides. In 1924 Horace and Ada Grocott, Caversham Baptists recently returned from Bolivia, where they had been missionaries, formed the first New Zealand branch of the Baptist Boys' Brigade, in order to provide idle youth with more constructive use of their leisure. Two years later they formed the first Baptist Girls' Brigade.[88] However, the leisure activities of boys and girls remained distinct and separate, as they had been in earlier times, when many parents largely ignored what children did in their free time.[89]

Despite the adult thrust to tame the playground and regulate children's leisure activities, children still enjoyed considerable freedom. Surrounding farms, empty paddocks and sections, extensive market gardens, sandhills and beaches provided ample opportunity for boys to play 'cowboys and Indians', build huts, help or harass the Chinese market gardeners, and fly kites. Others caught birds, shot rabbits and ducks, and one or two had a horse. Boys often used shanghais and played practical jokes.[90] Before the war, at least, larrikinism remained a problem, especially in the vicinity of David St. Gangs of 'rough' boys, most of them from South Dunedin (according to interviewees who grew up in Caversham), harassed those living in the area, breaking windows, scaring horses and generally making a nuisance of themselves. Bert Grimmett, who grew up on Fitzroy St, recalled that the local boys organised gangs and fought 'brick fights' with boys from neighbouring streets.[91] There were no girls' gangs as such, but the girls at the Lookout Point Industrial School feistily made their presence felt and helped to sustain a tradition of assertive femininity. In the 1900s *The Budget*, a local family journal, advertised courses in self-defence for young women. By the 1930s government departments often issued regulations and homilies instructing or exhorting children not to play on streets or play tricks on moving vehicles.[92]

Through most of our period the beach was more popular with young women than any organised sport, especially in the summer months. Many shops shut on Wednesday afternoon, all schools shut for the weekend, and prohibitions on using Sunday for peaceful and private leisure activities had largely been eroded by 1890. School children frequented the beaches and enjoyed paddling in the surf. It is unclear whether primary school children were taught swimming before the 1920s, although Otago Boys' High had a pool which was used by Girls' High pupils from the 1890s on. Rip currents at St Kilda and St Clair made the beach dangerous for swimming and in 1881 Caversham Borough opened a salt-water pool (at the south-western corner of St Clair beach). It was very popular with the citizens of the southern suburbs,

St Clair Lifesaving Club Pavilion. An earlier St Clair Pavilion, which contained dressing rooms, tearooms and a hall (in which weekly dances were held), burned down in 1914. These grand Surf Lifesaving club rooms came to dominate St Clair beach and signalled the growing popularity of the sport and its importance to safety for swimmers. *OTAGO WITNESS*, 28 FEBRUARY 1928, OTAGO SETTLERS MUSEUM

especially in periods when the beach itself was deemed unsafe for bathing. Rachel Grimmett regularly travelled from Fitzroy St to bathe there (men and women bathed at separate times). In the 1900s the beach became much more popular than the pool. Even in the 1890s the Dunedin Ocean Beach Domain by-laws were relatively undemanding, requiring that bathers over ten years of age wore 'decent' and 'proper' costumes (decency required that both sexes be covered from 'neck to knee', with the added requirement for women that their garment should be 'loosely fitting').[93] By the 1920s the definition of 'decent' and 'proper' had moved to accommodate greater areas of bare flesh and women's costumes usually now accented the breasts (the skirt, common until the 1950s, ensured that the female crotch was curtained).

The promenade put women and men on display, as did the beach itself when mixed bathing became more common in the early twentieth century. In 1910 the avant-garde magazine *Triad*, the influential local guardian of taste and standards, suggested that 'mixed bathing under decent conditions is a good thing for any community' and 'an excellent antidote for the folly of preening prudes'.[94] When a group of well-to-do men formed the Pacific Surf

Women lifesavers, at St Clair, c. 1920. It is not known when the first women's lifesaving groups formed, but they generally emerged within the framework of men's clubs that had spread around the country from 1910 onwards. The first national prize for men's six-man teams was launched in 1915, and became a club competition in 1922, but only in 1944 was the first six-place women's competition launched. St Clair women won that year. OTAGO SETTLERS MUSEUM

Bathing Club in 1910 and the St Clair Surf Lifesaving Club in 1911 – around the same time that other such clubs were being formed throughout the country – the modern beach was born. As the health benefits of sunshine and exercise came to be widely promoted, the beach burgeoned as a site of leisure activities. The lifesaving clubs, formed in the first instance by members of the city's upper middle classes, became dominated by men such as 'Duke' Gillies, a skilled worker and tradesman who designed the country's first four-man surf canoe in the 1930s.[95]

Between the wars the beach also came to symbolise physical freedom and independence for both sexes, a new frontier for self-expression. (The pre-war custom of promenading back and forth along the footpath to the tune of the Garrison Band began to lose favour.) The war's impact on women's fashions helped legitimise bathing costumes that emphasised bodily display, but with the advent of female beauty contests on beaches in the mid-20s bodily display reached new heights. Even before the war young 'roughs' indulged in voyeurism. It is not clear when the sandhills became a popular nesting-place for the sexually adventurous, but the availability of 'french letters' in the 1920s suggests the interwar period. Thus the beach offered recreational opportunities for those who wished to retain their respectability, and observe the new conventions, and for those who could not care less about such matters. Beach and beauty contests eclipsed all other recreations in summer, although, like organised sports, they were the preserve of the young and the single.

Private pleasures
Married women had little leisure, especially once the first baby was born. Indeed, as Langhamer suggests, the definition of the '"good" wife and mother as someone who devoted her time to the needs of other family members' made it difficult for women to prioritise their own pursuits without guilt.[96] Women's work created opportunities for the leisure activities of husbands and children. Some forms of women's work, such as knitting and sewing, easily taken up and put down, could be done while talking or listening to the radio.[97] Married women sometimes undertook these activities of an afternoon and during the First World War such activities were institutionalised. In St Clair, a Women's Club was formed in 1915 to knit and bake for 'our boys' (it survives still, although it has long outlived its original purpose). None of this should be taken to mean that married women could never relax or forget the world of domestic toil. 'Just to pop in and say gidday or . . . have a cup of tea . . .', chatting over the back fence, or in the interwar years going to the Plunket Mothers' Club, might provide social time beyond the demands of the

family.[98] Single women, even when kept at home, had more leisure than their married sisters (although some domestic servants would doubtless have dissented). At the start of the period, notions of respectability kept many young women in their homes, unless chaperoned. Male larrikinism or drunkenness, sexual danger and the lack of public toilets for women all added other constraints, especially for the disabled and the timid.[99] As Robin Law shows in chapter nine, however, women born in the 1910s and 20s felt relatively safe and comfortable going out at night.[100] No doubt the 1917 introduction of six o'clock closing transformed life on the streets 'after hours'.

The first survey of New Zealanders' leisure activities, taken long after our period had ended, discovered that reading and gardening were far and away the most popular.[101] Although we lack systematic data for our period, oral informants, male and female, often recalled their enthusiasm for both activities. Almost every woman interviewed remarked on the intense pleasure derived from reading. Many workplaces had libraries. The Hillside Railway Workshops established a library in 1885 and enlarged it further in the mid-1920s. It mainly provided engineering-related works and periodicals. The Wax Vesta Match Company, an important local employer of women, had its own library, containing mainly novels. Avid readers could pay to join the Athenaeum, a substantial circulating library with reading-rooms in the Octagon, or the Dunedin Book Club, which had rooms both in the city and in South Dunedin. Caversham Borough had its own library until it amalgamated with the city's new and free Carnegie Public Library in 1909, and various churches and lodges had their own reading and literary clubs. In March 1914 a public meeting launched St Kilda's library.[102] Bookshops and newsagents also dotted Hillside Rd, the Main South Rd and King Edward Rd. New books could be acquired relatively cheaply and in the interwar period the city boasted the country's largest second-hand bookshop.[103]

Newspapers and magazines were widely available. Apart from the *Daily Times* and the *Evening Star*, popular among workers, people could read such local journals as the *Otago Witness* and the Catholic *Tablet*. More specialised papers and periodicals catered for a fast-growing variety of interests, including pro-labour politics. In 1905 the first local edition of *Truth* hit the stands, with its mixture of sensationalism and muckraking. In the 1890s well-nigh universal literacy and new forms of cheap paper brought novels and magazines within the reach of a much larger audience. Magazines were consumed in quantity, and the colonial girl was said to read three-and-a-half magazines a month.[104] The dramatic explosion of novels and magazines for girls and boys both created and captured a new and youthful market. Boys were addicted to adventure stories and magazines, often devoted to scientific and mechanical matters.¹⁰⁵ Colonial girls were also apparently 'devoted to adventure books, often of the hair-breadth escape, somewhat bloodcurdling order'.¹⁰⁶ Apart from books, local magazines such as *The Budget*, C. N. Baeyertz's *The Triad*, Fred Rayner's irreverent and irregular *Sketcher* and the Sydney *Bulletin* (Otago's own Arthur Adams was a key figure), offered a choice of melodramas, short stories and comment.¹⁰⁷ Colonial editions of major British novels and a wide range of American fiction could also be readily obtained. Edna Lyall's freethinking *Donovan* and *We Two*, not to mention Louisa Alcott's feisty Jo from *Little Women*, engaged the imagination of the 'colonial girl'.¹⁰⁸ So, too, did the novels of such best-selling colonial writers as Edith Lyttleton and Louisa Baker, whose high-spirited heroines and reformed men had a lot of fun as they exemplified, finally, the dominant vision of a new domesticity.¹⁰⁹

Given the constraints upon women's access to public space, unless in a family or a peer group, it is not surprising that reading became enormously popular as a leisure activity for women. A private and individual activity, reading allowed women to enjoy their leisure without exhibiting themselves in public (although by the 1920s many did both). Compulsory schooling meant that, by 1900, almost all were able to read by the time they left school and most had access to some novels. From the 1890s the *School Journal* tried to whet the appetite for colonial stories while fostering Imperial citizenship. Many of the women interviewed remembered how important reading had been to them. Some boys read, but many 'never had much time for reading [as a child] . . . we were out raiding orchards and things'.¹¹⁰ Few could emulate Gertrude Shiel, who could read to her heart's content when she 'found out that I could . . . get way up into the ceiling' of her family's commodious two-storeyed house on Forbury Rd.¹¹¹ For some this stolen time cost them dearly, but most families appear to have encouraged reading. School prizes, if not birthday and Christmas presents, were almost invariably a book or membership of the Athenaeum.¹¹² Novels and contemporary plays, such as Ibsen's *The Doll's House* (available in English translation from 1889), could alert women readers to a critique of current domestic and social arrangements. Advice manuals and novels could also introduce women to new notions of sexual desire. Marie Stopes's *Married Love* (1918) proved to be phenomenally popular in New Zealand, perhaps even more so because of the publicity surrounding its censorship in 1924.¹¹³ Olive Schreiner, the South African author of the *Story of an African Farm* (1911), or New Zealander Jean Devanny's *The Butcher Shop* (1926), disrupted Stopes's romantic view of marriage. The destructive aspects of puritanism, or inherited moral codes, were everywhere under scrutiny if not outright attack.

The shorter working week and unprecedented levels of prosperity, well diffused in the southern suburbs, thanks to the level of job security provided by the railway workshops, allowed a fast-growing proportion of the population to pursue their individual interests. The rapid spread of hobbies first signified the new order. Hobbies could be completely idiosyncratic. Percy Godber, foreman in the tinsmiths' shop at Hillside in the mid-1920s, excelled in carving and painting Maori designs (he was also an outstanding photographer).[114] Others took up yachting and fishing. Pigeon-fanciers were fairly common. Many skilled men had workshops at home where they built model boats or trains, developed film or practised their craft purely for their own pleasure. In 1903 George Methven, a fitter, built the first locally made motor car, and Fred Cooke, one of the city's best-known motor importers, lived in St Kilda and regularly organised car rallies. Some men owned or took shares in a greyhound, a trotter or a racer. Such pursuits did not necessarily require much money. Sutton-Smith interviewed a Dunedin man who delighted in 'a good-sized scrapbook ... [in which he collected] crackers, attractive Christmas cards, and coloured advertisements from magazines'.[115]

By 1914 men and boys often collected cigarette cards, stamps and bottles. Scrapbooks were equally popular with girls, although they collected different things. Many girls also delighted in dolls, dolls' clothes and 'dress-ups'. Married women often got pleasure from practising their domestic skills. Embroidery and flower arrangement were especially popular. Bicycles, motor cycles and automobiles – both steam and petrol-driven – rapidly became the focus of a new frontier for male leisure, although a handful of women took part. Motor-cycle and automobile clubs became the new rage and the trolley became a mania among boys. The car now often replaced the train or bus as the means for reaching favoured picnic spots. By the 1930s the car had almost put the harbour ferries out of business.

More than any other medium, the moving picture created a new world of commercialised private fantasy aimed at women as well as men. From 1896, when a local Princes St theatre gave a Dunedin audience its first taste of this new medium, until the the First World War, Australian, American, French and British films provided cheap entertainment for a rapidly growing audience. The relationship between men and women was as central to this new medium as it had been for the novel. Early screenings took their place as a minor part of vaudeville and music shows, since the first films lasted less than a minute, but by 1905 you could enjoy an hour or more of entertainment – melodramas, actualites (early news and documentaries), historical dramas, romances and 'cinematic tourism'.[116] (Vaudeville, 'with the juggling acts and the dancing girls with their bare legs', remained popular.)[117] By the

The King Edward Theatre. The first moving picture theatre on the Flat, the Arcade Picture Palace, was destined for a short run. It opened at Cargill's Corner on 17 June 1911 and closed a month later. The Glasgow Theatre, in the South Dunedin town hall, opened on 1 July 1911, and had a similarly short life until reopened by Pathé Perfect Pictures in March 1912. The Coronation Hall in St Kilda was used as a cinema for a short time in 1912, 1919 and 1926. Residents of Caversham were more attracted to the purpose-built King Edward Theatre or the other picture theatres in town. Through the cinema, residents of the southern suburb were transported to other worlds.
KNEWSTUBB THEATRES, CINEMAS: DUNEDIN AND DISTRICTS, 1897–1974, DUNEDIN, 1974, P. 13

time the first theatre on the Flat opened at Cargill's Corner, in 1914, there were eight moving-picture theatres within five minutes' walk of the Exchange. By the end of the 1930s a local photographer and film enthusiast, Henry Gore, showed films in several local halls, including the St Kilda town hall.[118] The 'flicks' had already become the most popular form of entertainment for the working classes. From around 1914 the first purpose-built theatres, called 'palaces', created a world of glamour and escapism. Here every patron could briefly enjoy the privileges of royalty.

During the war, film became a universal attraction, appealing to men and women of all ages and classes.[119] Features about Gallipoli and the Somme drew enormous crowds. By 1916 it was estimated that around one-third of all New Zealanders attended the pictures each week.[120] By 1915 each permanent 'picture palace' offered two- to three-hour sessions, Monday to Saturday during the war years, while the Queen's Theatre on Princes St screened films continuously from midday until 10.30pm. (The city council would not permit screenings on Sundays, Christmas Day or Good Friday.)[121]

In the 1920s the Saturday matinée, here as elsewhere, became very popular with children. Boys and girls from the Flat attended more frequently than most of the city's children, many going at least once a week and sometimes more. In urban areas the social class of the parents was the most important factor in explaining the frequency of attendance. In 1927 some 44 per cent of children at Kensington Primary School were regulars at the pictures, compared to only 10 per cent from the school in Maori Hill, an upper-middle-class suburb. The ability to send children to the pictures gave harassed mothers living in cramped housing new leisure opportunities. As one child noted, 'When mother wants a quiet afternoon, she says "Off to the pictures".'[122] Matinées, like evening shows, usually provided a mix of features designed to appeal to the different interests of the two sexes. 'The pictures I like best,' wrote one 14-year-old boy, 'are the wild western romances.... It is exciting to see one of them [stars] in a fight, or galloping over the Praier [sic] on their fine horses.'[123] Most girls preferred romantic films and readily recalled Mary Pickford and Shirley Temple, though one 12-year-old said that she most liked 'a good comedy...' and Vera Horder adored westerns ('the music used to get faster and faster and faster as the film got... more exciting, more exciting').[124] Not everyone liked everything shown. 'I absolutely hate the love films,' one boy complained, 'for only subnormals would act the way those lovers do.'[125] You could hoot and holler if you didn't like what you saw, and in the days of silent film many boys and girls did just that. 'It's a wonder we didn't bring the roof off with the yelling and all that sort of thing,' Richard Perth recalled.[126]

Boys went to the pictures more regularly than girls, suggesting that they had fewer domestic chores and greater discretion as to how they used their leisure time.[127] On Saturday nights, in the interwar period, it became customary for families to attend together. Everyone dressed up in their best clothes for the occasion. The addition of 'sound' in the early 1930s made the movies the single most popular form of entertainment for women and men, boys and girls.

Film gave a powerful authority to certain ideas about the body, clothing and appropriate forms of behaviour. American film, which became internationally dominant after the First World War, was particularly explicit in exploiting sensuality and sexuality. Largely produced and controlled by 'new' immigrant groups, American films also subverted many Protestant norms concerning gender, appropriate behaviour and sex. Rendering sex and pleasure synonymous – and it was a theme in popular New Zealand novels at the time – was subversive in complex ways.[128] The comedians, especially Charlie Chaplin, were also subversive of modern conventions. Local moralists wailed, fearing the worst, and the New Zealand Educational Institute proclaimed that film was 'calculated to weaken the moral fibre' of young people.[129] Even conventional romances, such as Rudall Hayward's 1928 production, *Bush Cinderella*, could explore the meaning of respectability and competing notions of femininity and masculinity. It attracted large crowds in Dunedin (although it was set in Auckland).[130] Glamour and beauty were officially sanctioned in 1927, when the reigning Miss New Zealand, and former Miss Otago, Dale Austen, was awarded an acting contract in Hollywood as part of her prize. Thousands thronged the Dunedin railway station to farewell her on the journey to 'stardom'. Other young hopefuls jostled for a place in the limelight, parading before the cameras of local producers (these 'shorts' would be shown and patrons could cast a vote for their preferred choice before the main film was shown).[131]

Film helped to promote and legitimise beauty contests and a new standard of idealised femininity. Valued for their bodily modesty before the war, in the 1920s women were encouraged to put their bodies forward for assessment. Judgements based on outward appearance began to challenge those based on

Miss New Zealand comes home, 1927. The crowds gathered to greet the return to Otago of the reigning Miss New Zealand and former Miss Otago, Dale Austen, testify to the public's interest in beauty contests and the sense of civic pride that they fostered. Part of her prize was a Hollywood contract and locals looked forward to seeing a 'daughter of Dunedin' on the silver screen. J. T. PAUL PAPERS, HOCKEN LIBRARY

The Coronation of the Queen, Kensington Drill Hall, 1915. Rural communities, businesses, and suburbs selected candidates for the Queen's title and firms and individuals pledged money to a cause. In 1915 the first provincial Queen Carnival was held to raise money for the war and it proved enormously successful. In the interwar years many voluntary organisations, such as the South Dunedin Branch of the Labour Party, continued to run Queen Carnivals. *OTAGO WITNESS*, 1 SEPTEMBER 1915

inner character. The change occurred quite quickly. In 1915 Dunedin's 'Queen Carnival', a 'craze' designed to raise money for the wounded soldiers, saw various districts and firms choose a 'queen' to head their bid to raise money. Thousands paid handsomely to attend the coronation of Otago's queen in the new drill hall in Kensington. The contending queens were chosen for their virtuous character, not their looks, let alone their figures. None used Helena Rubinstein's new cosmetics. Most of the queens were married, or elderly unmarried women, or the daughters of well-known figures in the city, such as Eva Carson, whose father managed the Hillside Workshops.[132] By the late 1920s, partly thanks to the movies, the belief that virtue was more attractive than appearance had largely disappeared, especially among the young. Beauty contests, the preserve of the young and the single, saw contestants parade in bathing costumes, revealing vastly more naked flesh than hockey players had a mere twenty years earlier. Many of those disturbed by these rapid shifts provided an enthusiastic market for the community sings of the 1930s and 40s.

In the late 1920s and 30s local film producers successfully entered the market. Henry Gore of St Clair, who grew up in St Kilda and opened his own photographic studio in King Edward St at the age of eighteen, found in film a passion that dominated his life. So too did Jack Welsh, another resident of the Flat, who pioneered the first films of local news, including the visit by the Prince of Wales in 1920 and the St Kilda Band's famous quickstep march. In 1933 he began producing New Zealand's first weekly newsreel, 'New Zealand Soundscenes', and he made the first feature-length New Zealand talkie, *Down*

Bathing beauty competition, St Clair, 1928. By the 1920s, women were encouraged to put their bodies, rather than their character, forward for display. These young women all have the fashionably short hair that characterised the modern woman and perhaps all had hopes of a future in Hollywood. OTAGO WITNESS, 28 FEBRUARY 1928

on the Farm, which was exhibited in 1935 at Dunedin's Empire De Luxe. Nearly 20 per cent of the city's population went to see it during its two-week run.[133] Dedicated to 'the man on the land', the film charted the rivalry between two farming families, one New Zealand-born and the other recently arrived from England. Love between the Englishman's sons and the New Zealander's daughters brought the families together in the climax of a double wedding in Dunedin's First Church.[134] The success of such romantic themes reminds us that films often reaffirmed traditional expectations of daring men and demure women. Yet American films – like many of Rudall Hayward's – could also disrupt older conventions and constraints, and open imaginative pathways into other worlds. Hayward's uncle, Henry Hayward, the country's largest film distributor and theatre owner in the 1920s, often pushed films that reflected his own commitment to socialism and rationalism.[135]

The light fantastic
Dancing provided one of the strong continuities across the period. Dances had always been popular in the colony and they were an important leisure activity in which conventional heterosexual scripts were enacted. Even informal occasions might lead to exuberant dancing. Jess Whitworth, for instance, recalled

the arrival at her home of someone called 'Dr Budd', who quickly had Jess and her sisters 'all dance mad tripping round the floor [and] when business was slack in would come father and his face all smiles he would waltz and poker hop around . . . but if mother appeared he faded off'.[136] At weddings and other family festivities, the pleasure of the dance crossed generations. Before the First World War families often rolled up the living-room rug, someone struck up a tune on the family piano or a fiddle, and everyone joined in. Increasingly, however, demand grew for dances aimed specifically at young people.[137]

Friendly societies illustrate the growing enthusiasm of the young for heterosocial leisure. These societies were once the stronghold of workers and self-employed tradesmen determined to engage in convivial brotherhood, lubricated by copious draughts of alcohol, but in the 1890s younger members of the Flat's friendly societies began demanding that the meeting should be followed by a dance.[138] In the same period, some lodges debated admitting women, and one or two did, but in most cases women formed parallel organisations. The single young women of Miriam Rebekah Lodge, International Order of Oddfellows, like their male counterparts, sometimes felt embarassed at the unseemly speed with which they raced through the official business in order to start dancing. Such dances often went on until the early hours of the morning. By the early 1900s dance evenings had become well-nigh universal for the lodges.[139]

Dancing became so popular that by 1910 most voluntary organisations held at least an annual dance, often a ball (where people dressed more formally and the supper provided was most elaborate). Indeed, many organisations discovered that a well-organised dance was a simple means of raising money. By the 1920s many church Bible Classes held Saturday night dances (St Patrick's dance, by contrast, was on a Monday night).[140] Primary schools also began to organise dances and dancing lessons. Dances proved so popular that schools also began to organise parents' night dances.[141] Henry Gore organised several local dances to follow his film evenings, including a weekly one in the St Kilda town hall.[142] The Caversham Branch of the Labour Party, formed in 1919, ran a regular Saturday night dance until the 1950s and raised thousands of pounds in the process, enough to build the Harry Holland Hall. The Dunedin Women's Branch of the Labour Party – most of its members came from the Flat – also periodically ran a monthly dance in the South Dunedin town hall.[143] In the interwar period ballroom dancing became popular and the debutante ball became a major event on the calendar for the Catholic and Anglican churches.

Young lads and lasses walked to the Saturday night dance, often in small groups. Unless they were courting, in which case they paired off to come home, girls and boys often went home together as well. This seems to have been a matter of convenience rather than prudence, however, for some women recalled walking home alone for 3 or 4 kilometres through darkened streets in the wee hours of the morning.[144] On the dance floor, men led and women followed, symbolically enacting an expected future. Dancing was a socially sanctioned form of courting for the young that contained sexuality by strict rules of behaviour, rules that new dance crazes dangerously threatened to disrupt by centring on rhythm and physical contact.[145] Not everyone accepted dance as moral. Most devout Presbyterians and Baptists rejected the 'modern dancing' craze. A leading Presbyterian warned Bible Class leaders that dancing 'tends to destroy respect for the personality of others, and is based on a direct erotic appeal which makes self-control entirely difficult for some participants'.[146] Our interviews show, however, that teenagers of all denominations loved going to dances, and only in families where both parents were strongly of the view that dancing was wicked were the children kept away. In the late 1940s, the Caversham Presbyterians broke with convention and became the first in the country to allow their teenagers to organise their own Bible Class dance.

In the 1930s Joe Brown proved that, if you organised a big enough dance, and did it well, a living could be made. Joe Brown's Town Hall Dance catered to a Dunedin market, of course, although in the 1950s it was broadcast nationally.[147] The town hall dances, popularly known as 'Joe Brown's Matrimonial Bureau', became enormously popular. The atmosphere was, according to one ex-patron, 'slightly predatory but elegant'.[148] In the world of the dance we easily locate the shift from informal and impromptu entertainment, usually based on the household, to a more structured and predetermined leisure, where the dance, like the supper, was paid for and consumed.

Conclusion

In the southern suburbs, as in urban New Zealand more generally, 'the coming girl' enjoyed unprecedented freedom and independence – 'from being the pitied "old maid" of the Victorian and earlier eras to the envied bachelor woman of today'.[149] In this respect, young and unmarried women finally won many of the freedoms long enjoyed by their brothers. Once married, however, both women and men were likely to forsake organised sport for increasingly privatised family pursuits centred around home, car and crib. If the New Woman was a single working woman, free of family ties, practising her dance steps in her lunch hour, the new man was disciplined and sober, spending his free time in the Hillside library, learning to dance, or practising with the orchestra. By the interwar years he was far less likely to spend his weekends playing two-up or drinking than he was to be actively engaged in some form of organised sport, or, if married, working on his own home, in his own garden, or accompanying his family on an outing. The moves from homosocial to heterosocial entertainment, from the informal to the organised, and from communal to private pastimes signalled a reshaping of the uses of time. How that time was used became even more sharply demarcated by age. But, most of all, gender determined opportunity to participate in sport and the burgeoning commercial leisure market. Money and time for oneself, on the whole, remained male prerogatives, although single young women with jobs of their own enjoyed both until they married and had children.

These changes, together with the growing importance of such global cultural phenomena as the movies, made heterosexuality more central to leisure than it had been. Same-sex couples, especially men, were viewed with a new intolerance. Yet the meaning of leisure remained deeply gendered. Organised sports remained relatively unimportant for women, and most women still took what leisure they obtained within the rhythms of specific forms of work, especially knitting and needlework. Most of the new family-based forms of recreation probably required that the housewife do more work and do it with fewer amenities. Men, by and large, enjoyed a clearer demarcation of their work from their leisure, and throughout their lives had the right and the power to spend money on their own pastimes without anyone else's consent. Although single women made considerable progress in winning similar rights, the notion of leisure as a right remained fundamental to male, but not to female culture. Marriage and motherhood, increasingly, marked a critical transition in the lives of women.

The fact that leisure time was more available to men was rarely stated, perhaps not always understood, and in that sense parallels colonial egalitarianism. Yet public life interposed tensions or generated cross-currents. War required unprecedented levels of service from young single men, and did so twice on an awesome scale. At the same time women had become more attuned to pursuing their individual pleasures.

Seven Down and Out on the Flat: The Gendering of Poverty

ANNABEL COOPER AND MARIAN HORAN[1]

Maria St, one of South Dunedin's 'wee streets', sat among the noise and pollution of the Hillside Workshops, the coal-burning gasworks and (only a little further off) the railway running sheds. Its densely populated alleys ran through the backs of the King Edward Street shops and it had some of the southern suburbs' only examples of 'row' housing, a reminder of the slum-housing architecture immigrants had left behind. One of the Flat's least desirable addresses – in fact its name was later changed to Glasgow St partly in an attempt to clean up its reputation – Maria St housed a number of the area's poorest households.

In 1890, one of the worst years of the Long Depression, a number of Maria St's residents were at the point of destitution. Among them was Susan Westfold. A widow aged forty-six, she had five of her nine children still at home, including an illegitimate child a year old, whose father had disappeared. She got a little help from friends and her eldest son. She was getting by, but in mid-1890 she came down with typhoid.[2] A few doors along, Mary Ann Fleming, a single woman of about fifty in poor health, looked after the three McGarrigle children. Their widowed father, a miner, paid somewhat irregularly for their upkeep. She and the children were to move frequently over the subsequent years, but returned several times to Maria St and its vicinity, presumably because of its cheap rents.[3] Further along Maria St, Peter Lepper was unemployed and suffering from lumbago after a stint at stonebreaking on a public relief scheme. Mrs Lepper had a bad leg, but was earning a little through taking in a nurse (or foster) child, probably belonging to one of the daughters of the Hendrick family over the road.[4] Mary Jane Fraser, whose

Glasgow St (formerly Maria St), and the surrounding area, showing the sections in this part of South Dunedin and the alleys running between streets. King Edward St, South Dunedin's main retail area, runs down the right side of this detail. Glasgow Street's sections are in fact larger than those in the parallel street to its left. 1920 LAND VALUATION MAP, CITY COUNCIL ARCHIVES, DUNEDIN

husband went away to look for work, but seldom sent any money home, was attempting to support five of her six children.[5] None of these families was making ends meet; we know of their situations because they all came to the main provider of charitable aid in Dunedin, the Otago Benevolent Institution (OBI), to request assistance.

Some streets in the southern suburbs appear frequently in the OBI's 'outdoor relief' casebooks, with the streets of South Dunedin, Kensington and Caversham over-represented. Yet, by international standards, the suburbs of southern Dunedin at the turn of the last century constituted a very homogeneous settler society. The area's inhabitants might have thought the owners of the expansive properties in St Clair a world apart from the occupants of Maria St: Bert Grimmett, who grew up in Caversham, knew that the wealthy lived in St Clair and the 'poor place' was South Dunedin, with its 'wee back alleys' and its 'houses built right on the street'. The children down there would call you names, 'didn't hesitate to yell "what are you doing here?" ... So we kept to ourselves and fought among ourselves.'[6] But, as Clyde Griffen has shown, there was in fact a remarkable mixture of housing and occupation within a very brief circumference. To an extent this parallels the situation described by Paul Husbands in his study of Freeman's Bay in Auckland, although Husbands's picture is of rather more precise occupational distinctions, and a steady increase in wealth as you moved uphill.[7]

Indeed, it is hard to imagine that those familiar with nineteenth-century Dublin, Glasgow or London would have classed more than a very few of southern Dunedin's (or Freeman's Bay's) population as poor. There were no rooms housing five families, no backyards piled high with excrement for which there was no system of disposal and (as chapter ten shows), although tuberculosis and typhoid, diseases of poverty, made their appearance among the poor, they were not common, and there were none of the outbreaks of cholera familiar and feared in Old World slums.[8] For the immigrant generations, the comparison must have been powerful, and the 'absence' of ongoing poverty formed part of the colony's self-definition against the Old World. The authors of a school text on citizenship wrote as late as 1925 that:

> In Great Britain there have been in normal times large numbers of people living always in a state of semi-starvation. The condition of the poor of England's slums has been one of the greatest blots on her civilisation, and every thoughtful colonial who has seen it has returned with a determination to do something to prevent such a state of things from coming into existence in his own country.[9]

Yet, even in the plenty of a New World, there were real experiences of hardship, enduring over long periods of time as well as occurring during periods of economic depression. This chapter attempts to consider how poverty was distributed among the different inhabitants of the southern suburbs, and asks what made some people more vulnerable than others. It looks at what these different experiences of poverty can tell us about deeply embedded meanings of such gendered terms as motherhood, fatherhood and masculinity, dependence and independence, childhood, home and the shifting concept of old age, as well as the cultural and economic dispossession that could result from some of the understandings of these terms, and the practices and policies that arose from them. Exploring the gendering of poverty, we consider especially the gendered culture of demographic patterns and economic practices. Both meant that women and men frequently encountered poverty differently, as the people in the cases listed above did: the reasons for their poverty and the forms of aid they could gain access to were shaped by gender, life cycle, marital status and economics. We address the links between family life cycle and poverty, going on to consider the further implications of a gender analysis, and noting the specificities of the gendered ageing of the population over the period. Finally, shifting our focus to the gendered economic culture of the labour market and wage policy, we consider the significance of the male-breadwinner wage norm. Especially, we address the way that this practice meant that poverty was distributed unevenly, not only across a society, but also within families.[10]

The New Zealand historians who have studied poverty and welfare in recent decades are notable for their detailed and nuanced analyses of the way in which they intersect with gender. Comparison with the two key studies for our purposes reveals that the causes of poverty, the cultural understandings and practices associated with it and the policies developed to counter it, were similar in southern Dunedin to both the comparable inner-city suburb of Freeman's Bay in Auckland (the focus of Paul Husbands's study) and the national situation (Margaret Tennant's subject).[11] Consistently, poverty was affected by life cycle; women with young children, the sick, the disabled and the elderly were most at risk; the absence of an adult male wage brought penury; and charitable aid stopped well short of being a living allowance and was eked out with a close eye on the behaviour of its recipients. Our study reveals no great departures from the national pattern of urban poverty, or indeed that of many Western societies. This is hardly surprising, since one of the enduring – and the saddest – characteristics of the study of poverty internationally is precisely this pattern: the vulnerability of women, children, the sick, the disabled and the old.

One of the defining characteristics of the colonial state's attitude to poverty was its wish to deny it, a desire that sprang from two sources. First, the promise of a new land seemed almost synonymous with the banishing of poverty and – more pragmatically – the colony's own self-promotion to potential new immigrants in Britain relied on that assumption.[12] Second, as Margaret Tennant and David Thomson have pointed out, there was a powerful desire to avoid replicating the British Poor Law, which was understood to have created or perpetuated a class of dependent poor stuck in a poverty trap rather than to have alleviated poverty.[13] A number of commentators have discussed the responses of the state and private charities (which both had a hand in the charitable aid system) to poverty in New Zealand. Tennant's focus is on the policies of the charitable aid system (of which the Otago Benevolent Institution was a part) and the way in which aid was provided according to gender and age, with priority given to the care of children. Thomson, discussing old age pensions, argues that nineteenth-century New Zealand governments favoured a tight-fisted aid system, legislating for self-reliance and ensuring that a list of liable relatives must be applied to for assistance before the state would step in to help. In this respect, the colonial state reflected the bias of its population: through most of the nineteenth century, this was a 'young man's country', able – we would argue – to sustain gendered norms of 'independence' and 'autonomy'.[14] The high levels of masculine mobility, and the consequently high rates of desertion, were nevertheless recognised early in the new society. As Bettina Bradbury explains:

> Deserted wives were the first group of women whose property was protected by legislation. . . . Ordinances since 1846 had attempted to force men to fulfil their common law obligation to provide for wives and children by allowing a deserted wife to sue for a maintenance order and giving justices of the peace the power to chase down those in arrears, seize their property or imprison them if necessary.[15]

From 1860 the Married Women's Property Protection Act prevented absconding husbands from returning to claim savings that wives might have accumulated in their absence.[16]

Towards the end of the nineteenth century, and into the twentieth, the age and sex structure of the Pakeha population underwent a transition from an immigrant pattern to one of a settled society. There was a more even age and sex spread, forcing the plight of some women, children, elderly and disabled on to the national agenda. The Long Depression years of the 1880s and 90s brought the point home and showed that, despite the advantages of a new land, economic downturn could bring the families of even able-bodied men to penury. In 1885, levels of unemployment and destitution were – to a limited degree – recognised with the passing of the Hospitals and Charitable Institutions Act, which established a system of minimal welfare serving the country, in place of the locally developed systems that had existed previously. The new structure retained the emphasis on 'charity', with a bias towards the deserving and a preference for providing aid in the form of goods rather than cash.

Over the next half-century, roughly the period of our study, the state assumed increasing responsibility for its citizens, moving towards various kinds of entitlement and towards payment in cash, providing old age pensions (1898), widows' pensions (1911), family allowances (1926), benefits for unemployed men (1930), the guarantee of a minimum male-breadwinner wage (1936) and finally a wide net of social security provisions (1938).[17] With the arrival of the Great Depression at the end of the 1920s and then the election of the first Labour Government in 1935, the transition from 'charity' to 'entitlement' as the dominant character of assistance was complete.

The gendering of both private and state provision has been a matter of debate. Women could claim the old age pension at an earlier age than men; widows' pensions were available before the equivalent provision was made for widowers. Did this offer essential support to some women, or did it institutionalise their 'dependency'? Similarly, the role of government and the Arbitration Court in gendering state support – this time to men – through the wage-fixing process is a point of contention. Melanie Nolan has argued recently that, although a woman's minimum wage was a third to a half of a man's through the early part of the twentieth century, and Arbitration Court rulings do appear to favour the spirit of the 'family' or 'male-breadwinner' wage, the latter was nevertheless undermined by the Family Allowances Act of 1926, which supplemented the income of poorer, larger families through a payment made directly to the mother. In this way, she contends, government compromised between those lobbying for a male-breadwinner wage (which tipped economic authority in the family towards its male head) and those lobbying for motherhood and child endowment (which recognised the economic needs of children and the mother's primary responsibility for them).[18]

State policies and practices reveal much about colonial attitudes to poverty. They also shaped poverty in their uneven provision, which was weighted towards alleviation of categories of poverty considered acceptable – that which resulted from widowhood, sickness and old age, for example – but did less to assist those, such as unwed mothers or alcoholics, who were considered to be poor because of their moral inadequacies. Unemployment was also a 'difficult' cause of poverty to acknowledge, since its existence exposed the flaws in the colony's self-definition as a new, flourishing society with opportunity for all: nevertheless, the impact of the Long Depression of the 1880s and 90s was acknowledged by some provision of relief work.

Nevertheless, legislation and policy were only one determinant of the distribution of poverty. It is true that the records of welfare institutions provide the most complete and detailed evidence about the poor, and inevitably become the rather cloudy lens through which our information about poverty is refracted. However, it is the task of this chapter to concentrate, as far as is possible, on who experienced poverty, why some experienced it more frequently, and how people's experiences of poverty varied. We cannot – indeed we do not try to – ignore the welfare systems, but we seek to keep our attention on the people they variously served, managed, maintained or – the group most elusive to us because they do not appear in the records – neglected. We address welfare because of its role as one of the factors in the shaping, distribution and experience of poverty.

Because welfare records are our key source, they require some description. The first point to note is that one source is far more extensive and detailed than any other: the outdoor relief casebooks of the Otago Benevolent Institution.[19] In fact, the institution's records from the 1880s through to 1911

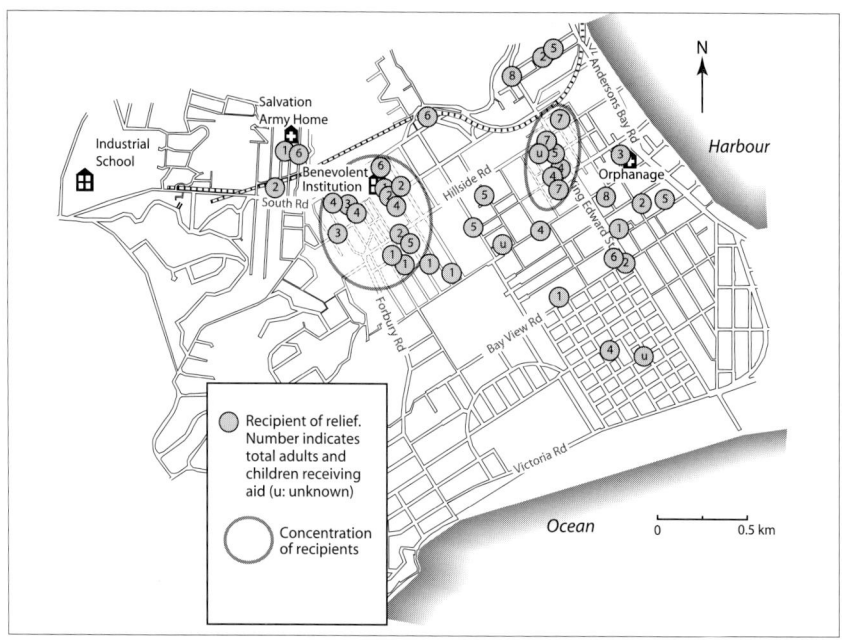

Map 7.1. Households receiving outdoor relief, 1905. By 1905, the region had returned to prosperity and the number of households receiving relief was less than half that of the 1890s. It is possible for us to map relief-receiving households in 1905 (though not for earlier years, because of the lack of street numbering). South Dunedin and Caversham account for almost all these households. The map reveals distinct concentrations. The cluster to the left shows that Caversham's relief-receiving households tend to occur in the streets surrounding the Benevolent. The smaller cluster to the right centres on Maria/Glasgow St, with its low rents (and reputation). It has more aid recipients than any other single street, and houses the largest families. There are clear gaps. Although we cannot precisely trace the location of every household, few fall within St Kilda, and none within Kew or St Clair. The map also shows the main charitable institutions of the area.

are the most complete and detailed outdoor relief records extant in New Zealand, and they allow us particularly privileged access to the lives of the southern suburbs' poor of this period. The OBI's successor in this role, the Otago Hospital and Charitable Aid Board (OHCAB),[20] did not keep records in anything like the same detail, nor did it often assist families over many years, as the OBI did for some families. The OBI records therefore allow us to say more about the earlier period, and particularly the 1890s, when they were especially detailed, than is possible for later decades, and more about people receiving outdoor relief than those supported by other forms of aid. The level of detail in the outdoor relief records reflects the fact that it was the most heavily monitored of the forms of aid, a fact undoubtedly connected to the level of public anxiety about it. In an era that privileged the arguably masculine qualities of self-reliance and 'independence', outdoor relief was seen as the most difficult form of aid to manage and was distinctive in supporting people – mainly women – in their own homes rather than directly under institutional eyes. But the resulting detail of the records has great value for us. To the extent that the case notes provide some data relatively consistently, they have allowed us to create a database using four 'slice' years (1889, 1895, 1900 and 1905).[21] Because they provide often considerable detail and a continuous narrative of some households over some years (up to twenty years for a few families), they allow us to consider the effects of family life cycle and economic change. Their detail also provides the basis for our discussion of the differing effects of poverty on women and men, and other more nuanced effects of gender and age. For this analysis, we created three edited volumes of transcripts of outdoor relief case reports, each taking a different type of sample.[22] We also use the more limited records of other institutions, and oral histories that refer mainly to the 1920s and 1930s.

Inspectors' entries in the Otago Benevolent Institution Outdoor Relief Casebook for 1890. Details of children, family circumstances and assistance provided are given, together with a narrative account of their current situation. ARCHIVES NEW ZEALAND, DUNEDIN

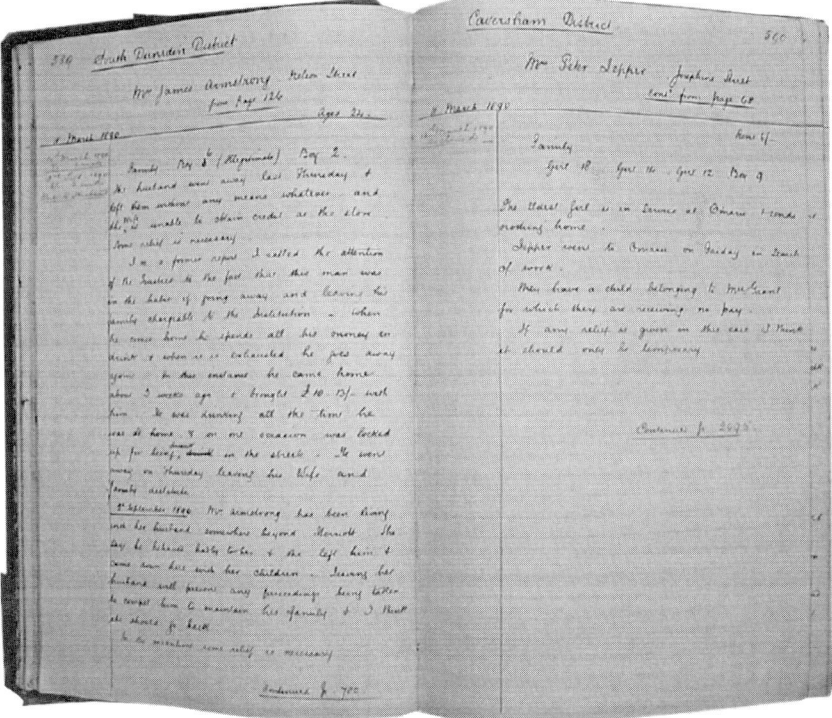

The second key point about our sources differentiates our study from many European studies of poverty, which use census returns (routinely destroyed in New Zealand) to establish levels of income and household composition.[23] Although the outdoor relief records do provide some similar information, such as occupation, income and family composition, they do not provide it for the whole population – the critical advantage of the census returns in analysing poverty within a larger society. The absence of the returns therefore has implications for the way we can define poverty. We cannot readily address 'relativist' definitions of poverty – that is, take a set percentage at the end of the income distribution.[24] It might be said that we have allowed – or had to allow – the Benevolent trustees and their successors to define poverty for us, but this is another way of saying that we have used a cultural definition, although, as we go on to argue, it is a partial one. That is, we have taken the aid agencies' recipients as a particular group of 'poor'. This group can be understood both to view themselves as poor – as unable to provide for their necessities of life – by virtue of the fact that they sought aid, and to be categorised as poor by others, because they came to be listed in these records. This does not mean, of course, that they were the only poor in the area – they were not – but they are the largest group for which we have evidence.

Using the welfare records available, in this chapter we explore the public face of poverty in the southern suburbs of the colony's major industrial and commercial city during the latter half of the Long Depression and the early part of the prosperous new century. Table 7.1 gives us a broad overview of the population receiving outdoor relief and how it changed through our four 'slice' years.

Table 7.1 Percentage distribution of outdoor relief study area population by number, age and sex, 1889–1905

Age	Sex	1889	1895	1900	1905
Number of Households		506	631	329	277
< 12	F	24	22	18	17
	M	25	20	17	15
	Unknown	2	2	3	3
13–20	F	7	10	12	7
	M	4	11	10	10
	Unknown	1	0	0	0
21–64	F	13	17	20	21
	M	4	8	8	6
65 and over	F	1	3	3	4
	M	1	2	3	3
Unknown	Unknown	18	5	6	14
Total		100	100	100	100

Source: Caversham Project Outdoor Relief Database.

The impact of the depression in the southern suburbs can be tracked through outdoor relief: in 1889, 506 people, 3.7 per cent of the population in the study area, received outdoor relief, rising to 631 (4.6 per cent) in 1895, then dropping to 329 (2.3 per cent) in 1900. As one might expect, given the lens through which the colonists viewed the problem of poverty, the outdoor relief records were dominated by children, and by women aged twenty-one to sixty-four years old.[25] Most of the children in the outdoor relief records belonged to women heads of household, that is, those without a male income. This was in part because, as we shall see, colonial society made separate provision for abandoned and orphaned children and for able-bodied men and so they tend not to appear in these records, but also because a sole mother's plight was indeed precarious. A woman might find herself in this situation for various reasons, most commonly because she had been widowed, deserted or left behind by a husband who travelled in search of work. If she was single and unable to find other work, prostitution might have resulted in dependent children. In this period, because the Victorian economy was buoyant, many husbands and fathers crossed the Tasman (some to return, others to vanish). Thus, able-bodied men appeared infrequently in these records; they received no assistance, for they were expected to be on the road in search of work. Old men who could neither earn enough nor manage their domestic arrangements appeared more often in another set of records, for they were usually institutionalised. Sick and disabled husbands, by contrast, do appear in the outdoor relief records, for this was a familiar explanation for a family's destitution. Otherwise, the families represented in these records were those without husbands and fathers. Outdoor relief existed largely to help such people.

Family life cycle
It has long been recognised that family life cycle is a significant factor in poverty. Households at risk of poverty shift from one side of the 'line of getting by' to the other as their families move through stages of vulnerability and relative ease. Traditionally, these shifts have been analysed in terms of the ratio of 'breadwinners' to 'dependants'. But, in the light of feminist critiques of this dichotomy, we argue that an analysis based on three economic categories of household members is preferable, and that it was the balance among these three categories of person in a household that was the crucial equation in the circumstances of a family.[26] Therefore, our three categories are 'dependants' (those who could contribute little or nothing to a household's resources, or who for reasons of age or illness constituted only a drain on its resources of cash and time); 'contributors' (who did not necessarily earn

money, but added to resources in the form of unpaid work, and supported the paid work of other members – a function characteristically gendered feminine); and 'earners' (those who brought in cash). Over time, most members of a family would occupy more than one of these roles, sometimes at once. It is clear from the outdoor relief narratives that the shifts in this balance frequently determined a household's movement in and out of poverty.[27] For instance, the family of Frederick Monson, a carpenter who suffered from paralysis and epilepsy and therefore often could not work, played a shifting part in the maintenance of the household. In 1890 all five children were under ten, including a newborn. The numbers of young children and a sick husband committed Mrs Monson to 'contributing', rather than to 'earning' activity. The family received regular relief as well as help from Frederick Monson's relatives, but could seldom bring in its own income. Nine years later, Mrs Monson earned some income nursing, but the children's income had become critical to the family economy. Though the eldest, a girl aged nineteen, was sometimes in ill health, she and her 18-year-old brother each brought in 7s 6d a week, and the third child, still only fourteen, earned 5s. A year later, the eldest girl's responsibilities were now 'domestic duties when her mother is out working'. Mrs Monson was therefore in a position to earn £1 a week, and her sons, now a little older, were bringing in 12s 6d and 7s 6d, making the family significantly better off: at this point their aid ceased.[28]

As the Monson family's case suggests, the early years of childbearing and rearing, when there were several dependent children, constituted a drain both on income and on the time of the mother, preventing her from engaging in other contributory or earning activity: they were the years of the first potential crisis. As the children grew and began attending school, they might demand less of their mother's time, releasing her for some income-earning activity, but it cost more to feed and clothe them. The cohort of families growing up through the beginning of our period were coming to terms with the effects of the Education Act 1877, which stipulated that children under thirteen had to attend school, thus taking them out of the productive life of the family for much longer than had previously been the case for poorer families. It was to benefit the children of this cohort, but in the years when families were still large (averages for fertile couples married in the 1880s ranged from 6.9 to 5.7 children)[29] it placed considerable demands on parents, as the family's ability to sustain itself increasingly devolved onto two people: a sole earner and a sole housekeeper. Inevitably, girls were often kept home to mind younger siblings, and boys had after-school jobs, especially in poorer families, but the emphasis had irrevocably shifted towards parents as earners and contributors and children as dependants.

Few photographers saw poor housing as a suitable subject for their art. The photograph above was taken after a child had died of abuse and neglect in this South Dunedin house. The figures are posed to suggest the story of the neglected boy, but the surroundings tell their own story of poverty. OTAGO SETTLERS MUSEUM

The balance began to shift as children completed compulsory education at thirteen (there was little prospect of children from these families continuing their education) and entered employment, but not dramatically at first, since wages were usually low for the first few years of employment. As they reached their later teens, their earnings approached an adult wage and could bring a significant shift in the household income. This was especially the case for boys who took up unskilled work, which did not entail years of low pay as an apprentice, and girls who took a factory job. The living circumstances of Amelia Broadley, a deserted woman with epilepsy who could seldom earn more than a few shillings, fluctuated from 1889, when her thirteen-year-old daughter earned only 3s a week in service, to 1890, when her next child, a son, began at the *Evening Herald* office earning 2s 6d. In later years the daughter lost her work, then found another job and contributed a little (but only earned 4s at most) and then at nineteen moved away to Christchurch, ceasing to contribute anything thereafter. The elder son's earnings increased gradually until at eighteen he earned 12s and gave his mother 6s. By then the younger son was thirteen and earning 5s: both boys still lived at home. The elder boy left home at twenty and was married at twenty-one.[30]

Children's capacity to help a household financially once they had left school, as these examples suggest, depended on a number of things: whether or not they were in full-time and regular work, whether they were doing an apprenticeship or were in an unskilled job (the former was poorly paid but promised greater long-term security and earnings), how much of their income was contributed to the family, and whether they were young men or young women. Their sex did not necessarily reflect only the higher labour-market value of men: although boys and young men doing unskilled work usually earned more than girls, they were also (in contrast to the Broadley family experience) somewhat more likely to leave home to work, with the common result that less of their earnings would come to the household, and then perhaps irregularly.[31] When neither James Proven nor his wife was able to earn as a result of increasing age and long-term illness, for example, the fact that all five of their sons lived and worked away from home – the farthest in Scotland, the closest in Wingatui on the Taieri Plains – meant that very little financial assistance arrived from them: promises were more frequent than remittances.[32] Nevertheless, the pressure on offspring to contribute was significant, required by law and, by today's standards, very high.[33] This expectation was undoubtedly a point of tension, however – many case notes record offspring who 'did not assist' – and attitudes underwent a generational change over the period. Mary Isabella Lee records her own unquestioning assumption, in the 1880s, that her earnings would go to her mother, but her grandson, growing up in the 1910s, was hampered by no such idea and spent his income freely on himself.[34]

Children's earnings as a source of income had a limited life. Once children married and set up their own households, their earnings were committed elsewhere. Sarah Sharp was able to do without relief between 1897 and 1900, because her son got full-time work with Mitchells' Carters. In April 1900, a week after he married and stopped providing support, she applied again to the Benevolent trustees.[35] Although they might be legally bound to help parents where they could, and the trustees certainly pursued adult children as well as other relatives in attempting to find family who could help support those in need, the children of the poor who turn up in the outdoor relief narratives tended not to have much to spare themselves. One can assume that, growing up in a household where money was tight and the pressure to hand over earnings high, most had limited opportunity to amass capital before marriage. The McGirrs had five adult children: two married sons, two married daughters and one single daughter in her early thirties. While the inspector recognised that the married children could not assist their parents, the single daughter, at various times reported to be 'out of a situation', 'ill for the last four months', 'not strong' and 'earning 15s' came under pressure to support her parents. Only when she married did she escape this responsibility.[36]

The departure of children from the home often coincided with the decreasing capacity of parents, especially fathers, to earn. This was especially the case with unskilled men. Most of the men in the outdoor relief samples were labourers who, once past their fittest and strongest years, were unable to command the wages of those years. Some in failing health found lighter but poorer-paid work.[37] This, combined with the loss of children's earnings, could pose a new economic threat as old age brought uncertainties of health and capacity. Clearly, as children established themselves, contributions, perhaps as much in kind as in cash, were made to many ageing parents. That this was common among the better off is indicated by one or two exceptions that appear in our samples. Robert McDonald's son, an engineer with an established career as a foreman, earning £3 10s a week, complied with a magistrate's order to pay 10s towards his elderly father's upkeep until April 1897, when he sold his property, left his job and disappeared: 'his father does not know where he is gone'. The fact that the son, at forty-eight, still had seven of his own eleven children to maintain may have made the extra burden of the father finally insupportable.[38]

The effects of life cycle could be exacerbated by specific family patterns. A large number of very young children plainly put a family at risk, as the case notes reveal repeatedly. This was also confirmed in our interviews. We are unable to compare the completed family size of study area families receiving aid with those who did not, but are able to arrive at some assessment of comparative family size through comparing the spacing of children and – a more complicated comparison – age of mother at first child among the relief-receiving mothers and age of women in New Zealand at first marriage. These analyses can only be suggestive, but are nevertheless striking. Among mothers in our outdoor relief sample, the average gap between children was 2.39 years (1889), whereas, among mothers in the national non-Maori population, it was 3.62 (1891).[39] The average age at which the first child was born among the outdoor relief-requesting mothers under forty in 1889 was 21.46. Although we do not have this figure for the study area or national populations, the national mean age for first marriage for women in 1891–96, which gives us a point of comparison, was 25.3.[40] Given that the younger a woman married, the more children she was likely to give birth to, these figures point to longer and busier childbearing lives for relief-requesting mothers, lives that took a greater toll on a mother's health and allowed her less time for earning activity.[41]

A large age gap between husband and wife, so that the husband was nearing or past the end of his effective earning life before children were independent, also posed a significant risk. To take one of a number of examples: in 1889 John Shaw was sixty-nine, with a 33-year-old wife and five children aged between two and fourteen. He worked as an engine cleaner on the Otago Central line, but after that work stopped he became unwell and was able to earn only 10s over two months 'hawking the "Japanese cleanser"'. Although the children contributed intermittent income over the following ten years, this family – and especially Mrs Shaw – was burdened by the combination of still-dependent children, an adult male who rapidly became an invalid and very limited sources of earnings.[42]

Life cycle and gender

Although the life cycle of the family unit must be fundamental in explaining movement in and out of poverty, if we deal only with the household as a unit we cannot address – indeed we conceal – the importance of gender. A gender analysis demands that we recognise that families are made up of individuals, whose expected functions within a household differ, and whose access to resources and the power to make decisions varies, largely according to the cultural value attached to their household position: gender and age are the key factors here. Viviana Zelizer observes that 'the distribution of money among family members is often as lopsided and arbitrary as the distribution of national income among families. Therefore [as Michael] Young argues, we should stop assuming that "some members of a family cannot be rich while others are poor".'[43] It is only relatively recently that the literature on poverty has paid attention to the way that gender interacts differentially with life-cycle effects.[44]

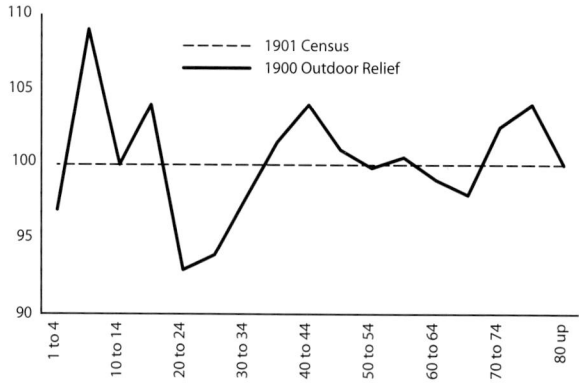

Figure 7.1 Age of outdoor relief female sample in 1900 compared to age of female population in southern suburbs from the 1901 Census. 1901 CENSUS, AND CAVERSHAM PROJECT OUTDOOR RELIEF DATABASE

DOWN AND OUT ON THE FLAT

The OBI data allows us to look at the connections between life cycle, gender and exposure to poverty. Women were over-represented in the outdoor relief records at a point in their life cycle when men were not. In each of our slice years, women aged 35–50 years are over-represented in comparison to the census record of the number of women of that age in the area's population. Figure 7.1 shows the comparison for 1900/1901.

The later childbearing and rearing years, therefore, put women at greater risk of poverty (as did old age, which we address later). When we take household type and marital status into account, a pattern that explains this begins to emerge, as Tables 7.2 and 7.3 demonstrate.

Table 7.2 Relief-receiving households by household type in selected years (percentage)*

	1889	1895	1900	1905
Number of Households	102	138	74	64
Couple with no children	6	6	7	0
Two parent nuclear family	25	27	16	25
Single parent nuclear family				
Female head	39	38	34	33
Male head	1	1	1	0
Multiple family	20	9	18	23
Single adult(s) only				
Female	8	13	16	16
Male	1	6	8	3
Total	100	100	100	100

* Percentage of all households receiving relief. Source: Caversham Project Outdoor Relief Database

Households headed by sole mothers constituted the most frequent household type in the outdoor relief books and sole fathers the least frequent. It should be noted, too, that the group 'multiple families' also includes a proportion of sole-mother families.

Table 7.3 Relief-receiving women aged over 20 by marital status in selected years (percentage)*

	1889	1895	1900	1905
Number	113	139	80	82
Never Married	10	9	14	12
Married	33	34	28	32
De facto	1	1	1	0
Widowed	18	22	40	39
Deserted	12	9	11	5
Separated	3	1	1	0
Unknown	23	24	5	12
Total	100	100	100	100

* Percentage of all women over 20 receiving relief. Source: Caversham Project Outdoor Relief Database

Widowhood and desertion, especially given the customary difference in women's and men's ages at marriage and the lower life expectancy of men (especially unskilled men), were increasing risks for mothers during their later childbearing and rearing years. The proportion of widows in our slice years ranged from 18 per cent in 1889 to 40 per cent in 1900 (probably reflecting the rapid growth of older cohorts as a percentage of the population) (see Table 7.3). Mary Mace was widowed at thirty-two with seven children aged seven months to fifteen years. Her two eldest children had begun earning, intermittently, but it was many years before she could do without aid.[45] Jane Steel at thirty-five had been widowed and then deserted: she had three children from her marriage and one from the subsequent relationship, but the father had gone to Melbourne and hadn't been heard of for six months. She later lived for a while with the father of a nurse child she had taken in, but he, too, drifted off.[46] Widows and deserted or separated women, taken together, are the most common group of relief-receiving household heads, and more so during the post-depression slice years (1900 and 1905), suggesting that, though many men and their families were at risk of poverty during periods of economic downturn, the situation of female-headed households posed more enduring difficulties, or, at least, difficulties that the Benevolent trustees were likely to see as insoluble. Widows were always the 'most deserving' category in the hierarchy of aid applicants, and the perception of their need was consolidating over the period. They were the most likely to be supported by their immediate community through fund-raising and similar forms of assistance, and the widows' pension was established in 1911. The vulnerability of sole mothers is confirmed by the narratives of the case records, which often tell of married women left in penury by absent men. This indicates that the figures for the category 'married' in Table 7.3 conceal a significant degree of effective desertion. Desertion was especially likely during the years of the depression, when some men took the opportunity of absence for work to abscond altogether, or to return only intermittent and partial pay packets. This last point directs our attention to an important but seldom discussed question: that of women's chances of poverty inside or outside marriage.

Until almost the turn of the century, New Zealand had a sex ratio that maximised the likelihood of women marrying.[47] This undoubtedly reduced the numbers of never-married women in the population as a whole. In European studies, women who never married are shown to be particularly exposed to poverty. Indeed, Joanna Bourke's study of Irish women's strategies of avoiding poverty is effectively a study of the ways in which women mitigated or avoided the state of being single.[48] In our sample, not many single women appear among the outdoor relief recipients. Those who do tend to be middle-aged and to have difficulty getting work, such as the three Gillespie sisters, who found intermittent housekeeping work, but always worked for poor wages and between them could only scrape a living.[49] To some extent, the infrequent appearance of single women undoubtedly resulted from the OBI's focus on children and their mothers, rather than on women in their own right, although it was probably also due to the high, and rising, demand for workers in Dunedin's clothing factories, and the ongoing need for domestic servants. The Sweating Commission of 1890 testifies to the existence of poverty among single women, and the Reverend Waddell, whose parish included Kensington, delivered his famous sermon on 'the sin of cheapness' – the evils of female sweated labour – not much more than a stone's throw from the edge of the southern suburbs.[50] However, conditions and pay for single women improved considerably following the Factory Act (1891) and it is likely that the cohort of young women coming into paid work in the 1890s were substantially advantaged over their older peers. The absence of unmarried mothers in the casebooks is also notable, reflecting the OBI's reluctance to 'encourage' these mothers and the greater likelihood of institutionalisation for their children. However, though the high number of women marrying reduced the numbers of a group of women historically vulnerable to poverty in the Old World, it may in some cases simply have shifted the nature and point of female vulnerability to poverty. Rather than the economic predicament of the unmarried woman, widowhood and desertion later in the life cycle became more significant in the New Zealand setting. Furthermore – and this is less quantifiable, but just as worthy of attention – marriage could pose the problem of lesser access to a household's resources combined with greater responsibilities within a family. As David Vincent has put it, 'the first priority of a poor man's wife was to put herself last'.[51] Others, too, would frequently allocate her this position. This is a point to which we shall return.

The other side of the gendered division of labour meant that single male parents could experience difficulty in looking after their families. The three single fathers in our sample (Table 7.2) are evidence that the loss of their wives made supporting their families difficult, but their scarcity on the outdoor relief records is also pertinent. The absence of a spouse was a major factor in a man's poverty, since it meant the loss of the key 'contributor', but it operated differently than for women. Few widowed men or sole fathers cared for their children themselves: usually, as was the strong expectation both of their community and the Benevolent Institution, they retained their gendered function as earners and remarried, or found a female relation or paid a housekeeper to care for the children. Unless they were disabled or ill, sole fathers turn up on the casebooks less as recipients of aid themselves than as the fathers of children being cared for in the households of other aid recipients – sometimes because they had not been able to pay the upkeep of the children being cared for. Maria Gandle and Mary Ann Fleming both cared for children whose fathers did not always pay for their upkeep.[52] More commonly, these fathers appear instead in the Industrial School admissions as their children are placed in institutional care. William Gammell, a widower, left his four children with his sister in South Dunedin for six years, sending her money for their upkeep. Once he lost his employment, however, she had to rely on charitable aid, which did not meet their expenses, and the children were admitted to the Industrial School.[53] Another widower, William Elliott, 'a lumper of good character in poor circumstances', employed a housekeeper to look after his children, but could not afford to keep her and had to admit them to the Industrial School.[54] For labouring men, the cost of paying, rather than being married to, a 'mother' for their children could prove impossible. This is testimony, of course, to the value of wives as 'contributors' to a household economy.

Outdoor relief was primarily directed at families. Those who for one reason or another did not form part of a unit that met the criteria of a home tended to be provided with 'indoor relief'. Institutional care was a minor industry in the southern suburbs, with two of the city's, and the region's, public institutions – one (the Benevolent) for the old and one (the Industrial School) for the young – located at either end of Caversham Valley. A church institution, the St Vincent de Paul Catholic Orphanage for girls, opened in 1898 in South Dunedin.[55]

Age, gender, the 'Benny' and the Industrial School

Old age had a very particular significance in the study area over this period, because of the presence in Caversham of 'the Benny' – the OBI's home for the aged – combined with Otago's demography. As Brian Heenan has shown, in the last two decades of the century, New Zealand's population underwent 'a strong pulse of demographic ageing': a sevenfold increase in those aged over sixty between 1874 and 1901. The new cohort of elderly was disproportionately male, a result of the large influx of gold-seeking male immigrants to Central Otago in the 1860s and 70s. In Otago as a whole, therefore, this increase in elderly, and especially in elderly men, was particularly pronounced: by 1901 elderly men greatly outnumbered elderly women, and the men were much more likely than the women never to have married.[56] Although, as younger men, the lack of a family to support might have given them relative freedom, now the disadvantages of their single state were more apparent. Without kin

One of the Flat's major landmarks. Nineteenth-century New Zealand may have wished to abandon Old World charity, but the imposing Benevolent Institution on Alexander St, Caversham, was testimony to the inability of many citizens to maintain their independence throughout their lives. BURTON BROTHERS, TE PAPA TONGAREWA, MUSEUM OF NEW ZEALAND

and, specifically, without a network of relatives who could be expected to support them in old age, they were vulnerable. In contrast to women's exposure to poverty during the late childbearing years, the over-seventy years are the only adult years when men constitute a significant proportion of outdoor relief recipients. Men unable to support themselves, however, were more likely to go into the Benevolent Institution – to receive indoor relief – than to receive outdoor relief. Men such as David Lister and Robert MacDonald, widowers whose children had maintained them, but could no longer do so, received outdoor relief for relatively short periods, but were then admitted to the Benevolent home.[57] More common were elderly men without families, who were usually admitted directly once they could no longer care for themselves. Through the Benny, Caversham in particular acquired a large population of elderly men from throughout Otago, mostly men who had never married and who, in the absence of an able-bodied wife or willing family, were understood to be without the minimum of domestic care needed in old age. By the 1890s the Benny's buildings and its extensive gardens on Eastbourne St were a landmark Caversham institution. Its mostly elderly male inhabitants were a recognised group and a symbol of community recognition that the prevailing 'young man's' values of self-reliance and independence were not always attainable for all members of society throughout their lives.[58]

The Benny was home to fewer elderly women than men.[59] There were a number of reasons for this: there were fewer women in this age group in the population, elderly women were much more likely to have married and therefore to have had children who might assist in their support, they were more likely to know how to undertake their own domestic care and also to look after others (it is probable that they were seen as more useful and acceptable inhabitants of, or nearby appendages to, the households of relatives or even acquaintances).[60] Undoubtedly, too, aside from such material differences, the powerful symbolic association between 'woman' and 'home' operated here: if a home was, almost by definition, a house with a woman in it, then even a widowed or single woman could be understood to 'have a home' in a way a man in a similar situation could not. Unlike the widowers who went into the Benny, Maria Lock, Mary Clint and Matilda Christie, elderly women without family support, were assisted over periods of fifteen years and more through outdoor relief, one in her own home and the others boarding in the houses of others.[61] Women who did enter the Benny were most likely to be unmarried mothers having their babies in the lying-in ward, or women who were so ill or otherwise incapacitated that they could not care for themselves, and had no family who could care for them. Mrs Duckett, who had eight children, the youngest aged one in 1890, was ill for the first few months of that year. Her husband, also ill and then out of work, began living away from home and she lived briefly with another man, but some months later was reported to be in hospital and the children living alone. The children were 'admitted', probably to the Industrial School, and Mrs Duckett was admitted to the Benevolent Institution.[62] This was an unusual case, however. Despite women's greater longevity, women with no family to care for them, and who could not care for themselves, were far fewer in the Otago population than were men.

Elderly Chinese men constituted a distinctive group of elderly men, since even fewer had wives, at least in New Zealand, than did European men of the same cohort. Most were ex-miners who had spent their working lives in Central Otago. The Chinese practice of sojourning (in which men could spend all or much of their working lives away from their families in China), combined with, from the 1880s, the New Zealand ban on Chinese women immigrating, effectively forced a single state upon them.[63] Although many miners did return to China, increasingly from the turn of the century they became a significant responsibility of the Benny, especially since they were by law not entitled to the old age pension. In 1896 thirteen Chinese men were admitted (out of 103 men in total), and during the first decade of the new century approximately 10 per cent of the Benny's admission each year were elderly Chinese men.[64]

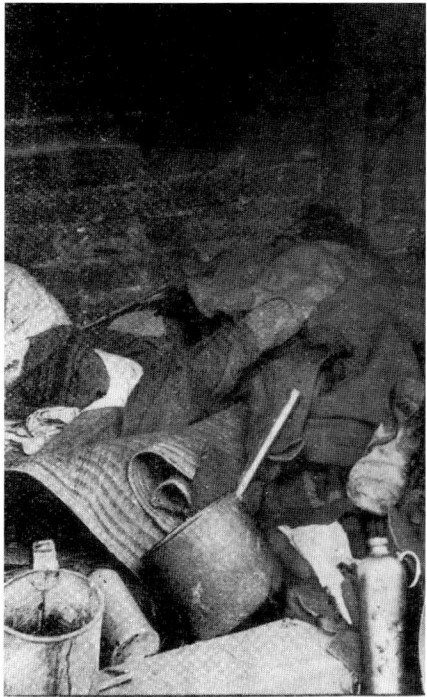

A CHINAMAN'S HAUNT.
The last picture taken was that of the home of a Chinaman recently removed to the Benevolent Institution. This was a fowlhouse, about 4ft high, but strongly and closely built. It had been the home of the late tenant for the past nine or ten months, and, like the man at the front, he had left a lot of little things behind him. Fortunately the camera does not show them all up.

'A Chinaman's Haunt.' The Chinese were the focus of colonial society's deepest anxieties, as this photograph and its caption reveal. The narrative encapsulated here also points us, however, to the conditions in which elderly single men with no family support might be living, and which might result in their admission to the Benevolent Institution. OTAGO WITNESS, 14 JUNE 1900

The plight of the non-'Asiatic' elderly was recognised in 1898 with the introduction of the Old Age Pension Act.[65] The numbers of elderly supported by outdoor relief might therefore have been expected to decrease after 1898: this did not happen, largely because of the criteria for the pension, which excluded newer immigrants or those who had no record of their date of arrival, the sizeable Chinese population, and those of questionable morality. In fact, numbers of elderly on outdoor relief increased, undoubtedly influenced by the new Act and the wider attitudes that had given rise to it: the Benevolent trustees seem to have accepted the idea that old age justified outdoor as well as indoor relief in the years following 1898 and were more likely to give outdoor relief on the grounds of age.

At the other end of the age range was another of the area's landmarks: the Industrial School at the top of Caversham Valley. It had been established in 1869 for neglected and delinquent children, but also to accommodate the increasing number of children then in the Benny: though it was one of the few places destitute children could be cared for, it was felt to be an inappropriate home for them. The school's admissions registers, extant from 1886 to 1897, enable us to distinguish between the kinds of cases helped through outdoor relief and those helped through admission of children to the Industrial School. Outdoor relief was given to families that the Benevolent inspectors saw as able to be maintained outside institutional care, whereas the Industrial School concerned itself with those families seen as unable to provide a home for children, even with financial aid. The concept of 'home', as Margaret Tennant has argued, was at the very heart of the question of welfare.[66] Our evidence shows how the definition of 'home' implicit in the effective allocation of cases to one or the other form of relief points once again to the gendered categorisation of poverty and the gendering of the forms in which relief was given. The meaning of 'home' here hinges on the presence or absence, not simply of a woman, but of a mother of an appropriate kind. Industrial School children all lacked an acceptable mother. In a breakdown of thirty-three cases related to the study area, most common (twelve) were illegitimate children whose mothers could not support them and had been able to make no claim on the father, then (nine) those whose mothers were dead and whose fathers could

Older girls help with the laundry at the Industrial School. OTAGO WITNESS, 27 MARCH 1901.

A HAPPY REUNION AT WINGATUI.
A brother and sister from different homes who see each other but seldom, and who were inseparable all the afternoon.

Many of the children in orphanages or the Industrial School were not 'true' orphans but children whose parents did not have the means or the ability to support them. This photograph tells of the emotional toll which poverty could exact on families.
OTAGO WITNESS, 18 MARCH 1930.

not both work and care for them, or who could not find a female relative or housekeeper to fill the mother's place. In other families (nine), one or both parents were in prison or the asylum. Some mothers (eight) were too ill or too poor to care for their children; another group (four) were not only indigent but 'drunken and immoral'; in two cases only, the mother, rather than the father, had deserted the family. Some cases belonged to more than one of these categories.[67] The situation of girls admitted to the St Vincent de Paul Orphanage reveals the under-representation of unmarried mothers in the OBI sample: of these admissions, 64 per cent were illegitimate and 6 per cent had mothers in prison. 'True' orphans with both parents dead made up only 3 per cent.[68]

The case of Mary Jane Fraser, mentioned earlier, illustrates the gendered distinction made between outdoor and indoor relief. Her second husband seldom provided for her and her children, and they were maintained for some years on outdoor relief. Her children were eventually committed to the Industrial School on the inspector's recommendation, but only after she appears to have given up trying to cope, probably began to engage in prostitution, and began drinking heavily. 'The mother is of intemperate habits and is immoral' is the note on the Industrial School's admission register.[69] This family fell first into the category of outdoor relief, and later into the Industrial School catchment: the difference was Mary Jane Fraser's performance and then failure as an acceptable mother.

The St Vincent de Paul Orphanage set out explicitly to provide a replacement home, with a community of women replacing 'lost' mothers.[70] Billie McLeod has argued that the Catholic girls who grew up there, most of whom were not strictly orphans, but rather the daughters of very poor single women, were better fed and had better access to medical care than most working-class children. For almost all, their institutional upbringing effected upward social mobility: 'St Vincent's girls left behind the indigence and poverty of their origins to join the respectable working class.'[71]

In summary, and at the risk of oversimplifying, it could be said that forms of relief both responded to the gendering of poverty and provided a gendered response. Broadly, outdoor relief stood in for absent or inadequate husbands (or at times sons, in the case of the elderly): its aid assisted with income. The Benny was most frequently a substitute for absent wives: it provided a 'home'. The Industrial School and – to a higher standard – the Catholic orphanage occupied the place of absent, inadequate or inappropriate mothers. Public

The St Vincent's Orphanage 'tinies', undated. Mostly the daughters of poor single women, these girls grew up in the only all-female community on the Flat – the Orphanage and the Sisters of Mercy Convent. SISTERS OF MERCY, SOUTH DUNEDIN

relief schemes and the work given to men by the OBI were also gendered, in that they were given exclusively to men and restored a central masculine function to these men (we explore this in more detail in the next section). On this reading, both the causes of and the responses to poverty were closely organised around gender and life cycle. This elaborate dovetailing of gender, poverty and state or community response had another, critical element, however, which we now explore: it was intimately connected to the dominance of the male-breadwinner wage in the organisation of the labour market.

The male-breadwinner wage and its absence
The concept of the male-breadwinner wage or family wage – which asserted that the wage of an adult male should be sufficient to support a family – structured the distribution of income in a way that ensured that gender profoundly shaped the experience of poverty. As Erik Olssen explains in chapter three, the male-breadwinner wage was already effective practice by the beginning of our period. The rulings of the Arbitration Court institutionalised it, and it became an explicit subject of debate and then increasingly normative through the early decades of the twentieth century. The Labour Government eventually enshrined it in legislation with the amendment of the Arbitration Act in 1936, confirming the practice as a kind of state assistance to the gendering both of the family and the labour market, in that it ensured that most of a household's income entered the family economy through a single member, its adult male.[72] As noted earlier, Melanie Nolan has argued that, despite this trajectory of increasing policy support for the practice, successive governments undermined the idea as much as they supported it. Specifically, she argues that the Family Allowances Act of 1926 subverted the family wage by directing a payment based on the number of children to the mothers of poor families, and by taking this path rather than increasing the minimum wage to all males. There is certainly validity in her depiction of the state's uneven and contradictory handling of the issue. But, as she points out, not until the mid-1930s were family allowances paid to more than a small proportion of households.[73] Margaret McClure, furthermore, notes the strength of the Pensions Department opinion that the allowance was to be a supplement only to the breadwinner's wage: a father had to sign the application and deserted women could not claim it.[74] All this aside, the fact remains that the family wage had implications for every wage-earner, male or female – and indeed for all those who relied on their income as well.

The lack, or loss, of a regular male wage was the most critical element in defining poverty in this society. In the outdoor relief casebooks, its absence took a variety of forms: men died, grew old, deserted their families, drank, or suffered accidents or illness and were unable to keep their old occupations or do a full week's work or 'proper' men's work. Some men who had lost regular work found bits and pieces of work – poorly paid and usually casual, an income that could not be relied upon. John Conn had only one arm, and his most lucrative work was fish hawking.[75] Hugh Reid, aged thirty-five, suffered from 'some complaint of the heart' and 'kidney and bladder trouble' and at his fittest could do only light work.[76] The families of John Conn and Hugh Reid received outdoor relief. Many other men were given work by the day, in accord with the OBI's policy of giving work wherever possible to male applicants, partly as a check on malingering applicants, but also as a means of restoring dignity to men who could not find employment. The importance of employment to masculinity is registered in the case of James Joyce, and in the inspector's ready understanding of what was at stake for this man. The inspector's initial reports on Joyce are conflicting: on the one hand he is 'subject to fits and can do very little work', but on the other hand is said by others in the area to be employed in breaking and training racehorses. Later, the inspector's inquiries lead him to revise his view: 'this impression however appears to have been given by the man's own boasting statements'. A discussion with the owner of the racehorses reveals that Joyce was given odd jobs of a very light nature and for minimal pay: both owner and inspector clearly recognise the symbolic value of this work and the reasons why a man capable only of little work might have inflated it for public consumption.[77]

During the latter 1880s and 90s, work was scarce. Public works relief schemes, as opposed to outdoor or indoor relief, constituted the state and community response to this cause of poverty, but provided work for men only. No figures for public relief specifically for our study area are available, but, for the district of Dunedin (rural as well as urban) over the period 1 April 1894 to 31 March 1895, 505 men were given work on government relief schemes.[78] The statistics also record dependants, indicating that these men were understood not simply as individuals but as the source of family income: 1972 people were dependent on the income of these 505 men.[79] Many men who went to labour on public works schemes in the Catlins, or on the railway in Central Otago during the Long Depression, would therefore have been married men. It is worth noting here that during the 1890s no one publicly questioned the idea that men might spend – or might be required to spend – long periods away from their families. This practice, and the associated assumption that men's duty to provide far outweighed any other of their masculine responsibilities, was understood and accepted. Some men did get work on local relief schemes, such those supported by the Unemployed Relief Association and the Pelichet

Bay Improvement Committee, and supervised by the OBI trustees.[80] Local relief work was seldom full-time, and all public relief work was paid at a low rate. It was hard physical work, frequently taking its toll on unemployed men whose previous jobs had not been as physically demanding. John Martin notes that in the 1880s half of the pay of men on relief schemes was remitted to their wives, and that men whose families were found to be in receipt of charitable aid were dismissed.[81] The system appears to have been less than watertight if these rules still obtained by the early 1890s, however, since men who sent nothing home, and men on relief whose families received aid, both appear relatively frequently among the outdoor relief cases.

The differential effects of the male-breadwinner wage on women and men within a household is a central question in a discussion of the gendering of poverty during this period. Its effects compounded existing beliefs about the relative value of men's and women's work. If adult women could expect to earn something between a half and a third of a man's wage, the family wage concept had far-reaching implications for households without a claim on a man's wage – the majority of those in the outdoor relief casebooks. Widows, deserted or separated wives, unmarried mothers, and women whose husbands did not pass on an adequate proportion of their pay packet were all confronted with the flip side of the wage differential: that a woman's wage was understood to be supporting her alone. The high proportion of female-headed households on the outdoor relief books reflects this anomaly. It also points to the fact that the female household head, although she was not particularly unusual, was culturally anomalous.[82] She was 'catered for' by outdoor relief, then by the widow's pension (for some) and later the Social Security Act of 1938, rather than through the wage structure.[83]

Women's low wage-earning capacity was compounded by responsibility for children, which fell as a combined blow on women who had no male breadwinner. The combination inevitably left women who had young children and little or no other source of income in a very precarious financial position. Tennant points out that the large gap between the average daily labourer's wage, or contemporary calculations of minimum living requirements on the one hand, and charitable aid agencies' allowances on the other, reveals the latter to be parsimonious in the extreme, giving something approximating a labourer's daily wage for a week's support to a family.[84] Outdoor relief, therefore, did not amount to a living allowance.

Even in couple-based households, the fact that the 'family' wage was paid not to the family but to its male head played a significant and related part, though a less readily quantifiable one, in the gendering of poverty. As we have suggested above, the high-marrying propensity of Pakeha women may not so much have reduced female poverty, in comparison with the Old World, as tended to shift it from outside to inside marriage and thereby altered its character. This question points to the importance of looking at individuals' access to resources as well as that of households, and to the distribution of poverty within the family as well as across a society. A wage paid to the wage-earner did not necessarily arrive in the household. There was evidently sufficient ambiguity about whose wage it was understood to be to provide grounds for some men to refuse to contribute enough of their wage to sustain the family. No doubt most of the hundreds of men who travelled back and forth in search of work during the Long Depression did send money home to support their families – those who appear on the outdoor relief books were distinguished by their failure to do so. Mrs O'Leary, for example, could hardly be said to have benefited economically from marriage. In 1891 Patrick O'Leary was away working at the Catlins and in Wellington, but she with her four children was applying for aid: 'He sends her no money. He is able to earn money but seems determined to do nothing for his family. When he left Catlins he drew between £5 and £6 [but] paid nobody there – not even for his food – but only gave his wife a few shillings. He bought her though a second hand Ball Dress. Mrs O'Leary is expecting to be confined every day . . . .'[85] Patrick O'Leary's occasional visits home invariably increased the size of the family, but not its income. Michael Condon, who had been reduced to hawking tea after an accident, earned 10s a week, but none of it reached his family: 'He has his dinner in town, which appears to be unnecessary, and his wife says he never takes a farthing home. He might do more for his family than he does,' noted the inspector.[86] Some men drank their pay, thereby preventing it from reaching the household. Of James Armstrong, the inspector noted that, 'In a former report I called the attention of the Trustees to the fact that this man was in the habit of going away and leaving his family chargeable to the institution – when he comes home he spends all his money in drink and when it is exhausted he goes away again. In this instance he came home about 3 weeks ago and brought £1 13s with him. He was drinking all the time he was at home and on one occasion was locked up for being drunk in the streets. He went away on Thursday leaving his wife and family destitute.' Six months later, evidently after a bout of violence, Mrs Armstrong and her two children had left James and taken a house in Maria St, but as the inspector noted this could hardly improve their situation, since her departure prevented her taking maintenance proceedings against him.[87] Bert Grimmett, speaking of his childhood in the 1910s and 20s, recalls the heavy drinking of men in the neighbourhood and his sense of women's powerlessness in this regard:

> . . . the man demanded that he drink if he wanted to drink. The woman didn't do that. She wasn't in a position to. She had to stay at home and look after the family and cook for the man and that. And I'm quite certain a lot of that went on . . . we used to go down and watch them coming out of the Waterloo Hotel at 6 o'clock closing time. There were all these men. There would be about 50 or 60 of them, all in a state of inebriation because they didn't start drinking until 5 when they knocked off work and they had to get thrown out at 6 and they drank and drank while they were there . . . I know a lot of the people down the road, Mr Page and Mr Scott and Mr Pollock and all those people, they just got what they wanted. So I don't know how on earth they paid for it some of them.[88]

Wally Seccombe has argued with regard to Britain that the male-breadwinner norm resulted in breadwinners assuming a right of ownership of the wage and what it purchased, and that, because the productive labour entailed in supporting a breadwinner's income-earning activity was not directly remunerated, its value could be effectively ignored: hence the view that non-earners were necessarily 'dependants'.[89] Hilda Maher recalled the common practice that:

> the best was always kept for the man, you know, even when it was dishing up the meals or anything, you can't have that piece, it's daddy's, you know, the best was always kept for the man, I think that women felt that was the thing to do, he had to go to work, so he got the best clothes and the best of food and that . . . that was the attitude in our home and lots of other places I knew of too.[90]

To the extent that this view prevailed in southern Dunedin, it points to one explanation for the behaviour of those recalcitrant men who simply refused to support their families. The issue of income distribution within the family was clearly recognised by the inspectors, and where they could they would apply pressure to men who did not pass on their wage or a sufficient amount of it. They also encouraged women to go to the courts for maintenance orders. There were also cases where a man's deficiencies, or stubborn refusal, were acknowledged (usually with a note to the effect that 'this is one of the cases where it is difficult to know what to do'), but aid was given to the wife and children in recognition that they had no other means of support.

The case notes' reports of financial relationships between couples can tell us something about understandings of domestic money and its gendering. Most of these relationships were going wrong: not only was there not enough money, but frequently it was not distributed according to custom. As Erik Olssen notes in chapter three, the most common practice among working-

Old World understandings of public charity are evident in this image, in which 'an eager and expectant crowd of children' clusters around the city's Salvation Army Barracks 'in joyful anticipation' of 'the treat to the poor children' on Coronation Day 1902. OTAGO WITNESS, 2 JULY 1902

class families in New Zealand was likely to have been the common British 'whole wage system', in which a husband handed over the wage packet to the wife to 'manage', perhaps first taking a cut for himself. But this pattern was undoubtedly subject to many variations, including the size of 'his portion' and, in less happy households, systems in which very little and/or highly varying amounts might be handed over.[91] The latter appears to have been particularly associated with heavy alcohol use and physical abuse. Jean Darby's memory of the exchange of money between husband and wife suggests a significant degree of variety:

> ... the men would ... come home and they'd give their wives an allowance, they didn't always give her their pay packet, they'd give what they thought she needed for housekeeping, well, it depended how much the man wanted to spend on his cigarettes and his drink and his gambling perhaps, and some men kept back a lot more than others, which meant the wife had to struggle on what she was allowed to feed the children and clothe the children, and some men were very selfish . . . .[92]

Furthermore, as in so many respects, the case notes reflect some mediation between middle-class and working-class values. Although many working-class households accorded the wife financial responsibility, if not necessarily control, the wives of wealthy or professional men were seldom entrusted with management of family money, but received either a regular allowance or asked for money to purchase specified items.[93] The Trustees of the Benevolent Institution, therefore, in providing goods much more readily than cash, followed a middle-class pattern of masculine 'giving' mostly to women, who had to make a case for specified items – boots, coal, food, rent – but not for cash about which they might make independent decisions. In this way, the Trustees could be seen as perpetuating the economic dependence forced upon many of these women by the refusal of some husbands to distribute their earnings within the family. Relief designed to assist men – work – earned them minimal amounts, but in cash, which could be spent according to a man's own decisions, playing a key part in the maintenance of 'independence' as a masculine attribute.

As we have noted, it was a common nineteenth-century pattern, more frequent during the Long Depression and reinforced by the provision of relief work at a distance, for men to spend sometimes long periods away from home for work. Our samples bear out the pattern noted by Paul Husbands, that poverty worked to make women less able to move, but precipitated men into high levels of transience.[94] This pattern of frequent absence raises questions about the distribution of income within families, the degree of consensus about it, and what relationship these absences had to charitable aid policies. One reason that a number of families ended up on the outdoor relief casebooks was that, when men spent long periods away, they were less likely to send the whole wage home than to consume what they needed first and send back what, if anything, was left, leaving their families with very little or nothing to live on. Some men transgressing the norms were more overtly abusive. The frequently absent Thomas Barlow supported his family intermittently at best, drank heavily over many years, physically attacked his wife regularly when at home, once with the result that he was imprisoned, and when drunk also broke up the furniture.[95] One question here is whether the frequent absences of men exacerbated existing tensions about income distribution, or whether the absence disrupted well-established 'whole wage' systems, thereby throwing the family economy into disarray.

This issue is complicated by the possibility that, in some cases, couples may have made strategic decisions about positioning themselves as candidates for outdoor relief or other aid. When a family applied for aid, an unemployed husband in residence was a disadvantage: his absence in search of work demonstrated efforts to earn, but also opened the possibility that he might retain enough of his earnings to 'deprive' his wife and family to a degree that would put pressure on the OBI to assist them. Even if he did in fact keep sending her money, the wife might say that she had had nothing from him. Or it might not be done with her collusion: a number of descriptions of the destitute condition of families suggest that some men, believing that the trustees would come to the party, made unilateral decisions to attend to their own needs first before sending anything home. These strategies were undoubtedly used, but how frequently is something we can only guess at. Desertion falls into a somewhat similar category. As Margaret Tennant notes, at least one Otago trustee suspected a few cases of strategic desertion.[96] Given the minimal amounts of outdoor relief payments, however, it is unlikely that it would have been worth the while of many couples to incur the cost of maintaining a breadwinner elsewhere simply in order to gain roughly one-fifth of a labourer's wage. This last point suggests that desertion or neglect was, usually, much what it seemed.

Having pointed to the defining nature of the male-breadwinner wage in a household's fortunes, however, we must also raise a question that reminds us of the limits of our sources in allowing us to form a definition of local poverty. Were there *no* households in receipt of a regular full-time male wage that were poor? Surely the combination of low unskilled wages and large young families would frequently produce hardship. Here is the limit of our key source: the OBI supported only certain categories of the poor through outdoor relief, those in the most destitute situations, and its primary method of defining them – consistent with the increasingly normative family wage concept – was 'no male support'. An able-bodied male was either found work through relief, or expected to find it himself. Although it is plain that even a regular labourer's wage must have been a significant asset to a household, it is also worth registering again the strength of the belief that New Zealand did not have a 'poverty problem'. If poverty was one of the key Old World evils that settlers sought to leave behind, there was inevitably considerable resistance to recognising its emergence here. Instead of accepting the biblical – and Old World – maxim that 'the poor ye will always have with ye', it was more tolerable to understand poverty as something temporary and/or anomalous: something that occurred only during 'hard times', and to non-normative categories of people. This is consistent with the comments that sometimes occurred in our interviews. People spoke of poverty as a *time* – for our cohort of interviewees, the depression of the 1930s. If there was a man in the house in 'steady work', this was a way, for Hilda Maher and others, of saying that the household was financially sound.[97]

Conclusion: the new century

The wealth of detail in the outdoor relief records declined after the end of the Long Depression, in part because poverty ceased to be so compelling a public issue until widespread unemployment emerged again in the 1930s. Breadwinners, by and large, could provide for families, and that kept poverty off the national agenda. Even some of the less quantifiable, intrafamilial, forms of poverty were undoubtedly mitigated by several important transitions documented in this volume. Perhaps the most significant was the fertility transition, which saw the average size of a completed family plummet from 6.9 for couples married in 1880, to 5.2 in 1891, 3.73 in 1913, and 3.2 in 1936. If large families, as we have argued, exposed people to poverty while children were dependent, the reduction in family size inevitably limited the number of families at risk.[98] The way in which women approached marriage may also have been changing. As other chapters show, women entering marriage in the new century were better educated, more likely to have participated in the paid workforce (and not just as domestic workers) and to have had some five to ten years earning. They were likely to enter marriage better off and, possibly, with a more confident sense of themselves and their entitlements: a little less likely, perhaps, to resign themselves to the position of the poorest within the household. For those who did not marry – an increasing percentage over the period, as the sex imbalance shifted in favour of women – labour market opportunities increased.

A further important change was the reduction in routine and widespread alcohol consumption by men (discussed in chapter six). Drinking (sometimes by women, but much more often by men) was noted frequently by Benevolent inspectors as a cause of familial poverty. Its economic impact on wives and children was often accompanied by physical violence. Over the period, drink retreated from the workplace, was (arguably) limited by six o'clock closing in 1917 and drinking to excess became less acceptable. Here, too, a key cause of the poverty of women and children was to some extent contained. This transition points to, and is part of, another key transition: the wider changes in the expectations placed on husbands and fathers and the emergence by the 1930s of the idea that a man's place, too, was 'at home'.[99]

For husbands and fathers, the role of breadwinner continued to be pivotal, but other masculine duties assumed much greater importance than they had in the 1890s. The provision of relief work in the Great Depression was attended by quite different assumptions than during the Long Depression. By the 1920s unemployment had increasingly come to be seen as unacceptable and wasteful, and unemployed men had come to be seen as legitimate recipients of assistance. The crystallisation of the male-breadwinner wage as public policy coincided with the emphasis on home ownership and the trend to suburbanisation, and doubtless fostered the growth of an increasingly domesticated and 'settled' concept of husband and father. Ideas about respectability both encouraged and legitimised the new domesticated man. These changes made it less acceptable for married men to leave home in search of work.

In 1930 public policy shifted to reflect these changing ideas. Whereas previously, as in the 1890s, governments and local bodies provided unemployed men with short-term labouring work around the country, now consideration was given to providing men with the minimum financial assistance to stay at home with their families. The Unemployment Act of 1930 formally marked this change (but, significantly, only men were entitled to the unemployment benefit). Unfortunately, this bold piece of welfare legislation had no chance of coping with the consequences of the Great Depression. Cheeseparing policies, termination of the dole and the use of unemployed men to do unskilled and often useless work made the new law a symbol of the government's heartlessness. Significantly, the Coalition Government's attempt to make relief for married men dependent upon moving to work camps in country districts met with such resistance that the policy was dropped: such resistance had never emerged in relation to similar schemes in the 1880s and 90s. Ironically – and, with hindsight, very misguidedly – the government's diffident first pilot

Our period began in the Long Depression, and ended in the Great Depression. The unemployed of the 1930s reacted angrily and publicly against government policies – something unimaginable in the 1890s. The food riot of January 1932, shown here, was successful in compelling the hospital board to provide extra relief. OTAGO DAILY TIMES, 11 JANUARY 1932

scheme of work camps was aimed at unemployed married men in St Kilda, the suburb that expanded in the 1900s and 1910s under the aegis of the new cult of masculine domesticity. Reaction was decisive: in March 1933, a 'large and vocal protest outside a St Kilda Borough Council meeting' objected on a number of grounds, among them that 'the men resented being compelled to leave their wives and homes with little prospect of being able to earn enough money to keep those homes together'. Following an agreed compromise that men would be medically examined, the following year 1343 Dunedin married workers were offered work in camps: the overwhelming majority presented certificates declaring them medically unfit![100] The new domestic man was voting for domestic life, in earnest.

Eight To and From, There and Back: Gender in Spatial Mobility

BRIAN HEENAN AND SARAH JOHNSEN[1]

Poor but not destitute in April 1889, Jane Steel turned for assistance to the Otago Benevolent Institution – the Benny – as she was to do time and again in coming years. Although just thirty-five years old, Jane was already a widow, a solo mother of four children. Three were the children of her late husband; the father of the fourth child had left Dunedin and had last been heard of in Melbourne, Australia. To the Benny's inspector she declared some income – a little from washing, sewing or perhaps knitting to order; a regular six shillings per week for the care of a 5-year-old nurse child. For six months, however, nothing had been remitted by the father of her youngest. Always renting, Jane was often on the move within southern Dunedin. During thirteen years from 1889 she reported as many as eight changes of address.[2] She may have come into conflict with landlords – she had one or two verbal standoffs with the Benevolent inspector – but frequent movement was not uncommon among the very poor.[3]

Jane Steel's situation contrasted with that of Rachel Grimmett, who lived for more than forty years in Faringdon Villa, a freehold house built by her husband in Fitzroy St in 1882. Fully-paid settlers under Vogel's 1870 Immigration Scheme, Richard (1839–1906) and Rachel (1835–1921) Grimmett sailed with their children from Plymouth, England, aboard the *Scimitar* in December 1873, arriving at Port Chalmers the following March. When the eight surviving children grew to adulthood, most established homes of their own nearby or elsewhere in New Zealand, although the oldest son later moved to Sydney via Wellington.[4] Faringdon Villa was the centre of an expanding and settled neighbourhood of Grimmett homes. But, as Rachel's personal diary demonstrates, the Grimmetts' stable home base was also the centre of a series of regular movement patterns. Some were visits to family lasting up to a few weeks, and others were trips completed within a single day. Rachel, an indefatigable member of the Salvation Army, may well have encountered Jane Steel in the course of her trips to the Sallies' 'supe' kitchen (Rachel's spelling),[5] her visits to the hot salt-water pool at St Clair, or as she walked the streets to present bills and collect payments, for she ran the finances of her husband's building business. For her part, Jane might have been making her visits to the Benevolent's trustees to wait for her weekly vouchers, or to the specified grocery store that had tendered to provide particular goods to those awarded aid.

In the contrasting stories of Jane and Rachel, we can discern several common themes spanning the continuum of different forms of spatial mobility, and revealing the significance of gender. Both their lives were shaped by the large-scale, cross-national migration flows so important to the colonial experience in the nineteenth century. In Jane's case, the movement of her fourth child's father to Australia – like that of so many Dunedin men who flocked to booming Melbourne in the 1890s – brought poverty and helped to precipitate her into a series of probably forced changes of residence. For Rachel the migration from England as part of a stable married couple brought comfort, modest prosperity and the beginnings of a local kin network. Both their lives, therefore, were also affected by their experiences of residential mobility (or stability) *within* southern Dunedin. Finally, for both women, their daily or weekly patterns of movement around southern Dunedin were shaped by their place in a gendered division of labour and a social world structured by gender – and class – norms and expectations.

In this chapter, then, we explore two dimensions of spatial mobility: residential movement within the local area ('local migration') and circular mobility involving trips that begin and end in the circulator's home ('circulation'). Our primary objective is to document and offer some explanation of the gender dimension of spatial mobility in the context of more general movement within the southern Dunedin suburbs from about 1890 to the later 1930s. Studying local migration and circulation together as aspects of a single continuum of mobility is relatively unusual; it is much more common for them to be treated as distinct academic topics. In the literature search for this paper we found no work that explicitly set out to address the two together, but, by recognising that these two forms of spatial mobility constitute a continuum, we demonstrate the full range of movement patterns within the local area that created the residents' experience of living in a particular place. To some extent, this experience was gendered, and we use what evidence is available to identify and interpret gender variations in local mobility. As Jane's and Rachel's stories suggest, the patterns of gender were inextricably linked to questions of class, and this, too, becomes central to our exploration.

The focus on gender dimensions of mobility at the local scale complements the historical research on the gendering of long-distance migration to colonial societies, a topic that has tended to attract more attention of late.[6] This chapter also complements the companion piece by Robin Law that follows it. Law's chapter addresses a specific aspect of the continuum of spatial mobility: the short trips undertaken within the urban space of Dunedin that form part of the broader category of circulation. Her focus is on the gendering of the transport technologies, the spaces in which they operated (notably the street), the cultural meanings of these trips, and how they changed over the study period. Law's chapter can be usefully read in conjunction with the section in this chapter that discusses circular mobility through an extended discussion of the Grimmett family in the early 1890s.

Conceptual framework: gender and spatial mobility
Gender has never been a strong dimension of empirical research on geographical movement, especially migration. The convention of using the household rather than the individual as a unit of analysis means that in the past gender differences were often obscured. Indeed, two widely referenced theoretical frameworks for geographical mobility – those of E. S. Lee and W. Zelinsky – devote little attention to gender.[7] Even by the early 1990s, the omission was evident in well-regarded, widely used texts on population in general and in one specifically on migration.[8] A scan of recent publications in relevant journals shows that, although rigorous empirical research on this topic is encountered with growing frequency, the topic remains comparatively undeveloped.[9] In particular, the prime focus among the majority of papers scanned was on the contemporary period; very few addressed spatial mobility in a historical context. Apart from recent research on the experience of nineteenth-century women travellers, and on gender in the history of urban transport and public space, historical studies are relatively sparse.[10] Consequently, this study appears to have few close precedents.

In historical studies of geographical mobility in New Zealand and elsewhere, the term 'transience' (or 'transiency') has been commonly used to describe 'the migration of households or of members of a household from one locality to another at some distance'.[11] This term fails to distinguish between specific dimensions of spatial mobility that are often qualitatively very different from each other in some combination of geographical scale, form, motivation, process and social connotations.[12] Instead of 'transience', we use two generic categories, formally defined by Zelinsky in 1971, that encompass all forms of geographical mobility, irrespective of their geographical or temporal dimensions. The two are *migration* (permanent shifting, including incessant wandering, and immigration) and *circulation*, that is, an absence of variable duration and distance from home (commuting, hawking, Hobsbawm's 'on the tramp' movement in search of casual paid work, and so on).[13] Unlike migration, circulation does not involve a shift in one's usual dwelling place: ready access to friends, relatives and resources close to home is maintained.

This conceptual framework enables a deeper understanding of mobility in its space–time rhythms, process, and meaning in community contexts than does the concept of transience. For most people who lived in southern Dunedin during our study period, whatever their class, gender or other social attributes, migration and circulation were complementary, even critical, and certainly closely intertwined components of the life course. On the one hand, such things as the need for paid work, or for a larger – or smaller and cheaper – house, drove migration; on the other, the pulsating ebb and flow of circular mobility maintained daily life in the context of extended family and neighbourhood support networks that remained intact unless broken by migration. When this occurred, the further a person or household moved, the greater the likelihood that established activity and relationship networks, and the patterns of circular mobility that enlivened them, would be disrupted and so require reconstitution.

Data, methods and context
In our analysis of local mobility we rely on quantitative data from the electoral rolls, supplemented by three different forms of qualitative evidence that reveal both migratory and circulatory movement: oral-history interviews (including three family residence histories), the Maria St cases (our Series II) from the record books of the Otago Benevolent Institution, and the personal diary of Rachel Grimmett.[14] The data sources available both constrain and enable the kinds of questions that can be asked about the gendered elements of local migration and circulation. For local migration, the electoral rolls allow us to establish differences in the patterns of such movement between adult men and women, although it is more difficult to put forward robust explanations for these differences.[15] The oral histories and the casebooks, nevertheless, provide us with enough evidence to go some way beyond speculation, and the oral histories also contribute to what we can establish

about circulation. It is a record made on a daily basis, however, which is of most help to us in our enquiry into circulation. Rachel Grimmett's diary of 1894–95, though limited as a social commentary on southern Dunedin, does allow us a privileged glimpse into the differing daily and weekly patterns of movement of the women and men of one family.

Although little historical work exists on circulatory mobility, we know quite a lot about migration, both for New Zealand and for the three boroughs – Caversham, South Dunedin and St Kilda – that constituted the study area. In 1901 the census reported that almost 37 per cent of all adults enumerated had been born in Britain and had migrated to the colony (about 2 per cent had been born in Germany, Lebanon or China). Even in 1921, when we have information only for St Kilda, just over 20 per cent of adults had been born elsewhere.[16] One might reasonably assume that a high proportion of the immigrants would have settled in the study area after moving around New Zealand, or even the Australasian colonies, although only about 5 per cent had also been born in one or other of these.

The project's earlier work on persistence and transience was based on data for Caversham Borough only. Although that study concluded that 'a simple dichotomy of stayers and leavers . . . is altogether *too* simple', it is noteworthy that roughly 65 to 70 per cent of all adults there at the start of any decade would be gone by its end (10 per cent had died in 1902–11 and 6 per cent in 1911–22). Nor did the persistence rates vary much between men and women, although overall persistence in Caversham Borough was lower than the rate reported for other New Zealand communities.[17] Married people – especially among the small employers, the business community and the skilled manual workers – were the ones most likely to persist, especially if they owned property. Brooking *et al.*, in the earlier study, concluded that 'a man's position in the life cycle and his marital status, then, determined the decision to stay or move more than occupation, class, wealth or place of residence, although there was a complex interaction between all these factors'.[18] Preliminary analysis of the extended study area – South Dunedin and St Kilda boroughs added to Caversham Borough – raised the persistence rate, not surprisingly revealing that only between 55 and 60 per cent left over any decade.

Our reconstruction of the gender dimension of local migration within the study area is rather limited, however, since what is possible is largely predetermined by conventions used in compiling the electoral rolls that constitute our primary source.[19] Apart from excluding anybody younger than twenty-one years old, a highly migratory population in the Otago region, the electoral rolls do not permit analysis of the movement behaviour of those who left the study area.[20] Despite an extensive (and expensive) record-linkage exercise to identify those who had left Caversham, almost no women were found. If families could be identified with any certainty, that might not matter, but the electoral rolls (and the street directories) only provide information about individuals rather than households. That said, however, we can reach certain tentative conclusions by establishing whether married or single persons were more likely to move within the study area, and whether they moved with others who shared the same last name and with whom they may well have formed a household unit.

In this chapter, evidence on local migration provided by the electoral rolls and street directories is supported by insights drawn from three other sources. The first is a sample of twenty-one oral-history interviews (with four male and seventeen female interviewees). For these informants, time and distance in geographical mobility were fluid, imprecise, if not indeterminate concepts, involving little respect for absolute dates, electoral roll periods or our sub-area boundaries. The second source consists of three residence-history profiles for related southern Dunedin households (we have called them the Walkers, the Jones and the Johnsons), covering the early 1900s to the 1930s.[21] Each profile gives details of the age, gender, kinship and residential movement of members of what were working-class nuclear-family households.

In addition we use data for a sample of thirty-five women and twenty-four men who applied for assistance or relief from the Otago Benevolent Institution between 1889 and 1911 (our Series II, the Maria St cases), a source that is particularly useful because it provides a perspective on gender-specific changes of residence.[22] Of those in our total sample, twenty-four of the female applicants and fourteen of the male applicants[23] had dependent children (0–13 years): 4.5 on average if a woman and four if a man.[24] In other words, the adults in our sample of applicants for outdoor relief were usually but a small fraction of the number actually moving when a household relocated.

Our final source, the personal diary of Charlotte Rachel Grimmett, an immigrant and long-term southern Dunedin resident, is used to define sites of gender linked by the space–time rhythm of circular mobility rather than local migration. Confined to just two years in the mid-1890s, the diary describes in remarkable and unusual detail the daily round of paid and unpaid work, family and social relations, and recreation among both male and female members of the household.

To and from: local migration

Between the elections of 1893 and 1938, local migration drove a continuous ebb and flow of people among the seven sub-areas or suburbs comprising the

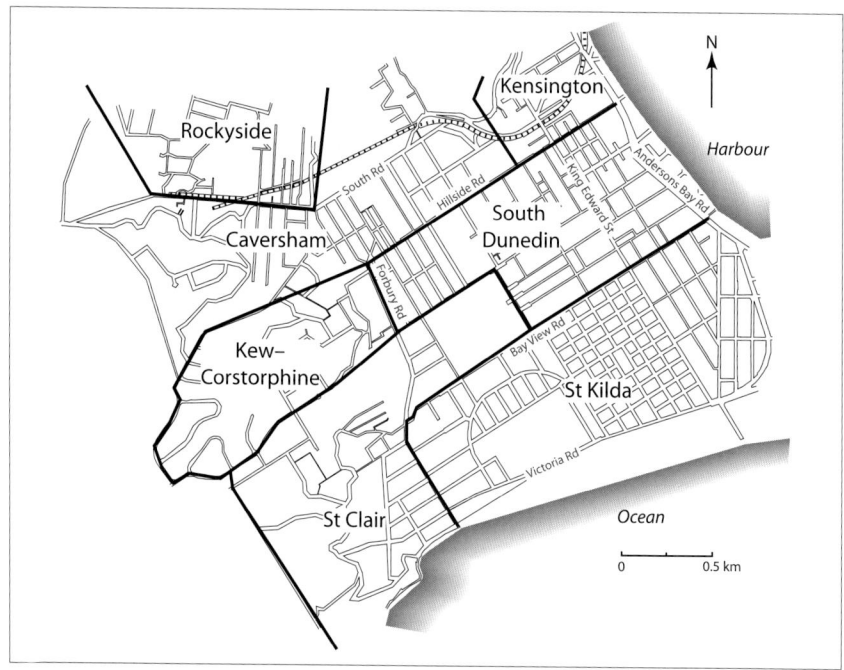

Map 8.1 Location of sub-areas

southern suburbs (Map 8.1). Migrants moved between densely peopled South Dunedin Borough, the initially sparsely settled St Kilda and a topographically diverse mosaic of five sub-areas – Caversham, Rockyside, Kensington, Kew–Corstorphine and St Clair – that defined the domain of Caversham Borough. As chapter two explains, although each was socially complex, our sub-areas differed broadly from one another in both employment structure and pattern of housing tenure.

The southern suburbs, then, offered a variety of opportunities for people who moved between them in pursuit of self-improvement or accommodation, at marriage or for other reasons. In all, the electoral roll yields a total of 6297 such moves between 1893 and 1938, a period during which each of the seven sub-areas exchanged movers with every other sub-area during most, if not all, of the five decadal slices from 1893–1902 to 1928–38.

Those who shifted – defined here as local migrants, because they began their shift in one suburb, but ended it in another within southern Dunedin – represented three of every ten persons alive at the start of our study period. Although the proportion of local migrants was always a minority of the study area's total population at the beginning of every decadal slice, nevertheless their importance varied between wide extremes across the period, from a low point of 21.8 per cent in 1893–1902 to double this in Edwardian times, 1902–11, when this form of mobility was easily at its most common.

Table 8.1 Males per 100 females among migrants within the study area by destination sub-area for decadal-slice periods from 1893–1902 to 1928–38

	1893–1902	1902–1911	1911–1919	1919–1928	1928–1938
Caversham	122	110	127	99	118
Kensington	500	107	125	114	102
Rockyside	300	192	157	100	135
St Clair	133	117	111	107	108
South Dunedin	109	113	122	135	119
St Kilda	200	123	122	120	103
Kew-Corstorphine		155	120	159	147
Study Area	163	116	123	118	113

Source: Caversham Electoral Roll Database 1893–1938

Our data from the electoral rolls reveal several points of difference between the patterns of local migration displayed by men and women. Despite there being more women than men in the total population throughout the study period, a gender ratio of 79.2 males per 100 females for those who did not move at all implies that women were much less likely than men to shift locally (see Table 8.2). Not only that, though most people who made both one move only, or two or more, were men, women were much more likely to shift only once – as implied by a gender ratio of 110.7 – than twice or more (a gender ratio of 138.3).

Table 8.2 Number of moves made by individual people present on sequential electoral rolls*

	No moves	1 move	2 + moves
Female	4603	2192	332
Male	3644	2426	459

*1893, 1902, 1911, 1919, 1928 and 1938 electoral rolls sampled. Source: Caversham database

A second point of difference is that a larger number and proportion of all males than all females took part in local migration in every decadal-slice interval and, with two small exceptions (Caversham and Rockyside, 1919–28; see Table 8.1), to every sub-area. Nevertheless, over the quarter-century or so between 1911–19 and 1928–38, male dominance among local migrants across the whole study area weakened progressively. In these years the total gender ratio fell from 163 to 113 (Table 8.1), a clear indication that, in proportion to males, local migration among the women of Caversham increased quite rapidly toward the end of our study period.

Not all of our seven sub-areas shared evenly in this trend, however (Table 8.1). For reasons that remain uncertain, three quite different sub-areas – posh St Clair and working-class Kensington, as well as mixed St Kilda – appear to have been crucibles of change in a longer-term shift in the gender balance of local migration within the study area. Gender ratios for each of the three suburbs imply that, compared with males, women who lived in them in the latter part of the study period were not only more likely to participate in local migration than were women in other sub-areas, but also appear to have done so at least as early as 1911–19. Indeed, as the ratios in Table 8.1 indicate, by 1928–38 closely matching numbers of males and females moved from other sub-areas to live in Kensington and St Kilda, and to St Clair (though somewhat less so). In other words, social and cultural circumstances in these sub-areas, and perhaps elsewhere in our study area, appear to have changed in a way that enabled (or obliged) women to undertake more residential movement in the years from about 1911–19 than they had before then.

Street analysis of local migration using electoral roll data for the southern suburbs provides us with finer detail on who moved and also points to some reasons why. Across the study area between 1893 and 1938, a little more than one in ten of both men (12.3 per cent) and women (11.7 per cent) transferred from one street to another *without* leaving the sub-area in which they lived, while a third of the men (34.9 per cent) and a quarter of the women (27.2 per cent) moved street *and* also changed sub-area. This means that, over the entire study period, almost half the men, but only two of every five women, changed their street address. Nevertheless, though men dominated local migration between sub-areas, as many women as men – signified by a gender ratio of 100.9 males per 100 females – shifted their place of residence, but remained living in the same sub-area.

Also according to our street analysis, it seems that single women were less likely to move than married women or single men, although in the period 1919–28 never-married women moved more frequently than never-married men. In that decade 45 per cent of married women and 38 per cent of single women shifted. It is also noteworthy that, in moving, 18 per cent of men, but a much smaller proportion (11 per cent) of women, left a household they shared with others who had the same last name to live in a household in which they were the only person of their surname. Although the number of those involved – 2011 men and 1157 women – was too small to allow much confidence in a disaggregation of these figures by decade, the evidence suggests that it became more common for women to move alone from a family home over time, a finding that confirms the interneighbourhood analysis discussed earlier.[25] It is also worth noting, perhaps, that, though one-time movers (or once-only movers) were more likely to be female than male, the latter were somewhat more likely to have made two or more moves (see Table 8.2). As will emerge in later discussion, however, there is no simple or obvious explanation for any of these changes, or for the gender differences identified.

Case studies of several Caversham families for which residential histories are available allow us a different kind of picture of local migration, though a more narrowly focused and specific one: in these cases, frequent shifts, always among rental properties, undertaken by working-class nuclear families in which the main income-earner, a male in each case, was seldom without paid work. One of these, the Walker family, was founded in 1902, when the wife and husband, a bootmaker by trade, married in Christchurch. Although the household was impressively mobile geographically, it was quite stable in social terms, since the main income-earner never moved out of the manual working class. Over their first nineteen years together, the couple had five children and changed residence as many as six times, a record equivalent to one move every 3.2 years.

In following years they made several more moves, but with, on average, a much longer interval (5.3 years) between each. Although the first three moves made by the Walkers occurred outside Dunedin, all of the rest began and ended somewhere in southern Dunedin. Most were very local and were made to take up alternative rental housing opportunities. For example, they lived for some years in Caversham township – first in Playfair St and then in nearby Marion St (later Thorn St) – and then moved less than half a mile away to one of the elegant new houses on Asquith St, Rockyside, just to the north of Caversham township. Later they moved to a neighbouring house in the same street. Their next shift came in 1936, when the husband and wife legally separated, taking up residence at different addresses within the study area, where they both benefited from a strong family support network. Mr Walker moved in permanently with their daughter, Doreen Jones, and his wife lived for a year in Christchurch with a sister before returning to Dunedin. She lived for a time in Ferguson St, St Kilda, and, finally, in a flat on the corner of Forbury Rd and Valpy St, St Clair. There she was often visited by grandchildren, who lived with their mother, Doreen Jones, and their father and grandfather a few miles away across the Flat, in Anderson's Bay Rd.

Only a little less mobile was the Johnson household. Created by marriage in 1901, it consisted of the husband (a labourer to 1919 and then a maltster), his wife and four children, the last born in 1909. Between 1901 and the husband's death in 1933, the Johnsons moved seven times, averaging one shift every 4.7 years. Apart from time spent in the mid-1920s in Gisborne, where Mr Johnson worked in a local brewery, the sequence of moves made as they shifted from one housing opportunity to another within the study area was also tightly circumscribed spatially. All moves made by both the Walkers and Johnsons began and ended in Kensington sub-area or nearby, in the vicinity of Anderson's Bay Rd and McBride St, and in and around Caversham township. It was more than coincidental that in both localities a large proportion of the housing stock was rental rather than owner-occupied.[26]

The twenty-one informants in the oral-history interviews reported sixty-six moves, involving more frequent changes of residence than is reflected in the electoral rolls: just as one would expect, given the tendency of the electoral roll method to understate migration. In all, seventeen of the twenty-one respondents who provided information about shifts made during the study period,[27] that is, four out of every five, gave details of a sequence of two or more local moves, some recalling as many as five or more. Across the whole sample of oral-history informants, the average was 3.1 shifts, most remembered by informants as children growing up in, and young adults leaving, a nuclear-family group made up of parents and their offspring. The electoral roll data, by contrast, indicate that some four-fifths of all adult women and men made only one move during the entire study period (1893–1938).

The people who sought assistance from the Benevolent Institution were among the poorest in the locality, and the women applicants among them were somewhat more mobile residentially than any other sub-population of women that we have identified in the southern Dunedin study area. Four out of every five of the women moved within the study area during the sixteen years covered by casebook records. In this mobile group, however, multiple movers appeared more often than they had among the sample of migrants drawn from the electoral roll or, as far as one can detect, from the oral histories. In fact, a large majority of these poor women – some 73 per cent – had shifted twice or more. Although eight of these women reported as many as four or more moves each, their husbands moved with even more remarkable frequency. As shown in chapter seven, unemployed able-bodied men usually left home in search of work in the earlier part of our period, usually with the understanding that they would send money back to support their families. Because their absence frequently impoverished wives still further – sometimes because a husband's initial circulatory intentions became migratory ones – the wives, too, could be precipitated into further, downwardly mobile, migration.[28]

Among these women, Jane Steel's record was unrivalled. Her eight moves in thirteen years meant that, on average, she shifted to a different address about once every twenty months. For care providers such as Jane, the large number of dependent (including fostered) children that moved with them would have severely limited opportunities for paid work, and that made it that much more difficult financially to make ends meet. Sparse income would have greatly constrained their housing choices, and therefore limited their migration destinations to neighbourhoods where rentals were cheapest. Like the Walker and Johnson households, all of those in our sample of applicants to the Benevolent Institution moved exclusively within the rental market. The proportion of the study area's housing stock available for rent varied from one suburb to another and declined over time. Even in 1937, the year when South Dunedin and much of Caversham township were surveyed as part of the national Housing Survey, just over 40 per cent of all houses in South Dunedin were rental, though the proportion was much lower in adjacent St Kilda.[29]

This pattern of movement was not peculiar to the poor, or those who hoped to obtain assistance from the Benevolent Institution. Local migration among southern Dunedin's Lebanese community followed a not dissimilar pattern. In the 1880s and 90s a number of families from Lebanon, most of whom travelled via Australia, had settled around Walker St in central Dunedin, just south of the Exchange. As noted in chapter two, between about 1905 and 1915, while the larger group of Catholic Lebanese families remained around Walker St, the Orthodox Lebanese families, who settled in Dunedin around 1890, left for Mafeking Terrace off Glasgow St, a predominantly rental district in South Dunedin's poorest neighbourhood, then relocated to a nearby neighbourhood, no larger than half a square kilometre, in the area between Anderson's Bay and King Edward roads.[30] Local moves made by Lebanese family members such as the Facoorys usually began and ended within this neighbourhood. Annie and George Facoory both moved often, and several rented houses in the Mafeking Terrace area appear to have passed from one Facoory to another. One address in Glasgow St, number 73, was occupied in turn by Annie (1913–15) and Kate (1916–18) Facoory, after the former moved a few doors to 55 Glasgow St (1916–17), where she lived for a short time before handing the dwelling on to Helena Facoory.[31]

Such spatially intense migratory behaviour reinforced the high level of residential propinquity and social bonding the Lebanese maintained over the entire study period. The opening in 1911 of St Michael's Orthodox Church on Fingall St both reflected their community strength and provided them with a focal point, while the inability of many of the immigrants, especially the housebound women, to speak English reinforced these bonds and helped sustain endogamous marriage.[32] For the Facoorys, and perhaps for other families in the Lebanese and wider community, the opportunity to own rather than rent residential property seems to have been denied for many years or entirely forgone, presumably because of lower income, or even, as with non-Lebanese families such as the Walkers and Johnsons, a broader working-class culture that preferred renting to owning. Among the Lebanese, however, it might well be that the commitment of many of them to long-term capital accumulation made home ownership economically nonsensical, at least until a certain level of material comfort had been achieved.

Describing the intricate ebb and flow of local migration within Caversham is one thing; identifying the cause of such complexity is quite another. In addressing this question, we need to bear in mind that the different sources have distinct strengths and weaknesses. The electoral roll data, though affected by a number of limitations, provide an accurate indication of the macro-patterns and allow us to investigate the relationships between local migration and occupation (for men only), as well as marital status (for both men and women). By linking the electoral rolls to the valuation records for 1921–22, we can also provide some analysis of the relationship between movement and an area's mean property values, and the proportions of rental and freehold properties.

The first questions that arise concerning the relationship between male occupation and local migration are whether households were likely to move when a man changed his job, and whether a man was likely to change occupation if the household moved. In general, it seems not. According to the electoral roll data for Caversham Borough, as few as 7.1 per cent of men in the paid workforce changed their occupation when they moved between sub-areas.[33] Of the men in the study area who moved from one street to another street, 23 per cent also changed occupational class; of those who changed occupational class, by comparison, 48 per cent moved to a different street. Although 21 per cent of those men who did not change occupational class also moved street, there was a clear tendency for shifts in occupational class to coincide with shifting house and street. Nevertheless, it needs to be borne in mind that, even in 1919–28, the most mobile decade, 85 per cent of men did not change occupational class.[34]

Whether the occupationally mobile man or his wife chose to move – almost all of these men were married – we cannot tell, but it seems likely that both financial and cultural reasons would have been important. Because a wife's key responsibilities concerned domestic matters, her voice would frequently have had added weight in decisions about moving house. The oral histories provide little mention of any relationship between the location of place of work and where people chose to live when they moved within southern Dunedin. Even the Housing Survey of 1937, which explicitly asked about this connection, usually failed to enter an answer (the handful who responded said because it was either close to work or cheap). The study area's compact size gave residents ready access, even on foot, to the numerous workplaces in Caversham and South Dunedin boroughs and, indeed, in adjacent parts of central Dunedin. For these generations of practised walkers (and cyclists), the Flat's distances posed few challenges.[35]

The second set of questions concerning migration and families occur in relation to class. In general terms, members of the upper-middle class – large employers, higher managers, professionals, semi-professionals – were substantially less likely to move than any class other than the self-employed/small employers. Manual workers, by contrast, were much more likely to move than any other class. Even if we take length of residence into account, and disaggregate by the nine occupational classes, the same pattern emerges. Presumably, manual workers had less access to credit and therefore had to 'leverage' themselves from a relatively cheap first house into a larger and newer one, assuming that is what they wanted to do. In some cases, especially among the skilled, couples may have chosen instead to add a room or two rather than move. John Sidey, a builder who became so successful as a storekeeper during the gold rushes that he was able to build a substantial farm on the Kew Rise, built one of the largest houses in the study area in 1863–64 – Corstorphine House – and extended it substantially in 1910. When his son inherited it, he added to the house still further. Except in the case of historically significant homes, however, we usually lack information about why such additions were undertaken and, in their timing, what connection they may have had with life-cycle factors. One possible factor – and here we can only speculate – is that, because of women's domestic responsibilities, the occupation or ownership of a certain kind of house may have been a marker of class status in a different way for women than it was for men. This is not to say that bricks and mortar did not signify class for men; more that it may have done so differently.

Evidence from the electoral roll on the connection between changing street address and a shift in marital status shows a stronger association than for occupation.[36] As might be expected, those people who shifted within the southern suburbs were also more likely to have changed their marital status than those who stayed in the same street.[37] By linking the electoral roll database to the information derived from marriage records, we can establish that most brides moved following their marriage, although 16.9 per cent of them remained at their pre-marriage address. Presumably, in these cases the husband moved to the bride's parents' address. It was more likely that people would move on changing marital status, in short, than it was for them to move on changing occupational status. Indeed – not surprisingly – the most mobile group were single people who married. Within Caversham Borough approximately one in three men (30.5 per cent) and one in five women (20.5

per cent) who married moved from one sub-area to another. An even higher proportion changed street. The oral-history informants also reported that creation of a new social unit by marriage usually, but not always, entailed, according to custom, a change of address for both parties.

One indication of the importance of family networks is the extent to which kin lived near one another. Elizabeth Roberts's English study suggests that women played a major part in maintaining affective ties with the extended family, while Young and Wilmott's study of Bethnal Green, London, in the 1950s noted that, 'the local kinship system . . . stresses the tie between mother and daughter'.[38] Of the 146 couples who married and lived within our study area, and whose parents can positively be identified in the area, only one couple set up their household in the same street as both sets of parents. Nine couples (5.49 per cent) lived in the same street as the bride's parents, and 28 (17 per cent) lived in the same street as the groom's parents. However, the great majority (108, or 65.85 per cent) who stayed within the study area did not live in such close proximity to their parents.[39]

The death of a spouse was also associated with relocation, but the effects of such an event on local migration were more pronounced for women. If we aggregate data for all interelectoral roll periods, 36 per cent of women whose status changed from married to widow shifted street location (compared with 19 per cent of married women who remained married to the same person). Some widows may have shifted to live with or near family members, as did Cecily Johnson, of the Johnson family discussed earlier. With Fred, her husband, she lived in Grosvenor St, but soon after his death in 1916 Cecily moved to a house in Vernal St, next door to her son Douglas and his wife Isa. Similar life-cycle adjustments appear to have been especially common among the Orthodox Lebanese, although there were notable exceptions. One was Sarah Hananeia, who, when widowed, became a successful itinerant hawker and head of household.[40]

The oral-history informants provide further evidence of life-cycle events that often drove local migration. Shifts linked to a change in living arrangements appear prominently in their accounts. Indeed, most of the sixty-six individual moves described by oral-history informants were linked in some way to a transition in family relationships, or to changing housing requirements and preferences, evidence providing strong support for the implied connection between marriage and migration drawn from the electoral roll data discussed above. A common life-course sequence among oral-history respondents began with the creation of a new social unit through marriage. At this point, both husband and wife usually (but not always) moved from their parental homes to independent accommodation. Most often this was a rented property, occasionally as close as next door to one or other set of parents, or at least often in the same neighbourhood. After renting for a few months, even for several years, or boarding for a short period in one or other parental home, another shift was initiated, this time usually to newly built or existing owner-occupied housing. Although we do not have data on age at first marriage, it appears that the north-west European marriage pattern, where a couple married only when they could afford to establish their own household, was normative behaviour in our study area.[41]

Marion Cooper's narrative of her residential experience during the early years of marriage closely followed this sequence. For the first thirty months she and her husband rented a flat in the front half of a widow's house across the road from where she had lived with her mother.[42] '[W]e [then] moved next door to my mother, a little cottage came up for sale there, so we moved there … we sort of did it all up.'[43] More mobile as renters were Beatrice Riddell and her husband, who lived in flats in St Clair, St Kilda, Caversham township and Cargill's Corner before buying a house in South Rd.[44] For some owner-occupiers, however, their movement on the housing market was in the opposite direction, from owner-occupier freeholder to renting. Overall the 1930s greatly reduced the amount of movement between streets, although, as noted earlier, this may be a function of the snapshot effect of the electoral rolls with their 3- to 5-year cycles. Anecdotal evidence indicates that quite a lot of 'flitting' occurred during the Great Depression.[45]

The process of family-building, and the need for more living space generated by a growing number of children, also saw families shift, according to the oral-history informants. So it was for Marjorie Scott's parents, whose first house was 'too small. As the children grew they had to get a bigger place because we didn't have enough bedrooms.'[46] Beatrice Riddell also recalled that her mother and father had moved within the study area for much the same reason, and so, too, did Doreen Jones and her family. Writing in 1935 to her mother, Mrs Walker of Asquith St, Rockyside, following her family's move to a much larger rented house in Anderson's Bay Rd, Doreen observed, 'it's a hell of a place to keep clean, and often wish it was the size of 17 Bathgate Rd. though how we all existed there beats me'.[47] In contrast, a desire for less rather than more living space also generated movement, as it did for Frances Kenny's elderly parents, who bought and moved to a smaller house on a more easily managed section.[48] Local migration was also driven by other factors, such as a change in neighbourhood land use, environmental transformation and a change in tenure arrangements. For example, Mavis Liverpool recalled how her parents were 'forced' to vacate their house in McGlashan St when this was 'taken over' by the Hillside Workshops.[49]

Over the course of years or decades, then, local migration within southern Dunedin, especially among the young and unmarried, and more clearly in terms of the family life cycle, generated distinctive gendered patterns of spatial mobility. In comparison, circulation involved similarly gender-specific differences among women and men moving around these same spaces, but on different time scales: a matter of weeks, days or hours, instead of the years encompassed by migration. With the exception of young and unmarried workers – most of whom never featured in an electoral roll – local migration usually involved entire households, whereas circulation usually involved individuals or smaller groups, perhaps from more than one household. One important element, kinship, links migration and circulation, as much in the general population of southern Dunedin as among small groups such as the Lebanese. As noted above, much local migration involved the splitting of households, most commonly when children grew up, married and established new homes, or when a spouse died. The electoral roll data indicate that most newly-wed couples – some 57.9 per cent – set up on their own account (25.1 per cent of couples moved in with a larger family household) somewhere within the study area. In the process of community-building, then, local migration also stimulated circulation, as members of the extended family remained within walking distance of each other, enabling them to maintain social contact readily through visiting, churchgoing and perhaps family outings.

There and back: circulation

Whether on foot, by bicycle, horse and cart, boat, tram, train or, as time passed, more and more by car, circular mobility was a critical enabling force in daily life in southern Dunedin. In public space, it took residents to, from, and perhaps around sites of paid and unpaid work, as well as social intercourse and recreation: sites that were, for the most part, the preserve of either men or women, but rarely of both. Sometimes, however, their domains momentarily converged in time and place, as they did in religious worship, as well as in picnicking and gardening, yet this did not mean that at these times male and female roles coalesced and their differences dissolved. Indeed, as chapters three and nine show, the rapid growth in employment opportunities for young and unmarried women meant that an increasing proportion of those between the age of school leaving and marriage went to work. Most young men worked in the study area, but most young women, even many of those employed in domestic service, went into the city by tram or train each day. Their new experience of circulatory mobility may have engendered the confidence – and the sense of freedom and growing economic independence

– that helped make them more likely to change street address than young men. It is possible, too, that the domestic skills that young women acquired as they grew up made them more able than their brothers to live independently. Few men, whether young or old, managed without a mother, a sister or a landlady to cook, wash and mend for them.

A narrow, but richly detailed, window on this relationship between people and place, as well as on its contribution to community-building in the study area, is provided by Rachel Grimmett's diary.[50] The movement of members of the Grimmett family – women and men, older and younger – between their home and their various personal activity spaces, both close by and further away, reveals largely gender-segregated patterns of circular mobility set in the intimate context of daily life. Covering just two calendar years (1894 and 1895) near the beginning of our study period, the diary records details of day-to-day events and activities involving Rachel herself, her husband Richard and those of their adult children still living at home. The diary also gives some information on occasional visitors and contacts with adult children no longer living at home or in Dunedin, and with relatives – presumably also immigrants – in Hampden, a small town 81 kilometres north of Dunedin.

The original Grimmett family consisted of the parents and their seven sons and a daughter, all born between 1862 and 1875. Before Rachel began recording details of daily family life in the mid-1890s, however, four of the sons had married and established independent households of their own, a process that in turn added another layer of circular mobility, expressed through visiting, shared outings and other activity within the extended family. Two sons, Ernest in Ardmore Drive, Kensington, and Ezra on Caversham Rise, still lived in the study area and are frequently mentioned by Rachel Grimmett. Another son, John, had earlier migrated to Nelson with his wife Mary and appears in the diary as a correspondent by letter (and as Rachel's host when she visited Nelson), making them passive and distant, rather than active local participants in ongoing family life. A fourth son, also married, lived in David St until the early 1890s, it seems, then shifted to Wellington, and later moved to Australia; but the diary makes no mention of this son. In addition, two other children – Roland and the youngest daughter, Leah – married in the later 1890s and lived for a time in houses on either side of their parents' Caversham home.[51] Richard Grimmett served his apprenticeship as a stonemason and bricklayer in England and worked primarily for himself until his sons joined him. Each of these became a building tradesman, but neither Mrs Grimmett nor Leah (unlike most of her peers) participated formally in the paid labour market, at least not according to Rachel's diary.

Charlotte Rachel Grimmett in 'Sally' uniform and wearing a neck clasp in memory of her daughter Leah.
COURTESY OF BERT GRIMMETT

The Grimmetts were modest property-owners well before the diary was begun in 1894. Indeed, they added to their holdings during the two years it spanned. Built by Richard Grimmett in 1882, the main investment and principal public display of their social status was Faringdon Villa, their smart, owner-occupied, two-storeyed brick house, a quietly imposing edifice that still stands in Fitzroy St. They also possessed a piece of land referred to by Rachel as the 'Bush'. Although its exact location remains unclear, it was certainly, for Rachel at least, within easy walking distance of home. There the family grew a variety of produce, from flowers and vegetables to berry, stone and pip fruits, as well as grapes.

Rachel's diary entries indicate a more or less mutually exclusive division of labour and social participation between males and females. Nowhere was this as clear as in paid and unpaid work (although, in Rachel's case, as noted earlier in this chapter and in chapter three, she in fact managed the financial side of the business). These differences in turn generated very different time-space patterns of activity and linking pathways of circular mobility for Rachel and Richard, but also, though much less elaborately, for Leah and other members of the household. Although men's work within the home, as portrayed in

TO AND FROM, THERE AND BACK

the diary, was limited (most often mentioned are house alterations and shoe repairs), paid work away from Faringdon Villa was almost entirely their preserve. The women, Rachel and daughter Leah, carried out the whole range of unpaid domestic toil. They did the housework, furbished the larder, did the cooking and, almost always on Mondays, the family's washing; they knitted stockings, too, and made or bought other clothes, both for themselves and for the men.

Role separation between men and women in the Grimmett household generated a procession of usually daily flows to and from Faringdon Villa. Strongly gendered, these differed markedly from each other in mix of purposes, or activity stimuli, so creating the quite distinctive gender-specific spatial patterns captured in Maps 8.2 to 8.4. Of the family members, Leah was by far the least mobile. In most weeks she left home no more than two or three times, most often in the evening and usually with a male escort. Sometimes Leah visited brother Ezra's wife, maybe attended some social event such as the Baptist flower show, went to the railway station to farewell a relative, perhaps

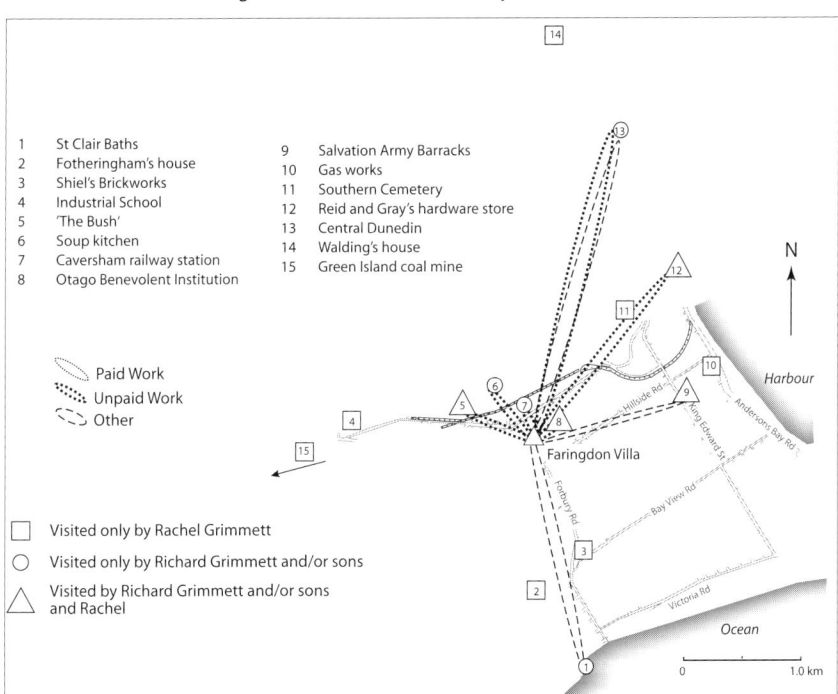

Map 8.2 A sample of circular mobility pathways traced by Rachel Grimmett between Faringdon Villa and selected activity sites in Dunedin

accompanied her mother to 'Ingles' and other shops 'in town', or with friends took a boat trip to the 'Heads'.[52]

For her part, Rachel Grimmett was much more mobile outside the home than Leah and seems to have moved as freely in the public arena as did her husband and sons. Mrs Grimmett's multi-dimensional role in the household frequently took her from the private world of Faringdon Villa onto the streets and through other public space in the study area – sometimes well beyond. Rachel was the principal manager of all accounts, both for the household and her husband's business. She prepared invoices for customers, collected payments, did the banking and paid all the bills. Much of this work involved her in interviews with debtors and creditors, and there is no doubt that her skill was critical to the success of the Grimmetts' contract building business.[53] She also oversaw family legal matters (for example, she liaised with the family lawyer about the purchase of a next-door section backing onto Surrey St, presumably as a capital investment). She spent considerable time gardening and – in a capacity that extended beyond household business – perhaps even more on community voluntary work. Most of the latter was in the name of the Salvation Army, or at least was motivated by religious conviction. Recreation took her out, too. Often in summer, sometimes with Leah or perhaps a friend, occasionally with Ezra and/or his family, but seldom with other male members of the household, Mrs Grimmett swam in the salt-water baths at St Clair, or spent time relaxing with family on the beach there.

Despite all this to-ing and fro-ing, Rachel was rather less peripatetic than the men of the household (see Maps 8.2 and 8.3). Whereas most of their daily mobility pathways were employment-related, Rachel's were mostly unrelated to paid work, although, of course, she handled many of the financial transactions generated by Richard's building business. Not only were the more important of her circular journeys less frequent than those of the men, but also, in contrast to them, her journeys were mostly on foot and rather more habitual in timing, duration, direction and activity site. This was certainly so of her regular outings to the St Clair beach and baths (Map 8.2/1); her trips to the 'supe' kitchen (Map 8.2/6); her weekly rounds of Caversham and St Clair, and to and from the 'Benny' in Alexander St (Map 8.2/8), distributing the *War Cry* and *Young Soldiers*, two Salvation Army publications; and, much less often, visiting private homes collecting 'self-denial' pledges. Indeed, circular mobility was critical to Rachel's zealous public testimony of the religious conviction that seems to have been a much more powerful driving force in her life than it was in Richard's, or in that of any of their children.

Somewhat more spasmodic, but nevertheless repeated many times, especially from spring through to autumn, were walks 'down' to and back from the 'Bush' (Map 8.2/5). There Rachel undertook a range of tasks: in season she weeded, planted and cut flowers for Faringdon Villa; thinned grapes, as she spent the whole day doing on New Year's Day 1894; picked red and black currants, as well as gooseberries, grapes, 'plumbs' and pears; 'took up' potatoes, usually with 'father'; and harvested other vegetables. Rachel Grimmett also records that she sometimes delivered, on foot and to order, quantities of some fruits – mainly grapes, plums and pears – to private homes. These are the only occasions on which diary entries signal that she herself received payment for her labour.

Rachel Grimmett's diary also allowed us to reconstruct the much more diffuse, much less predictable, map of employment-related circular pathways etched day by day over the two years by Richard Grimmett and his sons (see Map 8.3). Occasionally, one or more of them assisted their father, otherwise they tended to work alone. The frequency of movement and the amplitude of their pathways – in length, duration and location of activity sites – were largely determined by the success achieved in securing competitive contracts. Their jobs took the Grimmett men to many different sites in the city and, as

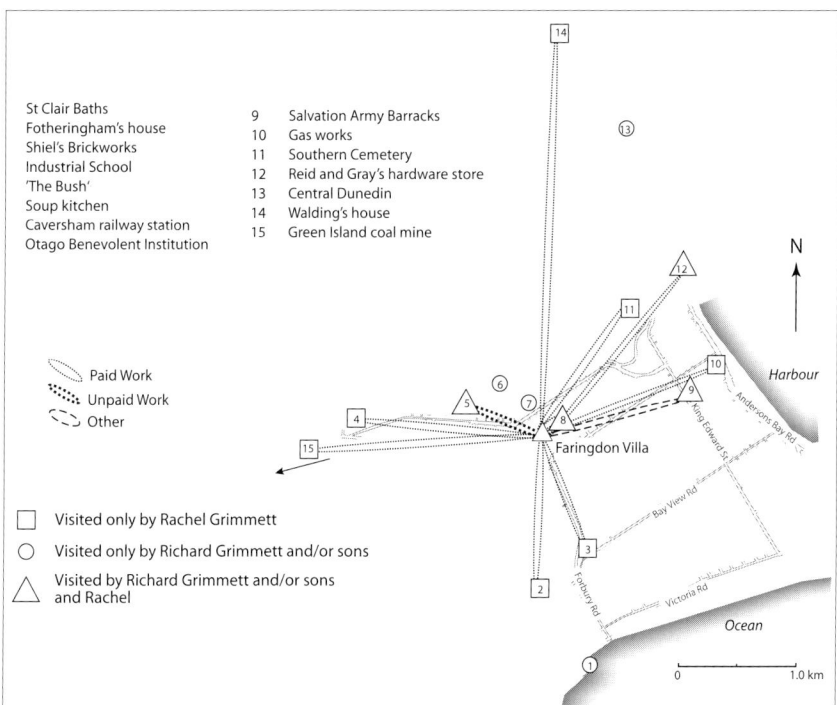

Map 8.3 A sample of circular mobility pathways traced by Richard Grimmett and sons

Richard Grimmett, stonemason, bricklayer, building contractor and father. COURTESY OF BERT GRIMMETT

discussed later, sometimes outside it. Some work was in private homes, such as Walding's in Roslyn and Fotheringham's on Allandale Rd in St Clair (Map 8.3/2 and 14), others were in public places such as the Southern Cemetery (Map 8.3/11). From time to time as well, much work was undertaken at the 'Benny' (Map 8.3/8) and at publicly owned utilities such as the gasworks (Map 8.3/10) and the Industrial School (Map 8.3/4): payment for tasks at the latter was by bank 'cheek' from Wellington. In fact, work for both central government and the local Caversham Borough 'counscell' appears to have been an important source of family income.

For Richard Grimmett and his sons, as this summary of their day-to-day job schedule implies, circular mobility was a generic trait. Journeying to and from their widely dispersed, varied and constantly changing places of work was one thing, assembling essential building supplies on site was quite another. Sons Ernest and Roland were almost always responsible for this 'young men's' heavy manual labour. Using the family's horse and cart, the sons carried a miscellany of goods between many different locations: bricks from the local works; sand from the beach; wood, window frames and roofing iron from 'town'; and cement, sand and rock aggregate from 'shiels' quarry

Faringdon Villa, a 'quietly imposing edifice' built by Richard Grimmett in Fitzroy Street in 1882. COURTESY OF BERT GRIMMETT

on Forbury Rd (Map 8.3/3). Ernest or Roland also used the family's horse and cart to run a small carrying business. For paying local customers they would often pick up and deliver a variety of goods, among them bricks and animal manure, but sometimes they ranged much further afield. Not infrequently, one or other drove over the hill as far as the Green Island mine (Map 8.3/15) to fetch coal, both for burning at Faringdon Villa and to sell.

On occasions, too, paid employment opportunities took 'father' and sometimes his sons to 'up country' work sites in provincial Otago (see Map 8.4). Such participation generated circular flows lasting much longer and covering a greater distance than the more usual daily intra-urban flows to and from Faringdon Villa. Tom spent time at Hyde, on the Central Otago rail line, and also at St Bathans, and both Ernest and Roland, as well as Mr Grimmett himself, worked for periods in Hampden. There, 'Messrs Grimmett and Sons of Caversham . . . thorough masters of their business', built the small town's new Roman Catholic church.[54]

When Richard Grimmett was working in Hampden, in January 1894, Rachel visited him, staying with maternal relatives for a week (see Map 8.4). Travelling by horse and trap between home and the Dunedin railway station,

Rachel journeyed to and from Hampden by express train. Within six months, on 19 June, however, she set out once more, again alone, on a much longer family expedition (Map 8.4). Sailing to Wellington on the *Mararoa*, she spent a few days there before boarding the *Penguin* for Nelson. After spending a month with son John and his family, Mrs Grimmett returned to Wellington for five days before embarking on the *Wairarapa*, Dunedin-bound via Lyttelton on 30 July. The diary yields no indication that Richard Grimmett took time from his paid labour to holiday, or to maintain family connections outside Dunedin, either with Rachel or alone. Our evidence on this aspect of family life suggests, classically, that the maintenance of such networks was primarily a female responsibility. Rachel was the family's fulcrum: her journeys and letters linked the extended family and kept them informed about each other. Only the oldest son and his family in Australia appear to have remained outside this network, for the diary does not mention any correspondence with him or exchange of visits.

The Grimmett family diary, then, provides unequivocal evidence of sharply gendered patterns of short- and longer-term circular mobility linking Faringdon Villa with activity sites in both private and public space.

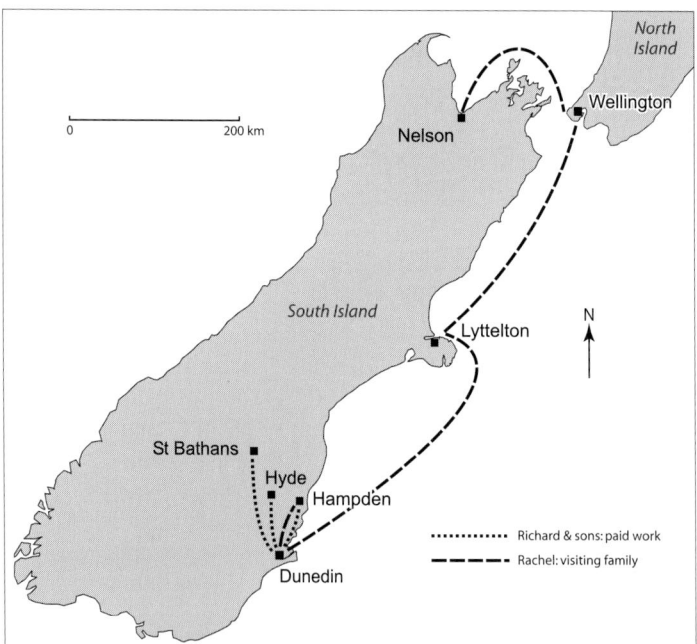

Map 8.4 A sample of circular mobility pathways between Faringdon Villa and selected activity sites outside Dunedin

Fundamentally, differences between pathways traced by the men on the one hand and by the women on the other were determined by the way in which paid and unpaid work, and social and family interaction, outside Faringdon Villa was distributed, and, on the few occasions when a male and female found themselves at the same destination, each was almost always there to engage in a different activity.

The 'Benny', places of religious worship, and the 'Bush' represent three such sites. Both Rachel and Richard went to the Benny, but did so at different times and for contrasting purposes, she in a voluntary capacity to disseminate the *War Cry* on behalf of the Salvation Army, he to undertake paid labour, and regularly to preach.[55] Sunday was clearly observed as a day of rest, diary entries for it being quite different to those for other days. Almost invariably, they are the shortest and make no mention of either paid or voluntary work, or visits to the 'Bush'. Instead, their content focuses on two aspects of family life – where and when Rachel Grimmett and 'father' worshipped on Sunday and who was and who was not home for tea that night. Sometimes the parents went together to 'knee drill' in the morning and/or at night, but as often they worshipped at different venues. While Rachel usually attended the 'Armey' service, Richard Grimmett went to the Industrial School, where he may well have been among those who led the service, as he did at the Benny every other 'Lord's Day'.

The 'Bush' was yet another site on which pathways tracked by individual members of the family converged, perhaps several times a week during the growing season. And yet gender differentiation was actually affirmed, if not enhanced, there, despite opportunities for close cooperative endeavour. This was a rare happening, however. Indeed, according to the diary, Richard and Rachel Grimmett's efforts in 'taking up' potatoes side by side in autumn was perhaps the most explicit of the few instances when work, waged or unwaged, at a site outside the walls of Faringdon Villa, coincided with an opportunity for close social interaction among male and female members of the family.

For the most part, then, the 'Bush' remained an activity site where the schedule of tasks remained sharply gendered. From time to time, Richard Grimmett and perhaps one or more sons, each usually alone, would spend half or rarely a whole day there between paid jobs. Sometimes they cleared scrub, chopped wood, cut hedges or fashioned fence posts; at other times the cultivated area was dug, drains cleaned and pathways repaired. In contrast, Rachel's visits tended to be more frequent and shorter, the tasks less onerous physically. She sowed seeds, planted out seedling cut flowers, weeded vegetables, thinned grapes and harvested vegetables as well as fruit for consumption at Faringdon Villa, or perhaps for selling on.

Although we have less evidence for them, the circulatory patterns of members of the Lebanese community offer a picture that in some respects mirrors, but in other respects contrasts, with those of the English-born Grimmetts. After their migration from the Walker St area to southern Dunedin, group cohesion and identity among the southern Dunedin Lebanese seems to have been sustained and reinforced by within-group marriage (Olga Barbara, née Facoory, for example, married a Lebanese man, as did her mother and grandmother); by the lifetime inability of at least some of the original adult migrants to speak English and their lack of naturalisation; by frequent reciprocal visiting among families; and, after 1911, by religious worship centred on St Michael's Orthodox Church in Fingall St, nearby the cluster of Lebanese households in the Anderson's Bay Rd/McBride St area.

Hawking – a specific form of circulation – was a common form of self-employment among the Lebanese and, in contrast to its common status among people of British descent as an occupation of last resort, taken up only by the incapacitated, appears to have been seen by the Lebanese as simply a form of trade: some Lebanese family fortunes were founded upon it.[56] The movement patterns of hawkers do not fit the conventional model of a short daily commuting trip to and from a stable site of employment; instead, their trips away from home involved days or weeks. George Facoory moved between home – the centre of gravity of his enterprise – his suppliers of clothes, household linen and other goods, and his customers. His circuit took him outside Dunedin, almost certainly to the south, for several days, a week, or even longer.[57] Jacob Facoory, another hawker, was usually away for several weeks, sending home earnings by money order to support his family. His circuit, which he travelled by horse and cart based at Hillgrove, in North Otago, was in rural north and eastern Otago.[58] There are fewer records of Lebanese women who hawked. The notable exception, well documented by Olga Barbara, is Sarah Hananeia (c. 1845–1927), who began hawking only after her six children were grown and her husband had died. Unlike Jacob Facoory, she hawked on foot, and she carried smaller goods, such as buttons, needles, socks and stockings, and handkerchiefs. She travelled to her circuit by train and, staying in boarding houses, spent the week selling in local towns such as Waikouaiti, Palmerston and Oamaru, returning to her family in Dunedin at weekends.[59] As hawkers, George, Jacob and Sarah all operated, in effect, within a multi-tiered circulatory mobility system: gathering goods for sale from suppliers in Dunedin; travelling to their country market-place and back to southern Dunedin; and moving around their respective selling circuits.

To and from, there and back in retrospect

The historical evidence reviewed in this chapter considerably enhances our understanding of space-time patterns of mobility expressed as local migration and circulation among the residents of Dunedin's southern suburbs during the period from the early 1890s to the late 1930s. Those like Jane Steel, at the bottom of the social order, found themselves on the move alongside the Sideys, other well-to-do locals and the middle classes. In some respects, movement and migration were colonial norms: people moved, and moved house, because movement and change seemed, for many of them, to be positive things in their own right.

Our evidence indicates that the propensity to shift residential location was unequally distributed among different groups. More mobile than most were the poor, with women in this category moving often within the study area, whereas poor men usually left it, sometimes even heading to Australia; and those immersed in critical life-cycle stages, whether just married, family-building or, especially among women, newly widowed. In addition the propensity of manual workers to move was somewhat higher than it was among the self-employed and small employers, while the less numerous upper-middle class was the least mobile of all social groups. Such a generally permissive pattern of social norms also assists our understanding of, but does not explain, the longer-term change in the gender composition of local migration based on electoral roll data. The large surplus of males so much in evidence from 1893–1902 to about 1911–19 gave way to a growing presence of women in gender ratios for the whole study area, and especially in Kensington, St Kilda and St Clair. This trend ensured that, by 1928–38, almost as many women as men were moving to homes within each of these suburbs, so significantly diluting the spatial pattern of widespread male numerical ascendancy in local migration that had persisted since 1893–1902.

Rachel Grimmett's diary, rather than the electoral roll database, or for that matter any of the other sources, provides the most compelling testimony about the connection between gender, activity site and personal mobility. In particular, evidence from the diary demonstrates that in southern Dunedin, and no doubt elsewhere, circular mobility rather than local migration supported and maintained extended family networks, as well as a sharp separation from day to day in the division of paid and unpaid work and in social roles among men (that is, Richard and his sons) and women (that is, Rachel and her daughter Leah). Gender-segregated circulatory paths also seem to have increasingly shaped the movement patterns of the young and unmarried.

The glimpse of late-Victorian middle-class family life afforded by the Grimmett diary also supports recent research by Gleeson[60] and others that contests the notion that nineteenth-century middle-class social space was rigidly gendered. In crude form, this view holds that the home was the domain of women, whereas public space was held by men in pursuit of economic gain and formal political participation. On the contrary, the reality in southern Dunedin, at least during the earlier part of our study period, appears to be more accurately captured by Law's dictum that 'activity space ... [was] not divided into a sterile dichotomy of (male) public and (female) private'.[61]

In the Grimmett household, it is true that the domestic terrain belonged, largely if not exclusively, to Rachel and her daughter. Nevertheless, Rachel Grimmett herself was a well-known figure around the streets of Caversham, St Clair, St Kilda and South Dunedin, as well as in parts of central Dunedin. In these public areas, Rachel must have had a very conspicuous presence: as accounts manager of the business, as Salvationist, as a volunteer worker and campaigner, and even as a beachgoer. Many of Rachel's activities in public space outside Faringdon Villa might be reinterpreted as a middle-class contribution to the material relief of less well-off households in the area while attacking the perceived causes of their poverty. Though hers was without doubt a rather more modest endeavour, Rachel's role in public philanthropy was not at all unlike that claimed by Gleeson for middle-class women working on behalf of the Melbourne Ladies' Benevolent Society in the last half of the nineteenth century.[62] Nor was it dissimilar to the voluntary work undertaken by the wives of businessmen and officials who belonged to the Ladies' Benevolent Committee of the Otago Benevolent Institution or the Auckland Ladies' Benevolent Society.[63]

Perhaps one should go somewhat beyond this, and ask whether Rachel Grimmett and others of her class in the 1890s, such as daughter Leah and Mrs McCracken (who sometimes did the *War Cry* round with or for Rachel and also helped at the soup kitchen), and, indeed, poorer people such as Jane Steel and hawkers such as Sarah Hananeia, were participants in a pattern of colonial social norms that considerably enhanced the ability of women to move about in the public arena. Industrialisation may have sharpened the separation of home and work among the middle classes in England and Scotland, and confined women more completely to their homes, but this had never been the case in the less industrial areas from which New Zealand had recruited most of its migrants. By the 1890s the question of women's occupation of public space was becoming an issue, as the call for the vote was supported by something as pragmatic as the call for public toilets for women.[64]

It is clear from the partial evidence presented here that Rachel Grimmett, Jane Steel, Sarah Hananeia and without doubt many other women who lived within the study area, circulated with relative freedom, though in ways quite

Hawking was a trade adopted by a number of Dunedin's Lebanese immigrants. Sarah Hananeia's son Nicholas is shown here with his horse and cart. CAVERSHAM PROJECT COLLECTION

unlike local men such as Richard Grimmett and his sons. Rachel Grimmett's diary suggests that differences between men and women lay less in their ability to be spatially mobile and rather more in the mix of movement stimuli and the collective nature of the activity sites visited by each. This is not to say that married women with small children and no baby-sitting available could move as freely as older women, whose children had grown up, or as freely as unmarried women. Household responsibilities also constrained both the freedom and circulatory mobility of married women – meals had to be ready at a precise time, clothes and laundry had to be washed and ironed each week. Unmarried women, unless they were running a household, evidently became freer to move in public spaces across the period, a process accelerated, as other chapters in this volume show, by free secondary education and the introduction of a technical college in 1908, no less than by the rapid expansion of labour-market opportunities for unmarried women. Travel to paid work, and – after 1902 – travel to secondary school, began to make being out and about a matter of normality for the cohort of young women maturing at the end of the century. Certain events, such as the war, may also have accelerated the growth in women's freedom to move. Film from the middle of the period suggests, however, that unmarried women usually moved in public with others of their sex, often friends or sisters. And, as Leah Grimmett's relatively contained mobility reveals, not all unmarried women, especially those primarily employed in the family home, spent much time beyond its confines. Indeed, our evidence points to significant differences between women on the basis of class, age, work and marital status.

Clearly, circulatory mobility underpinned the ability of people in sharply contrasting positions in society to participate in civic life and brought together quite different social and economic worlds across a range of spatial scales. Many of these relationships were shaped by imbalances of power and authority, and they transcended the boundaries of southern Dunedin, as they did from time to time in the Grimmett household (Map 8.4). At one extreme were the poor, women like Jane Steel, as well as men like Andrew Wigg and William Wright, both of whom claimed to inspectors from the Benny that to survive they had resorted to street hawking, a classic form of circulation, offering fish, 'Japanese cleanser', fruit and other goods for sale.[65] Somewhat further up the social ladder, their very mobility enabled self-employed hawkers like Sarah Hananeia and several of the Facoory men to move easily between home, relatives and friends in South Dunedin, and their provincial selling circuits in North Otago and elsewhere. Indeed, the Lebanese women, though they often moved short distances, undertook most of the circulatory movements, especially those related to building and sustaining kin (especially older Lebanese, who often could not speak English) and community networks. The heads of household, including the widow Sarah Hananeia, circulated throughout rural Otago and Southland. Circular mobility also underpinned the lifestyle of local MP Thomas Sidey, who sat at the top of the social ladder in southern Dunedin. Sidey and family spent part of the year at home in his electorate (Caversham and, from 1908, Dunedin South), attending to the needs of constituents in the industrial community that was the core of his suburban electorate, and the rest in Wellington when Parliament was in session, mixing there with the country's political elite.

Rather more problematic, as we have shown, is the identity of factors or stimuli that drove decisions to change address within the study area – in other words to make a local migration – and equally unclear is the direction of cause and effect in a number of other relationships revealed by the electoral roll data. Despite the identifiable factors of social mobility, changes in marital status and change in occupation, most moves were made for no reason now apparent. Perhaps it was simply that this society of migrants saw movement in terms of freedom and opportunity, and were well-disposed towards it. Our findings for Dunedin's southern suburbs are, moreover, in close agreement with those produced in research on more recent intra-urban mobility in culturally similar environments both in New Zealand and overseas.[66] These demonstrate that the primary stimuli of much intra-urban migration, such as occurred in southern Dunedin between 1893 and 1938, is transitional change in the life-course of families and households. Typically, such mobility takes place over relatively short distances, with households (including the newly wed) preferring to shift within the structure of their existing urban activity system(s), in order both to minimise life-course disruption, especially for children, and to maintain extended family networks and remain close to frequently used community institutions and facilities.

However, the family life-course, along with change in the micro living environment and other processes, offers a far from complete explanation of local migration within southern Dunedin. Left unexplained are intriguing nuances in the pattern of gender differentiation revealed, in particular, by the electoral roll data. Despite these lacunae, our testimony is suggestive. The data on both circulatory and migratory movement within the southern suburbs of Dunedin indicate that, over our study period, young and unmarried women became much more mobile. Their freedom to occupy public spaces undoubtedly presupposed the success of their mothers and grandmothers in quietly increasing the range of their journeys from home, to visit town, shop, work outside the home, attend the theatre or church, or involve themselves in public life. The debate over the need for toilets in Dunedin from the 1890s on provides a rhetorical marker of this shift.[67] The fact that the debate was conducted in terms of the rights of citizenship demonstrates the link to ideas of equality and freedom, ideas that had, in the Old World, been articulated to exclude women. Our evidence for southern Dunedin reinforces the contention that the newly emerging spaces of the New World were formed, as well as traversed, by women such as Rachel Grimmett.

Nine On the Streets of Southern Dunedin: Gender in Transport

ROBIN LAW

If you had been standing at the intersection then known as Ogg's Corner (later Cargill's Corner) early one morning in 1898, you would have seen throngs of people making their way to work, mostly on foot or by bicycle. To the onlooker, horsepower appeared to be the only alternative to human power as a way of moving people around the city – horses drew delivery carts, private carriages, hansom cabs, omnibuses and trams. Yet many of the men walking down the streets were local residents on their way to the Hillside Workshops, the largest industrial enterprise in southern Dunedin, where approximately 400 workers built and repaired rolling stock and steam-powered locomotives for all of New Zealand.[1] The people of southern Dunedin were thus centrally involved in a great transformation in transport technology, which involved the shift from almost total reliance on human and horsepower, to reliance on vehicles powered by steam, electricity, diesel and petroleum.

This chapter explores the gendered dimensions of that transformation.[2] As men and women, girls and boys took up new transport technologies, new social practices were formed around their use, and new cultural meanings were assigned to the technologies. Some of those transport practices and meanings were linked to shifts in gender relations over time, and the changing ways that masculinity and femininity were defined and performed. Like the previous chapter, this one explores the different ways that the men and women of southern Dunedin moved around the city, but it is distinguished by a focus on 'the street' as a setting and symbolic space, and by attention to changing transport technologies and institutions.

The last hansom cab driver in Dunedin – and, it is believed, in New Zealand – retired in 1938.[3] By this date, if you found yourself once again

Ogg's (later Cargill's) Corner, looking along King Edward St, early 1900s. A horse and cart shares the street with a tram. A bicycle leans against a post and children appear to be playing in the street. Ogg's Corner was the Flat's transport hub and one of its two commercial centres. MUIR AND MOODIE COLLECTION, TE PAPA TONGAREWA, MUSEUM OF NEW ZEALAND

on Ogg's Corner, you would have seen pedestrians, cyclists and occasional horse-drawn carts as before, but also electric trams, motor cycles, cars and lorries. Paving had been improved, electric lighting and telephones installed, public transport infrastructure extended, and the array of bustling shops along the street reflected new patterns of urban circulation. In the four decades from 1898 there was probably a greater variety in modes of transport available in Dunedin (as elsewhere in urban New Zealand) than at any other time before or since.

In popular writing, advances in transport technology are commonly deployed to denote the march of progress, often as part of a celebratory narrative tracing the triumph of human ingenuity over time and space. Scholarly attempts to define modernity have also been attentive to the impact of transport technologies on social life and culture in the twentieth century, noting, for example, the newly available pleasures of speed, artistic attempts to represent the visual appeal of machinery, and the role of transport in extending the power and influence of a metropolitan centre. More specifically, the subjective experience of moving through city streets as part of an anonymous urban crowd has been central to Western notions of individual consciousness in the 'modern' period.[4] A simple overview of urban transport this century suggests a narrative of ever-expanding opportunities for mobility and choice.

Yet, as feminist geographers and historians have argued, once the implications for men and women are examined separately, the story becomes more ambiguous.[5] The introduction of new modes of transport and corresponding changes in accessibility across the urban environment profoundly affected the spatial and temporal organisation of economic and social life, with different implications for men and women. By focusing our gaze on 'the street' as a setting where technology is deployed, it is possible to trace how gender and transport technology interacted over time to shape new patterns of gendered daily mobility. 'The street' is used here to include transport infrastructure and the spaces inside vehicles. Gender difference is expressed through subtle differences in where, when, why and how men and women travel, and what it means for them to be 'on the street', but gender is also crosscut by other forms of social difference, such as class and age.

In the first part of this chapter, a brief overview of the changing transport system in southern Dunedin from the 1860s to the 1940s is presented. This is followed by four sections that discuss changes in transport technology between 1898 and 1938, with reference to the street as a setting where gender difference is produced, and with attention to the worlds of work (both paid employment and unpaid labour) and leisure. The argument is not that technology 'caused' any particular social outcome, or that gender relations gave rise to a particular form of technology. Neither do I argue that the uses of transport technology simply reflected gender relations. Instead, I attempt to unpick the contested and complex processes by which technologies of transport were adopted, framed, given meaning and abandoned in a particular gendered historical context, and the sometimes unintended consequences that arose.

Changing transport technologies 1860–1940

In the 1860s, a range of horse-drawn contrivances passed along the streets of southern Dunedin: commercial carriers, private cabs for wealthy families and horse cabs for hire. Bicycles were introduced in the late 1860s, and prams with iron or rubber wheels appeared in the 1890s. The major streets of Dunedin were mostly formed of packed metal or loose gravel, but elsewhere the surface was plain earth – muddy in winter, dusty in summer.[6] These conditions presented challenges to pedestrians, too, though with slightly different implications for men and women. According to one writer: 'Princes Street in wet weather was a sea of mud, with crossings of "long flax" thrown down for foot passengers, and it was not an uncommon spectacle to see young ladies carried over by their men friends.'[7]

From about 1875 the growth of Dunedin's population stimulated attempts to introduce public transport services, often by developers such as David Proudfoot. Mass public transport was introduced to southern Dunedin in 1880, in the form of trams pulled by horses along tramlines laid in the road (a brief experiment with steam-powered trams was later tried but abandoned). Although intra-urban railway travel in Dunedin was never as important as in some other New Zealand cities, by 1901 the busiest railway line in Dunedin carried sixteen trains a day.[8]

At the turn of the century, two significant events took place that foreshadowed the future of transport on Dunedin's streets. The initial event was Dunedin's first electric tram journey in 1900. This set the scene for the subsequent electrification of the tram service, and its development into the substantial civic institution that was providing more than ten million trips each year just ten years later. The second significant event was the arrival in 1901 of the first car (a Locomobile), imported to Dunedin from the United States by W. L. Kempthorne, followed three months later by another American car, a Pope-Toledo.[9] The arrival of the car signalled the beginning of the trend towards the form of private transport that is the defining feature of our streets today.

Opening of the cycling season in Dunedin on 19 October 1901. This group relaxing at Second Beach, St Clair, indicates the popularity of cycling with both women and men. *OTAGO WITNESS*, 20 NOVEMBER 1901

Although the electric tram and the car both arrived on Dunedin streets at almost the same time, the trajectory of their adoption in the city was rather different. Electric trams (along with cable cars) became the dominant transport technology in the next three decades. The timing, routes and fares of the trams were such that access became available to a very wide segment of society. In fact, the historical evidence suggests that opportunities for mobility within the city were extended in a way that diminished social inequalities of gender (as well as age and class). During the first quarter of the century, the dominant modes of walking, cycling and 'tramming' were available to just about every able-bodied person, and they brought masses of urban residents into social contact with each other, thus creating shared experiences that strengthened the development of a sense of civic society.

In contrast, the private car was taken up much more slowly, and in a way that highlighted gender, age and class difference and removed individuals from communal urban experiences. Car ownership and driving expertise came to be associated with masculinity – specifically with a masculinity where Father sat firmly in the driving seat, encapsulated within the private space of the family car. Until after the Second World War, the high cost of vehicles and petrol tended to put cars beyond the reach of all but the affluent. In the long run, the rise of private transport had a dual effect, however: it not only improved the mobility of those with access to a car, providing a new indicator of wealth and status, but it also indirectly reduced the mobility of those without access to a vehicle, for, as car-owning individuals withdrew their patronage from public transport, the range and frequency of the service was diminished.

Thus we can understand the shift in transport technologies over the study period in terms of these two overlapping but contradictory developments. In the earlier part of the study period, the trend was towards increased mobility, greater opportunity and a more communal public life, brought about by improved transport infrastructure facilitating walking, cycling and tramming. In the later part of the study period, the trend was to even greater mobility and opportunity for a few (that is, those with access to a private vehicle), but, eventually, at the cost of reduced mobility and opportunity for others, in both absolute and relative terms.

By 1903 the city tramlines, now under the control of the City Corporation, were electrified and horses began to be phased out. An electrified tram system was introduced to Caversham, St Kilda and St Clair in 1905, soon followed by a service to Carisbrook.[10] Trams appeared every few minutes along the busiest routes. Tram fares were generally affordable at a penny a section; for threepence, one could travel the length of the city.

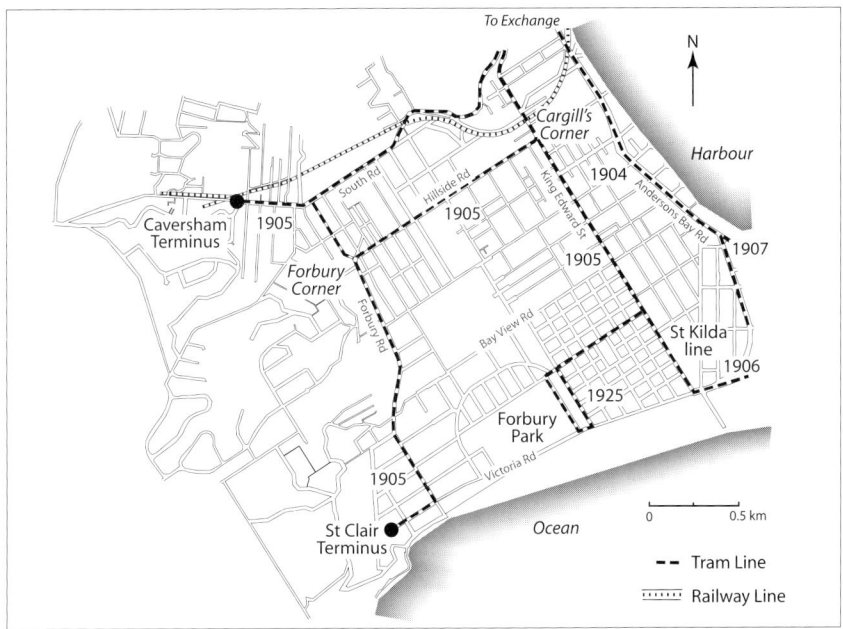

Map 9.1 Electric tramway routes and opening dates, 1890–1939

Concessions for special groups extended access to many. In 1911 the seventeen different kinds of concessions included reductions for volunteers (in uniform and out), for girl scouts and boy scouts, and for police and detectives.[11] 'Workers' cars' ran at peak times at a reduced fare, and apprentices and factory hands were eligible for cheaper tickets.[12] The chairman of the Tramways Committee noted in 1914 that, 'I have based concessions on a basis of encouraging cheap riding to the suburban termini – as the farthest off section is the least paying – and giving bona fide residents the advantage of being taken to and from work at the lowest remunerative price, and to include those younger members of the family who are learning trades.'[13] This suggests that the extension of mobility and access to a wide pool of citizens – particularly those in paid work – was seen as a civic goal.

By the 1920s bicycles thronged the streets at peak times. One resident recalled that 'it was just a stream of biking traffic in those days'.[14] Motor cycles were becoming more common, and those with sidecars could carry several people. The number of cars in New Zealand rose rapidly from 40,000 in 1920 to 71,000 in 1925.[15]

In Dunedin, the first cars were largely owned by doctors and wealthy business and professional people, such as Dr Emily Siedeberg, Thomas Sidey

George Methven sits astride the first car made in Dunedin, made by himself in his own backyard in Sydney St, Rockyside, in 1903. The car had a four horse-power petroleum engine and was about seven feet long. The motor-cycle proved more popular (and cheaper) than the automobile until, in the 1920s, the relative economies began to shift. In 1916 there were only 267 cars and 301 motor cycles registered in Dunedin; by 1924 private car registrations had risen to 946, a figure that does not include the vans and lorries that had begun to drive the horse from the streets. OTAGO WITNESS, 11 MARCH 1903

(who owned a series of Model T cars) and the McCracken family of grocers. Although men were more likely to be driving the first cars, women drivers (such as Dr Siedeberg) were not unknown. As early as 1901, an article in the *Lyttelton Times* (Christchurch) referred to Mrs Goodwin, the lady driver of a motor car.[16] By 1935 there were 143,000 cars registered in New Zealand, and this grew to 384,000 by 1955.[17]

Trams still dominated the streets during the 1920s. Table 9.1 shows the growth in population, passenger numbers and passengers per tram mile. It is notable that, although the estimated population served grew by only about 4 per cent between 1909 and 1912, the number of passengers carried grew by more than 20 per cent. On average, by 1912 each member of the population served by trams in Dunedin would have travelled on the trams more than

300 times a year. Passengers and the population served grew in the 1920s, but tram travel then declined somewhat. Nationally, the years of highest patronage were 1926 and 1927, when trams carried 167 million passengers. This total was not surpassed until the Second World War, when some 220 million passengers were carried in 1944 and 1945.[18]

Table 9.1 Selected aspects of tram travel in Dunedin, 1909–1943

	Estim Pop. Dunedin	No. passengers	Tram car miles	Average pass./mile	Average trips per person pa
1909	40,000	11,015,026	1,096,447	10.04	275
1910	40,000	11,380,473	1,104,245	10.3	285
1912	42,000	13,300,137	1,279,854	10.39	317
1926	76,000	22,434,073	na	12.51	295
1935	78,000	17,319,035	na	10.36	222
1943	73,000	19,000,174	na	12.35	260

Source: 1909, 1910, 1912 Annual Reports of Tramways Manager, Dunedin City Council Archives; Stewart, *Always a Tram in Sight*, for 1926, 1935, 1943 figures.

We turn now to a more specific question: how was gender produced on the streets of southern Dunedin? The first of four sections discusses work on the street.

The street as a workplace for men

Although the occupations related to transport changed over the decades (a decline in farriers, stablehands and coachbuilders being countered by a rise in engineering labourers, tram conductors and petrol pump attendants), men continued to predominate in the broadly defined transport sector. Modes of transport from horse carriages to bicycles to trams to taxis were largely built, sold, operated and managed by men. Hawkers, carters, delivery boys and messengers all spent a large part of their working day on the streets. For example, in southern Dunedin before the First World War, Chinese market gardeners sold all their produce by hawking it from door to door on baskets attached to a bamboo pole carried across the vendor's shoulders. On the whole, the street was a male site of work.

According to Stone's directories, the numbers of people employed in horse-related transport in Otago and Southland halved between 1903 and 1920, while the number who worked in the cycle trade doubled by 1912, subsequently declining somewhat (see Table 9.2).

The job losses associated with transition to new transport modes were not passively accepted. When the premises of David Proudfoot's tram service burned down in 1880, it was widely believed that angry hansom cab drivers had been involved. But new technology also offered entrepreneurial opportunities. For example, the present-day firm of Cooke Howlison began the century as bicycle manufacturers, but by 1907 Messrs Cooke and Howlison were importing and selling motor cars. The growing role of the car was signalled locally by the opening of a service station at the intersection of King Edward and Bridgman streets in 1928.[19] Apart from the Hillside Workshops, employment on the railway was particularly common in southern Dunedin; according to Stone's directory for 1884, clusters of railway workers lived near to each other on several streets.[20]

Table 9.2 Number of Otago and Southland businesses in transport-related occupations, 1903–20

Occupation	1903	1912	1920	1929	1939
Horse-related:					
Horse trainers and dealers	40	n/a	n/a	n/a	n/a
Livery stable keepers	39	74	27	11	4
Saddlers, harness makers and importers	92	75	60	54	41
Other:					
Cycle makers, importers and repairers	25	56	38	49	53
Motor Car Importers, Dealers and Repairers	0	26	112	187	183

Source: Stone's Trade Directories, 1903, 1912, 1920, 1929, 1938. NB that the category 'horse trainers and dealers' was incorporated in 'Livery stable keepers' from 1912.

The consistently masculine nature of this occupational realm presents a useful example of the construction of masculinity and how this changed over time. As transport technology changed and physical strength became less significant, new characteristics were incorporated into occupational definitions of transport-related jobs. But, because these occupations continued to be largely male preserves (in contrast to some other sectors, such as office work), the defining characteristics of the transport workforce tell us something about new constructions of masculinity emerging in this era, and how they intersect with other trends in workplace relations.[21]

Snowdon, writing about the railways in nineteenth-century Britain, argues that the railways 'crystallise quintessentially "modern" ideas, experiences, institutions and structures'.[22] He identifies strands of modernity (particularly bureaucratic domination) in the way that work was organised on the railways, including meticulous timekeeping, strict discipline, high levels of surveillance through a system of inspectors, visible hierarchies and authority marked by the widespread use of uniforms, and the provision of opportunities for rational recreation and self-improvement.[23]

A study of archived documents related to the Dunedin Tramways Department reveals the extent to which these strands of modernity were echoed

ON THE STREETS OF SOUTHERN DUNEDIN

Fred Cooke and Edward (Ted) Howlison test a Clement Garrard tricycle, Cooke driving and Howlison (16 stone) providing ballast, 1904. Frederick Augustus Cooke, son of a chemist in Christchurch, trained as a brass finisher and arrived in Dunedin in 1895 aged 25 having heard that there was 'a jolly good opening' here for a bicycle shop. Howlison, a crack cyclist, became Cooke's partner and they opened for business in 1895. Cooke built his own bicycles, named 'Record', and by 1903 was also making the Record Featherweight Motorcycle, 'Guaranteed to climb any hills in Otago without assistance'. Cooke Howlison also obtained the agency for several famous brands and in 1907 imported their first car. By 1930 Cooke Howlison had become one of the largest car importers and garages in Otago and had given up bicycles and motorcycles. Cooke had married in 1897 and settled in St Kilda, his daily trip back and forth to town a matter of obsessive interest to young devotees. See John Marsh's entry in *Southern People* and Mark Henderson, *History of the Motorcycle Trade in Dunedin 1900–1983*, Dunedin, 1983. COOKE HOWLISON PHOTO, COURTESY OF COOKE HOWLISON

locally. The documents also reveal traces of the ideal of masculinity current in that workplace. By 1909 the staff of the Tramways Department in Dunedin numbered 187, in occupations such as motormen, conductors and track repairers. Although occupations are not classified by gender in the archival records, the evidence suggests that the jobs (with the possible exception of the typist and some clerical staff) were overwhelmingly held by men. It was only during the First World War that New Zealand's first woman tram conductor was employed (in Oamaru).[24]

The Tramways Department (like those elsewhere in the country) was organised on a semi-military model, with uniforms and a clear hierarchical distinction among occupations. This is expressed in one annual report, where the tramways manager refers to his staff in military terminology as 'officers and men'. Men who worked for the department were also provided with opportunities to improve their physical fitness in appropriately manly ways, even as technology was reducing the need for physical strength. In 1912 a new recreation room was to be provided and a request was made for equipment, including boxing gloves, a punching ball, trapeze, ladder, rings and climbing ropes. The latter four were to be made by men in the department, revealing another dimension of masculine skill.[25]

The shifting patterns in the ways in which work defined masculinity, discussed in chapter three, are evident here also. Although many of the jobs in the Tramways Department were physically demanding, the notion of masculinity generated by the Tramways Department was not built solely on physical power and competence. In general in this period, as technological change reduced the need for brute physical strength and endurance in the workplace, other personal characteristics came to be highlighted, and used as the basis for promoting and disciplining staff, especially into positions involving control of machinery. According to the tramways manager, the key qualifications for a motorman were 'a cool head, nerve, and judgement'.[26]

The application of these standards did not go unchallenged. In 1911, a deputation of conductors who believed that they were being unfairly prevented from sitting the examination to become motormen visited the mayor. They put forward some reasons why they believed they were eligible, including

A group of men employed by the Dunedin Tramways Corporation, dressed in their working garb. HOCKEN LIBRARY

physical fitness, their status as married men with families, and length of service. In reply, the tramways manager argued that these issues were irrelevant, and that the key was whether or not the manager believed a man to be suitable to sit the exam. He argued that, 'You must remember that there is a responsibility in placing a man on a tram car. You are overlooking this point – that in the mind of the Manager he might not have nerve, which is the most important point.'[27] In this clash of definitions, the men were implicitly drawing on the new ethos of 'settled' suburban masculinity in arguing for what kind of man made a good worker; the manager's ideal worker is much more akin to a soldier. We might even suggest that, as technology 'demasculinised' occupations by reducing the need for strength, so military practices were brought in more powerfully to maintain their masculine nature and reinforce authority. Military echoes are evident in the manager's final comments, which stress his commitment to maintaining the line of command: 'If the men form the opinion that they can entirely ignore their Manager in matters of this kind, this would, in my opinion, have a disastrous effect on the discipline of the service, and it is well-known that no tramway service can be safely or profitably run without strict discipline.'[28]

The tramways provide a particularly interesting example of shifting notions of appropriate masculine behaviour in the context of changing technology and changing levels of militarisation during the study period. Because the work site for motormen, conductors and inspectors was so public, and because tramways staff tended to be seen as carrying a certain level of civic responsibility, changes in the gendered nature of these jobs were likely to carry some significance in the wider community, including southern Dunedin. We turn now to another aspect of the street as work site: its importance as the conduit for supplies of goods and services into the household, a process largely managed by women.

The street and the home as a workplace for women

Ruth Schwartz Cowan, in her important study of housework in the USA, identifies transport as one of eight key arenas of technological transformation.[29] This reminds us that responsibility for domestic work includes managing the movement of supplies into the home, and managing the movement of children. Most of the women with household responsibilities in southern Dunedin during the study period were reliant on walking and the tram service. In many ways, the transport system that served their domestic work was more efficient and less demanding than the system available to contemporary suburban housewives.

In the 1920s, when this photograph was taken, many goods were delivered to the household, or at least to the better-off. J. R. Brown's Hygienic Bakery delivered to Mary Redwood's mother, who rang in her order. As the twentieth century passed the truck became more economical than the horse for shorter and shorter trips until by the 1930s horse transport had become a rarity in urban areas. This picture shows the mix of transport modes still used, with the internal combustion engine now preeminent. The departing truck, probably delivering coal to the baker, is a Dennis, armed with an innovative system of gate gears, owned by McCracken Bros, one of Caversham's largest grocers. The delivery vans are Dodges. OTAGO SETTLERS MUSEUM

A key component of the transport arrangements pertaining to household work was the practice of delivering goods to homes. Milk was delivered daily in a 'billy outside the door' and coal was delivered regularly. Fruit and vegetables were initially sold by hawkers, who walked from door to door, and later sold from the back of a van. Households established accounts at local butchers, grocers, greengrocers and larger bakeries, and relied on deliveries by some butchers, chemists and grocers. If no one was at home, the delivery boy often simply took the goods into the house through the (usually unlocked) back door and unpacked them in the kitchen.[30]

Telephones could be used to order goods, but they remained relatively rare. By 1922 only 8 per cent of the households in Caversham had a telephone.[31] In its absence, children as messengers were an essential part of the household communication system. Children often repaid favours, or earned a penny, by running messages for neighbours. Mary Redwood, whose mother did use the telephone, recalled that:

> When I can remember my mother used the telephone. We had down Cargill Road, we had a lot of stores. We had a chemist, we had the butcher, Brown's the Baker, good vegetable shops, two butchers, a fish shop over the road. Mother had her regular butcher and things were ordered. The groceries were delivered.

Meat wasn't delivered so we were the ones who used to have to run down after school to get it. But there were no supermarkets. My mother never went down the shop with a basket to get messages. We were the runners. She had done all the ordering by phone in the morning.³²

Housewives needed to leave the house to pay bills and to do other kinds of shopping. Small children were taken out in a pram, which could be hooked to the front of the tram car. But children were also independently mobile from quite an early age. They walked alone or with other children to local primary schools, and took a tram to the more distant secondary schools, and they walked or cycled to other activities. As Mary Redwood again recalled: 'Mother didn't take us to town to get our hair cut, we were sent over with a sixpence or a shilling. We had to sit with all the old men at the barber shop.'³³

The spatial and temporal isolation of the housewife from the world of paid work was mediated by the widespread practice of a shared midday meal. Although some men took a cut lunch to work, others returned home for a hot meal, and schoolchildren and adult children in employment often rushed home by tram for a hurried meal before catching a return tram. Consequently, peak periods for tram use included the 12 noon to 2 p.m. period, as well as morning and evening journeys. Helen Wilson (born in 1909) remembers coming home from secondary school for the midday meal: they had to 'get that nine – nine minutes past twelve car home, and the dinner would be on the table, and then we'd all go back'.³⁴

At the beginning of the period, domestic work was largely reliant on deliveries, door to door sales, and goods and services that could be bought in the local area. In 1900, there were more than fifty businesses in Forbury Corner, Main South Rd and David St. Once the tram service became established, local shops located at major tram stops flourished, concentrating retail in distinct nodes. In southern Dunedin, the junction of the Ocean Beach tram route and the Caversham Valley lines helped the South Dunedin commercial centre to grow, and a small regional centre developed at the tram terminus in Caversham. However, the tram service also made the city centre more accessible. In the 1920s the large department stores attracted many women from all over Dunedin, and their role in providing handsome ladies' restrooms and places to eat suggested their importance in facilitating 'a day in town'.³⁵ This did somewhat constrain the growth of local shops. Only sixteen new premises were erected in South Dunedin's shopping precinct between 1905 and 1930, and food stores continued to predominate.³⁶

Although the circumstances of individuals may have varied, it seems that, over the first four decades of the century, housewives benefited from

Walking on Second Beach Road, St Clair, by the Salt Water Baths. While these people are walking for pleasure beside the sea, walking was, for many people, a primary and enjoyable means of getting around the town. Workmates often walked to their workplaces together. Young people might walk to and from evening dances in groups. OTAGO SETTLERS MUSEUM

an expansion in the variety of ways that goods could be acquired and transported into the house. Deliveries continued, sites of consumption in the local area and in the city centre grew more numerous (see chapter five), and shopping venues became more accessible to most housewives. It was only once car ownership became more pervasive that commercial enterprises in the local centres declined significantly.

Although it is useful to think of the street as an actual work site, or as part of the infrastructure supporting the home as work site, a more obvious use of the street is as the setting for movement between home and paid work. The choices that men and women made about how they travelled to and from work revealed the underlying gendered structure of labour markets in urban space, but also contributed to building up common-sense understandings of gender difference. We turn now to explore how gender was constructed in daily employment-related commuting by both men and women.

The street as the setting for the journey to paid work

Contemporary studies of Western cities repeatedly find that women tend to be employed closer to home than men, suggesting that they are constrained in their ability to seek work within a wider urban labour market by factors such as less access to private transport, relatively higher transport costs relative to wages, and less flexibility about time.[37] Did the same pattern apply to the employed men and women resident in southern Dunedin at the turn of the century? It is difficult to be sure, in the absence of comprehensive information linking home and work site. Since most employment in Dunedin was in small enterprises such as shops and workshops (many employing both men and women), it is important not to make generalisations on the basis of the records that exist for large enterprises. But it is worth noting that the high degree of occupational segregation in industry at the time meant that many Dunedin factories employed either predominantly men or women. In consequence, the specific mix of industries in an area could profoundly shape the gendering of the local labour market.

In southern Dunedin, there were several very large enterprises that recruited exclusively men, such as the Hillside Workshops and the gasworks, but only a few that recruited significant numbers of women: the Wax Vesta match factory is perhaps the best remembered. Dunedin's largest sites of female employment were all outside the Flat: Ross and Glendining knitting mills, the woollen mills at Mosgiel and Roslyn, Hallenstein's Clothing Factory, DIC and other stores and offices around the Exchange. Given this pattern of gender segregation among large enterprises, it is conceivable that the employed women of southern Dunedin might have faced journey-to-work trips that were, on average, about the same length as the commuting trips undertaken by the local population of employed men. In fact, it seems likely that a reversal of the general pattern occurred, where women living in southern Dunedin might have travelled longer average distances to their jobs than men did. Most of them also used public transport as they travelled into the Exchange, then the city's hub.

How did the modes of transport used change over time, and were there significant differences between men and women? Oral histories offer some useful – although partial – insights. In the early decades of the century, walking, cycling and tram travel were all common modes, and both men and women used them, although perhaps in different proportions. Informants in the Transport (Transcript Series Three) interviews for the Oral History Project who grew up in the southern suburbs recalled how their father went to work (this would have been between about 1915 and 1935). Of the ten men, two walked regularly, two cycled, one drove a car, three took the tram regularly, and the other two used the tram as well as walking or cycling on occasion. When the informants themselves began paid work (from about age fourteen – after 1925), they initially relied on walking (four) or the tram (six). Subsequently, three of them each bought a bicycle and began using that. Cars were not commonly used as a way of getting to work until much later. Christine King (born 1922) reports that, even when their family got their first car in 1938, her father did not take it to work: 'it wasn't usual for people to use that sort of transport'.[38] Those from more affluent families may have had access to a family motor car – in some cases, the car was bought by a father or grandfather and the younger members of the family (men and women) served as chauffeur.

Walking was regarded as the obvious mode to choose when distances were fairly short, and there were many work sites (especially for men) within easy walking distance of homes: 'We would see people regularly, droves of people you might say, walking to work in the morning at the same time.'[39] For longer distances, walking was often preferred for the penny or two tram fare saved. Young men and women would have both been earning fairly low wages, which might have encouraged walking or cycling. In fact, male apprentices would have earned even less than young women in shops and offices, and so young men might have been even more likely than women to walk to save money.

Walking also offered the benefits of exercise and social life. Mavis Liverpool (born 1923) remembers that from St Kilda 'there used to be groups of people walked to town every day and walk back home again. You know, office men did in groups.'[40] Distances were extensive by today's standards. As a young woman in her teens, Marion Cooper (born 1925) and a group of friends from Caversham would walk out to St Clair beach in the morning to swim, come home for breakfast, and then walk to work.[41] Over time, the importance of walking as a transport mode declined, as other transport modes became more accessible, and as local employment opportunities diminished.

But, though walking was available to men and women, bicycles – like the motor cycles and cars more common in the future – were much more likely to be owned by men. Four of five oral-history informants who were asked about gender differences replied that men were more likely to travel to work by bicycle than women. They also reported that men were more likely to own and ride bicycles all through their lives, and to use them for purposes apart from work trips. Every one of the six men who were asked about it remembers owning a bike in his youth, but only two-thirds (sixteen out of twenty-two) of the women said the same.[42] Of the ten informants questioned further about their parents' transport practices, four recalled their father using a bicycle, but not one reported their mother riding a bicycle in their lifetime.[43] Stuart Sidey reported that his mother had been a keen member of the University Bicycle Club in the 1890s before she was married, but had not cycled after marriage.[44] Cycling after marriage for women did not seem to be proscribed

This pair of young cyclists in 1917 pose outside a house in the suburb of Tainui, just outside the study area. While the matching poses and their merry expressions suggest younger women's enthusiastic adoption of cycling and the fun and freedom that bicycles offered, it was men who took up motorcycles, like the one the young man is seated on here. They are parked on a well-surfaced driveway with a garage in the background, suggesting that the household may have owned a motor car. HOCKEN LIBRARY

(some informants reported memories of married women and old ladies cycling around the neighbourhood), but was nonetheless not common.

Gender differences in cycling as a way of getting to work were probably not primarily due to variations in income. For the young men and women in their first jobs in the late 1920s and 1930s, weekly earnings were similar and bicycles were often their first major purchase when they 'got in the money'. Mavis Liverpool recalls that, 'It was the trend to get bikes when we got them', and remembers putting a pound down and paying it off at five shillings a week: 'Because a lot of places in South Dunedin had factories and they all walked and when you got at work a while, you got a bike and you biked.'[45]

More striking than gender differences in ability to pay were gender differences in self-perceived competence and interest. Women interviewed for the oral histories often recounted comical stories of their difficulties in learning to ride a bicycle. Christine King (born 1922) tells of her experience: 'I thought to myself, "I'll try the bike." Nobody was about . . . . I went down the hill. Halfway down I got so frightened and I was going so fast that I jumped off. I bowled across the road and hit somebody's fence. I never let on to everybody. The bike went careering down the hill on its own. It was terrifying.'[46]

Public teasing reinforced the theme of feminine fear and incompetence. After Phyllis Crossan (born 1922) had buckled her bicycle front wheel by riding into a lilac tree while employed in Central Otago, her family sent her a new bicycle through the post with a big sign reading, 'This bike is guaranteed to ride through people's gardens', evoking mirth among her co-workers.[47] A self-deprecating attitude to their mechanical competence pervades the interviews today, in phrases such as, 'I couldn't even ride a rocking horse.'[48] These differences in self-image probably had a considerable effect on gendered patterns of cycle use.

Over the study period cycling may have declined somewhat in popularity, as motor traffic increased and roads became more dangerous. But, perhaps more significantly, towards the end of the 1920s bicycles were overshadowed by the great rise in popularity of motor cycles. It is at this point that gender differences in access to transport resources began to establish themselves more strongly. Although motor cycles were rapidly acquired by young men and were used for commuting, there is little evidence in Dunedin of women riding motor cycles on their own, rather than as passengers.

Although cars were no longer a rarity by the end of the study period, relatively few people would have used them simply as a way of getting to work. More often the car was kept in the garage for weekends, and the workers in the household continued to commute by tram or on foot. Those who used a car in the course of their work might have commuted by car, and they tended to be older, more affluent business and professional men, especially doctors.[49]

By 1938, the end of the study period, gender differences in the journey to work were becoming embedded. Although tram, cycle and foot were still widely used modes of transport, they were now supplemented by the relatively costly private motor vehicles (motor cycle and car) that tended to be more closely associated with the men in the household. Men were more likely to learn to drive and were most involved as enthusiasts in the early years of motoring. Informants remembered their fathers' interest in motor vehicles: Helen Tweed (born 1914) recalled that her father was a founder of the Otago Motor Club[50] and Loma Kent-Johnston (born 1918) reported that her father was a foundation member of the local branch of the Automobile Association.[51] The following anecdote epitomises the cultural norm of men and women's different interest in vehicles, and the transgression involved when an object coded as male occupies a space coded as female: '... either my father or my brother bought a motorbike . . . . And they brought this bloody motorbike into the kitchen and they started it up inside, and the noise was something frightful, and my mother was saying, "Oh Rolf, dear, do you have to have that going?"'[52]

By the end of the study period, then, the relative equivalence between employed men and women in terms of daily mobility was on the brink of shifting decisively in men's favour as motor vehicles were confirmed as a largely masculine domain. Finally, we turn to examine the street as the locale for social life and the setting for trips not related to work.

The street as a setting for social interaction

At the beginning of the period, the poor conditions of the street and the limited transport system meant that streets did not function as particularly significant social settings. The provision of mass public transport in Dunedin, as elsewhere in the world, changed all that. The rise of mass public transport meant that males and females of all ages and a wide range of social classes were brought together in settings that were not highly regulated by traditional forms of social control.[53] To some extent this generated new forms of surveillance and social regulation, but it also opened up possibilities for new mobility and freedom.

At the start of the century, traffic levels in southern Dunedin were low enough that children could safely play in all but the main streets. Even in those streets with tramlines, the regularity of the tram service lent predictability to the street environment. Class inflected the connotations of playing on the

'Out for an "Airing".' While 'trolleys' were mainly a boys' preserve, here a young girl transports an infant with a look of delight. Handcarts and prams were used for carrying all sorts of goods and, as in this instance, children. Children had a great deal of fun assembling carts from whatever they could find and using them in their games. *OTAGO WITNESS CHRISTMAS ANNUAL*, 1941

The gender segregation space within trams is evident in this photograph, where men stand on the open middle section while women sit inside. Judging by the prams hanging on the outside of the tram, at least two of the women inside would have had babies on their laps. HOCKEN LIBRARY

street: someone who grew up in St Clair remembers that this definitely 'wasn't done'.[54] Children's games did indicate an expectation that boys would be more interested in transport technology, as in this recollection: 'Simple you know, girls playing skipping and hop scotch out in the street. Boys went round with a football and all that sort of thing.... Boys just had to have a trolley... well, most of the boys made it themselves. They managed to get some wheels from somewhere and most boys had a trolley in those days.'[55]

Once trams became common, they provided a social setting where class and gender boundaries might be breached by social contact. Children attending secondary school usually travelled on the tram. Although not supervised by parents, they came under the surveillance of the conductor and other regular travellers. Children were expected to give up their seats for older people, and many of the photographs of Dunedin trams show schoolchildren standing. Helen Wilson (born 1909) remembers that, 'We felt that the people on the cable cars watched us on the trams, they watched us, they watched to see if all the people were there. They sort of took us under their wing. You know when we'd stand in line, "Oh, the Wilson girls are not here", or somebody else is not here, they – it was very personal.'[56]

The spaces inside the trams were also clearly (though unofficially) demarcated by gender, providing a microcotago settlers museum of the 'separate spheres' of men and women. There were various kinds of tram carriages in Dunedin, and most of them seem to have been understood to be demarcated into an open area in the middle, where boys over about fourteen years of age and men stood, and the closed parts at the ends, where women and children could sit or stand. The seats on the outside were also usually occupied by men and boys. Although there were no formal rules, this division of space was well understood and maintained by social pressures. Marion Cooper remembers this with some amusement:

> The boys, bigger boys, would always sit outside. But I know one family, the boy you know was sort of a real 'mother's boy', you know. They always used to come and squeeze up in the seats beside their mother inside. We thought that was funny. Why didn't he sit outside with the men, you know? But he used to come and sit tucked up inside beside their mothers. Mother's boys. Isn't it awful what you think when you're kids?[57]

By the end of the study period this rule may have been less honoured, as photographs and film footage do show women (especially schoolgirls) sitting or standing in the open areas. Young women were regulated by norms of respectability that were distinctly gender-specific. Helen Wilson remembers coming home from school for the midday meal: 'We had to wear our hat and we wore gloves and we had to get properly dressed.'[58]

An established convention that regulated women's behaviour on the street persisted. By the 1930s, there was still some sense that the street was the appropriate space for male social interaction compared to the interior spaces of the shop, where women might converse:

> In those days the men didn't go into the shops [with] their wives or par – well, there weren't so many partners in those days, their girlfriends. They would stand right on the edge of the footpath and have a little conversation with their friends on the edge of the footpath while the rest of the world steamed along, but no, it was much more orderly, that I can recall.[59]

But of course these norms were not always followed. Over the course of the decades, the greater independence and mobility of young girls in factory employment challenged these conventions of respectability. Hilda Maher (born 1912) remembers some of her young women workmates from the Wax Vesta match factory getting into trouble: 'Ah well, they were up the street calling out. Friday night used to be a great night to go up the street. [It] was what they called Jacob's Corner, that was at the back of the Fitzjames, and um, I wasn't there this night, but there was a group of the girls and they were yahooing out or something and they got into trouble over that.'[60]

The degree of independent mobility that the tram services brought to young women is summed up in Phyllis Crossan's memory of going off to a dance: 'On a wet night – we used to wear long frocks in those days you see – you'd hitch your frock up, you'd have your evening shoes wrapped up in a parcel under your arm, and off you'd go flat stick to the tram. You'd get the tram into town.'[61]

Underlying the concerns about respectable behaviour on the street was some anxiety about the street as the site where all sorts of boundaries of social control were challenged, including sexual boundaries.[62] In 1909 a tour of inspection by the Tramways Committee found that 'indecent practices were much in evidence' in the shelter shed at St Clair.[63] A complaint was also received from Mrs Berwick, a shopkeeper on Main South Rd, Caversham, about 'larrikinism and bad language at the Shelter Shed, Glen Road'. The tramways manager commented that 'at present I do not think any lady would use the Glen Road Shelter Shed after dark'.[64]

The potential for sexual assault on women undeniably exercised some constraint on the mobility of women, as illustrated in this episode recounted by Emily Siedeberg: 'When walking at night, little incidents with stray men would occur and make my heart go pit-a-pat. One night I remember having to pass a man who was standing very stationary at a corner. I was preparing my thoughts to run if he advanced to me, but just at that moment he turned his policeman's lantern onto me, and I heaved a sigh of relief.'[65]

However, it is remarkable to note how many of the oral-history informants recalled an environment where women felt safe on the streets, even after dark. Frances Harris (born 1917) used to bike to Roslyn Mills from Concord: '. . . in fact I never ever had a light on my bike when I think of it, I started away early in the morning and nowadays, gosh, it would be quite dangerous really, apart from rather frightening'.[66]

To a large extent, the sense of safety was generated by the numbers of other people also on the streets. Mavis Liverpool remembers coming home from the Macandrew Road School committee dances in the 1930s: '[There were] crowds of young people walking because that was the only way they had to get there and see it was quite safe to walk home, nobody was ever touched or anything like that. And that was 12 o'clock, after 12 o'clock, and see you used to always walk home from town on a Friday night, because crowds did it.'[67]

Although men were more likely to cycle or walk alone at night than women, many women reported that they used to walk through the streets at night without fear:

> When I used to go home if I didn't have somebody to see me home I'd hop on the tram at quarter past twelve at night and go home. That was the last tram on a Saturday night. I'd walk down the street and never worry about anything. You'd pass somebody on the street and they'd say 'good evening' and you'd say 'hello, how are you?' and go on your merry way. I wouldn't go down the road here on my own now. But nobody worried.[68]

As private transport became more widespread later in the century, tram services declined in frequency, and fewer people went out on foot. Consequently, the perceived and probably the actual safety of the streets after dark would have diminished.

Of course, the issues of safety and protection for young women on the street at night were also bound up with conventions of courting: walking someone home was a well-understood courting practice, and it is difficult to untangle this motivation from others. Alison Abraham (born 1914) recalls that, at the end of a dance, the vicar would check that all the girls were accompanied – either with another girl or a boy – 'to make sure that there was no girl on their own'.[69] Although we can see this as a straightforward protective strategy, it also suggests a socially structured arrangement for initiating courting. The availability of trams and the presence of other young women made it relatively simple for girls to refuse an unwanted courting approach. Walking a girl home did impose considerable costs on young men, who often thereby missed the last tram to their own home. Bert Grimmett (born 1912) describes going to an ice skating party in one part of town that lasted from 11 to 2 a.m., then walking his partner home to another suburb (Mornington), leaving her at 3 a.m. to walk back to his home (in Anderson's Bay). The unaccustomed exercise of skating produced aching muscles, so he sat down to rest and fell asleep on a bench, to be woken by a concerned milkman at 6 a.m. He walked on home, then rose to be at work at 8 a.m. on Saturday morning – and did an 8-kilometre run in the evening![70]

As many scholars have noted, the adoption of new transport technologies of trams, bicycles, motor cycles and cars provided many opportunities for interaction between men and women outside social conventions and beyond the surveillance of their families. A full discussion of this topic is beyond the scope of this chapter, but some points are worth noting.[71] For secondary schoolgirls and schoolboys who had to travel beyond southern Dunedin each day, the trams provided considerable opportunities for interaction, and this appears to have been of some concern to parents. In a letter to the town clerk, one father wrote to complain about the restrictions on the times when school concession tickets could be used for travel over the lunch period, which was causing some inconvenience to his daughter at technical school. He assumed that the specific time restrictions were based on a recognised civic duty to segregate boys and girls, although later correspondence suggests that it was an attempt to avoid overcrowding. In his words: 'If report speaks true the hours have been arranged so that the High School Boys and the High School Girls and apparently the Technical School Girls will not meet; as they are rather free with each others (Possibly the effect of Higher education).'[72]

Bicycles and motor cycles provided many opportunities for social outings on weekends, but the car offered the greatest transformation in the privacy and mobility of courting couples. Families with cars regularly allowed sons to use the car to escort young women at night.[73] Rosanna Paul (born 1909) suggests that there was a fairly rapid transition in courting practices once cars became more common. When her older sisters were going off to dances, boys their age did not have cars, and they lived too far away for boys to walk the girls home. All that had changed when she began going out (in about 1928): she remembers that, 'if they didn't have motorcars they had their father's car'.[74] No doubt many young people welcomed the opportunities for unchaperoned contact offered by the car, but we might pause to consider what was lost. Instead of groups of men and women taking the tram from their homes and meeting up together at a dance, from which they could leave separately or together, they were now incorporated into a system based on 'the boy with Dad's car'. Gender inequalities in control over transport thus reinforced broader gender inequalities in social power and autonomy. In the shifts in the practice of courting over the study period, the mobility and autonomy offered by the tram service gave way to the even greater freedom and mobility offered by the motor car, but in a profoundly gendered form.

The widespread adoption of the private motor car in the period after the Second World War also reinforced the nuclear-family household as a significant site of commodity consumption. The family car provided a realm for the performance of the newly dominant form of suburban and familial masculinity.[75] The car demonstrated the financial success of the male breadwinner, it enabled family-based leisure outings with Father as driver, it offered the opportunity for men to acquire and practice mechanical skills that were becoming well-defined as a masculine domain, and it provided the focus of social groups, such as the Otago Motor Club.

For young women who had learned to drive and maintain cars in their youth, the shift to the passenger seat in the family car required a more passive expression of femininity. As a young single woman, Rosanna Paul had driven her father around and learned to cope with car trouble: 'We drove a Pontiac car. In those days the flywheels weren't very, it wasn't the strongest part, and

ON THE STREETS OF SOUTHERN DUNEDIN

It was only after the Second World War that car ownership became widespread among New Zealand families. Here a couple stand alongside what may have been a brand-new car parked in a residential street. HOCKEN LIBRARY

the teeth used to come off the fly wheel and get into the self-starter screw. I learned to take that self-starter to bits and put it together again and get the chips out of it so that the car would go. I thought that I didn't do too badly ... mechanically.'[76] But after her marriage, her husband always drove when they went out together. Her mixed feelings are evident in her words: 'Yes, I never drove unless I had to because – I enjoyed driving, I always loved driving – I was always quite pleased to sit back and be driven. [Interviewer: It's very relaxing, isn't it?] Well, it takes away any responsibility.'[77] In this interchange, the ambivalence of women's responses to the changing transport technology, and the shift from relative independence to dependence that accompanied the rise of the family car, are interwoven with ambivalence towards the shift from relative independence to formal dependence in the transition from a single to a married state. Each is expressed through the other, and they seem almost inextricable: the gendering of the technological change is plain.

Conclusion

Streets are the terrain of social encounters and political protest, sites of domination and resistance, places of pleasure and anxiety.[78]

Historians and geographers interested in gender have often marked out the social world into convenient spatially limited domains, such as 'home' or

283

'work' or 'public space'. In this chapter I have tried to link these domains through a focus on the space of the street and on the technologies of transport by which people undertook daily mobility in Dunedin in the early years of the twentieth century. Attention to daily mobility is productive, since in everyday discourse mobility typically carries multiple meanings and is recognised as simultaneously a constraint and opportunity. For example, a long daily commuting trip can be understood in terms of the high financial and time burden borne by the commuter – or, alternatively, it can be interpreted as a reflection of their freedom of movement and ability to access a wide spatial zone of employment opportunities. Also, although mobility is sometimes seen as simply a means to an end, everyday understandings also recognise the pleasures of independent movement for its own sake. These inherent ambiguities foreclose any simplistic conclusions about the implications of gendered mobility, making it easier to develop a nuanced interpretation that recognises cost and benefit in the lives of both men and women.

This chapter's review of changes on the streets of southern Dunedin shows that access to new technology in the form of bicycles and trams in the early years of the century did initially bring somewhat equivalent benefits for men and women. Both benefited from the combination of the old and the new. On the one hand, improved individual mobility through bicycles and trams brought easier access to more distant urban sites of work, shopping, education and recreation. On the other hand, for the first few decades at least, the organisation of paid and domestic work in time and space continued to be organised to suit a world where most people travelled on foot (so that, for instance, homes and work sites were typically fairly close, children walked independently, and deliveries to the home simplified domestic labour). The public transport system structured street life to some extent, providing a setting for the operation of social rules, and an institutional context in which some levels of public surveillance could operate, so providing a level of safety and respectability for women on their own.

Yet the technologies of the tram and bicycle, in opening up urban space, also began to destroy the viability of the local 'walking economy', with particular implications for domestic work. This process was reinforced with the rise of the motor car. Although there were clearly some gender differences in access to and use of bicycles, these became even more marked in the case of motor cycles and motor cars. In short, in the shifting parade of transport technologies that passed along the streets of southern Dunedin over the first four decades of the century, we can trace parallel processes of expanded and constrained mobility for men and women.

Ten The Risk to Life and Limb: Gender and Health

BARBARA BROOKES

On 17 June 1926, Donald Septimus Crossan, boilermaker at the Hillside Railway Workshops, had to climb to the ceiling of the building, more than 4.5 metres high, in order to turn off an air cock. On his way down:

> his clothing became entangled in the shafting and pulleys and Crossan was thrown round a shaft which was travelling at 160 revolutions a minute. After a few moments the clothing was completely stripped from the poor man's body, which then fell to the ground. Dr Lindon, who was sent for immediately, said death must have been instantaneous.[1]

Thirty-one-year-old Crossan, married with two children, had survived action in the First World War, only to die an untimely death in his workplace. Such dramatic accidents were rare, but they were a reminder of the risks men undertook on the job in the heavily industrialised southern suburbs of Dunedin.

A very different kind of risk was undertaken by the three women who testified at the trial of Ruth Kate Cranefield. In March 1923, two detectives visited Cranefield's house at 76 Main South Rd with a warrant for her arrest on two charges of procuring abortion. During the search of the house, the detectives found a syringe, a bottle of Lysol and a box of cotton wool. During the ensuing trial, witnesses gave evidence that Mrs Cranefield had a reputation as an abortionist. Two young single women and one married woman gave evidence that they had availed themselves of her services. Her Caversham address was well known, her skill apparently highly regarded and her service was relatively cheap: she charged £5 for inducing miscarriage.[2] Mrs Cranefield's business points to the risks women were prepared to take in order to prevent childbirth.

These stories of individual lives in southern Dunedin suggest that ideas about, and the experience of, health and ill-health were deeply gendered. Normative concepts asserted, in Joan Scott's words, 'a fixed binary opposition, categorically asserting the meaning of male and female, masculine and feminine'.[3] If to be a man, for example, was to be a worker and a provider, these social positions meant that protective legislation governing working conditions would unduly limit the rights of manhood. Donald Crossan expected that his work entailed risks and that, as the breadwinner for his family, he would bargain risk for reward. If to be a woman was to live under the future expectation of marriage and motherhood, these social positions would encourage protective legislation that limited women's access to the workplace and protected the health of the future generation.[4] But motherhood itself involved risks: the risk of social ostracism if it took place outside of marriage and the risk of death in childbirth at any time. Just as men made calculations about the extent of risk they wished to expose themselves to in the workplace,

Hillside Railway Workshops, 1927: men faced the risk of injury or death on the job in industrial workplaces. In addition to the dangers posed by working with machinery, men's health often suffered through breathing fumes and being exposed to cold, dampness and dirt. ARCHIVES NEW ZEALAND, DUNEDIN

so women, like those who called on Ruth Cranefield's services, made decisions about their readiness to have children and how many they would have. Although men were to provide the necessities of life for their families, women were entrusted with attending to the health of the rising generation.

The healthy or sickly lives of southern Dunedin residents were played out in a wider context of a community and a country that saw itself as building a new and better world than the one left behind. New Zealand has long regarded itself as *A Healthy Country*, the title of the important collection of essays on the social history of medicine in New Zealand, edited by Linda Bryder. The essays in that collection were concerned to place medicine in a wider social context in order to move beyond the useful, but limited, charting of trends traced by F. S. Maclean's 1964 *Challenge for Health*. Since the appearance of Bryder's volume, a number of valuable books analysing the evolution of children's health camps, the Department of Health and Maori health policies have appeared. So also have two fascinating biographies that have much to say about health: Jessie Munro's *The Story of Suzanne Aubert* and Fay Hercock's *Alice: The Story of a Woman Doctor*.[5]

Women, as health professionals or as mothers, have been the focus of a number of studies, but questions about gender and health have rarely been addressed in New Zealand historical work.[6] It is significant that, when they have been raised, it is most often in relation to mental health, as in Bronwyn Labrum's study of committal in Auckland.[7] Mental illness, due to the critiques of the anti-psychiatry movement of the 1960s and 70s, is more readily perceived as a cultural construction in which beliefs about gender play an important role. Yet, in studies of contemporary health statistics, sex ranks second only to age as an explanation for differential rates of illness and disability. 'Women's experience of daily symptoms,' wrote Lois Verbrugge in a 1990 study, 'their prevalence rates for many chronic conditions, their experience of short and long-term disability due to health problems, and their use of professional health services exceed men's within each age group. Nevertheless, women's rates of mortality are strikingly lower than men's.'[8]

Gender, it is clear, 'patterns how and why people become ill, and how differently they are judged – and judge themselves – in those processes'.[9] Such analysis is possible in recent years because of regular and accurate reporting on the health status of men and women. But what of the past? Can we determine how gender shaped the experience of health and sickness for individuals in the years 1890–1939? I would argue that a close examination of the texture of life in the southern Dunedin community allows us to interrogate the gendered meanings of the wider national trends of death, disease and accident. The questions raised here are twofold and informed by different sources.

First, popular advice books, advertising and oral history allow us to ask how, by the early decades of the twentieth century, women and men understood the causes of disease and what roles they played in the steps taken to maintain good health. Second, from the records of institutions that monitored people's ill-health in the late nineteenth century, we can ask how gender inflected the range and impact of ill-health experienced by individuals living in an urban community at that time.

National health patterns

In the nineteenth century New Zealand was upheld as an ideal land for settlers.[10] 'The death rate in New Zealand,' enthused the *Report on the Statistics of New Zealand 1889*, 'contrasts very strikingly with those in the other Australasian colonies and with European countries, and furnishes evidence of the great salubrity of the climate of the colony', a conclusion echoed by Dunedin's *Evening Star* the following year.[11] The *Report* did not focus on the picture behind the gross statistics: Maori were ignored; death rates from 'filth' diseases such as diarrhoea, dysentery, typhoid and scarlet fever remained high; and the fact that Pakeha men suffered consistently higher mortality rates than Pakeha women received little attention.[12] Pakeha men continued to have higher death rates through to the 1940s, although women in their mid-20s to mid-30s were more at risk of dying than men, because of the complications of childbirth, a differential that decreased, however, as couples limited their fertility and the dangers of childbirth slowly waned. Pakeha men were particularly vulnerable to violent death, whether by accident, drowning or suicide. In 1893 the proportion of violent deaths per 10,000 living males was 13.03; the comparable figure for women was 3.63. Dangerous occupations, such as blasting and tree-felling, usually male preserves, took their toll, although death rates from such accidents declined over the years. Male suicide rates remained markedly higher than women's.[13]

'The more strenuous occupations of males,' noted the 1916 national *Census Report*, rendered them 'much more liable to acquired ... infirmity'.[14] Age was a further consideration in that Pakeha men were older on average than Pakeha women and hence more liable to accident and illness. Higher male rates of infirmity (deafness, blindness and lunacy) were recorded in the 1896 and 1901 censuses. These figures are problematic because we do not know if women engaged in 'domestic duties' responded to the request to identify themselves as unable to carry out their usual occupation because of sickness.[15] A further source, hospital admission statistics, also suggests greater morbidity or ill-health among men, although it may be that women were more reluctant to leave their families and enter hospital for treatment, or that hospitals were more likely to admit men, placing greater value on them as workers.[16] By 1932 women outnumbered men in national hospital admissions for the first time, probably because childbirth was moving into general hospitals. The male death rate in hospital remained 'invariably higher', chiefly because of 'a higher average incidence of serious types of diseases and accident cases among male patients'.[17] Male vulnerability was also evident in the mental hospitals, where men consistently outnumbered women.[18]

Sea breezes and sanitation

The situation in the southern suburbs mirrored a number of the national health trends. As chapter two explains, the township of Caversham, at the foot of the Caversham Valley, began as a travellers' stop, but soon families seeking to escape the filth and congestion of inner-city Dunedin and its noxious industries settled the suburb and adjacent streets in South Dunedin. Although others came to reside close by the new industries, some of them as noxious as any in the city, that started up in Caversham and South Dunedin during the 1870s, the belief that seaside residential areas were healthier continued to exercise some hold on people's imagination. Many people believed that sea breezes promoted health, and this belief prompted health-conscious families to flee the disease-ridden streets of the central city.[19] Suburbs, with their parks and gardens, were regarded as paying a substantial health dividend and, in a world characterised by inadequate drainage and sewerage systems, low population densities alone probably contributed to lower rates of infant mortality and mortality generally. In the 1890s and 1900s, especially after Caversham and South Dunedin ratepayers voted to amalgamate with Dunedin city in 1904–05, modish ideas about town planning and garden cities increasingly shaped new subdivisions. The expansion of St Clair, the seaside suburb, reflected the new enthusiasm for parks, gardens and street verges. In the neighbouring seaside suburb of St Kilda, which remained an independent borough, similar ideas shaped suburban development and an effort was also made to escape the rectilinear model of street design. Tree-lined grass verges adorned curving avenues. Sports grounds and recreation areas abounded. The spread of single-unit houses, a national passion, contributed to the ubiquity of gardens.[20]

The state of the physical environment, coming under attention from the borough and city councils, was known to have an important impact on health. Sanitarians sought to provide clean water and effective sewerage, but such innovations spread slowly and unevenly across the city. The southern

St Kilda's first nightcart and Mr Hollander, a popular and respected 'nightman', 1910. Efficient removal of human waste was an important step in improving health and reducing the spread of infectious diseases such as typhoid. 'Nightsoil' was removed from the Flat between midnight and 5 a.m. and deposited in the St Kilda sand dunes. Progressively, however, indoor plumbing brought flush toilets to the households of southern Dunedin. OTAGO SETTLERS MUSEUM

Dunedin Flat, often referred to as 'the Swamp', was without an effective system of drainage until 1909 and it was not until about this time that a city-wide sewerage scheme was implemented.[21] Salubrity of surroundings within the study area varied according to topography, and families as a whole either enjoyed the grass verges of St Clair or inhaled the noxious fumes of the gas-works on Anderson's Bay Rd. Since for the majority of women the workplace was the family home, the condition and location of that house were of crucial importance. Workplace conditions for men could have a major impact on health, but were less likely to be subject to the individual's control.

The state of housing, and domestic hygiene, were crucial in women's efforts to sustain the health of their families. Until the 1930s, maternal mortality remained high in New Zealand, as elsewhere, while infant mortality rates dropped. Family size declined dramatically from the 1870s and, from that decade, thanks to the work of Pasteur and Koch, the germ theory began altering understandings of disease transmission. Nancy Tomes has argued in relation to the United States that the germ theory 'was easily incorporated into popular advice literature precisely because it seemed to justify widely accepted precautions of ventilation, disinfection, isolation of the ill, and general cleanliness'.[22] Her work reinforces the argument made by Ewbank and Preston that changes in domestic hygiene may have had an important impact on the decline in infant and child mortality in the USA and Britain.[23]

In the southern suburbs in the 1890s, two institutions, run by men, served the health needs of vastly different sectors of the population. Dr Millen Coughtrey came to Dunedin as the University of Otago's inaugural professor of anatomy and physiology, but soon left the university for private practice, including his own private hospital and sanatorium, said to be the most 'modern and extensive of its kind in the Southern Hemisphere'.[24] From his home in St Clair, Dr Coughtrey attended patients in his extensive establishment in Forbury Rd, which boasted two large wards, for men and women respectively, fourteen private rooms, an operating theatre and Turkish steam, lunge and spray baths, all set in grounds where tents could be erected in fine weather for patients to be 'aired in'. Those who preferred isolation could live in single huts. People who could afford such private care found luxurious surroundings, where the decorative work in some of the private rooms was said to approach 'very high art'.[25] A success in private practice, Dr Coughtrey also

Dr Coughtrey's private hospital offered private rooms and salubrious surroundings, unlike the public hospital facilities. While the wealthy might choose to pay to go there to convalesce, most of southern Dunedin's residents went to Dunedin Public Hospital when accident or serious illness struck. FROM G. N. STEDMAN, 'THE SOUTH DUNEDIN FLAT: A STUDY IN URBANISATION 1849–1965. VOL. 1.' MA THESIS, UNIVERSITY OF OTAGO, 1966

served as public vaccinator, and as surgeon-captain with the Otago Hussars, later promoted to surgeon-colonel on the staff of the First Regiment of the Otago Mounted Rifles. A 'lover of manly sports', he was president of the Otago Rugby Football Union from 1887–90 and, when not at the rugby in his leisure time, was to be found cheering on his racehorses. Millen Coughtrey was deeply involved in the Dunedin community as deputy chairman of the Drainage Board, vice-president of the Philharmonic Society and local secretary of the Royal Humane Society.[26] In southern Dunedin he epitomised a manly ethic of patriotism and civic duty. His public reputation, no doubt, brought patients to his private practice.

At the other end of the spectrum from Coughtrey's private and comfortable sanatorium lay a charitable institution, the Benevolent Institution, whose title reflected the intentions of its philanthropic founders. This Caversham home for the destitute first opened in 1866, funded by public support and government subsidy. Initially, the institution provided for orphaned children, but by the 1880s the focus had shifted to adults and, in particular, the elderly. In 1888, the Benevolent opened a lying-in ward that catered primarily to single women, although the obstetrical equipment was available to the wider Caversham community through its use by local medical practitioners at times of emergency.[27] By the turn of the twentieth century, medical staff at Dunedin Hospital were anxious to concentrate on short-term curative medicine and looked to the Benevolent Institution to provide for chronic and convalescent cases, particularly those suffering from tuberculosis. From 1907 Dunedin Hospital provided trained nurses to care for such patients in the Benevolent's renovated wards.[28]

Between the extremes of the private sanatorium and the institution for the indigent was a space women could occupy as less formal, but ultimately central, providers of health care for the community. As mothers, herbalists, midwives and daily nurses, women advised on how to keep healthy, dispensed potions and provided care in times of ill-health.

Household guardians: gendered responsibilities
Mothers were at the forefront of the battle against the 'invisible enemies' that spread disease, and their weapons for the health of the body consisted of good meals, fresh air and monitoring 'regularity'. Responsibility for health was gendered: women were expected to guard the health of their families through their daily rituals of cooking and cleaning. The formulation 'dirt equals disease',[29] given added weight in the early twentieth century by the new discipline of home science, haunted mothers who themselves had grown up

with the experience of infant deaths.³⁰ Domestic hygiene gave women a sense of control over the seemingly random action of germs. They were assisted in their campaign to raise healthy children by the advice of friends and relatives, by patent medicines that promised to promote their children's health and, from 1907, by New Zealand's Society for the Promotion of the Health of Women and Children (which became known as the Plunket Society). Protecting children's health took on a new significance in light of the decline in family size.

How women were best to perform domestic tasks became increasingly elaborated over the period. A small Whitcombe and Tombs booklet, *Housewifery for Use in School and Home*, made the link between the household and public health explicit, reminding its readers that, 'If personal cleanliness promotes individual health, civic cleanliness is absolutely essential for the health of the community.'³¹ Health manuals disseminated rules of health that advertisers reiterated, marketing products to assist the housewife in the pursuit of hygiene. In the early decades of the twentieth century, school medical officers (appointed from 1912) and Plunket nurses (from 1907) reinforced messages to mothers. Domestic science training was made compulsory for girls in 1917 and, in case the messages were in danger of being ignored, the covers of school exercise books carried the rules of health by the interwar years.³²

Oral-history informants suggest that mothers played a key role in the transmission of information about health in the early twentieth century and hence were looked to as the source of authority in the home on bodily wellbeing. The body was understood as a system that had to be kept in balance through a strict regimen, regulating intake and outflow, exercise and rest. These ideas were based upon ancient humoral understandings of the body as made up of different hot, dry, cold and wet elements that had to be kept in balance.³³ Old ideas, which gave a sense of control over the body, jostled alongside newer understandings of the disturbingly random nature of germs. Old regimens and new measures of cleanliness appeared to provide a ready way of prophylaxis against disease, the latter made more fearful by the knowledge of invisible microbes.

Cleanliness, involving washing and scrubbing, was a central rule governing health in the home. 'Dust,' declared Emily Siedeberg, New Zealand's first woman doctor and a widely respected Dunedin practitioner, was 'full of microbes [and] always carried infection'.³⁴ Her listeners, at a 1911 meeting of the Mothers' Union, were anxious to do whatever the doctor advised in order to do the best for their children. To ensure the health of the home, women engaged in scrubbing floors, beating carpets and boiling laundry. They were spurred on in such tasks by popular publications such as J. S. C. Elkington's

Health Reader, published by Whitcombe and Tombs, which verbally and visually contrasted the slovenly with the ordered housewife. Animals kept in dirty cages die, Elkington warned, and:

> Human beings are just the same as animals in this way, and a dirty or damp house, or one that is not properly ventilated, or that has dirty drains near it, makes the people in it more ready to catch any disease, than are other people who live in clean, dry, properly ventilated, and well-drained houses.³⁵

Charles Budden's *The Way of Health: Plain Counsels in Personal Hygiene* made the message to mothers even more stark: 'Without the knowledge of [natural laws] the mother's love too often finds its recompense only in a child's coffin.'³⁶ He warned that 'the air is full of germs. Houses, therefore, that are dirty are particularly dangerous.'³⁷ Advertisements for household products reinforced the cleanliness message. The 'Duncan Polish Mop' was marketed as 'A Great Boon to housewives and Mothers'. Not only was it

'The wrong place for rubbish' & 'The right place': Instructional texts, like Elkington's *Health Reader*, advised women how to guard against germs in the household and thereby maintain the health of their families. Health messages were inseparable from ideas about proper lifestyles and held the potential to induce guilt in mothers who failed to measure up. J. S. C. ELKINGTON, SOUTHERN CROSS SERIES *HEALTH READER*, WITH CHAPTERS ON ELEMENTARY SCHOOL HYGIENE, WELLINGTON, C. 1908.

THE RISK TO LIFE AND LIMB

Plunket Magazine advertisement for the Duncan Polish Mop: the promise of good health had potent appeal as this advertisement for a mop illustrates. In the early twentieth century, tuberculosis was a common and dreaded disease which all families wished to avoid. PLUNKET MAGAZINE, JANUARY 1915

clean and sanitary, a nurse recommended it as useful in 'the prevention of TUBERCULOSIS'.[38]

Robert Terry MD addressed his Auckland-published health manual, *How to Get Well and Keep Well*, to 'housewives and mothers', in the hope that by acquiring 'greater knowledge of the body and the keeping of it in health' the 'advance of the country' would be attained.[39] Vigilance in the household was necessary to ensure that family members had clean air to breathe, nutritious food, and that waste products were removed efficiently. Southern Dunedin residents recall that outside play and walks meant exposure to fresh air, and open windows in the house, particularly in bedrooms, encouraged the air to circulate. Kitty Brown recalled that 'plenty of vegetables and plenty of fruit' were regarded as the keystones of a good diet.[40] Plain but fresh food was important as well as, according to Phyllis Crossan, 'plenty of sleep'.[41]

295

Germs had to be eradicated from the household to protect children's health and boiling the washing was one way to ensure that the 'invisible enemies' didn't take hold.[42] Rosanna Paul remembered that, 'You boiled your clothes to kill the germs on them, the sheets, the pillow slips and the towels and anything like that.'[43] Mothers' lives were governed by the rituals of cleaning, through which, they believed, they could ward off tragedy. It is significant that Marion Cooper, born in 1925, recalled how anxious her mother was when Marion's children were young. 'Mother worried more than what I did. I just took it in my stride. It didn't bother me. Mum worried about the babies. When they were a bit older she was quite happy. But she said she was always nervous.'[44] The younger generation, coming to adulthood after the discovery of antibiotics in the 1940s, was no longer haunted by high infant-mortality rates and it may be that their mothers' care with domestic hygiene was one important factor in reducing those rates.

Cleaning rituals were supplemented by tonics, patent medicines and home-made remedies. Authors such as Dr Terry advised against the use of 'pills and purges', and at the same time promoted his own 'Robert J. Terry's Meal': 'evolved for the use of... patients who were deficient in mineral salts, also for pregnant mothers, rickety and backward children, and those large numbers who suffer from that "tired feeling"'.[45] Mothers made use of patent medicines for minor ailments. Phyllis Crossan recalled that Irish Moss cough mixture and Vicks Vaporub were commonly used for coughs.[46] Another woman recalled that her family were 'brought up on Wilson's malt extract... we also had Baxter's Lung Preserver and Lane's Emulsion'. Her mother dealt with 'the ordinary children's ailments. Chickenpox, measles, mumps' and had her own home health reference book to consult.[47] She also made up her own cough mixture, which contained liquorice and aniseed.

Patent medicines were widely advertised in newspapers for every ailment from simple colds, kidney and liver complaints, infections, fevers, bronchitis, asthma, pleurisy, consumption and nervous ailments to 'parched and scaly hair'.[48] The advertisements played upon women's fears about the health of their children and often promised different outcomes for women and men. Without Beecham's Pills, one advertisement proclaimed, 'no man can be his best, no woman can look her best'.[49] The emphasis on men's health and women's appearance was emphasised by an advertisement for 'Sulfarilla Tablets', which promised pure blood for men to cure 'eczema eruptions, boils, piles, and rheumatism, and all troubles caused by impure blood', while women were promised a 'Good Complexion'.[50] Some products, such as 'Fospherine!', which promised to give mankind 'NERVES like a Footballer', were specifically marketed to men. Mrs Louise Hawkins listed 'Female Pills'

THE RISK TO LIFE AND LIMB

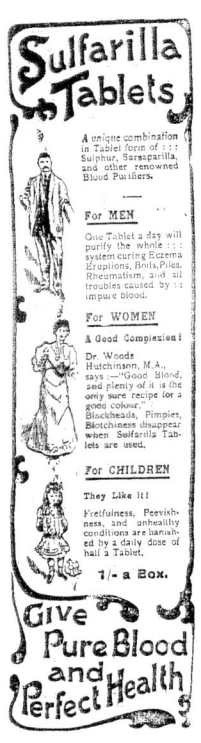
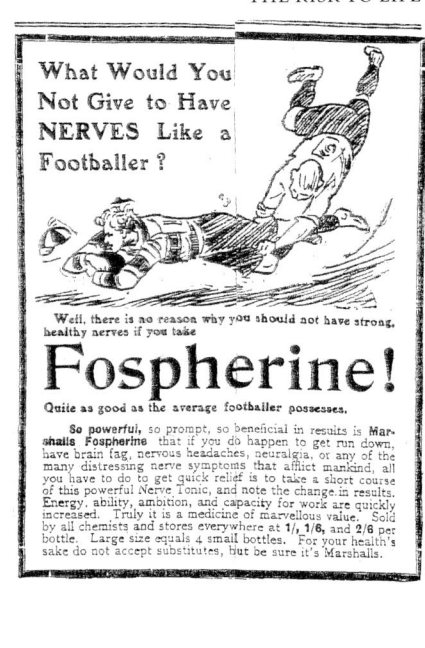

Fospherine 'Nerves like a footballer' and Sulfarilla ads: newspapers over the period contained numerous advertisements for many types of health remedies. Patent medicine manufacturers sought to attract clients by detailing their remedies for anything from constipation to weak hair, often aimed specifically at either women or men. The ubiquity of the advertisements suggests the ready market for such products. EVENING STAR, 2 JULY 1910; 4 JULY 1910.

among her 'French and American rubber goods, Barry's Pearl Cream and Spring Blossom Ointment and Pills'.[51]

A number of products, including 'Wahoo', promised to relieve the 'gloom and anxiety of spirits' suffered through constipation and many specifically appealed to mothers as guardians of children's health.[52] Excretion was closely monitored by mothers, who noted the regularity of children's bowel movements to ensure a regular 'clean out'.[53] 'The bowels and kidneys must be kept active,' advised Dr Siedeberg, 'by plenty of water & fruit & green vegetables; raisins figs dates'.[54] Dunedin orthopaedic surgeon and university lecturer J. Renfrew White declared in his *The Growing Body: Its Nature, Needs, and Training* that, 'More unhappiness of civilised folk is due to constipation than to any other single cause.'[55] *How to Get Well* reinforced the warning that constipation was 'the curse of civilisation', which sapped energy, retarded progress, wasted money and probably gave rise to cancer, while 'Internal Cleanliness' made for good health.[56] Mothers employed regular routines to ensure that families were free from constipation. Richard Perth's mother made sure that the family 'had your liquorice Friday night'[57]. In Marion Cooper's case, 'syrup of figs' or cod liver oil were administered.[58] Senna tea was another likely remedy or, 'in the case of stubbornness', an enema might be administered.[59] Just as dirt, allowed to collect in the home, was likely to become a playground for germs, so waste stored in the body might become a cause of disease. In spring Hilda Maher's mother used to give her children a big spoonful of 'treacle and sulphur together ... to purify the blood'.[60]

The ways in which the bodily system was held in balance might be seen in Rita Jory's recollection of the influenza epidemic that struck in New Zealand, as elsewhere, in 1918. The head hairdresser at the salon where she worked had caught influenza and advised the other staff to go the inhalation chambers set up in the town:

> I and Bessie, the two of us we packed up and went. There was a great long queue waiting to go in. All they had there for you to do was a wee acetylene lamp with a little glass tube and the steam coming out of this glass tube. You had to go and open up your mouth and let the steam go into your mouth . . . . So we went and did that and I went straight home and had the 'flu. Went straight to bed and I never went back for a week. The thing my mother reckoned that saved me was my nose bled a lot. Oh terrific bleeding nose I had.[61]

Bleeding the system in this case was thought to have restored the body's balance. Although long since banished from the repertoire of regular medicine, the idea of blood-letting as a restorative remained current in lay understandings of health.

Another type of imbalance was recalled by Verna Syme whose family friend had 'a milk leg after having one of her babies. The milk went to the leg and it left her lame the rest of her life.'[62] Misdirected bodily fluids could have serious implications. Even if the cause of a complaint was known to lie in some sort of strain, it still might be described in humoral terms. Marion Cooper and her mother both suffered from 'frozen shoulders' – joints that failed to work properly were understood to be 'frozen'.[63]

The limited supply of bodily nervous energy could be depleted in one mortal blow. Victoria Lake's mother 'got a dreadful fright' because of the fire at the Caversham brewery: 'her heart gave out, she just died like that, she got the shock of the fire, you see'.[64] And the fluidity of the body meant that one condition could transmute into another. Marina Mackenzie recalled that her

THE RISK TO LIFE AND LIMB

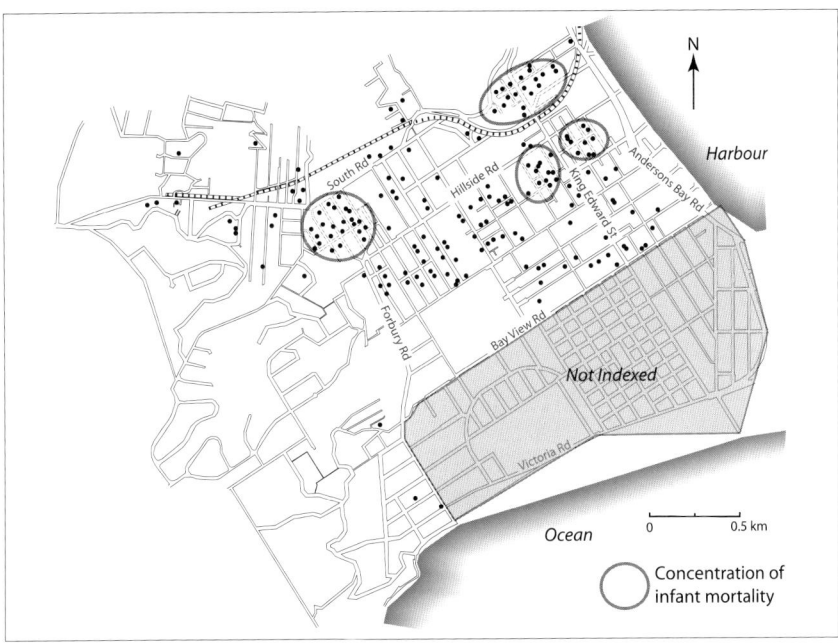

Map 10.1 Indexed locations of infant mortality, 1900–20. Infant deaths appear to be clustered in areas of older housing stock, notably Calderville, Kensington and the Rankeillor St and Maria/Glasgow St areas. The deaths of infants aged over one month and under one year declined more sharply than those of infants under one month over the period, suggesting that improvements in domestic hygiene may well have been the key to the transformation.

brother was 'left with TB' as a result of being badly gassed in the First World War.[65]

Alongside these older understandings of the body went newer beliefs in the causes of disease and how to control them. William Harris related the cause of his tuberculosis and that of four or five other family members directly to unpasteurised milk.[66] Kitty Brown recalled her good friend developing TB. When she went to visit her, 'I wasn't allowed to go anywhere near her. She was in a bed on one side of the room and I would be sat beside the fire on the other side. She must have died when I was in the fourth form I think, so that was that.'[67] When Louise Wellman developed diphtheria as a child, her mother refused to let her go to hospital and looked after her at home. 'She had to have a smock to cover her right up . . . . And a cap for her hair.' 'She had a shovel with sulphur burning on it in the room', 'a big wet sheet with Jeyes' Fluid over the door' and 'a big basin with disinfectant'.[68]

The idea that germs transmitted disease had a profound impact on the lives of women in the southern suburbs. Designated by the wider society as the guardians of the health of their families, they had to seek out and destroy dust and dirt where germs might lurk and endanger life. In the absence of the antibiotics that would transform the lives of generations born after the Second World War, women strove to prevent illness through energetic cleaning, monitoring their families' diets and imposing routines of cleanliness, sleep and exercise. Evidence of their success lies in the decline of the infant mortality rate in the Dunedin metropolitan area. Conrad Schumacher has shown that the deaths of infants under one month dropped less than the post-neonatal motality rate (infants aged over one month and under a year). The most significant decline in the post-neonatal mortality rate was in deaths from diarrhoea, which suggests that improvements in domestic hygiene may well have been the key to the transformation (whooping cough, less responsive to hygiene measures, remained a problem).[69] It may also be the case, as Randall Reeves has suggested, that family limitation caused an increase in the median age of infection for most infectious diseases, and thereby made an important contribution to lowering infant mortality.[70] The figures for deaths of infants under one month in the study area reflect the Dunedin-wide and national trend. From an average of 32.2 for the years 1905–09, they dropped to an average of 16.6 for the years 1915–19.[71]

Gender and risk

Men's work outside the home exposed them to the elements and to dangers in the workplace. The 'domestic duties' that occupied the great majority of women over the period involved heavy lifting, long hours and repetitive tasks, often in addition to casual work outside the home. Factory Acts attempted to limit women's participation in the workplace, in order to protect their reproductive role, reinforcing the idea that women's place was in the home. The conflation of masculinity with paid employment meant that men's work opportunities were unlikely to be regulated, but from 1900 they were able to seek some compensation for accident.

Around 10 per cent of the study area's male population were skilled metal workers and a good proportion of these were employed at Hillside. By 1919 approximately one in four of the workers there were likely to suffer an accident. Most, as Erik Olssen notes, were classified as 'minor': loss of a finger, eye injuries, bruises, sprains, cuts and burns. The men themselves made provision for sickness by forming, in 1882, the Hillside Sick Benefit Society, to which about 60 per cent of the workforce belonged at any one time.[72] From 1900 the Workers' Compensation for Accidents Act provided compensation for 50 per cent of the loss of earnings, with a maximum of £2 per week.

Compensation was not paid for the first fourteen days of incapacity, unless the incapacity lasted more than fourteen days.[73]

Other types of occupations held dangers, not so much in the work processes – as at Hillside – but in the chemicals used, such as the lead in paint or the phosphorous used in producing matches at the Wax Vesta Factory. Phosphorous, when absorbed into the bloodstream, caused disfigurement ('phossy jaw') and the often fatal phosphorous necrosis. The latter had been recognised as an industrial disease in Vienna in 1838, but it was not until 1894 that the New Zealand Factory Acts specified that children under sixteen years, and women, were not to work in the mixing or dipping of phosphorous matches.[74] Women, because they were viewed as the mothers of the nation, were subject to protective legislation held to be unnecessary for male breadwinners.[75] Few of the workers, however, were aware of the dangers of phosphoric poisoning that match-making entailed. The fact that young women moved out of the workforce to marry may have protected their health by preventing long-term exposure to phosphorus. Annie Norman recalled how her husband, who had worked in the factory's mixing and dipping room since at least 1900, said one night, '"Oh . . . there's something sticking out of me gum." So he pulled it out. It was a piece of bone, small piece, just like the end of a chop, where it's perforated.'[76] Since the family was dependent on his wages, Mr Norman continued to work at the Wax Vesta Factory until pain prevented him from carrying on. He died in 1918.[77]

Work in places such as the Phoenix jam factory, Mooney's furrier works, Cadbury Fry Hudson's and the Roslyn Woollen Mills provided young women from the southern suburbs with alternative employment to domestic service. A 1929 study of the health of women in industry in New Zealand noted that women were 'prone to be allotted poorly paid, monotonous work', while men were 'given more responsibility and room for initiative'. The author found that machinists and sedentary workers were 'particularly prone to menstrual troubles'. Standing occupations resulted in painful feet and varicose veins, and 'long continued close work, especially in artificial light' induced eye strain.[78] The Wax Vesta Factory was a distinctive institution in South Dunedin, in part because of the predominance of young women employed there. The Department of Labour Report for 1922 suggested that the factory had particularly high rates of absenteeism through accident and illness.[79] In more genteel workplaces, such as Ross and Glendining, workers could suffer from strain through repetitive work. Rose Goodall, aged sixteen, had to take a break from her work because of a sore arm.[80]

Severe illness among southern Dunedin working people might lead to their becoming in-patients at Dunedin Hospital and surgical intervention under chloroform. Men's rate of hospitalisation was approximately twice that of women during the years 1891–95, while women were more likely to attend the out-patients' department.[81] The majority of male labourers, skilled workers and factory operatives were admitted to hospital suffering from occupation-related injuries, with fractures and dislocations, strains, infected cuts and abscesses, and hernias from heavy lifting. George Mill from Kensington, sixty-four years old, fractured his ribs when he fell from scaffolding.[82] Caversham resident Alexander Dickie was kicked in the face by a horse. An operation to restore his nasal bones led to a post-operative infection, from which he died two days later.[83] A 33-year-old railway worker 'was squeezed between a railway truck and the wall inside the railway shed at Kensington'.[84] Common treatments patients received included hot fomentations, soap and water enemas, douches, charcoal poultices, belladonna and glycerin (for pain relief), boracic acid (used to wash wounds and inflamed tissue), liquorice powder (a purgative) and special diets: milk and brandy, arrowroot, and beef tea.

Women workers were also liable to fractures, abscesses and hernias and to the particular hazard of domestic service: 'housemaid's knee'. Twenty-six-year-old Mary Mullin from South Dunedin described the symptoms thus: 'About a year ago I felt pain at the left knee on walking, and noticed a slight swelling. The swelling gradually increased, and for the last two weeks has been very painful.' Dr Brown operated, making an incision at the side of the knee 'to prevent the scar from inconveniencing her in her future duties'.[85] Another 26-year-old suffering from the same complaint was treated with 'hot fomentations' and discharged after seven weeks in hospital.[86] The more exotic occupation of 17-year-old Agnes Tudelope, that of a circus and opera-company performer, had led to a fall in which she injured her back. She was encased in a plaster of Paris jacket and kept in bed.[87]

Even if an occupational accident was not the reason for a patient's admission to hospital, many believed it was the circumstances in which they worked that gave rise to health problems. A 42-year-old blamed her 'sedentary life' for her constant constipation, and another woman blamed her pelvic pain on 12- to 14-hour days at the sewing machine.[88] For men it was exposure to the elements while labouring that ruined their health. Quin Win, a 37-year-old, suffered pains in the back after having 'been exposed to all weathers'.[89] Another man, a wool scourer, 'constantly exposed to wet and cold', was admitted to the hospital with pain and stiffness in his joints.[90]

The stresses of women's and men's working lives took different tolls on their bodies and psyches and, for men in particular, one solace lay in drink. Men's leisure activities, discussed in chapter six, had serious implications for their health. Alcoholism was the primary reason for male admission to the Otago Asylum at Seacliff and it was always a far more significant reason for male committal than for women. From 1898 until 1902 'alcoholism' comprised over 16 per cent of male admissions to asylums throughout New Zealand.[91] Asylums were legally designated as places for the cure of 'habitual drunkards', a definition that included those who, through excessive drinking, neglected their business or insufficiently provided for their family.[92] It was not drinking alone, but the combination of alcohol with delusions or violence that led to committal. A 30-year-old tailor from St Kilda, William Allen, was admitted to Seacliff in June 1910 after having suffered four bouts of delirium tremens in twelve months. According to his mother, William believed she was poisoning him and 'caught her by the throat with intent to injure her'. He was, she stated, 'energetic when off Drink'. Five weeks in Seacliff put an end, at least temporarily, to his 'Alcoholic Delusional Insanity'.[93]

In 1903 southern Dunedin boasted one public house for every 404 adults in the population. Pubs clearly offered a centre of social conviviality for men and perhaps a welcome respite from home if they were failing in their breadwinning role. A balm for the discontents of men could, however, result in violence for wives and children, a risk that marriage entailed for women. Violence and alcohol were often associated. The *Otago Daily Times* reported the case of James Jennings, charged with assaulting his wife. He argued that his assault was justified, 'for she tormented him a great deal, especially by hiding his clothes and by bringing people into the house he objected to'.[94] Women and children suffered varying degrees of ill-treatment but, for the judiciary, concern with preserving marriage usually overrode the sufferings of women from domestic violence.[95]

The financial stress of the breadwinner's role told in the admissions to the Seacliff Asylum, where men were over-represented. At the national level, from 1893 to 1897, 'money-related causes' were responsible for more than 23 per cent of all environmental causes of insanity for men; for women, this cause made up only 3.6 per cent of admissions. Walter Southgate, a carpenter for forty-six years, was suicidal when admitted to Seacliff. He had recently sustained a bad injury to his hand, but tried to continue working because he wanted to provide for his family. He believed they were poverty-stricken, but his wife denied this, stating that his money worries were exaggerated.[96] Daniel Donovan, the father of nine children aged from one year and eight months to fourteen years, suffered from 'spinal and brain disease' and, by June 1889, he had been in the asylum for three weeks. His eldest child was crippled and therefore unlikely to find work.[97] Families in receipt of relief, such as these, were unable to pay the expected maintenance towards the upkeep of their institutionalised members. Some men were sent from the Benevolent Institution to end their days in the asylum when senile dementia developed and they became an annoyance to other residents, such as 76-year-old retired sailor Jack Wilson.[98]

Women's committal to asylums was more commonly assigned to 'interpersonal causes' ('domestic troubles', 'love disappointments') than was the case with men: an unsurprising outcome in a culture where the meaning of women's lives was closely bound up with personal relationships.[99] Maggie Duncan believed 'herself and her family to be very wicked' and had tried to kill herself with poison and her children with a rolling pin. Although her husband pointed to influenza as the cause of her trouble, her doctor blamed the menopause and 'religious excitement'. Maggie Duncan, a 45-year-old woman originally from Scotland, was sent from her home in Caversham to the Seacliff Asylum in 1900, where she died eleven years later.[100]

For women in paid employment, work in the homes of others, as domestic servants, remained the most significant paid occupation nationally until the Second World War. The risks involved in such work varied according to the whims of employers, but a number of witnesses before the Sweating Commission in 1890 commented on the toll domestic service took on health. Ellen Wilson, a shirt finisher who had worked from 9 a.m. to 11 p.m., did so because she was 'not strong enough' for domestic service.[101] When domestic servants became ill, they were often quickly dispatched back to their families. The Bridges family of a mother and five children was considerably worse off when the eldest daughter had to return home from her job in service because of her ulcerated throat.[102] Eighteen-year-old Mildred Willis had to leave her position in service at St Clair because of 'ill-health'. The later presence of an illegitimate child suggests a possible cause of her illness.[103]

It is significant that the only category of violent death where the rate for European women began to approximate that for men in the years 1880–89 was that of 'Burns and Scalds'.[104] Boiling water for washing and fires for cooking were dangerous household activities for both wives and domestic servants. A 25-year-old widow living in South Dunedin, who had three children to support, scalded her foot, which meant that she could not continue her Friday job of scrubbing the local fruiterer's shop.[105]

The risks unique to women as wives and mothers, and those that changed most dramatically over the period, were those involved in childbirth. Local women, as friends, nurses and midwives helped them face these risks at home. Only the poor or the single resorted to the Benevolent lying-in ward or the Forth Street Maternity Hospital. The reproductive history of Ellen Williams, admitted to Dunedin Hospital in 1890 suffering from piles and

These two unidentified family groups illustrate the dramatic drop in family size from the 1880s to the 1930s. The 1890s group consists of six children, while by the 1930s, two children had become the norm.
OTAGO SETTLERS MUSEUM

fistulas, suggests the problems due to repeated childbearing. She had had ten children, six of whom were stillborn. She was suffering great pain down her back, in the area of her womb and during defecation. She was found to have external piles and a prolapse of the posterior wall of the vagina. Surgery to remove the piles was undertaken.[106]

Women certainly had a great deal to gain by limiting births. First and foremost, the risks of death in childbirth increased with each successive birth. Second, repeated childbearing brought health problems, such as slit cervixes, prolapsed uteruses and varicose veins. Third, the emotional and physical burdens of child care fell directly on mothers, particularly with the advent of compulsory education and restrictions on child labour.[107] Maternal mortality remained high until the later 1930s, when the introduction of sulphonamide drugs, effective against puerperal sepsis, helped bring rates down.[108]

Southern Dunedin residents were, like the rest of the nation, limiting births. Families of six or seven, common in the 1880s, were less common by the interwar years. One preliminary study, based on the 1937 Housing Survey, suggests that couples waited over three and a half years between the first and second births and that only 21 per cent of households contained more than three children.[109] Family limitation was most successful when couples were agreed on the number of children they would have, but it was often left to women to taken the appropriate measures. Loma Kent-Johnston recalled how her husband, a Protestant minister, suggested 'it would be a wise thing if we didn't have children to start off with until we got to know one another first'. The burden of this decision fell on Loma: 'I had to take precautions every jolly time and he didn't like the condom.'[110] When Marjorie Scott fell pregnant with her second child, she felt she couldn't go through another birth like her first one. When she was told that ergot acted as an abortifacient, her husband purchased some for her to take. It had the desired result: a miscarriage.[111]

Anxiety about children's health was heightened as couples began to limit the size of their families: the conscious choice of limiting births also led to less fatalism with regard to infant death. As fathers of smaller families, men had fewer dependants to provide for, but perhaps they wished to provide more. In 1920 the *Evening Star* ran an article on health and holidays, signalling a new expectation that leisure time, the subject of chapter six, was essential to good health.[112] Parents, as suggested in chapter four, might well wish their children to achieve higher educational levels than they had themselves and this required financial support of children for a longer time.

Managing risk

Time off work due to illness and the costs of hospitalisation depleted the funds of families lucky enough to be able to pay. Men were better able than women to make provision for sickness through membership of Friendly Societies: in Jennifer Carlyon's opinion 'one of the most comprehensive forms of insurance against the calamitous effects of illness or accident to the wage earner'.[113] In order to claim a benefit, the lodge doctor had to examine the applicant and sign a certificate, and then monitor the patient's progress carefully. Those in receipt of benefits from the Court of Saint Andrews, Ancient Order of Foresters, had all sorts of ailments, from broken shoulders and poisoned fingers to chronic rheumatism, lumbago and heart disease. James Burton received five shillings per week from 1911 until at least 1922 because he was unable to work through insanity.[114] James Jackson, an engine cleaner who joined the Foresters in 1911, had one week and four days off work through an accident in 1912, for which he received £1 13s 4d. Of the thirty-four claims for benefits that year, ten were for accidents, twenty-three for sickness and one for insanity. In 1914 the proportion of accidents rose to nearly 50 per cent; eighteen claims were made for accidents, nineteen for occasional sickness and James Burton continued to receive support because of his long-term insanity.[115]

Women's independent access to this form of protection from risk was limited, since the majority of lodges in southern Dunedin catered for a male-only membership (though wives did receive benefits through their husbands). The exception was Miriam Rebekah, a lodge for women in Kensington. Another Dunedin women's International Order of Odd Fellows lodge with extant records gives us an insight into how women's lodges operated. The sixteen members of Ruth Rebekah No. 3, founded in 1895, organised a lodge doctor at the cost of sixteen shillings a year for married members and a chemist's services at two shillings a head.[116] The forty benefit and thirty honorary members were urged in 1898 to remember 'the necessity of going to the Doctor upon the slightest approach of illness [. . .] [to] prevent unnecessary expense to the Lodge and also save themselves from a long period of suffering'.[117] Members also debated the necessity of having a woman doctor, although there were few to be had, but eventually Dr Emily Siedeberg was on their list.

Health invariably deteriorated with age and, until the provision of the Old Age Pensions Act in 1898 (restricted and meagre as pensions were), the elderly depended on family to provide for them in the trials of old age. The state stepped in to ameliorate the problems of the aged as a reward for their contribution to building the new society. Men, on average, were older than women in the southern suburbs. Some aged and infirm men were resident in the 'Benny': the Otago Benevolent Institution. Age and stage of the life cycle, as chapter seven suggests, were factors in descent into poverty. The Old Age Pensions Act provided a small pension to morally deserving persons over sixty-five years who had been resident in New Zealand for twenty-five years. Yet many men and women had lost their ability to work well before sixty-five, as the demands of labouring and constant childbearing took their toll. A number of men in receipt of outdoor relief from the Benny were younger than sixty-five and regarded as 'Past Work'. This was the situation of Henry Wilson, who, at sixty-four, suffered from 'dropsy, heart disease and bronchitis'.[118] Both 61-year-old Patrick McCusker and his 58-year-old wife were categorised as 'Past Work' by the Benny inspector in June 1889 and therefore unable to support their partially crippled 24-year-old son, who could not find work. Patrick suffered from 'acute rheumatism' and chronic asthma, which made him bedridden and eventually, a year later, he died. Four months after Patrick's death, his wife was admitted to the Benevolent Institution.[119]

Male citizens were expected to fight for their country, a duty not required of women, and many men from the southern suburbs risked their lives and health in the service of New Zealand and the Empire. One study suggests that, of those who enlisted from St Clair and Macandrew Road schools for service in the First World War, around 20 per cent died.[120] Those who returned to the community might well be incapacitated in some way, bearing either external or internal scars. They were likely to die at a younger age than their contemporaries and to suffer chronic disability.[121] Although such men might no longer have felt they fulfilled their duty as independent breadwinners, the Dunedin Returned Servicemen's Association strove to promote the 'digger spirit' of duty, self-sacrifice and comradeship and to see in disablement 'honorable scars'.[122]

Scarlet fever was particularly virulent in 1903, a year in which 131 people in New Zealand died of the disease. Mothers dreaded the outbreak of such infectious diseases, which could devastate families. In January, six girls were quarantined and cared for in the Caversham scarlet fever hospital (the Government Immigration Barracks had been converted to a 'temporary' fever hospital in 1860). Accompanying the original photograph was a request from the doctor in charge 'for any old underclothing, such as nightgowns, for some of the patients. He does not want much and he does not care how old it is, as it will be burnt after being used. This will save any outlay for these articles at the expense of the community'. OTAGO WITNESS, 21 JANUARY 1903.

The difficulty of anticipating and managing risks to health was thrown into relief by the worldwide influenza pandemic coinciding with the return of servicemen from the First World War. Death rates in New Zealand were highest among men between the ages of thirty and thirty-four. One study of the southern suburbs found sixty-five deaths from the 'flu, which, contrary to the national pattern of more deaths among men, struck down thirty-four women and thirty-one men.[123] The 'flu drew attention to substandard housing and poverty existing in urban areas.[124]

Perhaps the most difficult health risks to manage were the infectious diseases that might indiscriminately affect men, women and children. They could spread quickly in families, despite the best efforts of mothers, particularly when housing conditions were poor and cramped. Rheumatic fever struck Alexander Simpson, who had to give up his bakery job as a consequence. Soon his wife was suffering from the disease and had to be hospitalised in July 1889. Fortunately, it seems that none of the four young children were infected, but the family became dependent on relief during this period.[125] Other infectious diseases, such as typhoid, scarlet fever and diphtheria, might affect families, but over the period to 1940 there was a downward trend in mortality in all cases.[126]

Tuberculosis, or consumption, was a major cause of death in New Zealand in the nineteenth century, exceeded only by deaths from heart disease in 1900. It was a disease associated with poverty and overcrowding, and the mortality rates increased nationally in the depression years of the 1870s and 1880s.[127] The causes and the infectious nature of the disease were not recognised at this time, so little was able to be done for sufferers. By 1910 the Otago Hospital Board had built a specialised facility at Pleasant Valley, near Palmerston, for tuberculosis patients.[128] David Fenby, an apprentice at Hillside, had to abandon his job for a time in 1926 while he sought treatment for his tuberculosis at the Pleasant Valley Sanatorium.[129] Though men were over-represented among tuberculosis sufferers by the interwar years, as young women moved into the profession of nursing, they risked exposure to the disease.[130]

The way in which risk was managed changed dramatically over the period, as the state stepped in, first with old age pensions, then widows' pensions, family allowances and the 1938 Social Security Act to provide a financial cushion in cases of need. The last of these Acts had the greatest impact on access to health care by providing free maternity and hospital care and subsidising visits to the doctor for all New Zealanders. Whereas Friendly Societies had provided maternity benefits and health insurance for women primarily as the dependants of male breadwinners, women were now entitled to health services because they were citizens. The state stepped in to act as a 'surro-

Sufferers from tuberculosis are exposed to one of the major contemporary therapies: fresh air. The Nordrach sanatorium was established at Flagstaff, a hill near Dunedin, in 1899 by Drs Ralph Stephenson and E. H. Alexander. Those who could afford private treatment went there for open air, good food and rest. Sanatoria preferred to take early cases. Those with advanced tuberculosis were cared for in crowded wards at Dunedin Hospital or in the hospital wards at the Benevolent Institution. In 1910 the Hospital Board opened the purpose-built Pleasant Valley sanatorium, just south of Palmerston. OTAGO WITNESS, 19 FEBRUARY 1902

gate husband or father', increasing the range of benefits available to women as of right, but perpetuating a moral code that upheld the nuclear family.[131] Maternity and health benefits were made available to all 'the mothers of the race'.[132] The perceived need for more births to prevent white population decline made women's health a state, rather than an individual, concern.

Conclusion

In 1901 the *White Ribbon* instructed its readers on 'The Home Maker and What She Ought to Know'. First and foremost:

> she must of course be an expert in hygiene. Why, the daily health of her children depends on her treating them rationally from the standpoint of hygiene; she must give them the right food at the right hours, she must know when it is wise to sleep and how much clothing should be worn.[133]

Women in the southern suburbs of Dunedin lived and were judged by such texts, acting out cleaning rituals in order to preserve the health of their families. Gender not only influenced how and why people became ill, it also determined responsibility for health, and that responsibility lay with women. Although improvements in sanitation and housing created a context in which outbreaks of disease were less likely, women's daily work within the home ensured that germs were kept at bay.

On the national level, the state attempted to regulate women's exposure to ill-health by restricting their participation in dangerous trades. Yet the main improvements in women's health came about through their own initiative, by restricting the number of children they had. Ruth Cranefield's customers were among the many women attempting to avoid the risks of childbirth and its consequences by whatever means available. By the 1930s the individual acts of such women were subject to intense debate, and they were accused of requesting an abortion as calmly as they would order a tube of toothpaste.[134]

The uneasiness about family limitation was accompanied by concern as to whether women's new employment aspirations, discussed in chapter three, were leading in the right direction. 'The Diary of a Doctor Who Tells' related a cautionary tale to the readers of the *Evening Star*. A businesswoman from out of town came to the doctor in distress. She was taking time out because she had had a nervous breakdown. The doctor quickly discovered that the root of her problem lay in the fact that she was a high-powered 'executive head of a big department, working alongside and on equal terms with the male executives'. The problem, he found, was that she really wanted a husband and family. 'We ambitious business women are fools,' she wept. 'We never really fit in. We won't work the men's way, and we're always trying to grab extra authority.'[135] Good health was perceived to lie, in this case, in a match between individual aspirations and the shared assumptions of the wider culture.

Shared assumptions equated masculinity with risk-taking and, in particular, with risk in the workplace, a view that was articulated by the Hon. John MacGregor in the Legislative Council. 'The artisan and the mechanic is [sic] like the soldier,' he stated in the debate on workers' compensation for accidents in 1900, in that 'both run a risk of death or horrid maiming, and that in the interests of others – of the community at large. The soldier has his pension, the industrial soldier should have his.'[136]

Men's sacrifice for their dependants, whether on the battlefield or in the workplace, should be rewarded. The 1900 Workers' Compensation for Accident Act took a halting step in this direction by providing compensation for injury in certain occupations. The Act was progressively amended to include compensation for occupational diseases and lump-sum payments for loss of function. Although historians, like most contemporaries, have focused on strikes and amendments to the Arbitration Act, most local unionists regarded the 1908 Amendment to the Workers' Compensation Act as a major step towards a more just society. By the time of Donald Crossan's death in 1926, his wife and two children were entitled to receive compensation to a maximum of £750. In 1936 the Labour Government increased compensation for the dependants of deceased workers.

The army of 'industrial soldiers' was kept fighting fit by the 'experts in hygiene' running the households of the southern suburbs, and the expectation that this should be so changed little over the period. The structural background against which individual encounters with sickness were played out, however, shifted dramatically over the years 1890 to 1939. In 1890 hospitals were mainly a place of last resort and mostly by labouring men who were lucky to have one sheet on their bed and had to assist in ward duties.[137] By the 1930s all classes sought the relief from pain, surgical remedies and recuperative potential that the hospital offered. Women began to outnumber men in the admission statistics as they chose to give birth there rather than at home. The hospital, as John Angus has noted, came to be seen 'as a centre of medical technology rather than as a charitable institution'.[138]

The taint of charity was removed completely with the advent of the first Labour Government. The 1938 Social Security Act introduced free hospital care, maternity benefits to cover the costs of childbirth, and a subsidy for the costs of visiting the doctor. What had once been needs became reinterpreted as rights, and wives stood to gain significantly as the state moved to provide for health care, perhaps more reliably than some husbands. Gains were offset by losses. The authority that women had exercised over health matters in the home was at risk of being undermined by new professional sources of advice and judges of home hygiene: school doctors and Plunket nurses.

Women's and men's experience of sickness and disability differed because they were exposed to different life events and these were largely determined by gender. Biology played a part, but it was one that became less marked as women limited their exposure to childbearing. Norms of masculinity ensured that men risked life and limb to provide for dependants, while norms of femininity resulted in women's responsibility for the health of their families. Intense anxiety over shifts in these norms surfaced in debates about 'race suicide' and the selfishness of the modern mother of the two-child family in the 1930s. But concerns that men were becoming effete and women frivolous were assuaged by the outbreak of the Second World War. War, once more, reasserted masculine commitment to risk and feminine dedication to the home front.

Eleven God, the Devil and Gender

JOHN STENHOUSE

Sunday morning in southern Dunedin in early May of 1901 dawned calm, clear and frosty. The quiet was broken only by the chirping of birds, the clang of bells and the scuff of feet as adults strolled and children scampered to church. Thomas Kay Sidey, lawyer, community leader and politician, together with his wife and son, joined the well-heeled worshippers entering Caversham Presbyterian in Manse St (now Thorn St), Scottish burrs echoing softly. Nearby, at Forbury Corner, working-class and lower-middle-class folk, many of them English-born, filed into a small, wooden Primitive Methodist church. Not far away, similar sorts trickled into Caversham Baptist. Rachel Grimmett, from a humble English background, donned uniform and bonnet before marching confidently and alone to 'knee drill' at the Salvation Army 'Barracks' in South Dunedin. Catholics of all sorts streamed into capacious St Patrick's Basilica in Macandrew Rd: Irish Catholic women with husbands and children in tow; prosperous descendants of the English Catholic aristocracy, such as F. W. Petre, an architect; and a few old Chinese men from the Benevolent Institution. By nightfall almost a third of the adult population of the three southern boroughs had attended church, while most of the community's children – around three-quarters – had been to Sunday School or Bible Class. Even the local freethinkers, critics of organised Christianity, sent their children to the Dunedin Lyceum, the secularists' Sunday School. Females significantly outnumbered males at most of these gatherings. What, this chapter asks, did religious beliefs and practices mean for the pattern of gender relations in southern Dunedin over the period 1890 to 1940? How did religion shape gender? And how did gender influence religious belief and behaviour?

This chapter makes two major claims. First, I argue that, in our study area, and by extension the nation, religion mattered, significantly shaping

Kensington Sunday School Class, 1913. Virtually all Protestant churches ran Sunday Schools. Most parents sent their children to Sunday School even when they did not go to church themselves. Children dressed up in their Sunday best to attend this small, neat Presbyterian-run Sunday School in Kensington, where they learned about the Bible, Christian teaching, and the golden rule. ST ANDREWS JUBILEE SOUVENIR BOOKLET, 1913, OTAGO SETTLERS MUSEUM

gender identities and relations. 'Secular New Zealand' – if by 'secular' we mean 'non-religious' – has existed more in the minds of historians than in reality. Yet, although religion mattered, 'it' had no single, unambiguous or monolithic meaning for gender identities and relations. This is my second point. Understanding the relationship between religion and gender requires taking diversity seriously.

For example, churchgoing Protestant women either led or numerically dominated the great social movements of the period 1880–1920: temperance and prohibition, Bible-in-Schools, and votes for women. These first-wave feminists set about transforming what many saw as a less than godly, male-dominated culture that paid too little attention to the concerns of women and children. They deployed Christian ideas and arguments to attack prevailing norms, obtain greater equality between the sexes and transform gender relations. Churchwomen in southern Dunedin, where evangelical Protestantism flourished, signed the 1893 suffrage petition in greater proportions than virtually any other urban area in the country, turning it into a stronghold of Christian feminism.[1] Yet Christian women could be found on the conservative as well as the liberal/progressive side of the great debates of

Laying the foundation stone of the Dunedin Lyceum, Dowling Street, 1881. Freethinkers, a diverse group united only by their hostility to the churches and a desire to secularise society, built their own Sunday School, the Dunedin Lyceum, near the city centre in 1881. Well-represented in southern Dunedin, freethinkers, mostly male, aimed to show that they were as committed as churchgoers to raising moral, upright children. OTAGO SETTLERS MUSEUM

the period, with many, probably most, taking middle-of-the-road positions. Many women, not especially interested in politics, dedicated their lives to husbands, children, community, church and nation in ways that, though problematic to many modern historians, have received little scholarly attention.

Diversity also characterised the relationship between religion and masculinity. Many New Zealand males looked with ambivalence upon organised religion, numerically dominated by females. Only a minority of men regularly attended church. Yet males dominated the pulpit and a significant minority could be found in the pew. Committed male Christians often led or supported the female-dominated social crusades of the period, though other churchgoing men, and many non-churchgoers, opposed or attacked female activists as wowsers and shrieking radicals. The fact that New Zealand males gave their religions – and anti-religions – diverse social meanings does not make them unimportant.

This chapter seeks to make sense of the small world of southern Dunedin by placing it in a series of broader contexts: patterns of gendered religiosity in Western Europe since the early modern period; the nineteenth-century British background; and the cultural patterns that emerged in colonial

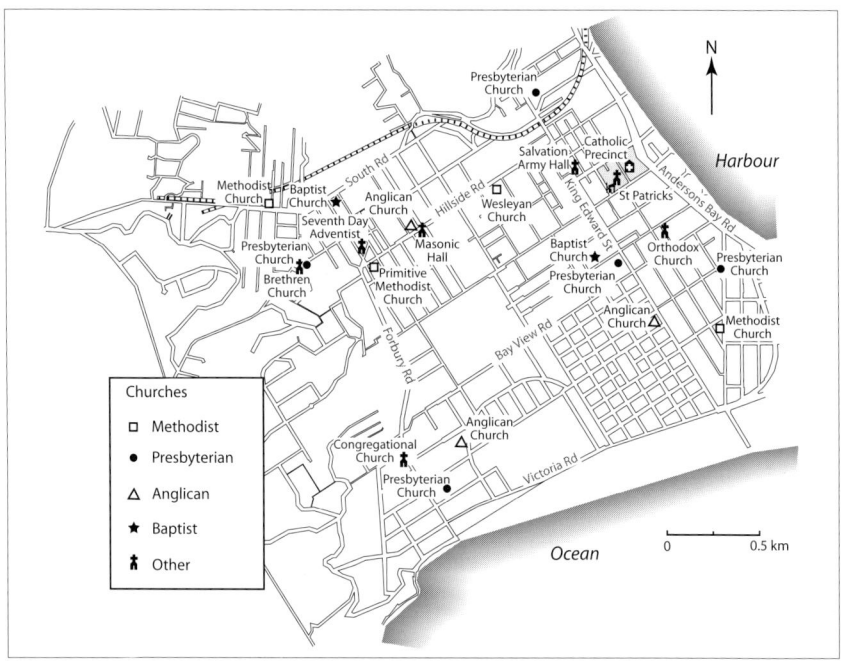

Map 11.1 Selected sites of worship, 1891–1939

New Zealand before 1890. It aims less to provide definitive answers than to speculate fruitfully and identify areas for further research. The primary sources on which I rely include census data; church records, such as membership lists, baptismal records, marriage registers and communion rolls; and oral histories. None proved an instant El Dorado. Census categories changed over time, for example, making it impossible systematically to trace changes in religious adherence in southern Dunedin's three main boroughs over the half-century of our study. Some groups, notably the Presbyterians, kept excellent records. Anglican data, by contrast, proved frustratingly patchy and incomplete. Oral histories, though posing their own interpretive problems, illuminated the mentalities of the inhabitants of greater Caversham in ways that mostly complemented other primary sources. The almost thirty people who spoke to us about religion represented a cross-section of the community: comfortably-off community leaders as well as working folk of modest means; committed believers from a range of denominations as well as atheists and everyone in between.

Brief explanations about perspective and definitions may help orient readers. My approach is broadly Weberian. I take seriously both the material and the spiritual (or symbolic) worlds that the citizens of greater Caversham created. Each context, material and ideal, shaped and was shaped by the other; I see neither as more basic or 'real'.[2] If I pay more attention in what follows to the latter, that is simply because previous researchers, led by Erik Olssen, have ably illuminated the worlds of work and politics.[3]

Second, when I use terms such as 'the churches', 'organised Christianity', and cognates, I am not simply referring to the views of the churches' mostly male leaders. To identify the churches with their male hierarchies constitutes a species of clericalism that fails to take sufficient account of the agency of ordinary New Zealanders, female and male, who did not invariably kowtow to bishops, priests and ministers. I focus here on popular religion, Christianity as ordinary New Zealanders created it, rather than on the 'top down' approach that once dominated church history. Furthermore, I do not identify 'religion' exclusively with organised Christianity and its institutions. Jews, adherents of Chinese religions, atheists, agnostics, theosophists and spiritualists all lived out their lives in southern Dunedin communities, numerically dominated by Christians. Faith flourished outside as well as within religious institutions. Although the rugby field, the pub, the lodge and the workplace constituted more popular places for many men than churches, we cannot assume that Christianity played no role in such places. Though local people did not generally wear their religion on their sleeves, the beliefs and values males learned in Sunday School and the family, often taught and reinforced by women, meant something, even in seemingly 'secular' masculine sites. Still, church records were accessible and this chapter relies substantially on them.

The American historian Joan Scott has argued that gender constitutes a primary way of signifying relationships of power.[4] It seems undeniable that in the Christian West males have often deployed religious discourse – and whatever else they could find – to legitimise a patriarchal social order that, in theory and to some extent in practice, sanctioned the subordination of females in church, state, society and family. Yet movements for the emancipation of women, led mostly by religious believers, also emerged out of the Christian West. Women (and men) found in Christianity not only subordination, dependency and oppression, but also power, authority, community and identity. This chapter eschews essentialist views of Christianity as either fundamentally oppressive, reactionary and patriarchal, or as essentially emancipatory, progressive and feminist. Both overly reductive interpretations fail to do justice to the complex reality of the past. Organised religion appears in the following narrative, then, neither as God – the fount of light, goodness and liberation – nor as the Devil – unmitigated darkness, evil and oppression – but as a bit of both, and mostly something in between.

Historiography

Before focusing on religion and gender in southern Dunedin, this case study must be set in the broader context of the evolution of New Zealand historical writing. The following sketch, brief and selective, picks out some significant patterns in the established historiography. For several reasons, I contend, religion has constituted a blind spot for many New Zealand historians. The rise of social history, of women's history, and of gender history has until recently tended to reinforce the secular perspective. The consequent marginalisation of religion, and especially of the moderate and conservative religious believers who existed in large numbers, impoverishes our understanding of our past, and of the ways in which gender has operated in our culture.

From the nineteenth century until the 1960s, general histories of New Zealand, written almost exclusively by men, focused largely on males, particularly those who wielded power and influence. War and politics commanded most attention. Women appeared only occasionally.[5] Few scholars noted a second, probably related, silence. Organised religion, numerically dominated by females, also received little attention. That some of our most influential male historians rejected Christian belief probably helps explain this. William Pember Reeves, arguably our most influential nineteenth-century historian, constituted one of several freethinking critics of organised Christianity in the Liberal Government of the 1890s. Although his histories depicted the missionary period rosily, religion virtually disappeared thereafter, and Pakeha males, the main actors, appeared largely secular in character and outlook – not unlike Reeves himself.[6]

In the twentieth century, Keith Sinclair made himself arguably the most influential New Zealand historian ever.[7] His historical writing, like that of Reeves, reflected the secular outlook of the post-Enlightenment religious sceptic, a type well represented among Pakeha intellectuals from the beginning of settlement. Few New Zealand readers expressed disquiet, perhaps because the Reeves–Sinclair tradition in certain respects echoed the Puritan mythistories of New England divines such as Cotton Mather. His *Magnalia Christi Americana* helped create a powerful and enduring sense of America as a light to the nations, a specially chosen land on which the eyes of the world were fixed.[8] The New Zealand of Reeves and Sinclair, though secular, outshone even Christian America as a world exemplar of enlightenment and virtue. Both historians depicted New Zealand as a post-Enlightenment 'city upon a hill', pioneering enlightened race relations, votes for women, industrial and labour legislation, old age pensions and other humane and progressive social policies. Their nationalist histories, celebrating the remarkable achievements of the New Zealand people, appealed greatly to their readers.

The nationalism of the Reeves–Sinclair paradigm also helps explain why its authors marginalised religion. In the Old World, religious differences divided nations. Englishmen spilled each other's blood in the mid-seventeenth century, religious divisions remained potent forces in British politics, and English, Scots and Irish settlers brought sectarianism with them to New Zealand. Reeves and Sinclair, seeking to construct historical myths of origins and identity around which New Zealanders could unite, played down religion, which they saw as a potential source of disunity, by secularising our past.

Sinclair also gave his historical writing a populist, masculinist flavour by celebrating the values of the 'ordinary bloke': mateship, egalitarianism, anticlericalism, rugby, racing and beer. 'Sunbathing and surfing, uninhibited striptease shows, the vast numbers of drinkers listening to singers or bands in suburban bars' illustrated the New Zealander's 'love of varied pleasures', he enthused. 'Many a "Kiwi" drinker must look into his nine ounce glass,' Sinclair observed in *A History of New Zealand*, 'only to discover there the disapproving face of his Primitive Methodist ancestor.' But the day of the wowser had gone, and a 'simple materialism' had replaced Christianity as the 'prevailing religion' of mid-twentieth-century New Zealanders. The 'pursuit of health and possessions' filled 'more minds than thoughts of salvation', Sinclair declared approvingly.[9] This view of the New Zealand past, celebrating a healthy, fun-loving, secular present displacing a puritanical religious past, reached a growing audience during the 1960s and 70s. As tertiary education boomed, left-leaning university-based historians, with Sinclair leading the way, constructed myths of origin that also constituted myths of national identity. Now secular historians, not Christian ministers or lay people, told New Zealanders where they had come from, and who they were.

The mainstream Protestant churches, which had traditionally seen themselves as critic and conscience of society, saw that role challenged, if not usurped, by university-based intellectuals during the 1960s, a decade in which internal conflicts divided the Protestant world. In 1967 the Presbyterian Church, which claimed the allegiance of almost one in four Pakeha New Zealanders, tried their own Professor of Old Testament, Lloyd Geering, for heretical views on the resurrection of Christ, attracting nationwide television coverage. New Zealand Christians could not agree among themselves, it seemed, about what constituted Christianity. *Time* magazine announced the death of God. Dwindling numbers of the ageing occupied gradually emptying pews in the mainstream Protestant churches, while young people flocked in record numbers to burgeoning universities.

There, many history students during the 1970s and 1980s encountered the views of E. P. Thompson, an English Marxist, whose *The Making of the*

English Working Class (1963) inspired a new wave of social history written 'from below'. The new social historians aimed to rescue previously neglected or marginalised groups – in Thompson's case the English working class – from the 'enormous condescension of posterity'.[10] New Zealand historians of women, influenced by the new politically commited social history and by second-wave feminism, soon argued that females, a majority of the human race, constituted perhaps the most neglected of those 'hidden from history'. Feminist historians made recovering the historical experience of women central to what became in the 1980s a larger project of rewriting general histories in new ways that recognised the importance of gender.

Yet one large group of New Zealanders remained at least as marginal in the new 'bottom up' histories as in the old 'top down' ones: lay religious believers, especially those who had some connection with Christian churches. This group constituted the great majority of the Pakeha population, and was dominated, as I shall show, by women. E. P. Thompson, who dismissed England's Anglican Establishment as 'Old Corruption' and despised Methodism as 'psychic masturbation', articulated a hostile attitude towards organised religion widely shared by the new breed of social historians. Their campaign to rescue the poor and marginalised from posterity's condescension turned out all too often, when it came to religious believers, to be highly selective.[11] Second-wave feminist antipathy toward Christian patriarchy (literally, 'father-rule'), which many feminists perceived as the root of much if not all evil, subjugating women and preventing them from achieving equality in the public sphere, exacerbated such hostility. Several leading New Zealand historians writing in the 1970s and 1980s depicted the churches as bastions of patriarchy. According to Erik Olssen and Andrée Levesque, writing in 1978 on the origins of the European family in New Zealand, the churches provided 'the principal justification for the patriarchal family'; the clergy were 'moral police', constituting 'eyes and agents of community control'.[12] Barbara Brookes, writing on abortion in the 1930s, depicted the churches as upholders of a repressive established order that, out of touch with the realities of women's lives, limited access to birth control, condemned abortion out of hand, and prevented recognition of women's 'individual autonomy' and 'their right to freely elect, or deny, motherhood'.[13] Margaret Tennant, reflecting on her earlier studies of female Christian reformers in late nineteenth and early twentieth-century New Zealand, noted how she then emphasised their 'social control and punitive morality'.[14] Such histories reinforced the established masculinist tradition of depicting organised religion as a restrictive, stultifying, repressive force – a Bad Thing – from which New Zealanders, particularly women, required liberation. Christian patriarchy functioned in such texts almost as the Devil, with the historian serving as exorcist. Such works illustrate the accuracy of David Harlan's recent contention that, in addition to their many other functions and purposes, historical texts have often constituted forms of moral discourse.[15] Collectively, the works discussed above established a particular perspective on the New Zealand past, which, during the 1970s and 1980s, became almost a new orthodoxy, though seldom recognised as such. Like all orthodoxies, it deserves careful scrutiny.

It was characterised by three features. First, the new historical paradigm, teleological, depicted nineteenth-century religious darkness giving way, gradually but inexorably, to twentieth-century secular light. Second, proponents generally characterised secularisation – the decline of religion and the rise of secular outlooks – as largely inevitable and unproblematic – a Good Thing. The American historian Anne Braude has criticised the secularisation thesis as both empirically weak and reflecting the world-view of secularising intellectual and political élites inclined to depict religious women as unenlightened reactionaries clinging to archaic and unscientific world-views.[16] Third, like other forms of advocacy history, the new orthodoxy, committed to opening up the public sphere to women, regularly fell prey to present-centredness. All too often the new social historians found in the past the regrettable absence of the present: late twentieth-century values regarding women's roles, gender relations and sexuality. All three assumptions, mutually reinforcing, discouraged historians from attempting to understand those New Zealanders – and they were many – who did not hold the desired contemporary values, or who held them insufficiently strongly. Many New Zealanders, too conservative, too religious, or simply too ordinary and unremarkable for historians' tastes, remained forgotten. Collectively, they constituted the mainstream New Zealand historians' 'Other'.

The new paradigm never entirely swept the field, however. The fullest and most empathic treatment of religion in the *Oxford History of New Zealand*, appearing in 1981, came – not surprisingly perhaps – from a female historian. According to Jeanine Graham, 'Christian faith and practice played a fundamental role in the shaping of colonial society', with the 'greater proportion of the population' acting according to 'what was essentially a Christian code'.[17] Feminist scholars such as Phillida Bunkle explored the evangelical origins, moral concerns and religious activities of first-wave feminist organisations such as the Women's Christian Temperance Union without, however, paying much attention to the interconnections between religion, social purity and politics.[18] Jock Phillips's pioneering study of New Zealand masculinities, *A Man's Country?*, noted the importance of religion to women and the social significance of the temperance movement, without exploring religion's meanings for manhood in much detail.[19] Historians such as Ian Breward, Hugh Jackson, Allan Davidson and Peter Lineham illuminated many aspects of New Zealand religious history, without having much impact on mainstream scholarship.

During the 1990s, however, religion began to edge back onto the agenda, thanks partly to impressive new scholarship in social, women's and gender history. Historians determined to understand women's lives sympathetically began to question the prevailing religion-as-false-consciousness assumption and to reveal how important religion had been to many women. Jessie Munro's award-winning biography of Mother Suzanne Aubert, for example, depicted a remarkable French Catholic nun whose traditional piety inspired a joyful zest for life and life-long dedication to loving and serving all, including the despised and rejected, without regard for colour, class or creed.[20] As a 'postgraduate researcher in the 1970s', Margaret Tennant reflected, she had written 'somewhat scathingly' about female Christian reformers. But by the late 1990s she had come to see 'the lives of females past' as 'more complex', the 'Christian frameworks within which many operated' as not only 'restrictive', but also 'enabling'.[21] Caroline Daley's study of gender in Taradale between 1886 and 1930 illuminated religion's importance to women, families, local communities and – by implication at least – the wider society. Taradale appeared markedly less atomised, bondless and anomic than Miles Fairburn's *The Ideal Society and Its Enemies* had implied.[22] James Belich, whose early work on war and politics tended to marginalise Pakeha religion, gave it slightly more space and significance in *Making Peoples* and *Paradise Reforged*.[23] Such evidence suggests that New Zealand historians may at last be developing a more complex, inclusive, and less teleological view of our past, in which religion receives the historical understanding routinely accorded to war, politics, class, race, health, sex and gender.

Southern Dunedin's religious landscape

Before developing this revisionist project in the context of southern Dunedin, a brief sketch of the local religious landscape is in order. Southern Dunedin was born modern, religiously speaking, in at least two respects. First, the state and the public sphere constituted secular domains. By 'secular' I mean simply that the state favoured no single church with the legal and political privileges enjoyed by established churches in the Old World; this does not imply that religion played no significant public role. In southern Dunedin, no church could establish effective *de facto* religious dominance because none had anything like a majority of even nominal adherents.

Second – and partly as a consequence of the first – a remarkable variety of churches, sects and religious movements bloomed in a diverse, open and pluralistic local religious economy. Small but lively groups of agnostics, atheists, rationalists, freethinkers, spiritualists, phrenologists, astrologers and fortune-tellers flourished in southern Dunedin, whose New Age dawned early. Males, as I shall show below, overwhelmingly dominated those groups – atheists, agnostics, rationalists and those professing 'no religion' – that were most distant from, and hostile to, orthodox Christianity. This lively assortment of religiously heterodox citizens lived and worked alongside small minorities of Jews from Britain and Europe, a few dozen Chinese Buddhists and Confucians, Lebanese Christians (Orthodox and Catholic), and English, Scottish and Irish Christians of all varieties.

Among Protestant Christians, an unusual concentration of evangelicals, many from English nonconformist backgrounds, made southern Dunedin religiously distinctive. Baptists, mostly of English origin, constituted almost 10 per cent of the population at the beginning of our period, four times as numerous as in the country as a whole. Small evangelical churches such as

Salvation Army Children, c. 1890s. By the 1890s women dominated the officer corps of the Salvation Army, which established a 'Barracks' in South Dunedin in the 1880s. The four female officers pictured here, including the formidable Rachel Grimmett (centre right), attracted a large group of girls and a few boys, mostly from working and lower-middle-class homes, most of the girls neatly dressed in hats and bonnets. *OTAGO WITNESS*, 7 MARCH 1922.

Laying the foundation stone of a new convent. Roman Catholics, mostly from working-class Irish backgrounds, established a strong presence in the southern suburbs, particularly in South Dunedin. The Church built a basilica, convent, and school, which attracted Catholic families to settle. By the 1890s, Catholics constituted about a fifth of the population of the borough of South Dunedin, and got on more and less well with their mostly Protestant neighbours. *OTAGO WITNESS*, 27 FEBRUARY 1901, OTAGO SETTLERS MUSEUM

the Congregationalists, the Church of Christ, the Brethren and the Salvation Army constituted another 5 per cent of the total. Evangelical Protestants combined, if we include Presbyterians in this category, made up about half the population of southern Dunedin in 1891. Church attendance rates in southern Dunedin were thus probably higher than in most other urban areas in the country.

Roman Catholics, mostly from Irish backgrounds, constituted a significant minority. Their numbers varied from just under 10 per cent in the borough of Caversham to more than 20 per cent in South Dunedin, well above their 14 per cent proportion in the nation. The presence in South Dunedin of a large Catholic church, St Patrick's, and associated infrastructure, notably Catholic schools, probably attracted Catholic families to settle in South Dunedin.

Little changed as the nation modernised between 1890 and 1939. The total of professing and churchgoing Christians declined slightly as a proportion of a growing population. The gradual entry of women into paid employment and higher education, together with the rise of new leisure and entertainment options, probably explains this mild downturn. The numbers of those professing 'no religion', or 'objecting to state' – overwhelmingly male – rose slightly, but remained minuscule. Believing without actively belonging

The Marlow family of South Dunedin, c. 1920. The Marlows, a devout Catholic couple, produced no less than ten children, a large family even by Catholic standards. Some historians have argued that Catholics began limiting their family size about as fast as most Protestants. Not the Marlows. As the photo shows, half of their ten children – three priests and two nuns – devoted themselves to the religious life, illustrating the attractions of and status attached to religious vocations in the Catholic world of the time. COURTESY OF THE MARLOW FAMILY, OTAGO SETTLERS MUSEUM

remained the dominant religious pattern in southern Dunedin, as in most parts of Britain and Western Europe. If secularisation is defined as the widespread abandonment of Christian belief and practice, it cannot be shown to have occurred on a significant scale during this period. Continuity rather than change constituted the most striking feature of New Zealand's socio-religious landscape during the first half of the twentieth century.

The feminisation of New Zealand religion?

What did religion mean to New Zealand women? In an article first published in 1974, Barbara Welter, an American feminist historian, argued that the years between 1800 and 1860 witnessed the 'feminization of American religion'. Welter used this term to describe a series of related processes: the growing numerical predominance of women in congregations and church-related welfare, reform, and missionary organisations; the rise of new American religious movements led by women, such as Seventh Day Adventism and Christian Science; and, in theology, the decline of strict Calvinism, hell and damnation, and the rise of kinder, gentler, allegedly more 'feminine' conceptions of God and forms of Christianity. Welter argued that the dignity, equality, sisterhood and spiritual strength women found in religion fired the nineteenth-century women's movement.[24] Can we see analogous processes at work in southern Dunedin between 1890 and 1939? Is it appropriate to speak of the feminisation of New Zealand religion?

We must begin answering this question by placing nineteenth-century developments in a longer and wider context. Women had dominated church membership and participation throughout Western Europe, in both Protestant and Catholic countries, since the seventeenth century, if not earlier. Clive Field analysed sex ratios in the English Free Churches – Baptists and Congregationalists – from 1650 to the present, and found that female members consistently and significantly outnumbered males over the entire period.[25] Historians of Western Europe see this pattern of gendered religiosity as a widely accepted division of labour within the household. Women took most responsibility for religious matters, while men offered support, often passively, an attitude exemplified by the London working man who, opening the door to the local vicar, said: 'Ah, you're from the church: you want to see the missus.'[26] Many Pakeha New Zealanders brought this pattern with them. It was 'mothers that always saw that children went to Sunday school or church', recalled a Caversham woman of her childhood.[27]

Statistically, the southern Dunedin situation is clear, confirming the broad outlines of the picture Caroline Daley has painted of religious life in Taradale.[28] Women outnumbered men in most Protestant churches, modestly among nominal adherents, and by a wider margin when it came to church attendance, taking communion and other measures of active religiosity. At St Peter's Anglican church, for example, a congregation in which unskilled working men were the only substantially under-represented occupational group, female communicants greatly outnumbered males. Between 1901 and 1909, an average of 278 Anglicans per year took communion. Of these, no less than 76 per cent were female. Of the 211 female communicants, only 72 were married, as against 139 singles. Half of all Anglican communicants, then, were single women, who constituted only about 29 per cent of the population of Caversham at this time.[29] Presbyterian communion rolls tell a similar story. Females constituted 67 per cent of communicants at Caversham Presbyterian Church in 1911, as against 33 per cent of males, among whom few unskilled or semi-skilled workers could be found. Single women again predominated, constituting almost half (46 per cent) of all communicants. A large majority were unmarried, with widows matching their proportions in the local community.[30] In 1915, with a proportion of Methodist men away as volunteers in the armed forces, 69 per cent of the members of Caversham Methodist church were female; by 1920 that had risen slightly to 70 per cent. Married women outnumbered married men by an almost two to one ratio; single women outnumbered single men almost three to one.[31] Caversham Baptist membership lists enable us to identify 59 members in 1892 and 164 in 1909. Sixty-seven per cent of Baptist members were female in both years.[32] The Methodist and Baptist churches, reflecting their British origins, attracted more skilled, semi-skilled and unskilled workers, and proportionally fewer from 'higher' occupational groups than either the Anglicans or Presbyterians. Yet all Protestant churches contained many skilled workers, constituting cross-class institutions. Active church involvement remained a predominantly female activity in the four Protestant churches studied, with women comprising between two-thirds and three-quarters of active members.

These statistics suggest that the gender gap in most Protestant denominations, narrow during childhood, when around three-quarters of all children in Otago and Southland attended Sunday School, widened from adolescence on. Oral histories suggest that teenage boys often ended church-related activities when they left school and started working, particularly if they were unskilled. Probably unskilled working-class males, following British patterns, were especially likely to see religion as women's business, to identify churchgoing with wowserism and sissiness, and to discourage active religiosity among the young men they socialised into their subculture. Single women, as the statistics show, dominated the pew, with married women some way behind.[33]

Why did single women outnumber the married among actively religious females? Oral histories suggest that the domestic demands imposed by marriage and childrearing curtailed churchgoing for some married women, at least temporarily. 'I had the first baby and then I had the second baby' and we stopped going to church so much, recalled Myrtle Caird.[34] Once her mother got married and 'had those children', recalled Victoria Lake, she 'couldn't very well be too involved'.[35] Probably cooking the Sunday roast as well as minding babies kept married women at home. Married couples who stayed at home while sending the kids off to Sunday School – and there must have been many of these – could obtain a few hours of rest, relaxation and intimacy in an otherwise hectic week. Probably Sunday School doubled as day care and baby-sitting. How many New Zealand babies were conceived on child-free Sunday mornings?

What about the second factor identified by Welter, the rise of female-led religious movements? Here, the success in southern Dunedin of the Women's Christian Temperance Movement, a religious movement as much as a political one, deserves attention. The suffrage petitions, supported by the WCTU, asked adult females to sign a petition calling on the House of Representatives to grant women the right to vote. As noted in chapter two, 57 per cent of the adult female population of southern Dunedin signed the third petition in 1893, a larger proportion than in any similar-sized urban area in the country.[36] Southern Dunedin constituted a hotbed of support for first-wave feminism. Why? In this chapter we can examine more closely the effects of religious denomination.

Previous historians have noted that the WCTU flourished in areas where Presbyterianism was strong.[37] Yet it was not especially strong in southern Dunedin. According to the 1891 census, in none of our three southern boroughs did Presbyterians constitute even a third of the population. What made southern Dunedin religiously distinctive, and helps explain the widespread support for the suffrage petition, was the overall strength of evangelical Protestantism. To a plurality of Presbyterians from Scottish backgrounds, we must add evangelical Protestants of English origins, notably Baptists and Methodists, who were far more numerous in southern Dunedin than in New Zealand as a whole. According to the 1891 census, in South Dunedin Baptists constituted 6.9 per cent of the population, in St Kilda 10.2 per cent, and in Caversham a whopping 12.2 per cent, more than five times their proportion in the nation as a whole of 2.4 per cent. Methodists, slightly below their national average of around 10 per cent in 1891, grew rapidly to constitute almost 15 per cent of the population of South Dunedin in 1901. Smaller evangelical denominations, such as the Congregationalists, the Church of Christ, the Brethren and the Salvation Army, all established effective presences, making up a combined total of almost 5 per cent of the population of Caversham and South Dunedin in 1891. All these evangelical Protestants combined constituted around half the population of our study area. They went more regularly to church, and showed greater zeal over a range of moral and social issues, public as well as private, than most non-evangelical Christians. At least 60 per cent, if not two-thirds, of the active members of these evangelical churches were female. We need go little further to explain the remarkable level of support for the 1893 suffrage petition.[38]

What is particularly interesting about the 1893 petition is that, although the patchiness of church records allows identification of the denomination of only a modest proportion of signatories, they include many Anglican women and at least eighteen Catholics.[39] Evidently not a few Catholic women made up their own minds to support votes for women, rejecting the advice of a Catholic hierarchy generally critical of first-wave feminists as yet another group of Protestants trying to tell Catholics how to behave. Were female Catholic signatories influenced by evangelical Protestant friends and neighbours?

Were women readier than men to ignore the Catholic–Protestant divide, and to practise a neighbourly ecumenism across the back fence?

Rachel Grimmett (1835–1921), who signed the suffrage petition, exemplifies the kind of evangelical Protestant woman too easily dismissed as a 'wowser'. Both she and her husband Richard embraced Salvation Army-style Christianity in the 1890s. By 1892 women constituted more than half the Army's full-time commissioned officers and commanded the five largest corps in the country, including Dunedin and Invercargill. For some, Army-style Christianity went hand in hand with militant feminism. 'I often feel like speaking my mind on the subject of women's rights,' declared Lieutenant Gertrude Gates in the *War Cry* in 1892. 'God has given us brains, then why should we not use them, particularly when it is for His honour and glory?' The Salvation Army had 'broken down the orthodox idea that woman's place is at home, and has given us what has long been needed – unrestrained liberty of action and thought'.[40] Rachel Grimmett practised what Gates preached, confounding contemporary – and some modern historians' – conceptions of Christian femininity. As Brian Heenan shows in chapter eight, she refused to confine herself to the private, domestic sphere and often marched alone through the streets to 'knee drill' (prayer and worship) at the 'Barracks', or to help out at the 'Benny', or at the soup kitchen run by the Army. Determined to carry the good fight to Satan's strongholds, God's Christian soldier invaded sacred male public space. Standing outside the Waterloo Hotel at Forbury Corner, as well as other pubs, Rachel stared down male drinkers as they came out, collecting money for the Army's charitable work and handing out copies of the *War Cry*. Some men reacted angrily. Understanding pubs, clubs and Parliament as sacred male space helps explain why. In boldly bringing female, family and Christian values into pub, club and politics, first-wave feminists were transgressing hallowed boundaries between sacred and secular, church and world, male and female domains. If the 'wowsers' had their way, it looked as though no autonomous male space would remain immune from female, family and religious values. Little wonder that male critics denounced first-wave feminists as a 'shrieking sisterhood' of interfering religious busybodies trying to turn the world upside down.

Rachel Grimmett not only carried family and Christian values into public space, she also – as chapter eight shows – brought the world of business into the home. Distinctions between a female-dominated private sphere of religion and family and a male public sphere of business and politics meant little in her household. Richard Grimmett might well have been surprised to learn that he was supposed to exercise supreme authority in household and family. Patriarchy meant little in this Salvation Army household. Decades later, her grandchildren remembered their matriarch with awe.[41]

Though Rachel Grimmett was a formidable character, her conviction that Christian women ought to exercise moral authority in a public sphere that could no longer be left exclusively to men was the kind that inspired thousands of like-minded women actively to support the great social movements of the period 1880–1920. Temperance and prohibition, votes for women, sabbath observance and Bible-in-schools attracted huge female interest and support. The churches' predominantly female membership and support base suggests that historians, who have hitherto focused largely on the male leaders of these movements, might reinterpret them as women's movements, expressing complex but powerful combinations of female, maternal, family and religious values. If a 'Great Tightening' transformed New Zealand during these years, 'moral evangelists' such as Grimmett powered it from below.[42]

Third, theological changes of the kind identified by Welter began to transform New Zealand as well as American Protestantism. During the last quarter of the nineteenth century, a growing number of Protestant ministers abandoned what they regarded as harsh, inhumane and exclusive conceptions of Christianity for warmer and more inclusive ones. In 1886, for example, the Reverend William Salmond, who had been Professor of Divinity at the Theological Hall, Knox College, and now occupied the chair of Mental and Moral Science at the University of Otago, published *The Reign of Grace*. In it he condemned traditional Calvinism for depicting God as a Cosmic Tyrant who tortured the damned for all eternity. Such horrendous theologies, declared Salmond, libelled the 'merciful Father' of Jesus Christ and encouraged 'tens of thousands' of thinking people to embrace 'speechless Atheism'. Salmond's sensational pamphlet ran quickly through five editions. Outraged conservative Presbyterians tried its author for heresy.[43] Three years later the Reverend James Gibb, the popular minister of Dunedin's First Church, publicly rejected the idea that non-elect infants would suffer eternal torment in hell. Painful personal experience informed Gibb's growing theological liberalism. He and his wife had suffered the loss of three of their own children in infancy. Both agonised over their post-mortem fate. The spiritual travails of Christian couples almost certainly reshaped the theologies publicly articulated by men.[44]

To conclude, then, Welter's feminisation thesis illuminates the gendered pattern of religious behaviour in southern Dunedin over our period, but only modestly. The gender gap in religious observance yawned wider on the colonial frontier than in Britain, thanks to the excess of single, non-churchgoing males until after the First World War. Women almost certainly did influence the warmer and broader theologies that arose in the nineteenth century and spread widely in the opening decades of the twentieth, though few contemporaries saw liberal Protestantism as 'feminised religion'.

Yet the discussion so far fails to answer several important questions. Why did New Zealand women go to church more frequently than men? What did they get out of religion? Should we see the churches as essentially patriarchal institutions that inculcated female subordination and self-sacrifice, turning girls and women into victims of Christian patriarchy? Or, as the example of Rachel Grimmett suggests, did they *also* constitute sites in which girls and women exercised agency, created community, and found moral authority and spiritual power?

The churches attracted women as public spaces that they could rightfully occupy. Just as pubs, sports clubs, Orange and Masonic lodges and other men's organisations offered men space apart from work and home that were sacred to the cause of male conviviality, the churches offered women sacred territory of their own. Though men dominated the pulpits and hierarchies of most of southern Dunedin's churches, women numerically dominated the pew, the choir, the Sunday School, Bible Class and the women's missionary society. Caversham Methodist Church, for example, ran a remarkable array of auxiliaries during the first two decades of the twentieth century. Those open to both sexes, most of which were numerically dominated by females, included a Sunday School, choir, Physical Culture Class, Junior Christian Endeavour Society, Young Worshippers' League, Wesley Guild, Band of Hope and a Bible and Literary Society. Those catering specifically for women included a Young Women's Bible Class, a Ladies' Auxiliary, a Nursing Society, a Ladies' Guild, and a Ladies' Sewing Guild.

In all the churches women raised often impressive sums of money by running bazaars, cake stalls, sewing circles and so on to finance church and school building programmes and foreign missionary work. Early in the twentieth century, for example, the Catholic laity of St Patrick's, women prominent among them, organised a ten-day 'nautical festival', which raised no less than £1300 – an impressive sum by the standards of the day – to pay for church and school renovations.[45] The religious and educational infrastructure of southern Dunedin, as throughout the West, owed a great deal to female philanthropy.[46]

Furthermore, as Erik Olssen has shown earlier, and as Rachel Grimmett illustrated, women played crucial roles in household economies. Female thrift, hard work and self-sacrifice – the so-called Protestant work ethic – might enable a family not only to avoid destitution but even to prosper. Southern Dunedin's stricter Protestant churches – Methodist, Baptist, Salvation Army, Church of

While young men sometimes stopped going to church during their teenage years, young women were more likely to remain actively involved. Here is the Caversham Presbyterian Church Girls' Bible Class in 1910, with their minister, the Reverend Daniel Dutton, a popular local identity. Presbyterian Bible Classes offered intellectual stimulation, with talks on hot topics by local notables, friendship and fun. OTAGO WITNESS, 1 APRIL 1930

Christ and Brethren – almost certainly appealed to local women for the same reasons that Methodism had attracted their mothers and grandmothers in Britain. Such churches' strict moral values appealed to women trying to train husbands and children and run households on tight budgets. According to the English historian Robert Moore, most women had 'an immediate interest in the behaviour of their menfolk', because a 'drunken, gambling father meant an ill-clad family, no new furniture, and growing debt at the store'. During Methodist missions in Britain, women could be seen 'running down the street, still wearing aprons, crying with joy, when hearing of their husband's conversion. Others attended chapel "to keep their husbands up to the mark"'.[47] Rachel Grimmett, wielding Salvation Army-style Christianity to keep local men in line, exemplified such attitudes. The hundreds of southern Dunedin women who signed the suffrage petition almost certainly saw the vote as a means to Christianise politics by making male politicians more attentive to the concerns of women, children and families.

The churches played central roles in the social lives of many young women, offering fun and friendship in a safe, structured environment. Her 'social life revolved around the church', recalled a Caversham Methodist of the lectures, socials and Bible Class dances she attended.[48] Two sisters joined other young people in the choir of the Caversham Baptist Church and 'had a very good time together', remembered another. They 'used to meet the choir people and go for picnics and all sorts of things like that'.[49]

Many young women wore denominational distinctions lightly. Presbyterian deaconess Mabel Cartwright enjoyed Christmas Eve of 1907 with the Catholic nuns at the St Vincent de Paul Orphanage. They had 'fun' packing 'all the little stockings' for the orphanage children with presents donated by the institution's 'many kind friends'.[50] Frances Kenny, a Catholic, reminisced that, after playing at a Catholic tennis club on Saturday, she and her friends would play tennis with non-Catholic friends on Sunday, and on Monday night Protestant and Catholic teenagers alike trooped to the dance that the Catholic boys organised at St Patrick's School.[51] A Catholic girl who worked in the Wax Vesta Factory had 'girlfriends who were very involved in other churches' and she 'went to all the functions with them', especially Salvation Army 'sing-songs' and 'speakers', which she 'loved'.[52] Girls who just wanted to have fun might find ways around the authority of male ministers. When St Peter's Anglican church ran a dance, they extended invitations to Caversham Presbyterian young people via their minister. But he, disapproving of dancing, refused to pass on the invitation. The girls ostentatiously 'obeyed', but turned up that evening at St Peter's anyway.[53]

Virtually all the churches ran sporting activities designed to retain or attract young people. Dunedin Catholics ran no less than four Catholic tennis clubs by the 1920s.[54] Even Caversham's Brethren, an evangelical sect inclined to suspicion of 'worldly' pleasures, ran a tennis club.

The churches played a major role in courtship, marriage and family formation. One Caversham couple met at St Peter's (Anglican) Sunday School and Bible Class. That was 'where we used to go for our entertainment, our dancing and our girls' clubs', she explained. 'Lots of girls met their husbands that way.'[55] For those married women who continued to attend, church often remained socially central. A Congregationalist woman recalled of Caversham in the 1930s that, though 'the wives went to church functions', their husbands 'did their thing' elsewhere, often playing bowls.[56] Married women almost certainly experienced in the churches more friendship, support and affirmation of maternal and family values than could be obtained in most other public institutions.

The more intellectually oriented churches helped educate and raise the social awareness of members, girls no less than boys. Presbyterian Sunday Schools conducted rigorous examinations and essay-writing competitions,

Christian Brothers ex-pupils' dance, 1935. The Catholic minority built their own subculture, complete with churches, convents, schools, sports clubs, friendly societies, and social events. Here ex-pupils of the Christian Brothers have a ball at the end of the Great Depression. This Catholic subculture was never as tight or exclusive as some clergy desired – some of the Catholics pictured here probably invited, and later married, Protestant partners. CAVERSHAM PROJECT COLLECTION

requiring extensive knowledge of the Bible and church history. Girls excelled, easily outnumbering boys in annual lists of prize- and award-winners. All southern Dunedin winners, for example, were girls.[57] Adolescence opened up further opportunities. Single women dominated the teaching staff of most Sunday Schools, creating a more humane classroom atmosphere, and a more child-centred pedagogy, than prevailed in the state school system. Several Sunday School teachers went on to outstanding careers in teaching and higher education.[58] Para-church organisations provided intellectual stimulation and heightened social awareness. A young Presbyterian woman regularly travelled from her home in St Clair to the St Andrews Literary and Debating Society begun by the Reverend Rutherford Waddell, where Dunedin's 'big lawyers' would speak to them on controversial topics, which she found 'awfully interesting'.[59] A Methodist remembered the Bible Class movement as a 'tremendous influence', helping her develop her God-given talents. Members discussed the economic causes of the Great Depression, the 'proper Christian attitude to money', war, marriage and sex.[60]

Overseas missions brought the churches in touch with the wider world and offered challenging and independent careers for young women. Annie Hancock, for example, daughter of a grocer and coal merchant who became mayor of Caversham, grew up in St Clair Congregational Church and was educated at Kensington Primary School, Otago Girls' High and Dunedin Teachers' College. She joined the Presbyterian Canton Village mission at Kong Chuen, where, from 1916, she trained Chinese women in kindergarten and primary school teaching and, later, taught English at Sun Yat Sen University in Canton. Living in south China enabled her to indulge her lifelong passion for natural history. She collected a herbarium of Chinese plants, which she later bequeathed to the Bishop Museum in Honolulu. Hancock completed her BA on leave at the University of California at Berkeley in 1927–28, assisted financially by the Presbyterian Foreign Missions Committee.[61]

What did all this have to do with religion? It might be argued that engaging in 'secular' activities constituted the churches' last desperate attempt to retain lay interest in a rapidly modernising and secularising world. There is probably some truth to the view that, by investing heavily in social relevance, the main Protestant churches (Anglican, Presbyterian and Methodist) made themselves vulnerable to social change. When, in the late 1960s and after, women sought new opportunities in leisure, sports, education, careers and politics, growing numbers looked outside the churches, now increasingly under fire from second-wave feminists as irredeemably patriarchal. The main Protestant churches, which had invested most heavily in social relevance, found lay women, previously their backbone, deserting. Numbers declined. As the British historian Callum Brown has argued, the decline of the main Protestant churches, which accelerated in New Zealand, as in many other parts of the West from the late 1960s, had a gendered dimension.[62] Scholars have often exaggerated this trend, however. Most twenty-first-century New Zealanders continue to identify themselves as adherents of particular Christian churches.

Furthermore, the assumption that the churches performed social rather than religious functions requires careful scrutiny. Those women who enjoyed socialising with friends and neighbours at church – and oral histories reveal that there were many – would almost certainly have been surprised to be told by a historian that they were engaging in social rather than spiritual activities. Were not helping and supporting one another practical expressions of Christian love? Reductive sociological interpretations of religious phenomena impose on past people explanatory categories that obscure the beliefs, values and intentions of those involved. Some sociologists have argued that sociological explainings-away of religion have constituted weapons in the campaign of secular Western political and intellectual élites to discredit Christianity.[63]

Religion and masculinity

The relationship between religion and masculinity constitutes largely unknown territory for New Zealand historians. Recent studies might lead us to think that few connections existed, that New Zealand men scarcely darkened the door of a church. Phillips, for example, writes of 'the weakness of traditional institutions like the church' in New Zealand, before characterising the 'decent bloke', a respectable, hard-working family man battling the 'boozer' in late nineteenth-century New Zealand, in largely secular terms as a 'social puritan'.[64] In her study of gender in Taradale between 1886 and 1930, Caroline Daley noted that men's oral histories talked 'about crime and disorder, alcohol and fighting', depicting 'a larrikin world where men were firmly in control'. Taradale's women, by contrast, 'told stories about home and family, religion and community, and presented themselves as home-loving, law-abiding, religious and tolerant citizens'.[65] Religion, it would seem, constituted women's business, with which New Zealand men had little to do.

The masculinisation of irreligion?

Phillips and Daley offer useful insights. Men, especially single, working-class men, were less likely to go to church than women. Yet the masculinisation of irreligion, like the feminisation of religion, constituted an old Western European pattern, not a nineteenth-century development. Males had long dominated the ranks of unbelievers and critics of established churches – atheists, agnostics and deists – in the Old World, largely because anti-religion constituted a political as much as a religious stance, and as such was a largely male prerogative. Although, for most Britons outside established churches, manly independence took Christian form in the ecclesiastical republics of nonconformity, a few fiery souls so detested 'Old Corruption' that they damned all forms of religion. In early nineteenth-century England, for example, republican journalists such as Richard Carlile hoped to see the last king strangled with the guts of the last priest, and a freer and more equal society emerge out of the ashes of the old.

Old World anticlericalism made its way early to New Zealand, where it flourished in rough-and-ready male-dominated frontier settlements, and became one of our earliest and liveliest cultural traditions. Charles Darwin, visiting the Bay of Islands with HMS *Beagle* in 1835, observed that many of the area's male inhabitants 'abused or sneered at' Protestant missionaries who criticised their drinking, violence and sexual liaisons with Maori women.⁶⁶ In the largely male settlement of O'Kain's Bay on Banks Peninsula in 1859, sawmillers organised dogfights to put an end to church services there.⁶⁷ Male anticlericalism reached fever pitch during the early 1860s, when the Taranaki war divided the colony. Those Anglican clergy, led by Bishop Selwyn and Archdeacon Octavius Hadfield, who blamed the government, not Maori, for the Taranaki war were condemned as traitors, not only to their race, but also to their gender, by angry male settlers. Hadfield, sneered the *Taranaki Herald*, allowed 'womanly weakness' to lead him astray; his emotional concern for Maori rights rendered him a strange, unmanly creature.⁶⁸

The 1880s saw the rise of an organised secularist movement heavily dominated by males. Freethinkers, who agreed on little apart from the evils of organised Christianity, flourished especially, as Peter Lineham has noted, in areas such as Palmerston North, Caversham and South Dunedin, where working-class men concentrated.⁶⁹ According to the 1891 census, South Dunedin contained no fewer than 75 freethinkers, 1.8 per cent of the population. A further 75 (1.8 per cent) 'objected to state' any religious views to the census-taker. Heterodoxy burgeoned more vigorously still in Caversham, where local Christians faced 19 freethinkers (0.4 per cent), 15 who professed 'no religion' (0.3 per cent), 83 who objected to state their religious views (1.8 per cent) and 36 'others' (0.8 per cent). In both the 'freethought' and the 'no religion' categories, males heavily outnumbered females. In the three boroughs of South Dunedin, Caversham and St Kilda combined, male freethinkers outnumbered females by 69 to 37, a ratio of almost two to one. Only a single female as against 15 males professed 'no religion'. By 1921 the gender gap among this varied group of secularists had widened. According to that year's census, among Dunedin city's self-defined agnostics, freethinkers, rationalists and adherents of no religion, males outnumbered females by 158 to 46, a 3.4 to 1 ratio. Men also dominated the 'object to state' category.⁷⁰

Samuel Lister was southern Dunedin's most outspoken atheist. Born in Edinburgh, he arrived in Dunedin in the late 1860s as a practising Presbyterian. He and his wife, Jane, lived in Bathgate Rd, South Dunedin. However, during the 1870s, following the death of his eldest son and the collapse of a business partnership, he began to drink heavily. Church authorities noticed and reproved him. Lister exploded, quit the church and declared war. The *Otago Workman*, the weekly paper he began in 1887, preached atheism, anticlericalism, republicanism and the values of brotherhood and democracy. 'The church of the present day is a gigantic fraud,' declared Lister. Its ministers, in it 'for gold and not for souls', do 'not believe what they teach'.⁷¹ He derided local clergy as too fond of 'wearing slippers' and 'gossiping' with the women of the congregation to be real men.[72] A great hater, Lister also despised wowsers, and in 1895 he libelled a leading male prohibitionist and received a 3-month jail sentence for his pains. A remarkably tolerant wider community, including many local Christians, rallied to Lister's defence, paying his fine. Like some other working men, Lister disliked first-wave feminism and votes for women, partly because the WCTU supported prohibition. As chapter two notes, however, his wife, who remained Presbyterian, signed the suffrage petition. An ardent unionist, Lister supported the labour movement, where he rubbed shoulders with Christian working men of various sorts, especially Methodists, Baptists and Catholics. Although they might not agree on religion, Christian and atheist labour supporters alike embraced the values of brotherhood, democracy and a fair go for the ordinary bloke.[73] Politics and morality provided common ground on which believer and unbeliever could unite; the religious differences that meant so much in the Old World seldom came between them.

Although those professing no religion and objecting to state a religious preference made up no more than 3.5 per cent of the population of Dunedin in 1921, it would be a mistake to underestimate the influence of this largely male group. Many of its leaders, brought up in evangelical Christian homes, retained the energy, activism, self-discipline and moral fervour of their backgrounds and forged successful careers. Freethought as an organised movement may largely have collapsed by the 1890s, as Lineham has noted, but that should not lead us to underestimate the influence that agnostics, freethinkers and rationalists exerted in such culturally influential institutions as government, the universities and the judiciary. Robert Stout, for example, a Scottish-born lawyer, became the country's leading freethinker during the 1870s and 1880s. The mostly Christian citizens of Dunedin, far from burning their local heretic, in 1884 elected him to represent them in Parliament as member for Dunedin East. Stout became Premier and, in the twentieth century, Chief Justice of the Supreme Court and Chancellor of the University of New Zealand. Male agnostics and freethinkers, such as Duncan MacGregor and T. J. Parker at Otago and A. W. Bickerton at Canterbury, played prominent roles in New Zealand universities from the 1870s on. In New Zealand, freethinkers enjoyed tolerance, respectability and status.[74]

The battle against Christianity was never an exclusively male affair, however. A few women also joined in. For example, Anna Stout, whose parents left the Presbyterian church after arguments over spiritualism, played a prominent role in first-wave feminism and the WCTU, while roving between agnosticism and Unitarianism.[75]

Christian masculinities

Conversely, organised religion was never an exclusively female domain. The great majority of New Zealand men professed some form of Christian faith throughout our period. Most – about three-quarters in Otago and Southland, according to David Keen – attended Sunday School as boys, and a modest proportion of these went on as teenagers to Bible Class, Boys' Brigade or the YMCA.[76] Most men got married either in church or at home under Christian auspices, and gave family members Christian burials. Although most adult males did not regularly attend church, many non-attenders encouraged their wives and daughters to go, and sent their children to Sunday School. This pattern probably suited those men who demanded more fidelity, self-sacrifice and virtue from wives and children than they themselves were willing to offer.

Male church attendance deserves brief attention. Hugh Jackson's fine studies of churchgoing in nineteenth-century New Zealand took insufficient account of gender in explaining why New Zealanders went to church less regularly than Victorian Britons.[77] Recent scholarship has shown that in England church attendance and social class correlated modestly between about 1850 and 1914. In general, the upper classes attended church more regularly than the middle classes, who went more often than working people, although recent studies have shown that historians have exaggerated the alienation of the working classes from the churches; skilled workers were numerous in most Protestant churches, and probably dominated the Baptist and Methodist churches. Yet, especially perhaps in working-class churches, women considerably outnumbered men, particularly among active, committed church members. This probably reflected the view, pervasive in English popular culture, that religion, intimately connected as it was with rites of passage such as birth, marriage and death, was largely women's business. Working-class adult males, especially unmarried and unskilled ones, constituted probably the least regular church-attenders in Britain. As we have seen, this working-class male subculture nurtured several varieties of unbelief.[78]

Such evidence as we can obtain from southern Dunedin suggests that this class-age-and-gendered British pattern of churchgoing carried over to New Zealand. Single males from unskilled occupational groups were distinctly under-represented among Protestant churchgoers as compared with the wider community. In Caversham Presbyterian Church, for example, married men (59 per cent of the male population of Caversham in 1911) constituted 78 per cent of male communicants. Single men (39 per cent of Caversham males) made up only 22 per cent of Presbyterian communicants, and a mere 6 per cent of church members.⁷⁹ Single males made up about 9 per cent of members of Caversham Methodist Church in 1915 and declined to about 7 per cent in 1920.⁸⁰ Yet single men of working and lower-middle-class origins abounded in nineteenth-century New Zealand, and the sex ratio did not equalise until after the First World War. The preponderance of single non-churchgoing males during the nineteenth century helps to explain New Zealand's modest levels of church attendance compared to Britain, North America and Australia over the same period. How far local Catholics followed this Protestant pattern has been difficult to determine. Preliminary research suggests that a considerably larger proportion of Catholic than of Protestant males were unskilled workers. We have not, as yet, been able to find hard data on mass attendance and other measures of active piety among Catholic males.

Southern Dunedin may offer clues as to why no radical reversal of nineteenth-century patterns took place between the 1880s and 1920s. During these years, as sex ratios began to equalise, churchgoing women and 'domestic men' began to battle the 'boozer' for cultural authority (for a more extended discussion of this battle, see chapter six). Churchgoers did their best in the great socio-religious movements of the late nineteenth and early twentieth century – temperance and prohibition, Bible-in-Schools and first-wave feminism – to Christianise the culture as they saw it, but they could shift established cultural patterns set by religiously passive or indifferent males only so far. In southern Dunedin, as throughout the country, active Christians rubbed shoulders at work and play, and often lived, with non-churchgoers. Often, as Dunedin oral histories attest, religiously active women lived with non-churchgoing men–father, husband, brother or son. Churchgoer and non-churchgoer alike sought to build good marriages, happy families and cohesive communities by avoiding quarrels about religion. Oral histories attest to a widespread popular determination to avoid what many saw as fruitless and divisive wrangling over differences in religious belief and practice. 'Mum liked the [Methodist] church' and used to sing in the choir, recalled William Harris, but 'Dad didn't go'. He worked 'very hard' all week and did not attend church, because he considered Sunday 'a day of rest'. Yet his parents 'never' argued about church.⁸¹ Christine King recalled that her mother belonged to Caversham Presbyterian church, but 'father never did'. This 'wasn't a problem', however, because 'the people around us weren't churchgoers' and most considered it 'completely okay for a man not to go to church at all'.⁸² The pattern of modest churchgoing established in nineteenth-century New Zealand was thus modified, but not reversed, by the arrival of growing numbers of active, often female, churchgoers late in the century, because the latter would not anger, and risk alienating, the former. Everyone, particularly women and children, had too much to lose. Clergy intent on building denominations sometimes denounced what they saw as the religious apathy and indifference of lay people, but there is no point in treating clerical jeremiads as gospel. Indifference there undoubtedly was, but many ordinary New Zealanders probably saw avoiding quarrels about religion, in order to build happy marriages, families and communities, as a practical expression of Christianity.

Privatising religion in order to avoid social conflict did not entail rejecting Christian belief or ethics, however, and cannot be seen as unequivocal evidence of secularisation. Southern Dunedin oral histories confirm what British research into male religiosity suggests: that 'implicit' or 'diffuse' Christianity more accurately describes the world-view and values of many non-churchgoing males than atheism or religious indifference.[83] 'I wasn't a disbeliever,' explained one Caversham man, but 'when you were working five and a half days a week, you didn't have much spare time', so sending family off to church 'let me get out into the workshop on Sunday morning!' Other working men known to him did likewise, he recalled. As a boy he attended Caversham Presbyterian Sunday School from the age of five until fourteen, where he found 'friendship' and a set of values that, at the age of ninety, he regarded as having been 'very' important for the rest of his life: 'the way you'd like to be treated, you treated them'. This was a colloquial version of the Golden Rule he learned in Sunday School.[84]

New Zealand historians have probably read too much into the fact that New Zealanders attended church somewhat less regularly than contemporary English, Scots, Irish and Australians. Phillips, for example, writes of the 'weakness' of 'the church', yet much of the evidence he cites in his discussion of the respectable classes' campaign to tame the 'boozer' suggests the opposite: that the churches played a significant though complex role in shaping New Zealand masculinities. The 'Anglican élite of Canterbury', Phillips argues, showing 'no great anxiety about the immorality of men', introduced what became New Zealand's Contagious Diseases Act of 1869, which enshrined in law the sexual double standard.[85] This argument suggests that Anglicans, who made up more than 40 per cent of the Pakeha population, played a major role in shaping a model of New Zealand masculinity that embraced the sexual double standard, and which the Christian women of the WCTU, and many evangelical men, condemned. Yet a careful reading of the 1867 Christchurch meeting suggests that the Church of England, never monolithic, divided over what constituted acceptable male sexual behaviour; no monolithic Anglican code of masculinity existed. At the crucial Christchurch meeting, the Reverend Lorenzo Moore, an ultra-evangelical Anglican, angrily opposed the proposal to introduce the CD Act, defying the Anglican dean of Christchurch, Dean Jacobs, in doing so. Moore embraced the strict sexual ethic upheld by those women, male evangelicals and others who played prominent roles in the campaign against the CD Act.[86] Furthermore, as Olssen notes, the CD Act was only enforced, half-heartedly and fitfully, in Christchurch and Auckland, indicating that, *pace* Macdonald and Phillips, 'the colonists were ambivalent about this Old World norm'.[87] That the churches articulated diverse behavioural norms for men, and that male (as well as female) Christians disagreed over issues such as sexual morality and drink, proves neither that the churches were weak, nor that religion was socially irrelevant. It simply demonstrates that historians must take religious diversity seriously in their search for the variety of sometimes conflicting Christian masculinities that emerged in late nineteenth-century New Zealand.

Why did males go to church? Church often served as the centre of social life for boys as well as girls. Sunday School picnics at Broad Bay, Green Island or Tomahawk Lagoon were 'wonderful', recalled Pat Donnelly of his Caversham boyhood; games, competitions and food kept everyone entertained for hours.[88] Ian Martin spent Saturday nights at a Presbyterian boys' club that kept him and his friends amused and 'off the street'. The next morning they met again at Presbyterian Bible Class, which he found 'interesting', and his teachers 'always very pleasant'. A national Bible Class conference held in Wanganui in 1938 attracted six or seven hundred young Presbyterians, he recalled, constituting 'a great matrimonial agency'. Church-run dances at Sidey Hall and in Caversham, where he met the girl who became his wife, attracted 'mostly Bible Class people', up to 300 in number.[89]

Many churches, concerned about boys falling away during their teenage years, sought to retain them by offering a range of activities they hoped would appeal. The motto of the Presbyterian Young Men's Bible Class captured their desire to project a compelling Christian masculinity: 'Be strong, and show thyself a man.' St Clair Congregational Church ran a gymnasium. Caversham's Brethren and Baptist churches also put on gymnastic classes that attracted boys from other churches. William Harris, a Methodist, went to both gym classes and also ran in a Baptist harrier club, which attracted between sixty and seventy boys from all over Dunedin every Saturday during the late 1920s.[90]

Young men's organisations such as the Bible Class movement, Boys' Brigade (established in South Dunedin in 1926) and YMCA aimed to produce muscular young Christian men who played hard but fair. It may be that, as Anne O'Brien has argued in the Australian context, the churches remained culturally influential in New Zealand precisely because Christian models

The Protestant churches tried to retain young men by organising sporting and social clubs and activities. Skilled working-class and lower-middle-class folk dominated the Baptist church, which was particularly strong in the southern suburbs. Here is a Baptist Young Men's Bible Class Camp, with Caversham Baptist boys flying their flag on top. *OTAGO WITNESS*, 20 APRIL 1926

of masculinity, far from rejecting everything the boozer stood for, related in more complex ways to more secular models.[91] The 'decent bloke', though condemning the violence, drunkenness and unrestrained sexuality of the 'boozer', remained a man's man. Winning respect in the community probably depended on doing so. Take the minister, the most visible representative of the churches. Maurice Gee's *Plumb*, based on the life of the Timaru Presbyterian minister J. H. G. Chapple, showed that Plumb's cricketing ability – he won respect as a tireless and accurate bowler – aided his acceptance and standing in the local community.[92] Michael Jones, a rugby superstar and devout Christian, illustrates the continuing vitality of this tradition of 'muscular Christianity', which, combining tough, fearless athleticism with chivalry, humility and respect for others, continues to attract admiration in 'secular' twenty-first-century New Zealand.

In southern Dunedin, those ministers who won the respect and affection of the local community, such as the Reverends Daniel Dutton and Charlie Sullivan, both Presbyterians, and Canon King, an Anglican, did so by displaying a Christian masculinity that combined intelligence, sensitivity and pastoral warmth with strength, manliness and courage. Dutton, who was the Presbyterian minister at Caversham between 1888 and 1922, exemplified the kind of manliness to which locals responded warmly. Many admired him for his learning: Dutton was a Fellow of the Royal Astronomical Society and of the Royal Geographical Society and his popular lectures on astronomy, geology and biology attracted large audiences in Dunedin, Otago and Southland. His courage and self-sacrifice also won respect: he served as chaplain with the South Island battalion in South Africa, proving so popular that, on the outbreak of the First World War, the community pressed a reluctant government to reappoint 66-year-old Dutton as chaplain. It eventually did, though it refused to let him near the front. Dutton's geniality, kindness and tolerance – he wore his dog-collar lightly and did not let clerical status come between him and ordinary folk – delighted his congregation and the wider community.[93]

Christian lay men learned to operate in similar ways. J. T. Paul arrived in Dunedin from Australia in 1899 to become the most influential labour leader in the city and a founder, in 1910, of the first New Zealand Labour Party. Paul's Methodist faith underpinned the moderation, courtesy and fairness with which he operated in both public and private spheres. A Christian socialist, Paul insisted on a fair deal for the worker, though in such a moderate, non-confrontational style that some of the hard men in the labour movement regarded him as a bit soft, particularly when he refused to abandon moderation during the divisive strikes of 1912 and 1913. As the accompanying photograph illustrates, Paul's Methodist-style manliness carried over into the private sphere as well. Devoted to his wife and children, he was a gentle, affectionate family man.[94]

T. K. Sidey, a lawyer, thrice mayor of Caversham, Liberal MHR for Caversham 1901–8 and Dunedin South 1908–28, and superintendent of Caversham Presbyterian Sunday School for almost half a century, provides a third example of the kind of Christian manliness that won favour locally. Sidey grew up in the 'Corstorphine' mansion built by his father, but never allowed either his relative affluence, or his devout Presbyterianism, to come between him and his constituents. He worked hard for all who asked, poor as well as rich, and during his first two terms spoke at virtually every public function run by the churches, Catholic as well as Protestant. He assiduously cultivated women's votes, forming a South Dunedin Ladies' Committee that visited local women in their homes. Most of his campaign workers were working-class folk. His reputation as a 'real gentleman' almost certainly helped him in political contests against 'ranting, table-thumping' boozers, especially with female voters.[95]

These three local men exemplified the kind of low-key, unostentatious Christian masculinity that almost certainly played a larger and more influential role in New Zealand culture than historians have acknowledged. The

J. T. Paul and daughter. Born in Victoria, Australia in 1874, Paul devoted his life to the Methodist church, the labour movement, and his family. As a labour politician determined to obtain a fair deal for the worker, Paul pursued a Christian socialist agenda in a moderate and gentlemanly manner that sometimes angered more secular radicals. He also expressed his Methodist-style masculinity as a husband and father devoted to the welfare of his family. Here he sits in the sunshine beside his daughter, their relationship seemingly intimate and affectionate. HOCKEN LIBRARY

fact that three of the most popular male community leaders in southern Dunedin were committed Christians suggests that the community was collectively forging new, inclusive, low-profile, modern forms of Christianity, well-adapted to the religiously diverse, pluralistic democracies of the New World. Devoting one's life to higher goods – family, team, church, community, nation, race, humanity – in a quiet, selfless way constituted a set of values deeply embedded in the psyche of many male (as well as female) New Zealanders. As Dutton's experience in the First World War illustrated, men as well as women embraced Christian values of self-sacrificing service; many southern Dunedin men gave their lives for God, King and country. This tradition of Christian masculinity was carried on in succeeding generations by such politicians as M. J. Savage, Walter Nash, Arnold Nordmeyer, Jack Marshall, David Lange and, in the Maori world, by men such as Sir Apirana Ngata and other members of the Young Maori Party, educated in the evangelical Anglican ambience of Te Aute College. Its central values of honesty, decency, kindness, responsibility and self-sacrifice for the common good, taught at Sunday School, church and home, to boys as well as to girls, helped families, churches, communities and the nation to cohere. Although it is no longer anchored so securely in Christian theology, this tradition has by no means disappeared in 'secular' twenty-first-century New Zealand.

Conclusion

New Zealand historians, especially in troubled recent decades, have often focused on the historical origins of the country's contemporary problems. Many have seen deep darkness in a past riddled with class, racial, ethnic, religious, generational, sexual and gender conflict and oppression. A country New Zealanders once praised as God's Own has gone rapidly, it would seem, to the Devil.

What held together such an allegedly dysfunctional, conflict-ridden society? What prevented it from flying apart completely? Many historians have dismissed religion as either too weak to provide social cohesion, or as exacerbating rather than curing the nation's ills. Few have paid attention to the quiet, unspectacular achievements of the forgotten people of New Zealand history: all those quiet religious believers, often, though not exclusively, female, from every ethnic and religious community. In home, church, school, and in the wider public sphere, such believers, whether regular or occasional churchgoers, sustained, transmitted and reshaped the Christian traditions that glued society together. The values and traditions they lived out, whether liberal, moderate or conservative, shaped the ways in which most people lived – however imperfectly. For believers, especially women, church offered a respite from the daily grind, quiet space to pray, and to think about life's larger meanings and purposes. Drawing strength, hope and identity from communities of faith, outside as well as within church walls, they knitted together marriages, families, local communities and the nation patiently, peaceably and without fanfare. Critical of their vices, we appear to be in danger of forgetting their virtues. Collectively, New Zealand's mostly Christian population created what for much of the twentieth century was one of the most prosperous, egalitarian, harmonious and stable liberal democracies in the world. By world standards, they handled their internal class, religious and racial differences, which tore other societies apart, remarkably well.

Inevitably, New Zealand's religious traditions also bequeathed problematic legacies to posterity. During the second half of the twentieth century, many New Zealanders debated inherited conceptions of the good life and the good society, and found much to criticise and reject, particularly in relation to sexuality, gender relations and notions of equality and authority.

Growing numbers of our university-educated intellectual and political élites repudiated Christian tradition as outdated, ethnocentric, puritanical and patriarchal – intellectually and morally bankrupt. Although I agree that New Zealand's religious traditions and practices require critical scrutiny, I have argued that the same goes for the intellectual tradition these cultural critics have forged since the 1960s. The fact that our ancestors built their world, not ours, is no reason not to respect their achievements. Perhaps twenty-first-century New Zealand is not so much nearer paradise as we like to think.

Endpiece Marriage: The Gendered Contract

BARBARA BROOKES

As the bells rang out and the steam whistles sounded at midnight to mark the dawn of the twentieth century, Emmeline Gallaway and her husband Thomas clasped hands and wished each other a happy New Year. Thomas said, 'I hope it will be a better one than usual.'[1] Like their neighbours in Bradshaw St, South Dunedin, they stood at their front gate to witness the celebrations. Rockets soared up from the exclusive Fernhill Club on the rise above the Flat and from the town hall simultaneously. The sky was alight with red, blue, green and yellow fireworks, roman candles were set off and 'crackers rattled in all directions'. The display was capped off by a splendid meteor that came out of the north, travelled in a horizontal direction, and faded out over the Otago Peninsula.[2] The pyrotechnics served to unite the community in anticipation of what the new century might hold.

Around two hours later, Emmeline Gallaway, clothed in her white nightdress and one stocking, lay dead on her bedroom floor, surrounded by a large pool of blood. Thomas Gallaway roused his neighbour, saying, 'Oh, do come. Someone has come in and half killed me and I believe my wife is dead.' Soon the whole street was roused as another neighbour was called to help look for the assailant, the local sergeant was called, a Mrs Irvine was asked to lay the body out, and the news of the tragedy spread from household to household.[3] The New Year dawned with news of 'murder in one of its most hideous forms'.[4]

New Year's Day was to see a number of celebrations: the Henry Dramatic Company at the Princes Theatre, sports at the Caledonian Ground and races at Waikouaiti. Thomas Gallaway's day, however, was marked by his arrest. The story of the mysterious intruder, who was supposed to have escaped through a narrowly opened window without leaving a trail in the uncut grass, appeared suspect. There were discrepancies in Gallaway's description of events and the search was on for the murder weapon. For the Crown, the question became one of motive: what would lead a man to kill his wife? As the trial unfolded, the community was called upon to elucidate the characters of Thomas and Emmeline Gallaway. The story became a morality tale about a particular site where gender is performed: the marital relationship.

The stories of the Gallaway household told by neighbours, friends, the local chemist and domestic servants indicate the permeability of private life at the cusp of the twentieth century. Communities, captured as individuals on electoral rolls on the Caversham database, were held together by the intimate knowledge people had of each other, sometimes welcomed, sometimes not. Intimate knowledge might derive from daily travel to work on the same tram, from a business relationship in which bodily measurements were necessary to make garments, the intimacy of tending to the sick, laying out the dead, or appraising deservedness for charity. Such knowledge might come from companionship at a work site, from close contact in the schoolroom, from shared leisure pursuits or shared worship. It was a knowledge formulated around ideas of sexual difference: that girls and women and boys and men brought complementary talents to the world and that these talents would be played out in very different ways. Applying these talents wisely made for good women and good men. An inability to meet society's standard of appropriate manhood or womanhood had numerous implications and could, at times, be fatal.

Baptism marked entry to community and their very names, Thomas or Emmeline, marked the road towards certain expectations. Clothing quickly became a further marker, exaggerated by class, as boys were put into breeches while girls remained in skirts. The schoolroom reinforced earlier lessons: girls were to be domestically oriented while boys might expect to engage with the public world. The world of work and its meanings was crucially divided by gender. Skill was something that many men aimed to acquire, and many women also, although the household tasks that women performed were not done for payment and were unmarked by the stages, such as 'journeyman' and 'master', that might apply in men's paid work.

Notions of work, home, and family were at the heart of the gender order. They gave meaning to lives and marked out those who were successful from those who were not. Marriage, as a public institution, was the place where the state most directly shaped gendered authority. Monogamy and heterosexuality were upheld, whereas bigamy and homosexuality were proscribed.

'Marriage itself,' Nancy Cott has argued, 'served as a form of governance.'[5] Householders, assumed to be male, had rights and responsibilities. And in marriage, unlike with other contracts, the terms of the partnership were not self-defined, but were enshrined in law.[6] Men had financial responsibilities to their dependants, and wives had the responsibility to carry out domestic duties. The very act of marrying, therefore, meant entry to a gendered contract, most forcefully signalled by women's abandonment of the name bestowed at their birth for the name of their husband. It was a contract witnessed by kin and friends and upheld by the community. As 'a voluntary union, based on consent', marriage was seen as a mirror image of the national political community.[7]

If the facade of the breadwinning man and domestically oriented wife hid a multiplicity of family circumstances in which all struggled to get by, it was a facade continually invoked and powerfully reinforced over the period 1890–1939. As its main buttress crumbled, with the decline in family size, rhetorical support for the ideal increased. The trial of Thomas Gallaway offers one insight into this story.

No evidence existed to corroborate Thomas Gallaway's assertion that an unknown assailant broke into his house early in the morning on New Year's Day 1900 and attacked him and his wife, leaving the latter dead. Thomas was portrayed by those who knew him as a good man. The first witness called at the trial was his near neighbour, Andrew Bain, who had known him for twenty-five years, and intimately for the last twelve. He described Thomas as being of 'a splendid character'. He was 'a gentle, kindly, good-tempered man', so much so that 'all the children in the street would run after him'. The main testament to his character lay, according to Bain, in the fact that, 'Not one out of a hundred men would stand what the accused had stood with his wife, and he was always patient and kindly, and would not quarrel with her.'[8]

Thomas Gallaway's 'calling' was as a fitter in the Hillside Railway Workshops, a workplace that employed many of the southern suburbs' skilled workers and one that linked masculinity, metal and speed in the production of trains. Part of the nineteenth-century transport revolution, it was a trade men were proud to be associated with, although the work was hard and conditions were poor. Sixty-one-year-old Thomas considered his work 'very hard'.[9] He was well thought of by his fellow employees. It was said that some years ago he had been addicted to drink, 'but had given the habit entirely up'.[10]

Emmeline Gallaway had no workmates to testify to her character. However, the state of her house, 'a well furnished and well kept appearance', signalled that she kept one part of the marital bargain.[11] She had also had employees – domestic servants – who observed her at first hand. Seventeen-year-old

Delia Gawn was in service to the Gallaways for four months in 1898. Delia had observed cracks in the marital relationship. She testified: 'They sometimes had quarrels.'[12] Thomas used to complain about his wife's taking chlorodyne, a medicine containing morphine, and spirits, which made her very quarrelsome. Delia reported Thomas as saying that, 'Emmeline was running [him] to death by taking chlorodyne and spirits.'[13] Delia had seen Emmeline throw a cup and a flatiron at Thomas, 'who was a quiet man who did not retaliate'.[14]

The evidence against the deceased Emmeline gradually grew. Margaret Beck, a neighbour of the Gallaways, testified that Emmeline 'was not a temperate woman, but took chlorodine'.[15] Gallaway had complained of this once or twice. Mrs Beck had seen Emmeline in a violent temper 'for want of chlorodine' and had been told by Thomas that her habit cost him from £6 to £6 10s monthly. When Thomas refused to get Emmeline what she craved, she would refuse to let him sleep. He had endeavoured to have her committed to Seacliff Asylum to break her habit, but the authorities 'refused to admit her'. Margaret Beck concluded by stating that Thomas 'behaved well to his wife in every respect, and was always an affectionate, kind, good man to her: and never exposed her, but hid her faults'. Emma Osmond, another resident of Bradshaw St, corroborated Margaret Beck's view. She had known Emmeline for about seven years and had seen her 'very violent at times', particularly when in need of brandy. She had never seen her violent towards her husband, 'although she did not give him any peace until she got what she wanted'.[16]

Neighbours were not the only ones aware of discord in the Gallaway household. William Wardrop, chemist of South Dunedin, had known the Gallaways for the seven or eight years they had been buying chlorodyne from him. Wardrop had warned the Gallaways about the addiction likely to result from continual taking of the drug, but Thomas had replied that his wife had an internal complaint. The chlorodyne meant that she, and therefore he, could rest at night, and he was prepared to take the consequences. They began buying half-ounce bottles, but reached the stage where Emmeline was consuming two 6-ounce bottles every seven days. As a result, Thomas was in debt to the chemist, a matter they had discussed. They had also discussed Thomas's attempt to have her committed to the asylum.

Emmeline Gallaway was not the only opiate addict on the Flat. The Dunedin papers might paint drug addiction as a particularly disreputable vice associated with the local Chinese population, but Thomas Wardrop's evidence suggested that white citizens had their own, perhaps less sociable, forms of opium addiction. 'There was a good deal of chlorodyne taken on the Flat and in the city,' stated the chemist. In fact, 'There was hardly a druggist in the city who had not several customers of this class.'[17]

Mr Wardrop advised Thomas to limit the quantity of chlorodyne Emmeline took. Thomas tried to do so, according to the chemist, although 'out of good nature' he could not compel her to break the habit. The chemist then 'reduced the strength of the preparation', but Emmeline noticed and Thomas requested that it be increased. A police inspection of the premises after the murder found fifty-eight large-size chlorodyne bottles, 150 medium, and seven small ones, with a large number of bottles outside, broken up and buried. The sergeant also found a bill from William Wardrop for £29 6s 6d.[18] At the time of his arrest, Thomas reportedly said, 'My wife was a good woman, only for one thing – she was ruining me through this chlorodyne.' He then shook his head and said, 'She is gone now, and I don't care what becomes of me.'[19]

On the first day of March 1900, the jury of twelve men assembled and were told by the Crown prosecutor that they should not be influenced by the sympathy they might feel for Thomas Gallaway because of his character references or his wife's addiction. He then went on to reinforce this sympathy by describing Emmeline as a 'morpho-maniac'. The prosecutor put forward the theory that New Year's Eve saw her in want of chlorodyne, that she then quarrelled with and assaulted her husband (Thomas bore an injury), he lost his temper and struck back, with fatal results. He then 'made up the improbable story of an attack upon them by a third party' – a story that the evidence, and in particular the discovery of a secreted tomahawk head likely to have caused the wounds to Emmeline's head, disproved. The prosecution, therefore, suggested accidental manslaughter, by a man of 'excellent character . . . subjected to heavy trials in connection with his wife', who 'bore his burden well'.[20]

Mr Sim, conducting the defence, claimed that all the evidence as to who struck the 'fatal blow' was circumstantial and that, although any intruder might have lacked a motive, such cases did occur, and he cited the Jack the Ripper murders in London's Whitechapel a few years previously. The Crown had only made the case that it was possible for Mr Gallaway to have killed his wife, but, if it was indeed him, 'Was he guilty of murder or manslaughter or was the act one of excusable homicide?'[21] Mr Sim recast the story as one of self-defence by a good man against a crazed woman:

> if the jury was convinced Mr Gallaway's hand had delivered the fatal blow to Mrs Gallaway they could do so . . . on the theory that Mrs Gallaway consumed a large amount of chlorodyne, making her homicidal. She then attacked Mr Gallaway in bed, who in his sleepy and dazed state caused by the blows, believed an intruder had come in and thus struck who he thought to be the intruder – who was actually his wife and thus the situation was entirely accidental – not manslaughter but in fact excusable homicide – which was not a crime at all.[22]

Emmeline Gallaway's headstone: Unlike other plots in the Southern Cemetery in which husbands and wives are buried alongside each other, or other headstones which note the attributes of a good woman (a faithful wife, a loving mother), Emmeline Gallaway's grave is a single one and her headstone merely records her name. The story behind this stark stone marking death is one of a life which failed to match expectations of the 'good woman'. PHOTOGRAPH COURTESY OF PAUL SORRELL

Despite the judge's warning to the jury that Mr Sim's suggestion that the murder was completely accidental was inconsistent with Gallaway's own statement about a struggle with an intruder in the passageway, the jury took only an hour to find Gallaway 'not guilty'. The community was in agreement that Thomas, a decent hard-working man, had been driven beyond endurance by a complaining, drug-addicted, violent wife who, despite his best efforts, was driving him into debt.

Emmeline Gallaway failed in the business of a wife. She failed to be docile, to be a good manager, and to keep her household out of debt. She was childless and it may well have been a uterine complaint that led to her addiction to chlorodyne. Her life, to some extent, was out of her control, as addiction drove her further on her path of failure.

The 1912 trial of Robert Turner for murdering his son, described in chapter three, illustrates the converse story: that of a man who failed in his breadwinning role. The Turner household had been brought to crisis by the refusal of the father to act as a breadwinner. The mother and children were forced to go out to work in order to support themselves and an idle man. Since his father would not, in his eldest son's eyes, act like a man by maintaining his breadwinnning obligations, he no longer deserved to be part of the household. Robert Turner dealt with his failings through drink and, fatally for his son, by self-defence.[23]

The violence with which the Turner family drama exploded and the Gallaway marriage ended meant they produced a unique body of evidence: the depositions of family and friends and trial records that closely document the words of domestic servants and Railway Workshop employees and their observations on family life. These records suggest that all marriages were open to public view and community assessment in ways that made them central to understandings of gender in society. Murder inscribed these judgements, perhaps altered by the trauma of death, permanently in the historical record.

Many of the other types of records on which our study is based are more resistant to readings about the texture of life. Surviving sources, by the very way in which they were created, establish, in Joan Scott's words, 'the authority of certain versions of the social order'.[24] Although women had gained one

Weddings were occasions for community celebrations. This photograph records the marriage of 18-year-old Lillian Bellett, daughter of Patrick John Bellett, hotel-keeper of St Kilda, and Mary Jane Bellett, whose 'domestic duties' were, no doubt, central to the running of the Pioneer Hotel. Lillian, who with her sisters, had attended Forbury school, married the 25-year-old Southland farmer, William Arthur Printz, in an Anglican service. The photo suggests how wedding celebrations brought together the generations and, in this instance, Maori and Pakeha. *OTAGO WITNESS*, 11 MARCH 1902

form of political citizenship in 1893, they were effectively disenfranchised in another. In electoral rolls, for example, work became identified with masculinity, while women's work was effectively written out and elided under 'domestic duties'. The male actor strides out from the historical record, apparently unmarked by ties of matrimony. As we note in Appendix II and in a number of other chapters, an important part of the Sites of Gender project has been to seek ways of retrieving women – and important aspects of men – from the records' blind spots.

Not all the omissions in this volume can be attributed to the historical record: as we complete our study, we are aware of the work that might still be done. Beyond the extremity of murder, we have not investigated crime records, which can be so revealing about everyday circumstances. Meanings surrounding sexuality remain opaque on the whole, although they are sometimes addressed obliquely in oral histories. We have not paid attention to men's involvement in, and the emotional costs of, the First World War, when motherhood and fatherhood became, for some, synonymous with mourning. Indeed, the family itself remains under-explored in this volume, though its presence is at the heart of all the investigations. So, too, is the public world of politics. These and other topics would repay further scrutiny.

Our aim in *Sites of Gender* has been to foreground the ways in which the system and meaning of gender relations was crucial yet contested in one community. The end of the Gallaway marriage, and the community's input into evaluating the partners' performance of their roles, illuminates this contestation in a particularly dramatic way. Family violence, though it comes within the frame of our examinations of work, poverty, health and leisure, is a story we have not told in itself. Much more typical within the boundaries of our study area, and indeed the nation as a whole, is the celebration of the wedding. On wedding days the community gave sanction to the gendered contract and witnessed an occasion on which a couple undertook to share their talents and to build a life together. Emmeline Gallaway had undertaken, in time-honoured tradition, to 'honour and obey', but her trials of life were such that Thomas Gallaway became enslaved to fulfilling his wife's needs. Emmeline's murder meant that the internal dynamics of gender relations were opened up for the community, in a courtroom in which authority lay with the all-male participants of judge, lawyers and jury. We have endeavoured to open up the wider social scripts of gender in the southern Dunedin community. As with the public scrutiny of the Gallaway marriage, the lens of gender, when brought to bear on a locality, suggests that initial impressions of social change can be deceptive.

Appendix I Chronology of Significant Events

COMPILED BY ROBIN LAW

International events are printed in boldface, *New Zealand* events are in italics, and events that occurred in Dunedin are printed in plain type.

1890
First moving-picture (film) shows open in New York.
Royal Commission of Inquiry reports on employment conditions ('Sweating' Commission).
Maritime Strike involves 8000 unionists.
Dunedin Tailoresses' Union formed.
Port of Dunedin shuts for 56 days.
'Labour Party' sweeps the city and neighbouring suburbs.

1891
John Ballance becomes Premier of first Liberal Government.
First of 14 Factory Acts passed during decade.
First women's franchise petition presented to Parliament.
Workingmen's Political Committee formed and Tailoresses affiliate.

1892
Second women's franchise petition presented to Parliament.

1893
Third women's franchise petition with more than 30,000 signatures is presented to Parliament.
Franchise is extended to women (Female Franchise Act) and first election is held in which women can vote.
Elizabeth Yates becomes mayor of Onehunga, first woman in British Empire to hold such a position.
Richard Seddon becomes Prime Minister.
Society for the Protection of Women and Children is formed in Auckland.
57 per cent of southern Dunedin women sign the suffrage petition.

1894
Advances to Settlers Act. Shop and Shop Assistant's Act. Industrial Conciliation and Arbitration Act.

1895
'Long Depression' ends in the mid-1890s.

1896
National Council of Women is founded.
Emily Siedeberg becomes the first woman to graduate in Medicine from Otago University.

1897
Queen Victoria's Diamond Jubilee.
Premier Seddon visits the United Kingdom.
Ethel Benjamin becomes the first woman to graduate in Law from Otago University.

1898
Old Age Pensions Act.
First cars imported into NZ.
Jubilee celebrations marking start of Otago Settlement in 1848.
Sisters of Mercy found St Vincent de Paul Catholic Orphanage for Girls in South Dunedin.
First pupils enrolled into what will become St Philomena's (secondary school).
Spring tides breach the St Kilda sandhills and flood much of the Flat.

1899
South African War begins.
NZ army contingent is sent to South Africa.
Southern Rugby Football Club is formed.
Otago Girls' High School forms a hockey team.

1900
Workers' Compensation for Accident Act. Public Health Act.

1901
Commonwealth of Australia formed and NZ stays out.
Nurses' Registration Act passed, making NZ the first country in the world to introduce registration for trained nurses.
First motor car arrives in Dunedin.
T. K. Sidey, Independent Liberal, wins the Caversham by-election.

1902
South African War ends.
Free secondary school education for two years introduced for those who pass Proficiency exam.

1903
First electric-powered trams run in Dunedin.
Salvation Army Home opened in Rockyside.

1904
Midwives Act.
Caversham Borough amalgamates with Dunedin city.

APPENDIX I

1905
Japan defeats Russia.
NZ Truth *magazine first published.*
New Dunedin railway station opens.
South Dunedin Borough amalgamates with Dunedin city.
Musselburgh School opens.

1906
Premier Seddon dies and is succeeded by Joseph Ward.

1907
NZ ceases to be a colony and becomes a dominion by royal proclamation.
The Society for Promoting the Health of Women and Children (Plunket Society) is founded in Dunedin, and first Karitane Hospital is opened.

1908
NZ population reaches one million.
Blackball strike (the first major industrial conflict since 1891).
Minimum wage rate for unskilled men in the public sector is set at eight shillings per day.
First purpose-built cinema opens in Auckland.
Free public library opens, thanks to a generous gift from Andrew Carnegie.
Carisbrook becomes the scene of major rugby matches.
King Edward Technical College opens.

1909
Compulsory military training introduced for all males aged 12 to 21 (later amended to 14 to 25 years old).
Dunedin's first public toilet for women is built at St Clair.
Little Sisters of the Poor, a home for the aged, is opened.
City-wide sewerage scheme implemented.

1910
King Edward VII dies and is succeeded by George V.
Women's employment as barmaids is curtailed by law.
Pacific Surf Bathing Club formed.

1911
Cost of Living Commission established. Widows' Pension Act.
Wolfenden and Russell open southern Dunedin's first department store.
Hallenstein Brothers erect a multi-storey store in the Octagon.
St Clair Surf Bathing and Lifesaving Club established.

1912
Reform Party wins vote of no confidence and William Massey becomes Prime Minister.
Public Service Act.
Waihi miners' strike.
St Kilda Municipal Band wins national championship.

1913
Workers in most ports and mines go on strike, and a general strike takes place in Auckland.

Massey's Otago Cossacks establish their camp at Tahuna Park.
NZ Wax Vesta Factory in Caversham burns to the ground.

1914
First World War begins.
NZ expeditionary forces dispatched to Samoa and Egypt.
Moving-picture theatre opens on Cargill's Corner.

1915
NZ forces take part in Gallipoli campaign.
National Coalition Government forms and six Labour MHRs refuse to join.

1916
Conscription introduced.
NZ Labour Party formed.

1917
Bolsheviks seize power in Russia and kill the Tsar.
Battle of Passchendaele: 3700 New Zealanders killed.
Six o'clock public house closing introduced.
Domestic science training in schools made compulsory for girls.

1918
End of First World War. Influenza pandemic.
NZ Labour Party wins two by-elections.
Influenza kills more than 200 in Dunedin (particularly bad in St Kilda and South Dunedin).
Electric Power Board Act provides framework for rapid development of hydro-electricity.

1919
Universal male suffrage introduced in the UK.
Only the soldiers' vote prevents prohibition from becoming law.
Women become eligible for election to Parliament.
First automatic telephone exchange opens.
Dunedin Branch of the second National Council of Women is founded.
Sidey defeats Labour's J. T. Paul by 84 votes to hold Dunedin South.

1920
Forty-four states establish the League of Nations (NZ a full member).
Immigration Act tightens restrictions on Asians and 'aliens'.

1921
NZ's commodity prices fall sharply and depression hits.

1922
Labour Party wins 23 per cent of the vote and elects 17 MPs, although Sidey retains Dunedin South.
Radio 4XD begins transmission in Dunedin.

APPENDIX I

1923
The General Secretary of the Labourer's Union, Jack MacManus of Caversham, becomes first Labour Party city councillor.
First woman candidate (Mrs E. F. C. Leech) stands for Dunedin City Council.
The 'great flood' swamps the Flat.

1924
Wiremu Ratana, leader of the Ratana church, petitions the King and the League of Nations to enforce the Tiriti o Waitangi.
Railwaymen's union strikes and is quickly beaten.
946 motor cars registered in Dunedin.

1925
Premier Massey dies and is succeeded by Gordon Coates.
Child Welfare Act.
Charleston dance craze sweeps UK and NZ.
NZ and South Seas International Exhibition held in Dunedin; 3.2 million attend.
NZ's first electric range is manufactured in Dunedin.

1926
Family Allowances Act.
National public radio broadcasts begin.
Telephone cable linking South and North islands laid.
St Kilda is the most densely populated borough in NZ.
Caversham Baptists form the first NZ branch of the Boys' Brigade and Girls' Brigade.

1927
Daylight saving introduced and adds an hour of daylight to summer evenings.
Miss Otago becomes Miss NZ and wins a trip to Hollywood.
DCC establishes NZ's first municipal restroom for women.

1928
Sir Joseph Ward leads United Party to victory, although dependent on Labour Party.
Kingsford Smith successfully flies across the Tasman and then tours NZ.
Opening of the new Hillside Railway Workshops, including a 'social block'.

1929
US stock exchange collapses and 'Great Depression' begins.
First 'talkie' movie arrives in NZ.
Woolworths (NZ) Ltd formed.
Radio Broadcasting Company begins local transmission.
DCC establishes first citizens' day nursery.

1930
Prime Minister Ward resigns, succeeded by Forbes.
Unemployment Act provides benefits for unemployed men.
Weekly air service begins between Christchurch and Dunedin.

1931
A new coalition of Reform and United parties wins the election.

Fred Jones wins Dunedin South seat for Labour Party.
Some 2700 men employed at relief rates by DCC on the No. 5 Scheme.

1932
Conscription introduced.
Unemployed riot in Auckland, Wellington and Dunedin.
800 food parcels distributed in Dunedin. Food riots in George St.

1933
Adolf Hitler appointed German chancellor.
Elizabeth McCombs becomes first woman MP in NZ.
'Mickey' Savage becomes leader of NZ Labour Party.
Southern Dunedin people protest against unemployment policies.

1934
John A. Lee anonymously publishes Children of the Poor.
Major C. H. Douglas propounds 'Social Credit' to the NZ Monetary Committee.
1343 married Dunedin men declare themselves medically unfit for unemployment camps.

1935
First Labour Government elected under Michael Joseph Savage.
New Dunedin City Council, Labour-dominated, places 800 unemployed men on full standard wages.
First feature-length NZ talkie film, *Down on the Farm*, shown in Dunedin.

1936
King George V dies and is succeeded by Edward VIII, who then abdicates.
Jean Batten flies from England to NZ in 11 days.
State housing programme launched.
National Party formed.
Committee of Inquiry into Abortion.
Compulsory arbitration reinstated and a minimum male-breadwinner wage established.
Pensions Amendment Act extends pensions to a wider population, including Chinese, Lebanese, invalids and deserted wives.

1937
Japan invades China.
National Housing Survey. First state house occupied.

1938
Savage leads Labour Party to landslide victory.
Social Security Act.
Labour city council defeated.

1939
Second World War begins.

Appendix II Qualitative and Quantitative Databases of the Caversham Project

DAVID HOOD[1]

Most of the chapters in this book draw mainly on traditional historical sources – newspapers, photographs (including film), diaries, letters, reports etc. But one of the distinctive ways in which the Sites of Gender project has been designed is in its use of both qualitative and quantitative methods and databases. It is fundamental to our understanding of gender (and indeed other categories of social analysis) that, as Joan Scott contends in an article significant for this volume, it is manifested in a series of diverse but tightly interrelated domains: through institutions such as schools and churches, through the labour market, through such phenomena as the accumulation of wealth and property, or voting patterns – but also through the ways in which individuals understand and express themselves, how they talk about their relationships with other people, the ways in which they understand important ideas such as work, family and home and so on, as well as the patterns of their daily lives.[2] The first few of these domains may often (but not always) be best illuminated by quantitative analysis, the latter by qualitative inquiry. This project has actively sought to explore the possibilities of deploying both kinds of data, and to bring together kinds of inquiry that are not always brought to impinge on each other.

Furthermore, the Caversham Project as a whole, and this phase, the Sites of Gender Project, are distinctive in that they draw upon the largest social historical database in Australasia (and one of the largest in the world). This database – or family of databases – was established initially to measure aspects of urban social structure central to what is now called Caversham Phase I. It became clear that the original databases – largely constructed from electoral rolls – were deficient in allowing us to track women, or the marital and familial status of men. The decision was taken to enlarge them in specific ways, in order to enable a larger research team to identify the ways in which gender both structured and was produced by urban society.[3]

By expanding the time period and the study area, we collected more data on women, and more data about men that would connect them back to their families. We also collected information from new records that both supplemented the information about women and provided assistance in reconstituting families: the women's suffrage petition of 1893, school records, marriage records, a series of trades directories, and the Housing Survey of 1937. The oral-history component of the project was also substantially enlarged, and most interviews were entered into a database, enabling it to be searched.

Relational databases have been central to the project by allowing this large volume of information, taken from a variety of different historical sources, to be rapidly combined, searched and synthesised.[4] Anybody who visits http://caversham.otago.ac.nz will quickly see how the automated linking of different instances of the same person, or different persons living at the same address, assists in family reconstitution, to take an important example.

In order to maximise the advantages of relational databases, most types of information, such as occupation, are given standard numeric codes, so that idiosyncratic variations in nomenclature can be recognised for what they are. Numeric codes have also been given to each occupation's class location, and to non-labour market descriptors such as retired, head of household with no occupation, woman-headed household etc. Numeric codes have also been given to any name-label that might change over time, such as street names. Although names have not been given a numeric code, they have been encoded in phonetic form to assist the identification of variant spellings. Encoding assists in identifying many of the messy confusions and imprecisions that haunt the sources, such as variant spellings of names ('James Kennedy', it was finally established, had been entered in the electoral roll as 'James Conheady', presumably by an English registrar).

Data linking also helps to establish the comprehensiveness of each source and the representative characteristics of a group. Some of our sources, particularly the Housing Survey, allow us to identify those adults living in the study area but not present on the electoral roll.[5] Data linking also allows us to follow an individual through linked sources from their parents' home, through schooling, and into their adult life. For those who spent much of their life in the study area, we can, for example, explore some of the opportunities present for that person and the path they followed. Or, by linking a source lacking occupational information, such as a church membership list, to a source with occupational details, such as the electoral roll, we can establish characteristics of the group not recorded in the first source.

Data linking also enables the identification of relationships between individuals within the records of interest. The individual fragments of information that each person contributes can be brought together to provide a more detailed description of the group. Historical records are often atomised because they are created at the level of the individual. By linking together individuals' records on the basis of shared criteria, such as address, representations of entire households can be made, even though the household was never directly recorded in the source(s) used.

Oral-history databases

The project's interview collection was constructed to serve as a major source of data on topics central to gender. It is an indexed and cross-referenced collection of 140 interviews. Most of these interviews were conducted in 1995–96 with residents of Dunedin's southern suburbs who had been born between 1894 and 1925. The research group devised a general questionnaire that explored several subjects then considered central to our projected inquiry. In 1995–96 Megan Cook, one of the project's senior research assistants, used these general questionnaires in interviewing forty-two persons who had grown up or resided for at least a decade in the study area. These interviews are generally known as Series One.[6] On the basis of those interviews, together with the customary 'snowball' technique, Megan undertook a further forty-eight interviews that focused on the following subjects: health, transport, wealth and poverty, and clothing/courtship/marriage. The interviews were transcribed, checked and edited, then entered by Megan into QSR NUD*IST, a type of textbase software that allows all mentions of any specified subject or combinations of words to be immediately viewed. NUD*IST also facilitated the quick generation of summative reports on any topic of interest, such as swimming around White Island, contraception, reading habits, dancing, and so on.[7]

APPENDIX II

Two further series of interviews were later conducted by Dr Shaun Broadley.[8] These interviews have also been incorporated into the NUD*IST textbase and Shaun produced two volumes of transcripts, the first containing his interviews with four respondents about religion and secondary schooling, and the second with members of the Lebanese community. In 2001–2 students in the Gender and Women's Studies Programme, University of Otago, also conducted interviews on the topic of work with women informants selected by the project. Termination of funding has prevented these being entered into NUD*IST. In 1995, as part of the research for her PhD, Catherine Smith also undertook three interviews relating to hairdressing, the transcripts and the tapes of which are held by the project. Tapes and transcripts of a further eight interviews, undertaken by Penny Isaac as part of the research for her thesis on South Dunedin during the 1930s, are also held by the project.

This text-based programme proved so useful that an earlier series of oral histories was entered into NUD*IST. In 1980–82 students enrolled in History 452, a research seminar on social history that focused on Caversham, had been required to undertake an interview as part of their course work. As a result twenty-six oral histories were completed that focused largely on memories of childhood. Most of the subjects had been born between 1890 and 1914 and were recruited on the advice of Alma Rutherford (whose *Edge of the Town* appeared in 1978). These interviews were subsequently transcribed by Paula Waby, who was afterwards employed to transcribe most of the later series. Shaun Broadley entered these into NUD*IST and produced two volumes. Six further interviews, including two that focused on childhood, were later incorporated into a third volume in the Childhood series (produced by Alison Holmes).

A series of interviews relating to men's skilled work, conducted in the mid-1980s by Dr Jeremy Brecher (sometimes in conjunction with Erik Olssen), also exists. These have not been transcribed or entered into NUD*IST, but are held, together with full indexes, at the Otago Settlers Museum.

All of the interviews conducted under the auspices of the project, with the exception of those by Jeremy Brecher, have been entered into NUD*IST. The original tapes and transcripts are held at the Otago Settlers Museum. The project holds an information sheet, containing biographical details, and a consent form for everybody interviewed from 1995 onwards. In those instances where interviewees requested anonymity, pseudonyms have been used. The pseudonyms used in this volume and other Caversham Project publications are listed in Appendix III.

The Caversham quantitative databases

Thanks to the Statistics Department's policy of systematically destroying the census enumerators' returns, the basis for social history and historical sociology in countries such as Britain and the United States, we have had to follow a long and expensive path to reconstruct the study area's adult population. In the first instance, the absence of these sources denied us the ability to recruit a national sample and compelled us to focus on a particular community. (The department also destroyed the raw data so that one cannot even ask new questions.) After investigating the value of using the local directories, *John Stone's Directory for Otago and Southland*, an excellent annual series (and part of a national series), it became apparent that, despite their considerable value, they were much less inclusive than the electoral rolls. (Their value is discussed later.) Family reconstitution, fundamental to many social inquiries, cannot be done by using electoral rolls or directories.

The project's databases have therefore been constructed to compensate for the absence of the enumerators' returns and the raw data. The original Caversham database (Phase I) includes everyone registered to vote resident within the boundaries of Caversham Borough and was constructed to examine patterns of social and geographical mobility, residential differentiation, and their interrelationships in the period 1902–22. (As a rule the electoral rolls provide the full name and address of every adult living in the electorate who registered to vote, the occupations of men, and the marital status of women.) This core data set was enhanced by using 'Intention to Marry' certificates to identify women's name changes on marriage, and death certificates to ascertain whether or not people had migrated or died. All records were transcribed, transposed into binary form, coded manually, then typed on to machine-readable cards by data-entry operators.[9] In 1998–99, thanks to improvements in optical recognition programmes, in order that the Sites of Gender project could be undertaken, we scanned every electoral roll for the period 1893–1938 and checked and coded all data for the new study area (South Dunedin and St Kilda boroughs as well as the old Caversham Borough).[10] This database now consists of more than 250,000 records, covering around 70,000 individuals. The database was specifically designed to allow interrogation of the meaning and importance of gender as a structural feature of urban society in the period between 1893, when women's suffrage was enacted, and the Second World War. It also increased our ability to analyse the significance of ethnicity and made analyses of social class more robust.

The databases consist of several major sets of records, and a host of minor records. In any form of record linkage, one of the major sources is normally involved, as they provide a comprehensive model of the residents of the area. The major data sources employed by the Sites of Gender Project are:

Electoral rolls (including supplementary rolls)

High-quality photocopies of the original printed electoral rolls for the study area were scanned onto the computer. The project would like to thank the Parliamentary Library for making this resource available. Corrections were made by manually checking the scanned text. The final form of the electoral rolls was then encoded, so that different names for the same occupation can easily be worked with as a unit. Stone's directories were used to establish the social class of ambiguous occupations.[11] Identifying common occurrences of names between different years of the electoral roll enables individuals to be traced through time.

The rolls were open to all adults, except for those deemed imbeciles, aliens, criminals yet to complete their sentences, or those not resident in the area for more than six months. Although participation in the electoral rolls decreased over time, they are still a near-complete representation of the adult population. The format of the rolls changed slightly over time; before 1911 no street numbers were included, and after 1902 women's marital status was listed instead of occupation.

The electoral rolls database contains:

1893 Caversham, City of Dunedin	1041 entries
1896 Caversham	5020 entries
1899 Caversham	5835 entries
1902 Caversham	6456 entries
1905 Caversham	6977 entries
1911 Dunedin Central, Dunedin South	13,035 entries

APPENDIX II

    1914 Dunedin Central, Dunedin South   13,075 entries
    1919 Dunedin Central, Dunedin South   14,937 entries
    1922 Dunedin Central, Dunedin South   14,485 entries
    1925 Dunedin Central, Dunedin South   15,242 entries
    1928 Dunedin Central, Dunedin South   17,665 entries
    1931 Dunedin Central, Dunedin South   18,481 entries
    1935 Dunedin Central, Dunedin South   18,300 entries
    1938 Dunedin Central, Dunedin South   18,685 entries

Marriage certificates and marriage registers

The marriage database consists of 5461 records of marriages that took place within the study area (that is, 5461 grooms and 5461 brides). These include both marriages among people dwelling within the study area and those living outside of it (though one of the parties was normally, or had been, resident within the area). In the first instance, 'Intention to Marry' certificates were collected for persons living in Caversham Borough in order to trace women whose name change on marriage had frustrated previous research, and to increase the numbers of persons whose age we knew.[12] With the extension of the project, we also set out to gather all actual marriage records from all churches, assuming that brides, at least, would marry near their normal place of residence.

Records of marriages normally contain evidence of the families of the bride and groom (that is, parents' names and fathers' occupations). Apart from their value in analysing marriage patterns, they can be used to: (a) link records of individuals between generations (some families had three generations of marriages within the study area and time period); (b) trace the continuity between spinsters and married women, with the attendant changes in name; (c) analyse intergenerational occupational mobility of males and connubial (or marital) mobility of both sexes; and (d) facilitate family reconstitution.

The sources for the marriage records are:

Registry Marriages 1893–1913. This ends in 1913, because at this date the registrar stopped entering suburbs. As only a very small proportion chose a civil ceremony, we have not tried to identify the study area registry marriages after this date.
St Patrick's South Dunedin 1881–1937
St Bernadette's Caversham 1934–37
St James South Dunedin Presbyterian 1880–1938
South Dunedin Salvation Army 1917–37
Caversham Presbyterian 1881–1936
Caversham Methodist (including the Primitives) 1919–28
St Clair Presbyterian 1911–38
Caversham Baptist 1933–37
Caversham Church of Christ 1907–38
St Peter's Caversham Anglican (includes St Peter the Less St Clair records) 1881–1937
St Kilda Methodist Church 1926–37
Holy Cross St Kilda Anglican 1918–44
St Kilda Presbyterian 1911–15

Given that half of all marriages collected took place in Presbyterian churches, we did not collect the marriage records for St Clair or Musselburgh Presbyterian churches. Due to difficulty in either locating or obtaining access, we have not collected the records of the following churches: St Clair Congregational, 1893–1923; the Kensington branch of St Andrews Presbyterian, 1926–32; the Greek Orthodox church in Fingall St, 1911– (when no patriarch was in residence, the nearest Anglican vicar officiated): or South Dunedin and Caversham Brethren, 1933–.[13]

At present the denominational breakdown of this database is: Civil, 344 marriages; Anglican, 956; Baptist, 144; Church of Christ, 71; Methodist, 436; Presbyterian, 2518; Roman Catholic, 966; Salvation Army, 26.

School records

The school records database was compiled from admission and withdrawal registers for all primary schools with surviving records. Although not complete, the records offer the richest available source of quantitative data on childhood. The inclusion of children in the schools' records documents their presence within the study area. Parental contact details are helpful in reconstituting families. Parental information shared between records establishes sibling relationships. These records were collected and entered into a database by Eleanor Leckie, a local genealogist. The project is deeply grateful to her for donating a set to us.

The specific schools collected are:

Caversham (1871–1920) 11,261 records
Forbury (1878–1920) 8568 records
Musselburgh (1905–20) 2851 records
St Clair (1896–1920) 2380 records.

The relevant records for Kensington Primary School have not survived and the records for the local Catholic primary schools were not collected.

Housing survey

The government launched the 1937 Housing Survey to identify the extent of the 'slum' problem in New Zealand. The focus of the survey was in areas where housing was believed to be a problem. According to those city council officials who made the decision locally, this included all of South Dunedin, Kensington, and a substantial area at the foot of the Caversham Valley.[14] The investigators recorded who was living in a particular dwelling, their ages and kin relationships, their occupations, whether or not the male(s) were employed, and details on the amenities, construction and condition of the buildings. The information, entered on note cards, has survived in the DCC Archives and was collected and entered into a database by Penny Isaac.[15]

Because of its detailed individual returns, the housing survey is the single source most akin to a census. It gives a range of information for the 10,815 people within the surveyed areas of the study area and provides the single largest source on families and households. The residential component of the survey notes descriptions of 2873 properties.

Land valuation records

The land valuation records were generated by the visits of DCC valuers to all rateable properties within Dunedin. The surviving records include all of the study area, except for the borough of St Kilda. The valuation details were recorded by a third party (the valuer). As a consequence, the occupier details may involve the variant spellings inherent in what the valuer thought they heard. Linking between the valuation roll and other sources needs to acknowledge this variation.

APPENDIX II

Although the valuation records contain land information, such as distinguishing between rental and owned property, the valuation for both the improved and unimproved values, together with information about such amenities as water supply and waste disposal, the main application of the records has been in identifying the physical point in space occupied by particular properties. By using details related to address to link to other sources, it is possible to draw maps and express spatial relationships between people of interest.

To make the records, the valuers paid three visits to the property over an annual period, estimating the property valuation on each visit. Two key periods have been transcribed and spatially indexed on the computer: the 1911/1912 period contains records of the valuers' visits to 3757 properties. The 1921 database houses records of visits to 4029 properties.

Other records

The minor sources comprise the collections of particular institutions. Major sources, through data linking, contribute to an exploration of questions unrelated to the original source material. Because of the more limited scope of the minor sources, they are normally employed to consider only questions related to that source.

Benevolent Institution records, register and casebooks

The Otago Benevolent Institution was the major provider of both 'indoor' and 'outdoor' relief to the poor until 1911. Its outdoor relief casebooks were the records of inspectors' visits to the homes of relief recipients, and constitute a relatively consistent collection of data, albeit one driven by the specific interests of the Benevolent's trustees. The project has two databases derived from the records relating to 'outdoor' relief. Marian Horan constructed the first database from the Otago Benevolent Institution's outdoor relief records for the southern Dunedin suburbs (South Dunedin, Caversham, Kensington, St Kilda and St Clair). From the inspectors' field notes, each individual who lived in a household that received relief at some time during the sampled years of 1889, 1895, 1900 and 1905 was given a record containing name, sex, age, occupation and several other details (if they were provided in the case notes, and for most they were). Each individual was also linked to other members of the household and to a separate table containing details of that household, such as address or the period of time for which the family received aid. This approach has allowed us to reconstruct age, sex, employment, and family size and composition for this period.[16]

The second database, constructed by Annabel Cooper with assistance from Marian Horan and Eva Lubcke, was produced from the same records, but as narrative samples rather than quantitative records. Three samples were taken: Series I: 'All Relief Cases for the Period 1889–90'; Series II: 'Relief Cases from Maria/Glasgow St 1889–1911'; and Series III: 'Cases of Persistent Relief Recipients 1889–1911'. For each case in each sample, all records were transcribed, with the exception of some records where the recipients moved permanently out of the area. Parts of the volumes are still subject to a 100-year privacy restriction. We therefore identify individuals only from records prior to 1903 in this volume, and the working paper transcripts will not be publicly available until 2012. Both the casebooks themselves and our transcripts are therefore given in references when authors cite this source.[17]

Friendly Society membership records

There were a number of Friendly Societies operating in southern Dunedin within the study period. The membership lists, part of each year's annual return, were located at

Archives New Zealand, and photocopied. Shaun Ryan undertook the work of constructing a database and coding categories such as occupation into standard forms.[18] The resulting 4305 entries were gathered from:

> Druids, Royal Oak Lodge, 1896–1922
> Druids, Enterprise Lodge No. 2, 1900–40
> Manchester Unity, International Order of Oddfellows (IOOF), 1907–40
> Unity, IOOF, 1875–1929
> St Kilda, IOOF, 1910–40
> Linda Rebekah, IOOF (women's lodge), 1903–40[19]
> Miriam Rebekah, IOOF (women's lodge), 1894–1940
> Foresters, Court of St Andrew, 1896–1940
> St Patrick's Hibernians, 1914–22
> Rechabites, Star of the South Tent, 1911–19

Infant deaths

The involvement of history students in the development of the project has seen the collection of a number of smaller, specialist, sets of records. These can be linked synergistically to the other sources of the project. One such collection of records, gathered by Conrad Schumacher, covered the 227 infant deaths that took place within the area in 1892, 1902, 1912 and 1922. Schumacher later expanded this database to include all infant deaths in the Dunedin urban area across the same period.[20]

Telephone subscribers

For 1910, 1913, 1916, 1919 and 1922 the telephone directories of Dunedin were searched for entries relating to the study area and the results compiled into a list of 2802 telephone subscribers. The 1928 telephone directory was added when optical character recognition software made it just as simple to take the entire Dunedin directory. When linked to the other sources, it produced 3683 residential and 2724 non-residential listings for that year.[21]

Directories: Stone's and Wise's

Two series of directories have been used, the first frequently so. The Stone's directories consist of three discrete directories, all of them invaluable. The first section, the streets directory, lists every household in a street in the order in which you would find it (after about 1911, street numbers were also given). The street directory provides the names and occupations of the heads of household. Income-earning children and boarders were listed below, indented to make the distinction clear. (In households created by married couples, which most were, the husband would invariably be identified as head, if he was alive and normally resident in the household, even if he was then absent). Women were listed only if they were single, or, if married, they were the owner of a business.

The second of Stone's directories was that for 'Trades & Professions', which listed most businesses of the region. Ordered by kind of business, the entries were transcribed by skilled typists and coded by David Hood to identify all businesses within the study area (many of which were owned and run by women). As well as showing patterns of business ownership, the directories offer some insight into women's employment. They also allow occupational labels that are ambiguous as to social class, such as baker or plumber, to be classified accurately. The number of entries (for Otago/Southland) by year is:

APPENDIX II

    1894 lists 6233 businesses
    1903 lists 7435 businesses
    1912 lists 8439 businesses
    1920 lists 7410 businesses
    1929 lists 8865 businesses
    1939 lists 9468 businesses

The third directory, the alphabetical one (which listed all entries for Otago and Southland), is mainly useful in trying to locate the destination of persons who left the study area (and therefore the electoral roll).[22] If a leaver had not died and could not be found in Stone's alphabetical directory for Otago and Southland, we searched Wise's Post Office Directory for New Zealand.

Death certificates (1893–1938)

Full death certificate information has been sought for residents of the original Caversham Borough who died between 1902 and 1928, in order to ensure that the dead were not counted as emigrants. This work was based on the original death certificates, which were organised into bound volumes in a chronological series. The key data collected were: (a) that death had occurred; (b) the year of death; and (c) the age of the deceased. At the end of the process, all the information on the certificate was collected. The result was a collection of 1299 complete death certificates and 1597 partial certificates.

The removal of the bound volumes of death registers to Christchurch – part of the Department of Internal Affairs' digitalisation project – meant that we no longer had access to this invaluable source when we extended the study area and the time period. Those individuals who left the electoral roll between any two elections have been checked in microfiche indexes of rolls to see if a death certificate exists.

1893 women's suffrage petition and the electoral rolls, 1893 and 1896

Kirsten Thomlinson entered the information from the 1893 petition and the electoral rolls for 1893 and 1896 into a database to identify signatories present in the study area. The names (and in some cases addresses) of 1726 petition signatories were recorded. She then linked these names to the electoral rolls for 1893 and 1896.

Railway workers, 1912, 1920, 1931, 1939

National lists of permanent railway workers were published by the government. As the Hillside Railway Workshops were a major employer of the area, representative years of these records were scanned in during 2001, and data linking was made to identify those workers in the study area.[23]

The Railway Classification Lists were scanned from the 1912 and 1920 *Appendices to the Journals of the House of Representatives*. Also scanned were the 1931 (Vol. 3) and 1939 (Vol. 4) volumes held in the *New Zealand Gazette*.

    The number of employee entries per year was:
    1912: 9445 entries
    1920: 10,328 entries
    1931: 10,012 entries
    1939: 11,440 entries

Appendix III List of Pseudonyms

The following are the pseudonyms used for oral-history informants who did not wish to be identified. The same pseudonyms are used in all Caversham Project publications.

Alison Abraham
Brian Abraham
Wilhemina Bassett
Kitty Brown
Marion Cooper
Jean Darby
Rachel David
Jocelyn Dean
Pat Donnelly
Jane Fraser
Nora Gain
Jennifer Glum
Maureen Judge
Christine King
Victoria Lake
Mavis Liverpool
Doreen Macbeth
Marina Mackenzie
Ian Martin
Yvonne Morris
Anne Moss
James Moss
Nora Olsen
Rosanna Paul
Richard Perth
Mary Redwood
Susan Ross
Marjorie Scott
Judith Silver
Paul Skipper
Georgina Terry
Elizabeth Thomson
Helen Tweed
Edward Waterman
Johanna Waterman

Notes

One Situating Gender

1. Donna Haraway, '"Gender" for a Marxist Dictionary: the Sexual Politics of a Word', in Linda McDowell and Joanne P. Sharpe (eds), *Space, Gender, Knowledge: Feminist Readings*, London, 1997, p. 64.
2. Kirsten Thomlinson, 'We the Undersigned: An Analysis of Signatories to the 1893 Women's Suffrage Petition from Southern Dunedin', MA thesis, University of Otago, 2001, p. 90. We discuss the 1893 petition in greater detail in chapter two.
3. Erik Olssen and Shawn Ryan, 'Jones, Frederick', *Dictionary of New Zealand Biography*, Vol. IV, 1921–1940, Auckland, 1998, pp. 255–56.
4. The publications arising out of this phase of the project have built up a rich description of the distinctive character and local history of the area. For the most recent account of the Caversham Project and its publications, see www.otago.ac.nz/nzpg/caversham.
5. Claire Toynbee, *Her Work and His: Family, Kin and Community in New Zealand 1900–1930*, Wellington, 1994, p. 9.
6. James Belich, *Paradise Reforged: A History of the New Zealanders from the 1880s to the Year 2000*, Auckland, 2001, pp. 181–86.
7. J. B. Condliffe, *New Zealand in the Making: A Survey of Economic and Social Development*, London, 1930, ch. 12, 'Maternal Legislation', attributes a range of social innovations to the influence of women's enfranchisement. In his revised edition, London, 1959, the chapter on 'Maternal Legislation' has been dropped and he is much more circumspect about the influence of suffrage, see p. 223.
8. Elizabeth Hanson, *The Politics of Social Security*, Auckland, 1980; Margaret McClure, *A Civilised Community: A History of Social Security in New Zealand, 1898–1998*, Auckland, 1998.
9. Melanie Nolan, *Breadwinning: New Zealand Women and the State*, Christchurch, 2000.
10. Jean Garner, 'McCombs, Elizabeth Reid', *Dictionary of New Zealand Biography*, Vol. IV, 1921–1940, Auckland, 1998, p. 303.
11. Erik Olssen, *Building the New World: Work, Politics and Society in Caversham 1880s–1920s*, Auckland, 1995, p. 1.
12. Thomas Lacqueur, *Making Sex: Body and Gender from the Greeks to Freud*, London, 1990.
13. Annabel Cooper and Maureen Molloy, 'Poverty, Dependence and "Women": Reading Autobiography and Social Policy from 1930s New Zealand', *Gender & History*, 9, 1, 1997, pp. 36–59.
14. Joan Wallach Scott, *Gender and the Politics of History*, New York, 1988, p. 31.
15. Notably, Joan Wallach Scott, 'Gender: A Useful Category of Historical Analysis', in *Gender and the Politics of History*, New York, 1988, pp. 28–50; Linda Nicholson, 'Interpreting Gender', in Linda Nicholson and Steven Seidman (eds), *Social Postmodernism: Beyond Identity Politics*, Cambridge, 1995; Haraway, '"Gender" for a Marxist Dictionary'; Linda McDowell, *Gender, Identity and Place*, Minneapolis, 1999.
16. Patricia Grimshaw, *Women's Suffrage in New Zealand*, Auckland, 1972; Barbara Brookes, Charlotte Macdonald and Margaret Tennant (eds), *Women in History: Essays on European Women in New Zealand*, Wellington, 1986, and *Women in History 2*, Wellington, 1992; Charlotte Macdonald, *The Vote, the Pill and the Demon Drink*, Wellington, 1993; Sandra Coney, *Standing in the Sunshine*, Auckland, 1993; Caroline Daley and Melanie Nolan (eds), *Suffrage and Beyond: International Feminist Perspectives*, Auckland and Annandale, 1994.
17. Scott, 'Gender', p. 31.
18. Appendix II provides an account of the various sources used in this project.
19. Olssen, *Building the New World*, ch. 4.
20. Jock Phillips, *A Man's Country? The Image of the Pakeha Male – A History*, Auckland, 1987; Robin Law, Hugh Campbell and John Dolan (eds), *Masculinities in Aotearoa/New Zealand*, Palmerston North, 2000.
21. Margaret Tennant, *Paupers and Providers: Charitable Aid in New Zealand*, Wellington, 1989.
22. Caroline Daley, *Girls & Women, Men & Boys: Gender in Taradale 1886–1930*, Auckland, 1999.
23. Scott, 'Gender', p. 42.
24. Scott, 'Gender', pp. 43–44.
25. Scott, 'Gender', pp. 44–45.
26. Caroline Daley and Deborah Montgomerie (eds), *The Gendered Kiwi*, Auckland, 1999; Bronwyn Dalley and Bronwyn Labrum (eds), *Fragments: New Zealand Social and*

Cultural History, Auckland, 2000.
27 Joan W. Scott, 'Experience', in Judith Butler and Joan W. Scott (eds), *Feminists Theorize the Political*, New York, 1992, pp. 22–40; Denise Riley, '*Am I That Name*': *Feminism and the Category of 'Women' in History*, Hampshire, 1988; Judith Butler, *Gender Trouble: Feminism and the Subversion of Identity*, New York, 1990; Caroline Daley, '"He Would Know But I Just Have a Feeling": Gender and Oral History', *Women's History Review*, 7, 3, 1998, pp. 343–59.
28 Doreen Massey, 'A Global Sense of Place', in Trevor Barnes and Derek Gregory (eds), *Reading Human Geography: The Poetics and Politics of Inquiry*, London, 1997, pp. 315–23; Tim Cresswell, *In Place/Out of Place: Geography, Ideology and Transformation*, London, 1996.
29 McDowell, *Gender, Identity and Place*, p. 30.
30 Louise Johnson, *Placebound: Australian Feminist Geographies*, Melbourne, 2000, p. 2.
31 McDowell and Sharp (eds), *Space, Gender, Knowledge*, p. 3.
32 Johnson, *Placebound*; Susan Hanson and Geraldine Pratt, *Gender, Work and Space*, London, 1995; McDowell, *Gender, Identity and Place*.
33 N. Laurie, C. Dwyer, S. Holloway and F. Smith, *Geographies of the New Femininities*, Harlow, UK, 1999.
34 Dean Wilson, 'Community and Gender in Central Auckland', *New Zealand Journal of History* (*NZJH*), 30, 1, 1996, pp. 24–42.
35 For the 'family man'; see also Phillips, *A Man's Country?*
36 A. R. Grigg, 'Prohibition and Women: The Preservation of an Ideal and a Myth', *NZJH*, 17, 2, 1983, p. 148.

Two The Landscape of Gender Politics
1 Mark Granovetter, 'Economic Action and Social Structure: The Problem of Embeddedness', *American Journal of Sociology*, 91, 1985, pp. 481–510; also Mark Granovetter and Charles Tilly, 'Inequality and the Labour Market', in Neil Smelser, *Handbook of Sociology*, New York, 1988.
2 David R. Reynolds, 'Political Geography: Thinking Globally and Locally', *Progress in Human Geography*, 16, 3, 1992, pp. 393–405.
3 G. N. Stedman, 'The South Dunedin Flat: A Study in Urbanisation 1849–1965', Vol. I, MA thesis, University of Otago, 1966.
4 The area between Anderson's Bay Rd and today's Portsmouth Drive is reclaimed land. Until the turn of the century, Anderson's Bay Rd skirted the harbour boundary. Most reclamation took place after the Second World War.
5 'Forbury' is not easy to define: 'The Forbury' was the name W. H. Valpy, the first of the area's settlers, gave to his 48-hectare farm. The name crops up all over the Flat: Forbury Rd runs from Forbury Corner, at the end of Hillside Rd, along the bottom of the Kew/St Clair hillside to the beach; Forbury School is securely in South Dunedin; and Forbury Racetrack (now Forbury Park) is in St Kilda.
6 The database is described more fully in Appendix II.
7 Stedman, 'The South Dunedin Flat', p. 26.
8 This track was used well into the period of European settlement and was still well-formed in 1870. Maarire Goodall and George Griffiths, *Maori Dunedin*, Dunedin, 1980, p. 17.
9 Goodall and Griffiths, *Maori Dunedin*, pp. 8–9.
10 Stedman, 'The South Dunedin Flat', p. 54.
11 Stedman, 'The South Dunedin Flat', pp. 54–55; Alma Rutherford, *The Edge of the Town: Historic Caversham As Seen Through Its Streets and Buildings*, Dunedin, 1978.
12 Stedman, 'The South Dunedin Flat', p. 167.
13 Stedman, 'The South Dunedin Flat', pp. 122–23.
14 Stedman, 'The South Dunedin Flat', pp. 132–37.
15 Apart from Stedman, 'The South Dunedin Flat', and Rutherford, *The Edge of the Town*, see K. C. McDonald, *The City of Dunedin: A Century of Civic Enterprise*, Dunedin, 1965, and H. J. A. Aitken, *St Kilda: The First Hundred Year*s, Dunedin, 1975.
16 Stedman, 'The South Dunedin Flat', pp. 128–29.
17 Stedman, 'The South Dunedin Flat', p. 129.
18 The various models of occupational structure used by the project have been explained, justified and outlined fully in Erik Olssen and Maureen Hickey, *Class and Occupation: The New Zealand Reality*, Dunedin, forthcoming.
19 This paragraph summarises many of the major conclusions of the first phase of the Caversham Project: see in particular Judi Boyd and Erik Olssen, 'The Skilled Workers: Journeymen and Masters in Caversham, 1880–1924', *NZJH*, 22, 2, 1988, pp. 118–34;

Erik Olssen, *Building the New World: Work, Politics and Society in Caversham 1880s–1920s*, Auckland, 1995, ch. 3; and, for movement between classes, Erik Olssen and Hamish James, 'Social Mobility and Class Formation: The Worklife Social Mobility of Men in a New Zealand Suburb, 1902–1928', *International Review of Social History*, 44, 3, 1999, pp. 419–49; and Erik Olssen and John Harraway, 'Pathways of Social Mobility: Worklife Occupational Mobility in Dunedin's Southern Suburbs, 1902–38', forthcoming.

20 Caversham 2 (for more information see Appendix II).

21 Lena Sommerstad, 'Welfare State Attitudes to the Male Breadwinning System: The United States and Sweden in Comparative Perspective', *International Review of Social History*, 42, 1997, Supplement, pp. 153–74.

22 The male occupational structure is a limited proxy for class in that it ignores both women's occupations and the fact that both women and men also achieved class status through other means, such as marriage, education and property ownership. See Erik Olssen, 'What Were Women Doing? Women's Marital Mobility in the Southern Suburbs of Dunedin, 1893–1938', forthcoming.

23 The population data has been taken from the censuses for 1881, 1891 and 1901. Later data has been retrieved from the meshblock maps that were developed as part of the census, and which are housed in a series relating to South Island boroughs, Statistics Department, Archives New Zealand. For an overview, see L. D. B. Heenan, 'A Population Geography of the Dunedin Urban Area', MA thesis, University of Otago, 1962, pp. 29–53.

24 For the period following 1901 we have relied on census data for St Kilda and the data for Dunedin city, summarised in Erik Olssen, 'Women, Work and Family: 1880–1926', in Phillida Bunkle and Beryl Hughes (eds), *Women in New Zealand Society*, Sydney, 1980, p. 161.

25 Brian Heenan, 'Population Ageing Among Non-Maori New Zealanders in Later Victorian Times: A Quirk of Immigrant Settlement History', *NZJH*, 35, 2, 2001, pp. 177–203.

26 For an analysis of the later nineteenth-century census data, see Catherine Wilson and Bruce Smith, 'Ethnic Origins in Caversham Borough and Surrounding Areas As Found in Census and Marriage Certificate Data 1880–1921', History 351 research essay, University of Otago, 2001. The figures from the marriage database were produced by David Hood. For a fuller description, see Appendix II.

27 In 1881, before the expansion of the Benevolent, only 8.9 per cent of the study area's males and 3.2 per cent of females older than forty-five had never married; in 1901 the figures were 12.3 per cent of males and 5 per cent of females. For the raw data, see *Census*, 'The Conjugal Condition of the People', Table IX, 'Showing the Numbers and Ages . . .', 1881, pp. 124–25 and 1901, pp. 268–69.

28 According to Miriam Gilson Vosburgh, *The New Zealand Family and Social Change: A Trend Analysis*, Occasional Papers in Sociology and Social Welfare No. 1, Victoria University, 1978, Table 2.1, p. 32a, the mean age nationally was 29.8 for men in 1881–86 and 25.3 in 1936–41; for women, the age fell across the same period from 25.8 to 22.4.

29 For the raw data see *Census*, 'The Conjugal Condition of the People', Table IX, 'Showing the Numbers and Ages . . .', 1881, pp. 124–25, and 1901, pp. 268–69. Vosburgh, *The New Zealand Family and Social Change*, pp. 32–35, identified a similar trend.

30 Brian Heenan, 'Rural-Urban Distribution of Fertility in South Island, New Zealand', *Annals of the Association of American Geographers*, 57, 4, 1967, pp. 713–35.

31 There are several techniques for measuring the level of fertility in a population. Some (often described as surrogate measures of fertility) entail calculating the ratio of children aged 0–4 years per 100 or 1000 women of reproductive age (usually from 15 or 16 years to 44 years) (e.g., the so called child:women ratio); other measures are based on the number of live births per 1000 total population (e.g., the crude birth rate), or the number of live births per 1000 total women, or married women only, aged 15 or 16 years to 44 years (e.g., the general fertility rate). We have calculated the child:women ratio (i.e., the number of children aged 0–4 years per 100 women aged 16 to 44 years) using the raw data in the table 'Showing the Ages of Persons . . . in each Borough', *Census* 1881, pp. 82–83; 1891, pp. 165–66; and 1901, p. 201. The crude birth rate confirms the trend shown by the child:women ratio.

32 Vosburgh, *The New Zealand Family and*

Social Change, chs 3 and 4. Although the Housing Survey provides only a snapshot at one point of time, rather than evidence of completed family size, little variation existed between social classes in the number of children at home. Felicity Speight and Amy Stapleton, 'Changes in Household Makeup: Occupation and Employment Status from the 1937 Housing Survey', History 351 research report, University of Otago, 1998.

33 For an account of the survey and a re-analysis of the data, see Penelope Isaac and Erik Olssen, 'The Justification for Labour's Housing Scheme: The Discourse of "the Slum"', in Barbara Brookes (ed.), *At Home in New Zealand: History, Houses, People*, Wellington, 2000, p. 119.

34 For an overview of the area, and greater Dunedin, in 1901 see W. A. V. Clark, 'Dunedin in 1901', MA thesis, University of Canterbury, 1961, especially ch. 5. Clark distinguished different residential areas on the basis of population density, the mean value of housing, the size of houses, the materials used to make the houses, access to amenities and the occupation of the male residents.

35 Roughly 53 per cent voted for continuance in both places, reduction was the next choice, and in St Clair 19 per cent voted no licence as against 14 per cent in Kensington.

36 For instance, see interviews with C. N. Ingram (b. 1900), interviewed by Sue Harkness, 1980, Caversham Oral History Project (COHP), Childhood Transcript Series Two, p. 15; and R. W. Maskell (b. 1912), interviewed by Margaret Wallis 1981, COHP Childhood Transcript Series Two, p. 65. Also Clark, 'Dunedin in 1901', pp. 94–97.

37 Isaac and Olssen, 'The Justification for Labour's Housing Scheme', pp. 115–19.

38 Statements about property values are derived from the project's database of property valuations in Caversham and South Dunedin boroughs for 1902–5, 1912 and 1922; see Appendix II. For South Dunedin, see also Clark, Dunedin in 1901, pp. 89–91.

39 In the interviews that focused on childhood memories, respondents were asked about perceptions of both Caversham township and neighbouring suburbs; see COHP, Childhood Series, Vols 1 and 2.

40 *Census* 1921, Appendix F, p. 7, and *Dwellings*, p. 57; *Census* 1936, Appendix A, p. 5, and Vol. XIII, *Dwellings and Households*, p. 3. For Dunedin – which included Caversham and South Dunedin by this time – the proportions were 20.8 per cent in 1921 and 16.4 per cent in 1936. For home ownership, see *Census* 1936, Vol. XIII, *Dwellings and Households*, pp. ii and 11.

41 See Clark, 'Dunedin in 1901', pp. 91–94, for St Kilda and St Clair. See also Aitken, *St Kilda*, and a brief life of J. J. Marlow, one of St Kilda's more prominent local body politicians across the period, D. G. Conly, *JJ's Dunedin*, Dunedin, 1951.

42 Clyde Griffen, 'The New World Working-Class Suburb Revisited: Residential Differentiation in Caversham, New Zealand', *Journal of Urban History*, 27, 4, 2001, pp. 420–44.

43 Olssen, *Building the New World*, p. 44.

44 M. C. Sanders, 'The Lebanese Community in Dunedin Before 1936', BA Hons research essay, University of Otago, 1980, pp. 44, 46, 65. See also Brian Heenan's longer discussion of the Lebanese in chapter eight.

45 Mabel Cartwright, Diary, 10 January 1908, Knox College Archives 3/279.

46 Atholl Anderson, *Race Against Time: The Early Maori–Pakeha Families and the Development of the Mixed-Race Population in Southern New Zealand*, p. 31.

47 Winston Cooper, *Always a Southern Man: The History of the Southern Rugby Football Club 1884–1984*, Dunedin, 1984, pp. 58–59.

48 Kenneth Denton (b. 1920), interviewed by Shaun Broadley, COHP, Religion, Identity and Community Series, unpublished.

49 Marion Cooper (b. 1925), interviewed 1996, COHP Transcript Series One, Vol. 4, pp. 213–14.

50 Susan Hanson and Geraldine Pratt, *Gender, Work and Space*, London, 1995.

51 Such practices are also documented by Dean Wilson in his discussion of gendered networks in Auckland, 'Community and Gender in Central Auckland', *NZJH*, 30, 1, 1996, pp. 24–42.

52 Erik Olssen, *A History of Otago*, Dunedin, 1984, ch. 8; Olssen, *Building the New World*, ch. 7; Bruce Scates, 'Mobilizing Manhood: Gender and the Great Strike in Australia and Aotearoa/New Zealand', *Gender & History*, 9, 2, 1997, pp. 285–309.

53 Kenneth W. Turner, 'Henry Smith Fish and the Opposition to the Female Franchise in Dunedin, 1890–1893', BA Hons research essay, University of Otago, 1985, p. 8.

54 In Auckland and Wellington, by contrast, unionism was weaker and more divided over philosophy and strategy.
55 Apart from Olssen, *Otago*, pp. 111–12, and *Building the New World*, ch. 7, see J. A. Salmond in Desmond Crowley (ed.), *New Zealand Labour's Pioneering Days*, Auckland, 1950, pp. 85–94.
56 Scates, 'Mobilizing Manhood', pp. 291, 293.
57 Scates, 'Mobilizing Manhood', p. 293.
58 Scates, 'Mobilizing Manhood', p. 287.
59 Because of changing electoral boundaries, the political history of the study area is very complex, and the complicated history of the labour movement in the period before 1922 makes it even more so; Olssen, *Building the New World*, ch. 8, canvasses the subject fully.
60 Turner, 'Henry Smith Fish', pp. 8–9 and *passim*.
61 *Otago Workman*, 12 September 1890, 13 December 1890, 22 August 1891, cited in Turner, 'Henry Smith Fish', pp. 22, 23 and 41.
62 See chapter three of this volume.
63 *Otago Workman*, 2 December 1893.
64 Patricia Grimshaw, *Women's Suffrage in New Zealand*, Auckland, 1972; rev. edition, 1987; Kirsten Thomlinson, 'We the Undersigned: An Analysis of Signatories to the 1893 Women's Suffrage Petition from Southern Dunedin', MA thesis, University of Otago, 2001, p. 125.
65 Thomlinson, 'We the Undersigned', p. 110.
66 Grimshaw, *Women's Suffrage*, pp. 3–4, 4–6, 30.
67 Occupational class and neighbourhood are not factors considered by Grimshaw.
68 See Grimshaw, *Women's Suffrage*, p. 30.
69 Thomlinson, 'We the Undersigned', pp. 96–97.
70 Thomlinson, 'We the Undersigned', p. 114.
71 Thomlinson, 'We the Undersigned', pp. 115–25.
72 Otago Benevolent Institute Outdoor Relief (OBIODR) Casebook, DAHI D 284 60-68, Archives New Zealand (ANZ), Dunedin. (References that follow are first to the Archives *volumes* and second to the individual *series* of the Caversham Project's edited transcripts of those volumes: Annabel Cooper with Marian Horan and Eva Lubcke (eds), 'Transcripts from the Otago Benevolent Institution's Outdoor Relief Casebooks', 3 vols, Caversham Working Paper (CWP) 2000–3. See Appendix II for more specific information on this source.) Vol. I, p. 20, Series I, p. 10; Vol. II, pp. 853, 981; Vol. III, pp. 1346, 1470, Series II, pp. 11–13; Suffrage Petition database, Caversham Project.
73 Suffrage Petition database, Caversham Project.
74 Patricia Grimshaw, 'Women's Suffrage in New Zealand Revisited: Writing from the Margins', in Caroline Daley and Melanie Nolan (eds), *Suffrage and Beyond: International Feminist Perspectives*, Auckland, 1994, pp. 25–41.

Three Working Gender, Gendering Work

1 Thanks to Megan Cook, Marian Horan, Annabel Cooper, Barbara Brookes and Robin Law for reading, criticising and assisting me to say what I have said.
2 I first used this idea to explore New Zealand history in 'Towards a History of the European Family in New Zealand', in Peggy G. Koopman-Boyden (ed.), *Families in New Zealand*, Wellington, 1978, pp. 1–26. See also Ruth Schwartz Cowan, *More Work for Mother: The Ironies of Household Technology from the Open Hearth to the Microwave*, New York, 1983; Wally Seccombe, *Weathering the Storm: Working-Class Families from the Industrial Revolution to the Fertility Decline*, London, 1993, pp. 29–32; and Joanna Bourke, *Working-Class Cultures in Britain 1890–1960: Gender, Class and Ethnicity*, London, 1994, chs 3 and 4.
3 For the relevant British background, see Thomas Laqueur, *Making Sex: Body and Gender from the Greeks to Freud*, London, 1990, and for the importance of urbanisation in generating apprehension about sex roles, Linda Colley, *Britons: Forging the Nation, 1707–1837*, New Haven, 1992, pp. 240–41.
4 The phrase is Joan Scott's, *Gender and the Politics of History*, New York, 1988, p. 2.
5 Erik Olssen and Maureen Hickey, *Class and Occupation: the New Zealand Reality*, forthcoming, [draft ch. 2, p. 36].
6 These ideas have been most fully explored in Judi Boyd and Erik Olssen, 'The Skilled Workers: Journeymen and Masters in Caversham, 1880–1914', *New Zealand Journal of History* (*NZJH*), 22, 2, 1988, pp. 118–34; Erik Olssen and Jeremy Brecher, 'The Power of Shop Culture: The Labour Process in the New Zealand Railway Workshops, 1890–1930', *International Review of Social*

History (*IRSH*), 37, 3, 1992, pp. 350–75; and Erik Olssen, *Building the New World: Work, Politics and Society in Caversham, 1880s–1920s*, Auckland, 1995.
7. For a history of the firm, see Neil Robinson, *James Fletcher: Builder*, Auckland, 1970, and Fletcher's unpublished autobiography, Fletcher Challenge Archives, Penrose, Auckland.
8. See Charlotte Rachel Grimmett, Diary, unpublished (kindly lent by the late Bert Grimmett). A copy is now held by the Hocken Library, Dunedin. For bootmaking, see Olssen, *Building the New World*, pp. 49–51.
9. This is the major argument of *Building the New World*. See ch. 9 especially.
10. Patrick Joyce, 'The Historical Meanings of Work: An Introduction', in Joyce (ed.), *The Historical Meanings of Work*, Cambridge, 1987, p. 2. There is an enormous literature on this issue now: see 'The Gendering of Work: Stitching Up the New World', Caversham Working Paper (CWP) 2000-6, Caversham Project, History Department, University of Otago, n. 5, p. 3.
11. In *Building the New World*, pp. 70–73, I have written more fully about work and the exclusion of women. In chs 7–9 I also analysed the consequences of that exclusion for politics and social life more generally.
12. Olssen and Hickey, *Class and Occupation*, ch. 4.
13. James Drummond, *The Life and Work of Richard John Seddon: Premier of New Zealand 1893–1906*, Christchurch, 1907, pp. 92–93.
14. For the bootmaking trade, see the testimony of Henry Rhodda, *Appendix to the Journal of the House of Representatives (AJHR)*, 1890, H-5, pp. 16–17. For the mobilisation, see Erik Olssen, *A History of Otago*, Dunedin, 1984, pp. 99–114, and *Building the New World*, ch. 7. There is nothing on bootmaking in New Zealand, but see Raelene Frances, *The Politics of Work: Gender and Labour in Victoria, 1880–1939*, Melbourne, 1993, chs 2, 5 and 8.
15. *AJHR*, 1890, H-5, p. 11.
16. *New Zealand Parliamentary Debates*, 95 (1896), p. 553. For sweating, see Olssen, *A History of Otago*, pp. 99–102 and Erik Olssen, 'Lister, Samuel'; Herbert Roth, 'Miller, John Andrew'; Ian Breward, 'Waddell, Rutherford', in *The Dictionary of New Zealand Biography (DNZB)*, *Volume Two, 1870–1900*, Wellington, 1993, pp. 272–73; 326–27; 558–59.
17. The Sweating Commission, 'Report of the Commission appointed to inquire into certain relations between the Employers of certain Kinds of Labour and the persons Employed therein', *AJHR*, 1890, H-5, p. v.
18. John H. Angus, 'City and Country: Change and Continuity: Electoral Politics and Society in Otago 1877–1893', PhD thesis, University of Otago, 1976, ch. 3; J. D. Salmond, *New Zealand Labour's Pioneering Days*, Auckland, 1950, ed. Desmond Crowley, pp. 104–7; Olssen, *A History of Otago*, pp. 109–12, and for developments and events on the Flat, *Building the New World*, pp. 171–86.
19. J. T. Paul, *Our Majority: Some Dark Shadows and High Lights of Industrial History*, Dunedin, 1910, p. 30, and Penelope A. E. Harper, 'The Dunedin Tailoresses' Union, 1889–1914', BA Hons research essay, University of Otago, 1988, pp. 26–35.
20. For Slater, see my essay in Jane Thomson (ed.), *Southern People: A Dictionary of Otago Southland Biography*, Dunedin, 1998, pp. 460–61.
21. Olssen, *Building the New World*, pp. 100–1.
22. For women's marginalisation see Olssen, *Building the New World*, pp. 187–94. See also Melanie Nolan, 'Employment Organisations', p. 196, and Melanie Nolan and Penelope Harper, 'Dunedin Tailoresses' Union, 1889–1945', p. 208, both in Anne Else (ed.), *Women Together: A History of Women's Organisations in New Zealand Nga Ropu Wahine o te Motu*, Wellington, 1993; and Penelope Harper and Melanie Nolan, 'Morison, Harriet', *DNZB*, Vol. 2, 1870–1900, pp. 336–37. I am very grateful to Dr Nolan for giving me all of her notes on the Tailoresses and on Jane Runciman, the long-serving secretary of the union.
23. *Otago Workman*, 13 September 1890. 'The Chiseler' pointed to a deeper domestic tension on 13 September 1890 when he remarked that his wife thought work good for him: 'My opinion is that all labour is a trouble . . . . I don't agree with labour, and labour does not agree with me.' He expected clean clothes and regular meals, however.
24. Bruce Scates, 'Mobilizing Manhood: Gender and the Great Strike in Australia and Aotearoa/New Zealand', *Gender & History*, 9, 2, 1997, pp. 285–309 (and p. 288 for the quotation).

25 *Evening Star*, 5 and 6 October 1893 (I am indebted to Linda Moore for this reference) and *Otago Workman*, 14 October 1893.
26 I have explored the role of the local Members of the House of Representatives, and the new ideological configurations on the Flat, more fully in *Building the New World*, pp. 188–99. For the concept of the wage workers' welfare state, see Francis G. Castles, *The Working Class and Welfare: Reflections on the Political Development of the Welfare State in Australia and New Zealand, 1890–1980*, Wellington, 1985, pp. 12–20 and Melanie Nolan, '"Politics Swept Under a Domestic Carpet"? Fracturing Domesticity and the Male-breadwinner Wage: Women's Economic Citizenship, 1920s–1940s', *NZJH*, 27, 2, 1993, pp. 199–217.
27 Marian Horan, 'Employing Gender in the New World: Factory Legislation in New Zealand, 1873-1901', MA thesis, University of Otago, 1999, pp. 182–3, and John E. Martin, *Holding the Balance: A History of New Zealand's Department of Labour 1891–1995*, Christchurch, 1996, pp. 68–69, 73–74.
28 See James Holt, *Compulsory Arbitration in New Zealand: The First Forty Years*, Auckland, 1987, chs 1 and 2.
29 Department of Labour, *Awards, Recommendations, Agreements, &c, made under the Conciliation and Arbitration Act*, 1, 1898, pp. 369 ff. for bootmakers; ibid., pp. 357 ff. for factory tailoresses; and 1 (1899), pp. 398 ff. for shop tailoresses. See also Holt, *Compulsory Arbitration in New Zealand*, ch. 2; Olssen, *Building the New World*, pp. 194–9; and Stephen Robertson, 'Women Workers and the New Zealand Arbitration Court 1894–1920', in Raelene Frances and Bruce Scates (eds), *Women, Work and the Labour Movement in Australia and Aotearoa/New Zealand*, Sydney, 1991, pp. 30–41.
30 For widows and widowers in the study area and New Zealand, see Janette Hart, 'Keeping the Family Together: A Study of the Persistence of Remarriage as a Survival Mechanism after European Colonisation', BA Hons research essay, University of Otago, 2001, especially ch. 3, and, for women without a breadwinner, see Annabel Cooper and Maureen Molloy, 'Poverty, Dependence and "Women": Reading Autobiography and Social Policy from 1930s New Zealand', *Gender & History*, 9, 1, 1997, pp. 36–59.

31 M. Sanders, 'The Lebanese Community in Dunedin Before 1936', BA Hons research essay, University of Otago, 1980, pp. 68–69 and 78–79.
32 See, for instance, Dorothy Page, 'Dissecting a Community: Women Medical Students at the University of Otago, 1891–1924', in Barbara Brookes and Dorothy Page (eds), *Communities of Women: Historical Perspectives*, Dunedin, 2002, pp. 111–28.
33 Seccombe, *Weathering the Storm*, p. 111.
34 Louise Tilly and Joan Scott, *Women, Work and Family*, New York, 1978.
35 Among other things, according to Seccombe, it allowed working-class households to keep the wife–mother at home, reduce the birthrate, and keep their children at school for longer; see Wally Seccombe, *Weathering the Storm*, pp. 71–81 and 115–17, and Sara Horrell and Jane Humphries, 'The Origins and Expansion of the Male Breadwinner Family: The Case of Nineteenth-Century Britain', *IRSH*, 42, 1997, Supplement 5.
36 The literature on this subject is now enormous. Among the key works are Seccombe's *Weathering the Storm*, especially pp. 111–23; Colin Creighton, 'The Rise of the Male Breadwinner Family: A Reappraisal', *Comparative Studies in Society and History*, 38, 2, 1996, pp. 310–37; Horrell and Humphries, 'Origins and Expansion of the Male Breadwinner Family', pp. 25–64; and Melanie Nolan, *Breadwinning: New Zealand Women and the State*.
37 Claire Toynbee, *Her Work and His: Family, Kin and Community in New Zealand, 1900–1930*, Wellington, 1995, ch. 5, and Olssen and Hickey, *Class and Occupation*, ch. 5, discuss self-provisioning.
38 As Creighton shows in 'The Rise of the Male Breadwinner Family', pp. 315–16, complex differences existed between countries in Western Europe and between regions in Britain. Horrell and Humphries, 'The Origins and Expansion of the Male Breadwinner Family', pp. 33–35, also show that the process varied considerably from one sector of the economy to another, being most developed among artisans and least developed among factory and agricultural workers.
39 Horan, 'Employing Gender', pp. 161–69 and 172–75, reported that neither the 1878 nor the 1889 Royal Commission found many married women in the workforce.

John E. Bartlett, 'Woven Together: the Industrial Workplace in the Otago Woollen Mills, 1871–1930', BA Hons research essay, University of Otago, 1987, p. 132, reported that even in 1875 only two out of 31 women employed by the Mosgiel Woollen Mill were married, although quite a few were middle-aged.

40 The major thinkers of the Scottish Enlightenment regarded the status of women, and their freedom from exploitation and degraded forms of labour, as key indicators of a civilised society. In Lancashire, where the marriage bar was not enforced, married women widely viewed it 'as a matter of social progress and of status to be able to give up wage-earning work'; E. Roberts, *A Woman's Place: An Oral History of Working-Class Women, 1890–1940*, Oxford, 1984, p. 137.

41 Bruce Smith and Catherine Wilson, 'Ethnic Origins in Caversham and Surrounding Areas as Found in Census and Marriage Certificate Data, 1880–1921', History 351 essay, University of Otago, 2001, and, for the carpenters, Olssen, *Building the New World*, p. 114.

42 Wally Seccombe, 'Patriarchy Stabilized: the Construction of the Male-breadwinner Wage Norm in Nineteenth-century Britain', *Social History*, 10, 1986, p. 57. See also Creighton, 'The Rise of the Male Breadwinner Family', pp. 310–37.

43 *Otago Workman*, 11 March 1893. Toynbee, *Her Work and His*, p. 163, described this as 'common practice among workers above subsistence . . .'. Karen Duder, 'Hegemony or Resistance? The Women of the Skilled Working Class and the Ideologies of Domesticity and Respectability', MA thesis, University of Otago, 1992, pp. 107–10, came to the same conclusion. Anecdotal evidence suggests that men increasingly kept any overtime they earned. For a useful discussion of gendered labour markets, see Mike Savage, *The Dynamics of Working-Class Politics: The Labour Movement in Preston, 1880–1940*, Cambridge, 1987, pp. 51–55.

44 It was only when the earnings of children began to flow into the family's economy that most working-class families achieved a comfortable margin against scrimping; see Cooper and Horan, chapter seven in this volume, and Olssen, *The Red Feds: Revolutionary Industrial Unionism and the New Zealand Federation of Labour*, Auckland, 1988, pp. 96–100.

45 Joanna Bourke, *Working-Class Cultures in Britain*, pp. 64–71, and Toynbee, *Her Work and His*, pp. 162–7.

46 As I remarked in *Southern People*, pp. 460–61, Slater 'was one of the most influential labour leaders never to sit in Parliament'. For Arnold and Sidey, see my essays in *DNZB*, Vol. 2, p. 12 and Vol. 3, pp. 471–72. Protective laws also contributed to labour-market segmentation; see Horan, 'Employing Gender', and Nolan, *Breadwinning*, ch. 2.

47 For the minimum wage for unskilled railway workers, see Olssen, *Building the New World*, p. 135. For Sim, see Holt, *Compulsory Arbitration*, p. 105, and Noel S. Woods, *Industrial Conciliation and Arbitration in New Zealand*, Wellington, 1963, p. 96. Sim also ruled that the court should 'endeavour to give the men fair remuneration for their work, regardless of whether employers got a profit or not'. See Henry Broadhead, *State Regulation of Labour and Labour Disputes in New Zealand*, Christchurch, 1908, p. 61 (and ch. 6 for a discussion of the minimum wage).

48 Over the years I have had several conversations with employers in the manufacturing sector, such as John McIndoe (of John McIndoe Ltd), who have claimed that this had been policy.

49 *Awards*, 3, 1902, p. 503, cited in Bartlett, 'Woven Together', p. 116. This did not prevent the companies from laying off large numbers of staff when a downturn occurred; e.g., *ibid.*, pp. 117–18.

50 Olssen, *Building the New World*, pp. 133–36, and John H. Angus, *The Ironmakers: The first hundred years of H. E. Shacklock Ltd.*, Dunedin, 1973, pp. 21–25.

51 Foremen and managers were usually male in all factories; see Bartlett, 'Woven Together', pp. 79–96. For the gendered composition of the workforce, see Bartlett, ibid., pp. 160–1. There are no studies of bootmaking in New Zealand, but about one-third of the workforce were women and they worked on stitching, an increasingly mechanised process undertaken in a separate room.

52 Marion Cooper (b. 1925), interviewed 2001 by Larissa Kindell, COHP, Gend 206 Transcripts: Women and Work, p. 7. Unless otherwise stated, all interviews were conducted by Megan Cook.

53 *ODT*, 13 November 1912, p. 5; criminal trial,

54 evidence of Robert Franklyn Turner, son of accused, p. 2, and evidence of William Ross, builder of St Kilda, DAAC/D256, 11/11/192, pp. 2–3, Dunedin Regional Office, Archives NZ. (I am indebted to Barbara Brookes for this material.)
54 Peggy Koopman-Boyden and Claudia Scott, *The Family and Government Policy in New Zealand*, Sydney, 1984, pp. 201–2; Melanie Nolan, *Breadwinning*, pp. 35–8, and 'Unstitching the New Zealand State: Its Role in Domesticity and its Decline', *IRSH*, 45, 2, 2000, pp. 251–77.
55 When the court set a minimum wage for women, it ranged between £1 5s a week for factory tailoresses and £1 7s 6d for shop tailoresses, whereas the minimum for tailors was £2 15s a week; see awards for the two categories of tailoress and for the tailors in *Awards*, 10, 1909, pp. 245, 646, 666 (these were minimum rates, of course). As Nolan points out, there was no national minimum for women before 1936: *Breadwinning*, p. 142.
56 It should be borne in mind that some societies, such as France, adopted this practice for both men and women, with employers differentiating wage rates on the basis of familial need; S. Pedersen, *Family, Dependence and the Origins of the Welfare State: Britain and France, 1914–1945*, Cambridge, 1993.
57 Shelley Griffiths, 'Feminism and the Ideology of Motherhood in New Zealand, 1896–1930', MA thesis, University of Otago, 1984, pp. 16–17.
58 Nolan, *Breadwinning*, p. 154, makes the point, but the entire issue has been ignored.
59 Woods, *Industrial Conciliation and Arbitration*, pp. 97–104 and ch. 4 for the post-1925 upheavals; Holt, *Arbitration*, pp. 153–58; and Nolan, *Breadwinning*, pp. 141–56 (only 16 per cent of married men had three or more children younger than 14 years old).
60 Nolan, *Breadwinning*, pp. 33–35.
61 The figures relating to property are derived from the Dunedin City Council valuation and rating records for 1911–12 and 1921–22. Unfortunately, these records do not exist for St Kilda. The proportion of businesses owned by women were higher in the study area than in either Dunedin or the province and rose slightly across the period (22.8 per cent in 1903, 23.8 per cent in 1920 and 25.1 per cent in 1939); see 'The Stone's Trades and Professions Database'. In Caversham Borough about 26 per cent of the properties were owned by widows; see Clyde Griffen, 'A More Egalitarian World? Residential Differentiation and Mobility in Caversham Suburb, Dunedin, 1902–1928', CWP 1997-8, pp. 28–29, 36.
62 Nolan, *Breadwinning*, pp. 33–35.
63 See Sister Mary Stephanie Glen, *Divide & Share: The Story of Mercy in the South 1897–1997*, Dunedin, 1996, chs 2 and 13.
64 Melanie Nolan, 'Runciman, Jane Elizabeth', in *DNZB*, Vol. 3, 1901–1920, Wellington, 1996, pp. 447–49.
65 For King, see Eileen Wallis, *A Most Rare Vision: Otago Girls' High School – The First Hundred Years*, Dunedin, 1972, pp. 88–89.
66 Olssen, 'Women, Work and Family', pp. 167–73, provides an account of the debate, and Nolan, *Breadwinning*, ch. 6, provides an excellent account of the 1930s debates over women's economic rights. For women's involvement in paid work, see Sandra Wallace, 'The Professionalisation of Nursing, 1900–1930', BA Hons research essay, University of Otago, 1987; Bronwyn Karran, 'She Stoops to Conquer: The Feminisation of the Clerical Workforce in New Zealand, 1890–1935', BA Hons research essay, University of Otago, 1991; Shannon Brown, 'Female Office Workers in Auckland: 1891–1936', MA thesis, Auckland, 1993; Louise Shaw, 'From Family Helpmeet to Lady Dispenser: Women Pharmacists 1881–1939', *NZJH*, 32, 1, 1998, pp. 23–42; and Patricia J. Sargison, '"Essentially a Woman's Work": A History of General Nursing in New Zealand, 1830–1930', PhD thesis, University of Otago, 2001.
67 B. A. Goyen, 'Truancy 1914–21', History 452 essay, University of Otago, 1983, pp. 13–14.
68 Cited by Patricia Grimshaw, *Women's Suffrage in New Zealand*, 2nd edn, Auckland, 1987, p. 6.
69 The manager of the NZ Clothing Factory told the 1878 Royal Commission that he knew of 'instances where the father does nothing'; *AJHR*, 1878, H-2, p. 12, cited Penelope Isaac, 'Stir, Bustle and Whir! A History of the New Zealand Clothing Factory 1873–1905 with Particular Reference to the Labour Process', BA Hons research essay, University of Otago, 1996, pp. 56–57. This was a major line of inquiry, however, and few cases were reported.
70 Declining fertility is discussed by Barbara

Brookes in chapter ten. Electricity was used mainly for lighting and heating water before the 1950s, but electric washing machines and vacuum cleaners were available from the 1920s; see Jean-Marie O'Donnell, '"Electric Servants" and the Science of Housework: Changing Patterns of Domestic Work, 1935–1956', in Barbara Brookes, Charlotte Macdonald, Margaret Tennant (eds), *Women in History 2*, Wellington, 1992, pp. 168–83.
71 Olssen and Hickey, *Class and Occupation*, ch. 4.
72 See S. O. Rose, *Limited Livelihoods: Gender and Class in Nineteenth-Century England*, London, 1992.
73 Rose Roberts (b. 1898), interviewed 1981 by Catherine Herries, Caversham Oral History Project (COHP), Childhood Transcripts, Vol. 1, pp. 185–89.
74 Both the 1878 and 1889 Royal Commissions found this; e.g., Mrs J., testimony to Sweating Commission, *AJHR*, 1890, H-5, p. 15.
75 In 'Employing Gender', pp. 47–50, Marian Horan discusses in particular the formative role of the 1842 Royal Commission into the mining industry in shaping Victorian attitudes.
76 This was a Western phenomenon; see Erik Olssen, 'Truby King and the Plunket Society: An analysis of a prescriptive ideology', *NZJH*, 15, 1, 1981, pp. 3–23.
77 Until the 1920s about 70 per cent of women employed in Dunedin's manufacturing sector were in the clothing and wool-milling trades (in 1901 the clothing industry employed 27 per cent of Dunedin's workforce, 80 per cent of whom were women). The best account of one of the major early companies is Penny Isaac, 'Stir, Bustle and Whir!', especially chs 3 and 4. Neither of the woollen mills, Mosgiel and Roslyn, has published histories, but, for valuable background, see Bartlett, 'Woven Together'.
78 For the industry, see *Cyclopaedia*, 1905, pp. 306–7, and interview with Laura Boulton, (b. 1911) interviewed n.d. [1985] by Carol Brown, COHP, Childhood Transcripts, Vol. 1. For Slater's views, *AJHR*, 1890, H-5, p. 14.
79 Bartlett, 'Woven Together', pp. 67, 79.
80 I first analysed the national figures in my essay on 'Women, Work and Family: 1880–1926', in Phillida Bunkle and Beryl Hughes (eds), *Women in New Zealand Society*, Auckland, 1980, Table 8.3, pp. 163–64.
81 For a more extensive discussion, see Olssen, *Building the New World*, pp. 76–83, and Dorothy Page, Howard Lee and Tom Brooking in chapter four of this volume.
82 For the declining proportion of women in skilled jobs, and their expanding numbers in white-collar and semi-professional occupations, see Olssen and Hickey, *Class and Occupation*, ch. 4.
83 Olssen and Hickey, *Class and Occupation*, ch. 3, and Nolan, 'Employment Organisations', in Else (ed.), *Women Together*, pp. 195–97.
84 T. A. Coghlan, the outstanding statistician, first for New South Wales and then the Commonwealth of Australia, and a key figure in developing a common Australasian policy, played a major role in this process in the 1890s and 1900s; see Desley Deacon, *Managing Gender: The State, the New Middle Class and Women Workers 1830–1930*, Melbourne, 1989, chs 5–7.
85 Roberta Nicholls, 'The PSC and the Equal Pay Campaign', in Alan Henderson, *The Quest for Efficiency: The Origins of the State Services Commission*, Wellington, 1990, pp. 247–48.
86 Alison Holmes, 'Occupational Mobility within the National Railway Classification (D-3) Lists 1912 and 1920', CWP 2002-2.
87 Angela Findlay, 'Widening Women's Sphere? Women, Work and Ideology in the New Zealand Post Office, 1900–1920', BA Hons research essay, University of Otago, 2000, chs 2 and 3; Bert Roth, *Along the Line: 100 Years of Post Office Unionism*, [Wellington], 1990, pp. 56–57, 74–75, 104–5.
88 Nicholls, 'The PSC and the Equal Pay Campaign', pp. 249–52 and Bert Roth, *Remedy for Present Evils: A History of the New Zealand Public Service Association from 1890*, Wellington, 1987, pp. 56–57 and 65–66.
89 Miss I. B. Paine became a senior official in the Housing Corporation, having started as accounts clerk: see interview with Miss I. B. Paine (b. 1922), interviewed 1981 by Alana Birchall, COHP, Childhood Series, Vol. 2, pp. 175–6. Jocelyn Dean became personal secretary to the Director of Rehabilitation: see Jocelyn Dean (b. 1922), interviewed 1983 [by Kaye Batchelor], COHP, Childhood Series, Vol. 1, pp. 20, 26. Personal communication from Dorothy Meder.
90 Jocelyn Dean (b. 1922), interviewed January

90. 1996 by Megan Cook, COHP, Transcript Series One, Vol. 1, p. 140, and Jane Thomson, 'Sidey, Thomas Kay' and 'Sidey, Helena' in *Southern People*, p. 454.
91. Billie D. McLeod, 'A Silent Testimony: St Vincent de Paul Catholic Orphanage for Girls, South Dunedin', PGDip research essay, University of Otago, 1992, Appendix 3, lists all the families that received girls.
92. Melanie Nolan, 'Runciman, Jane Elizabeth', *DNZB*, Vol. 3, p. 448.
93. Rose Roberts (b. 1898), interviewed 1981 by Catherine Herries, COHP, Childhood Series, Vol. 2, p. 189; Vera May Horder (b. 1911), interviewed n.d. [1982 or 83], Childhood Series, Vol. 1, pp. 292, 297, and various conversations with Dorothy Meder over several years.
94. Alexander Davidson (b. 1894), interviewed [1982?] by Tom Brooking, COHP, Childhood Series, Vol. 1, p. 193.
95. 'Cost of Living in New Zealand: Report and Evidence', *AJHR*, H-18, 1912, *passim*, and Dunedin Women's Branch of the New Zealand Labour Party (NZLP), Minute Book, 1, 20 November 1923 and 14 January 1924, AG 645 1, Hocken Library, Dunedin.
96. Cited by Isaac, 'Stir, Bustle and Whir!', p. 48. Although the actual number of domestics increased across the period nationally, the relative proportion kept falling and the proportion of all servants who were married women kept increasing; Olssen, 'Women, Work and Family', pp. 162–64. In the 1920s immigrants from Britain were recruited for domestic service; see Katie Pickles, 'Empire Settlement and Single British Women as New Zealand Domestic Servants During the 1920s', *NZJH*, 35, 1, 2001, pp. 22–44.
97. The multi-member city electorate of the period generated enormous electoral rolls. Extracting the names of electors living in the study area would be enormously costly, hence the figures for 1893 are much smaller than the others, including only those to the west of Forbury Rd. The increase in women listed under the category 'women at home' from 1903 to 1905 reflected the growing trend for women to be recorded by their marital status rather than their occupational status. By 1911 only a few women were not recorded on the rolls by their marital status.
98. For the national figures, see Olssen and Hickey, *Class and Occupation*, ch. 4.
99. Some 85 women also listed themselves as occupied with 'domestic duties'.
100. Olssen and Hickey, *Class and Occupation*, ch. 4.
101. Tony Bamford, 'The Wax Vesta Match Factory', History 452 essay, University of Otago, 1982, p. 13.
102. Kathryn Lucas, *A New Twist: A Centennial History of Donaghy's Industries Limited*, Dunedin, 1979, chs 4–5 (and especially pp. 54–90); Jodine Lyons, 'The "Grand Magasins" of the South: The World of Dunedin Department Stores 1890–1960', BA Hons research essay, University of Otago, 1999, pp. 12–14; and Louise Shaw, 'Hallenstein Brothers and Company 1876–1906: The Early Years of Mass Retailing in New Zealand', PGDip research essay, University of Otago, 1994.
103. Obituary, *ODT*, 13 July 2002, p. A35.
104. For the major firms at the start of the century, see the *Cyclopaedia of New Zealand*, Vol. 4, *Otago and Southland*, Christchurch, 1905, especially pp. 301, 306–7, and 336–43 for the clothing factories. There are no comparable later sources, but see the overview, including many brief accounts of particular firms, in the various anniversary issues of the *ODT*, especially 15 November, 1921, pp. 23–27 and 16 November 1936, pp. 22, 24–25, 29–30.
105. Gertrude J. Shiel (b. 1902), COHP, interviewed 1980 by Adair Bruorton, Childhood Series, Vol. 2, p. 279.
106. Margaret Galt, in 'Wealth and Income in New Zealand c. 1870 to c. 1939', PhD thesis, Victoria University, pp. 216–19, shows that this was a national trend.
107. Early film, collected by the Otago Gold Project, demonstrates this clearly. Indeed, it is unusual to see heterosexual couples together in public, even when congregations leave their places of worship. I am indebted to John Irwin for access to the film.
108. Gertrude Shiel, p. 263.
109. Mavis Liverpool (b. 1923), COHP, interviewed December 1995, Transcript Series One, Vol. 5, pp. 48–49.
110. Nicholls, 'The PSC and the Equal Pay Campaign', pp. 249–54.
111. Margaret Galt, 'Wealth and Income in New Zealand', pp. 214–16 and Nolan, *Breadwinning*, pp. 19–20, especially n. 40.
112. Rose Roberts (b. 1898), p. 185.
113. *Awards*, 6, 1905, pp. 175–77, and *ODT*, 15 February 1906. For wages in this industry, see also *Awards*, 14, (1913), p. 133; Penelope A. E. Harper, 'Dunedin Tailoresses', ch. 4;

and papers in the J. T. Paul Mss, Boxes 173, 696, Hocken Library, Dunedin.

114 R.W. Maskell (b. 1912), interviewed 1981 by Margaret Wallis, COHP, Childhood series, Vol. 2, p. 72.

115 See Bartlett, 'Woven Together', pp. 112–16, 134–37 and Appendix A; Isaac, 'Stir, Bustle and Whir!', pp. 54–59 (for the quotation see p. 56); Harper, 'Dunedin Tailoresses' ch. 4; and, for post-1914, developments J. T. Paul, *Our Majority*, Marion Cooper, p. 3. Many boys also worked in 'blind-alley' jobs: see Jerry White, *The Worst Street in North London: Campell Bunk, Islington, Between the Wars*, London, 1986, p. 163.

116 For an overview of trends in gendered wage rates, see Margaret Galt, 'Wealth and Income', chs 15 and 16, and, for the interwar period especially, Table 17.12, p. 272. I reviewed the evidence for the pre-1914 period in *Red Feds*, pp. 96–100. For the Arbitration Court's erratic policy, see Holt, *Compulsory Arbitration*, pp. 99–106.

117 Ellen Jordan, 'The Exclusion of Women from Industry in Nineteenth-Century Britain', *Comparative Studies in Society and History*, 31, 2, 1989, pp. 273–96, and Harriet Bradley, *Men's Work, Women's Work: A Sociological History of the Sexual Division of Labour in Employment*, Cambridge, 1989; both concluded that in Britain the newer the industry the more rigid the sexual division of labour. That also seems to be the case here. For the custom in the Wax Vesta factory, see Horan, 'Employing Gender', pp. 144.

118 Erik Olssen, 'The New Zealand Labour Movement and Race', in Marcel van der Linden and Jan Lucassen (eds), *Racism and the Labour Movement: Historical Studies*, Bern, 1995, pp. 373–92.

119 A point also made by Creighton, 'The Rise of the Male Breadwinner Family', p. 320.

120 'The Stone's Trades & Professions Database', 1902–38. In 1903 unmarried women constituted less than 20 per cent of business-owners in our study area and 35 per cent in Dunedin. By 1920, however, unmarried women constituted just over 40 per cent of women in business in the study area and over 50 per cent in Dunedin. Widows, of course, constituted something akin to a third sex; see Toynbee, *Her Work & His*, pp. 112–16, 119–22. See also Rebecca Smith and David Turner, 'Before the New World: Food Retail in Dunedin and Caversham 1890–1920', History 351 essay, University of Otago, Dunedin, 1998, pp. 6–7, 8–9, 13 (for butchers and fishmongers). See also Jane Adams and Karyn-Marie Piercy, '"Clothing the New World": The Clothing Retail and Manufacturing Industry in Dunedin and Caversham, 1890s–1920s', History 351 essay, University of Otago, 1999, pp. 11–12. For England and Wales, see Bradley, *Men's Work, Women's Work*, pp. 175–76. See also Wendy Gamber, 'A Gendered Enterprise: Placing Nineteenth-Century Businesswomen in History', *Business History Review*, 72, 1998, p. 203.

121 If we look at the occupations provided by the women who joined the Miriam Rebekah Lodge of the IOOF, we can see also that young women entered some trades, but never set up in business. Bookkeepers, clerks and bookbinders, even pressers and boot-finishers, not to mention a solitary photographer, appear as members, but have never been found listed in the *Trades Directory*.

122 See Marian Horan, 'The In-dependent Women? Women, Work and Charitable Aid in Otago, 1895 to 1905', BA Hons research essay, University of Otago, 1997, pp. 53–56. Some of women's entrepreneurial activities doubtless fell outside the law, or did so during this period. Bronwyn Dalley's work on one-woman brothels indicates that sex remained a saleable commodity, if an unlovely one: 'Lolly Shops "of the Red Light Kind" and "Soldiers of the King": Suppressing One-Woman Brothels in New Zealand, 1908–1916', *NZJH*, 30, 1, 1996, pp. 3–23. The Benevolent's records and some oral histories suggest that some women in the area of Maria (later Glasgow) St may have worked as prostitutes from their own homes. Fortune-telling was also illegal.

123 Catherine Smith, 'Business of Beauty: A History of Hairdressers 1920s–1960s', PhD thesis, University of Otago, 1998, pp. 35–37. In ch. 6, Smith discusses 'The Business of Ladies' Hairdressing' and, in ch. 7, 'The Technology and Training of Ladies' Hairdressers'.

124 Nenadic found in Edinburgh that many single women founded small family businesses, often with a sister. She also found that wives and husbands sometimes worked together in a business, in the clothing trades at least: see 'The Social Shaping of Business Behaviour in the

Nineteenth-Century Women's Garment Trades', *Social History*, 31, 3, 1998, pp. 626, 633–4, 636.

125 I tracked down the two daughters of Roland Grimmett when I interviewed Bert Grimmett, their brother. Over the next few months, they were both interviewed by Megan Cook, the project's research assistant for the construction of the oral-history database, and Catherine Smith.

126 When she was interviewed, Marion Cooper recalled the basketball team with particular pleasure, p. 2. (The team had just held a reunion.)

127 Caroline Daley, in *Girls & Women, Men & Boys: Gender in Taradale, 1886–1930*, Auckland, 1999, pp. 63–72, remarks on similar trends in Taradale, a semi-rural small town on the outskirts of Napier. Miriam Vosburgh, *The New Zealand Family and Social Change: A Trend Analysis*, Wellington, 1978, p. 48, noted that women who had worked were much more likely to use contraception. For the war's relation to these complex changes, see my discussion in Judith Binney, Judith Bassett and Erik Olssen, *The People and the Land Te Tangata me te Whenua: An Illustrated History of New Zealand, 1820–1920*, Wellington, 1990, pp. 308–11. For women's savings, see Duder, 'Hegemony or Resistance?', pp. 96–99.

128 Miriam Gilson, 'Women in Employment', in John Forster (ed.), *Social Process in New Zealand: Readings in Sociology*, Auckland, 1969, pp. 192, 194. In 1901 women constituted almost 19 per cent of the non-agricultural paid workforce, 25 per cent in 1926, and 21.5 per cent by 1936. In 1891 some 39 per cent of all women aged between 15 and 24 had paid work, by 1921 the proportion had grown to 50 per cent, and by 1940 to 60 per cent. It seems likely that by 1926 over two-thirds of unmarried women worked in the non-agricultural paid workforce. See Olssen and Hickey, *Class and Occupation*, ch. 4.

129 Obituary, *ODT*, 13 July, 2002, p. A35.

130 Michael King, *Wrestling with the Angel: a Life of Janet Frame*, Auckland, 2000, p. 36.

131 Bert Roth, *Along the Line*, pp. 74–75.

132 Independent Political Labour League, 1905–8; New Zealand Labour Party, 1909–11; the United Labour Party, 1912–14; the Otago Labour Representation Committee, 1914–16 (a powerful local alternative to the Social Democratic Party, 1913–21); and the New Zealand Labour Party, 1916– .

133 For the quotation, see *Otago Workman*, 14 October 1893.

134 For the quotation and the idea, see Scates, 'Gender and the Great Strike', p. 293.

135 Dunedin Women's Branch of the NZLP, Minute Book, 2, 27 January 1925, AG 645 2, Hocken Library, Dunedin.

136 Dunedin Women's Branch of the NZLP, Minute Book, 2, 26 May 1925.

137 A point made by Carol Pateman, 'Three Questions About Womanhood Suffrage', in Caroline Daley and Melanie Nolan (eds), *Suffrage and Beyond: International Feminist Perspectives*, Auckland, 1994, pp. 343–45.

138 The early minute books for this branch are missing: the first extant volume is for 1927–32 and the first membership book is for 1935–69; see Mss AG 573, Hocken Library, Dunedin.

139 For the death throes of the Tailoresses, see the correspondence between the DTU's officials in the J. T. Paul Mss, Boxes 278 and 590 (Paul had been president of the DTU since 1910). For Miss McCarthy's campaigns, see Annabel Cooper, 'McCarthy, Mary Ann Recknall', *DNZB*, Vol. 3, pp. 287–8; and Nolan, *Breadwinning*, pp. 150–51, 153. The papers of the South Dunedin WCTU and the Dunedin Women's Branch of the NZLP are both held in the Hocken Library, Dunedin. For an excellent analysis of a similar situation in Wellington, see Melanie Nolan, 'Gender and the Politics of Keeping Left: Wellington Labour Women and their Community, 1912–1949', in Brookes and Page (eds), *Communities of Women*, pp. 147–62. For the CP, see Kerry Taylor, 'The Communist Party of New Zealand from its Origins to 1946', PhD thesis, Victoria University, 1995.

140 This analysis is indebted to the work of Marilyn Lake, 'Socialism and Manhood: The Case of William Lane', *Labor History*, 50, 1986, pp. 54–62, and 'The politics of respectability: identifying the masculinist context', *Historical Studies*, 22, 1, 1986, pp. 116–31.

141 Olssen, *Building the New World*, pp. 194–9.

142 For the recruitment patterns of different classes, see Erik Olssen and Hamish James, 'Social Mobility and Class Formation: The Worklife Social Mobility of Men in a New Zealand Suburb, 1902–1928', *International Review of Social History*, 44, 3, 1999, pp. 429–37, and Olssen and John Harraway,

'Pathways of Occupational Movement', forthcoming.
143 C. J. Graham, 'Relief Camps in the Depression, 1931–35', PGDip research essay, University of Otago, 1976, pp. 15–16, 38.
144 A point also made by Jerry White, *The Worst Street in North London*, chs 6 and 7 (especially pp. 161–87, 188–218).

Four Schooling for a Gendered Future
1 *Caversham School Sixty-Fifth Anniversary Celebrations, 1861–1926*, Dunedin, 1926, p. 15. No date is assigned to this recollection of 'older ex-pupils', but the jubilee photos include a group of 18 from the first decade, 1861–70, and 94 from the second, 1871–80, so it is likely to be nineteenth century.
2 Erik Olssen, chapter three in this volume.
3 Kay Matthews, 'White Pinafores, Slates, Mud and Manuka', in Sue Middleton (ed.), *Women and Education in Aotearoa*, Wellington, 1988, pp. 20–21. As examples of mainstream educational history, Matthews cites A. G. Butchers, *Education in New Zealand*, Dunedin, 1930; John L. Ewing, *The Development of the New Zealand Primary School Curriculum 1877–1970*, Wellington, 1970; A. E. Campbell, *Educating New Zealand*, Wellington, 1941; Ian A. McLaren, *Education in a Small Democracy*, London, 1974; Ian Cumming and Alan Cumming, *History of State Education in New Zealand, 1840–1975*, Wellington, 1978.
4 Ruth Fry, *It's Different for Daughters: A History of the Curriculum for Girls in New Zealand Schools, 1900–1975*, Wellington, 1985, p. 25.
5 Anne-Marie O'Neill, 'The Gendered Curriculum' in Gary McCulloch (ed.), *The School Curriculum in New Zealand*, Palmerston North, 1992, pp. 74–101.
6 Margaret Tennant, 'Natural Directions: The New Zealand Movement for Sexual Differentiation during the Early Twentieth Century', in Barbara Brookes, Charlotte Macdonald and Margaret Tennant (eds), *Women in History*, Wellington, 1986, p. 99; Melanie Nolan, *Breadwinning: New Zealand Women and the State*, p. 136.
7 Colin McGeorge, 'The Moral Curriculum: Forming the Kiwi Character', in Gary McCulloch (ed.), *The School Curriculum in New Zealand*; Jock Phillips, *A Man's Country? The Image of the Pakeha Male – A History*, Auckland, 1987, p. vii and ch. 3; Greg Ryan, 'Rural Myth and Urban Actuality: The Anatomy of All Black and New Zealand Rugby, 1884–1938', *New Zealand Journal of History (NZJH)*, 35, 1, 2001, pp. 45–65.
8 Caroline Daley, *Girls & Women, Men & Boys: Gender in Taradale, 1886–1930*, Auckland, 1999. Kay Matthews's study, 'White Pinafores', is also a local one, and Rosemary Goodyear, 'Black Boots and Pinafores: Childhood in Otago, 1890–1920', MA thesis, University of Otago, 1992, has a chapter on primary schooling in the province, ch. 8; see also Joan Scott, 'Gender: A Useful Category of Historical Analysis' in *Gender and the Politics of History*, New York, 1988, p. 50.
9 Scott, 'Gender', p. 50.
10 Otago Education Board (OEB) Reports, 1890–97, Appendix F, Details of Inspection.
11 *Caversham School Sixty-Fifth*, pp. 11–13. Milne was headmaster from 1865 to 1906.
12 OEB Annual Reports. In 1900 the combined roll was 2015: Caversham had 538 pupils, Forbury 568, Kensington 360, Macandrew Road 435 and St Clair 114; OEB 1900, Appendix F, p. 40. The perceived characteristics of the schools have been supported by evidence from inspectors' reports and the composition of the school boards. See Tom Brooking, 'The Schools of Caversham', CWP 1990. Catherine Carter and Emma Liddell, 'Primary Education in the Caversham Area, 1890–1920', History 351 essay, University of Otago, 1998, reinforces the conclusion in relation to Caversham and St Clair schools. Records are not adequate to allow speculation in the case of Kensington and Macandrew Road. For location of schools, see Map 4.1.
13 Father P. R. Mee, *The Turn of the Tide*, Dunedin, 1977, pp. 19–21, 25, 32–33; St Patrick's had 200 pupils in 1883.
14 Colin McGeorge, 'Schools and Socialisation in New Zealand, 1890–1914', PhD thesis, University of Canterbury, 1985, p. 13.
15 OEB Reports, 1890–97; school rolls, Appendix B. At Caversham, 297 girls and 303 boys were listed (less than the reported total of 610, rising to 655 by the end of the year). Kensington had 206 boys and 146 girls and Macandrew Road had 288 boys and 228 girls. Forbury, in contrast, reported 195 boys and 217 girls; proportion of girls to boys, in *AJHR*, 1901, E-1, p. 2; Fry, *It's Different for Daughters*, p. 9; the attendance for Caversham School was assessed on

a roll halfway between the figures given for the beginning and the end of the year; Matthews, 'White Pinafores', p. 29; Howard Lee's research for 15 years from 1902 suggests that keeping girls from school was acceptable to the community. Although the rate of reported truancy was roughly the same for boys and girls, a ratio of 48:51, magistrates convicted more boys, in a ratio of 62:38: '"Playing the Wag": The Anatomy of Truancy: a Study of Truancy in Otago's Primary Schools from 1902 to 1917', MEd thesis, University of Otago, 1983, Table 27, p. 176.

16 The Education Act 1877 specified sewing and domestic science for girls and military drill for boys (*Statutes of New Zealand*, 1877); the Proficiency examination was introduced in 1899. Fry, *It's Different for Daughters*, ch. 2, pp. 104, 108; McGeorge, 'Moral Curriculum', pp. 48–49. The cadet scheme was wound up in 1912, to leave the way clear for cadet training at secondary school. *Macandrew Road School, South Dunedin, Jubilee 1883–1933: Souvenir Historical Sketch*, Dunedin, 1933.

17 *Caversham Sixty-Fifth*, p. 10.

18 Daley, *Girls & Women*, pp. 1–2; the line of demarcation was less rigid in small country schools: Fry, *It's Different for Daughters*, p. 10; *Caversham School Sixty-Fifth*, p. 9; McGeorge, 'The Moral Curriculum', pp. 48–9; Francis Raymond Gordon, in *St Clair Centennial Booklet, St Clair School, 1896–1996*, Dunedin, 1996, p. 88; Goodyear, 'Black Boots', p. 373; John V. Riach, *Forbury School, 75th Anniversary*, Dunedin, 1951; *Forbury School, 1875–1975, Souvenir of the Centenary*; *Musselburgh School, Dunedin, 75th Jubilee, 1905–1980*, all held in the Hocken Library, stress the violent nature of boys' play compared with girls'.

19 Fry, *It's Different for Daughters*, pp. 8–9. The leaving age was raised to 14 in 1901.

20 OEB Reports, 1882, Appendix F, II, p. 45. Other southern Dunedin schools also had a high pass rate in 1882: Forbury 82 per cent and Kensington 8 per cent; Macandrew Road opened in 1883 and the next year was proud to have a pass rate of 89 per cent. Two of the scholarship girls later graduated MA from Otago University and became teachers before marriage. Edith Pearce (later Bear), MA 1894, taught at Ashburton High School and Napier Girls' College. Jessie Rutherford (later Nimmo), MA 1896, at Balclutha and Caversham primary schools; Dorothy Page, 'The First Lady Graduates', in Barbara Brookes, Charlotte Macdonald and Margaret Tennant (eds), *Women in History 2*, Wellington, 1992, pp. 111, 114, 127; *Caversham School Sixty-Fifth*, list of former staff, pp. 11–13; *Macandrew Road Jubilee*, p. 10.

21 Rita Jory (b. 1902) and Louise Wellman (b. 1909), interviewed March 1996, Caversham Oral History Project (COHP), Transcript Series One, Vol. 5, pp. 139, 159; Victoria Lake (b. 1912), interviewed August 1996, COHP, Transcript Series One, Vol. 1, pp. 70–71; Marjorie Scott (b. 1909), interviewed January 1996, COHP, Transcript Series One, Vol. 2, p. 174. Unless otherwise stated, all interviews conducted by Megan Cook, Dunedin.

22 Hugh Mercer (b. 1900), in Goodyear, 'Black Boots', pp. 372, 410; Jessie McLaren (née Cumming;1901–90), in Goodyear, 'Black Boots', pp. 373, 374, 408; Henry Gordon Markham, in *St Clair Centennial*, p. 49; Caroline Daley, who interviewed men and women who had been pupils at the Taradale School before 1930, also noted that 'separate gendered experience gave rise to very different memories': *Girls & Women*, p. 10.

23 Sister Mary Zeta McEvoy, in *The Philomenian: Celebrating One Hundred Years*, Dunedin, 1997, p. 12.

24 Daley, *Girls & Women*, p. 139; *Zealandia*, 2, August 1889, p. 2, cited in McGeorge, 'The Moral Curriculum', p. 42; Kay Matthews describes as 'atypical' the action of a Hawke's Bay School Committee in 1886 in outlawing corporal punishment in the school after one little girl suffered severe bruising and bleeding around the arms and shoulders, having had three sticks broken on her ('White Pinafores', p. 25).

25 Hugh Mercer, in Goodyear, 'Black Boots', p. 375. He went to Forbury School; Lew Roebuck (b. 1910), interviewed by Tom Brooking, February 1981, Childhood Transcripts, Vol. 2, p. 207; William Rutherford (b. 1910), interviewed anon., July 1981, Childhood Transcripts, Vol. 2, p. 222; Richard Perth (b. 1903), interviewed by Melissa Reid, August 1981, Childhood Transcripts, Vol. 3, p. 25; Edward (b. 1904) and Johanna Waterman (b. 1905), interviewed October 1996, COHP, Transcript Series One, Vol. 1, p. 245; Henry Gordon Markham, a pupil from 1917 to 1924,

St Clair Centennial, p. 49, Margaret Newton and Isobel Spence, pupils 1932–9, *St Clair Centennial*, p. 99, Edna Drummond (née Jones), referring to Mr McMullan, *St Clair Centennial*, p. 61.

26 Fry, *It's Different for Daughters*, p. 92; J. A. Hanan, *Evening Star*, 16 March 1917, cited in 'Retrospect', *St Clair Centennial*, p. 14; Drummond, *St Clair Centennial*, p. 61.

27 Drummond, *St Clair Centennial*, p. 61, and Joyce Haigh (née Fox), *St Clair Centennial*, p. 63.

28 Fry, *It's Different for Daughters*, p. 25; Henry Gordon Markham in *St Clair Centennial*, p. 50.

29 Daley, *Girls & Women*, p. 3.

30 David McKenzie, 'The Growth of School Credentialling in New Zealand; 1878–1900', in Roger Openshaw and David McKenzie (eds), *Reinterpreting the Educational Past: Essays in the History of New Zealand Education*, Wellington, 1987, pp. 82–106; H. F. Lee, 'The Credentialled Society: A History of New Zealand Public School Examinations 1871–1990', PhD thesis, University of Otago, 1991, pp. 6–99; Page, 'The First Lady Graduates', pp. 113–20.

31 Erik Olssen, *Building the New World: Work, Politics and Society in Caversham, 1880s–1920s,* Auckland, 1995, pp. 125, 131. Hillside apprentices also had to be 15 years old. By 1930 the workshops employed 700 men.

32 For many school leavers, employment in the civil service was eagerly sought after, as it offered a reasonable income, security of employment and pension entitlements. It also exerted considerable influence over the rest of the labour market. See L. Lipson, *The Politics of Equality: New Zealand's Adventures in Democracy*, Chicago, 1948, pp. 157–58; R. J. Polaschek, *Government Administration in New Zealand*, Wellington, 1958, p. 100; McKenzie, 'The Growth of School Credentialling', p. 87.

33 Ian McLaren, 'Secondary Schools in the New Zealand Social Order, 1840–1903', PhD thesis, Victoria University of Wellington, 1965; Ian A. McLaren, 'Education and Politics: Background to the Secondary Schools Act, 1903. Part 11: Secondary Education for the Deserving', *New Zealand Journal of Educational Studies*, 6, 1, 1971, pp. 1–23; Ian A. McLaren, 'The Politics of Secondary Education in Victorian New Zealand', in Openshaw and McKenzie (eds), *Reinterpreting the Educational Past*, pp. 64–81; G. Lee, '"Open the Doors, Unbar the Doors" – The Development of Free Place Legislation and Its Effect upon Otago Boys' High School in the Years between 1900 and 1905', MEd thesis, University of Otago, 1983, pp. 35–40; G. Lee, 'From Rhetoric to Reality: A History of the Development of the Common Core Curriculum in New Zealand Post-Primary Schools 1900–1945', PhD thesis, University of Otago, 1991, pp. 1–34.

34 That is 5.4 per cent of the 132,262 children enrolled at primary school in New Zealand in 1902: *AJHR*, 1903, E-1, Table E.

35 Annie Norman (b. 1887), interviewed by Tom Brooking, February 1982, COHP, Childhood Transcripts, Vol. 2, pp. 99–100, 119–25. See Erik Olssen, chapter three of this volume, for further examples of children being called on to help the family, either by leaving school to help at home or to enter paid employment.

36 Pat Donnelly (b. 1910), interviewed by Shaun Broadley, March 2000, COHP, Transcript Series Two, Vol. 1, p. 30. His younger sisters went to OGHS, however, and his two brothers attended OBHS; Goodyear, 'Black Boots', p. 408.

37 Of Robert Rutherford's children, Robert William became manager of the match factory and a city councillor, John Robert, MA, became headmaster of Mornington School and Alfred James became a warehouseman. His two daughters, Jessie Hamilton, MA, and Violet, were both teachers before marriage. High educational and professional achievement was also a characteristic of the next generation.

38 Nolan, *Breadwinning*, p. 112.

39 An Anglican school, Selwyn College, limped along until 1911: R. P. Hargreaves, *Selwyn College's First Century, 1893–1993: A History and List of Residents*, Dunedin, 1993, pp. 16–18; Presbyterian John McGlashan College opened in 1918: *John McGlashan College: A History and Register*, Dunedin, 1971; *Diamond Jubilee of the Christian Brothers' High School, New Zealand, 1876–1936*, Dunedin, c. 1936; *King's High School Golden Jubilee Booklet, 1936–1985*, Dunedin, 1986.

40 Howard Baldwin, 'Educating the Elite? The Social Origins and Occupational Destinations of Otago Boys' High School Pupils, 1863-1903', MA thesis, University of Otago, 1996, pp. 98–100.

41 Eileen Wallis, *A Most Rare Vision: Otago Girls' High School – the First One Hundred*

Years, Dunedin, 1972, pp. 26–27. The curriculum included class singing and drawing and optional music, German, and knitting. Latin was taught from 1878.

42 Sir John Richardson, *Thoughts on Female Education*, Dunedin, 1870, cited in Page, 'The First Lady Graduates', p. 100.

43 Page, 'The First Lady Graduates', pp. 101–2; Appendix, p. 127–28.

44 Lucy Duncan, 'What Katy Did at School: A Study of Curriculum Development in Dunedin Girls' Secondary Schools, 1900–1920', BA Hons research essay, University of Otago, 1984; *St Patrick's School, South Dunedin 1878–1978 Centennial*, Dunedin, 1978; Bernard Cadogan, '"Lace Curtain Catholics": The Catholic Bourgeoisie of the Diocese of Dunedin, 1900–1920', BA Hons research essay, University of Otago, 1984; *The Philomenian*, Dunedin, 1997; Vida F. Shedden, *Columba College: The First Fifty Years, 1915–1965*, Dunedin, 1965; Muriel May, *St Hilda's Collegiate School: The First Seventy Years*, Dunedin, 1966.

45 Muriel May, *Freshly Remembered: Half a Century of School*, Christchurch, 1973, p. 38; Otago Boys' High School magazines, select issues, 1886–1901, Vol. XV, no. 1, April 1899.

46 Report and Prospectus, The Technical Classes Association (TCA), 1889–90, Report of First Year: Aims, p. 4: Professor George M. Thomson was secretary and Superintendent of Classes. These were held in the Normal School and students typically paid 5s a quarter for an hour's tuition a week. By the mid-1890s students could sit for qualifications in trades subjects from the City and Guilds of London Institute. Records of the daytime occupations, age and sex of the students tell us that, in that year, the majority (79) were clerks (a trend that would continue), that there was a sizeable group of school pupils under 16 who came for shorthand, and among the 75 who did not state their occupation were a number involved in 'domestic duties'. The report noted that the great majority of the students (259) came from Dunedin city, but there was a group of 26 from South Dunedin, Kensington and St Kilda.

47 David McKenzie, 'The Technical Curriculum', in McCulloch (ed.), *The School Curriculum*, p. 34.

48 Natalie Beath, Alison Holmes and Andrew Joel, 'Secondary Education of Cavershamians 1911–1921', History 351 essay, University of Otago, 1999.

49 Sandy Ehlers and Katie Tierney, 'Do Daughters Differ (From Sons in State Schools)? Gender and Education in Caversham', History 351 essay, University of Otago, 1999. Girls tended to stay at primary school longer than boys, although St Clair School is an exception to this pattern.

50 J. Irving, 'Co-educational or Single Sex Schools?' in *Set*, 1, 9, 1976; Eileen M. Byrne, *Women and Education*, London, 1978. In contrast, in both Australia and the USA, the preference for single-sex schooling gave way to a co-educational philosophy.

51 Robin Law, chapter nine in this volume.

52 May, *Freshly Remembered*, p. 37; Wallis, *A Most Rare Vision*, illustrations between pages 64 and 65 and opposite p. 113; Velda McCracken (b. 1920), interviewed October 1996, COHP, Transcript Sub-series Two: Wealth and Poverty, p. 236.

53 Anna Kathleen Frost, 'Exploring educational efficiency in New Zealand primary and post-primary schooling, 1900–1945', MA thesis, University of Otago, 1998; G. Lee, 'From Rhetoric to Reality'.

54 G. Lee, 'Open the Doors'; G. Lee, 'From Rhetoric to Reality'; H. Lee, 'The Credentialled Society'; David McKenzie, Gregory Lee and Howard Lee, *The Transformation of the New Zealand Technical High School*, Palmerston North, 1990.

55 Marchant to J. R. Sinclair (Chairman of Otago High Schools' Board of Governors), 7 April 1903, Otago High Schools' Board, *Files and Correspondence*, 1903; OGHS Annual Report, 1906, p. 5. The King Edward Technical College was due to open the following year; *ODT*, 13 December 1906; G. Lee, 'Open the Doors' p. 40, Table 3.

56 Marchant to Sinclair, 18 September 1907, Otago High Schools' Board, *Files and Correspondence*, 1907.

57 Wallis, *A Most Rare Vision*, p. 68.

58 Marchant to chairman, Otago High Schools' Board of Governors, 17 March 1908, 19 March 1908, 16 April 1908, 2 May 1908, in Otago High Schools' Board, *Minutes of Monthly Meetings*, Vol. 3, pp. 202, 210, 215, 222. In 1908, typing was not recognised by the department as part of the post-primary school syllabus.

59 Alexander Wilson, cited in Roy Shuker, *One Best System? A Revisionist History of State Schooling in New Zealand*, Palmerston North, 1987, p. 157; Morrell to Sinclair, 13

February 1908, Otago High Schools' Board, *Files and Correspondence*, 1908.
60 *ODT*, 17 February 1908. Two commercial courses were offered: a short three-hour course (comprising one hour each of bookkeeping, commercial geography and commercial correspondence) and a longer five-hour course (two hours bookkeeping, two hours shorthand and one hour commercial geography).
61 Ryan, 'Rural Myth', pp. 45–65. There were seven All Blacks from OBHS in the period 1881 to 1914. Phillips, *A Man's Country?*, suggests that the emphasis on sport had less to do with national identity than with prevailing fears of physical and moral degeneration, p. 105.
62 OBHS magazine, August 1918, May 1919; W. Somerville was the young soldier referred to, photo, opposite p. 96.
63 *AJHR*, 1910, E-6, p. 11; 1911, E-6, p. 12.
64 *ODT*, 22 May 1909; *Otago Witness*, 26 May 1909; Tennant, 'Natural Directions', pp. 93–4; Fry, *It's Different for Daughters*, pp. 36, 82–85; Ruth Fry, 'The Curriculum and Girls' Secondary Schooling, 1880–1925' in Middleton (ed.), *Women and Education*, pp. 33–36.
65 *ODT*, 22 May 1909; *New Zealand Gazette*, 1917, pp. 2769–73, 3029–34; *AJHR*, 1917, E-1, pp. 3–4, 9, 42–44, 49; E-6, p. 4; Nolan, *Breadwinning*, p. 110.
66 Wallis, *A Most Rare Vision*, p 82, p. 68.
67 Dunedin Technical Classes 1905–6, 17th Report. The typewriting class had 99 students, and all but two of those who gained a first-class certificate were women, as were 15 of the 21 who gained speed shorthand certificates. In addition to the 722 students in Dunedin evening classes, there were small classes at Mosgiel, Outram and Milton, and 291 students in Oamaru. A majority of the males (92) described themselves as clerks.
68 KETC Report and Prospectus, 1916.
69 KETC Report and Prospectus, 1916; KETC magazine (single copy only) 1916; newspaper clipping, n.d., day school break-up, 1916, Hocken Library.
70 Pat Donnelly (b. 1910), pp. 11–13; Ian Martin (b. 1912), interviewed by Shaun Broadley, March 2000, COHP, Transcript Series Two, Vol. 1, pp. 138–39; Caversham database and KETC rolls, 1911 and 1919. The numbers of males from Caversham School rose from six in 1911 to 22 in 1919. St Clair, which provided no evening-class students in 1911, had 25 (18 male) in 1919. Only Forbury numbers declined, from 20 (12 male) in 1911 to nine (six male) in 1919.
71 Stuart Sidey (b. 1908), interviewed October 1996, COHP, Transcript Series One, Vol. 5, p. 25; Ian Martin, pp. 139–142.
72 Caversham database, primary school records and OBHS rolls, 1911 and 1919.
73 M. H. King, 'Report of Committee appointed to consider the relationship between High and Technical Schools', 11 October 1926, Otago High Schools' Board, *Files and Correspondence*, 1926.
74 King, 'Report of Committee'.
75 Beath, Holmes and Joel, 'Secondary Education', Caversham database. Class rolls OBHS, OGHS, KETC. Frances Kenny (b. 1910), interviewed by Shaun Broadley, February 2000, COHP, Transcript Series Two, Vol. 1, p. 115, remembered that the community regarded OGHS as being more prestigious than KETC. Kenny also felt that some stigma attached to girls attending KETC to become mere typists and shop assistants; Christine King (b. 1923), interviewed by Shaun Broadley, February 2000, COHP, Transcript Series Two, Vol. 1, p. 71, remembered a sharp differentiation and considered herself to have been privileged in attending OGHS. Caversham database and KETC rolls, 1911 and 1919. The remainder of the girls in the 1911/1919 sample group took domestic.
76 Helen Wilson (b. 1909), interviewed May 1996, COHP, Transcript Series One, Vol. 5, p. 270; Alison Abraham (b. 1914), interviewed October 1996, COHP, Transcript Series One, Vol. 3, p. 7.
77 Frances Kenny, pp. 107–9: Frances Kenny arrived at school by 8 a.m. to be sure of getting a court.
78 Yvonne Morris (b. 1911), interviewed April 1996, COHP, Transcript Series One, Vol. 5, pp. 66–67.
79 Helen Wilson, p. 269.
80 Kitty Brown (b. 1905), interviewed December 1995, COHP, Transcript Series One, Vol. 1, pp. 119–20.
81 Helen Tweed (b. 1914), interviewed May 1996, COHP, Transcript Series One, Vol. 2, pp. 279, 286.
82 Erik Olssen, 'Towards a New Society', in Geoffrey W. Rice (ed.), *The Oxford History of New Zealand*, second edition, Auckland, 1992, p. 263.

83 'Let Us Advance Again', *National Education*, 7, 1, 1935, p. 459, cited in Rosemary Goodyear, 'The Individual Child: A study of the development of social services in education in relation to the first Labour Government's educational policy', BA Hons research essay, University of Otago, 1987, p. 2.
84 Lee, 'Playing the Wag'.
85 David McKenzie, 'The Proficiency Examination 1930–35: A Political Controversy', in John Codd, Richard Harber and Roy Nash (eds), *Political Issues in New Zealand Education*, Palmerston North, 1985, p. 194. Prime Minister George Forbes's comment is cited by McKenzie, p. 194.
86 Peter Fraser, Education Report, 1939, *AJHR*, 1939, E-1, pp. 2–3.

Five Producing and Consuming Gender

1 Helen Tweed (b. 1914), interviewed August 1996, Caversham Oral History Project (COHP), Transcript Sub-series One: Clothing/Courtship and Marriage, pp. 18–19. Unless otherwise stated, all interviews conducted by Megan Cook, Dunedin.
2 Mavis Liverpool (b. 1923), interviewed September 1996, COHP, Transcript Sub-series One, p. 202.
3 Angela McRobbie, 'Bridging the Gap: Feminism, Fashion and Consumption', *Feminist Review*, 55, Spring, 1997, pp. 73–89. A similar point is made in Susan Benson, 'Living on the Margin: Working-class Marriages and Family Survival Strategies in the United States, 1919–1941', in Victoria de Grazia (ed.), *The Sex of Things*, Berkeley, 1996, pp. 212–43.
4 McRobbie, 'Bridging the Gap', p. 78.
5 See, for example, John Fiske, *Understanding Popular Culture*, London, 1989; Mica Nava, 'Consumerism Reconsidered', in Morag Shiach (ed.), *Feminism and Cultural Studies*, New York, 1999, pp. 45–64.
6 For our purposes, class denotes relations of production and, in turn, affects relativities of income and expenditure.
7 Robert Bocock, *Consumption*, London, 1993, pp. 34–52; Peter Glennie, 'Consumption Within Historical Studies', in Daniel Miller (ed.), *Acknowledging Consumption*, London, 1995, pp. 164–203.
8 Pierre Bourdieu, *Distinction: A Social Critique of the Judgement of Taste*, London, 1984, *passim*; Gary Cross, *Time and Money: The Making of Consumer Culture*, London, 1993, p. 159.
9 Carolyn Steedman, *Landscape for a Good Woman*, London, 1986, p. 38; Grant McCracken, *Culture and Consumption: New Approaches to the Symbolic Character of Consumer Goods and Activities*, Indianapolis, 1988, pp. 57–70.
10 Joan Scott, 'Gender: A Useful Category of Historical Analysis', in *Gender and the Politics of History*, New York, 1988, pp. 28–50.
11 Scott, 'Gender', pp. 42–43.
12 We suggest that oral histories may be best regarded as sources of narratives, be they recollections or ideological positions, rather than all-knowing statements about social totalities. For a discussion of subjectivity, fashion and the limits of historical evidence, see Chris Brickell, 'Through the (New) Looking Glass: Gendered Bodies, Fashion and Resistance in Post-war New Zealand', *Journal of Consumer Culture*, 2, 2, 2002, pp. 241–69.
13 Grace Rogers Cooper, *The Sewing Machine: Its Invention and Development*, 2nd edition, Washington DC, 1976, p. 124.
14 Grace Neill, 'Reports of local inspectors of factories and agents of the Department of Labour', *AJHR*, 1895, H-6, p. 10.
15 Erik Olssen, *Building the New World: Work, Politics and Society in Caversham 1880s–1920s*, Auckland, 1995, p. 90.
16 Louise Shaw, 'Hallenstein Brothers and Company, 1876–1906', PGDip research essay, University of Otago, 1994.
17 Erik Olssen, *A History of Otago*, Dunedin, 1984, p. 122.
18 Report of the Sweating Commission, *AJHR*, 1890, H-5.
19 Otago Benevolent Institution Outdoor Relief (OBIODR) Casebook, DAHI D 284 60-68, Archives New Zealand (ANZ), Dunedin. (References that follow are first to the Archives *volumes*, and second to the individual *series* of the Caversham Project's edited transcripts of those volumes: Annabel Cooper with Marian Horan and Eva Lubcke (eds), 'Transcripts from the Otago Benevolent Institution's Outdoor Relief Casebooks', 3 vols, Caversham Working Paper (CWP) 2000–3. See Appendix II for more specific information on this source.) Volumes I–III; Series One. See also the discussion in chapter three.
20 OBIODR Casebook, Vol. I, pp. 389, 432, Series I, p. 50.

21 OBIODR Casebook, Vol. I, pp. 434, 531, Series I, p. 51.
22 Letter to the editor, *Evening Star* (*ES*), 13 December 1916, p. 7.
23 For example, *ES*, 26 December 1919, p. 2.
24 See Olssen, *Building the New World, passim*.
25 Marjorie Scott (b. 1909), interviewed January 1996, COHP, Transcript Series One, Vol. 2, p. 166.
26 Margaret Hanley, personal communication, 25 November 1999.
27 Another link between southern Dunedin and the Parisian fashion scene was provided by Helen Tweed's clothing teacher at school, who periodically departed for Paris and the workrooms of famous designers: Helen Tweed, p. 16.
28 Laura Boulton (b. 1911), interviewed by Carol Brown, COHP, Childhood Transcripts, Vol. 1, *passim*.
29 Laura Boulton, p. 45.
30 Jean Darby (b. 1918), interviewed September 1996, COHP, Transcript Sub-series Two: Wealth and Poverty, p. 27.
31 Jane Malthus, 'Dressmakers in Nineteenth Century New Zealand', in Barbara Brookes, Charlotte Macdonald, Margaret Tennant (eds), *Women in History 2*, Wellington, 1992, pp. 77–78.
32 Edward (b. 1904) and Johanna (b. 1905) Waterman, interviewed October 1996, COHP, Transcript Series One, Vol. 1, pp. 250–53 and 281.
33 Laura Boulton, p. 45.
34 Olssen, *Building the New World*, p. 90.
35 Karyn-Maree Piercy and Jane Adams, '"Clothing the New World": The Clothing Retail and Manufacturing Industry in Dunedin and Caversham, 1890s–1920s', History 351 essay, University of Otago, 1999, pp. 10–12; *Stone's Directory for Otago and Southland*, 1936, trades directory, pp. 866, 890, 904.
36 Only one advertisement for southern Dunedin was sighted in the entire sample of newspapers viewed for this chapter, and that was for a brewery.
37 For a more general discussion of women's economic activity in southern Dunedin from 1890, see Olssen, chapter three of this volume.
38 *Stone's Directory for Otago and Southland*, 1890, trades directory, p. 489. By 1884 a small nucleus of stores had developed along King Edward Rd (including general stores, chemists, saddlers and blacksmiths, as well as draperies), with a second, smaller shopping centre in South Rd, Caversham. See G. N. Stedman, 'The South Dunedin Flat: A Study in Urbanisation 1849–1965', MA thesis, University of Otago, 1966, pp. 149–52.
39 Piercy and Adams, '"Clothing the New World"', p. 9.
40 Piercy and Adams, '"Clothing the New World"', p. 9.
41 Piercy and Adams, '"Clothing the New World"', p. 18; see also Olssen, chapter three.
42 52 per cent in 1894, more than 70 per cent in 1903, 1912 and 1920.
43 53 per cent of drapers were listed as 'Mrs' in *Stones* in 1920. See also Piercy and Adams, '"Clothing the New World"', p. 22.
44 Stana Nenadic, 'The Social Shaping of Business Behaviour in the Nineteenth-Century Women's Garment Trades', *Journal of Social History*, 31, 3, 1998, p. 638.
45 *Otago Witness* (*OW*), 6 March 1890, p. 8.
46 *OW*, 6 March 1890, p. 44.
47 *Stone's Directory for Otago and Southland*, 1890, trades directory.
48 *ODT*, 19 May 1894, p. 2.
49 Jane Malthus, '"Bifurcated and Not Ashamed": Late Nineteenth-Century Dress Reformers in New Zealand', *NZJH*, 23, 1, 1989, pp. 32–46.
50 Angelique Richardson and Chris Willis, 'Introduction', in Richardson and Willis (eds), *The New Woman in Fiction and in Fact*, London, 2001, pp. 1–38; for a specifically Dunedin interpretation, see Catherine Smith, 'The Business of Beauty: A History of Hairdressers 1920s–1960s', PhD thesis, University of Otago, 1998.
51 See Robin Law's discussion in chapter nine.
52 Annabel Cooper, Robin Law, Jane Malthus and Pamela Wood, 'Rooms of Their Own: Public Toilets and Gendered Citizens in a New Zealand City 1860–1940', *Gender, Place and Culture*, 7, 4, 2000, pp. 417–33.
53 *OW*, 5 August 1908, p. 2; *OW*, 4 November 1908, p. 17.
54 *OW*, 4 November 1908, p. 73.
55 *OW*, 7 April 1925, p. 56.
56 Helen Tweed, p. 5.
57 The *Otago Witness* illustrated a 'frock for a matron' (5 January 1932, p. 60), while on a later date an advertisement for a 'Veet' hair removal agent was illustrated with three young women in swimsuits at the beach (*OW*, 2 February 1932, p. 56).
58 See, for example, *OW*, 5 January 1932, p. 60;

OW, 26 January 1932, p. 57; OW, 19 January 1932, pp. 57–58.
59 Mavis Liverpool, p. 176.
60 Mavis Liverpool, p. 176.
61 Maureen Judge (b. 1922), interviewed October 1996, COHP, Transcript Sub-series One, pp. 43–45.
62 Frances Kenny (b. 1910), interviewed August 1996, COHP, Transcript Sub-series One, p. 67; also Helen Tweed, p. 2.
63 Jean MacFarlane (b. 1909), interviewed August 1996, COHP, Transcript Sub-series One, pp. 101–2.
64 OW, 6 March 1890, p. 1.
65 OW, 6 March 1890, p. 3.
66 OW, 6 March 1890, p. 8.
67 Maria Constantino, *Men's Fashion in the Twentieth Century*, London, 1997, p. 20.
68 For example, Erik Olssen, *Building the New World, passim*; OW, 2 September 1903, p. 38.
69 Caversham Project photograph collection.
70 From advertisements cited in Jodine Lyons, 'The "Grand Magasins" of the South', BA Hons research essay, University of Otago, 1999, pp. 64, 70. See also Danielle Sprecher, 'Representations of Fashion and Modernity', MA thesis, University of Auckland, 1997, pp. 30–32.
71 Giles Dodson and Claire Gooder, 'The Basis of Dependency: Otago Soldiers' and Dependents' Welfare Committee 1918', History 351 essay, University of Otago, 1998.
72 William (b. 1916) and Frances Harris (b. 1917), interviewed June 1996, COHP, Transcript Series One, Vol. 2, p. 265.
73 For example, photographs on pp. 136 and 142 in Olssen, *Building the New World*.
74 See Mavis Liverpool, p. 183.
75 For a similar argument for the 1940s, see Brickell, 'Through the (New) Looking Glass', *passim*.
76 McRobbie, 'Bridging the Gap', p. 74.
77 OBIODR Casebook, Vol. I–III and V–X, *passim*; OBIODR Casebook, Vol. I–III, *passim*.
78 Phyllis Crossan (b. 1922), interviewed January 1996, COHP, Transcript Series One, Vol. 1, p. 192.
79 Jean Darby, p. 27.
80 Rosanna Paul (b. 1909), interviewed May 1996, COHP, Transcript Series One, Vol. 2, p. 84.
81 Megan Melville, '19th and 20th Century Sewing Machines in New Zealand', PGDip research essay, University of Otago, 1993.
82 OW, 6 March 1890, p. 44; OW, 4 September 1890, p. 9.
83 When the First World War broke out, however, boys as well as girls had to pick up khaki and navy wool and knit socks, balaclavas and scarves for the soldiers. See Edward and Johanna Waterman, p. 303.
84 Myrtle Caird (b. 1920), interviewed April 1996, COHP, Transcript Series One, Vol. 1, pp. 173–74; Rosanna Paul, p. 137; Jean MacFarlane, p. 103; Mavis Liverpool, p. 176.
85 McRobbie, 'Bridging the Gap', p. 74.
86 Kitty Brown (b. 1905), interviewed December 1995, COHP, Transcript Series One, Vol. 1, p. 127. Young women working in clothing factories would not necessarily have a full complement of skills, as factory dress production was broken into discrete tasks.
87 Maureen Judge, p. 30; Frances Kenny, p. 71; Yvonne Morris (b. 1911), interviewed September 1996, COHP, Transcript Sub-series One, p. 124.
88 Mavis Liverpool, p. 189.
89 Helen Tweed, p. 11.
90 Jean Darby, p. 23.
91 Frances Harris, p. 195.
92 OW, 4 September 1890, p. 6.
93 OBIODR Casebook, Vol. I, pp. 238–40, Vol. II, p. 752, Series I, p. 34.
94 OBIODR Casebook, Vol. I, pp. 245, 307, Vol. II, p. 838, Vol. III, p. 1607, Series I, pp. 35–36.
95 Victoria Lake (b. 1912) and Marina MacKenzie (b. 1908), interviewed August 1996, COHP, Transcript Series One, Vol. 1, pp. 62 and 104; Rosanna Paul, p. 137.
96 Maureen Judge, p. 43; Yvonne Morris, p. 121; Myrtle Caird, pp. 173–74; Rosanna Paul, p. 137.
97 Yvonne Morris, p. 126.
98 Mavis Liverpool, p. 173.
99 Myrtle Caird, p. 173.
100 Mavis Liverpool, p. 198.
101 Jean McFarlane, p. 111.
102 David Ausubel, *The Fern and the Tiki: An American View of New Zealand*, Sydney, 1960, pp. 27–32; Bill Consedine, 'Inequality and the Egalitarian Myth', in David Novitz and Bill Willmott (eds), *Culture and Identity in New Zealand*, Wellington, 1989, pp. 172–86. For a discussion of the place of egalitarianism in British working-class life, see Jerry White, *The Worst Street in North London: Campbell Bunk, Islington, Between the Wars*, London, 1986, p. 102 and *passim*.
103 Mavis Liverpool, p. 188.

104 Jean McFarlane, p. 104; also Yvonne Morris, p. 146; Ken (b. c. 1923) and Velda (b. c. 1920) McCracken, interviewed October 1996, COHP, Transcript Sub-series Two, p. 234.
105 Maureen Judge, p. 47.
106 Helen Tweed, p. 4.
107 Helen Tweed, p. 7.
108 Yvonne Morris, pp. 126, 153.
109 Pat Donnelly (b. 1910), interviewed September 1996, COHP, Transcript Sub-series Two, p. 33; Bert Grimmett (b. 1912), interviewed by Annabel Cooper, 1996, COHP, Transcript Sub-series Two, p. 65.
110 Mavis Liverpool, p. 209; Pat Donnelly, p. 38.
111 Laura Boulton, p. 44.
112 White, *The Worst Street in North London*, p. 191; see also Myrtle Caird, p. 173.
113 Jean Darby, p. 16.
114 See Cooper, chapter seven.
115 Laura Boulton, p. 45.

Six Spare Time? Leisure, Gender and Modernity

1 'New Social Hall at Hillside Workshops', *The New Zealand Railway Magazine*, 2 July 1928, pp. 50–51.
2 James Anthony Froude, *Oceana, or England and Her Colonies*, 2nd edition, London, 1886, p. 209. See also Claire Toynbee, *Her Work and His: Family, Kin and Community in New Zealand 1900–1930*, Wellington, 1995, pp. 134–37, 143–44.
3 E. P. Thompson, 'Time, Work-Discipline, and Industrial Capitalism', *Past and Present*, 38, 1967, pp. 56–97. John A. Lee, in *Children of the Poor*, New York, 1933, p. 85, recorded that the lack of a clock and the ensuing failure to be punctual constituted one of the defining characteristics of poverty in Edwardian Dunedin.
4 Claire Langhamer, 'Towards a Feminist Framework for the History of Women's Leisure, 1920–1960', in Anne-Marie Gallagher, Cathy Labelska, Louise Ryan (eds), *Re-presenting the Past: Women and History*, London, 2001, p. 200.
5 Clare Simpson has compiled a useful bibliography on *Women and Recreation in Aotearoa/New Zealand*, Department of Parks, Recreation and Tourism, Lincoln University, 1991. Caroline Daley, *Leisure & Pleasure: Reshaping and Revealing the New Zealand Body, 1900–1960*, Auckland, 2003.
6 Toynbee, *Her Work and His*, especially ch. 9.
7 Caroline Daley, *Girls & Women, Men & Boys: Gender in Taradale 1886–1930*, Auckland, 1999, chs 6–8 (especially pp. 124–26). See also Daley's essay, 'A Gendered Domain: Leisure in Auckland, 1890–1940', in Caroline Daley and Deborah Montgomerie (eds), *The Gendered Kiwi*, Auckland, 1999, pp. 213–34.
8 Cam Cummings (b. 1895), interviewed 1980 by Tom Brooking, Caversham Oral History Project (COHP), Childhood Transcripts, Vol. 1, p. 92. Unless otherwise stated, all interviews were conducted by Megan Cook.
9 James Belich, *Paradise Reforged: A History of the New Zealanders from the 1880s to the Year 2000*, Auckland, 2001, p. 122: Belich's phrase, 'The Great Tightening', captures a strong trend locally.
10 Pat Donnelly (b. 1910), interviewed 1996, COHP, Transcript Sub-series Two: Wealth and Poverty, p. 41; for drunkenness, see *Otago Workman*, 9 September 1893; 'The Seamy Side of Dunedin', *Evening Star*, 23, 24 and 31 October 1893; and, for gambling, David Grant, *On a Roll: A History of Gambling and Lotteries in New Zealand*, Wellington, 1994, pp. 66–68.
11 Mabel Cartwright, Diary, Monday 28 January 1908, reported one woman 'wringing her hands and frightened because there were Catholics . . . drinking next door'. We are grateful to Yvonne Wilkie for access to the Diary, which is now held in Knox College Archives, Dunedin.
12 See J. T. Paul, *Dunedin Operative Bootmakers' Union: Fifty Years of Effort, 1876–1926*, Dunedin, 1926, p. 11. For specific craft traditions of drinking in early Victorian Britain, see the temperance tract by John Dunlop, *The Philosophy of Artificial and Compulsory Drinking*, 6th edition, London, 1839.
13 Vera Horder (b. 1911), interviewed 1980 by Adair Bruorton, COHP, Childhood Transcripts, Vol. 1, p. 293, and Gertrude J. Shiel (b. 1901), interviewed 1980 by Adair Bruorton, Vol. 2, p. 286.
14 Daley, *Girls & Women*, p. 133. Daley came to similar conclusions about alcohol and gender, see pp. 143–50. Bert Grimmet (b. 1911), interviewed 1993 by Erik Olssen, COHP, Childhood Transcripts, Vol. 3, pp. 5–6.
15 Patricia Grimshaw, *Women's Suffrage in New Zealand*, 2nd edition, Auckland, 1987, p. 14.
16 Kenneth Turner, 'Henry Smith Fish and the Opposition to the Female Franchise

in Dunedin, 1890–1893', BA Hons research essay, University of Otago, 1985.
17 For the wider change, see Erik Olssen, *A History of Otago*, Dunedin, 1984, pp. 114–17, and Erik Olssen, *Building the New World*, Auckland, 1995, pp. 238–45.
18 Miles Fairburn concluded that alcohol consumption declined from the mid-1860s onwards to the late 1890s; a small rise occurred in the early twentieth century and another sharp decline took place from about 1918 to 1930: 'Violent Crime in Old and New Societies – A Case Study Based on New Zealand, 1853–1940', *Journal of Social History*, 20, 1986, p. 111.
19 Erik Olssen, 'Friendly Societies in New Zealand, 1840–1990', in Marcel van der Linden (ed.), *Social Security Mutualism: The Comparative History of Mutual Benefit Societies*, Bern and New York, 1996, pp. 191–93.
20 Bert Grimmett, p. 11.
21 A. R. Grigg, 'Prohibition and Women', *New Zealand Journal of History* (*NZJH*), 17, 2, 1983, pp. 148–51, discusses this campaign.
22 The best national study remains A. R. Grigg, 'The Attack on the Citadels of Liquordom: A study of the Prohibition Movement in New Zealand, 1894–1914', PhD thesis, University of Otago, 1977. Anna Blackman, 'The Righteousness which Exalteth a Nation: Prohibition in Dunedin 1919–1923', BA Hons research essay, University of Otago, 1987, provides an excellent local analysis.
23 *Otago Witness*, 26 May 1925, p. 33, and John E. Martin, 'Boreham, Charles Stephen', in *DNZB*, Vol. 2, pp. 50–51.
24 Unearned leisure was associated with the dissolute ways of the English aristocracy – summarised in Oscar Wilde's witticism: 'work is the ruin of the drinking classes'.
25 See the Registrar-General's caustic comments on the mania for halls: *AJHR*, 1890, H-2, p. 1; 1908, H-1, p. 6; 1910, H-1, p. 5. Some four local lodges built halls in the early 1900s. Other organisations followed suit.
26 Almost all the childhood interviews mentioned musical evenings at home, usually around a piano: e.g. (all from the COHP Childhood Transcripts), Frank Denford (b. 1906), interviewed 1982 by Lucy Duncan, Vol. 1, p. 217; Mr Donaldson (b. c. 1893), interviewed 1982 by Liz Sinclair, Vol. 1, p. 236; Mary Gilbert (b. 1901), interviewed 1982 by Gill Kaye, Vol. 1, p. 249; C. W. N.

Ingram (b. 1900), interviewed 1980 by Sue Harkness, Vol. 2, p. 23; Annie Norman (b. 1878), interviewed 1982 by Tom Brooking, Vol. 2, p. 101; and Vera Horder (b. 1911), Vol. 1, p. 294. On women and music more generally, see Andrea Deuchrass, 'Pushing Past the Confines of Femininity: Music for Women in Dunedin 1907–1950: A Vehicle for Agency, Recognition and Social Connections', BA Hons research essay, 2001.
27 For the crusade against gambling, in which Rutherford Waddell played a major part, see Grant, *On a Roll*, pp. 77–93.
28 No history exists of the Caversham Bowling Club, or either of the two tennis clubs, Caversham and St Kilda. See R. Maskell, *St Clair Bowling Club 1882–1982*, Dunedin, 1982, and J. B. Robertson, *The St Clair Golf Club 75th Jubilee*, Dunedin, 1940.
29 Hugh Trevor-Roper, 'The Invention of Tradition: The Highland Tradition of Scotland', in Eric Hobsbawm and Terence Ranger (eds), *The Invention of Tradition*, Cambridge, 1993, p. 16.
30 See the annual reports and the society's press clipping book, Caledonian Society Mss, Box 30, MS 1045, Hocken Library, Dunedin; the interview with C. W. N. Ingram, p. 30; and Shiobhan Alice O'Donnell, 'Dancing at the Auld Cale: A History of Highland Dancing in Dunedin between 1863 and 1900', BA Hons research essay, University of Otago, 1998, p. 64.
31 Louise Johnson, *Placebound: Australian Feminist Geographies*, Melbourne, 2000, p. 2.
32 See Brian Sutton-Smith, *A History of Children's Play: The New Zealand Playground 1840–1950*, Wellington, 1982, pp. 185–90 and ch. 12 (first published in Philadelphia, 1981). The Otago Education Board was to the fore in this process.
33 For the development of this ethos, nurtured in England's public schools, see J. Lowerson, *Sport and the English Middle Class 1870–1914*, Manchester, 1993, pp. 154–90, and Kenneth Sheard and Eric Dunning, *Barbarians, Gentlemen, and Players: A Sociological Study of the Development of Rugby Football*, Oxford, 1979, pp. 176–82. Professionalism was endemic in English cricket, which may help explain that game's failure to achieve popularity in New Zealand.
34 For a fuller discussion in the context of rugby, see Len Richardson, 'The Invention of a National Game: The Struggle for Control', *History Now*, 1, 1, 1995, pp. 1–8, and

34 G. T. Vincent, 'Practical Imperialism: The Anglo-Welsh Rugby Tour of New Zealand, 1908', *International Journal of the History of Sport*, 15, 1998, pp. 123–40.

35 Pirates and Southern used Carisbrook as their headquarters until Southern moved to Bathgate Park in 1914 (Pirates later moved to Tahuna Park). The Dunedin Club had its headquarters at the Caledonian.

36 Winston Cooper, *Always a Southern Man: The History of the Southern Rugby Football Club 1884–1984*, Dunedin, 1984; Sean O'Hagan, *Pride of the Southern Rebels*, Dunedin, 1981, pp. 88–91; and Stuart Thomlinson, 'The Classless Game: Myth and Reality', BA Hons research essay, University of Otago, 1999, pp. 58–74.

37 For the origins of these clubs and an analysis of the player base each recruited in the 1880s and 90s, see Thomlinson, 'The Classless Game'. By the 1940s, however, the game recruited more evenly from all social strata: see A. Lynch, 'Otago 17 – Southland 11: A Social History of Rugby in the 1940s', BA Hons research essay, University of Otago, 1984, pp. 20–24 (Southern was still more working than middle class, however); and Alan Manley, 'Antidote to Depression: Rugby and New Zealand Society 1919–1939', PGDip research essay, University of Otago, 1991.

38 O'Hagan, *Pride of the Southern Rebels*, pp. 27–28, 51–72.

39 Cooper, *Southern Man*, pp. 33–34, and Charles Little, 'The "Northern Game" in the South: The Rise and Fall of Rugby League in Otago, 1924–1935', BA Hons research essay, University of Otago, 1994, especially ch. 2.

40 Bill Milburn, 'From the Terrace', *ODT*, 10 July 1998 and 26 March 1999.

41 Cooper, *Southern Man*, p. 37, and pp. 32–33 for the events.

42 Little, 'The "Northern Game" in the South', ch. 2 (for Eckhoff, pp. 34–36, and sectarianism, pp. 45–46).

43 Bert Grimmett, pp. 4–5.

44 *The Big Game and Other Stories*, Caxton Press, Christchurch, 1947. Gaskell was a pseudonym for A. G. Pickard, a University player. For this period, see O'Hagan, *Pride*, pp. 92–94, and Cooper, *Southern Man*, chs 4 and 5.

45 Wallis, *A Most Rare Vision*, Dunedin, 1972, p. 86.

46 Cooper, *Southern Man*, p. 157.

47 Olssen, *Building the New World*, pp. 249–50, discusses rugby and egalitarianism at greater length.

48 Jock Phillips, *A Man's Country? The Image of the Pakeha Male – A History*, Auckland, 1987, chs 3 and 4.

49 The phrase is from Margaret Sievwright, 'The New Woman', *Lyttelton Times*, 30 April 1896, p. 2, reprinted in Margaret Lovell-Smith, *The Woman Question*, Auckland, 1992, p. 119.

50 The phrase is from the *Otago Witness*, 2 September 1914, p. 28, cited by Margaret Anderson, 'The Female Front: Attitudes of Otago Women towards the Great War 1914–1918', BA Hons research essay, University of Otago, 1990, p. 40. On dress reform, see Jane Malthus, '"Bifurcated and Not Ashamed": Late Nineteenth-Century Dress Reformers in New Zealand', *NZJH*, 23, 1, 1989, pp. 32–46.

51 For the pleasure of walking, see Cartwright, Diary, and interviews with Myrtle Caird (b. 1920), interviewed April 1996, Transcript Series One, Vol. 1, p. 177; Doreen Macbeth (b. 1920), interviewed May 1996, Transcript Series One, Vol. 2, pp. 13–14; Mary Redwood (b. 1924), interviewed March 1996, Transcript Series One, Vol. 2, pp. 68–69; Joyce Jones (b. 1926), interviewed January 1996, Transcript Series One, Vol. 3, pp. 100–1. For the cult of physical fitness, see Caroline Daley, 'Selling Sandow: Modernity and Leisure in Early Twentieth-Century New Zealand', *NZJH*, 34, 2, 2000, pp. 241–61.

52 Claire Simpson, 'Respectable Identities: New Zealand Nineteenth-Century 'New Women'– on Bicycles!', *The International Journal of the History of Sport*, 18, 2, 2001, p. 54.

53 *New Zealand Wheelman*, 19 October 1895, p. 4. For a fuller discussion of women's cycling, see Simpson, 'Respectable Identities'.

54 See also Robin Law's discussion of cycling and driving in chapter nine.

55 Charlotte Macdonald, 'Organisations in Sport, Recreation and Leisure', in Anne Else (ed.), *Women Together: A History of Women's Organisations in New Zealand: Nga Ropu Wahine o te Motu*, Wellington, 1993, p. 406. For Siedeberg as lodge doctor, see interview with Annie Norman (b. 1887), pp. 108, 116–17.

56 For further discussion of the idea that female sportswomen were 'an anomaly', see M. A. E. Hammer, '"Something Else in the

57. Susan Patullo, 'The cramming controversy in Otago, 1880–1908', BA Hons research essay, University of Otago, 1983.
58. 'Chronicles of the Enfranchised' by One of Them, *Otago Daily Times & Witness Christmas Annual*, December 1907, p. 44.
59. Fiona Farrell Poole, 'Amy Bock, 1859–1943', in Charlotte Macdonald, Merimeri Penfold and Bridget Williams (eds), *The Book of New Zealand Women/Ko Kui Ma Te Kaupapa*, Wellington, 1991, pp. 90–93.
60. Macdonald, 'Organisations in Sport, Recreation and Leisure', p. 405.
61. 'Chronicles of the Enfranchised', p. 34.
62. 'Chronicles of the Enfranchised', p. 33.
63. Cartwright, Diary, especially the entry for 3 January 1908.
64. Wallis, *A Most Rare Vision*, pp. 64–65.
65. According to Sutton-Smith, *History of Children's Play*, pp. 195–96, a Presbyterian youth worker, Reverend J. C. Jamieson, toured the main towns and introduced the indoor game – it was widely recognised that teenage girls lacked any game of their own. From there it spread to the primary schools as an outdoor game. Basketball is now known as netball.
66. Wallis, *A Most Rare Vision*, pp. 107–9. Several of those interviewed by Megan Cook in 1995–96, Transcript Series One, played sports at school; see Jennifer Glum (b. c. 1909), interviewed January 1996, Vol. 3, pp. 295–96; Frances Kenny (b. 1910), interviewed August 1996, Vol. 3, p. 206. Rachel David (b. 1921), interviewed March 1996, recalled Bible class tramps, Vol. 5, p. 147.
67. 'Chronicles of the Enfranchised', pp. 33–34.
68. Joyce Jones (b. 1926), interviewed January 1996, COHP, Medical History Transcripts, pp. 199–200.
69. Wilhemina Bassett (b. 1918), interviewed December 1996, COHP, Medical History Transcripts, p. 16; Louise Wellman (b. 1909), interviewed March 1996, COHP, Medical History Transcripts, pp. 366–67.
70. *New Zealand Medical Journal*, 18, October 1919, p. 263.
71. Hilda Maher (b. 1912), interviewed 1996, COHP, Transcript Series One, Vol. 4, pp. 46–48.
72. F. Truby King, *The Expectant Mother and Baby's First Month*, Wellington, 1916, pp. 18–19. (The three subsequent editions, issued by the Department of Health, greatly expanded the range of advice, but did not alter the message.)
73. See Anna K. C. Petersen, '"Signs of Higher Life": A Cultural History of Domestic Interiors in New Zealand c. 1814–1914', PhD thesis, University of Otago, 1998, p. 87. Scholars agree about the new importance of family and the construction of the family man: see Phillips, *A Man's Country?*, ch. 5; Toynbee, *Her Work and His*, p. 134; and other chapters in this volume.
74. Dr Bettina Hamilton (née Collier), 'A Sentimental Journey to St Clair', *ODT*, 8 May 1980, p. 17.
75. Bert Grimmett, p. 8; Richard Perth (b. 1903), interviewed 1996 by Erik Olssen, COHP, Medical History Transcripts, p. 275; Joyce Jones, interviewed 1996, Transcript Series One, Vol. 3, p. 100; Shirley Sparkes (b. 1925), Vol. 5, p. 132; and Rachel David, pp. 145–46, 148.
76. Not surprisingly the same was true in Taradale; see Daley, *Girls & Women*, p. 108.
77. C. W. N. Ingram (b. 1900), p. 24, and Johanna (b. 1906) and Edward Waterman (b. 1906), interviewed October 1996, Transcript Series One, Vol. 1, p. 245.
78. Jane Thomson (ed.), *Southern People: A Dictionary of Otago Southland Biography*, Dunedin, 1998, p. 313.
79. See 'Regulations', under 'The Government Railways Department Classification Act, 1896', *New Zealand Gazette 1896*, p. 1680.
80. *Mirror*, December 1936, p. 44.
81. Many interviewees discussed family leisure activities. For instance, Bert Grimmett, p. 12; Richard Perth, p. 34; Alison (b. 1914) and Brian (b. 1911) Abraham, interviewed October 1996, Transcript Series One, Vol. 3, pp. 29–32; Christine King (b. 1922), interviewed August 1996, Transcript Series One, Vol. 3, pp. 184–85; Shirley Sparkes, p. 132.
82. The importance of gardening, and its gendered nature, features in many interviews: e.g., Richard Perth, p. 281; William Campbell (b. 1913), interviewed 1981 by Mark Henderson, COHP, Childhood Transcripts, Vol. 1, pp. 60–61; Frank Denford, pp. 218–19; and Russell Grigg (d.o.b. unknown), interviewed 1982 by Tom Brooking, Childhood Transcripts, Vol. 1, p. 271; Rita Jory (b. 1902) and Louise

Wellman (b. 1909), interviewed 1996, COHP, Transcript Series One, Vol. 3, p. 170; Alison and Brian Abraham, 1996, Vol. 3, pp. 50–55; Beatrice Riddell (b. 1913), interviewed May 1996, Transcript Series One, Vol. 5, pp. 13–14.

83 For the new link between domesticity and a new aesthetic, see Petersen, '"Signs of Higher Life"', p. 107. See, too, Petersen, *New Zealanders at Home: A Cultural History of Domestic Interiors 1814–1914*, Dunedin, 2001, Parts 3 and 4.

84 W. J. Scott, *Reading, Film & Radio Tastes of High School Boys and Girls*, Christchurch, 1974, pp. 169–71.

85 For the quotation, see interview with Christine King (b. 1921), p. 187. Few interviewees recalled listening to radio as children; see Alison and Brian Abraham, p. 32.

86 Brian Sutton-Smith, *The Folkgames of Children*, Austin, 1972, pp. 10–13, 44–45, 215–21.

87 South Dunedin Presbyterian; Southern Bible Class; St Kilda Methodist; and Congregational; see A. G. Hebbard, *A History of the Caversham Harrier and Amateur Athletic Club: Fifty Years of Progress, 1905–1955*, Dunedin, 1955, and Angela Reid, 'The Harrier Movement', History 351 research essay, University of Otago, 2002, pp. 3, 6. The Civil Service Club, in which Andrew Melville of Hillside Workshops played a major role, recruited strongly among railway workers.

88 Michael Hoare, *Faces of Boyhood: An Informal Pictorial Record of the Boys Brigade in New Zealand, 1886–1982*, Wellington, 1982, p. 20. See also Alma Rutherford, *The Edge of the Town: Historic Caversham as seen through its Streets and Buildings*, Dunedin, 1978, p. 13.

89 Sutton-Smith, *The Folkgames of Children* (this work includes *The Games of New Zealand Children*, first published in 1959, which was based on interviews with adults recalling the games of their childhood).

90 Sutton-Smith, *A History of Children's Play*, p. 247, reported a Temuka incident in which a kite was found entangled in a 66,000 volt transmission line!

91 In the Childhood Transcripts, see especially the interviews with Grimmett, p. 4, and Ingram, p. 33.

92 For example, *The Budget*, 20 April 1910, p. 15, and *Education Gazette*, November 1934, cited in Sutton-Smith, *A History of Children's Play*, p. 247.

93 Dunedin Ocean Beach Domain Board, By Laws, Dunedin City Council Archives 4/1.

94 Cited in Stephen Barnett and Richard Wolfe, *At the Beach: The Great New Zealand Holiday*, Auckland, 1993, pp. 22, 25, and Douglas Booth, 'Healthy, Economic, Disciplined Bodies: Surfbathing and Surf Lifesaving in Australia and New Zealand, 1890–1950', *NZJH*, 32, 1, 1998, p. 45.

95 W. F. Kaler, *St Clair Surf Life Saving Club*, Dunedin, 1961, and obituary for 'Hugh Donald Gillies: Surf life-saving legend', *ODT*, 21 December 2002, p. A35.

96 Claire Langhamer, *Women's Leisure in England*, Manchester, 2000, p. 135.

97 See Heather Nicholson, *The Loving Stitch: A History of Knitting and Spinning in New Zealand*, Auckland, 1998.

98 Beatrice Riddell, p. 14.

99 E.g., Gertrude Shiel suffered a disability that made walking difficult; see her interview, pp. 286–87. For the increased provision of public toilets for Dunedin women, especially after 1910, see Annabel Cooper, Robin Law, Jane Malthus and Pamela Wood, 'Rooms of their own: public toilets and gendered citizens in a New Zealand city, 1860–1940', *Gender, Place and Culture*, 7, 2000, pp. 417–33.

100 See also Robin Law's innovative, 'Gender and daily mobility in a New Zealand city, 1920–1960', *Social & Cultural Geography*, 3, 4, 2002, pp. 425–45.

101 David Tait, *New Zealand Recreation Survey 1974–75*, Wellington, 1984.

102 H. J. A. Aitken, *St Kilda: The First Hundred Years. A Short History of the Borough of St Kilda 1875–1975*, Dunedin, 1975, p. 126.

103 *Aussie: The New Zealand Section*, 15 July 1924 and 15 December 1925.

104 See Kate Flint, *The Woman Reader 1837–1914*, Oxford, 1993, p. 161, and Betty Gilderdale, *A Sea Change: 145 Years of New Zealand Junior Fiction*, Auckland, 1982, especially the 'Chronological Bibliography', pp. 244–51.

105 Scott, *Reading, Film & Radio Tastes*, p. 87.

106 Constance A. Barnicoat, 'The Reading of the Colonial Girl', *Nineteenth Century*, 60, 1906, p. 943, cited in Kate Flint, *The Woman Reader*, p. 161.

107 See G. A. K. Baughen's essay on C. N. Baeyertz, the founder and editor of the *Triad*, who lived on Forbury Rd for several years, *DNZB*, Vol. 2, pp. 20–21; Nelson Wattie's essay on Adams, *DNZB*, Vol. 3, pp. 2–3; and J. O. C. Phillips, 'Musings in

397

Maoriland – or was there a *Bulletin* school in New Zealand', *Historical Studies*, 20, 1983, pp. 520–35.
108 Flint, *The Woman Reader*, p. 161.
109 Terry Sturm, 'Popular Fiction', in Sturm (ed.), *The Oxford History of New Zealand Literature in English*, Auckland, 1991, pp. 498–504.
110 See in particular Maureen Judge (b. 1922), interviewed April 1996, COHP, Transcript Series One, Vol. 3, pp. 79–80; and Rita Jory and Louise Wellman, pp. 162–3. The quotation is from the interview with John Wilkie (b. 1910), COHP, interviewed January 1996, Vol. 5, p. 241.
111 Gertrude J. Shiel (b. 1901), p. 291.
112 The oral histories never indicated the sort of conflict reported by Mary Lee: 'Sometimes my Sister would tell Mother that i had been reading Instead of wheeling them about & i would get a Wallopin', in Annabel Cooper (ed.), *The Not So Poor: An Autobiography*, Auckland, 1992, p. 58.
113 'Why the Rush?', *Aussie: New Zealand Section* 8, 15 January 1924; Barbara Brookes, 'Housewives' Depression. The Debate over Abortion and Birth Control in the 1930s', *NZJH*, 15, 2, 1982, p. 120.
114 Godber Mss, Alexander Turnbull Library, Wellington. For the contemporary context, see Anna K. C. Petersen, 'The European Use of Maori Art in New Zealand Homes c. 1890–1914', in Barbara Brookes (ed.), *At Home in New Zealand*, Wellington, 2000, pp. 57–72.
115 Cited by Sutton-Smith, *A History of Children's Play*, p. 219.
116 In 1898 the Salvation Army enlisted 14 one-minute films for a nationwide tour: Simon Price, *New Zealand's First Talkies: Early Film-making in Otago and Southland*, Dunedin, 1996, p. 5.
117 Richard Perth (b. 1903), interviewed 1981 by Melissa Reid, COHP, Childhood Transcripts, Vol. 3, p. 36.
118 Yvonne Morris (b. 1911), COHP, interviewed April 1996, Series 1, Vol. 5, p. 78.
119 James Moss recalled that, according to the Caversham Assembly, 'you'd be boiling in oil and hell' for attending the pictures before the war: James Moss (b. 1924), interviewed 2001 by Shaun Broadley, COHP, Religion Transcripts, unpaginated.
120 Daley, *Girls & Womens*, p. 110.
121 H. C. McQueen, 'A Preliminary Inquiry into the General Effects of Attendance at Moving Pictures by Children of Dunedin', MA thesis, University of Otago, 1927.
122 McQueen, 'A Preliminary Inquiry', p. 32.
123 McQueen, 'A Preliminary Inquiry', p. 39.
124 McQueen, 'A Preliminary Inquiry' p. 37, and, for the quotation, Vera Horder, pp. 297–8. See also interviews with Alison and Brian Abraham, pp. 31–32; Joyce Jones, pp. 102–4; and Jory and Wellman, pp. 155–56.
125 McQueen, 'A Preliminary Inquiry', p. 44.
126 Richard Perth, COHP, Childhood Transcripts, Vol. 3, p. 22.
127 Scott, *Reading, Film and Radio Tastes*, p. 115.
128 Some of those novels, notably Edith Lyttleton's *The Law Bringers* (1913), became popular Hollywood movies, in this case *The Eternal Struggle*: see Sturm, 'Popular Fiction', p. 502.
129 The view of the New Zealand Educational Institute in 1915, cited by Chris Watson and Roy Shuker in *In the Public Good? Censorship in New Zealand*, Palmerston North, 1998, p. 29. On juvenile delinquency and welfare officers concerned about the influence of film, see Bronwyn Dalley, *Family Matters: Child Welfare in Twentieth Century New Zealand*, Auckland, 1998, pp. 115–16.
130 Price, *New Zealand's First Talkies*, p. 46.
131 Rita Jory and Louise Wellman, the sisters of Bert Grimmett, recalled that once they had started earning money they had enough disposable income to spend on collating albums with movie-star pictures. They wrote to 'all these American actresses. All the women parts. We didn't bother about men.' Shirley Temple was also a favourite. Rita Jory recalled that Brown Ewing would make up frocks 'exactly like Shirley Temple's . . . just like what Shirley Temple wore in one of her films': Rita Jory and Louise Wellman, pp. 155–56.
132 See *Carnival Tit Bit Magazine*, 1915, and *Official Programme of Queen's Carnival, 27 and 28 August, 1915*, Dunedin, 1915.
133 Price, *New Zealand's First Talkies*, p. 52.
134 Price, *New Zealand's First Talkies*, pp. 47–48.
135 Henry Hayward, *Here's to Life*, Auckland, 1944, and Clive Sowry, 'Hayward, Henry John', *DNZB*, Vol. 3, pp. 203–4.
136 Jess Whitworth, *Otago Interval*, Hamilton, 1950, p. 26. See also Sutton-Smith, *A History of Children's Play*, p. 37, and Mary Lee, *Not So Poor*, p. 67, for similar impromptu dances.

137 The family of Charles Shiel, who had a large house, continued the custom of holding dances for young people at home. See Gertrude Shiel, p. 280. See also interviews, Transcripts Series One, Vol. 3, with Alison and Brian Abraham, pp. 26–28, 33–34; Maureen Judge, pp. 60, 66, 72–75; Rita Jory and Louise Wellman, pp. 140, 152, 157–58. Andrea Deuchrass, 'Pushing Past the Confines of Femininity', sets dance in a wider musical context, see pp. 31–50.

138 The social profile of the various lodges varied quite considerably, white-collar occupations being under-represented, except in Manchester Unity. For more detail, see Olssen, 'Friendly Societies in New Zealand', pp. 196–8.

139 Olssen, 'Friendly Societies in New Zealand', pp. 191–2.

140 Frances Kenny (b. 1910), p. 207.

141 Stan Allen (b. c. 1910), interviewed 1982 by Michelle Poole, COHP, Childhood Transcripts, Vol. 1, pp. 4–5.

142 Yvonne Morris, p. 77.

143 See the Minutes for 27 February, 28 May, 27 August 1924, Dunedin Women's Branch of the New Zealand Labour Party, Mss AG 645-1, Hocken Library, Dunedin.

144 E.g., Frances Kenny, p. 207; Rita Jory and Louise Wellman, pp. 157–8; Myrtle Caird, pp. 160–1.

145 Daley, *Girls & Women*, p. 108, notes that in her research on Taradale men and women later recalled quite different things (men tended to remember their larrikinism, whereas women recalled the dances, the clothes and the romance).

146 J. D. Salmond, *Recreational Activities of our Bible Classes*, Wellington, 1932, p. 27.

147 Rachael McDermott, 'Entertaining Ideas', pp. 10–18.

148 Cited in McDermott, 'Entertaining Ideas', p. 110.

149 "Konini" [Mona Tracey], 'The Voice of ENZED Women', *Aussie: The New Zealand Section*, 15 January and 15 August 1925.

Seven Down and Out on the Flat

1 The authors wish to thank other members of the Sites of Gender group for their comments, in particular, Barbara Brookes, Robin Law and Erik Olssen; and Brian Heenan for assistance with figures and tables. Another version of this chapter is forthcoming in the *Journal of Family History*.

2 Otago Benevolent Institute Outdoor Relief (OBIODR) Casebook, DAHI D 284 60-68, Archives New Zealand (ANZ), Dunedin. (References that follow are first to the Archives *volumes*, and second to the individual *series* of the Caversham Project's edited transcripts of those volumes: Annabel Cooper with Marian Horan and Eva Lubcke (eds), 'Transcripts from the Otago Benevolent Institution's Outdoor Relief Casebooks', 3 vols, Caversham Working Paper (CWP) 2000-3. See Appendix II for more specific information on this source.) Vol. I, pp. 163-64; Series II, p. 120.

3 OBIODR Casebook, Vol. I, p. 283, Series III, p. 31.

4 OBIODR Casebook, Vol. I, p. 68, Vol. II, p. 590, Series II, pp. 65–66.

5 OBIODR Casebook, Vol. I, p. 336, Series II, pp. 39–40.

6 Bert Grimmett (b. 1912), interviewed by Annabel Cooper, 1996, Caversham Oral History Project (COHP), Transcript Sub-series Two: Wealth and Poverty. All interviews conducted by Megan Cook unless otherwise noted.

7 Clyde Griffen, 'The New World Working-Class Suburb Revisited: Residential Differentiation in Caversham, New Zealand', *Journal of Urban History*, 27, 4, 2001, pp. 420–44; Paul Husbands, 'Poverty in Freeman's Bay 1886–1913', *New Zealand Journal of History* (*NZJH*), 28, 1, 1994, pp. 3–21.

8 Pamela Wood, 'Constructing Colonial Dirt: A History of Dirt in the Nineteenth-Century Colonial Settlement of Dunedin, New Zealand', PhD thesis, University of Otago, 1997; Jacinta Prunty, *Dublin Slums: A Study in Urban Geography*, Dublin, 1998.

9 E. K. Mulgan and Alan E. Mulgan, *The New Zealand Citizen*, 4th edition, n. p., 1925, p. 82.

10 Other studies, of New Zealand, Britain, the USA and Australia, are pertinent for setting the context of the picture we study in the southern suburbs. Most near to our research, Margaret Tennant discusses the provision of charitable aid in New Zealand, referring to charitable aid records in detail. Her *Paupers and Providers: Charitable Aid in New Zealand*, Wellington, 1989, deals with women, children and men in different

chapters, so marked is the distinction she sees between the circumstances of these groups. Paul Husbands's 'Poverty in Freeman's Bay' studies a comparable Auckland suburb. Miles Fairburn explores definitions of poverty and considers its causes in nineteenth-century New Zealand, attending in detail to the case of rural labourer James Cox in *Nearly Out of Heart and Hope: The Puzzle of a Colonial Labourer's Diary*, Auckland, 1995. David Thomson, *A World Without Welfare: New Zealand's Colonial Experiment*, Auckland, 1998, and Margaret McClure, *A Civilised Community: A History of Social Security in New Zealand 1898–1998*, Auckland, 1998, discuss the New Zealand welfare context. In the British context, David Vincent contends that the micro-economies of poverty have their own specificities and dynamics, in *Poor Citizens: The State and the Poor in Twentieth-Century Britain*, London, 1991. Jerry White argues persuasively for the gendering of opportunity, risk and social mobility, in *The Worst Street in North London: Campbell Bunk, Islington, Between the Wars*, London, 1986. Linda Gordon's history of single mothers in the USA, *Pitied But Not Entitled: Single Mothers and the History of Welfare 1890–1935*, New York, 1994, points to the systematic failure of recognition of this group of the poor and the consequent systematic disadvantage of single-mother families; with Nancy Fraser, she argues that the gendering of 'dependency' demands re-evaluation: Nancy Fraser and Linda Gordon, 'A Genealogy of Dependency: Tracing a Keyword of the US Welfare State', *Signs*, 19, 1994, pp. 309–36. For a discussion of this argument in the New Zealand setting, see Annabel Cooper and Maureen Molloy, 'Poverty, Dependence and "Women"': Reading Autobiography and Social Policy from 1930s New Zealand', *Gender & History*, 9, 1, 1997, pp. 36–59. Janet McCalman addresses many of these issues through oral history for the inter-war period, in her study of the Melbourne working-class suburb of Richmond, *Struggletown: Portrait of an Australian Working-Class Community 1900–1965*, Melbourne, 1984.

11 Tennant, *Paupers and Providers*; Husbands, 'Poverty in Freeman's Bay'.
12 McClure, *A Civilised Community*, p. 11.
13 Tennant, *Paupers and Providers*, p. 2; Thomson, *A World Without Welfare*, ch. 2.
14 For discussions of the gendering of 'independence' and 'dependence', see Fraser and Gordon, 'A Genealogy of Dependency', and Cooper and Molloy, 'Poverty, Dependence and "Women"'.
15 Bettina Bradbury, 'From Civil Death to Separate Property: Changes in the Legal Rights of Married Women in Nineteenth-Century New Zealand', *NZJH*, 29, 1, 1995, p. 51.
16 Bradbury, 'From Civil Death to Separate Property', p. 51.
17 With the Old Age Pensions Act 1898, the Widows' Pensions Act 1911, the Family Allowances Act 1926, the Unemployment Act 1930, the 1936 amendment to the Industrial Conciliation and Arbitration Act of 1894 and the Social Security Act 1938.
18 Melanie Nolan, *Breadwinning: New Zealand Women and the State*, pp. 137–63. McClure, *A Civilised Community*, also discusses family allowances, pp. 38–42.
19 The Otago Benevolent Institution was founded in 1862. Among its other functions, it provided outdoor relief for the Otago region from the late 1880s until the second decade of the twentieth century. Applicants for outdoor relief had to provide a referee and usually had to appear before the trustees for an interview in the first instance and thereafter on request. In addition, an inspector would irregularly visit their homes to enquire about their continued eligibility. The case notes kept regarding visits are extant from 1889–1911, with the exception of one missing volume.
20 For a discussion of this body, see John Angus, *A History of the Otago Hospital Board and Its Predecessors*, Dunedin, 1984.
21 See Appendix II, and also Marian Horan, 'The Outdoor Relief Database: An Introduction', Caversham Working Paper (CWP) 1999-1, for a more detailed account of this database.
22 Annabel Cooper with Marian Horan and Eva Lubcke (eds), 'Transcripts from the Otago Benevolent Institution's Outdoor Relief Casebooks', 3 vols, Caversham Working Paper (CWP) 2000-3. See Appendix II for a more detailed description.
23 See, for example, the studies in John Henderson and Richard Wall (eds), *Poor Women and Children in the European Past*, London, 1994.
24 For discussions of definitions of poverty, see Henderson and Wall, *Poor Women and*

Children, pp. 1–4, and Fairburn, *Nearly Out of Heart and Hope*, chs 8 and 9.
25 Compared to the census results for the study area in the closest years to our slices, both groups were greatly over-represented in the outdoor relief records.
26 For an account of the way in which women came to be seen as economically unproductive, see Nancy Folbre, 'The Unproductive Housewife: Her Evolution in Nineteenth-Century Economic Thought', *Signs*, 16, 1991, pp. 463–84.
27 For a general discussion of this question, see Henderson and Wall, *Poor Women and Children*, p. 5.
28 OBIODR Casebook, Vol. II, pp. 642, 829, Vol. V, p. 2563, Vol. VIII, p. 3934, Vol. VIII, p. 4008, Series III, pp. 45–47.
29 Miriam Gilson, 'The Changing New Zealand Family: A Demographic Analysis', in Stewart Houston (ed.), *Marriage and the Family in New Zealand*, Wellington, 1970, p. 51.
30 OBIODR Casebook, Vol. I, p. 20, Vol. II, pp. 719–20, Vol. VI, pp. 1896, 3027, 3370, Vol. VII, p. 3603, Vol. VIII, p. 4014, Series III, pp. 7–12.
31 Viviana Zelizer notes that in the USA also, girls were more likely than boys to hand over wages intact. *The Social Meaning of Money: Pin Money, Paychecks, Poor Relief, and Other Currencies*, New York, 1994, p. 59.
32 OBIODR Casebook, Vol. II, p. 962, Vol. III, p. 1263, Vol. VI, p. 2844, Series II, pp. 89–93.
33 Thomson, *A World Without Welfare*, ch. 1.
34 Mary Isabella Lee, *The Not So Poor: An Autobiography*, ed. Annabel Cooper, Auckland, 1992, p. 24.
35 OBIODR Casebook, Vol. VI, p. 3270, Vol. VIII, p. 3980, Series II, pp. 100–1.
36 OBIODR Casebook, Vol. VII, pp. 3841, 4090, Series II, pp. 78–79.
37 See chapter ten for further discussion of this point.
38 OBIODR Casebook, Vol. VII, p. 3367, Series II, p. 77.
39 E. Von Dadelszen (ed.), *New Zealand Official Yearbook 1986*, Wellington, 1987, p. 97.
40 Claire Toynbee, *Her Work and His: Family, Kin and Community in New Zealand 1900–1930*, Wellington, 1995, p. 219; we also draw here on the discussion in M. Lousberg and S. Williams, 'Children of the Caversham Poor', History 351 essay, University of Otago, 1999.
41 Miriam Gilson-Vosburgh, *The New Zealand Family and Social Change: A Trend Analysis*, Occasional papers in Sociology and Social Welfare no. 1, Department of Sociology and Social Work, Victoria University, Wellington, 1978.
42 OBIODR Casebook, Vol. I, p. 518, Vol. II, p. 755, Vol. III, p. 1400, Vol. V, p. 2581, Vol. VI, p. 3011, Vol. VI, p. 3235, Vol. VII, pp. 3369, 3467, 3690, Series II, pp. 102–9.
43 Zelizer, *The Social Meaning of Money*, p. 43. The reference to Young is, 'Distribution of Income within the Family', *British Journal of Sociology*, 3, 1952, p. 305.
44 See Henderson and Wall, *Poor Women and Children*; Tennant, *Paupers and Providers*; and Husbands, 'Poverty in Freeman's Bay'.
45 OBIODR Casebook, Vol. II, p. 1035, Vol. III, pp. 1135, 1460, Vol. V, p. 2230, Vol. VI, pp. 2794, 3241, Vol. VII, p. 3503, Series II, pp. 70–74.
46 OBIODR Casebook, Vol. I, p. 33, Vol. II, p. 883, Vol. III, pp. 1241–42, Vol. V, p. 3122, Vol. VI, p. 3286, Vol. VIII, p. 4219, Vol. IX, p. 4651, Series II, pp. 112–15.
47 Raewyn Dalziel, 'The Colonial Helpmeet: Women's Role and the Vote in Nineteenth-Century New Zealand', *NZJH*, 11, 2, 1977, pp. 112–23; Charlotte Macdonald, 'Too Many Men and Too Few Women: Gender's "Fatal Impact" in Nineteenth-Century Colonies', in Caroline Daley and Deborah Montgomerie (eds), *The Gendered Kiwi*, Auckland, 1999, pp. 17–35.
48 Joanna Bourke, 'Avoiding Poverty: Strategies for Women in Rural Ireland, 1880–1914', in Henderson and Wall, *Poor Women and Children*, pp. 292–311.
49 OBIODR Casebook, Vol. V, p. 2870, Vol. VII, p. 3810, Vol. VIII, pp. 4116, 4403, Vol. IX, p. 4728, Series II, pp. 43–46.
50 Report of the Sweating Commission, *AJHR*, G-5, 1890.
51 Vincent, *Poor Citizens*, p. 6.
52 OBIODR Casebook, Vol. I, p. 459, Series II, p. 41; Vol. I, p. 283, Vol. VII, p. 3696, Series III, pp. 31, 33.
53 Industrial School Register, 1892–1897 (DREPRO2 1B), Archives New Zealand (ANZ), Dunedin.
54 Industrial School Register, 1892–1897.
55 Billie McLeod, '"A Silent Testimony": St Vincent de Paul Catholic Orphanage for Girls, South Dunedin', PGDip thesis, University of Otago, 1992, p. 39. The Catholic diocese was under pressure when it brought in the Sisters of Mercy to found

the orphanage: Catholic children were dramatically over-represented among those under Industrial School care (in 1895, Catholics were 14 per cent of the national population, but 31 per cent of children in Industrial School care were Catholic). McLeod, pp. 18–19.

56 Brian Heenan, 'Population Ageing Among Non-Maori New Zealanders in Later Victorian Times: A quirk of immigrant settlement history?', *NZJH*, 35, 2, 2001, pp. 177–203. See also Tennant, *Paupers and Providers*, pp. 146–48.

57 OBIODR Casebook, Vol. VIII, pp. 3966, 4080, 4184, 4318, Series II, pp. 67–69; OBIODR Casebook, Vol. VII, p. 3367, Series II, p. 77.

58 Fairburn, *Nearly Out of Heart and Hope*, has shown that some younger men's lives did not fit the ideal either.

59 On 1 January 1896 the Benevolent Home contained 140 men 65 years and older. The national census taken on 31 March 1896 showed that 339 men aged 65 and over lived in Caversham. For women, the figures were 30 inmates 65 and over out of 219 in Caversham. OBI Inmates Register 1887–97, DAHI D281 1, ANZ, Dunedin.

60 Tennant, *Paupers and Providers*, p. 150.

61 OBIODR Casebook, Vol. I, p. 345, vol. II, p. 1583, Vol. V, p. 2721, Vol. VIII, p. 3897, Vol. IX, p. 4759, Series III, pp. 42–44; OBIODR Casebook, Vol. I, pp. 223, 341, Vol. II, p. 652, Vol. VII, p. 3349, Series III, pp. 19–22; OBIODR Casebook, Vol. I, pp. 101, 143, Vol. III, p. 1136, Vol. V, pp. 2238, 2648, Vol. VII, p. 3831, Vol. VIII, pp. 4070, 4340, Vol. IX, p. 4945, Series III, pp. 13–18.

62 OBIODR Casebook, Vol. I, p. 546, Vol. II, p. 609, Series II, pp. 34–35.

63 Brian Moloughney and John Stenhouse, '"Drug-Besotten, Sin-Begotten Fiends of Filth": New Zealanders and the Oriental Other, 1850–1920', *NZJH*, 33, 1, 1999, pp. 43–64.

64 Sarah Greenlees and Claire Smith, 'The Provision of Indoor and Outdoor Relief for the Aged in Caversham Through the Otago Benevolent Association: 1902–1922', History 351 research essay, 1996, p. 22.

65 Curiously, the Lebanese were also classified as 'Asian': McClure, *A Civilised Community*, pp. 54–55.

66 Margaret Tennant, 'The Decay of Home Life? The Home in Early Welfare Discourses', in Barbara Brookes (ed.), *At Home in New Zealand: History, Houses, People*, Wellington, 2000, pp. 24–40.

67 Industrial School Register, 1886–1892 (DREPRO2 1A) and 1892–1897 (DREPRO2 1B).

68 McLeod, '"A Silent Testimony"', p. 39.

69 OBIODR Casebook, Vol. III, p. 1155, Series II, p. 40; Industrial School Register, 1892–1897 (DREPRO2 1B).

70 See also Tennant, 'The Decay of Home Life?'

71 McLeod, '"A Silent Testimony"', p. 86.

72 See James Holt, *Compulsory Arbitration in New Zealand: The First Forty Years*, Auckland, 1986; Erik Olssen, *Building the New World: Work, Politics and Society 1880s–1920s*, Auckland, 1995, and Cooper and Molloy, 'Poverty, Dependence and "Women"'.

73 Nolan, *Breadwinning*, p. 160.

74 McClure, *A Civilised Community*, pp. 42, 54.

75 OBIODR Casebook, Vol. I, pp. 191, 493, Vol. III, pp. 1508, 1578, 1985, Vol. V, p. 2766, Vol. VI, p. 3167, Vol. VII, pp. 3510, 3708, Vol. VIII, p. 4127, vol. IX, p. 4521, Vol. IX, p. 4660, Vol. X, p. 188, Series III, pp. 23–30.

76 OBIODR Casebook, Vol. X, pp. 80, 238, Series II, pp. 94–95.

77 OBIODR Casebook, Vol. I, pp. 238–40, Vol. II, p. 752, Series I, p. 34.

78 *AJHR*, H-6, p. 34.

79 Although no direct comparison with outdoor relief is possible, we note that, in 1895, 631 people (including dependants) were provided with outdoor relief in the southern suburbs alone (see Table 1).

80 *Annual Report of the Otago Benevolent Institution for 1895*, Dunedin, 1896, p. 10.

81 John Martin, *Holding the Balance: A History of New Zealand's Department of Labour 1891–1995*, Christchurch, 1996, p. 26.

82 Nolan provides us with the evidence to show that the corollary was also true: although the man supporting children was the cultural norm assumed by the male-breadwinner wage, 60 per cent of men, according to the 1921 Census, were *not* supporting children! Nolan, *Breadwinning*, p. 155.

83 This point is argued at length in Cooper and Molloy, 'Poverty, Dependence and "Women"'.

84 Tennant, *Paupers and Providers*.

85 OBIODR Casebook, Vol. III, p. 1184, Vol. V, p. 2278, Vol. VI, p. 2808, Vol. VII, p. 3390, Series II, pp. 83–85.

86 OBIODR Casebook, Vol. VI, p. 3056.

87 OBIODR Casebook, Vol. I, pp. 114, 126, Vol. II, pp. 589, 780, Series II, pp. 8–10.
88 Bert Grimmett, p. 81. Bert Grimmett's own family's views – his grandmother was Salvationist Rachel Grimmett (see chapter eight) – would have alerted him to the adverse effects of drinking on families.
89 Wally Seccombe, 'Patriarchy Stabilized: The Construction of the Male-Breadwinner Wage Norm in Nineteenth-Century Britain', *Social History*, II, 1, 1986, pp. 53–76.
90 Hilda Maher (b. 1912), interviewed August 1996, COHP, Transcript Sub-series Two: Wealth and Poverty, p. 181.
91 Zelizer, *The Social Meaning of Money*, pp. 44 and 56–58, discusses the predominance of the whole wage system among American working-class families, but also the significant extent to which actual practice departed from the 'norm'. She cites a 1924 study of unskilled Chicago wage earners, which 'found that, when asked about their husbands' weekly earnings, over two-thirds of the wives gave lesser amounts than the actual earnings found on the payroll', p. 58.
92 Jean Darby (b. 1918), interviewed September 1996, COHP, Transcript Sub-series Two: Wealth and Poverty, p. 23.
93 This was the predominant British and American pattern. Although the high numbers of self-employed in New Zealand probably meant that more women in those families had financial responsibilities (see the discussion of the Grimmetts in chapter eight, for example), we have no reason to think that the pattern of greatly diminished female control over money in wealthier families did not apply here.
94 Husbands, 'Poverty in Freeman's Bay', p. 9. See also chapter eight for the relationship between poverty and mobility.
95 OBIODR, Vol. II, pp. 853, 981, Vol. III, pp. 1346, 1470, Vol. VI, p. 2885, Vol. V, p. 3251, Vol. VI, p. 3528, Series II, pp. 11–15.
96 Tennant, *Paupers and Providers*, p. 110.
97 Hilda Maher, p. 193.
98 These are the national figures, taken from Gilson, 'The Changing New Zealand Family', p. 51.
99 Ashley Hogan's study of shifts in the meaning of fatherhood in late nineteenth-century Victoria (a common destination, incidentally, for Dunedin's sojourning or absconding husbands) almost exactly mirrors the shifts evident here. Hogan argues that in 1880 fatherhood did not imply a responsibility of day-to-day care, but that by the end of the century this had changed, and it entailed a more intimate set of relationships. '"I Never Noticed She was Dirty": Fatherhood and the Death of Charlotte Duffy in Late-Nineteenth-Century Victoria', *Journal of Family History*, 24, 3, 1999, pp. 305–16.
100 Penelope S. Isaac, '"No Room for Luxuries": Aspects of Life in a Working-Class New Zealand Community in the 1930s', MA thesis, University of Otago, 1999, pp. 32–36, also citing Erik Olssen, *A History of Otago*, Dunedin, 1984, p. 184.

Eight To and From, There and Back

1 Thanks are due to Robin Law, Erik Olssen and Annabel Cooper, who each applied their skills over many days, and through successive drafts, to enable the production of this chapter; and to Karen Duder, Alison Holmes and David Hood, who also made substantial contributions.
2 Otago Benevolent Institution Outdoor Relief (OBIODR) Casebook, DAHI D 284 60-68, Archives New Zealand (ANZ), Dunedin. (References that follow are first to the Archives *volumes*, and second to the individual *series* of the Caversham Project's edited transcripts of those volumes: Annabel Cooper with Marian Horan and Eva Lubcke (eds), 'Transcripts from the Otago Benevolent Institution's Outdoor Relief Casebooks', 3 vols, Caversham Working Paper (CWP) 2000–3. See Appendix II for more specific information on this source.) Vol. I, p. 33, Series II, p. 112.
3 In his minutes of a meeting with Jane Steel on 23 March 1897, the Benny inspector described her as 'exceedingly rude and impertinent', OBIODR Casebook, Vol. III, p. 3122, Series II, p. 114.
4 Bert Grimmett (b. 1912), interviewed by Erik Olssen, 1993, Caversham Oral History Project (COHP), Childhood Series 3, p. 1. All interviews conducted by Megan Cook unless otherwise stated.
5 The kitchen was open during the winter of 1895, closing on 30 August. Although its location is uncertain, it appears to have been within walking distance of the Grimmett home. Rachel Grimmett, Diary 1894–95. Copy held by Caversham Project, History Department, University of Otago.
6 For example, Charlotte Macdonald, *A*

Woman of Good Character: Single Women as Immigrant Settlers in Nineteenth-Century New Zealand, Wellington, 1990.

7   E. S. Lee, 'A Theory of Migration', *Demography*, 3, 1, 1966, pp. 47–57; W. Zelinsky, 'The Hypothesis of the Mobility Transition', *Geographical Review*, 61, 1971, pp. 219–49.

8   H. R. Jones, *Population Geography*, 2nd edition, London, 1990; H. R. Barrett, *Population Geography: Conceptual Frameworks in Geography*, Harlow, 1992; G. T. Lewis, *Human Migration*, London, 1982.

9   In fact, disappointingly few papers on gender as a dimension of geographical mobility emerged from the contents scan. This covered a selection of recent issues of mainstream geographical journals (*Annals, Association of American Geographers; Area; Environment and Planning A and D; Progress in Human Geography; Transactions, Institute of British Geographers (New Series)*); two in population studies (*Demography* and *International Migration Review*); and several in women's/gender studies (*Australian Feminist Studies, Gender & History, Women's Studies International Forum,* and *Women's Studies Journal*). Between 1990 and 1999, papers on spatial mobility devoted to some dimension of gender numbered just 4 of 73 in the first group, 4 of 36 in *Demography*, 20 of 277 in the *International Migration Review* and, in the women's/gender studies collection, 15 of a total of 981 articles.

10 For writing on women travellers, see G. Robertson, M. Mash, L. Tickner, J. Bird, B. Curtis and T. Putnam (eds), *Travellers' Tales: Narratives of Home and Displacement*, London, 1994. Historical studies of gender and urban transport include C. McShane, *Down the Asphalt Path: The Automobile and the American City*, New York, 1994; Virginia Scharff, *Taking the Wheel: Women and the Coming of the Motor Age*, New York, 1991; and Martin Wachs, 'Men, Women and Wheels: The Historical Basis of Sex Differences in Travel Patterns', *Transportation Research Record*, 1135, 1987, pp. 10–16. Also see Lyndon Fraser and Katie Pickles (eds), *Shifting Centres: Women and Migration in New Zealand History*, Dunedin, 2002.

11 Tom Brooking, Dick Martin, David Thomson and Hamish James, 'The Ties that Bind: Persistence in a New World Industrial Suburb, 1902–22', *Social History*, 24, 1, 1999, pp. 55–73; Miles Fairburn, *The Ideal Society and its Enemies: the Origins of Modern New Zealand Society, 1850–1900*, Auckland, 1989; David Pearson, *Johnsonville: Continuity and Change in a New Zealand Township*, Sydney, 1979; Stephan Thernstrom, *Poverty and Progress: Social Mobility of a Nineteenth Century City*, Newburyport, Cambridge, 1964; Michael B. Katz, *The People of Hamilton, Canada West: Family and Class in a Mid-Nineteenth Century City*, Cambridge, 1975. The quotation is from Fairburn, p. 125.

12 Although Fairburn (*The Ideal Society*, p. 125) seems to single out 'habitual transience' among manual workers as a distinctive movement variant, and Pearson (*Johnsonville*, p. 103) highlights 'temporary transience' by 'the unemployed who went "on the tramp" [and] returned to "the village" [of Johnsonville], because of family and other local attachments', neither author attempts to impose further order. For further criticism of the word 'transient' (and by extension the concept of transience itself), see Brooking *et al.*, 'The Ties That Bind'. Also pertinent in this respect is Pearson's observation that 'temporary transience', for example 'on the tramp', was hidden by 'only looking at the beginning and end of the decade' when using sources such as the electoral roll and street directories (p. 103). We might also note that so-called persistence, the reciprocal of transience, also includes people who were, in a generic sense, circulators rather than migrants (for example, participants in Pearson's 'temporary transience').

13 E. J. Hobsbawm, *Labouring Men: Studies in the History of Labour*, London, 1964.

14 This chapter therefore exemplifies the utility of the multi-method approach to research on territorial mobility, and more generally in population geography, extolled recently by, among others, S. Openshaw, 'Towards a More Computationally Minded Scientific Human Geography', *Environment and Planning A*, 30, 2, 1998, pp. 317–32; A. Findlay and L. Li, 'Methodologies in Migration Research', *Professional Geographer*, 51, 1, 1999, pp. 50–60, and J. McKendrick, 'Multi-method Research: An Introduction to its Application in Population Geography', *Professional Geographer*, 51, 1, 1999, pp. 40–50.

15 The quantitative data on migration are

derived from the electoral rolls, generated by comparing changes of address by men and women of voting age who moved within the suburb from one to another of seven sub-areas of Caversham Borough (Map 8.1) between any two consecutive electoral roll years (e.g., 1902 and 1905) over the period 1893 to 1938. Data manufactured in this way are far from a complete record, since they miss people who moved twice between elections, or did not always (or ever) register, or who moved and then died, or who in moving did not cross a sub-area boundary and so on: therefore, the migration data from the electoral roll research inevitably understates the volume of local migration during any given period. For example, only one of the three moves made (1908–17) by Annie Facoory and one of the four recorded (1905–1912) for George Facoory involved an origin or destination that lay outside the South Dunedin sub-area: see Andrew Joel, 'The Facoory Family: A Report Prepared for the Caversham Project', Dunedin, 2000, pp. 2–3. Similarly, we cannot establish much about people who left or entered the area. Although we know that, over any decade, some two-thirds of all adults left Caversham Borough and were replaced by an even larger inflowing stream, our sources for tracking leavers – unless they died – only allow us to identify men who left. This limits our discussion of the gendering of out-migration.
16 Population *Census* 1921.
17 Brooking *et al.*, 'The Ties that Bind', pp. 63–64.
18 Brooking *et al.*, 'The Ties that Bind', p. 69.
19 Electoral rolls include women, but those who left the study area have to be traced in street directories. Virtually no women were ever found using this method, although it often proved successful in tracking men (see Brooking *et al.*, 'The Ties That Bind').
20 For migration within the province, see L. D. B. Heenan, 'The Urbanisation of New Zealand's Population: Demographic Patterns in the South Island, 1881–1961', in R. J. Johnston (ed.), *Urbanisation in New Zealand: Geographical Essays*, Wellington, 1973, pp. 108–31.
21 Because the Johnson household was initiated by marriage as late as April 1929, only the first decade of its lifeline falls within the Caversham study period.
22 See Appendix II for a discussion of this source.
23 The ages of these adults ranged from 16–72 and 23–72 for males and females respectively. Most men (17 out of 24) and women (31 out of 35) were younger than 60 years. (Note that women applicants were more likely than men to be sole parents.)
24 Though the two sets of data are not strictly comparable, it is intriguing that these figures, especially those for the women, compare closely with Gilson's estimates of average number of children per married couple with at least one child for marriage cohorts (various years) over the decade 1881–91. For those married in 1881 and 1891, and estimated to have completed childbearing between 1911 and 1921, the number of children produced ranged from 6.9 to 5.2 respectively: Miriam Gilson, 'The Changing New Zealand Family: A Demographic Analysis', in Stewart Houston (ed.), *Marriage and the Family in New Zealand*, Wellington, 1970, pp. 41–65.
25 See Brian Heenan, Sarah Johnsen and Hamish James, 'Intra-Urban Migration', Caversham Working Paper (CWP) 1998-1; and 'Local Migration', CWP 1998-3.
26 Clyde Griffen, 'The New World Working Class Suburb Revisited: Residential Differentiation in Caversham, New Zealand', *Journal of Urban History*, 27, 4, 2001, pp. 420–44.
27 The oral histories used in this analysis were selected from the project's oral history archives by an electronic search of all interviews for mentions of movement or shifting within the study area.
28 For a discussion of the relationships among poverty, gender and mobility, see chapter 7.
29 Penelope Isaac and Erik Olssen, 'The Justification for Labour's Housing Scheme: The Discourse of "the Slum"', in Barbara Brookes (ed.), *At Home in New Zealand: History, Houses, People*, Wellington, 2000, p. 116.
30 M. C. Sanders, 'The Lebanese Community in Dunedin before 1936', BA Hons research essay, University of Otago, 1980, chs 2 and 3; and Joel, 'The Facoory Family'.
31 Joel, 'The Facoory Family', p. 3. For the migration from Walker St to Mafeking Tce, see Sanders, 'The Lebanese Community', pp. 44–48.
32 For St Michael's, see Evans, *Southern See: The Anglican Diocese of Dunedin New Zealand*, Dunedin, 1968, pp. 195–96,

279–80; and on the community's social cohesion, see Olga Barbara (b. 1920) and Zita Ramsay (b. 1928), interviewed by Shaun Broadley August 2000, COHP, Oral History Interviews with Lebanese of Southern Dunedin, CWP 2001-3, pp. 45–46 and *passim*.

33 This observation is consistent with an apparently high level of occupational stability found in Caversham by Brooking *et al.*, and in particular with their argument that 'during their time in the suburb men did not tend to change their job, but it seems likely that if promoted they moved themselves and their family out of the suburb': 'The Ties That Bind', p. 73.

34 A three-class model was used; on a nine-class model, movement rates, predictably, increase; see Erik Olssen and Hamish James, 'Social Mobility and Class Formation: The Worklife Social Mobility of Men in a New Zealand Suburb, 1902–1928', *International Review of Social History*, 44, 1999, pp. 429–34.

35 For more on this point, see chapter nine.

36 Note that the statistics on marital status used here are drawn from the Caversham I Database, covering the period 1902–22.

37 In other words, those who did change residence from one sub-area to another during two consecutive electoral roll periods.

38 Elizabeth Roberts, *A Woman's Place: An Oral History of Working-Class Women 1890–1940*, Oxford, 1984, p. 180; Young and Wilmott, cited in Roberts, p. 178.

39 Couples and parents identified in the first electoral roll after marriage, upon which the married couple and both sets of parents are present.

40 Olga Barbara, 'Hananeia, Sarah', in Jane Thomson (ed.), *Southern People: A Dictionary of Otago Southland Biography*, Dunedin, 1998, p. 209.

41 Karen Duder, 'Hegemony or Resistance? The Women of the Skilled Working Class and the Ideologies of Respectability and Domesticity', MA thesis, University of Otago, 1992.

42 Marion Cooper (b. 1925), interviewed April 1996, COHP Series One, Vol. 4, Dunedin 1995–96, p. 198. This situation probably represents yet another example of adjustment to widowhood. Renting part of the house in this way would have provided income and company in lieu of living alone.

43 Marion Cooper, p. 198.

44 Beatrice Riddell (b. 1913), interviewed May 1996, COHP, Transcript Series One, Vol. 5, p. 7.

45 The street-level analysis of address changes in the electoral roll database fails to pick up any evidence of 'flitting', however, presumably because the filter provided by 3- to 5-year snapshots is too coarse.

46 Marjorie Scott (b. 1909), interviewed January 1996, COHP, Transcript Series One, Vol. 2, p. 168.

47 Personal communication (Jones family, described above).

48 Frances Kenny (b. 1910), interviewed August 1996, COHP, Transcript Series One, Vol. 3, p. 199.

49 Mavis Liverpool (b. 1923), interviewed December 1995, COHP, Transcript Series One, Vol. 5, p. 158. A variation on the theme of forced movement appears in one OBI casebook. As reported by Annabel Cooper, the inspector recommended that, for the Taylors (Mary Lee's parents) to continue receiving relief from the Benny, they would have to find accommodation away from the house occupied by Mary Lee and her children. Mary Isabella Lee, *The Not So Poor: An Autobiography*, ed. Annabel Cooper, Auckland, 1992, p. 29.

50 Grateful appreciation is expressed to Mr and Mrs H. W. Grimmett, Dunedin, for making available Charlotte Rachel Grimmett's diary, and for permission to use it in preparing this paper. Among close relatives and friends, Mrs Grimmett was known by her second given name (Rachel) rather than her first (Charlotte). She is referred to as Rachel throughout this volume.

51 Two other children died in their first year of life: one (Charlotte) before departure from England, the other (Frederick) after arrival in Dunedin. Leah, who died in 1900 within two years of her marriage, was also born in New Zealand.

52 The reference is to Taiaroa Head at the entrance to Otago Harbour.

53 Interleaved with the diary are several pages of accounts, in Rachel Grimmett's handwriting, of payments received from and made to various individuals and firms, mostly for the supply of goods and materials used in the family building business. Entries scattered through the diary also give details of money received for completed jobs and

54 of debt-paying trips by Rachel to the grocers (McCracken's), various building supply and other firms.
54 Undated and unsourced newspaper clipping in Rachel Grimmett's scrapbook.
55 Richard Grimmett had been a 'one time local preacher among the Primitive Methodists in the Old Land', according to an undated and unsourced newspaper clipping of an obituary for him in Rachel Grimmett's scrapbook.
56 See Dorothy Page and John Farry, *The Hawkers: A Family Story*, Dunedin, 1990, p. 20 and *passim*.
57 Joel, 'The Facoory Family'.
58 Joel, 'The Facoory Family'.
59 Olga Barbara, 'Hananeia, Sarah'.
60 B. J. Gleeson, 'A Public Space for Women: The Case of Charity in Colonial Melbourne', *Area*, 27, 1995, pp. 193–207.
61 Robin Law, 'Beyond "Women and Transport": Towards New Geographies of Gender and Daily Mobility', *Progress in Human Geography*, 23, 4, 1999, p. 574.
62 Gleeson,' A Public Space for Women', pp. 193–207.
63 Margaret Tennant, *Paupers and Providers: Charitable Aid in New Zealand*, Wellington, 1989, p. 15.
64 Annabel Cooper, Robin Law, Jane Malthus and Pamela Wood, 'Rooms of their Own: Public Toilets and Gendered Citizens in a New Zealand City, 1860–1940', *Gender, Place and Culture*, 7, 4, 2000, pp. 417–33.
65 OBIODR Casebook, Vol. VIII, p. 4255, Series II, p. 125; Vol. V, p. 2500, Series II, p. 131.
66 W. A. V. Clark, 'Locational Stress and Residential Mobility in a New Zealand Context', *New Zealand Geographer*, 31, 1, 1975, pp. 67–79; Kenneth Fairbairn, 'Population Movements Within the Christchurch Urban Area 1959', *New Zealand Geographer*, 19, 2, 1963, pp. 142–59; and B. A. Ramsay, 'Residential Mobility with Respect to Mosgiel', MA thesis, University of Otago, Dunedin, 1971; Paul L. Knox, *Urbanisation: An Introduction to Urban Geography*, New Jersey, 1994.
67 Cooper *et al.*, 'Rooms of their Own'.

Nine On the Streets of Southern Dunedin

1 Their numbers were to increase to about 700 by 1930. Erik Olssen, *Building the New World: Work, Politics and Society in Caversham 1880s–1920s*, Auckland, 1995, p. 27.
2 The focus is on the movement of people; movement of goods is not addressed in this paper, although it is a significant aspect of urban transport.
3 Hamish Keith, *New Zealand Yesterdays: A Look At Our Recent Past*, Sydney, 1984, p. 237.
4 James Donald, *Imagining the Modern City*, London, 1999; Marshall Berman, *All That Is Solid Melts into Air: The Experience of Modernity*, London, 1983.
5 Virginia Scharff, *Taking the Wheel: Women and the Coming of the Motor Age*, New York, 1991; Martin Wachs, 'Men, Women and Wheels: the Historical Basis of Sex Differences in Travel Patterns', *Transportation Research Record*, 1135, 1987, pp. 10–16; Robin Law, 'Beyond "Women and Transport": Towards New Geographies of Gender and Daily Mobility', *Progress in Human Geography*, 23, 4, 1999, pp. 567–88; Susan Hanson and Geraldine Pratt, *Gender, Work and Space*, London, 1995.
6 K. C. McDonald, *City of Dunedin: A Century of Civic Enterprise*, Dunedin, 1965, p. 180.
7 Eileen L. Soper, *The Otago of Our Mothers*, Christchurch, 1948, p. 60.
8 W. A. V. Clark, 'Dunedin in 1901: A Study in Historical Urban Geography', MA thesis, University of Canterbury, 1961, p. 57. There were four stations within the urban area (Dunedin, Pelichet Bay, Kensington and Caversham) and ten more in the vicinity. An attempt was also made to develop rail links across the Flat to serve commuters. In 1874, the Dunedin, Peninsula and Ocean Beach Railway Company was incorporated to establish a rail line to Ocean Beach, and a line to Ocean Beach (St Kilda) opened in 1876. One of the objectives of the company was to 'supply regular transportation for residents'. Cited in J. A. Dangerfield, *Dunedin's Matchbox Railway: the Dunedin, Peninsula and Ocean Beach Railway Company and Other Suburban Ventures*, Wellington, 1986, p. 9.
9 Graham Hawkes, *On the Road: the Car in New Zealand*, Wellington, 1990, p. 11.
10 Graham Stewart, *Always a Tram in Sight: the Electric Trams of New Zealand, 1900 to 1964*, Wellington, p. 149.
11 Minute Paper from Manager, Dunedin Tramways Department, 'Concession Tickets', 28 February 1911, Box P/1 1911, Transport, Dunedin City Council (DCC)

Archives.
12 Dunedin Tramways Committee Report, 19 June 1907, Box TC 1907, Transport, DCC Archives.
13 Minute Paper from Chairman (unspecified), Town Clerk's Department, 'Tramway Fares', 21 April 1914, Box F/1 1919, Transport, DCC Archives.
14 Mavis Liverpool (b. 1923), interviewed November 1996, Caversham Oral History Project (COHP), Transcript Sub-series Three: Transport, p. 368. Unless otherwise stated, all interviews conducted by Megan Cook, Dunedin.
15 Keith, *New Zealand Yesterdays*, p. 239.
16 *Otago Daily Times* Supplement, '100 Years of the Motor Vehicle in Otago', December 17 1999, p. 14.
17 M. H. Holcroft, *Carapace: the Motor Car in New Zealand: A Roadside View*, Dunedin, 1979, p. 28.
18 Hawkes, *On the Road*, p. 34.
19 G. N. Stedman, 'The South Dunedin Flat: A Study in Urbanisation 1849–1965', MA thesis, University of Otago, 1966, p. 203.
20 Stedman (p. 140) gives an example of two engine drivers and a signalman residing in Waverley St.
21 For more detail on the Hillside railway workers, see Olssen, *Building the New World*, ch. 6.
22 Trevor K. Snowdon, 'Railways, Rationality and Modernity', PhD thesis, University of Auckland, 1992, abstract.
23 See also George Revill, 'Trained for life: Personal Identity and the Meaning of Work in the Nineteenth-Century Railway Industry' in Chris Philo (ed.), *New Words, New Worlds: Reconceptualising Social and Cultural Geography*, Lampeter, Wales, 1991, pp. 65–77.
24 Graham Stewart, *The End of the Penny Section*, Wellington, 1973, p. 99.
25 Minute Paper from Manager, Tramways Department, 'New Recreation Room', 25 January 1912, Box TC33 T6 1912, Transport, DCC Archives.
26 Minute Paper from Town Clerk's Department (Mayor's Minute), 'Tramways Employees' (Conductors) Grievances', 24 August 1911, Box E/1 1911, Transport, DCC Archives.
27 Minute Paper from Manager, Tramways Department, 'Tramways Employees' (Conductors) Grievances', 26 August 1911, Box E/1 1911, Transport, DCC Archives.
28 Minute Paper from Manager, Tramways Department, 'Tramways Employees' (Conductors) Grievances', p. 5.
29 Ruth Schwartz Cowan, *More Work for Mother: The Ironies of Household Technology from the Open Hearth to the Microwave*, New York, 1983.
30 Ken McCracken (b. 1923) and Velda McCracken (b. 1920), interviewed October 1996, COHP, Transcript Sub-series Two: Wealth and Poverty, p. 77.
31 Mark Bailey and Thomas Ryan, 'Telephone Subscription in the Caversham Study Area 1910 to 1922', History 351 essay, University of Otago, 1998.
32 Mary Redwood (b. 1924), interviewed March 1996, COHP, Transcript Series One, Vol. 2, p. 74.
33 Mary Redwood, p. 74.
34 Helen Wilson (b. 1909), interviewed October 1996, COHP, Transcript Series One, Vol. 5, p. 270.
35 Annabel Cooper, Robin Law, Jane Malthus and Pamela Wood, 'Rooms of Their Own: Public Toilets and Gendered Citizens in a New Zealand City 1860–1940', *Gender, Place and Culture*, 7, 4, 2000, pp. 417–33.
36 Stedman, 'The South Dunedin Flat', pp. 202–3.
37 Hanson and Pratt, *Gender, Work and Space*.
38 Christine King (b. 1922), interviewed August 1996, COHP, Transcript Sub-series Three: Transport, p. 203.
39 Pat Donnelly (b. 1910), interviewed September 1996, COHP, Transcript Sub-series Three: Transport, p. 54.
40 Mavis Liverpool, p. 364.
41 Marion Cooper (b. 1925), interviewed April 1996, COHP, Transcript Series One, Vol. 4, p. 203.
42 Calculated from interviews conducted by Megan Cook for COHP, collected in Transcript Series One, Dunedin, 1995–96.
43 Interviews conducted by Megan Cook in 1996 for COHP, Sub-series Three: Transport Transcripts, Dunedin, 1995–96.
44 Stuart Sidey (b. 1908), interviewed in October 1996, COHP, Transcript Sub-series Three: Transport, p. 330.
45 Mavis Liverpool, p. 368.
46 Christine King (b. 1922), interviewed August 1996, COHP, Transcript Series One, Vol. 3, p. 157.
47 Phyllis Crossan (b. 1922), interviewed January 1996, COHP, Transcript Series One,

Vol. 1, pp. 201–2.
48 Rita Jory (b. 1902) and Louise Wellman (b. 1909), interviewed in March 1996, COHP, Transcript Series One, Vol. 3, p. 157.
49 Graham Cowie, writing about his childhood in Masterton as the son of two doctors, recalls the importance of transport. His father bought a motor cycle before 1910, and would occasionally tow his mother on her bicycle when both were going to see the same patient! But, once cars became more easily available, 'as both my parents were in medical practice, it was soon obvious that it was necessary to have two cars at a time': Cowie, *Yesterday's Motoring*, p. 11.
50 Helen Tweed (b. 1914), interviewed May 1996, COHP, Transcript Series One, Vol. 2, p. 296.
51 Loma Kent-Johnson (b. 1918), interviewed March 1996, COHP, Transcript Series One, Vol. 3, p. 240.
52 Bert Grimmett (b. 1912), interviewed January 1996, COHP, Transcript Series One, Vol. 2, p. 160.
53 Snowdon, 'Railways, Rationality and Modernity'.
54 Rosanna Paul (b. 1909), interviewed May 1996, COHP, Transcript Series One, Vol. 2, p. 128.
55 Joyce White (b. 1913), interviewed October 1996, COHP, Transcript Series One, Vol. 5, p. 203.
56 Helen Wilson, p. 294.
57 Marion Cooper (b. 1925), interviewed October 1996, COHP, Sub-series Three: Transport, p. 301.
58 Helen Wilson, p. 270.
59 Wilhelmina Bassett (b. 1918), interviewed November 1996, COHP, Transcript Sub-series Three: Transport, p. 222.
60 Hilda Maher (b. 1912), interviewed March 1996, COHP, Transcript Series One, Vol. 4, p. 48.
61 Phyllis Crossan, p. 198.
62 Peter Stallybrass and Allon White, *The Politics and Poetics of Transgression*, London, 1986.
63 Minute Paper from Town Clerk's Department, Dunedin, 'Visit of Inspection by Tramways Committee', 14 June 1909, Box TC33 01-T2 1909, Transport, DCC Archives.
64 Minute Paper from Manager, Tramways Department, 'Shelter Shed – Glen Rd', 16 August 1910, and Minute Paper from Manager, Tramways Department, 'Shelter Sheds', 14 July 1910, both in Box S/3 1910, Transport, DCC Archives.
65 Broadcast transcript, 'The Turn of the Century', MS 665-10, Siedeberg papers, Hocken Library.
66 Frances Harris (b. 1917), interviewed June 1996, COHP, Transcript Series One, Vol. 2, p. 190.
67 Mavis Liverpool, p. 373.
68 Phyllis Crossan, p. 200.
69 Alison Abraham (b. 1914) and Brian Abraham (b. 1911), interviewed October 1996, COHP, Transcript Series One, Vol. 3, p. 28.
70 Bert Grimmett, p. 145.
71 See James Watson, *Links: A History of Transport and New Zealand Society*, Wellington, 1996; Martin Wachs and Margaret Crawford, *The Car and the City: The Automobile, the Built Environment and Daily Urban Life*, Ann Arbor, 1992.
72 Letter to Chairman and Members of the Tramways Committee, Dunedin, from N. York, 12 February 1919, Box F/1, Transport, DCC Archives.
73 Ken McCracken (b. 1923) and Velda McCracken (b. 1920), interviewed November 1996, COHP, Transcript Sub-series Three: Transport, p. 270.
74 Rosanna Paul, p. 104.
75 J. O. C. Phillips, *A Man's Country? The Image of the Pakeha Male – A History*, Auckland, 1987.
76 Rosanna Paul, p. 82.
77 Rosanna Paul, p. 125.
78 Nicholas Fyfe, *Images of the Street: Planning, Identity and Control in Public Space*, London, 1998, p. 2.

Ten The Risk to Life and Limb
1 *ODT*, 18 June 1926, p. 8.
2 *Otago Witness*, 15 May 1923, p. 25.
3 Joan Scott, 'Gender: A Useful Category of Historical Analysis', in *Gender and the Politics of History*, New York, 1988, p. 43.
4 Marian Horan, 'Employing Gender in the New World: Factory Legislation in New Zealand 1873–1901', MA thesis, University of Otago, 1999.
5 Linda Bryder (ed.), *A Healthy Country: Essays on the Social History of Medicine in New Zealand*, Wellington, 1991; F. S. Maclean, *Challenge for Health. A History of Public Health in New Zealand*, Wellington, 1964; Derek A. Dow, *Safeguarding the Public Health: A History of the New*

Zealand Department of Health, Wellington, 1995; Derek A. Dow, *Maori Health and Government Policy 1840–1940*, Wellington, 1999; Raeburn Lange, *May the People Live: A History of Maori Health Development 1900–1920*, Auckland, 1999; Margaret Tennant, *Children's Health, Nation's Wealth: a History of Children's Health Camps*, Wellington, 1994; Jessie Munro, *The Story of Suzanne Aubert*, Auckland, 1996; Fay Hercock, *Alice: The Making of a Woman Doctor, 1914–1974*, Auckland, 1999.

6 Books that concentrate on women's experience include Phillippa Mein Smith, *Maternity in Dispute: New Zealand 1920–1939*, Wellington, 1986; Joan Donley, *Save the midwife*, Auckland, 1986; and Linda Bryder, *Not Just Weighing Babies: Plunket in Auckland, 1908–1998*, Auckland, 1998.

7 Bronwyn Labrum, 'Gender and Lunacy', MA thesis, Massey University, 1990; Bronwyn Labrum, 'Looking Beyond the Asylum: Gender and the Process of Committal in Auckland, 1870–1910', *New Zealand Journal of History (NZJH)* 26, 2, 1992, pp. 125–44.

8 Lois M. Verbrugge, 'Pathways of Health and Death', in Rima Apple (ed.), *Women, Health and Medicine in America: A Historical Handbook*, New York, 1990, p. 41.

9 Verbrugge, 'Pathways', p. 41.

10 The following two paragraphs are based on Barbara Brookes, 'Aspects of Women's Health, 1885–1945', in Bryder (ed.), *A Healthy Country*, pp. 149–51.

11 *Report on the Statistics of New Zealand 1891*, Wellington, 1891, pp. 46–47; *Evening Star (ES)*, 2 July 1890, p. 2.

12 Geoffrey Rice, 'Public Health in Christchurch, 1875–1910: Mortality and Sanitation', in Bryder (ed.), *A Healthy Country*, p. 88.

13 *New Zealand Official Year Book (NZOYB)*, 1942, p. 113.

14 *Census Report* 1920, p. 75.

15 M. Tennant, *Paupers and Providers: Charitable Aid in New Zealand*, Wellington, 1989, p. 165.

16 Derek A. Dow, 'Springs of Charity?: The Development of the New Zealand Hospital System, 1876–1910', in Bryder (ed.), *A Healthy Country*, pp. 49–50.

17 *NZOYB*, 1942, p. 113.

18 *Census Report* 1916, p. 75; C. Geiringer and R. McLennan, 'New Zealand Mental Health Statistics 1920–60', History 351 essay, University of Otago, 1988.

19 Pamela Wood, 'Constructing Colonial Dirt: A Cultural History of Dirt in the Nineteenth Century Colonial Settlement of New Zealand', PhD thesis, University of Otago, pp. 66–69.

20 For general background, see David Hamer, *New Towns in the New World: Images and Perceptions of the Nineteenth Century Urban Frontier*, New York, 1990; and, more particularly, G. N. Stedman, 'The South Dunedin Flat: A Study in Urbanisation, 1849–1965', MA thesis, University of Otago, 1966, pp. 170–74, 207–9; for recreational reserves, pp. 211–12.

21 Stedman, 'The South Dunedin Flat', pp. 75, 95; W. A. V. Clark, 'Dunedin in 1901: A Study in Historical Urban Geography', MA thesis, University of Canterbury, 1961, p. 28.

22 Nancy Tomes, *The Gospel of Germs: Men, Women, and the Microbe in American Life*, Cambridge, 1998, p. 57.

23 Douglas C. Ewbank and Samuel H. Preston, 'Personal Health Behaviour and the Decline in Infant and Child Mortality: The United States, 1900–1930', in John Caldwell *et al.* (eds), *What We Know about Health Transition: The Cultural, Social and Behavioural Determinants of Health*, Canberra, 1990, pp. 116–49.

24 *New Zealand Scenery and Public Buildings: Leading Business Establishments, Dunedin*, pamphlet, *Otago Daily Times* and *Otago Witness*, 1895, unpaginated.

25 *New Zealand Scenery and Public Buildings: Leading Business Establishments, Dunedin*.

26 Obituary, *Otago Witness*, 21 October 1908.

27 Adelheid Wassner, *Labour of Love: Childbirth at Dunedin Hospital, 1862–1972*, Dunedin, 1999, p. 20.

28 John Angus, *A History of the Otago Hospital Board and its Predecessors*, Dunedin, 1984, p. 102.

29 Nancy Tomes, 'The Private Side of Public Health: Sanitary Science, Domestic Hygiene, and the Germ Theory, 1870–1900,' *Bulletin of the History of Medicine*, 64, 1990, p. 152.

30 A chair of Domestic Science was established at the University of Otago in 1909 in response to fears about the declining birth rate and the changing position of women: Heath McDonald, '"This Educational Monstrosity..." A Study of the Foundation and Early Development of the School of Home Science, University of

Otago, Dunedin', BA Hons research essay, University of Otago, 1984.
31 Southern Cross, *Housewifery for Use in School and Home*, rev. edition, Auckland, undated, p. 5.
32 Margaret Tennant, '"Missionaries of Health": The School Medical Service during the Inter-war Period', in Bryder (ed.), *A Healthy Country*, p. 133.
33 These understandings are most apparent in regard to menstruation, where young girls were warned not to bathe or get chilled at the time of menstruation, in case the cold stemmed the flow of blood and resulted in illness. See Barbara Brookes, 'Hygiene, Health, and Bodily Knowledge, 1880–1940: A New Zealand Case Study', in *Journal of Family History*, 28, 2, 2003, pp. 297–313.
34 Emily Siedeberg Collection, 'Speeches', MS 655-10, Hocken Library, Dunedin.
35 J. S. C. Elkington, MD DPH (Chief Health Officer of Tasmania), Southern Cross Series *Health Reader,* with chapters on elementary school hygiene, Wellington, c. 1908, p. 7.
36 The sentence comes from a longer quote from Samuel Smiles, which begins, 'The physical health of the rising generation is entrusted to woman by Providence; and it is in the physical nature that the moral and mental nature lies enshrined. It is only by acting in accordance with natural laws . . . that the blessings of mind and morals can be secured at home.' Charles W. Budden, MD, *The Way of Health: Plain Counsels in Personal Hygiene*, London, 1920, p. 24.
37 Budden, *The Way of Health*, p. 100.
38 *Plunket Magazine,* January 1915; Royal Society for the Protection of Women and Children Collection, 1909–16, pamphlet, Hocken Library, Dunedin.
39 Robert J. Terry, *How to Get Well and Keep Well*, Auckland, 1933, p. 5.
40 Kitty Brown (b. 1905), interviewed December 1995, Caversham Oral History Project (COHP), Medical History Transcripts, p. 50; Marion Cooper (b. 1925), interviewed April 1996, COHP, Medical History Transcripts, p. 251: History Department, University of Otago. Unless otherwise stated, all interviews were carried out by Megan Cook.
41 Phyllis Crossan (b. 1922), interviewed January 1996, COHP, Medical History Transcripts, p. 72.
42 Frances Harris (b. 1917), interviewed June 1996, COHP, Transcript Series One, Vol. 2, Dunedin, p. 234.
43 Rosanna Paul (b. 1909), interviewed May 1996, COHP, Transcript Series One, Vol. 2, Dunedin, p. 116.
44 Marion Cooper, p. 247.
45 Terry, *How to Get Well,* p. 59.
46 Phyllis Crossan, p. 71.
47 Wilhemina Bassett (b. 1918), interviewed December 1996, COHP, Medical History Transcripts, p. 10.
48 See ads for Lane's Emulsion, *ES*, 2 January 1920; ads for Wine of Coca Leaves, Baxter's Lung Preserver, Paramo, Pure Vegetable Remedies, *ES*, 2 July 1895, p. 1; Radam's Microbe Killer, *ES*, 2 January 1895, p. 4.
49 *ES*, 3 January 1920, p. 5.
50 *ES*, 2 July 1910, p. 3.
51 *ES*, 4 July 1910, p. 2; *ES*, 2 January 1895, p. 4.
52 *ES*, 4 January, 1910, p. 2; Chamberlain's Tablets, *ES*, 3 January 1920, p. 4.
53 Wilhemina Bassett, p. 11; Richard Perth (b. 1903), interviewed May 1996 by Erik Olssen, COHP, Medical History Transcripts, p. 282.
54 Emily Siedeberg Collection, 'Speeches', MS 655-10, Hocken Library, Dunedin.
55 J. Renfrew White, *The Growing Body: Its Nature, Needs, and Training,* 2nd edition, Dunedin, 1932, p. 204. This book contained the system of physical training prescribed by the education department to be used in state schools.
56 Terry, *How to Get Well*, pp. 51–66.
57 Richard Perth, p. 282.
58 Marion Cooper, p. 252.
59 Wilhemina Bassett, p. 11.
60 Hilda Maher (b. 1912), interviewed April 1996, COHP, Medical History Transcripts, p. 220.
61 Rita Jory (b. 1902), interviewed March 1996, COHP, Medical History Transcripts, p. 370.
62 Verna Syme (b. 1918), interviewed April 1996, COHP, Medical History Transcripts, p. 320.
63 Marion Cooper, p. 245.
64 Victoria Lake (b. 1912), interviewed August 1996, COHP, Transcript Series One, Vol. 1, p. 58.
65 Marina Mackenzie (b. 1908), interviewed August 1996, COHP, Transcript Series One, Vol. 1, p. 72.
66 William Harris (b. 1916), interviewed June 1996, COHP, Transcript Series One, Vol 2, pp. 252–53.
67 Kitty Brown (b. 1905), interviewed December 1995, COHP, Transcript Series

One, Vol. 1, p. 110.
68. Louise Wellman (b. 1909), interviewed March 1996, COHP, Medical History Transcripts, p. 370.
69. Conrad Schumacher, 'Why Did So Many Babies Die? Infant Mortality and Causes of Death in Dunedin, 1900–1920', BA Hons research essay, University of Otago, 1998.
70. Randall Reeves, 'Declining Fertility in England and Wales as a Major Cause of the Twentieth Century Decline in Mortality: The Role of Changing Family Size and Age Structure in Infectious Disease Mortality in Infancy', *American Journal of Epidemiology*, 122, 1, 1985, pp. 112–26.
71. Infant death databases, compiled by Conrad Schumacher. Although every attempt was made to obtain accurate data, the addresses of those dying were not always complete and, if they died in an institution, the home address is not always given. The number of deaths within institutions increased over time. A further difficulty lies in connecting these addresses to the study area. For the methodological issues raised by such a study, see Schumacher, 'Why Did so Many Babies Die?'.
72. Erik Olssen, *Building the New World: Work, Politics and Society in Caversham 1880s–1920s*, Auckland, 1995, pp. 125–27.
73. Ian B. Campbell, *Compensation for Personal Injury in New Zealand. Its Rise and Fall*, Auckland, 1996, p. 16.
74. Barbara Harrison, *Not Only the 'Dangerous Trades': Women's Work and Health in Britain, 1880–1914*, London, 1996, p. 66.
75. Horan, 'Employing Gender', pp. 115–57.
76. Tony Bamford, 'The Wax Vesta Factory', History 452 essay, University of Otago, 1982, p. 13.
77. Annie Norman (b. 1887), interviewed 1982 by Tom Brooking, COHP, Childhood Transcripts.
78. A. Platts-Mills, 'Some Aspects Relating to the Health of Women in Industry in New Zealand', Fifth Year Preventive Medicine research essay, University of Otago Medical School, 1929, pp. 85–86.
79. *AJHR*, 1921–22, H-11, cited in Bamford, 'The Wax Vesta Factory', p. 13.
80. Otago Benevolent Institute Outdoor Relief (OBIODR) Casebook, DAHI D 284 60-68, Archives New Zealand (ANZ), Dunedin. (References that follow are first to the Archives *volumes*, and secondly to the individual *series* of the Caversham Project's edited transcripts of those volumes: Annabel Cooper with Marian Horan and Eva Lubcke (eds), 'Transcripts from the Otago Benevolent Institution's Outdoor Relief Casebooks', 3 vols, Caversham Working Paper (CWP) 2000-3. See Appendix II for more specific information on this source.) Vol. I, pp. 245, 307, Series I, p. 35.
81. Jean Marie O'Donnell, 'Female Complaints: Women's Health in Dunedin, 1885–1910', MA thesis, University of Otago, 1991, p. 100.
82. Medical Casebook, 1891–93, DAHI D267, ANZ Dunedin, p. 68. Thanks to Brooke Whitelaw for searching these casebooks.
83. Medical Casebook, 1891–93, DAHI D267, ANZ, Dunedin, p. 38.
84. Medical Casebook, 1891–93, DAHI D267, ANZ, Dunedin, p. 187.
85. Medical Casebook, 1891–93, DAHI D267, ANZ, Dunedin, p. 62.
86. Medical Casebook, 1891–93, DAHI D267, ANZ, Dunedin, p. 62.
87. Medical Casebook, 1891–93, DAHI D267, ANZ, Dunedin, p. 76.
88. Gynaecological Casebook, 1898–1900, DAHI D267, ANZ, Dunedin, p. 15.
89. Medical Casebook, 1891–93, DAHI D267, ANZ, Dunedin, p. 84.
90. Medical Casebook, 1899–1900, DAHI D267, ANZ, Dunedin, p. 77.
91. Hilary Haines, '"The Peculiarities of their Sex": An Analysis of the "Causes of Insanity" among New Zealand Women from 1878 to 1902', in Hilary Haines (ed.), *Women's Studies Conference Papers 1981*, Auckland, 1982, p. 178. See also Barbara Brookes, 'Men and Madness in New Zealand, 1890–1916', in Linda Bryder and Derek Dow (eds), *New Countries and Old Medicine: Proceedings of an International Conference on the History of Medicine and Health*, Auckland, 1995, pp. 204–210.
92. The Lunatics Act, 1882.
93. All names from the Seacliff Asylum files have been fictionalised to protect confidentiality. Case no. 4781, Medical Casebook 1910, Archives of the Seacliff Asylum, ANZ, Dunedin. I am grateful to Healthcare Otago for access to these records.
94. *ODT*, 8 June 1889, p. 2, ch. 2; cited in Susan Chivers, '"A Man's Home is His Castle": Domestic Violence in Dunedin, 1888–1914', BA Hons research essay, University of Otago, 1988, p. 32.
95. Chivers, '"A Man's Home"', p. 81.

96 Medical Casebook, 1915, case no. 5606, Seacliff Asylum, ANZ, Dunedin.
97 OBIODR Casebook, Vol. I, p. 47, Vol. II, p. 773, Series I, p. 12.
98 Medical Casebook, 1910, case no. 4783. See also Medical Casebook 1900, case no. 3443; case no. 3425, Seacliff Asylum, ANZ, Dunedin. All these men died at Seacliff.
99 See Barbara Brookes, 'Women and Madness: A Case-Study of the Seacliff Asylum, 1890–1920', in B. Brookes, C. Macdonald and M. Tennant (eds), *Women in History 2*, Wellington, 1992, pp. 129–47.
100 Medical Casebook, 1900, case no. 3403, Seacliff Asylum, ANZ, Dunedin.
101 'Report of the Royal Commission Appointed to Inquire into Certain Relations between the Employers of Certain Kinds of Labour and the Persons Employed Therein (Sweating Commission)', *AJHR*, 1890, H-5, pp. 23, 26.
102 OBIODR Casebook, Vol. I, p. 144, Vol. II, p. 812, Series I, p. 25.
103 OBIODR Casebook, Vol. I, pp. 188, 217, Vol. II, p. 831, Vol. IV, p. 1750, Series I, p. 29.
104 *Statistics of New Zealand 1889*, p. 65.
105 OBIODR Casebook, Vol I, p. 115, Series I, p. 21.
106 Dunedin Hospital Casebook, 1892–3, DAHI D267 1b, ANZ, Dunedin, p. 50.
107 For a discussion of this in the English context, see Barbara Brookes, 'Women and Reproduction, 1860–1939', in J. Lewis (ed.), *Labour and Love: Women's Experience of Home and Family, 1850–1940*, Oxford, 1986, pp. 149–71.
108 Mein Smith, *Maternity in Dispute*, p. 118.
109 Brooke Whitelaw, 'Women and Child-Spacing in the 1937 Housing Survey', History 351 essay, University of Otago, 1999.
110 Loma Kent-Johnston (b. 1918), interviewed March 1996, COHP, Medical History Transcripts, p. 161.
111 Marjorie Scott (b. 1909), interviewed January 1996, COHP, Medical History Transcripts, p. 155.
112 *ES*, 3 January 1920, p. 6.
113 See Jennifer Carlyon, 'Friendly Societies 1842–1938: The Benefits of Membership', *NZJH*, 32, 2, 1998, p. 124.
114 *Return of Sickness, Mortality and other Contingencies*, Court of Saint Andrews, Ancient Order of Foresters, 1911–1922. All names have been fictionalised in order to preserve confidentiality.
115 *Return of Sickness*, Foresters, 1911–1922.
116 Erik Olssen, 'Friendly Societies in New Zealand, 1840–1990', in M. van der Linden (ed.), *Social Security Mutualism: The Comparative History of Mutual Benefit Societies*, New York, 1996, p. 191.
117 Minutes of the Ruth Rebekah Lodge No. 3, 1 September 1898, IOOF Mss: cited in Olssen, 'Friendly Societies', p. 192.
118 OBIODR Casebook, Vol. I, p. 97, Vol. II, p. 1178, Series I, pp. 17–18.
119 OBIODR Casebook, Vol. I, pp. 129, 252, Series I, p. 23.
120 Evan Tosh, 'Caversham at War! An Examination and Analysis of Three Caversham Area Schools War Rolls of Honour', History 351 essay, 1998, p. 13.
121 See Peter Boston, 'The Bacillus of Work: Masculinity and the Rehabilitation of Disabled Soldiers in Dunedin 1919 to 1939', BA Hons research essay, University of Otago, 1993, pp. 72–73.
122 Boston, 'The Bacillus of Work', p. 74.
123 James Beattie and Brigitte Wright, 'The Impact of the 1918 Influenza Pandemic on Caversham', History 351 essay, 1999.
124 Martine Cuff, 'The Great Scourge: Dunedin in the 1918 Influenza Epidemic', PGDip research essay, University of Otago, 1980, pp. 67–68; Linda Bryder, '"Lessons" of the 1918 Influenza Epidemic in Auckland', *NZJH*, 16, 2, 1982, pp. 97–121; Geoffrey Rice, *Black November: The 1918 Influenza Epidemic in New Zealand*, Wellington, 1988.
125 OBIODR Casebook, Vol. I, pp. 250, 358, Series I, p. 37.
126 See Maclean, *Challenge for Health*.
127 Maclean, *Challenge for Health*, p. 360.
128 MacLean, *Challenge for Health*, p. 364.
129 Olssen, *Building the New World*, p. 133.
130 Natali Allen and Eve Brister, 'Nurses with Tuberculosis: A Preliminary Study', *Women's Studies Journal*, 5, 2, 1989, pp. 38–60.
131 Annabel Cooper and Maureen Molloy, 'Poverty, Dependence and "Women": Reading Autobiography and Social Policy from 1930s New Zealand', *Gender & History*, 9, 1, 1997, p. 45.
132 Neilson, Social Security Bill debate, 1938, *New Zealand Parliamentary Debates* (*NZPD*), Vol. 252, p. 397, cited in Cooper and Molloy, 'Poverty, Dependence and "Women"', p. 57. From 1905, the state-subsidised St Helens hospitals provided low-cost maternity care to the wives of men who earned less than £4 a week.
133 *The White Ribbon*, October 1901, p. 5, cited

in O'Donnell, 'Female Complaints', p. 24.
134 Barbara Brookes, 'Housewives' Depression. The Debate over Abortion and Birth Control in the 1930s', *NZJH*, 15, 2, 1985, p. 130.
135 *ES*, 1 July 1939, p. 3.
136 *NZPD*, 1899, 108, p. 528.
137 John Angus, *A History of the Otago Hospital Board and its Predecessors*, Dunedin, 1984, p. 102.
138 Angus, *A History of the Otago Hospital Board*, p. 101.

Eleven God, the Devil and Gender

1 Kirsten Thomlinson, 'We the Undersigned: an Analysis of Signatories to the 1893 Suffrage Petition from Southern Dunedin', MA thesis, University of Otago, 2001. I would like to thank the author for graciously sharing preliminary findings with me. See also the discussion in chapter two of this volume.
2 See also Patrick Collinson, 'Religion, Society, and the Historian', *Journal of Religious History*, 23, 2 1999, pp. 149–67.
3 Erik Olssen, *Building the New World: Work, Politics and Society in Caversham 1880–1920s*, Auckland, 1995. Although Olssen paid only brief attention to religion, I have found his observations useful in preparing this chapter.
4 Joan Wallach Scott, 'Gender: A Useful Category of Historical Analysis', in *Gender and the Politics of History*, New York, 1988, pp. 28–50.
5 Barbara Brookes, 'Women's History', in Colin Davis and Peter Lineham (eds), *The Future of the Past: Themes in New Zealand History*, Palmerston North, 1991, p. 76.
6 William Pember Reeves, *The Long White Cloud: Ao Tea Roa*, Auckland, 1973, *passim*.
7 Sinclair's works are too numerous to list. I draw in the following discussion upon *A History of New Zealand*, rev. edition, London, 1969, first published in 1959, probably the most widely read and influential history of New Zealand yet to appear.
8 On Mather and American Puritan historiography, see David Harlan, *The Degradation of American History*, Chicago, 1997, pp. 36–38.
9 Sinclair, *A History of New Zealand*, pp. 287–288.
10 E. P. Thompson, *The Making of the English Working Class*, London, 1963, p. 13.
11 Thompson, *The Making of the English Working Class*, pp. 385–410.
12 Erik Olssen and Andrée Levesque, 'Towards a History of the European Family in New Zealand', in Peggy Koopman-Boyden (ed.), *Families in New Zealand Society*, Wellington, 1978, p. 3.
13 Barbara Brookes, '"Housewives' Depression": The Debate Over Abortion and Birth Control in the 1930s', *New Zealand Journal of History* (*NZJH*), 15, 2, 1981, pp. 127, 131–34.
14 Margaret Tennant, 'Sister Mabel's Private Diary 1907–1910: Sisterhood, Love and Religious Doubt', *Women's Studies Journal*, 14, 1, 1998, p. 56.
15 Harlan, *The Degradation of American History*, pp. xxxii–xxxiii.
16 Anne Braude, 'Women's History *Is* American Religious History', in Thomas Tweed (ed.), *Retelling U.S. Religious History*, Berkeley and Los Angeles, 1997, pp. 87–107.
17 Jeanine Graham, 'Settler Society', in W. H. Oliver with B. R. Williams, *The Oxford History of New Zealand*, Wellington, 1981, pp. 112–39, p. 128.
18 Phillida Bunkle, 'The Origins of the Women's Movement in New Zealand: The Women's Christian Temperance Union, 1885–1895' in Bunkle and Hughes (eds), *Women in New Zealand Society*; see also R. Fry, *Out of the Silence: Methodist Women of Aotearoa 1822–1985*, Christchurch, 1987.
19 Jock Phillips, *A Man's Country? The Image of the Pakeha Male–A History*, rev. edition, Auckland, 1996.
20 Jessie Munro, *The Story of Suzanne Aubert*, Auckland, 1996.
21 Tennant, 'Sister Mabel's Private Diary', p. 56.
22 Caroline Daley, *Girls & Women, Men & Boys: Gender in Taradale, 1886–1930*, Auckland, 1999; Miles Fairburn, *The Ideal Society and Its Enemies: The Foundations of Modern New Zealand Society, 1850–1900*, Auckland, 1989.
23 James Belich, *Making Peoples: A History of the New Zealanders From Polynesian Settlement to the End of the Nineteenth Century*, Auckland, 1996; James Belich, *Paradise Reforged: A History of the New Zealanders from the 1880s to the Year 2000*, Auckland, 2001.
24 Barbara Welter, 'The Feminization of American Religion: 1800–1860', in Mary S. Hartman and Lois Banner (eds), *Clio's Consciousness Raised: New Perspectives*

25. Clive D. Field, 'Adam and Eve: Gender in the English Free Church Constituency', *Journal of Ecclesiastical History*, 44, 1, 1993, pp. 63–79.
26. On religion and gender in Western Europe, see Hugh McLeod, *Religion and the People of Western Europe*, New York, 1997, pp. 28–35.
27. Mavis Liverpool (b. 1923), interviewed December 1995, Caversham Oral History Project (COHP), Transcript Series One, Vol. 5, p. 192. Unless otherwise stated, all interviews conducted by Megan Cook, Dunedin.
28. Daley, *Girls & Women*, pp. 96–103.
29. M. Toomey, 'St. Peters Anglican Church: Parish of Caversham', History 452 essay, University of Otago, 1982, p. 11.
30. Justine Smith and Ali Clarke, 'Caversham Presbyterian Church 1911: An Analysis of the Gender, Marital Status and Class of Communicant Members', History 351 essay, University of Otago, 1998, pp. 9, 12–15.
31. M. Wallis, 'Kew Primitive Methodist Church 1900–1914 and Caversham Methodist Church 1914–1920', History 452 essay, University of Otago, 1983, p. 11.
32. M. Reid, 'Caversham Baptist Church: Sunday School 1890–1916 and Young Men's Club 1901–1907', History 452 essay, University of Otago, 1982, p. 6.
33. Gendered patterns of religiosity within the Catholic community await investigation. Data have so far proven difficult to obtain.
34. Myrtle Caird (b. 1920), interviewed April 1996, COHP, Transcript Series One, Vol. 1, p. 165.
35. Victoria Lake (b. 1912), interviewed August 1996, COHP, Transcript Series One, Vol. 1, p. 78.
36. Thomlinson, 'We the Undersigned', p. 98.
37. Dorothy Page, 'Introduction', *The Suffragists: Women Who Worked for the Vote: Essays from the Dictionary of New Zealand Biography*, Wellington, 1993, pp. 1–23, p. 7.
38. The statistics appearing in this paragraph are taken from the *New Zealand Census* 1891, 1906 and 1901.
39. Thomlinson, 'We the Undersigned'. I would like to acknowledge the invaluable work of Kirsten Thomlinson and Shaun Broadley in identifying the church affiliations of these signatories.
40. Cyril R. Bradwell, *Fight the Good Fight: the Story of the Salvation Army in New Zealand, 1883–1983*, Wellington, 1982, p. 123.
41. This description of Charlotte Rachel Grimmett is based on the following sources: her diary (mid-1890s), kindly lent by Mr and Mrs H. W. Grimmett, Dunedin; Olssen, *Building the New World*, pp. 182, 229; and Brian Heenan and Sarah Johnsen, in chapter eight of this volume.
42. 'Great Tightening' and 'moral evangelists' come from Belich, *Paradise Reforged*, pp. 121–25 and 157–88.
43. Peter C. Matheson, *'A Time of Sifting': Evangelicals and Liberals at the Genesis of New Zealand Theology*, Dunedin, 1991, pp. 7–8.
44. Lawrence H. Barber, 'James Gibb's Heresy Trial', *NZJH*, 12, 2, 1978, pp. 146–57.
45. E. M. Sinclair, 'The Catholics of Caversham, 1890–1920', History 452 essay, University of Otago, 1982, p. 5.
46. For the English background, see F. K. Prochaska, *Women and Philanthropy in Nineteenth-Century England*, Oxford, 1980.
47. R. Moore, *Pit-men, Politics, and Preachers*, Cambridge, 1974, p. 146.
48. Jean Smith (b. 1922), interviewed July 1996, COHP, Transcript Series One, Vol. 5, p. 55.
49. Kitty Brown (b. 1905), interviewed December 1995, COHP, Transcript Series One, Vol. 1, p. 108.
50. Mabel Cartwright, Diary 24–25 December 1907, Knox College Archives 3/279.
51. Frances Kenny (b. 1910), interviewed August 1996, COHP, Transcript Series One, Vol. 3, pp. 206–7.
52. Mavis Liverpool, pp. 168, 177.
53. Brian Abraham (b. 1911), interviewed October 1996, COHP, Transcript Series One, Vol. 3, p. 29.
54. Frances Kenny, p. 206.
55. Alison Abraham (b. 1914), interviewed October 1996, COHP, Transcript Series One, Vol. 3, p. 17.
56. Loma Kent-Johnston (b. 1918), interviewed March 1996, COHP, Transcript Series One, Vol. 3, p. 244.
57. David Stuart Keen, 'Feeding the Lambs: The Influence of Sunday Schools on the Socialization of Children in Otago and Southland, 1848–1901', PhD thesis, University of Otago, 1998, pp. 180–2, 329–44.
58. Keen, pp. 193–226, 254–86.
59. Rosanna Paul (b. 1909), interviewed May 1996, COHP, Transcript Series One, Vol. 2, p. 94.
60. Muriel Richards, 'Cargill Road Memories', in *Methodist Church of New Zealand*,

Centennial of Wesley Church Hillside Road, Dunedin (formerly Cargill Road, now Dunedin South) 1882–1982, (n.p., n.d.), Otago University Library, p. 12.
61 For biographical details, see Margery Blackman, 'Hancock, Annie Doidge', in Jane Thomson (ed.), *Southern People: A Dictionary of Otago Southland Biography*, Dunedin, 1998, p. 209; Rachel Gillett, 'Helpmeets and Handmaidens: The Role of Women in Mission Discourse', BA Hons research essay, University of Otago, 1998, pp. 56–76.
62 Callum Brown, *The Death of Christian Britain: Understanding Secularization, 1800–2000*, London, 2001.
63 See also Rodney Stark and Roger Finke, *Acts of Faith: Explaining the Human Side of Religion*, Berkeley and Los Angeles, 2000.
64 Phillips, *A Man's Country?*, p. 63.
65 Daley, *Girls & Women*, pp. 10–11.
66 Nora Barlow (ed.), *Darwin and Henslow: The Growth of an Idea, Letters 1831–1860*, Berkeley and Los Angeles, 1967, p. 114.
67 Belich, *Making Peoples*, p. 438.
68 *Taranaki Herald*, 24 November 1860.
69 Peter J. Lineham, 'Freethinkers in Nineteenth-century New Zealand', *NZJH*, 19, 1, 1985, pp. 61–81.
70 *Census*, 1891, 1921.
71 *Otago Workman*, 28 June 1889, p. 5; 5 December 1896, p. 11.
72 *Otago Workman*, 24 March 1888, p. 5.
73 Olssen, *Building the New World*, pp. 61–62, 250.
74 Lineham, 'Freethinkers'.
75 Raewyn Dalziel, 'Stout, Anna Paterson', in *The Dictionary of New Zealand Biography, Vol. Two, 1870–1900*, Wellington, 1993, pp. 482–84.
76 Keen, 'Feeding the Lambs', p. 136.
77 H. Jackson, 'Churchgoing in Nineteenth-Century New Zealand', *NZJH*, 17, 1, 1983, pp. 43–59.
78 McLeod, *Religion and the People of Western Europe*, pp. 23–35; for England, see Hugh McLeod, *Religion and Society in England, 1850–1914*, New York, 1996, pp. 11–70.
79 Smith and Clarke, 'Caversham Presbyterian Church 1911', p. 13.
80 Wallis, 'Kew Primitive Methodist Church', p. 11.
81 William Harris (b. 1916), interviewed June 1996, COHP, Transcript Series One, Vol. 2, p. 219.
82 Christine King (b. 1922), interviewed August 1996, COHP, Transcript Series One, Vol. 3, pp. 183–4, 185.
83 McLeod, *Religion and Society in England*, pp. 54–56.
84 Pat Donnelly (b. 1910), interviewed March 2000 by Shaun Broadley, COHP, Transcript Series Two, Vol. 1, pp. 46–49, 55, 60.
85 Phillips, *A Man's Country?*, pp. 63, 69–70.
86 This account is based on the description in Charlotte Macdonald, *A Woman of Good Character: Single Women as Immigrant Settlers in Nineteenth-Century New Zealand*, Wellington, 1990, pp. 179–81.
87 Erik Olssen, 'Families and the Gendering of European New Zealand in the Colonial Period, 1840–1880', in Caroline Daley and Deborah Montgomerie (eds), *The Gendered Kiwi*, Auckland, 1999, pp. 37–62, quotation on p. 48.
88 Pat Donnelly (b. 1910), interviewed March 2000 by Shaun Broadley, COHP, Transcript Series Two, Vol. 2, pp. 43–44.
89 Ian Martin (b. 1912), interviewed March 2000 by Shaun Broadley, COHP, Transcript Series Two, Vol. 2, pp. 165–66, 170–1.
90 *Four Square*, 1, 6, 1921, p. 1; Olssen, *Building the New World*, p. 39; William Harris, pp. 209, 227.
91 Anne O'Brien, '"A Church Full of Men": Masculinism and the Church in Australian History', *Australian Historical Studies*, 29, 3, 1993, pp. 437–57.
92 Maurice Gee, *Plumb*, Wellington, 1979.
93 For biographical information on Dutton, see Olssen, *Building the New World*, p. 39; 'Dutton, Daniel' in Thomson (ed.), *Southern People*, p. 143.
94 Olssen, *Building the New World*, pp. 214–25.
95 On Sidey, see Olssen, *Building the New World*, pp. 202–6, 210–12.

Endpiece Marriage

1 *ODT*, 12 January 1900, p. 7.
2 *ODT*, 2 January 1900, p. 4.
3 *ODT*, 10 January 1900, p. 7.
4 *ODT*, 17 January 1900, p. 3.
5 Nancy Cott, *Public Vows: A History of Marriage and the Nation*, Cambridge, 2002, p. 7.
6 Cott, *Public Vows*, p. 11.
7 Cott, *Public Vows*, p. 10.
8 *ODT*, 13 January 1900, p. 2.
9 *ODT*, 13 January 1900, p. 2.
10 *ODT*, 2 January 1900, p. 5.
11 *ODT*, 2 January 1900, p. 5.

12 *ODT*, 10 January 1900, p. 7.
13 ODT, 13 January 1900, p. 2.
14 *ODT*, 17 January 1900, p. 3.
15 *ODT*, 10 January 1900, p. 7.
16 *ODT*, 10 January 1900, p. 7.
17 *ODT*, 13 January 1900, p. 2.
18 *ODT*, 10 January 1900, p. 7.
19 *ODT*, 12 January 1900, p. 7.
20 *ODT*, 1 March 1900, p. 7.
21 *ODT*, 3 March 1900, p. 7.
22 *ODT*, 3 March 1900, p. 7.
23 Criminal Trial file, DAAC/D256, 11/11/192, Archives New Zealand, Dunedin.
24 Joan W. Scott, 'A Statistical Representation of Work', in Scott, *Gender and the Politics of History*, Columbia University Press, 1988, p. 115.

Appendix II

1 I wish to thank Erik Olssen and Annabel Cooper for their assistance with the introduction and the sections on oral histories and the Benevolent records.
2 Joan Wallach Scott, 'Gender: A Useful Category of Historical Analysis', in *Gender and the Politics of History*, New York, 1988, pp. 28–50.
3 A more detailed account of this process can be found in Erik Olssen, Tom Brooking, Brian Heenan, Hamish James, Bruce McLennan and Clyde Griffen, 'Urban Society and the Opportunity Structure in New Zealand, 1902–22: the Caversham Project', *Social History*, 24, 1, 1999, pp. 39–54.
4 For further discussion of the process of designing and operating a database comprising historical data, see David Hood, 'Past Lessons: Best Practice in Quantitative Historical Research', in Miles Fairburn and Erik Olssen (eds), *Class, Mobility and Voting in New Zealand, 1900–1954*, University of Otago Press, forthcoming.
5 For a discussion of this question, see David Hood, 'Matching Multiple Data Sources from New Zealand: The Experience of the Caversham Project', *History and Computing*, 12, 2, 2000, pp. 227–43.
6 The five volumes of transcripts, together with the sub-series, are held by the project, care of the History Department, University of Otago; the Hocken Library, University of Otago; and the Otago Settlers Museum. Sub-series One: Clothing/Courtship and Marriage (1996), five interviews; Sub-series Two: Wealth and Poverty (1996), nine interviews; Sub-series Three: Transport (1996), 10 interviews; Medical Series (1996), access restricted, 24 interviews.
7 While text in the database has extra subject terms associated with it to aid searching, these associated entries do not appear as part of the interviews. The text in the database is identical to the transcript.
8 Oral History Interviews [Religion and Secondary Education], Series Two, Vol. 1, four interviews, Shaun Broadley (ed.), Caversham Working Paper (CWP), 2000-1; Oral History Interviews with Lebanese of Southern Dunedin, six interviews, Shaun Broadley (ed.), CWP 2001-3. The University of Otago Research Committee also funded a series of interviews by Dr Broadley on religion, which have been added to the NUD*IST database.
9 Hamish James, 'A Database for All Seasons', *Archifacts*, October 1998, pp. 57–71.
10 For the year 1911 onwards, we scanned the entire electoral rolls for Dunedin Central and Dunedin South, but did not check or code information for people resident outside the study area.
11 The issue and the method are discussed fully in Erik Olssen and Maureen Hickey, *Class and Occupation: The New Zealand Reality*, University of Otago Press, forthcoming, ch. 4.
12 344 records relating to civil marriages and 2668 Intention to Marry certificates were gathered for the South Dunedin and Caversham area between the years 1893 and 1913; see Shaun Ryan, 'Intention to Marry Certificates: Preliminary Analysis, 1893–1912', CWP 1997-2, and 'Registry Marriages 1893–1920', CWP 1997-3.
13 See the comprehensive series of reports on church marriage records by Andrea Watson and Kate Smith, 'Marriage Records', and Shaun Broadley's series on extant archival sources, including evidence of membership, in 'Church Records', Caversham Project, History Department, University of Otago (these will be located in the Hocken Library when the project ends).
14 Penelope Isaac and Erik Olssen, 'The Justification for Labour's Housing Scheme: The Discourse of "the Slum"', in Barbara Brookes (ed.), *At Home in New Zealand: History, Houses, People*, Wellington, 2000, pp. 107–24.
15 Penelope Isaac, '"No Room for Luxuries": Aspects of Life in a Working-class New

Zealand Community in the 1930s', MA thesis, University of Otago, 1999.
16 See Marian Horan, 'The Outdoor Relief Database: An Introduction', CWP 1999-1. Marian Horan also drew on this work for her innovative study, 'The In-dependent Women? Women, Work and Charitable Aid in Otago 1895 to 1905', BA Hons research essay, University of Otago, 1997.
17 Annabel Cooper with Marian Horan and Eva Lubcke (eds), 'Transcripts from the Otago Benevolent Institution's Outdoor Relief Casebooks', 3 vols, CWP 2000-3.
18 Shaun Ryan, 'Friendly Societies: Caversham and South Dunedin', CWP 1997-1.
19 Linda Rebekah Lodge was not in the study area, but was collected in order to increase the number of women lodge members in the database.
20 Conrad Schumacher, 'Why Did So Many Babies Die? Infant Mortality and Causes of Death in Dunedin 1900–20', BA Hons research essay, University of Otago, 1998.
21 See also Mark Bailey and Thomas Ryan, 'Telephone Subscription in the Caversham Study Area 1910–22', History 351 research essay, University of Otago, 1998, and Kirsten Wilson, '"Who's That on the Line?" Telephone Subscription in the Caversham Study Area 1910–28, History 351 research essay, University of Otago, 2001.
22 Michael Hamblyn, *Down Every Street and Byway: Finding Your Family with Stone's New Zealand Directories*, Dunedin, 2001.
23 See Alison Holmes, 'Occupational Mobility within the National Railway Classification (D-3) Lists 1912 and 1920', CWP 2002-2.

Select Bibliography

A volume such as this, in which authors draw on a diverse range of disciplinary literatures, cannot hope to produce a full bibliography of manageable size. The list that follows is therefore selective, and includes only secondary sources. Information on the major primary sources that form the databases of the Caversham Project is included in Appendix II, Qualitative and Quantitative Databases. Many theses, dissertations and class essays or reports that have taken the southern suburbs of Dunedin and these databases as their subject are detailed in the endnotes to each chapter. A full list of these can be found at http://caversham.otago.ac.nz.

The general section below includes selected items cited in chapters one and two, items significant for the volume as a whole, or for several chapters, and selected publications arising from the Caversham Project. The following chapter sections identify the most important items for each chapter not already listed in the general section.

General

Aitken, H. J. A., *St Kilda: The First Hundred Years. A Short History of the Borough of St Kilda 1875–1975*, St Kilda, 1975.
Brookes, Barbara (ed.), *At Home in New Zealand: History, Houses, People*, Wellington, 2000.
Brookes, Barbara, Charlotte Macdonald and Margaret Tennant (eds), *Women in History: Essays in European Women's History*, Wellington, 1986.
Brookes, Barbara, Charlotte Macdonald and Margaret Tennant (eds), *Women in History 2*, Wellington, 1992.
Brooking, Tom, Dick Martin, David Thomson and Hamish James, 'The Ties that Bind: Persistence in a New World Industrial Suburb, 1902–22', *Social History*, 24, 1, 1999, pp. 55–73.
Bunkle, Phillida, and Beryl Hughes (eds), *Women in New Zealand Society*, Wellington, 1980.
Butler, Judith, *Gender Trouble: Feminism and the Subversion of Identity*, New York, 1990.
Butler, Judith, and Joan W. Scott (eds), *Feminists Theorize the Political*, New York, 1992.
Carnes, Mark C., and Clyde Griffen, *Meanings for Manhood: Constructions of Masculinity in Victorian America*, Chicago, 1990.
Clark, W. A. V., 'Dunedin in 1901: A Study in Historical Urban Geography', MA thesis, University of Canterbury, 1961.
Cooper, Annabel, Robin Law, Jane Malthus and Pamela Wood, 'Rooms of Their Own: public toilets and gendered citizens in a New Zealand city 1860–1940', *Gender, Place and Culture*, 7, 4, 2000, pp. 417–33.
Cooper, Annabel, and Maureen Molloy, 'Poverty, Dependence and "Women": Reading Autobiography and Social Policy from 1930s New Zealand', *Gender & History*, 9, 1, 1997, pp. 36–59.
Cooper, Winston, . . . *Always a Southern Man: The History of the Southern Rugby Football Club 1884–1984*, Dunedin, [1984].
Cowan, Ruth Schwartz, *More Work for Mother: The Ironies of Household Technology from the Open Hearth to the Microwave*, New York, 1983.
Cresswell, Tim, *In Place/Out of Place: Geography, Ideology and Transgression*, London, 1996.
Daley, Caroline, *Girls & Women, Men & Boys: Gender in Taradale, 1886–1930*, Auckland, 1999.
Daley, Caroline, '"He Would Know But I Just Have a Feeling": Gender and Oral History', *Women's History Review*, 7, 3, 1998, pp. 343–59.
Daley, Caroline, and Deborah Montgomerie (eds), *The Gendered Kiwi*, Auckland, 1999.
Daley, Caroline, and Melanie Nolan (eds), *Suffrage and Beyond: International Feminist Perspectives*, Auckland, 1994.
Dalley, Bronwyn, and Bronwyn Labrum (eds), *Fragments: New Zealand Social and Cultural History*, Auckland, 2000.
Deacon, Desley, 'Political Arithmetic: The Nineteenth Century Australian Census and the Construction of the Dependent Woman', *Signs*, 11, 1, 1985, pp. 27–47.
Deacon, Desley, *Managing Gender: The State, the New Middle Class and Women Workers 1830–1930*, Melbourne, 1989.
Else, Anne (ed.), *Women Together: A History of Women's Organisations in New Zealand/Nga Ropu Wahine o te Motu*, Wellington, 1993.

SELECT BIBLIOGRAPHY

Fairburn, Miles, *The Ideal Society and Its Enemies: The Foundations of Modern New Zealand Society, 1850–1900*, Auckland, 1989.
Fairburn, Miles, and Erik Olssen (eds), *Class, Mobility and Voting in New Zealand, 1900–1954*, University of Otago Press, forthcoming.
Gilson, Miriam, 'The Changing New Zealand Family: A Demographic Analysis', in Stewart Houston (ed.), *Marriage and the Family in New Zealand*, Wellington, 1970, pp. 41–65.
Granovetter, Mark, 'Economic Action and Social Structure: The Problem of Embeddedness', *American Journal of Sociology*, 91, 1985, pp. 481–510.
Granovetter, Mark, and Charles Tilly, 'Inequality and the Labour Market', in Neil Smelser (ed.), *Handbook of Sociology*, New York, 1988.
Griffen, Clyde, 'The New World Working-Class Suburb Revisited: Residential Differentiation in Caversham, New Zealand', *Journal of Urban History*, 27, 4, 2001, pp. 420–44.
Griffen, Clyde, and Sally Griffen, *Natives and Newcomers: The Ordering of Opportunity in Mid-Nineteenth-Century Poughkeepsie*, Cambridge, Mass., 1978.
Grimshaw, Patricia, *Women's Suffrage in New Zealand*, Auckland, 2nd edition, 1987.
Hamer, David, *New Towns in the New World: Images and Perceptions of the Nineteenth-Century Urban Frontier*, New York, 1990.
Hanson, Susan, and Geraldine Pratt, *Gender, Work and Space*, London, 1995.
Heenan, L. D. B., 'Rural-Urban Distribution of Fertility in South Island, New Zealand', *Annals of the Association of American Geographers*, 57, 4, 1967, pp. 713–35.
Holt, James, *Compulsory Arbitration in New Zealand: The First Forty Years*, Auckland, 1986.
Hood, David, 'Matching Multiple Data Sources from New Zealand: The Experience of the Caversham Project', *History and Computing*, 12, 2, 2000, pp. 227–43.
Horrell, Sara, and Jane Humphries, 'The Origins and Expansion of the Male Breadwinner Family: The Case of Nineteenth-Century Britain', *International Review of Social History*, Supplement 5, 42, 1997, pp. 24–64.
James, Bev, and Kay Saville-Smith, *Gender, Culture and Power: Challenging New Zealand's Gendered Culture*, 2nd edition, Auckland, 1994.
Johnson, Louise, *Placebound: Australian Feminist Geographies*, Melbourne, 2000.
Katz, Michael B., *The People of Hamilton, Canada West: Family and Class in a Mid-Nineteenth-Century City*, Cambridge, 1975.
Laqueur, Thomas, *Making Sex: Body and Gender from the Greeks to Freud*, London, 1990.
Laurie, N., C. Dwyer, S. Holloway and F. Smith, *Geographies of the New Femininities*, Harlow, UK, 1999.
Law, Robin, 'Beyond "Women and Transport": Towards New Geographies of Gender and Daily Mobility', *Progress in Human Geography*, 23, 4, 1999, pp. 567–88.
Law, Robin, 'Gender and Daily Mobility in a New Zealand City, 1920–1960', *Social & Cultural Geography*, 3, 4, 2002, pp. 425–45.
Law, Robin, Hugh Campbell and John Dolan (eds), *Masculinities in Aotearoa/New Zealand*, Palmerston North, 2000.
Lee, Mary Isabella, *The Not So Poor: An Autobiography*, Annabel Cooper (ed.), Auckland, 1993.
McClure, Margaret, *A Civilised Community: A History of Social Security in New Zealand, 1898–1998*, Auckland, 1998.
McDonald, K. C., *City of Dunedin: A Century of Civic Enterprise*, Dunedin, 1965.
McDowell, Linda, *Gender, Identity and Place: Understanding Feminist Geographies*, Minneapolis, 1999.
McDowell, Linda, and Joanne P. Sharpe (eds), *Space, Gender, Knowledge: Feminist Readings*, London, 1997.
Massey, Doreen, 'A Global Sense of Place', in Trevor Barnes and Derek Gregory (eds), *Reading Human Geography: The Poetics and Politics of Inquiry*, London, 1997, pp. 315–23.
Nicholson, Linda, and Steven Seidman (eds), *Social Postmodernism: Beyond Identity Politics*, Cambridge, 1995.
Nolan, Melanie, *Breadwinning: New Zealand Women and the State*, Christchurch, 2000.
Olssen, Erik, 'Friendly Societies in New Zealand, 1840–1990', in Marcel van der Linden (ed.), *Social Security Mutualism: The Comparative History of Mutual Benefit Societies*, Bern, 1996, pp. 177–206.
Olssen, Erik, *Building the New World: Work, Politics and Society in Caversham, 1880s–1920s*, Auckland, 1995.
Olssen, Erik, *A History of Otago*, Dunedin, 1984.

Olssen, Erik, Tom Brooking, Brian Heenan, Hamish James, Bruce McLennan and Clyde Griffen, 'Urban Society and the Opportunity Structure in New Zealand, 1902–22: The Caversham Project', *Social History*, 24, 1, 1999, pp. 39–54.
Olssen, Erik, and Maureen Hickey, *Class and Occupation: The New Zealand Reality*, University of Otago Press, forthcoming.
Olssen, Erik, and Hamish James, 'Social Mobility and Class Formation: The Worklife Social Mobility of Men in a New Zealand Suburb, 1902–1928', *International Review of Social History*, 4, 3, 1999, pp. 419–49.
Olssen, Erik, and Andrée Levesque, 'Towards a History of the European Family in New Zealand', in Peggy G. Koopman-Boyden (ed.), *Families in New Zealand Society*, Wellington, 1978.
Paul, J. T., *Our Majority: Some Dark Shadows and High Lights of Industrial History*, Dunedin, 1910.
Pearson, David G., *Johnsonville: Continuity and Change in a New Zealand Township*, Sydney, 1979.
Phillips, Jock, *A Man's Country? The Image of the Pakeha Male–A History*, 2nd edition, Auckland, 1996.
Reeves, W. P., *State Experiments in Australia and New Zealand*, Melbourne, 1968 (first published 1902).
Riley, Denise, *'Am I That Name?': Feminism and the Category of 'Women' in History*, Houndmills, 1988.
Roberts, Elizabeth, *A Woman's Place: An Oral History of Working-Class Women 1890–1940*, Oxford, 1984.
Rutherford, Alma, *The Edge of the Town: Historic Caversham As Seen Through Its Streets and Buildings*, Dunedin, 1978.
Scates, Bruce, 'Mobilizing Manhood: Gender and the Great Strike in Australia and Aotearoa/New Zealand', *Gender & History*, 9, 2, 1997, pp. 285–309.
Scott, Joan W., *Gender and the Politics of History*, New York, 1988.
Seccombe, W., 'Patriarchy Stabilized: The Construction of the Male-Breadwinner Wage Norm in Nineteenth-Century Britain', *Social History*, II, 1, 1986, pp. 53–76.
Seccombe, Wally, *Weathering the Storm: Working-Class Families from the Industrial Revolution to the Fertility Decline*, London, 1993.
Shapiro, Ann-Louise (ed.), *Feminists Revision History*, New Brunswick, 1994.
Sinclair, Keith, *A Destiny Apart: New Zealand's Search for National Identity*, Wellington, 1986.
Stedman, G. N., 'The South Dunedin Flat: A Study in Urbanisation 1849–1965', MA thesis, University of Otago, 1966.
Tennant, Margaret, 'Sister Mabel's Private Diary 1907–1910: Sisterhood, Love and Religious Doubt', *Women's Studies Journal*, 14, 1, 1998, pp. 43–59.
Thernstrom, Stephan, *Poverty and Progress: Social Mobility of a Nineteenth Century City*, Cambridge, 1964.
Thomlinson, Kirsten, 'We the Undersigned: An Analysis of Signatories to the 1893 Women's Suffrage Petition from Southern Dunedin', MA thesis, University of Otago, 2001.
Thomson, Jane (ed.), *Southern People: A Dictionary of Otago Southland Biography*, Dunedin, 1998.
Tilly, Louise A., and Joan W. Scott, *Women, Work and Family*, New York, 1978.
Toynbee, Claire, *Her Work and His: Family, Kin and Community in New Zealand 1900–1930*, Wellington, 1995.
Turner, Kenneth W., 'Henry Smith Fish and the Opposition to the Female Franchise in Dunedin, 1890–1893', BA Hons research essay, University of Otago, 1985.
Vosburgh, Miriam Gilson, *The New Zealand Family and Social Change: A Trend Analysis*, Wellington, 1978.
White, Jerry, *The Worst Street in North London: Campbell Bunk, Islington, Between the Wars*, London, 1986.
Wilson, Dean, 'Community and Gender in Victorian Auckland', *New Zealand Journal of History (NZJH)*, 30, 1, 1996, pp. 24–42.

Three Working Gender, Gendering Work

Bourke, Joanna, *Working-Class Cultures in Britain, 1890–1960: Gender, Class and Ethnicity*, London, 1994.
Castles, Francis G., *The Working Class and Welfare: Reflections on the Political Development of the Welfare State in Australia and New Zealand, 1890–1980*, Wellington, 1985.
Creighton, Colin, 'The Rise of the Male Breadwinner Family: A Reappraisal', *Comparative Studies in Society and History*, 38, 2, 1996, pp. 310–37.
Harper, Penelope, and Melanie Nolan, 'Morison, Harriet', in Claudia Orange (ed.), *The Dictionary of New Zealand Biography (DNZB), Volume Two, 1870–1900*, Wellington, 1993, pp. 336–37.

Lake, Marilyn, 'Socialism and Manhood: The Case of William Lane', *Labor History*, 50, 1986, pp. 54–62.
Lake, Marilyn, 'The Politics of Respectability: Identifying the Masculinist Context', *Historical Studies*, 22, 1, 1986, pp. 116–31.
Nolan, Melanie, '"Politics Swept Under a Domestic Carpet"? Fracturing Domesticity and the Male Breadwinner Wage: Women's Economic Citizenship, 1920s–1940s', *NZJH*, 27, 2, 1993, pp. 199–217.
Nolan, Melanie, 'Unstitching the New Zealand State: Its Role in Domesticity and Its Decline', *International Review of Social History*, 45, 2, 2000, pp. 251–77.
Nolan, Melanie, 'Employment Organisations', in Anne Else (ed.), *Women Together: A History of Women's Organisations in New Zealand/Nga Ropu Wahine o te Motu*, Wellington, 1993, pp. 195–207.
Nolan, Melanie, and Penelope Harper, 'Dunedin Tailoresses' Union, 1889–1945, in Anne Else (ed.), *Women Together: A History of Women's Organisations in New Zealand/Nga Ropu Wahine o te Motu*, Wellington, 1993, pp. 208–11.
Olssen, Erik, and Maureen Hickey, *Class and Occupation: The New Zealand Reality*, University of Otago Press, forthcoming.
Robertson, Stephen, 'Women Workers and the New Zealand Arbitration Court 1894–1920', in Raelene Frances and Bruce Scates (eds), *Women, Work and the Labour Movement in Australia and Aotearoa/New Zealand*, Sydney, 1991, pp. 30–41.

Four Schooling for a Gendered Future

Fry, Ruth, *It's Different for Daughters: A History of the Curriculum for Girls in New Zealand Schools, 1900–1975*, Wellington, 1985.
Goodyear, Rosemary, 'Black Boots and Pinafores: Childhood in Otago, 1900–1920', MA thesis, University of Otago, 1992.
Lee, G., 'From Rhetoric to Reality: A History of the Development of the Common Core Curriculum in New Zealand Post-Primary Schools 1900–1945', PhD thesis, University of Otago, 1991.
Lee, H. F., 'The Credentialled Society: A History of New Zealand Public School Examinations 1871–1990', PhD thesis, University of Otago, 1991.
McCulloch, Gary (ed.), *The School Curriculum in New Zealand*, Palmerston North, 1992.
Middleton, Sue (ed.), *Women and Education in Aotearoa*, Wellington, 1988.
Openshaw, Roger, and David McKenzie (eds), *Reinterpreting the Educational Past: Essays in the History of New Zealand Education*, Wellington, 1987.
Tennant, Margaret, 'Natural Directions: The New Zealand Movement for Sexual Differentiation during the Early Twentieth Century', in Barbara Brookes, Charlotte Macdonald and Margaret Tennant (eds), *Women in History: Essays in European Women's History*, Wellington, 1986, pp. 87–100.
Wallis, Eileen, *A Most Rare Vision: Otago Girls' High School – the First One Hundred Years*, Dunedin, 1972.

Five Producing and Consuming Gender

Brickell, Chris, 'Through the (New) Looking Glass: Gendered Bodies, Fashion and Resistance in Post-war New Zealand', *Journal of Consumer Culture*, 2, 2, 2002, pp. 241–69.
Consedine, Bill, 'Inequality and the Egalitarian Myth', in David Novitz and Bill Willmott (eds), *Culture and Identity in New Zealand*, Wellington, 1989, pp. 172–86.
Cooper, Grace Rogers, *The Sewing Machine: Its Invention and Development*, 2nd edition, Washington DC, 1976.
McRobbie, Angela, 'Bridging the Gap: Feminism, Fashion and Consumption', *Feminist Review*, 55, 1997, pp. 73–89.
Malthus, Jane, 'Dressmakers in Nineteenth Century New Zealand', in Barbara Brookes, Charlotte Macdonald, Margaret Tennant (eds), *Women in History 2*, Wellington, 1992, pp. 77–78.
Malthus, Jane, '"Bifurcated and Not Ashamed": Late Nineteenth-Century Dress Reformers in New Zealand', *NZJH*, 23, 1, 1989, pp. 32–46.
Nava, Mica, 'Consumerism Reconsidered', in Morag Shiach (ed.), *Feminism and Cultural Studies*, New York, 1999, pp. 45–64.
Nenadic, Stana, 'The Social Shaping of Business Behaviour in the Nineteenth-Century Women's Garment Trades', *Journal of Social History*, 31, 3, 1998, pp. 625–45.
Steedman, Carolyn, *Landscape for a Good Woman*, London, 1986.

Six Spare Time?
Daley, Caroline, 'Selling Sandow: Modernity and Leisure in Early Twentieth-Century New Zealand', *NZJH*, 34, 2, 2000, pp. 241–61.
Daley, Caroline, 'A Gendered Domain: Leisure in Auckland, 1890–1940', in Caroline Daley and Deborah Montgomerie (eds), *The Gendered Kiwi*, Auckland, 1999, pp. 213–34.
Hammer, M. A. E., '"Something Else in the World to Live For": Sport and the Physical Emancipation of Women and Girls in Auckland 1880–1920', MA thesis, University of Auckland, 1990.
Langhamer, Claire, 'Towards a Feminist Framework for the History of Women's Leisure, 1920–1960', in Anne-Marie Gallagher, Cathy Labelska, Louise Ryan (eds), *Re-presenting the Past: Women and History*, London, 2001, pp. 198–215.
Langhamer, Claire, *Women's Leisure in England: 1920–60*, Manchester, 2000.
Macdonald, Charlotte, 'Organisations in Sport, Recreation and Leisure', in Anne Else (ed.), *Women Together: A History of Women's Organisations in New Zealand/Nga Ropu Wahine o te Motu*, Wellington, 1993, pp. 405–16.
Price, Simon, *New Zealand's First Talkies: Early Film-making in Otago and Southland 1896–1939*, Dunedin, 1996.
Simpson, Claire, 'Respectable Identities: New Zealand Nineteenth-Century "New Women" – on Bicycles!', *International Journal of the History of Sport*, 18, 2, 2001, pp. 54–77.
Sutton-Smith, Brian, *A History of Children's Play: The New Zealand Playground 1840–1950*, Wellington, 1982 (first published in Philadelphia, 1981).

Seven Down and Out on the Flat
Fairburn, Miles, *Nearly Out of Heart and Hope: The Puzzle of a Colonial Labourer's Diary*, Auckland, 1995.
Fraser, Nancy, and Linda Gordon, 'A Genealogy of Dependency: Tracing a Keyword of the US Welfare State', *Signs*, 19, 1994, pp. 309–36.
Gordon, Linda, *Pitied But Not Entitled: Single Mothers and the History of Welfare 1890–1935*, New York, 1994.
Heenan, Brian, 'Population Ageing Among Non-Maori New Zealanders in Later Victorian Times: A Quirk of Immigrant Settlement History?', *NZJH*, 35, 2, 2001, pp. 177–203.
Henderson, John, and Richard Wall (eds), *Poor Women and Children in the European Past*, London, 1994.
Husbands, Paul, 'Poverty in Freeman's Bay 1886–1913', *NZJH*, 28, 1, 1994, pp. 3–21.
Rose, Sonya O., *Limited Livelihoods: Gender and Class in Nineteenth-Century England*, London, 1992.
Tennant, Margaret, 'The Decay of Home Life? The Home in Early Welfare Discourses', in Barbara Brookes (ed.), *At Home in New Zealand: History, Houses, People*, Wellington, 2000, pp. 24–40.
Tennant, Margaret, *Paupers and Providers: Charitable Aid in New Zealand*, Wellington, 1989.
Thomson, David, *A World Without Welfare: New Zealand's Colonial Experiment*, Auckland, 1998.
Vincent, David, *Poor Citizens: The State and the Poor in Twentieth-Century Britain*, London, 1991.
Zelizer, Viviana, *The Social Meaning of Money: Pin Money, Paychecks, Poor Relief, and Other Currencies*, New York, 1994.

Eight To and From, There and Back
Barbara, Olga, 'Hananeia, Sarah', in Jane Thomson (ed.), *Southern People: A Dictionary of Otago Southland Biography*, Dunedin, 1998, p. 209.
Clark, W. A. V., 'Locational Stress and Residential Mobility in a New Zealand Context', *New Zealand Geographer*, 31, 1, 1975, pp. 67–79.
Fraser, Lyndon, and Katie Pickles (eds), *Shifting Centres: Women and Migration in New Zealand History*, Dunedin, 2002.
Gleeson, B. J., 'A Public Space for Women: The Case of Charity in Colonial Melbourne', *Area*, 27, 1995, pp. 193–207.
Griffen, Clyde, 'The New World Working Class Suburb Revisited: Residential Differentiation in Caversham, New Zealand', *Journal of Urban History*, 27, 4, 2001, pp. 420–44.
Heenan, L. D. B., 'The Urbanisation of New Zealand's Population: Demographic Patterns in the South Island, 1881–1961', in R. J. Johnston (ed.), *Urbanisation in New Zealand: Geographical Essays*, Wellington, 1973, pp. 108–31.

SELECT BIBLIOGRAPHY

Sanders, M. C., 'The Lebanese Community in Dunedin before 1936', BA Hons research essay, University of Otago, 1980.
Zelinsky, W., 'The Hypothesis of the Mobility Transition', *Geographical Review*, 61, 1966, pp. 219–49.

Nine On the Streets of Southern Dunedin
Berman, Marshall, *All That Is Solid Melts into Air: The Experience of Modernity*, London, 1983.
Donald, James, *Imagining the Modern City*, London, 1999.
Fyfe, Nicholas, *Images of the Street: Planning, Identity and Control in Public Space*, London, 1998.
Hawkes, Graham, *On the Road: The Car in New Zealand*, Wellington, 1990.
Law, Robin, 'Beyond "Women and Transport": Towards New Geographies of Gender and Daily Mobility', *Progress in Human Geography*, 23, 4, 1999, pp. 567–88.
Revill, George, 'Trained for Life: Personal Identity and the Meaning of Work in the Nineteenth-Century Railway Industry', in Chris Philo (ed.), *New Words, New Worlds: Reconceptualising Social and Cultural Geography*, Lampeter, Wales, 1991, pp. 65–77.
Scharff, Virginia, *Taking the Wheel: Women and the Coming of the Motor Age*, New York, 1991.
Wachs, Martin, 'Men, Women and Wheels: The Historical Basis of Sex Differences in Travel Patterns', *Transportation Research Record*, 1135, 1987, pp. 10–16.
Wachs, Martin, and Margaret Crawford, *The Car and the City: The Automobile, the Built Environment and Daily Urban Life*, Ann Arbor, 1992.
Watson, James, *Links: A History of Transport and New Zealand Society*, Wellington, 1996.

Ten The Risk to Life and Limb
Angus, John, *A History of the Otago Hospital Board and its Predecessors*, Dunedin, 1984.
Brookes, Barbara, 'Hygiene, Health, and Bodily Knowledge, 1880–1940: A New Zealand Case Study', in *Journal of Family History*, 28, 2, 2003, pp. 297–313.
Bryder, Linda (ed.), *A Healthy Country: Essays on the Social History of Medicine in New Zealand*, Wellington, 1991.
Carlyon, Jennifer, 'Friendly Societies 1842–1938: The Benefits of Membership', *NZJH*, 32, 2, 1998, pp. 121–42.
Dow, Derek A., *Safeguarding the Public Health: A History of the New Zealand Department of Health*, Wellington, 1995.
Harrison, Barbara, *Not Only the 'Dangerous Trades': Women's Work and Health in Britain, 1880–1914*, London, 1996.
Labrum, Bronwyn, 'Looking Beyond the Asylum: Gender and the Process of Committal in Auckland, 1870–1910', *NZJH*, 26, 2, 1992, pp. 125–44.
Maclean, F. S., *Challenge for Health: A History of Public Health in New Zealand*, Wellington, 1964.
Reeves, Randall, 'Declining Fertility in England and Wales as a Major Cause of the Twentieth Century Decline in Mortality: The Role of Changing Family Size and Age Structure in Infectious Disease Mortality in Infancy', *American Journal of Epidemiology*, 122, 1, 1985, pp. 112–26.
Tomes, Nancy, 'The Private Side of Public Health: Sanitary Science, Domestic Hygiene, and the Germ Theory, 1870–1900,' *Bulletin of the History of Medicine*, 64, 1990, pp. 509–39.
Verbrugge, Lois M., 'Pathways of Health and Death', in Rima Apple (ed.), *Women, Health and Medicine in America: A Historical Handbook*, New York, 1990, pp. 41–79.

Eleven God, the Devil and Gender
Belich, James, *Paradise Reforged: A History of the New Zealanders from the 1880s to the Year 2000*, Auckland, 2001.
Braude, Anne, 'Women's History *Is* American Religious History', in Thomas Tweed (ed.), *Retelling U. S. Religious History*, Berkeley and Los Angeles, 1997, pp. 87–107.
Brown, Callum, *The Death of Christian Britain: Understanding Secularization, 1800–2000*, London, 2001.
Keen, David Stuart, 'Feeding the Lambs: The Influence of Sunday Schools in the Socialization of Children in Otago and Southland, 1848–1901', PhD thesis, University of Otago, 1999.
McLeod, Hugh, *Religion and Society in England, 1850–1914*, New York, 1996.
McLeod, Hugh, *Religion and the People of Western Europe, 1789–1989*. 2nd edn, New York, 1997.
Munro, Jessie, *The Story of Suzanne Aubert*, Auckland, 1996.
O'Brien, Anne, '"A Church Full of Men": Masculinism and the Church in Australian History', *Australian*

Historical Studies, 29, 3, 1993, pp. 437–57.
Prochaska, F. K., *Women and Philanthropy in Nineteenth-Century England*, Oxford, 1980.
Welter, Barbara, 'The Feminization of American Religion: 1800–1860', in Mary S. Hartman and Lois Banner (eds), *Clio's Consciousness Raised: New Perspectives on the History of Women*, New York, 1974, pp. 137–57.

Twelve Marriage: the Gendered Contract
Cott, Nancy, *Public Vows: A History of Marriage and the Nation*, Cambridge, 2002.
Scott, Joan W., 'A Statistical Representation of Work', in Joan W. Scott, *Gender and the Politics of History*, Columbia University Press, 1988, pp. 113–38.

Notes on Contributors

Emma Beer became retrospectively even more interested in leisure after a short stint in Japan working well beyond Samuel Parnell's '8 for work' each day. This is Emma's first co-authored publication, and she now lives in the UK, working for the Arts and Humanities Data Service at the University of London.

Chris Brickell has spent most of his life in Wellington, moving south in pursuit of opportunities to explore history, gender and sociology in new local settings. He has published an eclectic range of papers on consumption, gender, sexuality and New Zealand politics, with recent writing demonstrating a developing obsession for the 1940s. Chris now teaches in the Gender and Women's Studies Programme at the University of Otago.

Barbara Brookes lives in a male-dominated household, with a husband, three sons and a male dog. Her historical world, however, has been peopled by women and has centred on questions relating to health and fertility control. She teaches history at the University of Otago and enjoys the challenge of keeping her worlds in balance.

Tom Brooking is an old Caversham hand, having taught a course on the project with Erik Olssen in the early 1980s. Generally, he works on things rural and environmental, but he has learned much about the urban and suburban parts of New Zealand under Erik's expert guidance. Coming from a long line of teachers, Tom has also always been interested in the history of education and grew up hearing about the differences between his mother's and his father's experience of teaching. Occasionally, he has worked with Howard Lee on this area.

Annabel Cooper immigrated to Dunedin from Auckland when she was nineteen and now lives on the edge of Otago Harbour. Having completed two degrees, married one Anderson's Bay boy, and had one son and one daughter, her attachment to place is such that she considers herself almost a native. She is head of the Gender and Women's Studies Programme at the University of Otago, and has written on a number of topics (including war, autobiography and public toilets) relating to gender in New Zealand.

Brian Heenan did most of his growing up in North East Valley in the 1940s and 1950s, days when Caversham was a distant blur on his mental place map of Dunedin. And so it remained even after his marriage into a family that had enriched the project's database from the early 1900s and late 1930s. *Sites of Gender* research softened the blur, triggering a realisation that maleness had shaped virtually all activity domains of his youth and young adult life – in a household in which daughters, but not sons, washed, swept and dusted; in boy-only classes at senior primary and through secondary school; in the truly manly sports, his dad said, of rugby and cricket; and also with Father, often a brother, too, but never Mum or any sisters, holidaying at work on a bachelor uncle's farm at Maungatua, where, in late Victorian times, his dad had grown up with eleven brothers and four sisters.

David Hood was raised in Kew. A man of many hats, he looks after and expands the Caversham Project's computer resources, teaches computer courses, works on his doctorate, and tries to maintain a rich home life. His major research interest is in doing justice to the richness of the social world when representing information on the computer.

Marian Horan is an Aucklander by birth and a 'Dunedinite' by marriage. She first came to Dunedin in 1994, when she completed her Bachelors and Masters degrees in New Zealand history at Otago University. She now moves between the cities of London, Binghamton (where she is a doctoral student at 'SUNY-Bing'), and Dunedin, as she fulfills her commitments to family and research. She is following an interest in comparative research first developed at Otago, through her current research on working women and anti-prostitution campaigns in England and the United States.

Sarah Johnsen spent most of her childhood in a small farming community north of Dunedin, before moving to 'Dunners' to study at the University of Otago in 1992. She quickly grew to love the city and ended up staying for ten years, considering herself something of a 'local'. She now lives in East London, where she works as a research associate in the Department of Geography at Queen Mary,

CONTRIBUTORS

University of London. An ongoing interest in issues of gender and geographical mobility – first fostered when working on the Sites of Gender project – is central to her current research on homelessness in the United Kingdom.

Robin Law's first experience of Dunedin in 1994 (after a life spent in South Africa and Los Angeles) was renting a small wooden and scrim cottage in Bathgate St, South Dunedin, with her husband and small daughter. Waiting for the bus by the memorial to the war dead in Hillside Rd, pushing a pram past the tightly packed picket fences of the neighbourhood, and listening to the neighbour's reminiscences about her pub-owning grandfather gave Robin a rich sense of the layers of gendered history on 'the Flat' and led to her involvement in the Caversham Project. She taught urban geography at Otago University and published research on a diversity of topics, including public toilets, masculinity and gendered transport planning.

Howard Lee lives in a (slightly) male-dominated household with a wife, daughter, two sons and a stray (possibly female) cat. Dunedin born and bred, his parents owned and operated businesses in South Dunedin for 32 years. Howard's own teaching and research interests are predominantly in the fields of comparative education, curriculum history and policy, educational assessment and public school examinations, history of New Zealand education, and education policy analysis. Being an identical twin (his brother is also an education academic) has profoundly influenced his views on the importance of individuality and identity. Howard and his brother also share a passion for fine (and expensive-to-maintain) motor cars.

Jane Malthus grew up in a villa in Musselburgh on the Flat, with the beach and the foreshore reclamation as her playgrounds. Interested in dress and fashion from an early age, she and her sister made dolls' clothes, then their own minis, midis and maxis. Jane taught in Clothing and Textiles Sciences at the University of Otago for twenty-one years, but is now following her dreams by embarking on a fine arts degree. She maintains her dress interests as Honorary Curator of Costume at the Otago Museum.

Erik Olssen's parents ensured that he grew up on the edge of the study area and attended King's High School on the Flat. As the eldest of four boys, he was trained to dust and vacuum, feed the chooks and do dishes, although rugby and athletics were his passions. After completing his MA at Otago, he did a PhD at Duke University, returning after six years with a French-Canadian wife, who became a second-wave feminist. They had two sons, and Erik learned to cook things that couldn't be grilled, but proved inept at needlework. Some twelve years after that marriage ended, he remarried an Aucklander and a third-wave feminist, who now lectures in Gender and Women's Studies. They have young twins, a girl and a boy, who bring together the scholarly and the private realms in all sorts of surprising ways.

Dorothy Page, now retired after many years of teaching history and researching women's history and biography at the University of Otago, remembers being brought on childhood visits from flat, open Invercargill to the cramped noisiness of her mother's cousin's place in Bathgate St, South Dunedin. The house was small, dark, solid and well-maintained, and its owner, who worked all his life at Hillside, was proud that it stood on a double section, where he cultivated an excellent vegetable garden. She still remembers vividly the sights and sounds on the short-cut through a crowded industrial area to Cargill's Corner, on the way to catch a tram to town, and she later married a St Clair boy.

John Stenhouse lives in a female-dominated household where he and his son Sean are learning to love, honour and obey! Members of his family lived in Caversham, and several oral histories recorded detailed memories of his great uncle, the Reverend Charlie Sullivan, minister of Caversham Presbyterian Church. The study of religion and gender in southern Dunedin has permanently altered his vision of the past.

Kirsten Thomlinson grew up in Harwood on the Otago Peninsula, enduring a winding 45-minute bus ride into the Flat every day, where she attended high school. The school gates represented the boundary to her southern Dunedin experience, and only very occasionally did she skive off to enjoy the beauty of St Clair beach and a swim in the hot salt-water pools. Kirsten has now opted for new surroundings – moving to Edinburgh, Scotland. Still surrounded by suburbs such as Musselburgh and Corstorphine, and streets such as Grosvenor St and Caledonian Rd, her connections to Dunedin, and indeed the Flat, remain strong.

Index

abortion, 285-6, 306, 311, 361
Abraham, Alison, pseud., 118, 281, 371
accidents, industrial, 285, 288, 300-1, 302; compensation and insurance, 300, 306-7, 309-310, 311-12, 357
aged, and health, 307-8; and poverty, 193, 203, 208-211; old age pensions, 3, 194, 211, 307, 309, 357
alcohol, changing attitudes to, 58-9, 340; health issues, 302-3; men's leisure activity, 153-6, 302-3; rugby and, 165; six o'clock closing, 155-6, 179, 359; *see also* prohibition; Women's Christian Temperance Union
Alex Thompson & Son Ltd, 68
Allen, William, 303
arbitration system, 3, 58, 356; and eight-hour day, 151; and gendered division of work, 64, 65-6; and wages, 80, 215; *see also* Industrial Conciliation and Arbitration Act
arithmetic, gendered teaching of, 97, 103
Armstrong, James, 218
Arnold, James, 62

Barlow, Jessie, 47
Barlow, Thomas, 221
barmaids, work in pubs curtailed, 14, 358
Basham, 'Aunt Daisy', 174
Batchelor, Ferdinand, 59, 115
beauty contests, 178, 184-5, 186, 360
Beck, Margaret, 351
Bellett family, 354
Bennett, Agnes, 59
Bible-in-Schools, 314, 330, 340
Bickerton, A.W., 338
Bock, Amy, 166
body, and clothing changes, 135-8, 140, 165; bodily difference, 50-52; films and, 183; respectability and physical activity, 165, 166, 168; reproductive duties, 166; swimming at the beach, 178; wellbeing of, 293-300; *see also* beauty contests
Boreham, Steve, 88, 155-6
Boulton, Laura, 128, 129, 147, 149
bowls (game), 157-8
brass bands, 170-1, 358
breadwinner, *see* male breadwinner wage
Bridges family, 304
Broadley, Amelia, 47, 201
Brown, Joe, 188
Brown, Kitty, pseud., 119-120, 145, 299, 371
Brown Ewing & Co., 76, 132, 133, 134, 144
Brownlie, Misses, 134, 144
Budden, Charles, 294
Burgess, Mary Ellen, 1

Cadbury Fry Hudson, 76, 301; sports teams, 168-9
Caledonian Games, 158-9
Caledonian Grounds, 27, 158
Cameron, Sir Donald, 89
Campbell, Flora, 168
Cardno, Catherine, 85

Carson, Eva, 185
Cartwright, Mabel, 36, 154, 166-7, 333
Cavanagh, 'Old Vic', 163, 164
Cavanagh, 'Young Vic', 163, 164
Caversham, 16, 27; borough amalgamates with Dunedin, 357; demographic change, 24-6; description, 28-30, 36, 39; female occupations, 23-4; history of development, 19-22, 289; library, 179; male occupations, 22-3; map, 28; migration to, 230; poor in, 191; suffrage petition and, 48-9; tramline, 262; transience, 230; *see also* the Flat; Forbury
Caversham Baptist Church, 323, 327, 328, 333; Bible Class, 343; dances, 188; Girls' and Boys' Brigades, 175, 360
Caversham Industrial School, 14, 20, 73, 212-14; children of widowers, 208
Caversham Methodist Church, 331, 340
Caversham Presbyterian Church, 332, 339-40
Caversham Primary School, 94, 95, 96, 99, 100; break-up day, 91, 103; choir, 172; destinations of Std 6 pupils, 105; pupils going to secondary school, 111-12; school cadets, 101
Caversham Project, vii, 2, 10, 17, 26, 230; qualitative and quantitative databases, 362-70
Child Welfare Act (1925), 360
childbirth, 290, 304-6; *see also* midwives
children, as recipients of outdoor relief, 199; child-centred families, 175; contribution to family economy, 60, 120, 200-203; films and, 183; leisure activities, 175-6; mobility, 271; play, 13, 175, 277-8; use of trams, 278; *see also* education; family size; playgrounds
Chinese, 36, 351; employment, 55, 80; in Otago Benevolent Institution, 36, 210-11, 313; market gardeners, 20, 33, 265; pensions for, 361; religions, 323
Christie, Matilda, 210
churches, and suffrage, 46; attraction for men, 342-3; attraction for women, 331-2, 346; campaign for prohibition, 155; education activities of, 333-4; feminisation of NZ religion, 325-336; gender and attendance, 313, 324-5, 326-7, 330-1, 339-341; Grimmett family and, 251, 313; on the Flat, 316, 323-5; sports clubs, 175, 333, 342; youth activities, 332-3, 335, 342; *see also* evangelical churches; Protestant churches; religious belief; Roman Catholics; specific churches e.g. Caversham Baptist Church
circulatory mobility, 229-230, 242-57, 283-4; gender differences, 246-51; 253-6; young single women and, 242-3; *see also* mobility; migration
class, *see* social class; occupations
cleaning, 293-6; 310-11
clerical work, 71-2, 76-7; popularity of, 116-7, 121-2; school education for, 92, 113, 116-17; *see also* white collar/blouse workers
Clint, Mary, 210
clothing, as signifier of gendered identity, 149-150; as status symbol, 141-2, 146-9; bathing costumes, 138, 149, 177-8; changes in men's dress, 140-3; changes in women's dress, 134-140; clothes swapping, 145-6; homemade, 144-5; respectability and, 279; *see also*

428

INDEX

corsets; hats; rational dress
clothing trade, factories and workshops, 125-30; gender and, 124-5, 127-9; production and consumption in, 123-5, 143, 146; retail outlets, 130-3; women in, 76; *see also* dressmakers; tailoresses; tailors
Conn, John, 216
consumption, in clothing trade, 123-5, 143, 146; in the household, 67-8; in transport, 271-2; motor car and, 282
Contagious Diseases Act (1869), 341-2
Cooke, Fred, 181, 267
Cooke Howlison, 266, 267
Cooper, Marion, pseud., 38, 64, 83, 84, 241, 274, 279, 296, 298, 371
corporal punishment, 100-1
corsets, 134, 138, 139
Cost of Living Commission, 62, 358
Coughtrey, Dr Millen, 291-2
Cranefield, Ruth Kate, 285-6, 287, 311
Crossan, Donald, 163, 285, 286, 312
Crossan, Phyllis, 143, 276, 280, 295, 296
Cumming, Jessie, 100, 104
curriculum, school, gender and, 97-8, 102-3, 113; in secondary schools, 112-20; manual training, 97, 100
cycling, 260, 261, 263; cycle trade, 265, 267; gender and, 274-6; transport to work, 274-5, 280; women and, 165-6, 275

Daley, Caroline, and Taradale research, 7, 11, 93, 97, 100, 103, 152-3
dancing, 186-8, 280, 281, 360; organised by churches, 333, 342
Darby, Jean, pseud., 128, 145, 148, 220, 371
Davidson, Alexander, 73-4
Dean, Jocelyn, pseud., 72, 77, 371
department stores, and women workers, 76-7, 131; clothing trade, 125-6, 130-1; *see also* specific stores, e.g., DIC
Depression, *see* Great Depression; Long Depression
deserted wives, 194, 206, 207, 217, 226; pensions for, 361
DIC, 76, 126, 131, 273
Dickie, Alexander, 302
Direct Distributing Co., 76
domestic science, becomes compulsory in schools, 115-6, 117, 293, 359; cooking, 97, 100, 117; health care, 292-3; sewing, 97; unpopular at King Edward Technical College, 116-7, 122; *see also* cleaning; dressmakers; health
domestic service, 67, 73-4; health problems in, 302, 304; schools and, 92, 113; Violet Watson, 136; *see also* housework
domestic violence, 303, 355
Dominion Tailoring and Mercery Co., 76
Donaghy's, 21, 31, 55, 61, 76
Donald, Miss, 95
Donaldson, 'Weasel', 163
Donnelly, Pat, pseud., 104, 117, 147, 342, 371
Donovan, Daniel, 303
Drapery Supply Association, 123, 144
drapery trade, 131-2
dressmakers, 127, 128, 130, 132-3, 134; home dressmaking skills, 139, 144; working from home, 143-4; *see also* tailoresses

drugs, 351-2
Duckett, Mrs, 210
Duncan, Maggie, 304
Dunedin Lyceum, 313, 315
Dunedin Public Hospital, 291, 301
Dunedin Tailoresses' Union, 41, 56-7, 65, 67, 86, 87, 356; and wages, 79
Dutton, Rev. Daniel, 332, 343-4, 345

Earnshaw, Bill, 62
Eckhoff, E., 163
education, becomes compulsory, 60, 95-6, 121, 200-1, 305-6; development of employment-related education, 121; free secondary education, 104-6, 112-3, 121, 357; importance of, 95, 96, 121-2; technical, 113, 121-2; *see also* corporal punishment; curriculum; primary schools; secondary schools
Education Act (1877), 60, 95, 200, 305-6
egalitarianism, 124; among skilled workers, 47-8, 53-4; as expressed by clothing, 146-9; in schooling, 105-6, 122; in sport, 164; on the street, 12-13
Elkington, J. S. C., 294
Elliott, William, 208
'embeddedness', 15, 16, 40
employment, *see* work
Employment of Females Act (1873), 69, 70, 151-2
evangelical churches, 46, 47, 323-4, 328, 331-2; and dancing, 188

Facoory family, 237-8, 252
Factory Acts, 69, 207, 300, 301, 306, 311, 356
factory work, women and, 23, 50, 55, 64, 69, 70-1, 75-6, 77, 125-7
family, 3, 51; becomes more child-centred, 175; kinship networks, 240, 250; leisure activities, 156, 170-8; lifecycle and poverty, 199-204; *see also* children
Family Allowances Act (1926), 3, 66, 194, 195, 215, 309, 360
family economy, 60, 67-8, 69, 90, 120, 200-3, 215; *see also* gardening; wages
family size, reduction in, 3, 4, 35-6, 91-2, 120, 175, 223, 290, 305-6, 311; impact on deaths in childbirth, 285, 305; *see also* childbirth
family wage, *see* male breadwinner wage
family violence, 303, 355
Faringdon Villa, 249; s*ee also* Grimmett family
Female Franchise Act (1893), *see* suffrage
femininity, 2-3; beauty contests, 184-5, 186; clothing and, 135, 139, 150; compliance in schools, 100; driving and, 282-3; first-wave feminism, 314-15; health issues, 286-7, 312; leisure and sport, 165-70; religious belief and practice, 325-36; respectability, 165, 166, 279-82; role of wife, 12, 353; school curriculum, 115-6; *see also* women
Fenby, David, 309
Ferguson, Lindo, 115
films, *see* motion pictures
Fish, Henry Smith, 43-4
Flat, the, 16-17, 19; character, 20-1, 39; demographic character, 24-6, 95; industrialisation, 21-2; infrastructure development, 20, 289-90; rise of amateur sport, 260-1; workplaces mapped, 53; *see also* Caversham; Kensington; St Clair; St Kilda;

429

INDEX

South Dunedin
Fleming, Mary Ann, 190, 208
Fletcher Bros Construction Co., 22, 52
floods, 35, 357, 360
Forbury, 17
Forbury Primary School, 95, 96; destinations of Std 6 pupils, 105; pupils going to secondary school, 111-12
Fraser, Mary Jane, 190-1, 213-4
freethinkers, 313, 315, 324, 337-8
friendly societies, 153, 156, 187, 306-7; membership records, 368-9; women's access to, 307; *see also* Miriam Rebekah Lodge

Gallaway, Emmeline, 348-9, 350-54, 355
Gallaway, Thomas, 348-9, 350-54, 355
gambling, 153, 154, 156; in sport, 156-7, 159, 160, 161, 162-3
Gammell, William, 208
Gandle, Mary, 208
gardening, 172-3, 246, 247; gendered activities, 251; in suburbs, 289
germ theory, 290-1; control of germs, 293, 296; impact on women's lives, 299-300, 310-11; *see also* health
Gillies, 'Duke', 178
Glanvill, Rebecca, 75
Glasgow Street, *see* Maria Street
Godber, Percy, 89, 181
Godber family, 89
Goodall, Rose, 301
Gore, Henry, 33, 182, 185, 187
Great Depression, 25, 64, 66, 77, 173, 194, 223-5, 360
Grimmett, Bert, 163, 175, 191, 218-9, 281
Grimmett, Louise, 82-3; *see also* Louise Wellman
Grimmett, Rachel, 49, 177, 226-7, 229-30, 231, 313, 323, 329, 331, 332; as businesswoman, 52, 244, 246, 330-1; circulatory mobility, 242-51, 254-6, 257
Grimmett, Richard, 52, 243-4, 247-8, 250, 329
Grimmett, Rita, 82-3; *see also* Jory, Rita
Grimmett family, 242-51, 253-4
Grocott, Ada & Horace, 175

hairdressing, 78, 82-3, 132; short hair for women, 82, 138, 139, 149
Hallensteins, 71, 76, 125-6, 131, 273, 358
Hananeia, Nicholas, 255
Hananeia, Sarah, 240, 252, 254, 256
Hancock, Annie, 335
Hancock, John H., 158
handicraft trades, 22-3, 50, 51, 52-3, 68-9; *see also* workers, skilled
Hardie, J. & Co., 140-1
Harris, Frances, 280
Harris, William, 299, 340
hats, for men, 142; for women, 140, 279; milliners, 128-9
Hatton, Marion, 44-5
hawking, 252, 255, 256, 265
health, gendered nature of, 285-8; government provision for, 312; health manuals, 293, 294-5, 297-8; national health patterns, 288-9; patent medicines, 296-8; women and healthcare, 292-300, 310-11; *see also* abortion; accidents; germ theory; hospitals; infectious diseases; mortality rates
Henry Potts Mission, 70

Herbert Haynes & Co., 140
Hillside Workshops, 11, 14, 21, 50, 52, 63-4, 273, 286; accidents, 285, 300-1; clothing worn, 141-2; library, 179; lists of workers, 370; opening of social block, 151, 360; rugby and league teams, 160, 163; school qualifications needed, 104; Sick Benefit Society, 300; streets nearby, 190; war service of employees, 1-2
historiography, of gender, 4-10; gender in schooling, 92-3; health, 287; historical geography, 10-14; leisure, 152-3; poverty, 193; religion, 318-22; spatial mobility, 227-9; women's history, 5-6
hobbies, 181
hockey, 167, 168, 357
Hogben, George, 112-3
holidays, family, 172, 173
Hollander, Mr, 290
Hooper, Maude, 1
Hopkinson, Ellen, 1
Horder, Vera, 73, 154, 183
Hore, Jack, 164
hospitals, changing nature of, 312; Dr Coughtrey's private hospital, 291-2; hospitalisation of men and women, 301-2; tuberculosis and, 310; *see also* Dunedin Public Hospital; Pleasant Valley Sanatorium; Seacliff Asylum
housework, 23, 54, 73-4, 143-4; and technological change, 269-70, 28
housing, and hygiene, 290-1; and ill-health, 309; and poverty, 201; State housing, 361

Industrial Conciliation and Arbitration Act (1894), 3, 58-9, 63, 64, 65, 80, 151, 195, 215, 311, 356; amended (1936), 215, 312, 361
Industrial School, *see* Caversham Industrial School
industrialisation, 21-2, 125-130
infectious diseases, 308, 309; *see also* tuberculosis
influenza epidemic, 298, 309, 359
Irish, in South Dunedin, 31

Jack, Robert, 173
Jackson, James, 307
Jennings, James, 303
Johnson family, pseud., 231, 235-6, 237, 240
Jones, Doreen, pseud., 235, 241
Jones, Frederick, 2, 361
Jones, Joyce, 168
Jory, Rita, 298; *see also* Grimmett, Rita
Joyce, James, 216

Kempthorne, W.L., 261
Kenny, Frances, 119, 139, 333
Kensington, 16; description, 27-8, 31, 39; female occupations, 23-4; history of development, 19-22; local migration to, 234; male occupations, 22-3; map, 27; poor, 191; suffrage petition, 48-9; *see also* the Flat
Kensington Primary School, 94, 95
Kensington Sunday School, 137, 314
Kent-Johnson, Loma, 276, 306
Kew, 16; development of, 20, 32, 33, 34, 35; female occupations, 22-3; male occupations, 23-4; suffrage petition, 48-9

430

King, Canon, 343
King, Christine, pseud., 175, 274, 275, 340, 371
King, Frederick Truby, 59, 115, 166, 169
King, Mary, 66, 118
King Edward Technical College, 107, 108-9, 114, 118-9, 358; curriculum, 116-8; typing class, 119
King Edward Theatre, 182

Lake, Victoria, pseud., 298, 327, 371
Lebanese, in South Dunedin, 31, 36, 59; circulatory mobility, 252, 256; local migration, 237-8, 240; pensions for, 361; religion, 323
Lee, Mary Isabella, 202
leisure activities, gendered, 151-3; of children, 97-8, 175-6; of family, 170-8, 189; of married women, 178-9, 188, 189; of men, 156-165; of women, 165-70, 189; of young single women, 83-4; *see also* alcohol; gambling; gardening; hobbies; reading; sports; walking
Lepper family, 190
Lister, David, 209
Lister, Jane, 47
Lister, Samuel, as atheist, 337-8; *Otago Workman* and, 41-2, 55; women's suffrage and, 43-4, 155, 338
Little, Walter, 99
Liverpool, Mavis, pseud., 78, 123, 139, 145-6, 147, 241, 275, 280, 371
Lock, Maria, 210
Long Depression, 25, 54-5, 56, 71, 190, 198-9, 216-7, 221, 357

Macandrew Road School, 95, 97, 100
McCarthy, Mary, 86-7
McCusker, Patrick, 307-8
McDonald, Robert, 203, 209
McCracken family, 264
Mace, Mary, 206
McFarlane, Jean, 146
McGarrigle family, 190
McGirr family, 202-3
MacGregor, Duncan, 338
MacGregor, Hon. John, 311
McIndoe, Mabel, 66
McKenzie, Marina, pseud., 298-9, 371
McKenzie, Robert 'Whang', 172, 174
McKinlays Bootmaking Factory, 21, 52, 64, 76
McMillan, Elizabeth, 76, 84-5
Maher, Hilda, 169, 219, 222, 279-80, 298
Maher family, 77
male breadwinner wage, 3-4, 23-4, 43, 51, 53-4, 59, 60-9, 87, 88, 90, 120; 156; impact of loss of, 59, 63, 215-22, 233-4; *see also* wages
Maori, 36-8; *see also* Ngai Tahu
Marchant, Maria, 113-4
Maria (Glasgow) Street, 190, 191, 229
Maritime Strike, 40-3, 56, 57, 356
Marlow family, 325
marriage, age of, 24-5; as gendered relationship, 348-54; changes, 223; clothing for, 139-40; courting practices, 282, 282, 333; equality within, 69, 84; local migration, 239-41; rates of, 24-5; trousseaux, 84, 123-4; *see also* women, married
Married Women's Property Protection Act (1860), 194

Martin, Ian, pseud., 117-8, 342, 371
masculinity, 2-3, 7, 42, 87-8; alcohol, 5, 8-9, 88, 153-6; male breadwinner wage, 3-4, 23-4, 43, 51, 53-4, 59, 60-9, 87, 88, 90, 353-4; Christian masculinity, 342-6; employment, 51-2, 53-5, 60-9, 88, 216, 221, 300, 303, 311; family car, 282; family man, 12, 51, 88-9, 90, 120, 156, 188-9, 224-5; health issues, 286, 311-12; home handyman, 89, 172; 'macho' man, 87-8; military service, 1-2, 89, 115; NZ studies of, 6-7; religion, 315, 336-46; rugby, 115, 160-5; school behaviour, 100-1, 115; sport, 89, 115, 156-65; transport occupations, 266-9; *see also* men
Maskell, R.W., 79-80
May, Muriel, 108
meals, at midday, at home, 271
mechanisation, in clothing trade, 126-7; in workplace, 52, 70-1
Meder, Dorothy, 73, 77
men, 12-14, 39; accident compensation, 300-1; and alcohol, 153-6, 332-3; attitudes, 43-4, 46-7, 60-2, 64; church attendance, 339-40, 342-3; clothing, 140-3; domestic responsibilities, 12; education, 97, 98, 100-1, 102-3, 105-6, 109-10, 114-5, 118, 121; health, 288-9; in asylums, 303-4; leisure activities, 153-6, 188-9; local migration, 233-4, 238, 253; occupations, 22-3, 265-70; organised sport, 156-65; political mobilisation, 40-3, 54-5; religion, 323, 327, 336-46; travel to work, 272-6; workplace accidents, 285, 301-2; *see also* masculinity
menstruation, and physical activity, 168
Mercer, Hugh, 100
Methven, George, 21-2, 50, 181, 264
midwives, 85, 304, 357; *see also* childbirth
migration, 227, 229, 230-42; among Lebanese, 237-8; family networks, 240; for work, 238-9; lifecycle changes, 239-42; local migration, 256-7; men and women, 233-4; poor, 236-7; single women, 234-5; social class and, 239; *see also* circulatory mobility; mobility; transience
military service, 1-2, 308, 309; compulsory military training, 358; links with rugby, 164; links with transport industry, 268-9; school cadets, 97, 98, 101, 114
Mill, George, 302
Milne, William, 95
Miriam Rebekah Lodge, 75, 166, 187, 307
mobility, 253-7; among poor women, 236-7, 253; as part of employment, 247-9, 252; cars and, 262; gender dimensions of, 226-9, 284; of children, 271; trams and, 262; *see also* circulatory mobility; migration; transience
modernity, in New Zealand, 3, 49, 91-2, 120-1; and clothing for women, 150; gender and, 4; role of young, single women, 69, 90; transport and, 266-7
Mollison, Mills & Co., 134
Morison, Frederick, 200
Morison, Harriet, 56-7
Morrell, William, 114
Morris, Yvonne, pseud., 119, 145, 147, 371
Morrison, Arthur, 62
mortality rates, 287, 288, 289; infant, 290, 291, 296, 299, 300; maternal, 290, 306

INDEX

Mosgiel Woollen Mills, 64, 70, 126, 273
motion pictures, 156, 169-70, 181-6, 189; first 'talkies', 360, 361; theatre opens in Cargill's Corner, 359
motor cars, 261-2, 263-4, 357, 360; and courting, 282; family car, 282-3, 284; men and, 276-7; travel to work, 274, 276; women and, 264, 282-3
motor cycles, 275, 276
Mullin, Mary, 302
Musselburgh Primary School, 95, 102, 358; destinations of Std 6 pupils, 105; pupils going to secondary school, 111-2

National Council of Women, 65, 66, 357
National Provident Fund, 3
native-born New Zealanders, 24, 60-2
navvies, 51-2, 90
'New Woman', 3, 135-6, 165-70, 188
New Zealand Clothing Factory, 71, 76
New Zealand Labour Party, 86-7, 356, 359
Ngai Tahu, 18; see also Maori
Norman, Annie, 104, 301
nursing, 72, 75, 309, 357; Plunket nurses, 293, 312; see also midwives

occupations, male, 23; employers, 22, 23, 28, 29, 32, 35, 52, 109-10; professionals, 32-3, 35, 109; self-employed, 22-3; skilled, 22, 23, 28, 29, 31, 34, 46, 47, 48, 50, 52-3, 68-9, 109-10; unskilled, 22, 28, 29, 30-1, 34-6, 46, 52, 87-9, 111-12; white collar, 22-3, 28, 29, 31, 34-5, 52, 88, 90, 109-10
occupations, female; factory work, 23, 50, 55, 64, 69, 70-1, 75-6, 77, 125-7; paid domestic service, 67, 73-4, 92, 113, 136, 302, 304; professional, 59, 75, 80; self-employed, 23, 69, 80-3, 132-3, 143-4; semi-professional, 52, 71-2, 75, 77-8; skilled, 72, 75, 127-9; unpaid domestic service, 23, 54, 73-4, 143-4; white-blouse, 23, 52, 71-3, 74-5, 76-8, 80, 84, 86, 92, 131
Ogg, John, 158-9
Ogg's (Cargill's) Corner, 21, 158-9, 258-9
Old Age Pensions Act (1898), 3, 194, 211, 307, 309, 357
O'Leary, Patrick, 218
Osmond, Emma, 351
Otago Benevolent Institution, 4, 11, 12, 19, 20, 24, 73, 143, 191, 208-11, 214-15, 226, 229, 231, 236-7; as provider of health services, 292, 304, 307-8; Chinese residents, 36, 210-11; Grimmett family and, 251; outdoor relief casebooks, 195-7, 368; women residents, 209-10
Otago Boys' High School, 106-8, 109-10, 114-15, 117, 118; sport, 161, 176
Otago Girls' High School, 106-8, 164; curriculum debates, 113-14, 115-16, 118-19; sport, 167, 168, 176, 357
Otago Motor Club, 282
outdoor relief, 196-9, 206-8, 211, 213-14

Paine, Miss I. B., 73
Parker, T. J., 338
Paul, J. T., 79, 344, 345, 359
Paul, Rosanna, pseud., 144, 145, 282-3, 296, 371
pensions, 3, 361; and health care, 309; deserted wives, 361; family allowances, 3, 66, 194, 195, 215, 309, 360; gendering of, 194-5; old age, 3, 194, 211, 307, 309, 357; unemployed, 194, 224, 360; widows, 3, 65, 194, 206, 217, 309, 358

Pensions Amendment Act (1936), 361
Perth, Richard, 298
Petre, F.W., 313
Pinkerton, David, 43
place, as part of study of gender, 10-14, 15, 16, 40-9
playgrounds, 157, 277-8
Pleasant Valley Sanatorium, 309, 310
Plunket Society, 293, 295, 358
poverty, 191-2, 198; and alcohol, 218-19, 220; and clothing, 124, 145; gendering of, 192-3, 194-5, 199, 204-8, 217-18; government and, 193-5, 224; impact of loss of breadwinner's wage, 59, 63, 215-22; life cycle and, 199-204; see also Otago Benevolent Institution; outdoor relief; pensions
primary schools, as microcosms of gendered society, 95, 97; community events, 171-2; curriculum, 97, 102-3; organised sport, 102, 175; playground activities, 97-8; see also specific schools, e.g., Caversham Primary School
Printz, Lillian and William, 354
private schools, 108, 109, 114
Proficiency examination, 98-9, 103, 104, 105
prohibition, 28, 32, 155, 314, 330, 340, 359; see also alcohol; Women's Christian Temperance Union
protective legislation, see Employment of Females Act; Factory Acts; Shop and Shop Assistants' Act; Sweating Commission
Protestant churches, 326-7; 330-1; 335-6
Proudfoot, David, 265-6
Proven, James and Mrs, 202
public service, and women, 72-3, 86

radio broadcasting, 359, 360; family recreation, 173-5
railways, 51, 261, 358; and modernity, 266; employment, 266
rational dress, 134-5, 137, 165
reading, 179-80; free public library, 358
Redwood, Mary, pseud., 270-1, 371
Reeves, William Pember, 43, 318-19
Reid, Hugh, 216
religious belief, feminisation of, 325-36; importance of, 313-15, 317, 335-6; men and, 339-46; numbers of professed and practising Christians, 324-5; see also churches
respectability, 165, 166, 168, 279-282
Reynolds, Rachel, 145
Riddell, Beatrice, 241
Roberts, Rose, 73, 79
Roberts family, 69
Roman Catholics, 313, 324-5, 334, 340; and suffrage, 46, 328-9; and temperance, 155; schools, 95, 108, 175; sports clubs, 161, 163, 333; see also St Vincent de Paul Catholic Orphanage for Girls; Sisters of Mercy
Roslyn Woollen Mills, 53, 63, 64, 70, 79, 126, 273, 280, 301
Ross and Glendining, 63, 76, 126, 140, 163, 273, 301
rugby, and masculinity, 115, 160-5; at Carisbrook, 358; links with war, 164; see also Southern Rugby Union Football Club; sports
rugby league, 163
Runciman, Jane, 66, 67, 73
Rutherford, Robert, 104

St Andrews Literary and Debating Society, 334

432

St Clair, 16, 191; description, 32-4, 35, 147; development of, 20, 27, 289; female occupations, 23-4; local migration to, 234; male occupations, 22-3; sports, 175; suffrage petition, 48-9; surf lifesaving club, 176, 177; tram-line, 262
St Clair Primary School, 33, 95, 100-1, 101-2, 103; pupils going to secondary school, 111-12
St Kilda, 16; brass band, 171, 358; demographic change, 24-6; description, 34-6; development of, 20, 27, 289, 360; female occupations, 23-4; flu epidemic, 359; library, 179; male occupations, 22-3; migration to, 230, 234; suffrage petition, 48-9; tram-line, 262
St Patrick's School, 95, 100
St Vincent de Paul Catholic Orphanage for Girls, 208, 213, 214, 333, 357
Salvation Army, 83, 220, 227, 246, 313, 323-4, 329, 357; see also Grimmett, Rachel
Scott, Joan, 4, 5, 8-9, 12, 93, 124-5, 286, 317, 354
Scott, Marjorie, pseud., 127, 241, 306, 371
Seacliff Asylum, 303-4
secondary schools, 103, 104-5; curriculum, 92, 112-20, 121; free education at, 104-6, 112-13, 121; single-sex schooling, 110; sports, 159-60, 167; uniforms, 112; see also Otago Boys' High School; Otago Girls' High School; King Edward Technical College
service class, 71-2, 75
sewing machines, 126, 144
sexuality, double standards, 341-2; in film, 183-4
Shacklocks, 50, 52, 63-4, 360
Sharp, Sarah, 202
Shaw, John and Mrs, 204
Shiel, C.W., 22, 33, 81
Shiel, Gertrude, 72, 77, 78, 81, 154, 180
Shop and Shop Assistants' Act (1894), 356
Sidey, Helena, 66, 73
Sidey, John, 239
Sidey, Stuart, 118, 274
Sidey, T.K., 43, 62, 87, 151, 256, 263-4, 313, 344, 357, 359
Siedeberg, Emily, 59, 115, 280, 293, 297, 307, 357; owns car, 165-6, 263
Sim, William, 62
Simpson, Alexander, 309
Sisters of Mercy, 73, 75
six o'clock closing, 155-6, 179, 359; see also alcohol; temperance
Sixpenny Clothing Club, 145
Slater, Bob, 56, 57-8, 62
Smith and Fotheringham, 21
social class, and church attendance, 339; and clothing, 146-9; and leisure activities, 166; and support for suffrage, 46-8; and transportation, 262; see also occupations
Social Security Act (1938), 3, 194, 217, 309-10, 312
Society for the Protection of Women and Children, 4, 356
South Dunedin, 16-17, 20-2, 27, 30, 31, 61, 289; borough amalgamates with Dunedin, 358; demographic change, 24-6; description, 30-2, 39; female occupations, 23-4; flu epidemic, 359; housing, 237; male occupations, 22-3; migrants to, 230; poor, 191; suffrage petition, 48-9
Southern Rugby Union Football Club, 161-5, 357
Southgate, Walter, 303

spatial mobility, *see* circulatory mobility; migration; mobility
sports, amateurism in, 159-63, 165; churches and, 333; codified and organised, 157-60, 161-2; community events, 171-2; for children, 175; for women, 84, 137, 165-70; gambling, 156-7, 159, 160, 161, 162-3; in schools, 102, 115; masculinity and, 89, 115, 156-65; *see also* specific sports, eg, hockey; rugby
Stanley, Thomas Litchfield, 19
Steel, Jane, 226-7, 236-7, 253, 254, 256
Stout, Anna, 338
Stout, Robert, 43, 338
suffrage, 4, 356; attitude to alcohol, 154-5, 340; petitions, 1, 2, 15-16, 69, 43-7, 314, 356, 370; religious denomination and, 46, 314, 328-9, 332; social class and, 46-8; *see also* Women's Christian Temperance Union
Sullivan, Charlie, 37-8; *see also* Tipene, Charlie
surf lifesaving, 176, 177-8, 358
Sutherland, Minnie, 98
Sweating Commission, 41, 47-8, 55-6, 207, 356; and clothing trade, 127; and domestic service, 304; and wages, 65
swimming, at beach, 135; 176-8, 246, 274; bathing costumes, 138, 149, 177-8
Syme, Verna, 298

tailoresses, 147; factory, 127-8; shop, 127-8; *see also* dressmakers; Dunedin Tailoresses' Union
tailors, 127, 130, 142; bespoke, 130
teaching, 72, 75
telephones, 270-1, 359, 360; subscribers, 369
Terry, Robert, 295, 296
Thompson & Son Ltd, 68
Tipene, Charlie, 37-8; *see also* Sullivan, Charlie
Todd, Margaret, 77
Todd & Brown, 130
toilets, outside, 290
toilets, public, for women, 136, 179, 257, 358
trade unions, 15, 39, 40-3, 54-9; and women, 55. 56-8, 86; attitude to alcohol, 155; *see also* Dunedin Tailoresses' Union; Maritime Strike
Trades and Labour Council, 42-3
tradesmen, skilled, 22, 23, 28, 29, 30-1, 34, 46, 50, 52-3, 68-9, 86; at Hillside, 41, 50; attitude to women's suffrage, 47-8; competition from women workers, 68-9; education and, 109-111; radicalism, 40-3; women workers, 72, 75, 127-9; *see also* handicraft trades
trams, 20, 242, 264-5; electric, 261-3, 357; facilitate secondary education, 112, 278, 281-2; gendered seating arrangements, 278-9; give mobility to women, 242-3, 262, 280-1; horse-drawn, 261; masculinity and, 266-9; modernity and, 266-8; opportunities for social interaction, 281-2; retail businesses and, 271-2; tram workers, 267-9
transience, 228-9; among men, 216, 221-2, 224-5, 236; among poor, 226, 227, 236-7; in Caversham, 230; *see also* migration; mobility
transportation, impact on domestic work, 269-70, 284; technological change and gender, 258-60, 262, 272-7, 282-4; *see also* cycling; motor cars; motor cycles; railways; trams

INDEX

Trevathan, Dave, 164
tuberculosis, 309, 310
Tudelope, Agnes, 302
Turner, Robert, 64-5, 353-4
Tweed, Helen, pseud., 120, 123, 139, 147, 276, 371

unemployment, 223-4, 361; benefits for unemployed, 194, 224, 360; controls, 63-4; public works relief schemes, 216-7, 224-5, 361
Unemployment Act (1930), 194, 224, 360

Valpy, W. H., 19

Waddell, Rev. Rutherford, 55-6, 207, 334
wages, in clothing trade, 127; control of pay packet within family, 61-2, 219-21; gendered wage system, 58, 78-80; government controls, 62; male minimum, 358; women's wages, 65-6, 78-80, 87, 217; *see also* male breadwinner wage; family economy; work, paid
Walker family, pseud., 231, 235-6, 237, 241
walking, as leisure activity, 165, 170; to work, 273-4
Ward, Mrs Percy, 166
Waterman, Johanna, 129
Wardrop, William, 351
Watson, Violet, 136
Wax Vesta Factory, 13, 14, 21, 39, 75-6, 77, 78, 80, 273, 279-80, 333; fire, 359; health problems at, 301; library, 179; sports teams, 169
Wellman, Louise, 299; *see also* Grimmett, Louise
Welsh, Jack, 185-6
Westfold, Susan, 190
White, J. Renfrew, 297
White, W.M., 21
white-blouse workers, 23, 52, 71-3, 74-5. 76-8, 84, 86, 131; education, 92; wages, 80; *see also* clerical work
white-collar workers, 22-3, 28, 29, 31, 34-5, 52, 87-9, 90, 109-10
Whitworth, Jess, 186-7
widowers, 59, 207-8
widows, 59, 206, 207, 217
Widows' Pension Act (1911), 3, 65, 194, 206, 217, 309, 358
Wigg, Andrew, 256
Williams, Charlie, 37-8
Williams, Ellen, 304-5
Willis, Mildred, 304
Wilson, Alexander, 114
Wilson, Ellen, 304
Wilson, Helen, 118, 119, 278
Wilson, Henry, 307
Wilson, Jack, 304
Wilson, 'Stringy', 100
Win, Quin, 302
Wolfenden and Russell, 131, 358
women, 12-14; and alcohol, 154-5; and reading, 180; as recipients of outdoor relief, 199, 205-7; changes in clothing, 134-40, 177-8, 278; citizenship rights, 4, 43-8; domestic responsibilities, 12, 350-1, 353; education, 59, 97, 102-3, 105-6; education at high school, 109-110, 113-4, 118-120, 121-2; health, 288-9, 301, 302, 311;

health insurance, 307, 309-10; historiography of women's history, 5-6; impact of reduced family size, 3, 4, 25-6; in asylums, 304; increased mobility, 135, 242-3, 254-7, 262, 280-1; involvement in church, 313, 324-5, 326-7, 331-2; leisure activities, 151-3, 165-70; local migration, 233-4, 253; Maritime Strike and, 42, 43; networks, 39-40, 48-9, 240, 250; occupations on the Flat, 23-4; public toilets for, 136, 179, 257, 358; rugby and, 163-4; safety in streets, 280-1; sports, 189, 165-70; *see also* femininity; 'New Woman'; suffrage; women, married; women, single
women, employment of, 69-85, 120-1; attitudes to, 51-2, 56, 59, 66; businesswomen, 80-3, 132-3; changing occupational patterns, 74-8; codes of behaviour, 78; department stores, 76-7, 131; health problems, 301, 302; impact of mechanisation, 52, 70-1, 126-7; impact on gender relationships, 77-8, 84, 85-90; married women and, 60-2, 63, 66, 69, 73, 81, 84-5, 86, 133, 143-4; options, 120; protective legislation, 301, 311; travel to work, 76, 272-6; wages, 65-6, 78-80, 87, 217; working conditions, 69-70; young single women and, 66-8, 69-85, 92; *see also* clerical work; dressmakers; tailoresses; white-blouse workers; work, paid; work, unpaid
women, married, 223; childbirth risks, 304-5; church involvement, 326-7, 333; circulatory mobility, 246, 253-5, 271; consumption patterns, 271-2; cycling, 274-5; driving, 282-3; employment, 60-2, 63, 66, 69, 73, 81, 84-5, 86, 133, 143-4; family networks, 39-40, 48-9, 240, 250; leisure activities, 178-9, 188, 189; local migration, 239-41; obligations of wives, 350-1, 353; role in domestic hygiene and health, 12, 292-300, 310-11; *see also* childbirth; family; family size; marriage; widows
women, single, 83-4, 120; as Sunday School teachers, 334; circulatory mobility, 242-3, 245-6, 255-7; dancing and, 84, 187-8; employment, 66-8, 69-85, 92; involvement in church, 326-7, 332-3; local migration, 234-5; poverty, 206-7; sport, 84, 165, 188
Women's Christian Temperance Union, 154-5, 321, 327-8
work, paid, changes in occupational structure, 22-3, 52-3, 74-8; consumption and, 123-4; gender conflicts, 54-6, 68-9; gendered division of labour, 50-1, 52, 59, 63-4, 80, 82, 85-90, 127-9; government control measures, 58-9, 65-6, 69-70; local migration and, 238-9; public works relief schemes, 216-7, 224-5; transport occupations, 265-9; travel to work, 39-40, 273-4; *see also* handicraft trades; navvies; occupations; trade unions; tradesmen, skilled; wages; white-blouse workers; white-collar workers; women, employment of
work, unpaid, 54, 178; by daughters, 67-8, 73-4, 92, 104, 105; dressmaking, 124, 144-5; in Grimmett family, 245; *see also* cleaning; housework
Workers' Compensation for Accidents Act (1900), 300, 306-7, 309-10, 311-12, 357
Workers' Political Committee, 56, 57-8, 86, 356
World War I, 101-2, 308, 359
Wright, William, 256